The Cultures of the West

A History

Volume 1: To 1750

Clifford R. Backman
Boston University

New York   Oxford
OXFORD UNIVERSITY PRESS

Oxford University Press is a department of the University of Oxford.
It furthers the University's objective of excellence in research,
scholarship, and education by publishing worldwide.

Oxford   New York
Auckland   Cape Town   Dares Salaam   Hong Kong   Karachi
Kuala Lumpur   Madrid   Melbourne   Mexico City   Nairobi
New Delhi   Shanghai   Taipei   Toronto

With offices in
Argentina   Austria   Brazil   Chile   Czech Republic   France   Greece
Guatemala   Hungary   Italy   Japan   Poland   Portugal   Singapore
South   Korea   Switzerland   Thailand   Turkey   Ukraine   Vietnam

For titles covered by Section 112 of the US Higher Education Opportunity Act,
please visit www.oup.com/us/he for the latest information about
pricing and alternate formats.

Published by Oxford University Press
198 Madison Avenue, New York, New York 10016
http://www.oup.com

Library of Congress Cataloging-in-Publication Data
Backman, Clifford R.
  The cultures of the West : a history / Clifford R. Backman.
    p. cm.
  ISBN 978-0-19-538889-3 – ISBN 978-0-19-538890-9 – ISBN 978-0-19-538891-6
  1. Civilization, Western.   2. Religion and civilization.   3. Science and civilization.
  4. Philosophy and civilization. I. Title.
  CB245.B324 2013
  909'.09821--dc23
                        2012033151

9 8 7 6 5 4 3 2

Printed in the United States of America on acid-free paper

---- ✦ ----

This book is for
Graham Charles Backman
Puero praeclaro, Scourge of Nations;

and for my mother
Mary Lou Betker,
with my best love;

and in memory of my brother
Neil Howard Backman, USN (ret.)
(1956–2011)
who found his happiness just in time.

---- ✦ ----

BRIEF CONTENTS

CONTENTS

By recognizing the Fertile Crescent's connective role—that is, its nature as a commercial center or meeting-point for the central Asian and eastern Mediterranean economies—Sargon highlighted what was to become perhaps the dominant trait of Middle Eastern history, its strategic significance as the connection-point between East and West.

The Greeks themselves, and especially the Athenians, came to regard the mid-5th century BCE with a determined awe, recalling it as a lost halcyon era that outshone anything that came before it or since. Through the centuries, much of Western culture has continued the love affair and has extolled "the glory that was Greece" as one of the two or three pinnacles of human achievement.

The western world had never seen a military juggernaut like this: in 622 Muhammad and his small group of followers had been forced from their home in Mecca, yet within a hundred years those followers had conquered an empire that stretched from Spain to India, an area twice the size of that conquered by Alexander the Great.

Like the humanists who
sought to restore ancient
morals, Luther sought to
re-create what he believed to
be Christian belief and
practice as they had existed
in the apostolic Church. He
saw himself as a restorer, not
a revolutionary, a liberator
rather than an
insurrectionist.

When Western science revived in the 16th century, it did so once again hand in hand with Christian faith. It is a modern conceit that science advanced only when it divorced itself from religion; that divorce became finalized only in the 19th century. The Scientific Revolution therefore needs to be understood as an offshoot of religious history.

14. From Westphalia to Paris:

The whole of society became obsessed with rule-making and breaking. Rules of etiquette, standards of spelling and usage, norms for musical composition and visual art, academic curricula, domestic architecture, even the subtle social demands of fashion—all these felt the pressure to conform.

List of Maps

Introduction:
Why History?

Through most of my school years I hated history; it seemed a dull exercise in memorization, a slightly sophisticated version of the game of trivial pursuit. Names and dates, followed by more names and dates. *The Battle of Actium was fought in what year? 31 BCE. Name the three ships that sailed to the New World with Christopher Columbus in 1492. The Niña, the Pinta, and the Santa María. Who fought in the Battle of Lepanto? The Holy League (Spain, Venice, the Papal State) and the Ottoman Turks, in 1571. Who delivered the sermon entitled "Sinners in the Hands of an Angry God"? Jonathan Edwards, in 1741. When was the Interstate Commerce Commission established? 1887. Whose assassination in 1914 triggered the start of World War I? Archduke Ferdinand of Austria.* And so on. Important facts all, but deadly boring when treated, as they invariably were, merely as data points to be learned by rote and recited on demand. Occasionally my teachers assigned map quizzes, usually pertaining to battles, which pleased the part of me that enjoyed pretending to be a field commander drawing up my forces to launch brilliant attacks on incompetent enemies. But then all pleasure disappeared when we were subsequently given photos of paintings and sculptures that "illustrated what life was like" in whatever time period was then under discussion. My failure was total. Try as I might, I never could find much to say, or think, or feel, or care about in 17th-century Dutch still lifes ("Oh, look! A loaf of bread!") or 18th-century French rococo landscapes filled, to my jaded eye, with prissy aristocrats in fake settings. No, history bored me, but I was good at it and so kept at it. (Good grades mattered.) My breakthrough moment came in college, when, with the help of my then-girlfriend, I realized that what I hated was not history itself but most of my history teachers—those dry, pinched souls who crushed everything that was vital, interesting, and important out of the great drama of human life. Out of my life, at any rate. History, after all, is the story of people, and anyone who finds people interesting ought therefore to find history interesting. If a person finds history boring, the problem lies either with him, as an unimaginative lout, or with the way in which the history is presented. Rejecting immediately, of course, the former as impossible in my case, I decided firmly on the latter. Blame the messengers, in other words, not the message. Over the years, I have become increasingly convinced of the correctness of this view. In their desire to present all the facts, most of my teachers—and most of the historians they had us read—simply drained all the life out of the subject.

Part of the problem lay in method. Teaching and writing history is difficult, in large part because of the sheer scope of the enterprise. Should one barrage a student or a reader with facts, clearly and objectively stated, and expect her to see the meaningful patterns in them, or should one discuss the patterns, the Big Ideas, and the deeper questions of human life confronted by any particular society in the past, and then allow her to teach herself enough factual details to corroborate and illumine those larger themes? Both approaches have value, and each has its own weaknesses. Most large-scale history books tend to choose the first option and make a fetish of their factual comprehensiveness and strict objectivity of tone. The problem with this approach is that it too often works only for those few who are already true believers in history's importance and leaves most students and readers yawning in their wake. I knew a fellow in college who was one of these true believers; he could recite the names and dates, in order, of every king of England and every archbishop of Canterbury from 1066 to the present. Impressive, in a nerdy way. But he had no idea at all how to explain the causes of England's civil war in the 17th century, or why the British voted their national hero, Sir Winston Churchill, out of office immediately after the end of World War II. Probably for both good and ill, I choose the latter option—to teach and write history by emphasizing ideas and trends, and the values behind them; to engage in the debates of each age rather than to narrate who won them. Once people are genuinely interested in a topic and can see the reasons to care about it, it seems to me, they can pick up the essential facts by themselves. Moreover, experience has taught me that they will do so.

Four years ago, when Oxford University Press invited me to write a general history of the Western world, I warned them that my approach to the topic would be a bit out of the ordinary. I wanted to write a book that would irritate people, inspire them, confuse them, make them question themselves, and sometimes enlighten them, but certainly always engage them. There are enough books already published to make bored readers fall asleep over. My first eccentricity, if that is what it is, is that I wanted to write a book that had opinions and argued with readers. No one falls asleep in an argument, I figured. My second eccentricity, I warned, is that I do not believe in Western civilization as it is usually defined. I believe instead in what I call—and what nearly became the title of this book—the Greater West. It's time to explain.

There are as many histories of any society as there are historians willing to write them. The shape, themes, and degrees of detail in each result from whatever each author considers of greatest importance—politics, social development, technology and science, economics, gender relations. A focus on any particular theme produces a different understanding of who we have been and therefore who we are. Like the changing patterns in a child's kaleidoscope, the smallest shift of attention or emphasis reveals new configurations of ideas and insights into the way we see ourselves. No single vantage point can claim primacy; as Albert Einstein (1879–1955) theorized and subsequent scientists affirmed, the truths revealed by every perspective in the cosmos are equally true to each observer. But that does not mean one cannot be wrong. "Facts are stubborn things," wrote the American statesman John Adams (1736–1826), in a very different context, "and whatever may be our wishes, our inclinations, or the dictates of our passion, they cannot alter the state of facts and evidence." Historians can disagree, for example, about the specific causes of an event like the Franco-Prussian War (1870–1871), or about its consequences for subsequent generations; but the factual realities of those specific people in those specific places, performing those specific actions, cannot be tampered with. The challenge of writing history, but also its deepest value and most enduring purpose, is in the selection and assemblage of those facts, and the conclusions one draws from them.

To follow a single theme, or a clutch of them, is one way to mediate between comprehensive factuality and meaningful interpretation, and hence the preference by most writers of large-scale histories to select discrete vantage points, to trim the material in such a way that emphasizes, for example, political events. Seen this way, the history of the Greater West emerges as a centuries-long march toward the development of the modern democratic nation-state. A focus on social themes traces the evolution of social classes, the family, interethnic relations, and dominant moral codes. An economic approach emphasizes the everyday common struggle to survive in the world—the production of food, developments in manufacture and commerce, the passing on of property—and culminates not only in modern prosperity but in the belief in a fixed set of economic laws that govern human life. The unspoken corollary of this approach is that it is the recognition of this set of laws to which modern prosperity owes thanks; capitalism thus appears not as a customary practice or an ideology but as a subdiscipline of natural science.

This book too adopts a thematic approach, but a theme seldom utilized in contemporary histories. While paying due attention to other aspects of Western development, it focuses on what might be called the history of values—that is, on the assumptions that lie behind political and economic developments, behind intellectual and artistic ventures, and behind social trends and countertrends. Consider for example, the achievements of the Scientific Revolution (1500–1750). The advances made in fields like astronomy (Nicolaus Copernicus, Johannes Kepler, Galileo Galilei), chemistry (Robert Boyle), and medicine (William

Harvey) did not occur simply because individuals smart enough to figure out new truths happened to come along. Harvey's discovery of the circulatory system was possible only because the culture in which he lived had begun, albeit hesitantly, to allow the dissection of human corpses for scientific research. For many centuries, even millennia, before Harvey's time, cultural and religious taboos had forbidden the desecration of bodies. But the era of the Scientific Revolution was also the era of political absolutism in Europe, a time when prevailing sentiment held that the king was all that stood between mankind and barbarism. Any enemy of the king—for example, anyone convicted of a felony—therefore deserved the ultimate penalty of execution and dissection. No king worship, no discovery of the circulation of the blood. At least not at that time.

Similarly, the search for underlying value assumptions illuminates the effort to explain the gloomy outlook, bordering on nihilism, of the modernist movement of the early 20th century. For the preceding hundred years Europe's traditional Christianity had wavered and withdrawn in the face of industrialism, migration, economic despair, and the intellectual assaults of Darwinian evolution, the so-called higher criticism of the Bible, and the radically new physics of quantum theory and relativity. The trauma of World War I simply was a bloody culmination of the longer trend of the loss of religious belief. A godless universe might still have an underlying order and purpose, but quantum theory and relativity demolished any hope of finding them. For the most stubborn holdouts determined to retain a belief in a meaningfully ordered cosmos, though, World War I crushed any last shreds of hope. If nothing is permanent, true, and purposeful, the modernists thought, then human life is a wasteland of pointless impressions, blind desires, and empty hopes.

> What are the roots that clutch, what branches grow
> Out of this stony rubbish? Son of man,
> You cannot say, or guess, for you only know
> A heap of broken images, where the sun beats,
> And the dead tree gives no shelter, the cricket no relief,
> And the dry stone no sound of water. Only
> There is shadow under this red rock,
> (Come in under the shadow of this red rock),
> And I will show you something different from either
> Your shadow at morning striding behind you
> Or your shadow at evening rising to meet you;
> I will show you fear in a handful of dust.
> (T. S. Eliot, The Waste Land, 1922)

On the other hand, the collapse of order was liberating to some. Just as modernist poets like Eliot freed themselves from rhyme and meter, so too did modernist music (Arnold Schoenberg, Paul Hindemith, Igor Stravinsky, Alban Berg) discard traditional compositional structure and tonality. In painting, movements like Dadaism and cubism explored nonrepresentational forms and played with the very idea of visual sense.

A history that emphasizes the development of values inevitably distorts the record to some extent, for obviously not every person living at a given time held those values. Medieval Christians did not uniformly hate Jews and Muslims, believe the world was about to end, support the Inquisition, and blindly follow the dictates of the pope. Not every learned man and woman in the 18th century was "enlightened" or even wanted to be. The young generation of the 1960s was not composed solely of war resisters, hippies, drug aficionados, feminists, and rock-music lovers who celebrated free love in the muddy fields at Woodstock (although many people now of a certain age like to pretend that they were then). With this caveat in mind, however, it remains possible to offer general observations about the ideas and values that predominated in any era. This book privileges those ideas and sensibilities and views the events of each era in relation to them.

And it does so with a certain amount of opinion. To discuss value judgments without ever judging some of those values seems cowardly and is probably impossible anyway. Most large-scale histories mask their subjectivity simply by deciding which topics to discuss and which ones to pass over; I prefer to argue my positions explicitly, in the belief that to have a point of view is not the same thing as to be unfair. Does this risk confusing the reader who might mistake my opinion for accepted fact? Possibly, I admit. But education is as much about teaching students to evaluate arguments as it is about passing on knowledge to them, and students cannot learn to evaluate arguments if they are never presented with any. Or if they are asleep.

In a second departure from tradition (which in this case is really just habit), this book interprets Western history on a broader geographic scale than other historians do. All full-scale histories of Western civilization begin in the Fertile Crescent, the ancient region made up of Mesopotamia (in modern-day Iraq), Palestine (modern-day Syria, Lebanon, and Israel), and Egypt—but after making a quick nod to the origins of Islam in the 7th century they focus almost exclusively on western Europe. Attention moves like the sun ever westward, through ancient Greece to Rome, thence to Britain, France, and Germany (with a bit of Italy and Spain thrown in when unavoidable), and finally embraces America once it emerges from its international isolation in the 20th century. The Muslim world thereafter enters the discussion only when it impinges on European actions. This book overtly rejects that view and insists on including the region of the Middle East in the general narrative, as a permanently constitutive element of the Greater West. For all its current global appeal, Islam is essentially a Western religion, after all, one that has its spiritual roots in the Jewish and Christian traditions and the bulk of whose intellectual foundations are in the classical Greco-Roman canon. To treat the Muslim world as an occasional sideshow on the long march to western European and American world leadership is to falsify the record and to get the history wrong. Most textbooks touch repeatedly on the Islamic world, of course, but do so only in episodic fashion—and those episodes are invariably whenever Europe and the Middle East are in conflict.

A simple analogy shows the poverty of this approach. Consider any long intimate relationship you have had—perhaps a romantic tie, a family connection, a work colleague, or a long friendship. If someone were to write the history of that relationship but in the process examined only the arguments you had, it could not possibly (no matter how detailed and "objective") be an accurate history of the relationship. It could not possibly be even an accurate history of the arguments, since it would view them entirely out of context. That is the situation with the Greater West. The "European world" and the "Middle Eastern world" have been in a continuous relationship for millennia, buying and selling goods, sharing technologies, studying each other's political ideas, influencing each other's religious beliefs, learning from one another's medicine, facing the same challenges from scientific advances and changing economies. We cannot explain who we are if we limit ourselves to the traditional scope of Western history; we need a Greater Western perspective, one that includes and incorporates the whole of the monotheistic world. Nearly every one of the fundamental turning points in European history (the developments of agriculture, literacy, urban life, monotheistic religion, religious heresy; debates over tolerance, over intellectual freedom, over the rights of women; the Black Death; the invention of gunpowder; the discovery of the larger global world; the challenge of secularism, the debate over reason, the Enlightenment (called *al-Nahda* in Arabic); the catastrophic conquests of Napoleon Bonaparte; the changes brought by rapid industrialization; the First and Second World Wars, the Cold War; and the rise of modern feminism, liberalism, and conservatism) have been experienced jointly by the European and Middle Eastern societies. And not only have we confronted the same challenges, we have interacted with each other intimately in our responses to each new development. Only by broadening our focus can we do justice to each other and to the reality of how our histories have played out. This expanded view introduces a rafter of new difficulties, for apart from the unfamiliar nature of much of the new material, it forces the additional compression and selection of more traditionally mainstream matters.

I am very much aware of the risks involved by this approach. In order to discuss, for example, the campaigns to reform and modernize Islamic understandings of women's roles in society in the early 20th century, this book gives less attention to many of the most significant activists for women in Europe and the United States. A woman like Aletta Jacobs (1854–1929), the first university-trained female physician in the Netherlands, a champion of women's health and the right to suffrage, deserves more space than she receives here (although I point out that she is discussed at greater length here than in any other book of this sort). I wanted to make room, however, for women like Huda'i Sha'arawi (1879–1947), the pioneering Egyptian feminist. The payoff seems worth it, if the end result is a broader recognition that the Islamic world's development has closer parallels with the European and American society than has generally been thought or acknowledged.

Since religious belief has traditionally shaped so much of Greater Western culture—whether for good or ill is every reader's responsibility to determine—I have placed it at the center of my narrative. Even for the most unshakeable of modern agnostics and atheists, the values upheld by the three great monotheisms have had, and continue to have, a profound effect on the development of our social mores, intellectual pursuits, and artistic endeavors. The history of religion does not explain all of Greater Western history, but it is as useful a handle as any to grasp the whole, as are politics, economics, society, and intellectual life. It seems to me to be worth trying, especially since religious misunderstanding and friction dominate so much of our current attention.

In another break with convention, the book incorporates an abundance of primary sources into the narrative. I have always disliked the boxed and highlighted source snippets that pockmark so many of today's textbooks. Any teacher who is honest knows that most students do not read them. It seems to me that any passage worth quoting is worth working into the text itself—and I have done so, with some brio. But a word about them is necessary. For the first three chapters I have needed considerable help. I am ignorant of the ancient Middle Eastern languages and have relied on the current version of a respected and well-loved anthology from my own undergraduate days.[1] When discussing the sacred texts of Judaism, Christianity, and Islam I have used their own authorized translations. Simple courtesy, it seems to me, calls for quoting a Jewish translation of the Bible when discussing Judaism; a Catholic, Orthodox, or Protestant Bible whenever discussing those main branches of Christianity; and the English version of the Qur'an prepared by the royal

---

[1]   Nels M. Bailkey and Richard Lim, *Readings in Ancient History: Thought and Experience from Gilgamesh to St. Augustine*, 7th ed. (Wadsworth, 2011).

publishing house in Saudi Arabia when discussing Islam.[2] Last, some of the political records I cite (for example, the Cairo Declaration of Human Rights) are quoted from their official English versions. But apart from these special cases—all duly noted—every translation in this book, from chapter 4 onward, is my own.

SUPPORT MATERIALS FOR *THE CULTURES OF THE WEST*

The Cultures of the West comes with an extensive package of support materials for both instructors and students.

- **Companion Web Site (www.oup.com/us/backman):** For students, the site includes quizzes, flashcards, documents, interactive maps, and links to YouTube videos. Access to the student site is unrestricted. For instructors, the site includes an instructor's resource manual that provides for each chapter, a detailed chapter outline, suggested lecture topics, learning objectives, suggested Web resources and digital media files. It also includes, for each chapter, approximately 30 multiple-choice, short-answer, true-or-false, and fill-in-the-blank questions as well as approximately 10 essay questions.
- **Instructor's Resource DVD:** Includes PowerPoint slides and JPEG and PDF files for all the maps and photos in the text; an additional four hundred map files, in PowerPoint format, from *The Oxford Atlas of World History*; and approximately 250 additional PowerPoint-based slides organized by theme and topic. The DVD also includes the Instructor's Resource Manual, and the test questions can be customized by the instructor.
- **Sourcebook for *The Cultures of the West*, Volume One: To 1750:** Edited by Clifford R. Backman and Christine Axen, it includes approximately two hundred text sources in Western civilization, organized to match the chapter organization of *The Cultures of the West*. Each source is accompanied by a headnote and reading questions. Free when bundled with the text.
- **Sourcebook for *The Cultures of the West*, Volume Two: Since 1350:** Edited by Clifford R. Backman and Christine Axen, it

---

2   *Tanakh: The Holy Scriptures,* by the Jewish Publication Society; *New American Bible,* published by the U.S. Conference of Catholic Bishops; *New Revised Standard Version,* published by Oxford University Press; and *The Orthodox Study Bible.* For the Qur'an I have used *The Holy Qur'an: English Translations of the Meanings, with Commentary,* published by the King Fahd Holy Qur'an Printing Complex (A.H 1410).

includes approximately two hundred text sources in Western civilization, organized to match the chapter organization of *The Cultures of the West*. Each source is accompanied by a headnote and reading questions. Free when bundled with the text.

- **Mapping the Cultures of the West, Volume One: To 1750:** Includes approximately forty full-color maps, each accompanied by a brief headnote. Free when bundled with the text.
- **Mapping the Cultures of the West, Volume Two: Since 1350:** Includes approximately forty full-color maps, each accompanied by a brief headnote. Free when bundled with the text.
- **Now Playing: Studying Western Civilization Through Film:** (available in both student and instructor editions) is a concise print supplement that provides synopses, recommended scenes, and discussion questions for thirty of the most commonly assigned films in Western Civilization classes. Qualified adopters can receive a Netflix subscription with their adoption. *Now Playing* can be bundled with *The Cultures of the West* at no additional cost.
- **E-book for *The Cultures of the West* (both volumes):** An e-book is available for purchase at **http://www.coursesmart.com.**

BUNDLING OPTIONS

The Cultures of the West can be bundled at a significant discount with any of the titles in the popular Very Short Introductions or Oxford World's Classics series, as well as other titles from the Higher Education division world history catalog (**http:// www.oup.com/us/catalog/he**). Please contact your OUP representative for details.

ACKNOWLEDGMENTS

Working with Oxford University Press has been a delight. Brian Wheel is the person who talked me into attempting a new history of the Greater West. I am grateful for the confidence he showed in me and for all the encouragement he offered. Charles Cavaliere, Brian's successor, served as point man, guiding me through the entire project with grace and kindness. His cheery enthusiasm kept me going through many a difficult hour. If the prose in this book has any merit, please direct your compliments to John Haber, prince of editors. I shall miss working with him. Lauren Aylward, Theresa Stockton, Lisa Grzan, Eden Kram, Meg Botteon, Kim Howie, and the rest of the staff shepherded me through the marketing and production phase and deserve all the credit for the wonderful physical design of the book—images, captions, layout, and font.

Some two dozen external reviewers, anonymous to me, read various chapters of this book as they emerged from my printer. Those who did not wish to remain anonymous include Robert Brennan, Cape Fear Community College; Gregory S. Brown, University of Nevada–Las Vegas; Scott G. Bruce, University of Colorado–Boulder; William Caraher, University of North Dakota; John Cox, University of North Carolina–Charlotte; Jason Coy, College of Charleston; Lynda Pinney Domino, Simpson College; Steven Fanning, University of Illinois at Chicago; Irina Gigova, College of Charleston; Laura Hutchings, University of Utah; Andrew Jenks, California State University–Long Beach; Erik N. Jensen, Miami University; Andrew Keitt, University of Alabama–Birmingham; Thomas A. Mason, Indiana University–Purdue University Indianapolis; David Matz, St. Bonaventure University; Charles A. Maxfield, DeSales University; Martin Menke, Rivier College; David A. Messenger, University of Wyoming; Peter J. Myers, Palo Alto College; Stephen Norris, Miami University; Devin Pendas, Boston College; Michael Redman, University of Louisville; Pete Rottier, Kent State University; Mark Edward Ruff, Saint Louis University; Wendy Sarti, Oakton Community College; Thomas J. Schaeper, St. Bonaventure University; Linda Bregstein Scherr, Mercer County Community College; Stuart Smyth, University at Albany–SUNY; Laurie Sprankle, the Community College of Allegheny County; Jane Strother, Campbell University; Victoria Thompson, Arizona State University; Hans P. Vought, SUNY–Ulster County Community College; Janet M. C. Walmsley, George Mason University; David White, McHenry County College; and Matthew Donald Zarzeczny, the Ohio State University. Reading their criticisms felt at times like falling face-first into a threshing machine. (You know who you are, reader no. 6!) I am grateful nonetheless for every comment they offered; our profession depends on people offering honest criticism of one another's work. If I have not accepted every one of their suggestions, they should still feel proud of the work they did. This is a better book, and I hope that I am a better teacher, because of their unsung efforts.

My doctoral student at Boston University, Christine Axen, has been a support from the start. She has taught with me, and occasionally for me, through the last three years, and I appreciate the time she took away from her own dissertation research to assist me on this project—pulling books from the library, running down citations, suggesting ideas. Now that Oxford has asked me to prepare a companion volume of primary texts for this book, Christine has proved such an immense help that she will share the title page with me when that volume appears.

To my wife, Nelina, and our sons, Scott and Graham, this book has been an uninvited house guest at times, pulling me away from too many family hours. They have put up with it, and with me, with patience and generosity that I shall always be thankful for. Their love defines them and sustains me.

With so many good people supporting me, I should have finished sooner. I'll do better next time.

About the Author

Clifford R. Backman is Associate Professor of History at Boston University, where he has taught since 1989. He is author of *The Decline and Fall of Medieval Sicily: Politics, Economy, and Religion in the Reign of Frederick III, 1296–1327* (1995) and *The Worlds of Medieval Europe* (Oxford University Press, 2003). His current projects are a biography of King James II of the medieval Crown of Aragon and a study of Arnau de Vilanova, the infamous heretic who was the personal physician to four successive popes.

A Note to the Reader

I follow a few basic conventions. Instead of the old BC (Before Christ) and AD (Anno Domini) designations for centuries, I use the new norms of BCE (Before the Common Era) and CE (Common Era). Dates are given, whenever possible, for every figure mentioned in the book. Political leaders are identified by the years they were in power—hence (r. 0000–0000) means that he or she *ruled* during those years, and, in the modern era, (g. 0000–0000) means that he or she *governed* during them. All other dates, unless otherwise noted, are life- and death-dates.

One of the chief difficulties of the "Greater Western" approach is the sheer number of unfamiliar names. The history of the Islamic Middle East, this book argues, has to take into account national or ethnic differences, as much as the more familiar distinction between Sunni and Shia Muslims. To help with this, I have indicated wherever possible the ethnicity of an individual. [A] denotes an Arab. [K] indicates an ethnic Kurd. [P] identifies a Persian (Iranian). [T] signals that the person is a Turk. The reasons for these designations will be clear as the chapters unfold.

The Cultures of the West

A History

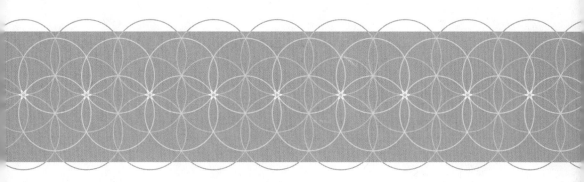

CHAPTER 1

Water and Soil, Stone and Metal

10,000 BCE–2100 BCE

The origins of Western civilization lie in southern Iraq. The region was called Sumer five thousand years ago, and it was the site of the first consistent use of agriculture, the domestication of animals that made farming possible, the construction of cities, and the invention of writing. At first glance it seems an unlikely place for civilization to begin: the soil is sandy, summertime temperatures regularly surpass 110°F (43°C), and the dull flatland receives a scant eight inches of annual rainfall. (By comparison, most of the Mediterranean basin receives nearly four times as much.) There was no stone to quarry, no metal ores to mine, and little timber with which to build. Bordered by the relatively low-lying Zagros Mountains of Iran to the east, it nevertheless lay exposed to raiding groups from the Iranian steppe.

THE ANCIENT NEAR EAST

But it was first in Sumer that true civilization began. It brought early agriculture, trade, and an empire. It brought writing, ancient songs, and ancient deities. When Egypt became a second cradle of civilization, its firm social hierarchy extended even to the kingdom of the dead.

THE TIGRIS AND THE EUPHRATES

Sumer lay in the narrowing plain between the lower reaches of the Tigris and Euphrates rivers. The Sumerians had access to the Persian Gulf, whose headlands reached about one hundred miles further inland in ancient times than they do today. Yet they never developed a maritime tradition and remained resolutely bound to

◀ **Sumer** Sumerian noblewoman wearing a shawl, possibly denoting preparation for a wedding. ca. 2100 BCE.

the soil. Sandy though that soil was, it was made fertile by the flooding of the two great rivers, as the winter rains of Syria and the spring thaws of the snows of the Taurus Mountains to the far north brought layer upon layer of silt to fertilize the land. Twisting slowly eastward through narrow defiles until they reached the high plains of Syria and Kurdistan, the rivers plunged dramatically southward, picking up speed as they approached the site of today's city of Baghdad. The Tigris River, with its deep bed, flooded less broadly but with a strong current. The Euphrates, on the other hand, was broad and shallow, overran its banks easily, and scattered highland silt over a wide expanse. The faster-flowing Tigris usually reached its high-water mark in April, while the Euphrates generally reached full flood about a month later. By managing this water via an elaborate network of levees, reservoirs, and irrigation canals, the Sumerians were able to produce abundant yields of summer grains for themselves and prairie grasses for their herds. Crop yields may have reached ratios as high as 30:1—that is, thirty bushels of grain harvested for every bushel of seeds planted, a ratio comparable to that produced by American farms in the first half of the 20th century.

Archeological evidence suggests that the Ubaids—the first identifiable group to settle in the region—began farming in Sumer perhaps as early as 7000 BCE. Remnants of irrigation tunnels, built of stone, date at least to 5900 BCE and possibly earlier. Archeologists in the last hundred years have discovered even older settlements involving agriculture in other sites throughout the Middle East. At Jericho in Palestine, for example, evidence of grain storage—though not necessarily of grain production—reaches back to 9000 BCE. Agriculture also developed in northern Mesopotamia only two hundred years later, then on the south-central Anatolian plateau around 7500 BCE, and finally in southern Russia and along the banks of the Black Sea ca. 7000 BCE, after the geological shifting of continental plates opened the Dardanelles and let the saltwater of the Mediterranean pour in, to create the Black Sea out of what used to be a freshwater lake. But only Sumer gives evidence of continuous settlement, systematic agriculture, developed urban

CHAPTER TIMELINE

ca. 9000 BCE
Evidence of grain
storage, Jericho

ca. 5500 BCE
Appearance of cities in
Eridu and Ur (Sumer)

ca. 7000 BCE
Earliest evidence of
farming in Sumer

ca. 4000 BCE
Beginning of
Bronze Age

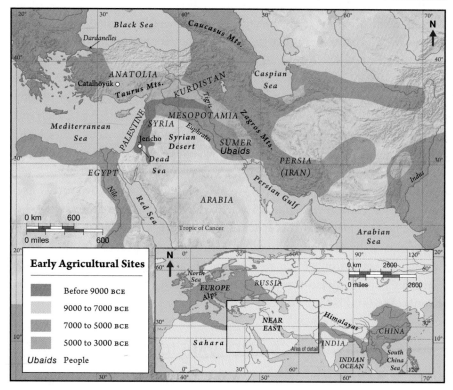

MAP 1.1 Early Agricultural Sites

life, and the use of writing. From there the technique of farming spread eastward into India, westward to the coastal plains of the eastern Mediterranean, and even as far as western Europe (see Map 1.1).

Archeology and guesswork are our only guides to these developments. Early agriculture depended on collective labor, and lots of it: until native animals such as oxen were domesticated, the brutal work of cutting open the soil, planting seeds, weeding, pruning vines, cutting stalks, and grinding grains had to be done by hand. Skeletal remains of early agriculturalists—chiefly women—display agonizingly

Women

ca. 3500 BCE
Earliest evidence
of writing (Sumer)

ca. 2350 BCE
Reign of Akkadian
King Sargon I

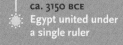

ca. 3150 BCE
Egypt united under
a single ruler

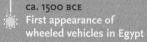

ca. 1500 BCE
First appearance of
wheeled vehicles in Egypt

curved spines. Men, on the other hand, hunted, gathered, and ruled. Villages began to appear, some of them rather large; for safety, the people at most sites constructed stone or earthen walls to protect them from attack. The early settlement at Jericho had a population of roughly two thousand people by 7000 BCE and a fortification wall that may have reached thirty feet in height. In west-central Anatolia, at about the time Jericho was completing its wall, cattle breeders settled at Çatalhöyük, where their population swelled to between eight and ten thousand. They built a village of closely placed mud-brick homes that, interestingly, were entered via holes in their roofs.

Primitive metal tools appeared around 7000 BCE as well, when small bits of raw copper were hammered into shape with stones. By 5000 BCE early settlers had learned how to smelt copper ore into the pure metal, which they then either cast into molds or, by 4000 BCE, mixed with tin in order to produce bronze. Bronze was significantly stronger than its component parts, and its use in weaponry and farm implements spread throughout the Near East quickly—inaugurating the **Bronze Age** (4000–1500 BCE).

EARLY SUMER: KINGS AND WARRIORS, PRIESTS AND SCRIBES

Rich in potential for grain-producing but lacking the stone and metal needed to bring it about, the Sumerians had to develop trade relations. These reached to the ore-rich but grain-poor settlements along the upper Tigris River and westward into Palestine and lower Anatolia. Sumerian grain traveled well in the arid atmosphere of the Near East, and the masses of heavy stone and metal they needed to produce it were easily transported down the strong current of the Tigris. But maintaining these important commercial ties over such long distances compelled the Sumerians to develop writing. With it they could keep records of orders, shipments, revenues, and obligations.

The origins of the Sumerians are unknown since their language is unrelated to any other known tongue, whether ancient or later. It is likely that they entered the Tigris-Euphrates plain, as did most of their subsequent invaders, from the Zagros Mountains in Iran.[1] Sumerians were not the only inhabitants of Mesopotamia, of course, but they were the dominant group until their conquest by the Akkadians around 2500 BCE. Their founding myths identify Eridu and Ur as their first cities; archeological evidence confirms that these appeared as early as

---

[1]   This region is also known as Mesopotamia, which derives from the ancient Greek name for the area. It means "between the rivers."

languages

5500 BCE and contained as many as fifty thousand inhabitants at their peak, and were followed soon by settlements at Uruk, Lagash, Nippur, and Kish; Sumerian cities were considerably larger and more complex than the rural villages in Palestine, Syria, and Anatolia.[2]

While most people worked the land, economic specialization developed quickly. Stonemasons, merchants, rivermen, weavers, dyers, civil and hydraulic engineers, metalworkers, potters, and scribes—all emerged as distinct occupations. In the first centuries, these cities were governed by clan elders, who perhaps worked in concert as a primitive form of municipal council. They could not, however, defend the Sumerians against invaders or satisfy the whims of the deities who controlled the natural forces of heat, wind, and water. These constant needs resulted in the rise of new twin nodes of power—militarily backed monarchies and divinely appointed priesthoods.

Kingship and priesthood commonly emerge together in Western societies, sometimes in contest with one another and sometimes elided into each other. Military action was most efficiently directed by a single commander to whom everyone owed obedience—the king, whose formal title was **lugal**. Protection against the gods, especially the unpredictable deities that the Sumerians believed in, required the priests. This large and permanent caste was charged with anticipating the gods' desires, interpreting their actions, and above all propitiating their wrath through prayer and sacrifice. Given their joint responsibility for protecting the people from harm, kings and priests have traditionally worked together: kings stand as bulwarks and standard-bearers of the priests' institutionalized religion, while priests serve to consecrate kings and bless their actions. In the ancient Near East, and well into Europe's own history, the worst crises frequently occurred when the secular and religious powers were at cross-purposes.

king

est

The Sumerians' own king list, written around 2100 BCE but reflecting a much older oral tradition, fancifully boasted that an unbroken string of monarchs had governed Sumer for well over two hundred thousand years. This tradition reached back even before the worst crisis of all: a mythical Great Flood sent by capricious gods that covered the entire earth and all but annihilated mankind. Much like the Biblical tale of Noah and the Ark, for which it served as a model, the Great Flood

---

[2]   Settlements were also heavily fortified. Uruk had a full six miles of battlements surrounding it.

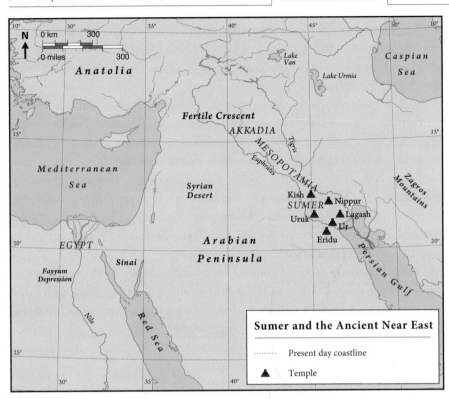

MAP 1.2   Sumer and the Ancient Near East

never happened but retained its mythic power because of the peoples' genuine fear of actual flooding. The Tigris and Euphrates occasionally swelled to unusual size and covered farms, fields, and flocks.[3] This legend, told in the great Sumerian poem the *Epic of Gilgamesh*, served to remind the people of the unpredictability of the gods while creating a reference point for the start of their own history.

Sumer consisted of a sprawl of independent city-states, each governed by a lugal, a priestly caste, or an uneasy combination of the two (see Map 1.2). The earliest king we can identify with any certainty was En-Mebaragesi, who ruled over Kish, near the site of the later city of Babylon, around 2600 BCE. His most significant achievement was the construction of the temple in Nippur, the home of the great sky god Enlil. En-Mebaragesi ruled during the so-called Early Dynastic Period, which lasted from 2900 to 2350 BCE. The king list relates that political dominance in Sumer temporarily passed from Eridu and Shuruppak, in the south, to Kish, in the north, and that after Kish's brief ascendance, southern Sumer once again took the lead (though with power then centered on Ur, Uruk, and Lagash). Some enthusiasts take this assertion literally

---

3   It seems likely that the legend of the Great Flood, if it had any basis in historical fact at all, originated with the creation of the Black Sea.

and suggest that the Great Flood legend refers to an actual event. They try to synchronize it with the unusually large layer of silt deposits that settled over part of lower Sumer at some point between 3000 and 2900 BCE. But the chronologies of the king list and the archeological record disagree with one another by many centuries.

The Sumerians invented writing during this age, starting with primitive early pictograms, or drawn representations of objects. These gave way to a sophisticated system of ideograms, which represent concepts, and phonograms, or marks indicating syllabic phonetic values. The latter are similar to the shortcuts used by today's text messengers. Sumerian writing used nearly two thousand symbols, which meant that literacy remained a tightly held monopoly of professional scribes, who consequently enjoyed positions of great significance in society. Without them, kings and priests could not compile records, issue decrees, or establish legal or liturgical canons. By far the most famous of the Early Dynasts was Gilgamesh, who ruled Uruk around 2600 BCE. Tradition credits him with building the battlements surrounding that city and claims that after his death the grateful people of Uruk gave him a magnificent burial: they diverted the Euphrates River, buried his body in the exposed riverbed, and then released the waters once again into their original channel so their ruler would lie forever beneath the great river.[4] But Gilgamesh is best known as a literary figure, the hero of the later Babylonian epic that bears his name.

A Semitic people called the Akkadians overwhelmed the Sumerian city-states around 2350 BCE and established the Akkadian Period, which lasted until about 2100. They had lived for several centuries along the upper Tigris, trading with the Sumerians and the peoples of Syria. Although they were foreigners, the Akkadians respected Sumerian culture and adopted its language, institutions, and religion. The most successful of the Akkadian kings was Sargon I (ca. 2350 BCE), who conquered everything from lower Sumer to northern Syria, all the way to the Mediterranean (see Map 1.3). This fierce conqueror boasted constantly of his cruelty as a matter of policy, making him perhaps the first ruler who found that simply maintaining a reputation for savagery can hold a large population in check as effectively as actual savagery can.

THE IDEA OF EMPIRE

Sargon placed family members in control of the territories he conquered, thereby governing a knitted-together empire.[5] This was a surprisingly new idea. The Sumerians had fought plenty of wars over the centuries, but their custom had always been to

---

[4]   In 2003 a team of German archeologists discovered what they believe to be the ancient city of Uruk. The excavation is still underway; Gilgamesh's grave has yet to be located.

[5]   Sargon installed one of his daughters as high priestess of the temples to the Sumerian moon goddess. Her name was En-Heduanna, and she is history's first known female author. Several of the hymns she wrote have survived.

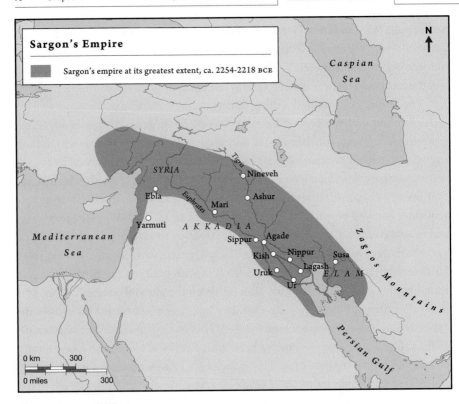

Sargon's Empire

Sargon's empire at its greatest extent, ca. 2254–2218 BCE

MAP 1.3   **Sargon's Empire**

defeat a neighbor and then to withdraw and receive annual tribute from the conquered. The notion of actually governing the lands they conquered seems never to have occurred to them. Sargon, however, saw that a hitherto unimagined level of wealth and power could result not only from controlling grain-rich Sumer but also from commanding the trade routes of upper Mesopotamia. Through this region Sumerian grain traveled northward, while textiles, metalwork, and animal products of the northern portions of the **Fertile Crescent** moved south. His empire far exceeded any earlier kingdom in its magnificence, but its real significance lay in the model of strategic authority that it established. By recognizing the Fertile Crescent's connective role—that is, its status as a commercial center or meeting point for the central Asian and eastern Mediterranean economies—he highlighted what was to become perhaps the dominant trait of Middle Eastern history, its strategic significance as the connection point between East and West.

> By recognizing the Fertile Crescent's connective role—that is, its status as a commercial center or meeting point for the central Asian and eastern Mediterranean economies—he highlighted what was to become perhaps the dominant trait of Middle Eastern history: its strategic significance as the connection point between East and West.

The Sumerians had commonly referred to their rulers as shepherds of the people. The Akkadians, however, would have none of that. An inscription from the reign of one of Sargon's successors—his grandson Naram-Sin—describes him as "the Strong, the Ruler of Akkad":[6]

> Even when the four corners of the earth were united in opposition to him, [he] emerged victorious . . . and took captive all the kings who had united against him. Because he had saved Akkad in time of crisis, all the people of the city begged of the gods—of Ishtar, in Eanna; of Enlil, in Nippur; of Dagan, in Tuttel; of Ninhursaga, in Kesh; of Enki, in Eridu; of Sin, in Ur; of Shamash, in Sippur; and of Nergal, in Kutha—that Naram-Sin might be worshipped as a god in Akkad. Accordingly, they built a temple for him in the center of the city.

Sargon's empire collapsed roughly one hundred years after his death, and control of the region was restored to a series of native kings known collectively as the Third Dynasty of Ur (ca. 2100–2000 BCE). This was the last period of Sumerian history, since the Ur dynasts were ultimately displaced by new waves of invaders who poured over Mesopotamia (or simply through it en route to Palestine) after 2000 BCE: the Semitic Amorites from southern Iran (2000–1600), the Hittites, an Indo-European group from central Anatolia (1600–1400), the Mitanni (1500–1300, also Indo-Europeans), and the Assyrians (1500–600, a Semitic-speaking group) from the northernmost reaches of the Tigris River. There were others, too. But these groups generally disdained Sumerian culture and did their best to suppress or supplant it. Their interests lay more in the northern and western reaches of the Fertile Crescent, from Syria and Anatolia down through Palestine and approaching Egypt. As Sumer declined, the priestly caste went into elegiac mode, writing and preserving sad hymns to their gods and laments for the lost glories of the early city-states.

There is some evidence that economic decline contributed to the invaders' disdain for the Sumerian way of life. Centuries of flooding and irrigation had left high quotients of mineral salts in the farm fields. Since these salts rose to the surface as the water was absorbed into the land, the quality of the soil deteriorated, reducing productivity. Local farmers attempted to stop the decline by introducing new grains, but it seems clear that the gradual corrosion of the alluvial plain, which worsened the further south one went toward the confluence of the two great rivers, brought an end of Sumerian life. It was no coincidence that the Amorites, the group to succeed the Akkadians, built a new capital for themselves

---

6   The Akkadians thus appear to have introduced the cult of king worship.

considerably further to the north, a city that remained the dominant Mesopotamian city for many centuries thereafter: Babylon.

MESOPOTAMIAN LIFE: CITIES AND SLAVES, LETTERS AND NUMBERS

So much for the political framework. But what do we know about how people in early Mesopotamia lived, what they believed, and how they understood the world?

Since agriculture is what brought them there in the first place, it is right to start with their working of the land. Farming occupied probably 90 percent of the population, who used wooden plows, bronze-tipped seed drills, and stone-bladed hoes. Mesopotamia comprised roughly eight thousand square miles (twenty thousand square kilometers) of land fed by a network of major stone canalways and an elaborate sprawl of subsidiary smaller channels, which divided the land into relatively regularly spaced and equally sized plots. While the largest estates belonged to the kings and temple priests, most farmland was held privately. Whole clans, rather than individuals, owned each plot of land, and they worked out for themselves the distribution of tasks and profits. In most cases the consent of the whole clan was needed before any parcel of land could be sold. Yet it remains unclear how that consent was achieved—whether by all the adults equally, solely by the men, under the leadership of the clan elders, or by some other means. Clans who wanted to relinquish their landownership, perhaps to migrate northward into Syria or into Palestine (as did the Hebrew patriarch Abraham around 1800 BCE), resorted to adopting would-be buyers into their clan in order to facilitate the sale of their property. Inheritance practices were **patrilinear**, through male heirs, although, in the absence of one, women could own property and give evidence in courts.

A barter economy predominated, with farmers giving grain portions to the various craftsmen—carpenters, smiths, potters, and weavers—who produced the tools they needed to work the land. Payments in kind were likewise made to the priests in the local temples. Commoners also owed a certain amount of labor to their communities, usually for the all-important tasks of maintaining the irrigation canals and urban fortifications. All adult men fought to defend the city-state from attack and were responsible for supplying their own weapons and equipment. Law allowed for divorce and remarriage, although women were not considered equal partners of their husbands.

The cities that dominated Sumer were built of sun-baked brick and surrounded by deep moats and fortified battlements. The major streets within each city ran from the gates to the market squares and then to the temples and the royal palace. These streets could accommodate two-way traffic of chariots and ass-drawn wagons and carts; branching off these were tangles of narrow byways and alleys where the bulk of the people lived in cramped, low-roofed huts. Open space came at a premium; the wealthy displayed their status and good fortune by building interior courtyards in their palaces. Larger towns like Ur, Uruk, Lagash, Kish, and Nippur held populations as large as forty or fifty thousand, but five to ten thousand was more common. Rank and filthy, these towns had no sewers; human waste was simply dumped into the unpaved streets, where it was foraged (and added to) by crowds of swine, goats, oxen, and dogs. Clean water to drink was a luxury, which accounts for the Sumerians' early invention of beer—the alcohol in it forestalled the proliferation of pathogens.

Temples dotted the cityscape. Sumerians believed in and sacrificed to hosts of deities, but each city observed the formal recognition of a particular patron god, for whom they erected vast terraced pyramid-like mounds called **ziggurats**, atop which stood lavishly decorated temples that served as the earthly home of the god or goddess. Sumerian religion maintained that the gods had invented humans in order to serve them and perform the labor that they would otherwise have to do for themselves; hence temple worship involved prayer, the singing of hymns, and offering the deities an array of gifts. Priests received a percentage of every farmer's produce and of every manufacturer's wares. In return, they presided over the temples' rites and kept the gods appeased. Human life was subject to the whims of the gods. The Sumerians believed that their deities commanded the forces of nature; and while the deities were generally benevolent (hence Sumerian prosperity), they could nevertheless act capriciously and were easily roused to anger.

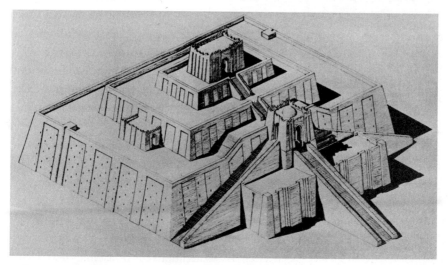

Artist's Reconstruction of the Ziggurat of Ur, ca. 2500 BCE   Worshippers ascended the long stairs to the first platform, where there stood a gatehouse through which they gained admittance to the upper levels. At the top of the ziggurat was the shrine, in which the priests conducted their rituals.

Priests often worked alongside the king to govern the city-state, creating a de facto theocracy. To aid in that work, and to keep a careful tally of payments made or yet owed to the deities, the priestly caste invented writing—Mesopotamia's greatest single contribution to the world. The earliest surviving documents (records of payments received from votaries, primarily) come from Uruk and Kish around 3500 BCE. Sumerian scribes wrote by pressing figures into mud or clay tablets that were then either sun-dried or baked until hardened; the script they developed is called **cuneiform**.[7] Cuneiform markings represented ideograms and groupings of letters in syllables, rather than individual letters. The first alphabet developed two thousand years later, in Palestine, among the Canaanites and the Phoenicians.

Once the syllabary code had become established, Sumerian scribes set to work recording economic transactions, astronomical charts, religious poems and prayers, medical regimens, legal decrees, arithmetical calculations—all manner of things. Among the most interesting are early word lists. These lists were not dictionaries, but rather groups of related nouns—four-legged animals, birds of various sizes, types of flowers and other plants, species of fish, and varieties of precious stones and metals. Such lists probably originated as study guides for learning the cuneiform script.

Yet they also represent mankind's first documented efforts to make sense of the world, by classifying its components and seeking order among its bewildering variety.

A second set of markings depicted numbers. Sumerian mathematics used place-value numerals, with both base-ten and base-sixty notations. (The latter survives in our division of time into sixty-minute hours and sixty-second minutes.) By 2300 BCE they had either invented or imported the abacus. They used arithmetic to keep financial accounts and for studying the constellations and the movement of the planets in the night sky. Since their survival depended on knowing when to expect the spring floods, they paid close attention to measuring time. They

Early Writing   A clay receipt, ca. 2300 BCE, tallying the number of sheep and goats in a particular herd; perhaps part of a bill of sale, but also perhaps a record for taxation purposes.

---

7   Cuneiform literally means "wedge-shaped" in Latin, after the indentation made into the clay by a reed stylus.

followed a solar calendar but divided it into twelve lunar months, which necessitated the insertion of a thirteenth month every third year. The flooding of the rivers eroded the Sumerians' mud-brick buildings and boundary markers, so they quickly became adept at basic geometry in order to re-create their washed-away property lines.

Slavery appeared early in Sumer. Two principle sources of slaves existed: debt bondage and the taking of captives in war. People who owed money to landlords or merchants seldom sold themselves into slavery; instead, they sold their family members. The practice may have begun as the offering of a child as collateral for a loan or as a ransom against a promise to repay a debt. Failure to pay resulted in the child's permanent loss of freedom. War captives and their descendants, however, probably represented the larger portion of the slave population. The Sumerians generally avoided using slave labor in the fields, since the opportunities for escape were too great. Instead, slaves remained in the cities, working as domestic servants, laborers in workshops, and concubines. The frequent warring between the city-states, and between the Sumerians and their invaders, resulted in a steady supply of new slaves—which was a necessity in ancient times, since the harshness of slave life meant that slave populations were seldom self-sustaining. Their mortality rates almost always exceeded their birth rates. Given the vulnerability of this population, therefore, the Sumerians kept their slaves from the backbreaking work of tilling the land and maintaining the irrigation canals. Slaves were used instead to help around the house and the work yard.

Oral custom and written law structured Sumerian life, and as early as 2300 BCE at least one ruler, Ur-Ukagina of Lagash, had brought these laws into a single, published code that articulated the pursuit of justice, not the preservation of inherited right, as the aim of government. Economic specialization in the cities had created a degree of social stratification that ancient custom could neither address nor restrain, leaving thousands vulnerable to exploitation in every city. Written law emerged from this as an effort to reform society by restricting the rights of the powerful. Ur-Ukagina's law code survives only in fragments and in references found in later texts. The portions that survive limit the rights of the priestly caste and wealthy landowners to evict tenants and seize their property, exempt widows and orphans from paying taxes, and oblige the government to meet the funeral expenses of the poor. One inscription reads: "[Ur-Ukagina] freed the people of Lagash from usury, burdensome controls, hunger, theft, murder, and seizure of their property. He established freedom. Widows and orphans were no longer at the mercy of powerful individuals."[8] This effort to relieve oppression did not last long, however: the Akkadians conquered Sumer shortly after Ur-Ukagina's reign. Subsequent rulers,

---

8   This inscription contains the first known use of the word for "freedom" in any Western language: *ama-gi.*

however, continued to produce reformist codes, the most famous of all being that instituted by the Babylonian ruler Hammurabi (ca. 1700 BCE).

RELIGION AND MYTH: THE GREAT ABOVE AND GREAT BELOW

Sumerian religion, as reconstructed from myths and ritual prayers written in Babylonian times, consisted of a complex web of relations. It encompassed at least three strata of existence: Heaven, the Great Above, and the Great Below.

The Sumerians regarded the day and night sky as the high overarching bowl of Heaven, a fixed semisphere where dwelt Anu (meaning "sky," literally, but representing the divine force itself) and a group of spirits known as the Igigi. The Great Above consisted of the space from the dome of the sky down to the surface of the Earth; this was the dwelling of the Annunaki—the assemblage of gods and goddesses to whom the people of Sumer sacrificed and offered prayers, and whose aid they invoked. Enlil, the god of the air, reigned supreme here; the other chief gods were Utu, the sun god (called Shamash by the Akkadians), Nanna Suen, the moon god (Sin to the Akkadians), Nin-Khursaga, the Earth goddess (Akkadian Ishtar), and Enki, the god of waters (later identified with the Babylonian god Ea); but the names of at least fifty other Annunaki survive. Mankind was the creation of Enki, who had made humans specifically to provide food and comfort for the gods. People, in other words, were the servants of the gods in the most literal sense. Interestingly, the deities in the Annunaki did not create the world but were in fact created by it.

The world itself came about through the movement of two primordial forces—the male and female principles (Abzu and Tiamat, respectively)—which resulted in the creation of the physical world and then of the gods themselves. But the Annunaki feared the creation of even more gods, who presumably might have supplanted them, and so Enlil killed their mother, Tiamat, and Enki slew Abzu. The murdered parents thus descended into the Great Below, the world beneath the surface of the Earth. Also beneath the Earth was Kur (Ersetu to the Akkadians), which was the Land of No Return, the place to which all humans went after death. The Sumerians believed there were two separate entrances to the world of the dead, one in the caves of the Zagros Mountains and another in a secret staircase hidden in the city of Uruk. After dying, all Sumerians entered Kur by one of these portals, whereupon they received judgment from a council of six hundred gods. It is hard to say what the purpose of such judgment was, however, since all the dead were consigned equally to spending eternity wandering naked and exposed through an endless expanse of darkness, dust, and heat.

Each city-state possessed its own unique patron deities, and it was the joint responsibility of the lugal and his corps of priests to lead their societies in ritual

The Standard of Ur, ca. 2500 BCE   This plaque, made of lapis lazuli embedded in wood, portrays farmers, carters, scribes, merchants, and priests en route to offer their sacrifices to the deities.

worship. Sumerian gods numbered more than three thousand, but most of them remained unknown outside their local cult centers. Only the major deities like Enlil, Enki, and Ishtar enjoyed wide recognition, through the stories that made up Sumerian mythology. Each deity represented a force of nature and was anthropomorphic in form and all too human-like in behavior. But the gods stood well beyond human understanding. A crude barter characterized human-divine relations: the Sumerians courted favor from the gods by offering them prayers and appeasing them with gifts, while the gods blessed the people (when it suited them) by sending favorable conditions for the growing of abundant food.

The gods were capricious, though, and could lash out in anger by sending a burning drought, a devastating flood, a plague of crop-eating insects, or a wave of foreign invaders. Sumerian priests guarded against such divine fickleness by reading omens in the organs of animals sacrificed in the temple, by interpreting dreams, or by seeing coded messages in the flight patterns of birds. Religious life in Sumer thus consisted largely of maintaining favorable but distant relations with the gods and goddesses. Heavenly interaction with humans spelled doom as often as it brought delight.

> Religious life in Sumer thus consisted largely of maintaining favorable but distant relations with the gods and goddesses. Heavenly interaction with humans spelled doom as often as it brought delight.

Sumerian mythology consisted of an intricate web of tales. Their gods, it turns out, were energetically incestuous, making it all but impossible to work out their genealogy. To illustrate with just the first generations: Anu, the great god principle in Heaven, fathered Tiamat and Abzu, who then consorted with one another and produced two mud deities named Lahmt and Lahamu. These siblings then paired off to produce Kishar, a fertility goddess, and her brother Anshar, the god of the North Star, and these two then somewhat predictably came together—but unpredictably they somehow gave birth to Anu, their own great-grandfather. From this point on, the family tree becomes impossibly tangled.

In earliest times the tales lacked a strong moral element; the gods exhibited the same self-interest that humans did and pursued their pleasures and whims accordingly. By the start of the second millennium, however, many myths bear witness to a heightened interest in justice and a sense of rational moral order. A hymn to the goddess Nanshe of Lagash, for example, lauds her as the deity who "sees the oppression of man over man, who is the guardian of orphans, . . . the caregiver of widows, who seeks justice for the poor, . . . who comforts the homeless and shelters the weak."

The best-known of the moralized Sumerian hymns comes from the Babylonian period. Known as the Shamash Hymn after the Babylonian name for the sun god Utu worshipped in the city-state of Sippur, it offers praise for the god's relentless protection of the weak and troubled:

> You care for all the peoples of the lands,
> And everything that Enlil/Ea . . . has created is entrusted to you.
> All that draws breath you shepherd without exception. . . .
> The whole of mankind bows to you,
> Shamash, the universe longs for your light. . . .
> You stand by the traveler whose road is difficult,
> To the seafarer in dread of the waves you give [comfort]. . . .
> You save from the storm the merchant carrying his capital;
> The [boatman] who sinks in the ocean you equip with wings;
> You point out settling places to refugees and fugitives, and
> To the captive you point out [escape] routes known only to you.

The hymn goes on to praise Utu/Shamash for punishing corrupt judges and dishonest merchants, for granting long life to those who work for justice, and for rewarding the honest and kindly. The lugals, too, came to be valued as much for the extent to which they provided justice, since their temple duties of leading sacrifices and observing the chief festivals of the religious year gained in significance.

A contrary tradition in Sumerian myth laments the unpredictability of the gods' affections and care to protect the righteous. "The Poem of the Righteous Sufferer" expresses the agonies of an unnamed Sumerian who despite his strict ritual observance has nevertheless suffered the loss of his wealth and social position:

> I gave my attention to supplication and prayer:
> To me prayer was discretion, sacrifice my rule.

The day for reverencing the god was a joy to my heart;
The day of the goddess's procession was profit and gain to me.
The king's prayer—that was my joy,
And the accompanying music became a delight for me. . . .
Who knows the will of the gods in heaven?
Who understands the plans of the underworld gods?
Where have mortals learnt the way of a god?
He who was alive yesterday is dead today.
For a minute he was dejected, suddenly he is exuberant.
One moment people are singing in exaltation,
Another they groan like professional mourners.
Their condition changes like the opening and shutting of the legs,
When starving they become like corpses,
When replete they vie with the gods.
In prosperity they speak of scaling heaven,
Under adversity they complain of going down to hell.
I am appalled at these things; I do not understand their significance.

A later Babylonian writer reworked the myth and turned this poem into a song of praise for the god Marduk. This patron deity of Babylon comes to the sufferer's aid and restores him to happiness, ending with a paean to traditional teaching and ritual.[9] In the original tale, however, the dominant tone is despair. The narrator seeks not an end to human suffering but merely an explanation for it. Why do the wicked prosper? Why are the lives of the righteous filled with want, fear, violence, and confusion? Why will the gods not spare humans from the pain of life?

To judge from their literary remains, the people of Mesopotamia thought deeply, almost obsessively, about these matters. The parlous nature of life almost demanded it. After all, the land they inhabited had many natural blessings but was vulnerable to invasion by raiders seeking to snatch away the very blessings the Sumerians worked so hard to procure. Moreover, the rivers that gave such abundant life to the region also destroyed it by unpredictable and uncontrollable flash flooding. The more the Sumerians prospered, the more likely they were to be attacked. These were ironies of a most soul-searching kind. If the gods could alternately bless and batter humans so capriciously, is it vain to regard the world as being in any way ethically ordered? And if life lacks moral sense, is it worth the agony of living it? Can we have trust in heaven? Attitudes shifted with time and fortune, but the Sumerians, while not unremittingly gloomy, recognized

---

[9]   The Babylonian tale may have provided a model for the Hebrew author of the biblical Book of Job.

that life is serious business. They had deep souls, gave thanks for small blessings, but kept a wary eye open for all manner of the world's senseless agony. Among their many extraordinary contributions to Western culture was the invention of the conscious search for meaning in life. And that may be their most important contribution of all.

ANCIENT EGYPT

Southwest of the Fertile Crescent, along the banks of the Nile River in Africa, lay the second cradle of Western civilization. The Nile originates in two sub-Saharan tributaries—one in northern Ethiopia, fed by Lake Tana, and the other stretching all the way south to Lake Victoria in Uganda. They meet near today's Sudanese capital city of Khartoum. From there the Nile flows northward, dropping through a series of dramatic cataracts, or waterfalls, before reaching the gentle sloping plane of Egypt itself.

For six hundred miles it meanders slowly northward, cutting a green swath of fertile land on either side of the riverbed, until about a hundred miles shy of the Mediterranean it branches out in a delta with no fewer than seven major openings to the sea, spread over nearly two hundred fifty miles of coastline. This delta region forms "Lower Egypt," and the six-hundred-mile-long river valley directly south of it comprises "Upper Egypt." Together, the two regions made up approximately twelve thousand square miles (thirty-one thousand square kilometers) of arable land, and they were home to human communities dating back to 5000 BCE.

Egypt thus consisted of two extremely long strips of land on either side of the Nile, between four and twelve miles across, and a vast triangular delta. The waters of the Nile swelled annually, beginning in August. At their peak in September, they reached nearly twenty feet above their low ebb in April and May, bringing more than one hundred million tons of rich sediment to replenish the banks. Spring planting thus began when the greatest amount of land was exposed, and the harvest was brought in just before the next replenishing flood began. People lived in small communities along the river's edge as early as 5000 BCE but did not begin to farm the land until approximately 3500. Until then, they tended their flocks, living off the plants and trees that grew naturally along the shores.

Away from the cultivated shores of the Nile, the rest of Egypt was all but uninhabitable, with nothing but arid desert to the east, west, and south. The relatively small land bridge of the Sinai Peninsula, the only point of contact between the African and Asian continents, narrowed to a span of only forty miles as it approached Egypt proper. Controlling the movement of peoples through so small an area posed little trouble through most of Egypt's history. Nature thus blessed Egypt with a concentrated abundance of fertile soil, an easy means of communication and transport, and a protective surrounding that kept invaders out for nearly fifteen hundred years. The marshy delta's port cities comprised Egypt's only exposure to other peoples, and hence the fortification of the harbors represented the only significant military expense of her rulers. Soldiers were well paid by the affluent government, and with no enemies to contend with they could devote all their energies to policing their own people. Moreover, and unlike Sumer, Egypt had abundant resources in stone and metal ores and hence could engage in impressive building projects, like palaces and pyramids. Timber was the only vital natural resource unavailable, but this was easily procured via trade through the delta cities and then shipped upriver. By such natural advantages Egypt unified early, developed a strong central government, and enjoyed more lasting peace and prosperity than any other early culture.

Human settlements based on agriculture appeared as early as 5000 BCE. The first languages used in the region belonged to the Hamitic and Semitic families. These suggest that the earliest settlers arrived from the northern coast of Africa to the west and from Palestine and Syria to the northeast. By 4000 BCE the construction of rafts made of papyrus reeds, which grew abundantly in the marshlands, enabled the groups stretched along the river to be in continuous contact. Technologies of tool making, copper mining, irrigation, swamp drainage, and stone carving spread accordingly (see Map 1.4).

Given the ubiquity of arable land along the river, the earliest Egyptians did not congregate in cities but instead spread out more or less evenly in hundreds of small villages; hence the first organized states emerged as regional groupings, called **nomes**, along segments of the river. These nomes eventually coalesced into larger units, until finally, around 3150 BCE, the entire kingdom was unified under a single ruler. Tradition credits a man named Menes with the feat; after him Egyptian kings wore a crown that joined the characteristics of crowns of the earlier rulers of Lower Egypt and Upper Egypt.[10] (Many scholars have replaced the semilegendary Menes with Narmer, whose position as first ruler of a united Egypt is corroborated by an engraved palette that illustrates the combined kingship.) The division of Egypt's history into thirty dynasties was the invention of a native historian of the Hellenistic era named Manetho, after Alexander the Great had conquered the kingdom in 332 BCE. Scholars have since tinkered with the details but have kept Manetho's general scheme.

---

[10]   The word pharaoh, which means "palace" or "great house," did not come into general use until 1500 BCE or so. Since the Egyptians believed their ruler to be a god, to speak his name aloud was blasphemy.

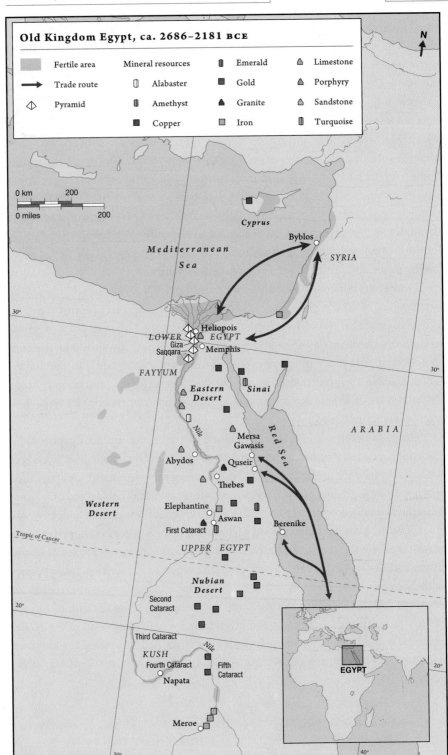

Old Kingdom Egypt, ca. 2686–2181 BCE

Fertile area	Mineral resources	Emerald	Limestone
Trade route	Alabaster	Gold	Porphyry
Pyramid	Amethyst	Granite	Sandstone
	Copper	Iron	Turquoise

N

Cyprus

Byblos

Mediterranean
Sea

SYRIA

30°

Heliopois
LOWER   EGYPT
Giza
Saqqara   Memphis

30°

FAYYUM

Eastern
Desert   Sinai

Nile

ARABIA

Mersa
Gawasis

Red Sea

Abydos   Quseir

Thebes

Western
Desert   Elephantine

Berenike

Aswan

Tropic of Cancer   First Cataract

UPPER   EGYPT

Nubian
Desert

Second
Cataract

20°

Third Cataract

KUSH
Fourth Cataract   Fifth
Cataract

EGYPT

20°

Napata

Meroe

30°   40°

MAP 1.4   Ancient Egypt, ca. 2686–2181 BCE

Narmer Palette   This plaque commemorates King Narmer (a.k.a. Menes—Old Kingdom pharaohs had as many as five names each), the first ruler to unite Lower and Upper Egypt. The front image *(left)* portrays Narmer as he prepares to smash the skull of a rival with a mace. To the right the god Horus, in the shape of a falcon, brings him captives. Narmer wears a kilt, with the tail of a bull (symbolic of strength) attached to his backside. The reverse side of the plaque *(right)* shows another bull, at the bottom, breaking through the fortifications of a city and trampling a victim, while above, servants attend to two great beasts whose long necks are entwined, a scene that presumably represents the union of the Lower and Upper Kingdoms. On top, a ruler with his servants carries banners and the spoils of war.

An identifiable Egyptian civilization thus took shape at roughly the same time that organized Sumerian society began—around the start of the third millennium BCE. This corresponds with the appearance of writing in both societies. The Egyptians—who had established trade relations with the Sumerians by that early time—may have acquired the idea of writing from Mesopotamia. Unlike the Sumerian cuneiform, however, the Egyptians developed a system of **hieroglyphs** (literally, "sacred carving"), based on a combination of pictograms and phonetic

Ancient Egypt
Archaic Period: 3150–2686 BCE (Dynasties 1–2)
Old Kingdom: 2686–2134 BCE (Dynasties 3–6)
First Intermediate Period: 2134–2035 BCE (Dynasties 7–10)
Middle Kingdom: 2035–1640 BCE (Dynasties 11–12)
Second Intermediate Period: 1640–1570 BCE (Dynasties 13–17)
New Kingdom: 1570–1070 BCE (Dynasties 18–20)
Third Intermediate Period: 1070–664 BCE (Dynasties 21–26)
Late Period: 664–332 BCE (Dynasties 27–30)

signs. The Egyptians wrote on a kind of paper made of woven strips of papyrus reed that was much easier to use than the Sumerians' clay tablets, and which made it possible for Egyptian scribes to devise two cursive scripts (known as demotic and hieratic scripts) that made record keeping considerably easier. As a result, the written records of Egypt vastly exceed those of Mesopotamia in both number and variety, and the arid condition of the local environment enabled them to survive the long centuries more or less intact. For the first four dynasties, in fact, more of their writings survive than the buildings they lived in, for the latter were made of baked mud brick, which erodes rapidly even in Egypt's dry climate. They reserved expensive stone for the palaces and tombs of the wealthy and for the temples presided over by the influential priestly caste.

SOCIAL STRATA IN EGYPT

Society was strictly stratified, and social distinctions were expressed by dress codes. Most Egyptians worked the land. Slavery existed but was not as widespread as in Mesopotamia. Egypt's relative insulation from outsiders deprived it of the main source of slaves: prisoners of war. Besides, the pharaoh had an unquestioned right to force his subjects to join labor crews for public-works projects. Slightly above the farmers in social status were the simple artisans: brewers, weavers, stonemasons, bricklayers; even higher were the makers of luxury items for the elites: goldsmiths, jewelry makers, perfumers. A smaller corps of professionals stood above these: physicians, scribes, architects, priests, and civic officials. In theory, all Egyptians were equal under the law regardless of class or sex, and even the lowliest farmer could hope to petition the vizier for redress of a legal complaint; but that was theory, not reality.

Monogamous marriage was the norm for Egyptians, although it was not required by law, and men of all classes frequently took additional wives or concubines. Women, however, were subject to harsh legal punishment and social ostracism for engaging in sex outside of marriage to a single husband. Both sexes, though, could own property, enter contracts, and settle disputes in court.

The basic Egyptian diet consisted of varieties of grain—whether as bread, gruel, or beer—supplemented with a few vegetables (leeks, garlic, squash, and lettuce, especially), along with figs, dates, and fish. Meat was a rare treat for commoners, as was wine. Two other food practices date back to the Old Kingdom: the keeping of bee colonies, for honey and wax, and the netting of wild geese as they followed their own food trail along the river's edges.[11] June to September was the

---

[11]   The Egyptians learned early the trick of fattening the geese by feeding them large quantities of raw bread dough.

flooding season, October to February saw the growing of the grain fields, and March to May was the harvest. Given the brutal heat, most Egyptians wore little clothing. Children, in fact, generally went naked until they entered puberty, and it was common for men to shave and oil their entire bodies. Most peoples' homes, too, were designed to offset the heat: simple mud brick, often painted white, remained relatively cool throughout the day, and all cooking was done in small open-air patios. They covered their homes' packed-earth floors with reed mats. Egyptians followed a solar calendar but never developed the technological tools or scientific expertise of the Sumerians. Even wheeled vehicles did not appear until the New Kingdom, ca. 1500 BCE.

Ruler worship dominated Old Egyptian life—or at least it was the dominant characteristic of the regimes that produced the evidentiary record. The pharaoh was a living god, the source of justice and stability, the munificent owner of the whole of Egypt and its people, and the embodiment of the people's hopes and love. This official adoration was ubiquitous, endless, and drearily constant for nearly two thousand years. Officials who wanted to remain in the pharaoh's good graces had to adopt a fawning, obsequious tone that makes a modern reader squirm:

> To the great King, my Lord, the Sun-God from Heaven, thus I, Prince Zatatna of Acre, Your servant, the most humble servant of the Great King—indeed, the very dirt beneath Your feet, the ground upon which You tread—sends greeting. Seven times, O Great King, seven times, O Sun-God from Heaven, I fall, prostrate and helpless, at Your feet.

So began a typical piece of provincial administration. The unremitting glorification given to the pharaoh in the third and second millennia BCE, much of it on a colossal scale, would have brought an envious tear to the eye of many a 20th-century fascist dictator. The great pyramids and the monumental sculptures in the Valley of Kings tell only part of the tale. In the New Kingdom era the priests wrested power from the pharaoh and tried to govern independently. Consequently—or possibly not, depending on how one reads the evidence—Egyptian wealth and power diminished considerably. For now, though, statues of the pharaohs adorned every temple; inscriptions praising their magnificence appeared in every city; hymns in their honor rang out in every religious service.

From their palace at the capital city of Memphis, strategically and symbolically located at the point where the Delta joined the long river valley of Upper Egypt, the pharaohs controlled every aspect of public life through cults of personality backed up by armies of bureaucratic and military officials. Each nome was administered by a nomarch appointed by the king, and they all reported to a central official called a vizier. The nomarchs oversaw all public works projects, coordinated food distribution, heard appeals, and dispensed justice. Assisting all these was an army of scribes who kept census records, tallied tax revenues, noted expenditures, and issued the government's decrees. Members of the royal family held many of these posts.

Few states in Western history have experienced such completely centralized rule. Despite its invention and wide use of writing, however, Egypt never bothered to write down the laws of the land. Since the pharaoh, a living god, walked the earth, whatever he said at any moment was, in effect, the law. When he, in a carefully calculated moment, summoned the Nile to begin its annual rise, the river duly responded; the sun shone at his command; the earth produced its bounty because he willed it. And a ruler mighty enough to command the very Earth's obedience did not hesitate to demand the submission of its inhabitants. Slavery was thus regular but not widespread, for the common people were in fact expected to obey the pharaoh's every expressed whim without hesitation or complaint. The pharaoh was understood to be the god Horus. When he died he became an even greater deity by being absorbed into Osiris, an amalgam of all pharaohs merged into one, the ruler of the underworld where his absolutist authority never ended. Royal officials received estates from the pharaoh in return for their service, rather than salaries. The pharaohs likewise endowed mortuary cults and temples in order to promote the worship of themselves after their deaths on earth.

> Few states in Western history have experienced such completely centralized rule. Despite its invention and wide use of writing, however, Egypt never bothered to write down the laws of the land. Since the pharaoh, a living god, walked the earth, whatever he said at any moment was, in effect, the law.

It was an efficient way to govern, to be sure, and under benevolent rulers and judicious officials ancient Egypt enjoyed a material standard of living that vastly exceeded that of any contemporary society, until the end of the Old Kingdom (ca. 2100 BCE). By then, the pharaohs had alienated so much of their land that they began to have trouble meeting their vast administrative costs, prompting the nomarchs to challenge royal power for the first time and thereby inaugurating the First Intermediate Period. Old Kingdom glories should not be overstated, though. In the early centuries, contentment among the population often consisted simply of the absence of famine and the presence of peace, with little more to enrich daily life. By those standards pharaonic Egypt succeeded beyond expectations, but the achievement was nature's rather than the Egyptians'. Safe from foreign aggression because of the surrounding deserts, easily unified by the quiet-flowing Nile, and fed by the abundance of grain and fruit sprouting along its banks, Egypt had only not to disturb nature's rhythms in order to reap its rewards.

Accordingly, the supreme virtue of Egyptian culture was **ma'at**—a recognition of the world's ordering and a commitment not to upset it. Scholars commonly translate ma'at as "justice," which is too generous. Ma'at, in practice, was a kind of moral stasis, an acceptance of the world as it is, a reluctance to change anything for fear that the result might be worse than the reality already experienced. Early Egypt thus embodied a conservative principle that may be its most significant legacy to Western culture.

The contrast between it and the tumultuous but dynamic societies of Mesopotamia is striking. In Sumer, a messy congeries of cultures was in perennial conflict—challenging, experimenting, wondering, often failing, but always adapting to new circumstances and incessantly searching for meaning in the apparent jumble of it all. In archaic Egypt, the theocracy held power for two thousand years by feeding its subjects' stomachs while starving their minds by turning passivity into the supreme civic virtue.

THE KINGDOM OF THE DEAD

Old Kingdom Egypt lacked much of the variety and sophistication of the Middle and New periods; its life revolved obsessively, and monotonously, around the pharaoh. Even its religious life proved to be another aspect of pharaoh worship. Egyptian religion was a mix of local myths and traditions that defies easy description. Each nome revered a specific local deity, most of them animal-shaped, and a statue of whom stood in the local temple, and whose cults formed the center of village religious life. The temple statue was believed to be the god or goddess, not merely to represent him or her; individual homes often would have small statuettes to the deity in a corner, to whom the people offered small gifts of grain, oil, or wine at mealtimes.

A company of major deities ruled over the local gods, and probably served to create a sense of a shared culture among the peoples of Lower and Upper Egypt. One of these major gods, named Ptah, was credited with creating the world, but beyond this he played little role in Egyptian mythology. The most important deities by far were the incestuous brother and sister Osiris and Isis, whose love for each other set the whole cosmology in motion. Osiris became the first god-king of the earth that Ptah had created; but his brother Seth, jealous of Osiris's kingship and possibly of his relations with Isis, killed Osiris, chopped him up, and scattered bits of his body all the length of the Nile. Distraught, Isis searched out every piece and with the help of Anubis, the god of mummification, reassembled Osiris's body, bringing it miraculously back to life just long enough for Isis to enjoy one last sexual union with her brother, who promptly died again after completing the deed. But the job was done: Isis became pregnant and in time gave birth to the

A Section from a Book of the Dead Scroll   The scroll was prepared for—and possibly
even by—a royal scribe named Hunefer. Thebes, ca. 1275 BCE. The god Anubis brings Hunefer
(*far left*) into the judging chamber, watched over by Isis and Osiris (*far right*). In the middle
scene Hunefer's heart is weighed in the scales against the feather that symbolizes ma'at.
The weighing is successful, and Hunefer then approaches the enthroned Osiris to receive
his reward. Isis stands behind the throne. The Hunefer Scroll is among the best known of
surviving Book of the Dead texts. Since the outcome of the judgments was seldom in doubt,
it was not unusual or blasphemous for a well-placed scribe like Hunefer to prepare his own
scroll and depict his own salvation after death.

god Horus—who eventually grew to manhood, avenged his father by killing Seth,
and took over the rulership of the world. Every pharaoh was thus believed to be a
new incarnation of Horus, the god himself walking the earth. And upon his death
every pharaoh transformed into Osiris, who ruled over the realm of the dead for
eternity.

The Isis-Osiris myth remained central to Egyptian culture for thousands of
years, until it was supplanted by Christianity in the early centuries CE—which
was itself replaced by Islam in the 7th and 8th centuries CE. As a tale of resurrection, of life defeating death, it leaves something to be desired. Osiris, after all,
was revived only briefly. He came and he went. Nevertheless, his tale expressed
at least the notion of life's renewal, a cycle of generation, death, and regeneration that paralleled the rhythm of flood, planting, and harvest along the great
Nile's banks. Temples and statues to Isis and Osiris were erected all throughout
the kingdom and reminded people everywhere of the universality of the pharaoh's authority. In the afterworld Osiris judged the souls of the dead pharaohs
before admitting them to his realm—a realm that was remarkably similar to
life along the Nile. Not a better life but simply *more* life, which the Egyptians
seem to have regarded as blessing enough. Common people in the Old Kingdom
received vastly simpler burials, the arable land on the bank being too precious
to use for commoners' graves. Buried well away from the great pyramid valleys

and far from the Nile itself, they were assumed to move easily into the afterworld—where they continued to farm, mine, and manufacture, in service to the redeemed pharaohs forever.

Admission to the afterworld was not automatic for a pharaoh, yet neither was it tied closely to ethical behavior in his lifetime. Their religion held that the soul of the deceased wandered through a dim wasteland, beset by various demon-spirits, in search of the House of Judgment where Osiris, along with forty-two other judges, would decide whether or not the dead soul could enter. One could in theory remain lost in the wasteland for eternity, but the ancient Egyptians fortunately possessed a canon of helpful texts that led one to paradise. These incantations, magic spells, proclamations, and hymns were inscribed on the walls of the royal tombs—hence their collective name of Pyramid Texts. These texts guided the dead through the wasteland and provided sets of prayers and incantations that could be used against the demons. Moreover, they supplied the answers needed to satisfy the questions posed by Osiris and the other judges. With such scripted clues, the pharaoh's eternal reward was assured. After passing the examination, the dead ruler then made a final solemn declaration:

> I have not done evil to mankind.
> I have not oppressed the members of my family. . . .
> I have not brought forward my name for exaltation to honors.
> I have not ill-treated servants.
> I have not belittled a god.
> I have not defrauded the oppressed of their property.
> I have not done that which is an abomination to the gods. . . .
> I have made no man to suffer hunger.
> I have made no one to weep.
> I have done no murder.
> I have not given an order for murder to be done for me.
> I have not inflicted pain. . . .
> I have not committed fornication. . . .
> I have not encroached on the fields of others. . . .
> I have not cut into a canal of running water. . . .
> I have not obstructed a god in his procession
> *I am pure! I am pure! I am pure! I am pure!*

After which the god Anubis weighed the dead pharaoh's heart on a scale, and if the purified heart weighed no more than a feather, the soul was admitted to the eternal presence of Osiris.

Religion thus had little, perhaps nothing, to do with ethics. Whether one received reward or torment in Osiris's realm depended not on the quality of one's life but simply on whether or not the pharaoh received the proper send-off; hence the obscene expense on pyramids, tomb-temples, and burial gifts. The departed pharaoh's confession before Osiris lacks any positive spirit of morality; virtue consists of not performing evil rather than actively doing good. Just as ma'at did not equal justice, so too did the spiritual purity that entitled one to enter paradise imply nothing more than formulaic correctness. In the earliest centuries only members of the royal family could receive the supreme reward, but the privilege of salvation was extended to the nobles in the Middle Kingdom period, and to all Egyptians generally—although only in the New Kingdom many centuries later.

While it lacked the emotional complexity of Sumerian religion, Egyptian religion possessed an attractively hopeful belief in the unstoppable resilience of life. Death, while not exactly a thing to be yearned for, did not need to be feared. It represented only a rite of passage—not into an Eden but back to the shores of the Nile, where time would run as endlessly as the great river itself.

WHO, WHAT, WHERE

Bronze Age	ma'at
cuneiform	nomes
Fertile Crescent	patrilinear
hieroglyphs	ziggurats
lugal	

SUGGESTED READINGS

Primary Sources

The text of Ur-Ukagina's law code on pages 15–16 is adapted from Nels M. Bailkey and Richard Lim, *Readings in Ancient History: Thought and Experience from Gilgamesh to St. Augustine*, 6th ed. (Boston, 2002), p. 20. The Shamash Hymn is found in Bailkey and Lim, p. 22.

"The Poem of the Righteous Sufferer" is found in W. G. Lambert, *Babylonian Wisdom Literature* (Oxford, 1960), pp. 31–35. The Book of the Dead and The Pyramid Texts can be found in *Ancient Egyptian Literature* (Berkeley, 2006) by Miriam Lichtheim.

Anthologies

Bailkey, Nels, and Richard Lim, eds. *Readings in Ancient History: Thought and Experience from Gilgamesh to St. Augustine* (2002).

Bryce, Trevor. *Letters of the Great Kings of the Ancient Near East: The Royal Correspondence of the Late Bronze Age* (2003).

Foster, John L., trans. *Ancient Egyptian Literature: An Anthology* (2001).

Glassner, Jean-Jacques. *Mesopotamian Chronicles* (2004).

Lichtheim, Miriam. *Ancient Egyptian Literature: A Book of Readings* (2006).

Vanstiphout, Herman. *Epics of the Sumerian Kings: The Matter of Aratta* (2004).

Studies

Anthony, David W. *The Horse, the Wheel, and Language: How Bronze-Age Riders from the Eurasian Steppes Shaped the Modern World* (2010).

Aruz, Joan. *Art of the First Cities: The Third Millennium BC from the Mediterranean to the Indus* (2003).

Assmann, Jan. *The Mind of Egypt: History and Meaning in the Time of the Pharaohs* (2003).

———. *The Search for God in Ancient Egypt* (2001).

Bottéro, Jean. *Everyday Life in Ancient Mesopotamia* (2001).

———. *Religion in Ancient Mesopotamia* (2004).

Brewer, Douglas J., and Emily Teeter. *Egypt and the Egyptians* (2007).

Charvát, Petr. *Mesopotamia before History* (2002).

Crawford, Harriet. *Sumer and Sumerians* (2004).

Foster, Benjamin R., and Karen Polinger Foster. *Civilizations of Ancient Iraq* (2010).

Glassner, Jean-Jacques. *The Invention of Cuneiform: Writing in Sumer* (2003).

Harris, David R. *Origins of Agriculture in West Central Asia: An Environmental-Archaeological Study* (2010).

Hodder, Ian. *The Leopard's Tale: Revealing the Mysteries of Çatalhöyük* (2006).

Kemp, Barry J. *Ancient Egypt: Anatomy of a Civilization* (2006).

Leick, Gwendolyn. *Mesopotamia: The Invention of the City* (2003).

———. *Sex and Eroticism in Mesopotamian Literature* (2003).

Liverani, Mario. *Uruk: The First City* (2006).

Robins, Gay. *The Art of Ancient Egypt* (2008).

Silverman, David P., ed. *Ancient Egypt* (2003).

For additional resources, including maps, primary sources, visuals, web links, and quizzes, please go to **www.oup.com/us/backman**.

CHAPTER 2

Law Givers, Evil Emperors, and Dangerous Gods

2100 BCE–486 BCE

NEAR EAST AND EASTERN MEDITERRANEAN

The second millennium BCE can hardly be topped for drama. Droughts, famines, civil wars, foreign invasions, frightful new weapons, and brutal empires—all these characterized the age and marked its major turning points. Four empires dominated the era: Egypt's Middle and New Kingdoms, the Babylonian (and later Persian) Empire in southern Mesopotamia, the Assyrian Empire of northern Mesopotamia, and the Hittite Empire in Asia Minor. Between these powerful kingdoms lay a sprawl of smaller states along the eastern Mediterranean coastline and skirting the southern edges of the Anatolian mountains. Once established, this patchwork of big and small states lived in relative harmony, in a dense web of commercial, cultural, and diplomatic connections that inspired some remarkable advances in each society.

Around 1200 BCE, however, newcomers appeared—outsiders loosely related by their dialects of a new language family known as Indo-European. Their waves of invasion set off a chain reaction of political collapse and economic ruin that wiped out nearly every state in the Near East. It left the peoples adrift and unsure, vulnerable to new regimes, and exposed to new ideas about human fate, man's relationship with the divine, the purpose of government, and the essence of morality. By 1000 BCE, or thereabouts, Western history had taken on a radical realignment that would have been unthinkable only two hundred years earlier. This realignment led to the birth of Western culture's first two great religions, Judaism and Zoroastrianism.

◀ **Imperial Warrior** A Persian archer, part of a procession, in glazed brick. From the palace of Darius the Great in Susa (550–486 BCE). These elite soldiers served as the king's personal bodyguards.

Moreover, the interaction of the Indo-European groups and the primarily Semitic

- Old Babylon
- Middle Kingdom Egypt
- The New Kingdom Empire
- The Indo-European Assault
- The Age of Iron Begins, ca. 1200 BCE
- Persia and the Religion of Fire

CHAPTER OUTLINE

peoples of the Fertile Crescent opened the way for the development of the **Greater West**—a world that bridged Europe and western Asia. This Greater West was composed not of a single hybrid culture but rather of the sense of a shared destiny in a large matrix of individual cultures. Europe and the Middle East have remained bound into and with one another ever since, by bonds of trade, intellectual cross-fertilization, cultural overlap, and religious rivalry.

OLD BABYLON

The city of Babylon was founded around 1950 BCE by the Semitic-speaking Amorites, who seized control of Sumer soon after the turn of the second millennium. Its location at the nexus of several trade routes through the northern Mesopotamian plain made it a strategic base for extending power out of Sumer itself and northward toward Syria, from which the Amorites themselves had come. The most famous of the early Babylonian rulers was Hammurabi (r. 1792–1750 BCE), the first great lawgiver and liar in Western history. A large archive of his diplomatic records survive, which document his crafty rise to power. At the start of his reign Babylon was simply one among many Amorite kingdoms and was by no means the largest or strongest. Unable or unwilling to challenge his neighbors on the battlefield, he instead managed to persuade all of them of the existence of numerous conspiracies against their crowns. He passed endless false rumors, usually of his own making and reiterated in person by his many ambassadors. They warned each city-state of a plot supposedly being hatched in another. Believing the lies, the other Amorite kings continually attacked one another for nearly twenty years and exhausted themselves in the process. Hammurabi then went on the offensive and in less than a decade conquered them all. He emerged as the sole ruler of virtually the entire Tigris-Euphrates region; thus was built the great Babylonian Empire (see Map 2.1).

Shortly thereafter, he issued a set of laws known as the Code of Hammurabi, texts of which presumably were distributed throughout the empire. He likewise

CHAPTER TIMELINE

2035–1640 BCE
Middle Kingdom
Egypt

ca. 1950 BCE
Amorites seize
control of Sumer

ca. 1640–1570 BCE
Hyksos ascendancy
in Egypt

ca. 2000 BCE
Beginning of
Indo-European migrations

1792–1750 BCE
Reign of
Hammurabi

1570–1070 BCE
New Kingdom
Egypt

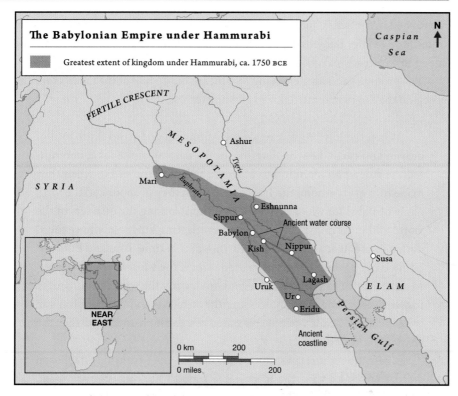

The Babylonian Empire under Hammurabi

Greatest extent of kingdom under Hammurabi, ca. 1750 BCE

Caspian Sea

FERTILE CRESCENT

MESOPOTAMIA

Ashur

Tigris

SYRIA

Mari

Euphrates

Eshnunna

Sippur

Ancient water course

Babylon

Kish   Nippur

Susa

Uruk   Lagash

Ur

Eridu

ELAM

Persian Gulf

NEAR EAST

Ancient coastline

0 km   200

0 miles   200

MAP 2.1   The Babylonian Empire under Hammurabi

had the entire Code engraved upon an eight-foot column of basalt, as a permanent record of his greatness as a ruler. As propaganda, the Code could hardly have been more successful, since scholars have credited Hammurabi as the first great lawgiver in Western history ever since. Ironically, though, the Code is not in fact a true law code: it contains only 282 clauses, addressing issues like property rights, water rights, marriage, violent crime, and wage regulations. It neglects to mention many equally vital aspects of Babylonian life, such as the commercial marketplace that formed the lifeblood of the economy. More significantly, the Code is never

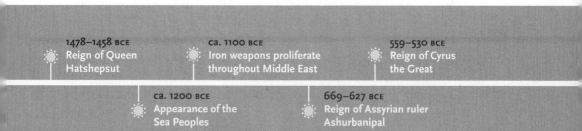

1478–1458 BCE
Reign of Queen Hatshepsut

ca. 1100 BCE
Iron weapons proliferate throughout Middle East

559–530 BCE
Reign of Cyrus the Great

ca. 1200 BCE
Appearance of the Sea Peoples

669–627 BCE
Reign of Assyrian ruler Ashurbanipal

mentioned in the actual judicial records that survive from Hammurabi's reign or from those of later Babylonian kings. Its statutes may simply represent new laws added to an already-existing body of legislation.[1]

The prologue and long epilogue together make up half of the Code's text and proclaim the king's magnificence in glowing terms:

> When the lofty Anu, king of the Anunnaki gods, and Enlil, lord of heaven and earth, he who determines the destiny of the land, committed the rule of all mankind to Marduk, the chief son of Ea; when they made him great among the Igigi gods; when they pronounced the lofty name of Babylon; when they made it famous among the quarters of the world and in its midst established an everlasting kingdom whose foundations were firm as heaven and earth—at that time, Anu and Enlil appointed me, Hammurabi, the exalted prince, the worshiper of the gods, to cause justice to prevail in the land, to destroy the wicked and evil, to prevent the strong from oppressing the weak, to go forth like the sun over the black-headed people, to enlighten the land and to further the welfare of the people. . . .
>
> These are the just laws which Hammurabi, the wise king, established and by which he gave the land stable support and good government. Hammurabi, the perfect king, am I. . . . The great gods called me, and I am the guardian shepherd whose scepter is just and whose beneficent shadow is spread over my city. In my bosom I carried the people of the land of Sumer and Addad; under my protection they prospered; I governed them in peace; in my wisdom I sheltered them. . . . The king who is pre-eminent among kings am I. My words are precious, my wisdom is unrivaled. By the command of Shamash, the great judge of heaven and earth, I make justice to shine forth on the land. By the order of Marduk, my lord, no one may scorn my statutes, and my name shall be remembered with favor in Esagila forever. . . . In the days that are yet to come, for all future time, may the king who is in the land observe the words of justice which I have written upon my monument! May he not alter the judgments of the land which I have pronounced, or the decisions of the country which I have rendered! May he not scorn my statutes! If that man have wisdom, if he wish to give his land good government, let him give attention to the words which I have written upon my monument! And may this monument enlighten him as to procedure and administration, the judgments which

---

[1]   Could Hammurabi have created the Code primarily as a monument to himself?

I have pronounced, and the decisions I have rendered for the land! And let him rightly rule his black-headed people; let him pronounce judgments for them and render for them decisions! Let him root out the wicked and the evil from his land! Let him promote the welfare of his people! Hammurabi, the king of justice, to whom Shamash has committed truth, am I. My words are weighty; my deeds are unrivalled; only to the fool are they vain; to the wise they are worthy of every praise.

The actual statutes of the Code seem an afterthought in comparison.

Despite its cultic bluster, the Code tells us much about how Babylonian society differed from the Sumerian one it supplanted; in fact, the bluster itself tells much of the tale. As we saw in chapter 1, the Sumerian chief military executive (or lugal), assisted by scribes and priests, had supervised a battery of local officials—with a complex web of traders, craftsmen, and farmers. The Babylonians replaced this norm with a top-heavy and decidedly heavy-handed plutocracy. Hammurabi's conquests had resulted in the monopolization of wealth by his royal court and armed supporters. Vast estates and commercial concerns controlled by the Babylonian elites took the place of the more diverse economy of the Sumerians. Most of Babylonia's inhabitants remained legally free but were nevertheless land tenants or commercial dependents of the nobles who dominated the palaces and temples. The Babylonians also expanded the use of slave labor on their estates and began to buy and sell slaves on the international market.

Social stratification was more rigid as well, and the penalties for offenses against one's superiors were severe. Women of all classes, except for slaves, had the right to divorce abusive husbands and to receive financial support from husbands who divorced them without good cause. Capital punishment was meted out unhesitatingly for any number

Propaganda Device   The top portion of the stele on which is inscribed the Law Code of Hammurabi, ca. 1700 BCE.

of crimes—murder, assault, rape, theft, and adultery (applicable to women only) were the most common—but the means varied according to sex: men were killed by the blade, women by drowning.

Hammurabi also introduced a form of religious imperialism that both paralleled and legitimated his political oppression. The worship of Marduk, the patron god of the city of Babylon, became required throughout the empire; Hammurabi's subjects could continue to worship their old gods only if they accepted Marduk as the supreme Babylonian deity. Interpreting his military conquests as the worldly enactment of Marduk's spiritual victory over all other gods and goddesses, Hammurabi stands at the beginning of a long Western tradition of justifying warfare as a religious duty. If the Divine Authority demands that His followers engage in warfare—and indeed if He in some sense needs them to do it in order to fulfill His own cosmic aims—then what else can pious followers do? Such warfare is not only morally justifiable, because divinely sanctioned, but is in fact an act of religious devotion itself.

> Interpreting his military conquests as the worldly enactment of Marduk's spiritual victory over all other gods and goddesses, Hammurabi stands at the beginning of a long Western tradition of justifying warfare as a religious duty.

It is striking how frequently religious warfare, like Hammurabi's conquests, occurs throughout Greater Western history. We shall see it again and again in later chapters: the milhemet mitzvah ("war of religious obligation") that inspired the Hebrews to seize their Promised Land from the Canaanites, Philistines, and Amalikites; the jihad-stoked conquests of the medieval Muslims and the Crusades of medieval Christians; the Wars of Religion of 16th-17th century Europe; the efforts to tame the "Godless heathen" of the New World or "to bring Christianity to the savages" of Africa in the 18th and 19th centuries; the fight for "God and country" in World War I; and the struggle against "Godless communism" in the second half of the 20th century. In each case, when it comes to war and religion, each justifies and inspires the other. Western culture is not unique in this regard, of course, and wars without an explicitly religious motive have been equally numerous, but religiously based conflict is a notably recurring element in Western history. Hammurabi is our first religious zealot, and the society he created, though it lasted only two centuries after his death, left a bitter legacy of lies, greed, and smug brutality. Few people mourned the passing of the Old Babylonian Empire.

It did produce a literary masterpiece, however. An anonymous Babylonian scribe gathered a number of folktales about the semimythical Sumerian king Gilgamesh—ruler of Uruk some eight hundred years before the Babylonian conquest—and wove them together into an epic of remarkable sophistication. The *Epic of Gilgamesh* relates the adventures of a powerful but egotistical king whose arrogance leads him to offend the gods. Unexpectedly, the gods' subsequent plot to kill him fails when Gilgamesh tames the savage half-man half-beast Enkidu, whom they had sent to destroy him, and the two become friends and pursue a series of heroic adventures. When the gods strike again by slaying his beloved new friend, Gilgamesh is filled with panic at the inevitability of death. He spends the rest of the epic on a doomed quest for enlightenment and the secret to eternal life.

The poem notably credits women for their civilizing influence on men. Enkidu, for example, is tamed by an encounter with a temple priestess:

> The lass beheld him, the savage man,
> The barbarous fellow from the depths of the steppe....
> [She] freed her breasts, bared her bosom,
> and he possessed her ripeness.
> She was not bashful as she welcomed his ardor.

They spend six days and seven nights in nonstop passion; then Enkidu undergoes a transformation that estranges him from the other animals of the steppe:

> After he had had his fill of her charms,
> He set his face toward his wild beasts.
> On seeing him, the gazelles ran off,
> The wild beasts of the steppe drew away from [him]....
> His [legs] became motionless.... Things were not as they were before.
> Now he had wisdom, broader understanding.
> Returning he sat at the feet of the harlot.... She says to him,
> "Thou art wise now, Enkidu; thou art become like a god."

Gilgamesh himself, seeking to drown his sorrows after Enkidu's death, receives some sensible advice from a kindly barmaid who is actually the grain goddess Sippur in human form:

> Gilgamesh, ... the life thou pursueth, thou shalt not find.
> When the gods created mankind,
> Death for mankind they set aside,
> Life in their own hands retaining.
> Thou, Gilgamesh, let full be thy belly,
> Make thou merry by day and by night.
> Of each day make thou a feast of rejoicing,
> Day and night dance thou and play!

Let thy garments be sparkling fresh,
Thy head be washed; bathe thou in water.
Pay heed to the little one that holds on to thy hand,
Let thy spouse delight in thy bosom!
For this is the task of mankind!

Gilgamesh, however, obsessively continues his quest and learns of a magic plant growing on the floor of the sea. Whoever pulls the plant from its root and eats it will in fact gain eternal life. Eventually Gilgamesh locates the plant by tying heavy stones to his feet and walking the ocean floor. When he arrives back on shore and is about to eat the plant, however, a giant serpent emerges from the sea, snatches the plant from his hand, and pulls it back to the depths. Gilgamesh is left alone and hopeless on the shore, doomed to the death he could not avoid.

The poem depicts old Sumerian culture but was written down, in the full version in which it survives, in Babylonian times and in the Babylonian tongue. Little seems added to the original Sumerian folktales. The Babylonian compiler merely changed the names of several of the characters and of the gods into Babylonian ones. Thus the figure who tells Gilgamesh about the Plant of Life is named Ziusudra in the Sumerian fragments that survive but is called Utnapishtim, a Babylonian name, in the full compiled version. Was the compiler merely trying to make the text more appealing to a Babylonian audience?[2]

A more subversive aim is possible too: perhaps the poet or compiler hoped the epic could inspire the Babylonians to strive after something more than the wealth and power they hoarded so single-mindedly. Gilgamesh at the beginning of the poem is arrogant, self-centered, and boastful. He sounds more than a bit like Hammurabi in the bombastic claims of the Code. At the end he is broken, fearful, and sad beyond expression, but he has grown into spiritual maturity. He has become deserving of pity and even forgiveness.

MIDDLE KINGDOM EGYPT

The erosion of royal authority, beginning in the Fifth Dynasty of the Old Kingdom, brought about the First Intermediate Period in Egypt (2135–2034 BCE). In this relatively brief but turbulent period, the local nomarchs usurped royal power, plundered farmers' property, and engaged in widespread lawlessness. Mentuhotep II, the first pharaoh of the Eleventh Dynasty, however, was able to subdue the nomarchs and restore central authority from Thebes. It was the start of several

---

2   Was the compiler of *Gilgamesh* trying to depict Babylonians as something more than greedy, venal, boorish oppressors?

periods of empire, including reigns of the most active and powerful pharaohs and the origins of a new religious tradition, monotheism.

Mentuhotep II's reign ushered in the Middle Kingdom (2035–1640). Thebes lay in Upper Egypt, roughly three hundred miles south of the traditional capital at Memphis. Moving the capital there allowed for closer oversight of the nomarchs. It also provided a base for launching new military expeditions southward, up the great river, into Nubia, in order to secure control of the strategic cataracts and to acquire the vast stone quarries and gold deposits found there.

With restored fortunes, the pharaohs of the Middle Kingdom were able to renew public building programs—such as land reclamation in the delta and the extension of irrigation networks and reservoirs along the river. They could even pursue military expansion beyond Egypt's natural borders, into Sinai and along the Syrian coast. These projects required more laborers than the local population could provide, however, which led the pharaohs to recruit groups of foreigners (hyksos in Egyptian) to work in the mines and fields. As the number of foreigners grew, especially in the delta, where they were concentrated, and as resistance to their presence grew among the native population, tension arose. This tension eventually resulted in an overthrow of the government by the foreigners, an uprising that inaugurated the Second Intermediate Period (1640–1570 BCE), which is sometimes referred to as the **Hyksos ascendancy**.

Egyptian religion continued to be a myriad of local cults rather than a single organized faith. The cults remained *henotheistic*: while they recognized the existence of other deities, each locale proclaimed allegiance to a particular god or goddess as their special protector. In the case of the pharaoh's court, new prominence was won by Amon-Ra, the patron deity of the city of Thebes. The most significant development in religion, however, was the extension of salvation (that is, entry to the House of Judgment) to the nomarchs, other nobles, and wealthy commoners. The heavenly reward was no longer a monopoly of the pharaohs. The cause of this development is unknown, but the means of it is clear: the contents of the Pyramid Texts began to circulate among the well-to-do. They were also inscribed onto papyrus books, or coffin texts, placed alongside the bodies in their tombs.

By the end of this period, the various coffin texts had been consolidated into the **Book of the Dead**, the only full-length text of any sort that Egypt contributed to Western literature until the 19th century. This book, when placed in a casket, theoretically opened the gates of paradise, such as it was, to anyone who died with it in his or her possession. The Book of the Dead, though, is not a work of literary art; it is an anthology of incantations, magical spells, boilerplate praise poems, and cribbed solutions to the riddles put to one by Osiris at the entrance to the House of Judgment. Although of great historical interest, these writings are negligible as poetry or prose musings. Ma'at, acceptance of the world's right ordering, remains the dominant

Middle Kingdom

Voyage to the Next World   This wonderfully preserved wooden coffin held the remains of a Middle Kingdom priest named Nekhtankh. The hieroglyphs invoke the gods Osiris, Isis, Nephthys, and others to provide Nekhtankh with all the food and comforts he will need in the afterlife. The vivid eyes represent the priest's soul looking expectantly to the voyage into the next world.

focus and the supreme virtue. To the extent that Osiris and his council truly judged anyone's ethical behavior in life, they did so according to the dead soul's record of sustaining ma'at, which in most cases meant not performing injustice.

The Middle Kingdom did produce an exceptionally large body of writing—mythological stories, folktales, handbooks of practical advice, medical regimens, travelogues, some earnest love poetry, personal letters, and professional treatises (on being a successful merchant, civil administrator, estate manager, or whatever). Few of them interest anyone other than specialists, however. The mix suggests that the intellectual tenor of the age was above all else pragmatic and hardworking—no nonsense about theoretical or abstract notions, no deep introspection, no intellectual playfulness or even curiosity. Egypt never produced anything remotely like the *Epic of Gilgamesh* or the works of the ancient Hebrew psalmists and prophets. It never matched the philosophers, tragedians, or epic and lyric poets of ancient Greece. The popular father-to-son advice handbooks—usually called "Instructions"—display a genuine if somewhat formulaic concern for ethical behavior. They urge the recipient to work hard at his trade, to obey his

superiors, and to cultivate a modest demeanor; they praise charitable acts and denounce corruption and exploitation of the poor.[3] Should one fall short of the moral standard, the Book of the Dead was there to help.

The Instructions left behind by several Middle Kingdom pharaohs have an altogether different tenor, one that reflects the less elevated general position they held in comparison to their godlike Old Kingdom predecessors. In his Instruction to his son, Amenemhet I, for example, urges "hold yourself apart from those subordinate to you . . . and be on guard even when you are asleep." Trust no one, neither family nor friend, and be especially watchful of the treacherous nomarchs, he warns. The advice, in this case, was sound: Amenemhet left his Instruction unfinished, and a later scribe completed it with a wry note that the great king had been assassinated by one of the officials in the royal court before he could finish the memo.

Middle Egypt's great arts were architecture and sculpture—practical arts both, since most of the works produced served the purpose of promoting or

---

[3]   The Instructions were not intended for general audiences, which may account for their vaguely memo-like quality.

Ushabti   Funerary figures who accompanied the new dead on their journey were called *ushabtis*. They were the servants of the dead, charged with providing food and water, performing physical labor, and in some cases providing sexual amusement. The hieroglyphs found most frequently on ushabtis quote a passage from the sixth chapter of the Book of the Dead: "Hail, ushabti! If [the deceased] be decreed to do any work in the afterlife, let every task that stands in his way be removed—whether plowing fields, tending the water channels, or carrying sand."

extending the might of the pharaoh. Painting and sculpture followed stylistic and iconographic norms that dated to the Old Kingdom with simple lines, flat surfaces, and a modest palette of colors. Funerary figurines made of clay or wood were exceedingly common. Though simple in design, these figures (called **ushabti**, or "those who respond") represented the servants who continued to work for one in the afterlife. Science and technology mattered little, since Egypt's technological needs were simple and were amply met by the might of the river and the availability of the virtual slave labor of the masses. Mathematical knowledge was not widespread. Government officials probably understood and used all four computational operations—addition, subtraction, multiplication, and division. They employed fractions to a limited extent and were able to estimate the area of a circle by measuring the diameter, subtracting one-ninth of its value, and squaring the result. (Since the area of a circle is in fact πr^2, they in effect approximated p to about 3.16.)[4] Egypt also did not develop wheeled vehicles until the New Kingdom and relied on oxen and donkeys (for plowing and carting, respectively) long after the Babylonians had already domesticated horses for farming and for pulling wheeled chariots.

---

[4]   Only a handful of engineers could handle simple geometry or algebra.

The modest stability of the Middle Kingdom collapsed quickly when the Semitic-speaking foreigners admitted to the realm suddenly rose in revolt and took control of most of the delta region around 1700 BCE. The precise identity of this group is still debated, and Egyptian sources refer to them only as the Hyksos ("foreigners"). Whoever they were, they were aided by the arrival of thousands of their countrymen who had raced across Sinai on light, horse-drawn chariots. Armed with simple bows, long lances, and swords made of bronze, the Hyksos quickly seized control of the Nile delta and forced the rulers in far-southern Thebes to recognize their overlordship. The Hyksos style of warfare unnerved the Egyptians, who used neither cavalry nor archers (since trees to make bows were relatively rare) and had traditionally relied on swarms of infantrymen armed with copper-tipped spears and stone-headed clubs.

For seventy years, from 1640 to 1570 BCE, the Hyksos dominated Egypt while building extensive commercial and diplomatic links with Palestine, Syria, and the islands of the Aegean Sea. During that time the Nubians to the far south broke away from the rulers in Thebes and established an independent kingdom called Kush. The Theban rulers thus found themselves trapped between foreigners at each end of the Nile, but they capitalized on the direness of the situation by inspiring their soldiers to pursue the noble cause of national liberation—which they promptly did, after quickly studying the new techniques of war. With their modernized army, they drove the Hyksos from Egypt around 1570 BCE and pursued them all the way to Palestine, a campaign that inaugurated Egypt's golden age—that of the New Kingdom (1570–1070 BCE).

THE NEW KINGDOM EMPIRE

The embarrassment of the Hyksos conquest proved to the Egyptians that the defense provided by their surrounding deserts no longer sufficed. Realizing that Egypt's relative isolation was at an end, the pharaohs of the New Kingdom decided to seize the initiative by extending their might to other lands. They subdued the Nubians to the south, which guaranteed Egypt's access to the gold mines of the region—a necessity now that gold had been established as the international standard for commerce throughout the Near East. From this vantage point they opened new trade routes down the western shores of the Red Sea and as far away as present day Sudan and Somalia (see Map 2.2).

Militarily, the reinvigorated army—now led on the battlefield by the pharaoh himself—conquered all of Palestine and advanced into Syria as far north

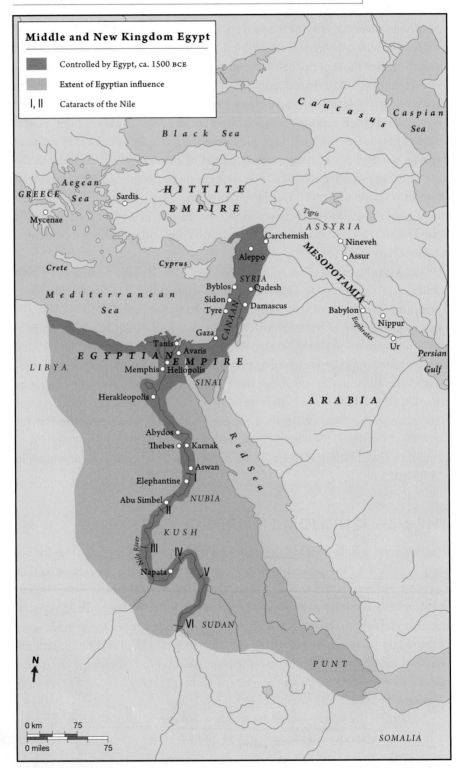

MAP 2.2 Middle and New Kingdom Egypt

as the city of Aleppo. The most aggressive of the new Eighteenth Dynasty rulers was Thutmose I (r. 1504–1492 BCE), who was also the first pharaoh to be entombed in the new necropolis of the Valley of the Kings. Thutmose led his army into Syria until he reached the banks of the upper Euphrates, where he erected a victory plaque and proclaimed himself the greatest of Egypt's rulers. He had "surpassed the achievements of all the kings who lived before me. . . . The gods have delighted in my reign, and their temples have been filled with celebration. . . . I have pushed the boundaries of Egypt as far as the sun shines, . . . and I have made her triumphant over every land." His victories consisted more of looting raids than true conquests; nevertheless, his reign marked Egypt's transition into a fully militarized society in which army officers replaced civil officials as the backbone of the administration. Booty and tribute poured into the royal coffers, as did the gold from the recaptured Nubian mines, and the increased wealth allowed him to construct scores of luxurious palaces for the high military caste and a network of new temples to gods both old and new. The god of military victory, named Amen, predictably rose in religious prominence during this period. His main temple at Karnak, just across the river from Thebes, received a series of massive additions and embellishments until it became a vast complex of halls, temples, administrative buildings, and storehouses, making it by far the largest religious compound in the ancient world.

Valley of the Kings   Though grander than most, the temple complex of Queen Hatshepsut is characteristic of the Middle Kingdom period.Instead of remote pyramids, notable Egyptians constructed elaborate malls with administrative offices, altar rooms, libraries, treasuries, and living quarters.

The reign of Queen Hatshepsut (r. 1478–1458 BCE) was notable for its prosperity and peace, but is best remembered for the spectacular mortuary temple she
had constructed at Deir el-Bahri—a series of terraced gardens and broad colon-
nades carved into the high cliffs of the river valley. All the pharaohs of the New
Kingdom after Thutmose I chose to be buried in this Valley of the Kings. The
burial sites were separate from the mortuary temples themselves. They hoped
that this manner of entombment—in deep caves whose entrances were then
concealed—would foil grave robbers.

The royal family practiced traditional brother-sister marriage, the idea behind
it being that only the daughter of a pharaoh was sufficiently exalted to be the
queen of another pharaoh. These marriages were usually but not always asexual.
Every pharaoh, however, had dozens if not hundreds of wives in his harem, by
whom he produced his heirs. Hatshepsut was the daughter of Thutmose I, the
queen of Thutmose II (r. 1492–1478), and the bane of her stepson Thutmose III
(r. 1458–1425). He was thus the half sister of Thutmose II and the stepmother of
Thutmose III.[5]

Although Thutmose III officially began his reign upon his father's death in
1478, he was a child and lived for twenty tense years under the firm control of
his stepmother. Once he took control for himself, he ordered his stonemasons to
deface Hatshepsut's images and erase her name from all monuments. He dedicated his reign to extending Egypt's might even further into Palestine and Syria,
personally leading as many as sixteen campaigns. He left a network of client kings
to do the actual work of governing the empire, taking their sons with him back
to Thebes in order to be indoctrinated in Egyptian law and custom. In this way,
when these children grew to maturity, they could govern their lands in an increasingly Egyptian context. Diplomatic marriages between the daughters of the client
kings and the Egyptian royal sons were also common; but no Egyptian princess
was ever wedded to a foreign king.

The goal of "Egyptifying" the broader Near East had less to do with aiding
the development of civilization than with simply bringing more people, whether
slave or free, into the service of the pharaoh. If Egypt could no longer retain its
splendid isolation, then the rest of the world should at least recognize the need
to sustain the ma'at that only passive acceptance of pharaonic rule could effect.
Driving the point home were the huge reliefs of Egyptian armies and their victorious generals that bedecked palace and temple walls everywhere they went. Additions to the temple complexes at Karnak and Luxor further attest to the grandeur
of imperial Egypt at its height.

---

[5]   Egyptian law allowed for a woman to rule in her own right, although the occurrence was rare enough that
royal monuments portrayed her with a fake beard.

The reigns of Amenhotep III (r. 1390–1352 BCE) and his son Amenhotep IV (r. 1352–1338 BCE) mark both the pinnacle of the New Kingdom and the point at which it began a downturn. The priests who presided over the temples now controlled roughly a quarter of the empire's land. Concerned about their growing power—especially about the priests at Karnak, home of the sun god Amon-Ra—Amenhotep IV instituted a radical change: renaming himself Akhenaten, he elevated a minor solar deity called Aten to supreme status among the gods. Egyptian mythology in fact maintained separate cults for different phases and aspects of the sun. The god of the sunrise was different from the god of the sun at noontime, for example, and the god of sunset was yet another distinct entity. Amon-Ra was thought of principally as the heat energy of the sun.[6] Akhenaten closed the temples to Amon-Ra, violently suppressed their cults, and promoted Aten as the sole true and universal deity.[7] (He even had Amon-Ra's name chiseled out of royal inscriptions.) He hoped to forestall popular reaction by emphasizing that it was the royal family's obligation to worship Aten, while the obligation of the Egyptian people was to continue worshipping the pharaoh as always.[8] He abandoned the palace at Thebes and erected a new capital some three hundred miles to the north at a place called Akhetaten, now known as el-Amarna.

The belief in a single, supreme deity—or **monotheism**—was a novelty, and it did not go over easily with the people. They still craved the consolation of their all but certain eternal blessedness in the old faith. Akhenaten and Nefertiti, though, while undoubtedly motivated in part by a desire to break the power of the priests, were genuine enthusiasts for the new religion. Tradition credits the pharaoh with composing the heartfelt Hymn to Aten:

> Thou appearest beautifully on the horizon of heaven,
> Thou living Aten, the beginning of life!
> When thou art arisen on the eastern horizon,
> Thou hast filled every land with thy beauty.

Whatever its limitations as poetry, it conveys genuine passion, a devotion quite unlike the tired formulaic chants of the Book of the Dead.

---

[6]   The new god Aten was originally the physical sphere comprising the sun. Under Akhnaten's imposed monotheism, though, Aten incorporated all the many aspects of the sun.

[7]   The pharoah's new name meant, literally, "the one dedicated to Aten."

[8]   Akhenaten's queen was Nefertiti, the famous beauty.

Family Hour at the Pharaoh's   Bas relief, ca. 1350 BCE, portraying Akhenaten and Nefertiti along with three of their six daughters. Akhenaten is best remembered for his effort to replace traditional Egyptian religion with a new cult devoted to a single god called Aten. In this scene, the royal family offers prayers to this sun deity. The image continues a little-understood artistic tradition that portrays Akhenaten in androgynous fashion. Note that his body is more curvy than that of his queen, a famous beauty.

Akhenaten's plans went awry, however, for he underestimated both the popularity of Amon-Ra and the priests' determination to hold onto their lofty position. Akhenaten gradually became something of a religious recluse, isolated at el-Amarna and ignoring the needs of the empire. His successors on the throne—Tutankhamen, Ay, and Horemheb—quickly suppressed the new cult and restored the old faith. Eventually, a new pharaoh arose from the ranks of the military and restored the empire's fortunes. Ramses II (r. 1279–1212 BCE), Egypt's only ruler known as "the Great," repulsed the Hittite advance on the Syrian territories and built temples, palaces, and statues on a colossal scale. Perhaps one-half of all the Egyptian monuments that survive today belong to Ramses II's reign.[9] Tradition associates him with the evil pharaoh in the story of the Biblical book of Exodus, but Hebrew enslavement in Egypt and a subsequent release under the messianic leadership of Moses is not supported by any surviving Egyptian documentary or archeological evidence. Nevertheless, the reign of Ramses II was a last gasp of glory before Egypt once again fell to outsiders. Peoples from far away swept through the Aegean Sea, over Egypt, and rampaged through the rest of the Near East around 1200 BCE.

THE INDO-EUROPEAN ASSAULT

The newcomers were a motley crew, related to one another by language: each spoke one of a family of languages known today as **Indo-European**. In 1786 an Englishman named Sir William Jones (1746–1794), then serving as a judge in colonial India, delivered a paper to the Asiatic Society in which he observed that

---

[9]   Statues and temple-pillars were not the only erections of Ramses II. He reportedly fathered nearly two hundred children by his various wives and concubines.

Great Temple of Ramses II   Ramses ordered the construction of this massive temple to hold his remains, ca. 1250 BCE. The colossal statues on the façade are all representations of Ramses himself (whom no one ever accused of subtlety). Statues and paintings of the pharaoh, often showing him receiving the worship of various gods and goddesses, are situated throughout the temple.

ancient Sanskrit (the ancestor from which the major languages spoken in northern India are derived) shared an exceptional number of word roots and grammatical forms with ancient European tongues like Greek, Latin, Gothic, and the Celtic languages; from this he argued that they must therefore be related. This common ancestor soon came to be called Proto-Indo-European and is now believed to have originated somewhere north of the Black Sea.[10] The idea had been put forth in a more general way a hundred years earlier by a Dutch philologist, but Jones (who spoke thirteen languages fluently and could read another fifteen) produced enough data to make the theory rightly his own.

The Indo-European peoples, an extremely numerous horde of nomadic shepherding nations, began to radiate from their homeland near the Black Sea as early as 2000 BCE. Several groups moved into western Europe, the forerunners of the Celts and the Goths. One strain migrated into the Aegean Sea, where they established the base for what was to become the Greek-speaking world. Many other groups—most notably the Hittites and the Mitanni—settled throughout Asia Minor and the Iranian plain.

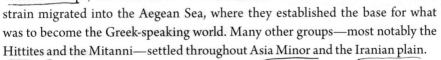

---

10   Proto-Indo-European is the source from which sprang the family of languages from Ireland to India.

The **Hittites** initially settled in north-central Anatolia in a sprawl of small states, but by 1700 BCE they had united into a single kingdom (see Map 2.3). From the time they appeared on the scene, they were an aggressive, war-loving society. Although they raided Mesopotamia regularly (they even sacked Babylon in 1595 BCE), the Hittites focused their military efforts on the Egyptian-held portions of Syria and Palestine. They advanced slowly. Though superior in arms, the Hittites could not put as many soldiers on the field as the Egyptian army could. The turning point came in 1286–1285 BCE, when Egypt, under Ramses II, and the Hittites, under their king Hattusilis III, declared a truce after an inconclusive battle at Qadesh and established the first written peace treaty in Western history:

> Behold: Hattusilis, the great chief [of the Hittites], has made a treaty with [Ramses], the great ruler of Egypt, beginning this day, to establish good peace and brotherhood between us forever. . . . And the children of the children of the great ruler of the Hittites shall live in brotherhood and peace with the children of the children of Ramses, . . . and hostilities between them shall cease forever.

The peace did not last long. The Hittites, it turned out, had a gift for conquest but none for government, and their unified kingdom faced continual challenges from regional warlords who preferred their own local despotism to the national brand. When yet another wave of Indo-European invaders swept through the area, the Hittite kingdom collapsed.

Called the **Sea Peoples** by the Egyptians, this new group attacked swiftly throughout the Aegean and eastern Mediterranean seas, setting off shockwaves of dispossessed war refugees much farther inland than the Sea Peoples themselves ever advanced. The Sea Peoples appeared in the Nile delta in 1207 and within twenty years had gained control of most of it. They effectively ended the Egyptian empire in Palestine, since the pharaohs no longer had access to the sea and hence could not engage in trade or diplomacy.

The Sea Peoples fought on land as an infantry, bearing double-edged swords made of bronze and javelins; they also had an innovation: plate armor. Bronze was easily shaped into close-fitting armor that protected their soldiers far more reliably than any earlier type of protective covering. The Hittites and the Egyptians who slowly learned from them had relied on lightly clad archers who rode lightweight chariots; their greater speed and agility could wreak havoc on most ancient infantries, armed as they mostly were with clubs and spears. But the bronze armor of the Sea Peoples gave them enough protection against archers that they could hold their formations and defeat the Egyptian and Hittite forces.

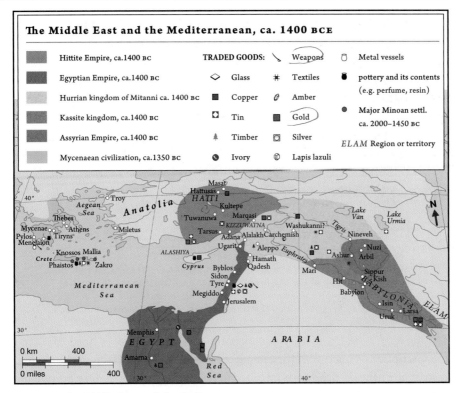

The Middle East and the Mediterranean, ca. 1400 BCE

Hittite Empire, ca.1400 BC	TRADED GOODS:	Weapons	Metal vessels
Egyptian Empire, ca.1400 BC	Glass	Textiles	pottery and its contents (e.g. perfume, resin)
Hurrian kingdom of Mitanni ca. 1400 BC	Copper	Amber	
Kassite kingdom, ca.1400 BC	Tin	Gold	Major Minoan settl. ca. 2000–1450 BC
Assyrian Empire, ca.1400 BC	Timber	Silver	*ELAM* Region or territory
Mycenaean civilization, ca.1350 BC	Ivory	Lapis lazuli	

MAP 2.3   The Middle East and the Mediterranean, ca. 1400 BCE

No one knows who the Sea Peoples were. Obviously they arrived by sea and most likely spoke an Indo-European language, or group of languages, but these facts suggest only that they came from the northern shores of the eastern or central Mediterranean. Theories abound. Were they the Philistines described in the Hebrew Bible? Were they a rival tribe of the Mycenaean Greeks, or the Trojans, or the Hebrews, or the Siculi (the indigenous people of Sicily)? Egyptian records occasionally identify specific subsets among the Sea Peoples, which suggests that they used the name as a catchall for a whole swarm of different ethnic groups.[11] Whoever they were, and wherever they came from, they left behind a trail of annihilation so great that virtually no records survive to describe their wreckage until they reached Egypt. In Greece alone, 90 percent of the population was obliterated.

In Egypt, our first written and pictorial evidence of the Sea Peoples comes from an inscription set up by Ramses III in 1176 BCE to commemorate a rare victory over the intruders. The carved relief shows attackers of many varieties, wearing distinctive clothing and headdresses and carrying an assortment of weapons. The text of

---

[11]   Among the specific peoples named by the Egyptians were the Habiru, whom some believe to have been the Hebrews.

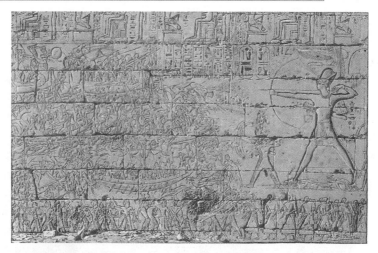

The Sea Peoples Defeated   This wall engraving from the mortuary temple
of Ramses III, ca. 1180 BCE, at Medinet Habu, shows the pharaoh, at right,
leading an ambush of the Sea Peoples. Ramses had blocked the channels of
the Nile Delta, which prevented the Sea Peoples' advance, and then unleashed an archery assault on the ships as they struggled to turn course and
escape to the sea.

the inscription—it is part of the temple complex at Medinet Habu in the western
district of Thebes—clearly was intended to revive flagging hopes. One portion depicts Ramses III in his war chariot, leading his brave troops to battle; its caption
reads in part:

> The king, rich in strength as he rides forth, filling the hearts of the
> [Sea Peoples] with fear and awe; sole lord, whose hand is capable, con-
> scious of his strength, like a valiant lion lying in wait for wild cattle, freely
> going forward, his heart confident, smashing thousands into heaps in the
> space of a moment. His power in the fray is like a fire, making all who
> assail him to collapse in ashes.

Another wall depicts Ramses in the midst of the battle, scattering an army of
terrified Sea Peoples:

> Behold him, as when Set rages, overthrowing the enemy, . . . tram-
> pling down the plains and hill-countries; the enemy lies prostrate, beaten
> from head to tail before his horse. His heat burns up their bodies like a
> flame. Hacked to pieces are their bodies, throughout eternity.[12]

---

[12]   Set (also spelled Seth) was the wrathful god of the desert.

The destruction caused by the Sea Peoples was vast. In southern and southeastern Europe, they annihilated whole cities. Few Near Eastern or Egyptian cities disappeared altogether, by contrast, but the invaders smashed old trade routes and splintered the diplomatic connections that had kept the region relatively stable from 1500 to 1200 BCE. The three major states of the era—New Kingdom Egypt, Hittite Anatolia, and Babylonian Mesopotamia—had generally managed to keep the wider region peaceful and had kept commerce moving. Even the smaller states that provided a sort of buffer zone between the major empires had thrived for those three centuries. But the destruction caused by the Sea Peoples sent shockwaves of displacement and despair through all three empires (see Map 2.4).

The disappearance of the Sea Peoples is as much a mystery as is their origin. Despite Ramses III's fanciful inscriptions, no evidence exists of an annihilating defeat of them or of their continued horrific progress through the Near East to afflict other nations elsewhere. Hence it is likely that they were absorbed into the indigenous populations. This assumption helps to explain the unusual degree of cultural innovation, economic realignment, political reconfiguration, and religious change that occurred in the Sea Peoples' wake. And an important part of that change was the perfecting of an old technology: the refining of iron.

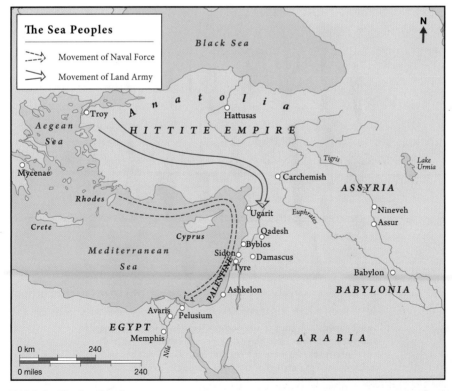

MAP 2.4   The Sea Peoples

THE AGE OF IRON BEGINS, ca. 1200 BCE

Iron ore is plentiful in the Near East, and people had been mining it for a long time. Objects made of iron have been dated as early at 5000 BCE. By 1200 BCE, metalworkers had begun to perfect their methods. By repeating the process of heating, quenching, hammering, they also could produce iron objects of ever greater strength. With new weapons and new trading goods, power shifted again and again. The changes culminated in a new model of statecraft under the Persians and a new religion of fire, Zoroastrianism.

Iron ore was not an obvious choice. It is brittle and will produce a usable metal only after it is melted and its impurities burned away. The process, while simple to describe, is difficult to master. Iron melts at a much higher temperature than copper (the main constituent element in bronze) and must remain in its melted state for a considerably longer time. The constant temperature needed is difficult to achieve with primitive wood fires. Moreover, iron, ironically, is a weaker metal than bronze and is more susceptible to deterioration by moisture. Even in the dry climate of the Near East, iron can easily oxidize (that is, rust). A clash between an iron sword and a bronze sword would invariably end with the iron sword shattered.

Iron Weapons   Armies in the ancient Near East fought primarily with spears, arrows, and knives, rather than swords. Limited metal-ore resources were the reason. Swords did not become common until the arrival of the Indo-European peoples.

Given these disadvantages, what was gained by producing iron weapons and tools? Simply put, mass production. Iron ore is abundant throughout the region, and, consequently, once the production process was perfected, people of all walks of life could afford iron implements.[13] By 1100 BCE iron weapons began to proliferate; by 800 BCE most common homes were well supplied with iron pots, tools, and utensils. The problem with bronze was that its two constituent parts—copper and tin—are both considerably rarer and are seldom found in the same region. In order to maintain a constant supply of bronze, the Near East had to maintain steady commercial relations; any disruption in the long-distance movement of these metals and the available supply of bronze disappeared. This is precisely what happened with the invasions of the Sea Peoples and the mass waves of refugees they set in motion. Trade networks that had proliferated during the years from 1600 to 1200 BCE simply disintegrated. The abrupt decline in the availability of bronze gave the advantage to the iron-brandishing Sea Peoples (whoever they were).

With the Hittite empire destroyed, Assyria and Babylon set reeling, and Egypt sent into yet another Intermediate Period (the Third, 1070–664 BCE), the political map of the ancient Near East changed dramatically. New peoples and states arose, some of them of old provenance, others of newcomers. The ethnic jumble of the turn of the millennium exacerbates the problem of identifying the Sea Peoples and tracing their movements. The region resembled a busy intersection whose traffic lights have gone out at rush hour. Groups like the Phoenicians, the Canaanites, the Philistines, the Amalikites, the Kassites, the Amorites, the Aramaeans, the Mitanni, the Moabites, and the Hurrians—to name only the best known—appeared on the scene in a bewildering tangle.

The **Phoenicians**, to pick just one, were particularly successful, since they took to the sea and established a network of trading colonies that stretched across the major Mediterranean islands (Cyprus, Sicily, Sardinia, the Balearics) and along the northern coast of Africa. Their name, which the ancient Greeks picked up from a West Semitic dialect, meant "the purple people"—a reference to their expertise in dyeing.[14] Later writers like the Greek historian Herodotus reported that Phoenician sailors claimed to have circumnavigated Africa, although this is doubtful. The Phoenicians' most important contribution to Western history was the dissemination of its alphabet, which simplified the task of writing. Theirs was among the first alphabets in Western history, but since it

---

[13]   Iron is actually the sixth most abundant element in the universe. It makes up roughly 5 percent of the earth's crust.

[14]   The waters off the shore of ancient Phoenicia (roughly, today's nation of Lebanon) had large populations of murex snails, from whose shells a distinctive reddish-purple dye was made.

provided the model for the alphabet later adopted by the Greeks, it led directly to the development of the alphabet used in the Western world today. The most famous of Phoenician cities was Carthage, which they founded sometime in the 9th century BCE, in present-day Tunisia, and which later challenged Rome for mastery of the entire Mediterranean.

The **Philistines**, by contrast, settled in the territory just south of Phoenicia. They are best known as the villains in the Hebrew conquest of the Promised Land, the barbarous people whose champion was the giant Goliath. Possibly an offshoot of the Peleset (one of the groups singled out by the Egyptians as being among the Sea Peoples), they in fact were an urban, commercial people who practiced little agriculture—just enough to put them at odds with pastoralist groups like the Hebrews.[15] Their origins likely lay in Mycenaean Greece. Little is known of their language, but archaeological remains link them with ancient Greek culture. The Philistines introduced grape and olive vines to the Holy Land, which are indigenous to the Greek archipelago, for example. Their architectural styles—as exemplified by the great citadels at Ashdod, Ashkelon, and Gaza—likewise resemble the fortified palaces of the Mycenaeans. The Philistines lived in the cities but controlled the agricultural hinterland and the regional trade routes. Most important, the Philistines occupied the region of Palestine that provided much of the copper and tin needed to produce bronze. Their control of such strategic sites and their access to superior weaponry, while making it impossible for their foes to forge similar weapons of their own, is what made the Philistines so substantial a foe to the advancing Hebrews.

> Phoenicians' most important contribution to Western history was the dissemination of its alphabet, which simplified the task of writing. Theirs was not the first alphabet in Western history, but since it provided the model for the alphabet later adopted by the Greeks, it led directly to the development of the alphabet used in the Western world today.

The disruptions caused by the Sea Peoples inspired a radical militarization of the **Assyrians**, who lived along the upper reaches of the Tigris. Terrified of attack from the strangers to the west, and unsure of the Hittites and Babylonians to their north and south, respectively, Assyrian culture turned militant and relied overtly on the use of violence and terror to maintain order. Their political fortunes rose and fell, depending on the relative ruthlessness of subsequent rulers, but from the mid-12th century BCE Assyria earned a well-deserved reputation for savagery that lasted for at least six centuries. From their imposing capital at Nineveh, the Assyrians maintained a large standing army of more than one hundred thousand soldiers

---

[15]   Traditionally, societies based on permanent settlement do not get along well with nomadic groups. Think of the conflicts between the cattle ranchers and farmers of the American West in the 19th century.

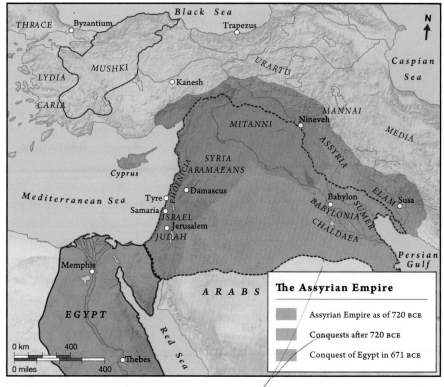

MAP 2.5   The Assyrian Empire

divided into specialized units (infantry, cavalry, archers, engineers, and so on) that, uniquely among ancient armies, trained to work in concert (see Map 2.5).

The Assyrians were the first army to use iron weapons extensively and may also have pioneered another technological advance: they added carbon and nickel to refined iron, to produce steel. Steel blades were significantly stronger than both iron and bronze blades and resisted decomposition. Producing it was expensive, however, which meant that many centuries would pass before steel production became widespread. The Assyrians knew the value of broadcasting their fearsome strength at arms, though. The victory monuments they erected depicted brutal scenes of slaughter, decapitation, rape, and torture, often in chilling detail. Their goal was to frighten people into submission, and it usually worked. When warnings failed, the army did its dirty work with gusto—going so far on occasion as to annihilate entire populations. This was the fate of the "ten lost tribes of Israel," who fell to the Assyrians in 722 BCE. Assyrian law dictated corporal

> The Assyrians knew the value of broadcasting their fearsome strength at arms, though. The victory monuments they erected depicted brutal scenes of slaughter, decapitation, rape, and torture, often in chilling detail.

Assyrian Cruelty The Assyrians were among the most feared of ancient peoples. Through most of the 8th century BCE they were ruled by a series of bloody-minded and ruthless kings who employed sadistic violence as a means of commanding obedience, and they commemorated their worst atrocities with sculptures, engravings, and paintings of all sorts, to remind people of what could happen to them if they opposed the king. This relief, from the palace at Nineveh of the ruler Sennacherib (r. 705–681), shows the torture and slaughter of Jews after the battle of Lachish.

punishments for hosts of crimes, resulting in thousands of publicly performed mutilations a year. On the other hand, at least one Assyrian ruler (Ashurbanipal, r. 669–627 BCE) built the first known library in Western history. Archeologists have recovered thirty thousand clay tablets from its ruins in Nineveh. Most of this treasure store consisted of foreign literary works preserved in Assyrian cuneiform. For example, many modern editions of the *Epic of Gilgamesh* are based on Assyrian redactions unearthed at Nineveh.

Assyria's cruelty had earned it the furious hatred of its neighbors. In 612 BCE an alliance led by the Medes and the Chaldeans stormed into Nineveh and reduced it to ashes and dust. Within another decade all vestiges of Assyrian might were destroyed. The new victors did not introduce an era of good feeling, however. The Medes, an Indo-European people, were happy to return to Iran, knowing that the Assyrians were gone once and for all. That left the Chaldeans, the Semitic-speaking residents of southern Babylonia (known also as neo-Babylonians), in control of all of Mesopotamia and much of the Levant, where they adopted Assyrian methods and ruled by brute force. One of the neo-Babylonian kings, Nebuchadnezzar II (r. 605–562 BCE), led his army into Jerusalem, destroyed the Hebrew Temple, and carried tens of thousands of Hebrews into slavery back east, in Babylon.

PERSIA AND THE RELIGION OF FIRE

Still another group arose in the middle of the 6th century BCE, a people who toppled the neo-Babylonians and brought some stability to this near-hopeless situation that had continued, off and on, since 1200 BCE. These were the Persians, an Indo-European nation whose origins are unknown. Led by an energetic and charismatic ruler named Cyrus (r. 559–530 BCE), they lived near the midpoint of the eastern shore of the Persian Gulf. Suddenly and unexpectedly, the Persians united their various tribes, freed themselves from the overlordship of the Medes, and defeated their next neighbor, the Lydians. They then invaded Mesopotamia so quickly that Babylon surrendered without a fight.

Cyrus was the undisputed master of the east, the largest empire the Western world had yet seen. He freed the Hebrews and allowed them to return to Jerusalem, where they quickly established a semiautonomous vassal state. Such largess was typical of Persian rule, but it resulted from strategic, not altruistic, thinking. The Persian Empire was simply too large for a central government to administer effectively. It was a land empire that, in contrast to Egypt, did not have a grand reliable waterway running through its center to allow easy unification. Cyrus thus portioned out his empire with care and forethought. Why govern a group like the Hebrews, when they could do so themselves? So long as they recognized Persian overlordship, caused no trouble, and sent payments of tax and tribute on time, Cyrus was wisely content to let them go their own way. The Hebrews were not the only people treated in this manner.

Cyrus' son and heir, Cambyses (r. 530–522 BCE), conquered Egypt herself and advanced far into Anatolia, uniting the entire Near East for the first time. The great Persian Empire ultimately stretched from the Hellespont in the west to the Indus River in the east, from the upper Nile in the south to the middle reaches of the Black, Caspian, and Aral Seas in the north. It covered well over two thousand miles on an east-west axis and more than a thousand miles from north to south. The ancient world had seen nothing like it (see Map 2.6). The Persians instituted a single

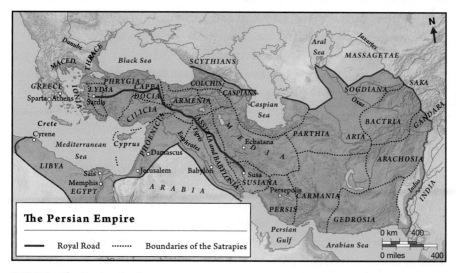

MAP 2.6   The Persian Empire

currency and a standardized system of weights and measures, but otherwise allowed their subject peoples to govern themselves according to their own traditions. After centuries of Egyptian, Hittite, Assyrian, and Babylonian brutality and imperialism, the light-handed approach of the Persians was a welcome relief—which explains the relative absence of rebellion against the new rulers. The conquered could consider, and perhaps even admire, Persian culture, science, and religion.

The death of Cambyses triggered a dynastic crisis, since he died young and without an heir. Eventually a cousin named Darius carried the day. His reign lasted from 521 to 486 BCE, during which time he reformed the administration and undertook an extensive campaign to improve the empire's infrastructure. His projects included the famed Royal Road, a 1,600-mile roadway from Sardis (near the Aegean coast, in Anatolia) to Susa (near the Persian Gulf, in modern-day Iran) that became the main artery for moving goods, capital, services, information, and soldiers through the heart of the empire. Darius also cut a canal that connected the Nile with the Red Sea, to facilitate trade with Egypt, and brought systematic irrigation to the Iranian plateau for the first time, which dramatically increased the agricultural production of the land. Last, he built a vast new capital in Persepolis, two hundred miles east of Babylon. The move calmed people's concerns about having an emperor breathing down their necks and brought the eastern half of his empire, which extended to India, within his gaze. With a calm and peaceful interior at last, with a single currency, and with physical barriers to efficient interaction removed, the economy of the Near East roared to new life. The material standard of life improved for most people, and for most of those it improved dramatically. The Persians had created not just a new state but a new model of statecraft: imperialism via accommodation and tolerance.

The stunning political and social success of the Persians paved the way for a revolution in religious life, for they brought with them a new religion that spread rapidly throughout the Near East and remained the dominant faith of that part of the world until the rise of Islam in the 7th century CE.

The Persians originally had a polytheistic religion not unlike the ancient Sumerian faith, with deities of various types representing natural elements and forces. In what may have been a self-conscious effort at reform, a man named Zoroaster began to preach the supremacy of a single god and the requirement of an ethical basis of life as the proper way of worshipping him. It was the beginning of **Zoroastrianism**, the first transnational Western religion.

We know little of Zoroaster (which is the Greek version of his Persian name, Zarathustra); he lived sometime around 1300 BCE and claimed to have received a vision of this "Wise Lord," **Ahura Mazda**. Ahura Mazda, he preached, was the one true and eternal God, altogether wise, just, and good; significantly, though, Ahura Mazda was not all-powerful—for he had an adversary named Angra

Persepolis   Persian nobles on their way to the imperial court.

Mainyu, later known as Ahriman. "Truly there are two primal spirits, twins renowned to be in conflict. In thought, word, and act they are two: the Good and
the Bad" (Yasna 30.3). It was in order to defeat Ahriman, Zoroaster taught, that
Ahura Mazda created the world and all living things, to provide a battleground
for the cosmic struggle.

Zoroaster composed a sequence of hymns to Ahura Mazda. These seventeen
poems—known as the Gathas—were passed on orally for many centuries until
the Persians acquired writing. By the time the Gathas were finally written down
in the 3rd century CE, a great number of other holy texts had been produced by
other Zoroastrian priests. These were combined with the original Gathas, and
the result was the **Avesta**—the holy book of the Zoroastrians.[16]

The creation myth of this new faith maintained that Ahura Mazda disseminated his spirit in seven unique forms called spentas, or "Holy Immortals," who
created the seven principal elements: Sky, Water, Earth, Plants, Cattle, Man, and
Fire. Ahriman brought death into the world, but Ahura Mazda so ordained that

---

[16]   The Avesta consisted of twenty-one books, but only fragments remain, since the Muslim conquerors of
the Middle Ages searched out every copy they could and destroyed them.

the first five elements are self-regenerating, always bringing more life and therefore more good into the world. Man alone bears the responsibility of choice. The ethical quality of our lives determines not only our own fates but the fate of the world.

Zoroaster wanted to emphasize the unity of mankind, the fact that all peoples regardless of ethnicity are linked by moral necessity and that all lives have value. Indeed, our lives have a vast purpose—not merely, as in the Sumerian and Egyptian religions, an obligation to serve—that ennobles us and gives meaning to our suffering. God's final element, Fire, exists to inspire and assist us. It represents God's righteousness and truth, his purifying strength, and our hope. Living righteously meant regular prayer (five times daily) always in the presence of fire, performing various temple rituals, and following a high ethical standard of honesty, charity, cleanliness, and respect for nature. In this way, Zoroastrians had every hope of personal salvation, which meant joyous reunion with Ahura Mazda in paradise and the satisfaction of playing a role in God's ultimate victory over Evil. The Gathas enjoined believers to love all peoples, to aid the poor, to practice generous hospitality. They showed respect for nature by not eating animals before the animals had attained maturity and could reproduce. Persian temples drew freely on Sumerian, Akkadian, Babylonian, Assyrian, and Egyptian architectural styles to emphasize that Ahura Mazda was the god of all nations and tribes.

> Zoroaster wanted to emphasize the unity of mankind, the fact that all peoples regardless of ethnicity are linked by moral necessity and that all lives have value. Indeed, our lives have a vast purpose—not merely, as in the Sumerian and Egyptian religions, an obligation to serve—that ennobles us and gives meaning to our suffering.

Zoroastrian priests were called **magi**. Their primary responsibility was to tend the sacred fires in the temples, where various rituals central to Zoroastrian life were conducted: marriage, initiation rites, burial rites. Special study was required to become a magus, mostly involving study of the fast-multiplying Avesta texts and memorization of liturgical prayers, but the magi, while highly respected, were not regarded as possessing supernatural powers. Priests and laity remained distinct, but they interacted socially and even intermarried. Priests wore white garments that represented purity; initiated laity were identified primarily by wearing a lengthy cord called a kusti. Zoroastrianism recognized differences between the sexes. It had special temple rites, for example, to help women conceive and to purify them after childbirth. But it allowed all men and women, boys and girls, equal access to the temples and performed the same initiation rites for them all. Away from the temple, women believers could lead the family in prayers and even perform certain rituals. Women wore saris but not veils.

Zoroastrian belief spread rapidly. The state did not forbid other religions or attempt to suppress them, which may have been the key to Zoroastrianism's success. For many subjects of the empire, Ahura Mazda became a kind of benevolent overlord, while their traditional deities were left as immortal spirits in service to the great God. But the ethical element of the faith needs emphasizing. Before Zoroaster, early religions posited no connection between religion and morality. The Sumerian gods, for example, cared only how people treated them, not how they treated each other. The Egyptians were required to obey the divine pharaoh and never upset the order of ma'at—but the only moral expectation placed on them by their religion was not to do harm. Zoroastrian faith gave people

Keeping the Flame Alive   A ring of Zoroastrian priests celebrate their New Year festival with a ritual dance around the sacred flame. Once the most widespread religion in the ancient world, Zoroastrianism today has only two hundred thousand followers worldwide. Low birth rates and high rates of conversion to more mainstream religions are contributing to their rapid decline.

the luxury of feeling that their actions mattered: the way they treated each other helped to create a better world. It appealed to the millions who wanted meaning in life. It assured them that they were good, that their deeds and strivings had purpose, and that a higher ethical standard made life more tolerable for everyone.

WHO, WHAT, WHERE

Ahura Mazda	Indo-European
Assyrians	magi
Avesta	monotheism
Book of the Dead	Philistines
Epic of Gilgamesh	Phoenicians
Greater West	Sea Peoples
Hittites	ushabti
Hyksos ascendancy	Zoroastrianism

SUGGESTED READINGS

Primary Sources

The best translation of *The Epic of Gilgamesh*, quoted on pages 39–40, is found in *Myths from Mesopotamia* by Stephanie Dalley.

The Instruction of Amenemhet I is found in Parkinson, R. B., ed. and trans. *The Tale of Sinuhe and Other Ancient Egyptian Poems, 1940–1640 BC* (2009), pp. 206–208.

The text of the inscription at Medinet Habu is adapted from Bailkey and Lim, *Readings in Ancient History: Thought and Experience from Gilgamesh to St. Augustine*, 6th ed. (2002), p. 54.

Source Anthologies

Hoffner, Harry A., Jr., trans. *Letters from the Hittite Kingdom* (2009).

Black, Jeremy, trans. *The Literature of Ancient Sumer* (2004).

Chavalas, Mark W, ed. *The Ancient Near East: Historical Sources in Translation* (2006).

Luckenbill, Daniel David, ed. *Annals of Sennacherib* (2005).

Moran, William L., ed. and trans. *The Amarna Letters* (2000).

Studies

Akkermans, Peter M. M. G., and Glenn Martin Schwartz. *The Archaeology of Syria: From Complex Hunter-Gatherers to Early Urban Societies, ca. 16,000–300 BC* (2003).

Aubet, Maria Eugenia. *The Phoenicians and the West: Politics, Colonies, and Trade* (2001).

Boardman, John. *Persia and the West: An Archaeological Investigation of the Genesis of Achaemenid Persian Art* (2000).

Briant, Pierre. *From Cyrus to Alexander: A History of the Persian Empire* (2006).

Brosius, Maria, ed. *Ancient Archives and Archival Traditions: Concepts of Record-Keeping in the Ancient World* (2003).

Bryce, Trevor. *The Kingdom of the Hittites* (2005).

———. *Life and Society in the Hittite World* (2004).

Day, John V. *Indo-European Origins: The Anthropological Evidence* (2001).

Fleming, Daniel E. *Democracy's Ancient Ancestors: Mari and Early Collective Governance* (2004).

Galil, Gershon. *The Lower Stratum Families in the Neo-Assyrian Period* (2007).

Grajetzki, Wolfram. *The Middle Kingdom of Ancient Egypt: History, Archaeology, and Society* (2006).

Holloway, Steven W. *Aööur Is King! Aööur Is King!: Religion in the Exercise of Power in the Neo-Assyrian Empire* (2002).

Joannès, Francis. *The Age of Empires: Mesopotamia in the First Millennium BC* (2005).

Leick, Gwendolyn. *The Babylonians: An Introduction* (2002).

Meskell, Lynn. *Private Life in New Kingdom Egypt* (2004).

Morris, Ian, and Walter Scheidel, eds. *The Dynamics of Ancient Empires: State Power from Assyria to Byzantium* (2009).

Oates, Joan, and David Oates. *Nimrud: An Assyrian Imperial City Revealed* (2001).

Oren, Eliezer D. *The Sea Peoples and Their World: A Reassessment* (2000).

Ray, John. *Reflections of Osiris: Lives from Ancient Egypt* (2001).

Roehrig, Catharine H., ed. *Hatshepsut: From Queen to Pharaoh* (2005).

Silverman, David P., Josef W. Wegner, and Jennifer Houser Wegner. *Akhenaten and Tutankhamun: Revolution and Restoration* (2006).

Tyldesley, Joyce A. *Ramesses: Egypt's Greatest Pharaoh* (2001).

Van de Mieroop, Marc. *King Hammurabi of Babylon: A Biography* (2005).

Wiesehöfer, Josef. *Ancient Persia from 550 BC to 650 AD* (2001).

Yasur-Landau, Assaf. *The Philistines and Aegean Migration at the End of the Late Bronze Age* (2010).

For additional resources, including maps, primary sources, visuals, web links, and quizzes, please go to **www.oup.com/us/backman.**

אֱלֹהִים אֵת הַשָּׁמַיִם וְאֵת הָאָרֶץ: וְהָאָרֶץ הָיְתָה תֹהוּ וָבֹהוּ

וְחֹשֶׁךְ עַל־פְּנֵי תְהוֹם וְרוּחַ אֱלֹהִים מְרַחֶפֶת עַל־פְּנֵי הַמָּיִם: וַיֹּאמֶר

אֱלֹהִים יְהִי אוֹר וַיְהִי־אוֹר: וַיַּרְא אֱלֹהִים אֶת־הָאוֹר כִּי־טוֹב וַיַּבְדֵּל

אֱלֹהִים בֵּין הָאוֹר וּבֵין הַחֹשֶׁךְ: וַיִּקְרָא אֱלֹהִים לָאוֹר יוֹם וְלַחֹשֶׁךְ

קָרָא לָיְלָה וַיְהִי־עֶרֶב וַיְהִי־בֹקֶר יוֹם אֶחָד: פ וַיֹּאמֶר אֱלֹהִים יְהִי

רָקִיעַ בְּתוֹךְ הַמָּיִם וִיהִי מַבְדִּיל בֵּין מַיִם לָמָיִם: וַיַּעַשׂ אֱלֹהִים

אֶת־הָרָקִיעַ וַיַּבְדֵּל בֵּין הַמַּיִם אֲשֶׁר מִתַּחַת לָרָקִיעַ וּבֵין הַמַּיִם אֲשֶׁר

מֵעַל לָרָקִיעַ וַיְהִי־כֵן: וַיִּקְרָא אֱלֹהִים לָרָקִיעַ שָׁמָיִם וַיְהִי־עֶרֶב וַיְהִי־

בֹקֶר יוֹם שֵׁנִי: פ וַיֹּאמֶר אֱלֹהִים יִקָּווּ הַמַּיִם מִתַּחַת הַשָּׁמַיִם אֶל־מָקוֹם

אֶחָד וְתֵרָאֶה הַיַּבָּשָׁה וַיְהִי־כֵן: וַיִּקְרָא אֱלֹהִים לַיַּבָּשָׁה אֶרֶץ

CHAPTER 3

The Chosen People

1200 BCE–538 BCE

Sometime between 1800 and 1700 BCE, a tired old man in the city of Ur, near the confluence of the Tigris and Euphrates rivers, began to hear a voice in his head.[1] His name was Abram, and according to the stories passed on about him he was then seventy-five years old, poor, and childless. The voice came from heaven, and it told Abram to take his family—which consisted of his wife, Sarai, his nephew Lot, and their servants—and to leave Ur and go where God would lead him. "The LORD said to Abram, 'Go forth from your native land and from your father's house to the land that I will

show you. I will make you a great nation, and I will bless you; I will make your name great, and you shall be a blessing. I will bless those who bless you and curse him that curses you; and all the families of the earth shall bless themselves by you'" (Genesis 12.1–3).

It is a tale filled with complex meanings and the promise of a great nation. It is a part of the library of books now called the Hebrew Bible, but also a tale of the unwitting founding of two great nations and three religions.

A GREAT NATION

Being a pious man, Abram and his family obeyed without hesitation. Their trek followed the course of the Fertile Crescent. God led them

◀ **In the Beginning** This beautiful page of the opening of the book of Genesis—here showing its Hebrew name "Bereshit" ("in the beginning") in enlarged letters—comes from a multivolume edition of the Bible planned for publication in Germany in the 1930s. This first volume appeared just before Hitler's rise to power in 1933; the rest of the project was never completed. By long-standing Jewish tradition the text of the Scriptures is never adorned with representational imagery, in order not to distract attention from the holy word. Decorative elements consist almost entirely of the beautiful presentation of the script itself.

northward through the Mesopotamian plain, westward across Syria, then southward into the land of the Canaanites in Palestine. At Shechem, which was roughly in the center of Canaan, the Lord actually appeared to Abram and promised to give all the surrounding land to his offspring. That promise is only the beginning of the tale's complex relationship to history.

Abram built the Lord an altar as a way of giving thanks, but he may have wondered whether the gift was such a blessing. The land was then suffering from a horrific famine, which forced Abram and his family to continue travelling southward in search of food, past the Negev desert, then westward across Sinai and into Egypt. This was a dangerous move, because Abram's wife was an exceptionally beautiful woman, and he believed the Egyptians to be so lecherous that someone might kill him in order to get to her. Pleading his self-concern, he persuaded Sarai to pose as his (presumably unmarried) sister. Pharaoh's agents saw her beauty and sent her to the royal palace as a new addition to his harem. "And because of her, it went well with Abram; he acquired sheep, oxen, asses, male and female slaves, she-asses, and camels" (Genesis 12.16). But the Lord sent a plague upon the pharaoh because of the wrong done to Sarai, and so the pharaoh sent her and Abram packing. They returned to Palestine, where the Lord repeated his promise of dominion over the land and descendants as numberless as the stars in the night sky.

A decade passed without either promise being fulfilled. When Abram was eighty-six, Sarai sent her own servant, an Egyptian maiden named Hagar, into his bed in order that he might produce a child by her. Hagar became pregnant, and Sarai, embarrassed at the ease with which Hagar had achieved what she herself had never been able to accomplish, beat her harshly. Hagar eventually gave birth to a son to whom Abram gave the name Ishmael. Another dozen years passed. The Lord appeared to Abram again and repeated his promises, but this

---

[1]   According to the Bible, Abram came from "Ur of the Chaldeans." But by the time the Chaldeans appeared in Mesopotamia (around 700 BCE) the city of Ur had long since ceased to exist.

CHAPTER TIMELINE

ca. 1750 BCE
Abram/Abraham

1005–965 BCE
Reign of King David

ca. 1200 BCE
Hebrews begin to
move into Palestine

965–928 BCE
Reign of King
Solomon

time he told Abram to change his name to Abraham, while Sarai was henceforth to be called Sarah. Moreover, God ordered Abraham to circumcise himself and Ishmael and to promise to circumcise all their male offspring on the eighth day after their birth. Abraham did indeed cut off his own foreskin, and some short time later, remarkably, the ninety-nine-year-old Abraham and the ninety-year-old Sarah did conceive a child—a son. They named him Isaac and duly circumcised him on the eighth day. Sarah was joyful to have a child at last but could not help resenting the continued presence of Ishmael and his mother, Hagar, so she ordered them to leave the household. The story takes a bittersweet turn when the Lord speaks to Hagar for the first time and assures her that he has a plan for Ishmael as well: "I will make a great nation of him" (Genesis 21.18).

Whether or not it accords with historical truth, the story reflects a tradition that this one man, Abram/Abraham, was the patriarch of two great nations. Through Sarai/Sarah he fathered the nation of the Hebrews, out of which developed the religion of Judaism, while with his Egyptian concubine Hagar he produced the line that resulted in the Arab nation and their faith of Islam.

The tale bristles with difficulties: why was Abram/Abraham chosen? Why was his family led to the land promised to them at a time of famine, when they could not live there? How did Abram/Abraham justify handing his beloved wife over to the pharaoh's lust? After their release from Egypt, why did God repeat his promise to Abram/Abraham's family, only to let another ten years go by before fulfilling it? After Hagar produced Ishmael, why did he let another twelve years pass before allowing Isaac to be born? And why he did make Hagar endure twelve years of Sarai/Sarah's bullying before extending any consoling promise to her?

But even this is only the beginning of the complexities that dog the effort to know the origins of the children of Abraham. Political and religious ideologies play an important role in this problem, of course, but even more fundamental is the vexing question of the Bible itself and its usefulness as a historical source. The debate is as old as the Bible itself.

950 BCE
Composition of first
biblical texts

ca. 721 BCE
Assyrians conquer Israel

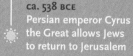
ca. 587 BCE
Fall of Jerusalem to the
Chaldeans; beginning
of Babylonian Captivity

ca. 538 BCE
Persian emperor Cyrus
the Great allows Jews
to return to Jerusalem

THE BIBLE AND HISTORY

To begin, it is not a book but a library. The Hebrew Bible consists of twenty-four books written over a period of nearly one thousand years. According to Jewish tradition, the entire set of books was finally established, ordered, and canonized around 450 BCE by a group remembered as the "Men of the Great Assembly" (Anshei Knesset ha-Gedolah). Most scholars, however, would regard that as too early a date and prefer something around 250 or 200 BCE—and they place the composition of the first biblical texts as early as 1100 BCE.

Many Christians will be surprised by a first look at the Hebrew Bible, since it organizes the books in a way unfamiliar to Christian tradition. The Hebrew Bible is commonly known as the **Tanakh**—an acronym based on the letters *T* (for **Torah**, meaning "Instructions"), *N* (for Nevi'im, or "Prophets"), and *K* (for Ketuvim, or "Writings")—and it groups its books accordingly. It has the five books attributed to Moses under the first heading, the prophets from Joshua to Malachi under the second, and all the remaining writings under the third. Moreover, there are two distinct versions of the Jewish Bible: the Masoretic text compiled in Hebrew in the 2nd century CE, and the Greek text, the **Septuagint**, compiled around 200 BCE for the Greek-speaking Jews of the Hellenistic era. Jewish tradition, supported by textual criticism, regards the Masoretic text as a definitive recreation of the lost version put together by the Men of the Great Council. It thus has priority over the Greek version, which is actually five hundred years older.

The Dead Sea Scrolls   The scrolls are a collection of 972 ancient texts found in a dozen caves near Qumran, by the Dead Sea. The scrolls consist largely of Hebrew biblical texts (roughly 40 percent of the total), with a somewhat smaller number of apocryphal biblical writings. The rest of the collection consists of legal and devotional texts. Most of the scrolls are on parchment and are written in Hebrew, Aramaic, Greek, and Nabataean.

TABLE 3.1 **Comparing the Canons of the Jewish Bible**

	HEBREW VERSION	SEPTUAGINT [GREEK]	
Torah	Genesis	Genesis	**Pentateuch**
	Exodus	Exodus	
	Leviticus	Leviticus	
	Numbers	Numbers	
	Deuteronomy	Deuteronomy	
Nevi'im	Joshua	Joshua	
	Judges	Judges	
	1 Samuel	Ruth	
	2 Samuel	1 Samuel (called 1 Kingdoms)	
	1 Kings	2 Samuel (called 2 Kingdoms)	
	2 Kings	1 Kings (called 3 Kingdoms)	
	Isaiah	2 Kings (called 4 Kingdoms)	
	Jeremiah	1 Chronicles	
	Ezekiel	2 Chronicles	
	12 Minor Prophets[1]	1 Esdras	
		2 Esdras	
		Job	
Ketuvim	Psalms	Psalms	
	Proverbs	Proverbs	
	Job	Ecclesiastes	
	The Scrolls[2]	Song of Solomon	
	Daniel	Isaiah	
	Ezra	Jeremiah	
	Nehemiah	Lamentations	
	1 Chronicles	Ezekiel	
	2 Chronicles	Daniel (includes material not in the Tanakh)	
		12 Minor Prophets	
		Tobit	
		Judith	
		Wisdom of Solomon	
		Ecclesiasticus	
		Baruch	
		1–2 Maccabees	
		3 Maccabees	
		Prayer of Manasseh[3]	
		4 Maccabees (appendix)	

Notes:

[1]The Minor Prophets are Hosea, Joel, Amos, Obadiah, Jonah, Micah, Nahum, Habakkuk, Zephaniah, Haggai, Zechariah, and Malachi. The Tanakh regards these as a single book; the Septuagint prints them as individual books.

[2]The Scrolls (also regarded as a single book) consist of The Song of Songs (called the Song of Solomon in the Septuagint), Ruth, Lamentations, Ecclesiastes, and Esther.

[3]The last seven texts are not part of the Hebrew canon.

The Septuagint text varies from the Masoretic in some significant ways, most especially in its acceptance of certain additional books that do not appear in the Hebrew tradition.[2]

The variations in the canon are important: the Hebrew scriptures evolved over time rather than emerging fully formed and perfect at a single moment in history.[3]

The problems are obvious. For one, they ascribe impossibly long lives to the early leaders of the Hebrews. Abraham, we are assured, died in his 175th year, and his son Isaac died aged 180. We are told that Isaac's son Jacob died when he was very old, although a precise age is never given, but Jacob's son Joseph reportedly lived to be 110. A second problem is that the Scriptures coopt stories from other ancient Near Eastern cultures as if they had occurred uniquely to the Hebrews. The legend of Noah and the Ark clearly derives from the Sumerian tale of the Great Flood, to pick the most obvious example. Even the single most important episode in defining the Hebrews as a people presents a problem. Here, Moses leads them out of Egyptian bondage, receives the Torah on Mount Sinai, and guides them to the Promised Land. The story establishes the Hebrews' special **covenant** with God, and yet there is virtually no archeological or documentary evidence for it outside of the Bible itself.

> These difficulties hardly negate the Bible's value as a historical source. Rather, we must read the texts on their own terms: they portray not an earthly history in the usual sense but the development of a relationship—the growth of a people's understanding of their connection to a transcendent deity.

These difficulties hardly negate the Bible's value as a historical source. Rather, we must read the texts on their own terms: they portray not an earthly history in the usual sense but the development of a relationship—the growth of a people's understanding of their connection to a transcendent deity.

Whatever the Bible may lack in exact historical accuracy, it makes up with a searing depiction of a difficult, demanding, and inscrutable God. He places extraordinary obligations on a small, persecuted minority from whom he expects the highest degree of ethical behavior. And their failures to live up to that standard are narrated again and again. The Hebrews are depicted as the **Chosen People**—but that status confers more obligations than rewards. They are Chosen, but not in the sense of favored. Rather, they are held responsible for maintaining a standard of moral behavior and pursuing justice on earth. How else can one interpret the travails of Abraham? Along with the repeated promises and the constant requirement of waiting for fulfillment, he must undergo tension and division within his own household. God tests Abraham far more frequently than he rewards him, and those tests are severe.

---

2   The Roman Catholic and the Orthodox churches regard the Septuagint version as normative. Protestant churches usually print the Septuagint's extra books (which they call the Apocrypha) as a type of appendix.

3   As historical sources, the Hebrew scriptures are both uniquely valuable and uniquely problematic.

Most cruelly of all, God tells Abraham to take his son Isaac to the top of a hill outside Moriah, pin him on a rock slab that serves as a crude altar, and sacrifice him. Abraham brings him there, ties him up, draws his knife, and begins to plunge it toward his own son, who is old enough to speak and hence to understand what his father is doing. Only when the knife is about to slit Isaac's throat does God intervene and stay Abraham's hand. The Lord then says to Abraham:

> Because you have done this and have not withheld your son, your favored one, I will bestow My blessing upon you and make your descendants as numerous as the stars of heaven and the sands on the seashore; and your descendants shall seize the gates of their foes. All the nations of the earth shall bless themselves by your descendants, because you obeyed My command. *(Genesis 22.16–18)*

We are never told Isaac's reaction to the episode, but we can infer it. He comes across as a passive, almost doddering, figure throughout his own brief part of the Genesis narrative.

The origins of the Bible remain subject to debate even after three thousand years of intense study. The first books to be composed, scholars agree, were the five books of the Torah, which began to appear, in various forms, around 950 BCE and perhaps a bit later than that. What makes dating the texts so challenging is that several authors and editors had a hand in the process. Most Biblical scholars hold to the so-called **Documentary Hypothesis**, which holds that the texts as they survive result from the intertwining of several writers' work, writers known by the initials J, E, D, and P. These indicate, respectively, the Yahwist author (ca. 950 BCE), the Elohist Author (ca. 750 BCE), the Deuteronomist author (ca. 650 BCE), and the Priestly author (ca. 550 BCE). Some scholars add a still later figure known as R, for the Redactor.

The Yahwist (J) is believed to have been the first, and his writings can be identified by his use of the term **YHWH** to stand for God. J is presumed to have written most of Genesis, and certainly those parts of it that relate the stories of Abraham and his descendants. J's God is always YHWH in Hebrew (which English-language Bibles represent by the all-capitals word LORD), and as we have seen, YHWH frequently intervenes directly in his human characters' lives.

The Elohist (E), by contrast, uses a different word[4] but never depicts any direct human encounters with him. In Genesis, the long final section telling the tale of Joseph and his brothers comes from E. (Joseph is the first human being in the Bible who never sees or hears God personally, yet still believes.) E's handiwork is the patchiest, with few long passages apart from the Joseph story, which suggests that it reflects an oral as opposed to written tradition, something interwoven

---

4   Elohim, meaning simply "god" or "deity."

TABLE 3.2 **Chronology of Composition of Hebrew Bible**

DATE	THE TORAH	THE PROPHETS	THE WRITINGS	DEUTEROCANONICAL
1300s				
1200s				
1100s				
1000s				
900s	The Yahwist "J" author			
800s	The Elohist "E" author	Amos Hosea Isaiah Micah		
700s		Zephaniah Nahum Habbakuk Jeremiah	Joshua Judges 1–2 Samuel 1–2 Kings	
600s	Middle portion (ch. 12–29) of Deuteronomy. Priestly "P" author.	Obadiah Ezechiel Isaiah, I–II Haggai Zechariah		
500s	Later portions of Deuteronomy	Isaiah, III	Job Ruth	
400s		Malachi Obadiah Joel Jonah Ezra-Nehemiah	Proverbs Esther Ecclesiastes 1–2 Chronicles Lamentations	
300s				
200s			Daniel	Sirach Ecclesiastes
100s				Tobit Wisdom 2 Maccabees
1				1 Maccabees

All dates are approximate and BCE

here and there throughout the J narrative. Around 750 BCE, the argument goes, as the Assyrian armies marched toward the Hebrew lands, E set to work, trying to preserve the tales handed down among those who settled in the northern part of Palestine as a counterbalance to J's heavy emphasis on the Hebrews in southern Palestine. This desire to preserve the traditions of the northern Hebrews may explain why E so frequently tells stories of sibling rivalry, such as that between Jacob and Esau (Isaac's sons) and between Joseph and his brothers.

The Deuteronomist (D) is the most controversial of the authors. Some scholars consider him to be the author of the book of Deuteronomy but of little else, whereas others regard him as the most critical figure in Biblical transmission. The latter see evidence of his influence throughout the whole of Torah and throughout the historical narratives from Joshua to 2 Kings. In 621 BCE, during repair work on the Temple in Jerusalem, laborers uncovered a long-lost manuscript that consisted of Deuteronomy and (presumably) the rest of the Torah, plus new historical material. D insists on the absolute centrality of allegiance to Torah and worship in the Jerusalem Temple, but also relentlessly describes the crisis of the Assyrian conquest and the approach of the Babylonians as the result of a national failure of morals and observance.

Finally, the Priestly Author (P), or more likely authors, set to work after the fall of Jerusalem to the Babylonians in 587 BCE, inserting a vast body of priestly ordinances from the time of the First Temple into the traditional material of Torah. P's handiwork is woven throughout the first books of the Bible but is especially evident in the book of Leviticus and in the first ten chapters of Numbers. P is also responsible for the first chapter of Genesis (J's version of Creation had begun with chapter 2), for a priestly version of Abraham's covenant with God (Genesis 17), and the story of Moses's death (Deuteronomy 34).

Not all Biblical scholars adhere to the Documentary Hypothesis. Many prefer other explanations for the Bible's abrupt shifts, inordinate repetitions, and frequent contradictions. Everyone agrees, however, that the Bible is a patchwork of many writers' hands—as well as the product of considerable revision, expansion, editing, and rearrangement. It is above all a testament to the Jews' perseverance, their faithful determination to make sense of their experience, and their longing for God. As we shall see, much of that experience consisted of repeated persecution and oppression.[5]

> Everyone agrees, however, that the Bible is a patchwork of many writers' hands—as well as the product of considerable revision, expansion, editing, and rearrangement. It is above all a testament to the Jews' perseverance, their faithful determination to make sense of their experience, and their longing for God.

THE LAND OF CANAAN

Whatever their legendary origins, the Hebrews began to move into Palestine sometime around 1200 BCE. This is a long time after their supposed arrival under Abraham in 1800 BCE. The Bible tells of four hundred years of enslavement in Egypt, followed by a heroic march of liberation and the conquest of Canaan.

In the Bible the march of liberation was led by Moses, to whom was given the first elements of the Torah. As mentioned before, however, no non-Biblical evidence exists for a large Hebrew presence in Egypt at any time during the New Kingdom. Nor is there evidence for a dramatic Hebrew rebellion and subsequent release from bondage. It seems unlikely that events of such magnitude would

---

5   The Jews' experience makes the Bible above all else a map of human pain.

go utterly unmentioned in the hundreds of thousands of Egyptian records that survive from the New Kingdom era. Yet it seems equally unlikely that a nation would invent a legend of their own humiliating enslavement if it had no basis in fact. All that can be said with certainty is that when the Hebrews moved into Palestine, around 1200 BCE, they brought with them an unshakeable conviction: God, they believed, had vouchsafed the land to them. In return, they felt a special obligation to live according to an exacting ethical and ritual code, to care for the poor and downtrodden, and to serve the cause of justice.

They were not necessarily a single people and may instead have been a loose assemblage of speakers of related dialect groups. The Bible describes the Hebrews' division into twelve tribes. Figures known as **judges** held a combination of religious and political authority over each tribe, together with military leadership in times of war. The Hebrews could communicate with the other Semitic groups who had already settled the land—the Amalekites, Amorites, Aramaeans, Canaanites, and the Phoenicians—but the Hebrews were overwhelmingly a pastoral people. Their movement over the land with their herds put them at odds with the other Semites who were chiefly farmers and town dwellers. While they remained seminomadic, the Hebrew tribes had carved out certain zones for themselves by 1000 BCE. Those in the hilly south called themselves the people of **Judah**, while the northern-based tribes took the name of **Israel** (see Map 3.1).

Religious life centered on the family, with daily prayers and rituals to observe the emerging body of Torah. The judges and a caste of priests drawn from the tribe of the Levites led communal services that frequently involved some form of animal sacrifice (the "burnt offerings" referred to in the Bible). The Hebrews did not proselytize to non-Hebrews and focused instead on broadening the acceptance of YHWH among their own. Indeed, the Bible tells repeatedly of the people returning to the worship of Golden Calves and other idols.[6]

The Hebrews maintained the political autonomy of each tribe for as long as they could, but when the Philistines conquered the southern coastal plain of the Levant, they were forced to mount a united defense against annihilation. They entered the alliance thinking it would be temporary, and internal bickering made concerted action difficult. In 1050 BCE, or thereabouts, the Philistines demolished the main Hebrew sanctuary at Shiloh and carted off the **Ark of the Covenant** as a war trophy. After that military catastrophe, the bulk of the people called out for the creation of a Hebrew monarchy. Only a clear central command under a charismatic figure with military skill, they argued, could hold the confederation together and destroy the Philistines.

---

6   Many Hebrews still felt pulled to the polytheism of their Semitic neighbors—which suggests that the strict monotheistic faith in YHWH was of relatively recent origin. Indeed, many scholars suggest that the development of Jewish monotheism owed something to the westward conquests of the Zoroastrian Persians.

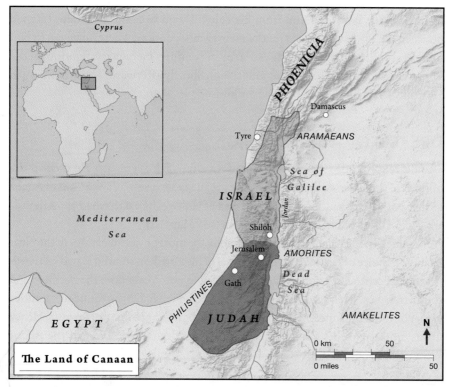

MAP 3.1   The Land of Canaan

One of the tribal Judges, named Samuel, advised against it but in the end he agreed, and he selected a military officer named Saul to be the first king of all the Hebrews. Samuel acquiesced after getting this message from YHWH:

> Heed the demand of the people in everything they say to you. For it is not you they have rejected; it is Me they have rejected as king. Like everything else they have done ever since I brought them out of Egypt to this day—forsaking Me and worshiping other gods—so they are doing to you. Heed their demand; but warn them solemnly, and tell them about the practices of any king who will rule over them. *(1 Samuel 8.7–9)*

Saul stopped the Philistine advance into the hills but was unable to push them back to the coast. The stalling of the war effort, coupled perhaps with Saul's personal shortcomings, led Samuel to withdraw his already tepid support and to promote a new leader to take his place. This was David, an ambitious member of Saul's court. David launched a campaign of his own against the Philistines, paralleling that of Saul, and scored a series of quick victories that won him the popular support of the Hebrews. Saul, jealous of David's success and envious of his popularity, banished him from his court. David became an outlaw, trapped between the Philistine coast and the Hebrew hill country, where he began to plot his takeover of Saul's throne. He did so by becoming a mercenary, fighting for the Philistines in the final battle that killed Saul. Shortly afterwards—by tradition, in 1005 BCE—David took the throne for himself.

DREAMS OF A GOLDEN AGE

David's reign (1005–965 BCE) is noted for three achievements. He pushed the borders of the Israelite kingdom to their greatest expanse, from the Gulf of Aqaba in the south to fifty miles north of the Sea of Galilee; he established Jerusalem as the capital city; and he composed psalms (see Map 3.2).

Politically, the Israelites were now among the most powerful nations in the Near East. The choice of Jerusalem for the capital of his kingdom showed David's shrewdness, for its central location made it well placed to watch over both the northern and southern tribes. Even more important, the city, which had been founded centuries earlier by the Canaanites, had no prior religious significance for the Hebrews. Hence it was unlikely to fuel tribal competition for privilege. David brought the Ark of

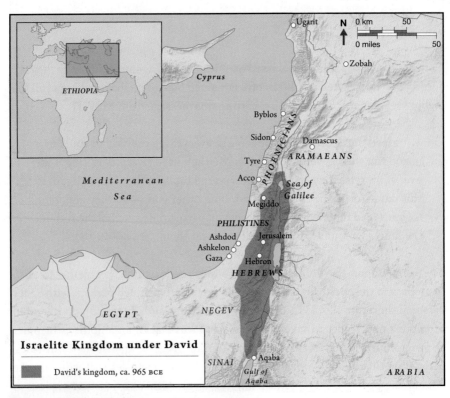

MAP 3.2   Israelite Kingdom under David

the Covenant into the city and began to construct a magnificent palace for himself (which he financed with a combination of heavy taxation, forced loans, and slave labor). As for the psalms, 1 Samuel 16.23 describes David as a musician of talent. Yet if David indeed wrote any of them, they are only Psalms 1 through 41.

David's son Solomon (r. 965–928 BCE) succeeded him and threw his considerable energy into enlarging his father's palace complex. He also began construction of a temple to house the Ark of the Covenant. The Bible devotes three entire chapters to describing the Temple (1 Kings 6–8). Everything about it deserved mentioning, starting with its size—thirty feet wide, ninety feet deep, with three stories. It had latticed windows, inlaid wood paneling, carved cherubim, chains that secured double doors leading into the inner sanctuary where the Ark was placed, and statuary embossed with gold leaf. This was, the Bible assures us, a house fit for the Lord. Solomon also expanded the royal palace until it formed a vast complex with the Temple.

Moreover, he built the Israelites' first commercial fleet, which sailed out of the Gulf of Aqaba at the kingdom's far southern tip on the Red Sea. It put Israel in direct contact with Upper Egypt, Ethiopia, and the coastal peoples of the Arabian peninsula. The Israelites sold the copper that they (or their slaves, actually) mined from the rich veins found in the southern Negev. The trade was highly lucrative and helped to finance the palace and Temple projects.

The Bible portrays Solomon, like his father, as a wise and great ruler who championed the causes of justice and piety.[7] Solomon wrote psalms, too, and is credited with writing the books of Proverbs and the Song of Songs. Both men, however, could be selfish and despotic, and despite their genuine positive traits were nowhere near as popular in their lifetimes as in later centuries. Their sexual appetites were tireless: David pursued married women as well as servant girls, and Solomon, we are told, had seven hundred wives and three hundred concubines, including "the daughter of Pharaoh, women of the Moabites, Ammonites, Edomites, Zidonians, and Hittites" (1 Kings 11.1). They had cruel streaks, too. In the story of the beautiful Bathsheba, David intentionally ordered her husband into battle so that he could then claim the widow for himself. After a victory over the people of Zobah, David took over twenty thousand Canaanite soldiers captive as slaves and had all their horses hamstrung. Solomon's consorts were of an exceptionally large number, but his bed-hopping was not intrinsically wrong. Polygamy was common among the early Israelites, especially among the elites.

Most likely, the overwhelmingly flattering nature of the Bible's portrayal of these men resulted from the role they played in strengthening the cult of YHWH. All their conquests, their building projects, their artistic endeavors, their efforts to provide justice for the people—everything was done in service to the God whose great Temple

---

7   "King Solomon excelled all the kings on earth in wealth and in wisdom. All the world came to pay homage to Solomon and to listen to the wisdom with which God had endowed him" (1 Kings 10.23–24).

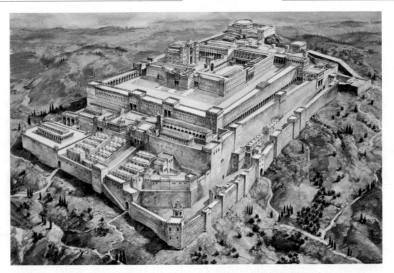

The Temple of Solomon   Artist's reconstruction of Solomon's palace and the Temple in Jerusalem, built in the middle of the 10th century BCE.

they had raised in Jerusalem. Compared to this, what did some sexual peccadilloes matter? The Bible's compilers gladly held up the David-Solomon era as the Golden Age of ancient Israel, and the tales of these two kings entered Jewish folklore.

The romanticization of David and Solomon introduced an entirely new element into Western culture, or at least one for which no earlier evidence survives—namely, the popular belief in a past paradise, a lost era of former glory, when humanity had attained a perfection of happiness. This is more than mere nostalgia, and it has been a hallmark of Western life ever since. Throughout the centuries Western societies have attempted to evoke or re-create a golden age—a past from which we have declined and to which we hope to return. Our reformations therefore tend to be *reformations*, efforts to restore past glories rather than to create new ones. It might be the Jews' struggle to reestablish themselves in the Promised Land. It might be American mythmaking about the Founding Fathers, the old West, or a pristine game of baseball before Astroturf and the designated hitter. In each case, Western culture has sought to return to a perfection we have lost.

> Throughout the centuries Western societies have attempted to evoke or recreate a golden age—a past from which we have declined and to which we hope to return. Our reformations therefore tend to be *reformations*, efforts to restore past glories rather than to create new ones.

According to the Bible, the northern tribes refused to accept Solomon's son Rehoboam as their king and broke away to form a separate realm. Hence from 937 to 721 BCE there were *two* Hebrew kingdoms—the kingdom of Israel in the north, with its capital at Shechem, and the kingdom of Judah in the south, still centered on Jerusalem. Judah, though smaller, had the advantage of its relatively isolated

TABLE 3.3   **More Dreams of a Golden Age**

We encounter many romanticized ideals of past greatness in history, including these:

The Jews	A Greater Israel
Greece	Periclean Athens
Imperial Rome	The glories of the Republic
Feudal Europe	An Arthurian Camelot
Renaissance Italy	The perspective, harmony, and virtue of classical Rome
Protestant Reformation	The spiritual and communal perfection of the first Christians
Islam	The fabled tolerance and high culture of the medieval caliphate
Ottoman Empire	The magnificence of Suleiman the Magnificent
France	The First, Second, or Third Republics; the First, Second, or Third Empires
England and America	The reign of Queen Victoria
America	The Founding Fathers The cowboy gunmen of the Old West The common man (e.g., Frank Capra films, Norman Rockwell paintings) Slain leaders (Abraham Lincoln, John F. Kennedy)

position in the hills. As a state and, more importantly, as a people, Israel disappeared with the arrival of the Assyrians in 732 BCE. These brutal conquerors annihilated tens of thousands and sent the rest off into slavery throughout the Assyrian Empire, where they vanished—the famous Ten Lost Tribes of Israel. The people of Judah, henceforth known as Jews, held out until they were overwhelmed by the Chaldeans, or Neo-Babylonians, under their ruler Nebuchadnezzar, in 587 BCE. This began the **Diaspora** ("exile" or "scattering"). The Chaldeans destroyed the Temple at Jerusalem and took the Jews eastward into the **Babylonian Captivity**.

WOMEN AND THE LAW

Fixing the status of women in ancient Jewish society is no easy task, but not, as with other Near Eastern peoples, because of a dearth of evidence. The Bible devotes hundreds of pages to describing, praising, criticizing, legislating, berating, lamenting, and expressing gratitude for the women of the Hebrew world. The image that emerges from it is complex and sometimes self-contradictory, and yet it is clear that Jewish society gave its women more social autonomy, legal rights, education, and respect than any other ancient group, with the possible exception of the Persian Zoroastrians—whose treatment of women remains far less understood because of the paucity of sources. (Most of the archives and libraries of the Zoroastrians were destroyed, often intentionally, during the Islamic conquests of the 7th and 8th centuries CE.)[8]

---

[8]   No other ancient people has left such varied and detailed records about how they regarded their mothers, wives, sisters, and daughters.

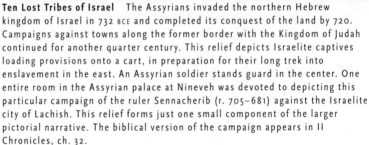

Ten Lost Tribes of Israel   The Assyrians invaded the northern Hebrew kingdom of Israel in 732 BCE and completed its conquest of the land by 720. Campaigns against towns along the former border with the Kingdom of Judah continued for another quarter century. This relief depicts Israelite captives loading provisions onto a cart, in preparation for their long trek into enslavement in the east. An Assyrian soldier stands guard in the center. One entire room in the Assyrian palace at Nineveh was devoted to depicting this particular campaign of the ruler Sennacherib (r. 705–681) against the Israelite city of Lachish. This relief forms just one small component of the larger pictorial narrative. The biblical version of the campaign appears in II Chronicles, ch. 32.

The legendary and narrative passages depicting the pre-Mosaic era invariably describe women as having been created in order to help, if not to serve, men. From Sarai/Sarah on, Hebrew women appear overwhelmingly in the roles of dutiful daughters, obedient wives, and loving mothers. Enough exceptions to the pattern exist, however, to suggest that many women did carve out different paths for themselves. Moses's own sister, the prophetess Miriam, helped to guide the Hebrews across the Red Sea and led their celebration of thanksgiving once they had reached the other side. Another prophetess, Deborah, actually governed one of the twelve tribes during the era of the Judges. And a married woman named Huldah was so respected for her knowledge of Jewish Law that King Josiah of Judah (r. 641–609 BCE) entrusted her with validating a newly discovered Torah-scroll fragment found in Jerusalem. Two other women, whether historical or not, were deemed significant enough to deserve entire Biblical books devoted to their stories: Esther, a young Jewish girl who becomes queen of Persia and uses her position to forestall a plot to annihilate the Jews within the empire, and Ruth, the main character (and a convert to Judaism) in a charming story about long-suffering love, faithful friendship, and fulfillment.[9]

The Torah established the framework for women's roles in Jewish society. As usual, the discrepancies between male and female prerogatives are first to draw one's attention. The Law strictly demands virginity of girls before marriage but lays no comparable burden on boys; women cannot give testimony in civil or criminal cases; a husband can divorce his wife for cause, but not vice versa unless the husband agrees to the split. On the other hand, tradition gave girls the right to a basic education (usually enough to allow them to read the Scriptures and guide their own children's early religious education), guaranteed their entitlement to inherit property, allowed them limited economic autonomy, and accorded protection to widows. The bans on women entering the Temple or performing other liturgical rites during menstruation or immediately after giving birth, times when they are labeled "impure" or "unclean" (Hebrew *tumeh*), may seem misogynistic but appear less so when one considers the more numerous conditions that rendered a man tumeh—such as touching the carcasses of proscribed animals, experiencing nocturnal emissions, developing a rash or sore on his skin, or even just acquiring a bald patch in his beard. To be tumeh did not denote sinfulness or a loss of self-worth; it meant only that one was not ceremonially fit for certain religious rites and needed to undergo a ritual purification or cleansing. Nevertheless, women of all ages were generally regarded as individuals needing higher degrees of protection and guidance.

The fifth commandment given to Moses on Mount Sinai enjoined all Hebrews to honor their mothers and fathers equally, and a later rabbinical judgment declared—rhetorically, not juridically—"Death to him who strikes or curses his own mother." But the tenth commandment forbade men from coveting their neighbors' wives, houses, work animals, "or any other thing belonging to your neighbor," a command that would seem to regard wives as possessions rather than people. Within marriage, the Law required husbands to honor, support, and work on behalf of their wives at least to an extent that matched the value of the property a woman brought into the marriage by her dowry. Wives who brought no domestic servants into their marriage were expected to perform six specific household tasks for their husbands: grinding grain, cooking, cleaning, spinning and weaving, bed preparation, and child nursing. A Jewish wife was entitled to relinquish one of these essential labors for every servant provided by her dowry.[10] Wives were exempt from an obligation to perform fieldwork. The Law expected women as well as men to make annual visits to the Temple in Jerusalem, especially

---

[9]   To this day, Jews in Iran are referred to colloquially as Esther's children.

[10]   Mothers led the prayers that preceded the main daily meal, and in pre-Temple times they participated in performing ritual sacrifices.

at Passover, and provided special bathing spaces for women to prepare themselves for entering the House of the Lord.

Among the most popular of Biblical books is the **Song of Songs**, also known as the Song of Solomon, which consists of a poetic dialogue between a bride and bridegroom that celebrates married love in all its emotional and physical intimacy. Centuries of religious commentary have interpreted the text as an allegory of the covenant between God and his people, but a simpler reading sees in it a hymn to the joy that married union brings in equal measure to man and wife. The bride speaks first:

> Oh, give me the kisses of your mouth,
> For your love is more delightful than wine.
> Your ointments yield a sweet fragrance,
> Your name is like finest oil—
> Therefore do maidens love you.
> Draw me after you, let us run!
> The king has brought me to his chambers.
> Let us delight and rejoice in your love,
> Savoring it more than wine. *(Song of Songs 1.2–4)*

To which the bridegroom sings in reply:

> You have captured my heart,
> My own, my bride,
> You have captured my heart
> With one glance of your eyes,
> With one coil of your necklace.
> How sweet is your love,
> My own, my bride!
> How much more delightful your love than wine,
> Your ointments more fragrant
> Than any spice!
> Sweetness drops
> From your lips, O bride;
> Honey and milk
> Are under your tongue;
> And the scent of your robes
> Is like the scent of Lebanon. *(4.9–11)*

Sexual delight is an intrinsic element of married love, and the Law recognizes the woman's full enjoyment of it. But pleasure is not the only reason for marriage. God's first instruction to Adam and Eve in the Garden of Eden was to reproduce: "Be fertile and increase, fill the earth and master it." Every Jewish man therefore was expected to marry as early as possible, which most priests and rabbis interpreted to mean the onset of puberty. The Torah not only declines to praise celibacy, it never even mentions it.[11] A girl could not be forced into marriage before puberty and retained a limited right to refuse a marriage partner proposed by her father after she had reached it. The Law does not demand marriage of all females as it does of males, but rabbinical tradition advises women not to remain single, lest they come under suspicion by their neighbors as sexual adventuresses.

Women in ancient Israel and Judah, on the whole, were better off than most of their contemporaries: they could own and inherit property, received at least a basic education, enjoyed legal rights in marriage, participated actively in the religious life of the community, and received the respect of their peers and the veneration of their families so long as they obeyed the Law.

Women in ancient Israel and Judah, on the whole, were better off than most of their contemporaries: they could own and inherit property, received at least a basic education, enjoyed legal rights in marriage, participated actively in the religious life of the community, and received the respect of their peers and the veneration of their families so long as they obeyed the Law.

PROPHETS AND PROPHECY

The splitting of the Hebrew kingdom and the subsequent disappearance of the successor states prompted the arrival of the age of the great prophets. Samuel, last of the Judges, was the first of the great prophets. After him came Elijah and Elisha (both mid- to late 9th century BCE), Amos and Hosea (mid-8th century), Isaiah and Micah (late 8th century), Jeremiah (late 7th to early 6th centuries), and Ezekiel (early 6th century). The Minor Prophets—so called for the length, not the significance, of their prophetic books—came too. Allowing for differences between them as individuals, the prophets as a group shared a calling to warn the Hebrews of the approaching Assyrian and Babylonian dangers and to interpret those dangers as signs of YHWH's growing displeasure. By failing to uphold standards of justice, decency, and observance of the Torah, they warned, the people had placed themselves in both mortal and spiritual peril; as Jeremiah put it in his Temple sermon:

> Thus said the LORD of Hosts, the God of Israel: "Mend your ways and your actions, and I will let you dwell in this place. Don't put your trust

---

[11]   The prophet Jeremiah is the only Jewish figure in the Hebrew Bible known to have been celibate (see Jeremiah 16.2).

in illusions and say, 'The Temple of the LORD, the Temple of the LORD, the Temple of the LORD are the [buildings].' No, if you really mend your ways and your actions; if you execute justice between one man and another; if you do not oppress the stranger, the orphan, and the widow; if you do not shed the blood of the innocent in this place; if you do not follow other gods, to your own hurt—then only will I let you dwell in this place, in this land that I gave to your fathers for all time." *(Jeremiah 7.3–7)*

In casting the blame for their misfortunes upon themselves, the Jews introduced the essential notions of self-criticism and moral responsibility into Western culture. It hardly seems possible to imagine a Sumerian interpreting a calamity like the Hittite invasion as anything other than divine whim, or to picture an Egyptian interpreting the Hyksos catastrophe as the consequence of a moral failing on Egypt's part. Earlier societies had senses of morality, but those morals had little to do with their religions. The Jews, however, went even further and conflated faith and morals to a degree that they could not be separated or distinguished.[12] **She'ol** was the Biblical underworld, and yet the ancient Hebrews did not believe in separate places of reward and punishment in the afterlife. A good life of devotion to YHWH, ethical behavior, and commitment to justice was desirable for its own sake, not as a means to a heavenly end. Ethic and action were necessary components of each other, intrinsic and inextricable.

> A good life of devotion to YHWH, ethical behavior, and commitment to justice was desirable for its own sake, not as a means to a heavenly end. Ethic and action were necessary components of each other, intrinsic and inextricable.

This was a revolutionary development in Western life, but one that hardly made the Jews any happier a people. Joy and agony are both present on every page of the Bible, and indeed the Scriptures are often at their greatest expressive power when crying out in pain. Among the psalms attributed to David, one that has entered Jewish liturgy as a daily prayer for supplication is the following:

> O LORD, do not punish me in anger,
>   do not chastise me in fury.
>   Have mercy on me, O LORD, for I languish;
>   heal me, O LORD, for my bones shake with terror.
>   My whole being is stricken with terror,
>   while You, LORD—O, how long!

---

12 Among ancient Near Eastern cultures, only the Zoroastrianism of the late-coming Persians connected ethics with religious observance.

O LORD, turn! Rescue me!
>   Deliver me as befits Your faithfulness.
>   For there is no praise of You among the dead;
>>   in Sheol, who can acclaim You?
>>   I am weary with groaning;
>>   every night I drench my bed.
>>   I melt my couch in tears.
>   My eyes are wasted by vexation,
>>   worn out because of all my foes.
>>   Away from me, all you evildoers,
>>   for the LORD heeds the sound of my weeping.
>>   The LORD heeds my plea,
>>   the LORD accepts my prayer.
>   All my enemies will be frustrated and stricken with terror;
>>   they will turn back in an instant, frustrated.   *(Psalm 6)*

Few ancient texts expressed comparable sentiments; only the Sumerian "Song of the Righteous Sufferer" comes close to such power.

PRIESTS AND RABBIS

The loss of Jerusalem, the Temple, and the land of their fathers, and the Jews' captivity in Babylon represented crises of the highest order. Had YHWH abandoned the Jews, turned his back on them, and revoked the promises he had made to Abraham and Moses? These concerns motivated the prophets to call the Jews to stricter observance of Torah, to stamp out immoral behavior, and to turn their hearts and minds to YHWH. But how was stricter observance of Torah possible when the Jews no longer lived in a Jewish society? The question prompted a shift in authority from the priestly caste to rabbis and the Bible itself. When the Persian emperor finally allowed the Jews to return from captivity, the same questions divided Jewish society.

For nearly five hundred years Jewish religious life had centered on the home and the Temple. To live an observant Jewish life, while ethically challenging, was logistically simpler in a mostly Jewish realm: the distances involved were, after all, not so great. The daily disciplines of prayer, charity, fair dealing, and hospitality were practiced in the home. The ritual demands of communal worship could be observed by intermittent journeys to the Temple in Jerusalem. The high priests controlled Temple life, performed the rituals, resolved disputes, and represented the community of the Chosen. The king administered the realm, defended the people, and worked to keep the economy afloat.

Now the Jews were shorn of centuries of tradition—exiled from their beloved Temple, the ritual prayers, ceremonies, and sacrifices that provided spiritual sustenance and communal identity. They were in captivity and in the minority, facing day-to-day situations that had never occurred in their own kingdom. In these times, established law no longer clearly applied. Does the prohibition of a Jew eating under the roof of a non-Jew apply to a Jewish slave of a Babylonian master? May a Jew indentured to a Persian employer obey his boss's commands on the Sabbath? Under what conditions may a Jew enter a business partnership with a non-Jew? If no Jewish physician is available, may an ill or wounded Jew seek care from a Gentile physician? Such problems had been addressed to some extent in the past, but usually in the abstract. These questions, and others like them, were now urgent.

Compounding the difficulties, the priestly caste had been largely eradicated or marginalized. To whom, then, could the Jews turn for answers? During the fifty years of their Babylonian Captivity, they turned increasingly to their rabbis. The status of **rabbi** had a long lineage going back centuries. Originally an honorific term, the word meant something like "master," in the sense of a person of skill: a man who learned a craft from an expert might call that expert his rabbi, just as a person might honor a special tutor. By the 6th century BCE, however, a rabbi was specifically a teacher of Jewish law. Shorn of their Temple lives, the Jews turned to the rabbis, who became the de facto leaders of the Jews in exile. Rabbis continued to teach Torah but also increasingly became religious judges. Their role was to extrapolate from the principles of Torah, so as to redefine an authentic Jewish life in radically changed circumstances. The incremental growth of a body of rabbinical law—analogous to the tort law of modern societies—came to heavily influence Jewish life and identity, even to the point where legal scholars started to refer to rabbinical judgments as the expression of an Oral Torah that supplemented the written Law. In response, groups of exiled priests began to revise the codified Torah, inserting laws and rituals associated with the P author and reemphasizing the centrality of priestly worship in Jewish life.

In 538 BCE the Persian emperor Cyrus the Great (r. 576–530 BCE) released the Jews and allowed them to return to Jerusalem. His decision triggered a predictable conflict. Must the new generations of Jews, who never knew Temple worship or the authority of the priests, relinquish rabbinical teaching and leadership? Was rabbinical Judaism merely a temporary measure in an emergency, or was it a new and authentic way of being a Jew? Moreover, who would decide—the priests? The rabbis? The people themselves?

The prophets Haggai and Zechariah, whose books appeared at just this time, urged the rebuilding of the Temple and reestablishment of priestly authority. Did the construction of a Second Temple on the ruins of the First mean the restoration of the old order, or could rabbinical tradition somehow embrace and even subsume the traditions of the past? This conflict motivated much of the compiling, editing, and rewriting of the Bible described earlier in this chapter. The territory of Judah remained under Persian control for another two hundred years, until Alexander the Great began his conquest of the entire Near East around 330 BCE, but the situation remained in flux.

As late as 458 BCE, the prophet Ezra came to Jerusalem from Babylon with his own edition of the Torah, promoting reform along rabbinical lines. Ezra, indeed, is the essential source for rabbinical Judaism, a second Moses in his authority. While the book emphasizes Ezra's charisma to establish his authority, it relies even more on a decree by the Persian emperor Artaxerxes I (r. 465–424 BCE):

> Artaxerxes king of kings, to Ezra the priest, scholar in the law of the God of heaven, and so forth. And now, I hereby issue an order that anyone in my kingdom who is of the people of Israel and its priests and Levites who feels impelled to go to Jerusalem may go with you. For you are commissioned by the king and his seven advisers to regulate Judah and Jerusalem according to the law of your God, which is in your care, and to bring the freewill offering of silver and gold, which the king and his advisers made to the God of Israel, whose dwelling is in Jerusalem. . . . And you, Ezra, by the divine wisdom you possess, appoint magistrates and judges to judge all the people in the province of Beyond the River who know the laws of your God, and to teach those who do not know them. Let anyone who does not obey the law of your God and the laws of the king be punished with dispatch, whether by death, corporal punishment, confiscation of possessions, or imprisonment. *(Ezra 7.12–15, 25–26)*

A GENIUS FOR REINVENTION

Judaism's genius for reinvention helped it to survive tumultuous changes in its social and political fortunes. Whatever their earliest origins, the Hebrews entered Palestine with a developing understanding of their uniqueness. Rare monotheists in an overwhelmingly polytheistic world, they sustained a faith in their responsibility to God and in their exclusive rights to a particular homeland. Its dissolution and loss was only the first of many catastrophes that prompted them to reengage with tradition, to reinterpret their past and present lives, and to chart new paths for their development.

The result of this reinvention is the Bible itself, as it took shape after shape. Where tradition before had been primarily oral, the Hebrew Scriptures gradually emerged as a canon. It and the centuries of commentary that followed represent a uniquely fascinating archive of a people's dreams and disappointments.

Factions of Jews debated not only the proper ways of worshipping YHWH and adhering to his laws but even the fundamental issue of who exactly was a Jew.

The Babylonians, after all, did not forcibly relocate every single Jew to the east. A rigid social group, or caste, may make religious, social, or economic distinctions. The Babylonians had carted off primarily the higher-caste Jews in *all* those senses, in an effort to decapitate Jewish society and render it more pliant.[13]

The numbers involved are small. The population of Judah before the Exile had been perhaps as low as thirty thousand, one-quarter of whom were sent into captivity. Certainly that was enough to end Judean life as it had existed. The economy of the fifty-year Persian era declined to mere subsistence level; effective government ended and was replaced by Persian overseers whose chief interest was the collection of tribute. The biblical book of Lamentations vividly depicts the despair felt by the people who interpreted Judah's fall as a sign of God's rejection of them:

> The Lord has laid waste without pity
> All the habitations of Jacob;
> He has razed in His anger
> Fair Judah's strongholds.
> He has brought low in dishonor
> The kingdom and its leaders.
> In blazing anger He has cut down
> All the might of Israel;
> He has withdrawn His right hand
> In the presence of the foe;
> He has ravaged Jacob like flaming fire,
> Consuming on all sides. *(Lamentations 2.2–3)*

Adding to the misery, many Jews had decided to reject the YHWH cult altogether and had assimilated into the culture and religion of their captors. Jeremiah, who was among the Jews who went to Egypt, prophesied YHWH's further wrath upon the apostates who gave themselves over to foreign gods:

> And now, thus said the LORD, the God of hosts, the God of Israel: 'Why are you doing such great harm to yourselves, so that every man and woman, child and infant of yours shall be cut off from the midst of Judah, and no remnant shall be left of you? For you vex me by your deeds, making offerings to other gods in the land of Egypt where you have come to sojourn, so that you shall be cut off and become a curse and a mockery among all the nations of earth. . . . I am going to set my face against you for punishment, to cut off all of Judah. I will take the remnant of Judah

---

[13]   Except for professionals and artisans, the majority of the population in the Persian era remained behind.

The Second Temple   Reconstruction model of the Second Temple, built after the return of the Hebrews from the Babylonian Captivity, after 547 BCE.

who turned their faces toward the land of Egypt, to go and sojourn there, and they shall be utterly consumed in the land of Egypt. They shall fall by the sword, they shall be consumed by famine; great and small alike shall die by the sword and by famine, and they shall become an execration and a desolation, a curse and a mockery. I will punish those who live in the land of Egypt as I punished Jerusalem, with the sword, with famine, and with pestilence. Of the remnant of Judah who came to sojourn here in the land of Egypt, no survivor or fugitive shall be left to return to the land of Judah. Though they all long to return and dwell there, none shall return except [a few] survivors.' *(Jeremiah 44.7–8, 11–14)*

The Temple, then nothing but ruins, remained at least a site of symbolic significance. It is possible that some sort of communal religious life had taken place there during the Exile, but the records are unclear. But when the emperor Cyrus decreed that the Jews were free to return to Judah and to rebuild their Temple, surprisingly few chose to do so. Life in Babylonia and Egypt had been better than the captives had expected. The general tolerance with which they were treated, together with the Jews' own adaptive skills, brought them a level of material prosperity that they had not been able to achieve in remote Judah. The small minority of exiles who returned to Jerusalem consisted primarily of those associated in one way or another with the Temple and palace. Their efforts to reestablish their old authority in Jerusalem left the

The "Wailing Wall"   All that remains of the Second Temple today.

Diaspora communities free to develop their rabbinical traditions without resistance.

Few of the Jews who had remained behind in Judah welcomed the idea of re-installing the old hierarchy, so relations between the population and the return-ees remained tense. The elites, widely suspected of collusion with the Persian overlords, made matters worse by refer-ring to themselves as "the children of the Exile" while dismissing the rest of the population as "the people of the land." Intentionally or not, the Temple faction implied that they alone were the true bearers of Jewish tradition. Ezra and Nehe-miah, the two most prominent prophets of the mid-5th century BCE and ardent champions of the Temple party, railed against Jews who had married outside the faith and those who undeservingly claimed the traditional self-identification of "children of Israel" and "children of Abraham."

Economic factors played a role in this conflict too. Many of the returnees had put up their old properties as collateral for loans: they needed cash to recapitalize their business concerns. When some of those concerns failed, their property was often seized.

With so much at stake, it hardly comes as a surprise that so much effort at recording, revising, expanding, editing, and reinterpreting the Scriptures took place in this era. The Jews of the 6th and 5th centuries BCE were in a crucible of intense political and economic heat that compounded and aggravated the painful struggle to define Jewish identity. YHWH was proving to be a harsh taskmaster, and his people were learning that to be chosen was not necessarily to win.

WHO, WHAT, WHERE

Ark of the Covenant	Israel
Babylonian Captivity	rabbi
Chosen People	Septuagint
covenant	She'ol
Diaspora	Song of Songs
Documentary Hypothesis	Tanakh
Judah	Torah
judges	YHWH

SUGGESTED READINGS

Primary Source

Berlin, Adele, and Marc Zvi Brettler, eds. *The Jewish Study Bible: Jewish Publication Society Tanakh Translation* (2004).

Anthologies

Arnold, Bill T., and Bryan E. Beyer, eds. *Readings from the Ancient Near East: Primary Sources for Old Testament Study* (2002).

Hallo, William W., ed. *The Context of Scripture* (2002).

Studies

Bartor, Assnat. *Reading Law as Narrative: A Study in the Casuistic Laws of the Pentateuch* (2010).

Esler, Philip F. *Ancient Israel: The Old Testament in Its Social Context* (2006).

Finkelstein, Israel, and Neil Asher Silberman. *The Bible Unearthed: Archaeology's New Vision of Ancient Israel and the Origin of Its Sacred Texts* (2002).

———. *David and Solomon: In Search of the Bible's Sacred Kings and the Roots of the Western Tradition* (2007).

Flusser, David. *Judaism of the Second Temple Period*. Vol. 1, *Qumran and Apocalypticism* (2007).

———. *Judaism of the Second Temple Period*. Vol. 2, *The Jewish Sages and Their Literature* (2009).

Halpern, Baruch. *The First Historians: The Hebrew Bible and History* (2003).

Hays, J. Daniel, and Tremper Longman. *The Message of the Prophets: A Survey of the Prophetic and Apocalyptic Books of the Old Testament* (2010).

Hendel, Ronald. *Remembering Abraham: Culture, Memory, and History in the Hebrew Bible* (2004).

King, Philip J., and Lawrence E. Stager. *Life in Biblical Israel* (2002).

Liverani, Mario. *Israel's History and the History of Israel* (2007).

Pardes, Ilana. *The Biography of Ancient Israel: National Narratives in the Bible* (2000).

Person, Raymond F., Jr. *The Deuteronomic History and the Book of Chronicles: Scribal Works in an Oral World* (2010).

Schiffman, Lawrence H. *Qumran and Jerusalem: Studies in the Dead Sea Scrolls and the History of Judaism* (2010).

———. *Understanding Second Temple and Rabbinic Judaism* (2003).

Smith, Mark S. *The Memoirs of God: History, Memory, and the Experience of the Divine in Ancient Israel* (2004).

Stavrakopoulou, Francesca, and John Barton. *Religious Diversity in Ancient Israel and Judah* (2010).

Van der Toorn, Karel. *Scribal Culture and the Making of the Hebrew Bible* (2009).

Weinfeld, Moshe. *Normative and Sectarian Judaism in the Second Temple Period* (2010).

———. *The Place of the Law in the Religion of Ancient Israel* (2004).

For additional resources, including maps, primary sources, visuals, web links, and quizzes, please go to **www.oup.com/us/backman.**

CHAPTER 4

Greeks and Persians

2000 BCE–479 BCE

G reek history begins around 2000 BCE, when the first Indo-European settlers appeared around the Aegean rim. In the Mycenaean age, those on the mainland grew wealthy—and in the epic poetry of Homer, the Greeks took them for their ancestors. The Greeks themselves drew up armies, established colonies, and developed the first philosophers. They founded the city-states of Miletus, Sparta, and Athens, and they came into collision with a great empire in Persia. But their origins lie in legends.

GREECE AND PERSIA

◀ **Koure** Starting in the Archaic Age, Greek sculptors popularized the use of figures called *kouros* ("youth") and *koure* ("maiden"), in worship of Apollo. The purpose of the statues is still debated. Male *kouroi* are usually nude, beardless, and standing erect in a posture reminiscent of Egyptian statuary. This statue of a *koure* was produced in the mid-6th century BCE and was used to mark the grave of the woman who modeled for it. The artist's inscription at the base gives her name, Phrasikleia. It reads: "The grave marker of Phrasikleia. I shall be called a maiden *[koure]* forever, since the gods allotted me this identity instead of a marriage. Aristion of Paros carved me."

FROM CHAOS TO TRAGEDY

The legends are not always pretty: the cosmos began with primordial Chaos, out of which emerged the elemental forces of Gaia (Earth), Eros (Love), Tartarus (Abyss), and Erebus (Darkness). Earth brought forth, through self-gestation, Uranus (Sky)—which is when the trouble began. Uranus took his own mother, Gaia, as his wife, and they produced the twelve Titans. One of them, Kronos castrated his father, overthrew his mother, and took up lordship of the heavens, subjecting his Titanic brothers and sisters to his rule, except for his sister Rhea (Fertility), whom he took as his queen. Fearing that one of his children might do to him what he had done to his own father, Cronos took each child that Rhea produced and ate it. Rhea, we are told, disliked this; so she took the next child that came along (Zeus, the god of Thunder) and hid it and gave Cronos a stone wrapped in a blanket to eat instead. When Zeus grew to manhood, he drugged Cronos with a potion that made him vomit all his children. Zeus then rallied his revived siblings to join him in killing Cronos and seizing control of heaven.

The Birth of Athena   The patron goddess of Athens, Athena was said to have been born, fully grown, from the head of her father, Zeus. In this image from ca. 500 BCE, Athena springs from Zeus's skull. Hephaistos, the forger god who had cracked Zeus's head open with his axe, to speed up the delivery, has apparently fled the scene. Apollo and Hermes appear on the left; Ares and Aphrodite on the right.

All this was just the beginning of the story. Greek mythology consists of hundreds of tales regarding the great **Olympian deities** (Zeus and his siblings, who lived on the mythical Mount Olympus), demigods, and heroes, whose adventures display astonishing creative power and vitality. Themes of incest, patricide, and rebellion occur with unnerving frequency. Like some of their Near Eastern peers, Greek gods and goddesses can be petulant, vain, and full of self-importance, but they also embody virtues of honor, justice, and love. They do not always act admirably, but they do not act without reason. If anything, the myths portray life as an intricate web of passionate feeling and reaction. Each myth leads into and influences the next. A spurned wife here emerges as a wrathful harridan there. A proud king in one story becomes the humbled fallen in another. Greek mythology presents a

CHAPTER TIMELINE

2500 BCE Beginning of Minoan Culture on island of Crete	
	1600 BCE Appearance of Mycenaeans in Greece; use of Linear B script
1375 BCE Mycenaeans seize Knossos	
	1450 BCE Mycenaeans destroy and/or take over most cities in Crete, with exception of Knossos
776 BCE First Olympic Games held	
	1200 BCE Dark Age begins; Mycenaean Greece destroyed

universe of emotion, ambition, and a search for justice—but it also portrays, often with horrifying effect, the unexpected consequences of every action. Life began with Chaos, as the Greeks saw it, and it usually ends in tragedy.

THE MYCENAEAN WORLD: HEROES AND KINGS

Although the first settlers may have been of diverse origins, they quickly developed a sense of a cultural unity and began to refer to themselves as a single people—the Hellenes.[1] They inhabited a larger territory than the Greek mainland itself. In ancient times, the term Greece meant the rough circle of land consisting of the Greek peninsula to the west, the coasts of Macedonia and Thrace to the north, coastal Asia Minor to the east, and the island of Crete to the south, plus the scores of smaller islands throughout the Aegean Sea. The climate is magnificent, with year-round sun and modest rainfall, but the land itself is harsh. Greece proper has a wild, jagged coastline with few harbors broad and deep enough for mooring large vessels. Inland the countryside is mountainous and irregular: less than 20 percent of the land is arable. The land was covered with forests in the Neolithic Age, but by the time the Hellenes arrived most of the trees had long since disappeared. Making matters worse, mineral ores were scarce, rivers even scarcer, and the waters of the Aegean Sea were not particularly well-stocked with fish.

What made the Aegean rim so attractive was the sea: sailing through the calm waters was easy at any time of the year. Distances were short, and the sheer abundance of islands meant that one never risked getting lost. (Ancient mariners navigated by landmarks rather than by the stars.) Hundreds of coastal communities could thus be in constant contact with one another. The Hellenes may have settled in a vast sprawl of isolated sites, but by devoting themselves to trade they could prosper. Although they were generally able to feed and clothe themselves, the

---

[1] The English words Greece and Greek derive from the Latin names for the region and its people: Graeca and Graeci, respectively.

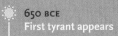

750 BCE		499 BCE
Dark Age ends; beginning of Archaic Age	650 BCE	Ionian cities revolt against Persian Empire; end of Archaic Period
	First tyrant appears	

700 BCE	594 BCE	494–479 BCE
Homer composes the *Iliad* and *Odyssey*	Solon established as leader in Athens	The Persian Wars

effect

ancient Greeks never developed much of a manufacturing base; they shipped goods from one site to another rather than producing goods of their own. Transport, not industry, made their fortunes. Their high degree of contact with other cultures meant more than a strong economy as well; it also exposed them to ideas, technologies, value systems, political institutions, artistic styles, and religious practices. The result was an exhilarating cultural adaptivity—a willingness to criticize old ideas and to experiment with new ones. The physical chaos of the Aegean rim gave birth to a brilliant civilization that lived passionately, sought order and justice, and questioned the meaning of life, of time, and of death. And like many of the plays for which it is renowned, ancient Greek culture ended tragically.

> The physical chaos of the Aegean rim gave birth to a brilliant civilization that lived passionately, sought order and justice, and questioned the meaning of life, of time, and of death. And like the most renowned of the plays it produced, ancient Greek culture ended tragically.

The first signs of Aegean prosperity and creative energy emerged in Crete. In 1899 a British archaeologist, Sir Arthur Evans (1851–1941), unearthed a magnificent palace complex at Knossos—with three stories and nearly thirteen hundred rooms. Evans mistakenly identified it as the

Knossos   Artist's reconstruction of the Minoan-palace at Knossos. A massive, labyrinthine complex, the palace was built and rebuilt throughout the years 1700–1400 BCE. It had nearly 1,300 separate living spaces, work rooms, storage areas, galleries, and halls. There was, however, only one toilet connected to a drain, although an efficient sewer system carried off waste water poured into it at various collection sites. The one working toilet was in the queen's bedroom.

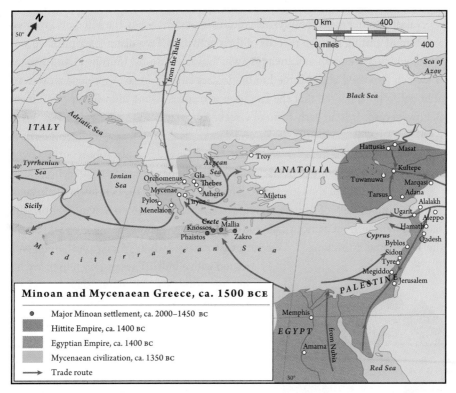

MAP 4.1 Minoan and Mycenean Greece, ca. 1500 BCE

palace of the Greeks' legendary ancient king Minos and gave the name **Minoan** to a culture that had its heyday from 2000 to 1500 BCE (see Map 4.1). The palace actually belonged to an exceptionally wealthy trader and shipping magnate, who ruled over Knossos itself but not the entire island. Subsequent excavations have found numerous other palaces, though none quite so splendid. Vibrant decoration—murals, statuary, frescos, tiling, pottery, textiles, and metalwork—characterized them all, which suggests that Minoan wealth was widely spread. Moreover, none of the palaces had fortifications of any kind, which likely means that naval defenses were sufficient to keep marauders away. Homes of town dwellers have been found, too—more modest, but still more attractive and comfortable than common urban homes in Middle Kingdom Egypt or Hittite Anatolia.[2] Minoan ships carried tons of Egyptian wheat, Greek olive oil and wine, Palestinian metalwork, Anatolian textiles, and Babylonian spices.

---

[2]   Rural peasants constituted the bulk of the Minoan population, but few traces of their lives have been found.

Like the other great commercial cultures of ancient times, the Minoans invented a system of writing to keep records of their activities. Two distinct scripts have survived, which are known as **Linear A** (which was in use by 1800 BCE) and **Linear B** (which appeared about three hundred years later). Linear A remains a mystery, although scholars agree that the language it records is not Indo-European. Linear B, however, records an early form of Greek. Apparently the trader culture on Crete predated the arrival of the Hellenes, and the success of that earlier culture may have been what attracted the Hellenes into the Aegean in the first place. Numerous Greek legends, after all, describe their fascination with Minoan life and magnificence.

The stories about the Greek hero Theseus are among the best known. Theseus, a prince from the city of Athens, traveled to Crete to pay tribute to King Minos, who sent the hero into the famous Labyrinth. Minos had built the maze in order to hold the monstrous Minotaur (a freakish beast created when Minos's lecherous wife mated with a bull). Theseus, keen to prove his heroism, finds the Minotaur, slays it, and retraces his path out of the Labyrinth and into the arms of Minos's daughter.[3] The Greek fascination with Crete thus seems well documented; their arrival on the island around 1500 BCE coincides with the transition from Linear A to Linear B. Minoan Crete taught the Greeks seafaring, commerce, writing, and the rudiments of government. By 1400 BCE, though, disaster struck. Whether it was an invasion or a natural calamity like an earthquake, the island of Crete was devastated, and their social and commercial empire—now in the hands of the Hellenes—began to fade.

The Phaistos Disk   This disk was found in 1908 by archeologists working at the Minoan palace of Phaistos, which is on the island of Crete. Nearly six inches (15 cm) in diameter, it has a spiral of various symbols stamped into the clay on each side. All efforts to decipher the code have failed, leading some individuals to suggest, predictably, that the disk is a hoax. Other interpretations argue that it is a calendar, an astronomical chart, or even a game board. Take your pick.

The Hellenes living on the Greek mainland then began to dominate the Aegean. The years from roughly 1600 to 1200 BCE are known as the age of **Mycenaean Greece**, after the city of Mycenae, which according to tradition was the city ruled by the legendary king Agamemnon. Like their mythical king, the Mycenaeans were haughty, cocksure, and militaristic. What kept them from becoming a powerful empire was their internal division. The Greek mainland consists of hundreds of highland valleys and plains separated by irregular mountains and deep defiles; by controlling a handful of mountain passes, a tribal

---

[3]   Legend has it that the god Zeus, when hiding from his cannibalistic father, went to Crete and hid inside another labyrinth until he was ready to rebel against Cronos.

leader could effectively seal off an entire plateau area and create an autonomous, if isolated, miniature kingdom for himself. Once in control, these leaders governed through a tightly centralized royal court made up of military officers and bureaucrats, who lived and worked in the enormous citadel-palaces constructed from large stone blocks. Common peasants, nominally free but little better off because of it, and slave teams worked the land and tended the herds. Peasant women weaved fabric, minded children, and prepared food. Handfuls of artisans engaged in leatherwork, winemaking, and metalsmithing.

Virtually all of the surviving Linear B tablets consist of supply lists for the kings' armies. They detail grain rations, wine allowances, clothing, and armor allotments. Larger kingdoms engaged in mass manufacture. The palace at Pylos, on Crete, for example, maintained over four hundred bronzesmiths on site. Since that many workers would produce vastly more armor and weapons than their king needed, it seems clear that Mycenaean Pylos specialized as an arms manufacturer.

The intense competition for raw materials, markets, and control of trade routes kept the Mycenaeans in more or less constant conflict with one another—which, in turn, validated their militarism. A king kept his position of dominance by acquiring the things his people needed, which he did by trade when possible but by force

Mycenaean Warrior Vase The "warrior vase" was named by Heinrich Schliemann, the 19th-century archeologist who discovered it. It is a mixing bowl (*krator* in Greek) used for mixing wine and water and dates to the 12th century BCE. The armor and weaponry are characteristic of the Mycenaean Age—nobleman warriors in short tunics with breastplates and greaves (leg armor). Helmets, shields, and spears complete the look.

when necessary. Conquest and gain were self-justifying. These are precisely the conditions and perhaps the only conditions that can turn figures like Agamemnon and Achilles into heroes. Royal tombs, shaped like inverted beehives, were veritable display-houses of weaponry and armor, to which were added miniatures of chariots and battleships, all surrounded by wall drawings of war scenes and the slaughtering of captives.

Little is known of Mycenaean religion. Various texts mention the names of several gods—most notably Zeus, Poseidon (the god of the sea), and Demeter (the goddess of grain). Since the Mycenaeans built no temples, which might have left some record of their activities, however, we know nothing about communal religious life, or indeed if any existed at all. Homes had individual shrines within them, either for the worship of ancestors or for petitioning the few gods whose names have survived. Yet no prayers or inscriptions survive to describe the content of their faith. The beehive tombs and their grim contents tell us more about Mycenaean life than any afterlife they might have believed in. In this way, at least, the first Greeks resemble the Old Kingdom Egyptians: states of great wealth and power, possessed of technological skill and access to other cultures, and with developed literacy, but with no intellectual or literary heritage of any note. Two hundred years, from 1400 to 1200 BCE, is a long time for a literate people to go without to producing anything worth remembering.

> The beehive tombs and their grim contents tell us more about Mycenaean life than about any afterlife they might have believed in. In this way, at least, the first Greeks resemble the Old Kingdom Egyptians: states of great wealth and power, possessed of technological skill and access to other cultures, and with developed literacy, but with no intellectual or literary heritage of any note.

THE END OF AN AGE AND MYTHIC ANCESTORS

The later Greeks insisted on claiming the Mycenaeans as their ancestors, though, and ascribed to them the epic adventures of their mythical heroes. When Homer composed the **Iliad**, sometime around 750 BCE, he chose a tale set in Mycenaean times—the events of the Trojan War. In reality, the war occurred as one of the many struggles by the newcomer Greeks to seize part of the Aegean rim; but in Homer's reimagining, the tale becomes one of Greek honor and military destiny.[4] The son of King Priam of Troy, named Paris, has been appointed the judge of a beauty contest between three goddesses. Each goddess bribes Paris, who ultimately selects the goddess (Aphrodite) who offered him the most beautiful mortal woman on earth.

---

4   Troy was an important trading city in northwestern Asia Minor.

That woman was Helen, the wife of King Menelaus of Sparta (and the brother of Agamemnon), who is promptly delivered to Troy as Paris's prize. The war then begins when all the Mycenaean kings join forces to avenge the injury done to Menelaus's honor. Homer assuredly based his epic on ancient oral traditions, but the *Iliad* can hardly be taken to represent Mycenaean culture accurately. If anything, it describes aspects of the Dark Age (1200–800 BCE) that separated Homer's world from Agamemnon's. But telling tales of Mycenaean heroes, powerful rulers, and their origins in a murky distant era of violently contending gods gave the Greeks a sense of rootedness. It tied them to their new Aegean home and tried to make sense out of the chaos of their lives.

The Mycenaean age ended abruptly with the invasion, around 1200 BCE, of the Dorians, one of the groups sometimes associated with the Sea Peoples who caused so much damage in Egypt and the Levant. The Dorians spoke a dialect of early Greek and may well have been present in the Aegean rim for some time. The Mycenaeans had thrown up a considerable number of new fortifications (and reinforced existing ones) around 1250 BCE, which suggests they saw trouble coming. But the Dorians, by themselves, could hardly have brought about the decline of the Mycenaeans and the start of the Dark Age, for the calamity that hit Greece proved so monumental that it must have resulted from other factors as well— whether plague, famine, civil strife, emigration, or a combination of them all.

> A single, astonishing fact drives the point home: between 1200 and 800 BCE Greece lost 90 percent of its population. This was perhaps the worst single scenario in the general upheaval caused by the Sea Peoples through the eastern Mediterranean and the Near East.

A single, astonishing fact drives the point home: between 1200 and 800 BCE Greece lost 90 percent of its population. This was perhaps the worst single scenario in the general upheaval caused by the Sea Peoples through the eastern Mediterranean and the Near East. The agrarian peasants in Greece were the least well-off farmers of the ancient Near East, given the harshness of their land, and were therefore least able to survive the catastrophe. The town dwellers of the Aegean cities were in a better position, but once the demographic hemorrhage interrupted the trade cycle, there was little they could do to compensate. Hence everyone presumably fled or was cut down by war, famine, or disease before they could flee. By the time the Dark Age ended, around 800 BCE, the Greeks had not only declined in dramatic numbers but had also shifted tenancy. A majority of those who survived had moved from the inland plateaus to the coastal towns, where they attempted to take up new trades. The days of isolated rural kingdoms were over.

And that is precisely what Homer laments in the *Iliad* and *Odyssey*. These epic poems, like all great art, work on many levels; on the political level, they are conservative, romanticized nostalgia, another instance of lament for a lost, idealized past. The *Iliad*'s heroes are all kings, and the conflicts dramatized by the poem all center on the issue of the honor due to them:

- The need to avenge Menelaus's honor starts the war.
- Achilles feels a seething rage when Agamemnon is awarded one of his maidservants, which Achilles regards as a shameful trammeling of his honor.
- Only one common soldier among the Greeks is given a speaking part in the epic: Thersites, who in Book 2 urges his comrades to give up the fight and return to Greece. Odysseus humiliates him for dishonoring his king and beats him with his staff in front of all the soldiers.
- Achilles brings dishonor to King Priam of Troy by desecrating the corpse of Priam's slain son.

The long, loving descriptions of each Greek king's noble mien, battlefield bravery, magnificent armor, and stately speech—everything, then, serves Homer's goal of lauding the halcyon past of Mycenaean monarchy. In an early scene in the *Iliad*, as the Greeks take the field to prepare for yet another battle, Priam leads Helen to the ramparts that surround Troy so that she can identify the Greek leaders for him.

> "Come, Helen," said Priam, "and tell me who is that great and powerful
> man over there? Others are taller than he, but never have I seen a warrior
> more finely formed, more noble in bearing; surely he is a king."
> Beautiful Helen replied, . . . "That is Agamemnon, the son of Atreus,
>   the lord
> of the Argos plain, a noble ruler and dread warrior." . . .
> Then old Priam looked out again, and this time he beheld Odysseus,
>   and asked,
> "And who is that one? He is a head shorter than Atreus's son, but has
> broader shoulders and a more powerful chest. He has laid his
>   armor and
> weapons on the ground, and strides commandingly up and down
>   the ranks
> like a burly ram keeping a flock of silver-fleeced sheep in line."
> And Helen, the heavenly beauty, answered him, "That is Odysseus,
>   the son

of Laertes, the skillful mastermind, Ithaca-born (that raw, stony
    island!),
who knows every trick and stratagem of war." *(Iliad 3.150–220)*

Homer laments the passing of the heroic age of landed kings and dreads the coming
of the new, diminished Greece of coastal cities with their petty concerns.

    Another famous passage, toward the end of the poem, describes the impos-
sibly ornate new armor made for Achilles by the forge god Hephaestus when
Achilles finally gets over his anger at Agamemnon and decides to reenter the fighting. Hephaestus finishes the suit of armor with a splendid new shield, on which he
casts fantastically precise scenes—including an image of two cities, contrasting the
effete mundane present with the manly heroic past:

> [Hephaestus] forged two cities also, fair and bustling: in one there were
> wedding scenes and feasts, crowds with torches leading brides
> from their chambers and escorting them through the streets.
> Loud wedding songs broke out and young men danced
> while flutes and lyres played; women stood in their doorways and
>   watched.
> A crowd stood in a market, for there was a quarrel over the
>   compensation
> one man owed another for a murder he had done. The first man
> swore to the crowd that he had paid all, and the other denied it. . . .
> The town elders sat on chairs of stone set in a circle, holding staves
> put into their hands by heralds; with the help of a staff
> each elder rose in turn to voice his judgment. Two talents of gold
> lay at the circle's center, a payment for the one whose judgment
>   would be
> the most straightforward and true.
>
> Around the other city, however, two besieging armies in shining
>   armor,
> Divided on what to do: whether to sack the city or to spare it in
>   return for
> half the citadel's treasure. The townsfolk would not concede to either
>   plan,
> and secretly armed themselves to break the siege. . . .
> They filed out, led by Ares and Pallas Athena, who were clad in golden
>   robes. . . .

> When the besieging armies, meeting in council, heard [the citizen-
> soldiers, lying in ambush]
> They mounted their horses and sped towards where the sound was
> coming from.
> The armies drew up in battle lines by the riverbanks and hurled
> their bronze-tipped javelins. Then Strife and Riot joined the fray,
> and dreadful Fate too—who dragged a wounded man, an unwounded
> one,
> and a dead one as well behind Her. [Fate's] tunic was soaked with
> blood,
> and She, Strife, and Riot joined the battle and fought like living men,
> and dragged their dead away. (*Iliad, 18.490–500, 509–512, 516–518, 530–540*)

The contrast is clear: a society of shallow merrymakers, pettiness, decrepit officials, and justice for sale, and a society of manliness, resolve, and bold action. Greece, Homer wails, once the home of heroes, has become a nation of whiners.

The Trojan Horse   This is one of the earliest representations (ca. 670 BCE) of the stratagem that supposedly ended the Trojan War. Greek soldiers hid inside the wooden sculpture that was given as a parting gift to the victorious Trojans and emerged from it at night and opened the city gates to the entire Greek army. The story does not appear in the Iliad but is mentioned in the Odyssey. In this image, taken from an amphora (a large storage vessel for wine, oil, or water) found at Mykonos, the Greeks are shown as though peering through windows.

The *Odyssey* treats the same theme. With the end of the Trojan War, wily Odysseus, the king of Ithaca, spends ten years struggling to get home to his devoted wife, Penelope, and his loving son, Telemachus.[5] In the meantime, his royal palace has been taken over by "suitors"—young upstarts from the town who try to persuade Penelope that Odysseus is dead and to get her to choose one of them as a new husband. Hence we have the noble king's adventure, in which he proves his superiority to every challenge, and a society, Ithaca, paralyzed with self-doubt. The suitors represent the "new" society of Homer's own time—brash, pushy, self-interested, and ignoble. The poem is a lament: *When, oh when, will our king come back? Oh, if only our king were here, we would then see justice and right order restored!*

But if Homer romanticizes the long past, he mistakenly attributes to it many of the qualities of his own time. The Mycenaean kings were vastly wealthier than any of the royals on display in the epics—not through any particular merit of their own, but simply because they hoarded their societies' money more brutally than those of Homer's own time did. Moreover, the ancient kings did not necessarily stand in the thick of the fray the way Agamemnon, Ajax, Menelaus, Odysseus, and others do in the poems; they directed the fighting from a safe distance instead. And much of the armor, weaponry, and tactics described in the poem differed profoundly from those used by the Mycenaeans.

The Dark Age obviously had its share of calamities. Still, once the demographic collapse had occurred and the migration of the survivors to the coasts had taken place, Greece was not a place of unrelenting misery. The decreased population meant that the amount of food needed to maintain it also declined, to the point where the mainland was able to feed itself unaided by imports from Egypt and Asia Minor. Since the foodstuffs produced in Greece—grain, oil, wine, and meat—were difficult to preserve in the bright heat, the rulers of Homer's time tended to distribute surpluses among the people, thus ensuring at least an absence of famine. The upland villages and coastal towns were small enough to be self-governing, which inspired a sense of independence among the people; identifying themselves as the sustainers of their own communal lives, they gradually coined a new word—**polis** (plural poleis)—for their communities. The polis referred to the physical town, the people who resided in it, and the group identity they shared. To belong to a polis meant more than happening to reside in a particular locale; it meant being a constituent element of something larger than oneself, participating in a web of mutual obligations, responsibilities, and rights.

---

[5]   Odysseus battles giant beasts, survives shipwrecks, is seduced by a goddess, visits the underworld, taunts the sea god Poseidon, encounters witches, and outwits one foe after another.

COLONISTS, HOPLITES, AND TYRANTS

As the Homeric era gave way to the **Archaic period** (750–500 BCE), the poleis of Greece began to extend their reach by establishing networks of colonies. These networks extended around the Aegean rim, then into the Black Sea, and ultimately westward into the Mediterranean. With the expanded reach of the poleis came other changes as well—including a society built for war. This brought with it highly trained armies, periods of political reform under tyrants, a cult of masculinity, more constraints on women, and ritualized homosexual contact among the aristocracy.

The colonies were not military expansions. The Greeks generally searched out uninhabited harbors, established small coastal settlements around them, and then opened trade relations with the populations further inland (see Map 4.2). Inheritance practices lay behind this growth. Greek custom dictated that a man's estate was divided by his legitimate heirs—an easy enough matter when it comes to cash, flocks and herds, and portable property. But what about a man's farmland? A farm may be large enough to survive subdivision among a man's sons, but what happens to those subdivisions when the next generation comes along? At a certain point (and usually an early one), the portions of land received by individual heirs cannot support a family. This forced many heirs to sell their land, usually to a sibling but in theory to anyone with available funds. With the money, they would then relocate to a colony and set up anew.

The colonists, in other words, were neither military adventurers nor impoverished exiles but landholders—specifically, landholders who had cashed out their equity and were looking for new investments. An entrepreneurial spirit, not an exploitative one, drove Greek colonization. Given that fact, it is not surprising that groups of these entrepreneurs from a single polis would set out together in search of new settlement. Personal connections and a sense of shared identity also caused them to establish commercial ties with the polis from which they had come. In this way, the Greek colonies established were not just dependencies of the home city-state, to be exploited for domestic gain. Rather, they took on the character of smaller reproductions of the home city. They were independent and self-governing, yet united in identity with the original polis.

Between 750 and 500 BCE, the Greeks established hundreds of colonies around the Aegean rim, the Black Sea, and the entire perimeter of Asia Minor, across southern Italy and Sicily, and along the southern coast of France and the eastern coast of Spain (see Map 4.2). A handful of colonies appeared along the North African coast as well.[6] This explosive growth coincided almost exactly with the collapse of

---

[6] There were two types of colonies: apoidikiai and empora, the first self-governing, the second governed from the mainland as trading outposts.

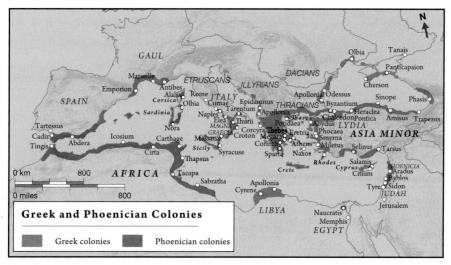

MAP 4.2   **Greek and Phoenician Colonies**

Israel under the Assyrians (722 BCE) and the conquest of Judah by the Babylonians (587 BCE). The coincidence was not entirely coincidental, for the turmoil in the Holy Land interrupted the commercial activity of the Phoenicians, who had previously been the main actors on the sea-lanes. The Greeks thus had few competitors for control of the sea-lanes, and certainly none with the geographical advantages they had. Because of the opportunities abroad, most Greek cities maintained fairly stable population levels in the Archaic period, and many colonies outstripped their home cities in size.

Steady home population levels contributed to two contradictory developments: the involvement of individuals in the public life of their communities and the concentration of wealth (and consequently of power) in a small coterie of families. Greek democracy was never fully democratic in the modern sense of the term. However, it did encourage, and result from, the active involvement of skilled workers, merchants, shippers, and financiers in the life of their poleis and corresponding colonies. As for the colonists themselves, they actively sought out contact with their neighboring or host populations, but were careful not to assimilate. Ethnic pride forbade that—for the Greeks, like many other ancient cultures, regarded themselves as superior to other nations. Moreover, the ease and speed of contact with the mainland kept the colonists' cultural identity as Greeks strong. Panhellenic religious festivals and celebrations like the Olympic Games (the first of which took place in 776 BCE) helped to keep the scattered Greek colonists in close contact with one another. But because the overseas Greeks encouraged contact with their non-Greek neighbors, a steady exposure to new ideas, technologies, and practices helped promote innovation. It is no accident that many of ancient Greece's greatest thinkers and artists came from the colonies rather than the mainland.

But because the overseas Greeks encouraged contact with their non-Greek neighbors, a steady exposure to new ideas, technologies, and practices helped promote innovation. It is no accident that many of ancient Greece's greatest thinkers and artists came from the colonies rather than the mainland.

One did not have to be a prominent merchant, civic official, or intellectual to serve one's polis. Every male between the ages of sixteen and sixty served in the polis's military force. The use of trained infantry did not originate with the Greeks, but with the Assyrians—although there is no clear evidence that the Greeks learned the technique from them. Earlier military strategy, if it can be called that, consisted of mass swarmings of foot soldiers under the leadership of chariot-riding kings or generals. Once the battle lines were drawn up, the fighting quickly devolved into a free-for-all. The Greeks, however, perfected fighting in trained units. They had to, since their depleted population meant that they could never count on having superior numbers on the field. What they came up with was the notion of groups of foot soldiers holding tight formation as a block, eight horizontal lines of ten to twenty men each, who stood shoulder to shoulder and moved as a single unit. Called a **phalanx**, such a unit rushed at the enemy and smashed through them, like a kind of foot-powered armored tank. Each soldier wore a breastplate and helmet, had a short sword at his belt, and carried a round shield (called a hoplos in Greek) and a thrusting spear. By combining their weight and momentum, they made up a powerful force.[7]

It required long hours of training to develop an effective phalanx, for each soldier had to overcome the instinct to fend for himself by swinging his sword at everything that moved. Instead, the soldiers had to hold formation and fight as a single group. This had two important consequences. First, since all men fought in their polis's army, all had to attain a degree of physical conditioning—and hence the Greek emphasis on exercise. Athletic games (such as the Olympics), public training facilities, sporting events, and the like all played important roles in Archaic Age culture, a fact we can see in the artwork of the time. Greek painting, sculpture, and poetry emphasize the beauty of a fit male physique more so than any other ancient culture. To be fit and strong, they believed, was more than to be beautiful: it was freedom itself. Second, the hoplite army underscored and confirmed the

---

[7]   The name for these soldiers, hoplites, derives from the shields they carried.

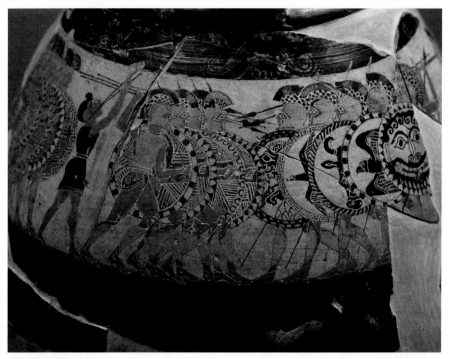

Hoplites The circular shield of Greek infantry was called a *hoplon*, hence the soldiers'
name. Hoplites were literally "shield bearers," and even though their principal weapon
was a spear, it is fitting that they were named for their defensive gear. The circular
shields held by rows of footmen overlapped one another and presented thus a solid wall
of defense. The company, like the civil societies they represented, depended on group
action to survive. Their discipline and group-mindedness are evident here in the uniformly faceless soldiers, the perfect alignment of their marching feet, and the parallel
lines formed by their spears.

interdependence of the polis. It was the body politic, the community that literally
stood together as one or perished. A phalanx was living proof that people are stronger together than apart.

And this led to trouble. The more the Greek cities relied on the new armies,
the more important the commoners who made up their ranks became. These soldiers paid for their own equipment and took battlefield instructions from one another through a combination of verbal and manual signals. The aristocrats who
made up the charioted officer class declined in importance accordingly, which had
important repercussions for political life. A city that depends on its common men
for survival cannot deny them political power. This is why the Archaic Age was
filled with social strife—and why Homer's great epics are politically significant.
The stratified society ruled by noble kings and aristocratic heroes was giving way

to a primitive but encouraging egalitarianism, a world of merchants, craftsmen, teachers, colonists, and workers.

Powerful aristocracies, however, do not go away quietly. Popular demands for a greater voice in government usually inspired a conservative reaction of some sort, and the stridency of the debate intensified in boom-and-bust cycles. An early effort at social revolution occurred at Athens in 632 BCE, when a popular athlete named Cylon tried unsuccessfully to rouse the masses against the nobles and wealthy merchants who ran the polis as an oligarchy. A dozen years later the city council gave extraordinary authority to a fellow aristocrat named Solon, to institute reforms that might free the city from class strife. His efforts ultimately failed, which resulted in a more populist figure named Pisistratos seizing power around 560 BCE. He was Athens's first tyrant.

> A city that depends on its common men for survival cannot deny them political power. This is why the Archaic Age was filled with social strife—and why Homer's great epics are politically significant. The stratified society ruled by noble kings and aristocratic heroes was giving way to a primitive but encouraging egalitarianism, a world of merchants, craftsmen, teachers, colonists, and workers.

The word tyrant carries a pejorative meaning in English, but in ancient Greek a **tyrant** (*tyrannos*) was simply a person who seized power temporarily in order to bring about dramatic reform in a politically deadlocked state. In terms of social class, the tyrants were aristocrats but were allied with the masses. Some Marxist historians have seen them as the first "dictatorships of the proletariat," which is not entirely wrong. The difference between Solon and Pisistratos was that Solon had been the nobles' candidate for temporary dictatorship, while Pisistratos was the popular champion. The Archaic Age is peppered with occasional tyrannies, among the best known of which was the tyranny at Thebes of a semilegendary figure named Oedipus. (It ended badly.) Tyrannies seldom lasted longer than a decade or two, since the reasons for it had either been achieved by that time or else were deemed hopeless. In either case the tyrant lost the popular support of the hoplites, which put an end to his power.

Tyrants were installed in order to reform the state and were judged good or ill according to that standard alone. The methods they employed were of less significance. Pisistratos went so far as to wound himself with a spear, so that he could ride his chariot into the Athenian marketplace, blood dripping from his injury, and claim to have survived an assassination attempt from his rivals. All this was to whip the crowd of his supporters into a frenzy and quiet his rivals. Solon, it should be noted, became one of Pisistratos's closest advisors.

Here is how the historian Herodotus described the education of one tyrant, Periander of Corinth (r. 627–587 BCE), by another, Thrasyboulos of Miletus (d. 388 BCE):

> Periander was initially a kinder tyrant than his father [Cypselus] had been, but after he had absorbed the lessons of Thrasyboulos, the tyrant of Miletus, he became even more bloodthirsty than Cypselus had been. . . . [After Periander sent an ambassador to Miletus] Thrasyboulos led this messenger into a grain field outside the city. . . . Over and over again, whenever he saw a wheat stalk growing higher than its neighbors he cut it down and threw it away, until he had at last done away with all the strongest and most flowering of the wheat stalks. He spoke no words as he passed through the entire field, and then dismissed the messenger. After [the messenger] returned to Corinth, Periander asked him eagerly what Thrasyboulos had said. The messenger replied that Thrasyboulos had said nothing and that he thought Periander had sent him to deal with a madman who destroyed his own property. . . . But Periander, interpreting Thrasyboulos's actions well, understood right away that his [Thrasyboulos's] advice was to kill Corinth's leading citizens. From this point onward Periander inflicted every imaginable type of brutality on his people.

Not all tyrants were as vicious as Periander, but most Greeks were glad to see the days of the tyrants pass—even if they remained darkly fascinated by them in their histories and stage tragedies.

A CULT OF MASCULINITY

Archaic Greece developed a cult of masculinity that distinguished it from other ancient cultures. Theirs was a society built for war, in which every man sixteen to sixty was expected to serve in the hoplite army. Women, they were persuaded, were inferior creatures who contributed nothing to the public life of the community and hence did not deserve the social or political advantages of citizenship. Except for slave girls and women of the lowest working class, who might work as cleaners or seamstresses, women were essentially unseen in Greece. Girls received little or no education and were raised with the idea that their sole function in life was to marry, produce children, and care for their household. At marriage a young woman became the legal dependent of her husband, having the same rights as (and no more than) the children she would produce. Apart from going to the market or the public well, visiting family members, and attending funerals and a handful of religious ceremonies, women (that is, all females above the age of twelve) were never to appear alone in public. Doing so would bring shame upon the household and give the father or husband leave to punish her severely.[8] Most homes in fact were physically divided into male and female zones, often with the female rooms enclosed behind a locked door to which the husband kept the key.

Except for slave girls and women of the lowest working class, who might work as cleaners or seamstresses, women were essentially unseen in Greece. Girls received little or no education and were raised with the idea that their sole function in life was to marry, produce children, and care for their household.

Citizenship in a polis, like ownership of property, was hereditary and a right so precious as to inspire an obsession with legitimate birth. A woman's seclusion, the Greek male insisted, was an essential measure to protect her from harm but more especially to ensure that any child she bore was indeed his own. Maintaining a woman's invisibility was the best way, men determined, to maintain her chastity before marriage and fidelity within it. Female virginity was an absolute requirement for marriage, except for cases of a man wedding a widow. Before a wedding, young brides typically offered special prayers and presented gifts at a temple to the virgin goddess Artemis; these gifts often consisted of the toys enjoyed by the bride in her girlhood. As a sexually experienced wife, she would no longer have need of them.

Since men in the Archaic period commonly did not marry until they were thirty years old, they thereby placed substantial sexual strains upon themselves.[9] Only three outlets for this pent-up energy existed: the use of female slaves as forced sexual partners, recourse to prostitutes, or sex with another man. The culture tolerated all three practices within certain limits. Slave girls had little hope of escaping sexual persecution. As the property of the man of the house, they had no choice but to submit to his attentions. In many cases, though, slave girls faced more violent treatment from the wives of their masters, particularly if the husband took a particular liking to a servant and favored her over sexual play with his wife.

Prostitutes were another option. Called *hetairai* in Greek ("companions," literally), these women were professional hostesses who offered meals and music in addition to sex; they received customers in their own residences, for the most part, but higher-priced hetairai also offered a kind of catering service, attending aristocratic symposia (drinking parties) and entertaining guests with music, dancing, and

---

[8]   A man who caught his wife committing adultery was legally entitled to kill her. A man who suspected his wife of adultery, but lacked proof, could beat her with impunity.

[9]   Girls were married soon after they reached the age of menstruation—somewhere around fifteen—in order to get maximum use of their fertile years.

Love for Sale   The Greeks enjoyed drinking cups with comic or bawdy scenes portrayed at the bottom—an ancient equivalent of today's thermally sensitive drinking glasses on which an image of a clothed beauty turns naked once the ice goes in—cheap frat-boy humor. Here an older man propositions a young "beautiful lad" (as the inscription *pais kalos* has it) with a sack of coins. Their robes, finely trimmed, mark them as members of the upper classes, for whom such homoerotic play was considered a unique privilege.

some practiced banter, in addition to the expected sexual couplings. These more expensive escorts were usually foreign-born, which added an element of exoticism to the otherwise tawdry business.

Homosexual contact was accepted, and even approved of, by society so long as certain norms were followed. First, it was a unique privilege of the aristocracy. Middle-class or working-class men who engaged in it received ridicule and hostility—ridicule because they were assumed to be too poor to afford a hetaira or not manly enough to rape a slave girl, and hostility because they were usurping an aristocratic right. Second, aristocratic homosexuality was regarded as an aspect of love, not merely as sexual release. Older men took noble youths, usually aged twelve to fifteen, under their protection, to guide them in the ways of society, government, and elite culture. Sexual relations were understood to be a part of this tutoring, with the young partner servicing the desires of the elder. To have intercourse with such a youth brought no shame. It was understood to be a right of high position in society. Call it "mentoring with privileges." But the vision of an enlightened Greek world in which mature and sophisticated men initiated compliant, elegant, noble youths into the joys of same-sex love without any shame on either part is a utopian fantasy. The culture simply gave its aristocrats free rein to penetrate anyone they wanted, except for other men's wives. There is no doubt that genuine love existed between many noble elders and their mentored youths; but there is no reason to regard all these arrangements as mutually and freely chosen.

What the Greeks despised was the inversion of sexual roles. For a grown man to receive intercourse, rather than to perform it, was a disgrace. Likewise, the exclusive enjoyment of sex with other males, whether one was in the active or passive role, they found repellent. The ancient Greek language has no words corresponding to the English word homosexual—either as a noun or an adjective. Having sex with another man was something that one did, a socially sanctioned rite of passage for the elites; but it did not define a human type.

SPARTA: THE MILITARIZATION OF THE CITIZENRY

Evidence (not all of it absolutely convincing) attests to roughly nine hundred poleis in the Archaic period, including the Black Sea, Aegean, and Mediterranean colonies. In order to appreciate the variety of forms "political" life could take, three examples should suffice. Sparta, Miletus, and Athens were the most powerful city-states of the age. And each was powerful in a different way.

Sparta boasted the most impressive military. It was a brutally efficient city—a large community in which an exceptionally large slave population (as much as three-quarters of the city's inhabitants) performed the labor of producing food, building homes, tending animals, weaving cloth, and doing basic craftwork. The slaves' labor freed the Spartan citizens to pursue the solitary goal of preparing for war. They did so neither to repel foreign invasion nor for overseas conquests of their own but simply to keep their enormous slave population in check. A revolt by the slaves, called **helots**, in the mid-7th century BCE had nearly toppled the Spartans and persuaded them to stay on their guard.

The militarization of the citizenry in the mid-7th century was nearly absolute and began at childbirth. City officials examined every infant born, to judge if it was healthy enough to keep; those who failed to pass muster were abandoned in the nearby mountains. Military training began at age seven for both boys and girls, with group exercise, marching drills, and athletic competitions, especially wrestling and javelin hurling. The sexes separated at age twelve, with girls taught elementary reading and writing and domestic economy, while boys were handed over to live in military barracks and instructed in fighting with weapons.

Diets were sharply restricted—not to combat obesity, but in order to inspire the boys to become effective thieves. Food thieves were punished harshly, not for the crime of theft but of getting caught. The food they stole was from their own farms. When training began at age seven, each boy was awarded a farm by the state. This farm was run for him by slaves. A hungry Spartan lad was expected to sneak from his barracks, dash to his own farm, steal his own food, and make it back without being caught or observed at either end. The idea was to acquire real-life experience of enduring the pains of hunger, of learning to move about without being seen, and of becoming self-reliant. Plutarch (d. 120 CE) describes an episode in which a young Spartan, having gone off in search of food, caught a fox. On the way back to his barracks, some older Spartans came upon him in the dark. Rather than face the humiliation of being caught, the young man hid the live fox under his cloak and never gave a hint of it to the elders, even as the fox bit and clawed its way into his entrails.

Boys were taught basic literacy, but the bulk of their training was military. At age twenty they began active service in the hoplite army. If they served ten straight years, they were granted full Spartan citizenship, which involved the right to speak in the assembly and to hold leadership positions in the polis. If a Spartan married while in his twenties, he still lived in his barracks—and had to sneak out at night to visit his wife. He was then punished, if he was caught, for the crime of being caught.

The superhuman rigor of Spartan training is obviously overstated, and one may wonder why so many historians take seriously this claim to severe self-denial and principled masochism. Disciplined people often boast of their self-denial, and often enough they amplify it in the boasting. Moreover, undisciplined people often exaggerate the discipline of others. It is significant that the only detailed contemporary description of Spartan life comes from Xenophon (427–354 BCE), an Athenian who witnessed the humiliating defeat of his city by the Spartans in the Peloponnesian War (431–404 BCE), as we will see in chapter 5. He dramatizes Spartan life in his book *Hellenica* ("Greek History"), in which he narrates the failure of Athenian democracy and his own disillusionment with his city. A later work, *The Constitution of the Lacedaemonians*, written in 388 BCE, provides the colorful detail. And the better known *Life of Lycurgus* by Plutarch draws heavily on Xenophon's treatise but adds considerable amounts of gossip and hearsay.[10]

Xenophon blamed Athens's defeat on its lack of order and discipline, the very traits he so admired in his adopted Sparta. All Spartan men, he insists, had the right to beat any Spartan youth for misbehavior; and the father of that youth, after learning of the beating, would beat the child again in order to show his solidarity with his peers. To discourage materialism and greed, he reports, Sparta forbade the use of gold and silver and instituted a new coinage made of iron— which was so valueless that it would require a wagonload of cash to make even

---

[10] When the war ended, Xenophon went into voluntary exile and ultimately ended up in Sparta, where he lived for twenty years before finally returning to Athens in 366.

Spartan Youths   The popular cult of Sparta as the site of practical discipline, order, and commitment was largely a creation of the Enlightenment. In the 19th century the painter Edgar Degas (1834–1917) portrayed Spartan youths as happy, grounded, playful, and, above all, purposeful. Here he imagines a group of spirited girls challenging some boys to a wrestling match.

a modest purchase. A Spartan man who was too old to satisfy his wife's sexual longings and produce children, he says, was required by law to appoint a young stud to be his wife's lover—which the elder Spartan always did with equanimity, knowing that he was doing what was best for the polis. Xenophon's description of the relentless rigor of Spartan life can hardly be believed, but it is the beginning of a tradition—one that the Spartans were keen to propagate. It was also a tradition that the Athenians wished to elaborate, since it lessened the embarrassment of their defeat in the Peloponnesian War. Who could blame them for falling to such superhumans?

Despite such exaggerations, Sparta was a notably disciplined and austere place. The artwork and music that had characterized its earlier history all but disappeared. Spartan life aimed at a single goal—keeping its citizens strong and resolute enough to keep the helots in place. The deadening effect on the society of this frightened narrowness of vision might well have been the undoing of Sparta, had it not been for a slow-gathering threat—a Persian invasion of Greece. Military dangers justify military precautions and give their founders an aura of foresight. The enormity of the Persian danger enhanced the perceived wisdom of Sparta's military reformers and added to their reputation for superhuman fortitude.

MILETUS: A MERCHANT OLIGARCHY AND THE FIRST PHILOSOPHERS

Miletus offered a sharp contrast to Sparta. Located on the western coast of Asia Minor, it was a commercial and cultural hub, involved equally in mainland Greek and Anatolian affairs. Miletus (modern Milet) originated in the Mycenaean period, declined during the Dark Age, and then reemerged as one of the Archaic Age's most vibrant cities. It had as many as a hundred colonies, most of these in the Black Sea region, like Sinope and Trapezus, its two most important colonies and the Turkish cities of Sinop and Trabzon today.[11]

Located on a small but strategic peninsula, Miletus was one of the principal way stations for Greek goods entering Asia Minor. There was also a fair-sized harbor, although accumulating sediment from the Maeander river—Büyük Menderes today—has since filled it, and it now lies roughly three miles (five kilometers) from the sea. It was also close to the inland city of Sardis, the western terminus of the Royal Highway built by the Persians as the main thoroughfare running through the heart of their empire. This made it a natural distribution point for Persian goods throughout the eastern Mediterranean. In constant contact with the Greek, Hittite, Phoenician, and Egyptian worlds in addition to the Lydian and Persian ones, Miletus was among the most cosmopolitan of cities in the 7th and 6th centuries BCE. It acquired a reputation producing for high-quality ceramics and eccentric intellectuals—like the philosophers Thales (624–546 BCE), Anaximander (610–546 BCE), and Anaximenes (585–528 BCE), and the early historian Hecataeus (550–476 BCE).

MILETUS AND THE AEGEAN, ca. 550 BCE

Governed by a merchant oligarchy, the people of Miletus saw greater potential for growth in the Mediterranean than in the land trade with Persia, and so they organized the other coastal cities of Asia Minor into an alliance called the **Ionian League**. A reputation for rebelliousness reached far back in the city's history.[12] The Persians took control of Miletus when they conquered the whole of Asia Minor and set up a series of tyrants to govern the city in their stead. Herodotus relates that the first of these, Histiaeus (d. 494 BCE), joined in the Persian campaign against the Scythians in southern Russia (what is now Ukraine), using his city's service to the empire as a means of extracting the right to colonize throughout the Black Sea. Given the extraordinary number of Miletus's colonies in the area, Herodotus's tale may be true. Even so, doubts about the city's truest loyalties continued, whether eastward with Persia or westward with the Greeks.

---

[11]   Miletus's colonies focused on shipping slaves, timber, and wheat from the region of southern Russia. All were in short supply in the Aegean.

[12]   As early as 1320 BCE, in the first recorded reference to the city, Miletus was cited as a center of rebellion. The Hittite king Mursili II ordered it to be razed as a consequence.

When the Ionian League finally broke with Persia in 499 BCE, Miletus (and its new tyrant, Aristagoras) joined the revolt and became its leader. Persia exacted a terrible revenge, however, leveling the city shortly thereafter. The destruction of the city was so great that it inspired Phrynichus, one of the earliest Greek tragedians, to compose a play on the theme in 492 BCE. *The Capture of Miletus,* we are told, won first prize in the dramatic competition of that year but upset the audience so severely that the judges forbade any playwright in future to compose another tragedy on the theme. And, for good measure, they hit Phrynichus with a heavy fine. The play survives only in small fragments.

Miletus's greatest claim to fame, however, is as the birthplace of philosophy. The first three true philosophers in Western history—Thales, Anaximander, and Anaximenes—all appeared there. The city's essence as a cultural crossroads no doubt contributed much to this development, although evidence of a heightened appreciation for **rationalism** is present in Greek culture going back to Mycenaean times. What Thales and his followers began was the effort to systematize the observations one draws from everyday experience. Cause and effect surround us at all times, of course, and to notice that fact does not take genius. We observe the world's workings everyday: seeds buried in soil grow into plants; wood placed in fire is itself inflamed, whereas metal or stone is not; wine, when drunk, produces lightheadedness; the shadow produced by a stick placed vertically in the ground lengthens, shortens, and changes direction as the sun moves through the sky. To explain the relation of cause and effect, when discussing details of the natural word, is the realm of science. Thales and his followers, however, went further: they tried to ascertain whether all of nature followed a rational order. Was nature in fact a system? Was there, or is there, a set of universal truths that hold together the material world—and if so, how can we learn them? Does human life exist within an eternal code of truths larger than anything our cultural traditions or religions teach us? This is the realm of philosophy.

Thales, the first philosopher, never wrote a word. Philosophy, he believed, is best explored in conversation. The answer to every question, after all, raises another question (at least if the answer is at all interesting). A written text, however, is finite and fixed and therefore cannot possibly be completely right. Anaximander, his student, disagreed on that point and wrote reams. Their conclusions may seem unimpressive now but, if looked at correctly, seem remarkably insightful. Consciously or not, they and Anaximenes all began with an assumption that provides the foundation of all of modern physics—the conservation of matter. Everything came from somewhere, and since the complexity and variety of the world is obviously increasing as we move forward in time, then everything must be traceable to a single point, a single element, if we move backward through time.

What was this universal source? For Thales it was water, the primordial substance from which everything derives. Anaximander posited the existence of a single infinite ether, a malleable goo that took different forms when subjected to opposing forces of heat and cold, wetness and dryness. Anaximenes went even further and added the complicating factor of air, which affects the shape-shifting of the ether by its relative density or lightness. What is interesting about these speculations is the way they hint at a theory of evolution. If the entire physical cosmos has a common beginning, and if the world we observe is still constantly changing, then surely we ourselves came to be through a process of change in the past.[13]

Nothing like this had ever quite been attempted before. The mutability of the physical world has always been known. The Sumerians complained about it incessantly, and the Egyptians saw it as a deviation from the stability offered by obedience to the pharaoh. The Hebrews initially regarded it as the fulfillment of YHWH's design, then later feared that he had turned his back on them and his plan. The Ionian Greeks, however, were the first to approach the mutability of the physical world as a rational problem and to test their interpretations of it with logical arguments. This was to be one of the ancient world's greatest legacies for Greater Western culture—a sense of order, a search for meaning, and a tradition of submitting one's ideas to critical inspection.

The Ionian thinkers even submitted religion to critical analysis. The boldest figure of all was Xenophanes of Colophon (570–480 BCE), who noted that deities in every culture tend to have the physical characteristics of the culture: thus Ethiopian gods and goddesses have black skin and curly hair, while Greek artists portray their divinities with olive skin and dark wavy hair, and the barbarians of Thrace (a region well to the north of Greece) worship deities with fair skin, reddish hair, and blue eyes. His conclusion? Humans make gods in their own image—not, as the Hebrew Bible says, the other way around. If cattle could speak, Xenophanes quips, they would pray to gods who look like cattle. His main concern was to turn people away from the Olympian-deity cults, which he regarded as poetic nonsense, and to examine life through critical reason.[14]

---

[13]   Anaximenes even asserted that humans must have been, at one time, fish.

[14]   Xenophanes held that reason can guide us toward the truth. It is impossible to know the truth with absolute certainty—but the point, he insists, is to make the effort.

Radical speculation like this declined in Ionia after the Persians conquered Lydia in 494 BCE and acquired control of Miletus. The philosophers either fled or joined the resistance. The mode of critical thinking begun in Miletus spread quickly to the Greek mainland, however, where it took root especially in the city of Athens.

ATHENIAN DEMOCRACY

Athens is older than Jerusalem, older than Nineveh, older than Thebes. Perhaps only Jericho, of all the cities of the Western world, has a longer history of continuous human settlement. As early as 3000 BCE, Neolithic tribesmen built a fort atop the Acropolis, and people have lived there ever since. Geography favors it: the hilltop provides a natural defensive position from which to control the nearby plains, which provide farmland and pasturage. The Eridanus river flowed through the center of the town (it has long since dried up), and the port of Piraeus lies only six miles (ten kilometers) away. Athens thus had ready access to natural resources and communication links but was also sufficiently isolated to enjoy natural protection. Athens was already a leading city in Mycenaean times and was able to hold out against the marauding Sea Peoples, although it then went into the same sharp decline as the other cities of the Dark Age. As the clouds cleared by 700 BCE, Athens stood ready to take advantage once again of its uniquely strong position, and under the leadership of the landholding aristocracy the city slowly seized control of the entire region of Attica.[15] By the mid-600s BCE, however, so many new people had been added to the roster of Athenians that they began to challenge the authority of the aristocrats. The clash between the privileges of the few and the demands of the many is what led to the tyrannies of Solon and Pisistratus mentioned before.

Like other Archaic Age cities, Athens experimented—at times against its will—with a variety of constitutions, some democratically created, some imposed by occasional autocrats. Legal distinctions between classes, tribes, and precincts (called demes in Greek) were redrawn, laws were drafted and redrafted, and both executive and judicial institutions were reorganized. The system as established in 510 BCE remained more or less in place until Alexander the Great conquered Athens in 338 BCE, and it provides the model for our understanding of Athenian democracy.

We should begin by understanding that democracy's limitations. Full participatory citizenship was restricted to somewhere between 5 and 10 percent of the population: slaves, women, the working poor, and most lesser craftsmen and artisans were denied the right to vote in the assembly and to hold municipal office. The

---

[15] Athens grew by bringing smaller neighboring towns into its jurisdiction—what classical historians call *synoikismos* ("gathering together in a single home"). "Urban sprawl" works just fine.

numbers come from Thucydides, who reckoned the number of actual citizens as forty thousand. He put the number of slaves in Athens as high as four hundred thousand, and the number of noncitizen residents at seventy thousand. Called metics, they had no democratic rights and had to pay for the privilege of residing in the city.

Still, no other ancient society placed power in the hands of so many of its people. It may be more accurate, statistically speaking, to regard Athens as an unusually large oligarchy rather than as a true democracy, but the real accomplishment of the constitution lay not in the size of the electorate; it was in its strict definition and supervision of the powers of civic officials. Officeholders in Athens served the city and its constitution, unlike those in other ancient societies who served a king or regarded their own will as the constitution. An Athenian-style democracy today would not be admitted to the European Union and would even come under criticism by the Organization of African States, although it would probably get a favorable nod from Russia and China. But in the context of its time, Athens's experiment with government by (some of) the people was a rare and beautiful thing.[16]

The main body of the government was the citizens' Assembly (*ekklesia* in Greek), which met to consider new legislation, adjudicate trials, and set policies. As many as five to six thousand men comprised the assembly at any one time, which was obviously too cumbersome a group for any effective governance; hence most day-to-day government was performed by a smaller group called the council (*boule*). Chosen by lots, the members of the council selected the leading magistrates; these were not elections in the modern sense, but an actual lottery. Elections were reserved for the positions of *strategoi*—the military commanders in charge of the citizen army. Magistracies and command positions were for one-year terms, and while popular strategoi could serve an unlimited number of consecutive terms, all magistrates were removed from office after a single term.

THE PERSIAN WARS

By the 490s BCE Sparta, not Athens or Miletus, was the strongest polis in Greece. Most other cities of the time would have named it as their leader, if asked. As tensions rose with the advancing Persian Empire, more and more poleis turned to the Spartans for guidance; not only was their army the strongest in Greece, but Sparta—alone among Greek cities—did not have overseas colonies. This assured people that Sparta's leadership in a Panhellenic military force would play no favorites. Few people trusted the Athenians to be so selfless.

---

[16]   The bulk of the Athenian constitution was the work of a reformer named Cleisthenes, who established the new system in 508 BCE.

The Persian Wars (494–479 BCE) did not have to happen. Persia had been eager enough to conquer all of the Near East and to bring Zoroastrianism to the world, but the empire initially showed no signs of determination, or even desire, to add Greece to its dominion. Doing so, after all, would require the Persians to develop maritime skills that they neither had nor needed. The Greeks controlled the sea-lanes throughout the eastern Mediterranean and the Black Sea. Since the Persians controlled everything else, the Greeks had no one else with whom to trade. Conquering the people would have been a waste of resources.

Revolt by the Ionian Greeks changed all of that. The trouble started in Miletus, which had been governed by a brief series of Persian-affiliated tyrants. The Greek colonies along the Ionian coast (Ionia being the westernmost province of Asia Minor) tired of sending their taxes and tribute eastward and waited only for a leader to organize them into a full-scale rebellion. The rebels' chance came when the tyrant of Miletus, Aristagoras, gambled that the Greek mainland would come to the Ionians' assistance and that the Persians, lacking a navy, would let the Ionian colonies go. He was right and wrong in equal measure. The coastal colonies did unite in seceding from Persia, and the mainland Greeks did come to their aid; but Persia refused to let the challenge to their authority go unanswered.

When Sparta balked at sending its troops to Miletus, the Athenians, sensing an opportunity, leaped in. In 499 BCE they led a smallish force that sacked the Persians' provincial capital at Sardis (modern Sart). But then the Athenians declared victory and went home, leaving the Ionian cities to face the Persian emperor's wrath alone. That emperor was Darius (r. 521–486 BCE). He decided to teach the Athenians a lesson, and in 490 BCE he sent an army of twenty thousand elite troops across the Aegean with orders to land on the mainland and to march on Athens and destroy it. The armies met on the plain at Marathon, where the Athenian phalanx smashed through the Persian infantry line. The Greek writer Herodotus records that 6,400 Persians were killed, while the Athenians lost only 192. Darius, humiliated, withdrew. Athens rejoiced in its victory and its new standing as the champion of all of Greece (see Map 4.3).

One of the city's leading politicians, Themistocles (524–459 BCE), advised the polis that the Persians would undoubtedly come back and that the Athenians should therefore prepare. They did so by investing in a fleet of two hundred new warships called **triremes**, thereby turning Athens into a major naval power. Introduced, according to Thucydides, in the 8th century BCE, they were oared warships, with three tiers of rowers. Constructed of pine or fir, they were relatively light ships that, with a well-trained crew, could attain very high speed. With a bronze-tipped hardwood prow, they were extremely effective at ramming into the hulls of opposing ships.[17]

---

[17]   Another favorite tactic was to build up speed, approach alongside an enemy ship, withdraw the oars, and let the momentum of the trireme shear away the oars of the foe, leaving him helplessly adrift.

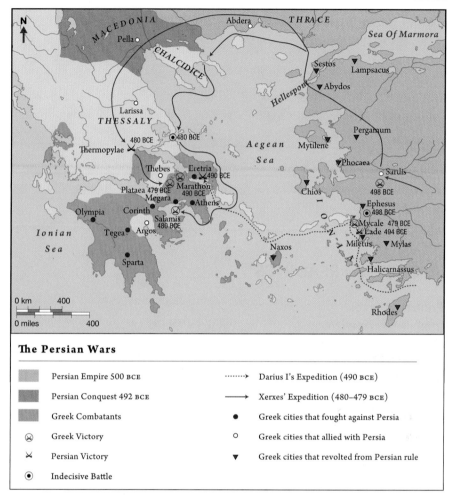

The Persian Wars

▨ Persian Empire 500 BCE	┈┈┈▶ Darius I's Expedition (490 BCE)
▨ Persian Conquest 492 BCE	⟶ Xerxes' Expedition (480–479 BCE)
▨ Greek Combatants	● Greek cities that fought against Persia
⊗ Greek Victory	○ Greek cities that allied with Persia
⤫ Persian Victory	▼ Greek cities that revolted from Persian rule
⊙ Indecisive Battle	

MAP 4.3   **The Persian Wars**

The empire did strike back, in 480 BCE. Darius's son Xerxes (r. 486–465 BCE) was then in charge, and he assembled the largest army in ancient history for a land assault. Herodotus reckoned it at 1.7 million soldiers, but most historians estimate the real figure was about one-tenth of that. The Persians marched north from Sardis, crossed the Hellespont, moved westward across Thrace and Macedonia, and prepared to invade Greece from the north. The Persian threat finally persuaded most of the Greeks to unite in defense. Sparta fought a heroic frontline action at the battle of Thermopylae (480 BCE), while the Athenians harried the Persians supply ships. Greek victories at Salamis (480 BCE)—a naval battle—and at Plataea (479 BCE) finally forced Xerxes to give up and return to Persia. Greece was poised to enter its golden age.

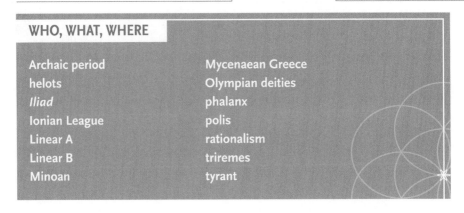

WHO, WHAT, WHERE

Archaic period	Mycenaean Greece
helots	Olympian deities
Iliad	phalanx
Ionian League	polis
Linear A	rationalism
Linear B	triremes
Minoan	tyrant

SUGGESTED READINGS

Primary Sources

Herodotus. *The Persian Wars.*

Hesiod. *Theogony.*

———. *Works and Days.*

Homer. *The Iliad.*

———. *The Odyssey.*

Thucydides. *The Peloponnesian War.*

Xenophon. *Hellenica.*

———. *Constitution of the Lacedaemonians.*

Anthologies

Buckley, Terry. *Aspects of Greek History, 750–323 BC: A Source-Based Approach* (2010).

Lefkowitz, Mary R., and Maureen B. Fant, comps. *Women's Life in Greece and Rome: A Source Book in Translation* (2005).

Nagle, D. Brendan, and Stanley M. Burstein. *Readings in Greek History: Sources and Interpretations* (2006).

Rice, David G., and John E. Stambaugh. *Sources for the Study of Greek Religion* (2000).

Studies

Bagnall, Nigel. *The Peloponnesian War: Athens, Sparta, and the Struggle for Greece* (2006).

Brunschwig, Jacques, and Geoffrey E. R. Lloyd, eds. *Greek Thought: A Guide to Classical Knowledge* (2000).

Camp, John M. *The Archaeology of Athens* (2002).

Cartledge, Paul A. *The Spartans: An Epic History* (2003).

De Souza, Philip. *The Greek and Persian Wars, 499–386 BC* (2003).

Dickinson, Oliver. *The Aegean from Bronze Age to Iron Age: Continuity and Change between the Twelfth and Eighth Centuries BC* (2007).

Ducat, Jean. *Spartan Education: Youth and Society in the Classical Period* (2006).

Gere, Cathy. *Knossos and the Prophets of Modernism* (2009).

Graham, Daniel W. *Explaining the Cosmos: The Ionian Tradition of Scientific Philosophy* (2006).

Hall, Jonathan M. *A History of the Archaic Greek World, ca. 1200–479 BCE* (2006).

Holland, Tom. *Persian Fire: The First World Empire and the Battle for the West* (2005).

Langdon, Susan. *Art and Identity in Dark Age Greece, 1100–700 BCE* (2010).

Pedley, John. *Sanctuaries and the Sacred in the Ancient Greek World* (2005).

Pomeroy, Sarah B. *Spartan Women* (2002).

Pomeroy, Sarah B., Stanley M. Burstein, Walter Donlan, Jennifer Tolbert Roberts, and David Tandy. *Ancient Greece: A Political, Social, and Cultural History Third Edition* (2012).

Schofield, Louise. *The Mycenaeans* (2007).

Snodgrass, Anthony M. *The Dark Age of Greece: An Archaeological Survey of the Eleventh to Eighth Centuries* BC (2000).

Thomas, Rosalind. *Herodotus in Context: Ethnography, Science, and the Art of Persuasion* (2002).

Waterfield, Robin. *The First Philosophers: The Presocratics and the Sophists* (2009).

For additional resources, including maps, primary sources, visuals, web links, and quizzes, please go to **www.oup.com/us/backman.**

CHAPTER 5

Hellenism and Second Temple Judaism

499 BCE–142 BCE

THE CLASSICAL AND HELLENISTIC WORLD

The Classical and Hellenistic Ages witnessed all the best and worst of ancient Greek life. The first, the Classical Age, ran from the defense of Greece against Persia to the conquest of Persia by the Greeks under Alexander the Great (479–323 BCE). The Hellenistic Age that followed ran from Alexander's death to the conquest of the East by the Romans (323–327 BCE). A sense of euphoria swept through the people after their victory over Xerxes, and the Athenians felt more euphoric than any. Their bravery at Marathon and their decision to build a fleet of triremes had led directly to the Persians' defeat. Now, with the exception of Sparta and a few outliers, every polis in Greece recognized Athens's new position of leadership.

Its leadership meant more than military achievements. Athens embodied a life of ritual and restraint, the birth of medicine, and the search for a meaningful life. Yet it seems only right that one of its greatest achievements, along with epic and lyric poetry, was tragedy, for its golden age ended with the disastrous war between Athens and Sparta. The Peloponnesian War lasted twenty-seven years and consumed much of the Greek peninsula. As it happened, of the period's greatest philosophers—Socrates, Plato, and

◀ **Medical Science** This sarcophagus from the 1st century BCE shows a physician—recognizable from the surgical implements hanging on the wall behind him—who perhaps moonlighted as a veterinarian (hence the horse).

Aristotle—the last taught the military heir to the disaster, Alexander the Great. The ensuing Hellenistic Age also coincided with a time of Jewish rebirth and Hellenization.

THE CLASSICAL AGE

Despite their celebrations, none of the Greeks believed they had seen the end of the Persian threat. Athens argued successfully for the creation of a military alliance among all the poleis, one dedicated to maintaining a strong defense and, if possible, even pressing the offensive into Persian territory. The alliance was called the **Delian League**, named for the Aegean island of Delos where the group's treasury was kept. By 470 BCE, in other words, Greece was victorious, independent, organized, self-confident, and quickly amassing wealth. The Greeks could be forgiven if they felt a bit of pride. They could be forgiven, too, if they did not foresee that the next great conquests, following their downfall, were to come from peoples they knew as little more than barbarians. They could have noticed even earlier the return of the Jews, freed by the Persians, to Jerusalem.

Golden ages seldom last very long, and the Greek one was no different. They also are seldom as golden as people believe them to have been. The start of the Persian Wars in 499 BCE and the end of the Peloponnesian War in 404 BCE mark the **Classical Age**, when Greece witnessed an impressive vitality in civic life, economic prosperity, artistic expression, and literary achievement.

The Greeks themselves, and especially the Athenians, came to regard the mid-5th century BCE with a determined awe, recalling it as a lost halcyon era that outshone anything that came before it or since. Through the centuries, much of Western culture has continued the love affair and has extolled "the glory that was Greece" as one of the two or three pinnacles of human achievement.

The Greeks themselves, and especially the Athenians, came to regard the mid-5th century BCE with a determined awe, recalling it as a lost halcyon era that

CHAPTER TIMELINE

499 BCE	490 BCE	478 BCE
Start of the Persian Wars	Darius of Persia invades Greece	Delian League established
	479 BCE Persian Wars end	

outshone anything that came before it or since. Through the centuries, much of Western culture has continued the love affair and has extolled "the glory that was Greece" as one of the two or three pinnacles of human achievement. A more sober viewer can admire the brilliance of the time without overlooking its less praiseworthy elements.

Most of the great achievements of the age were connected in some fashion to Athens. That city, in the heady atmosphere of patriotic victory over Persia and its newfound prosperity, had ample material and spiritual resources to devote to education, urban development, artistic expression, and religious ritual. Moreover, Athenian ties to the Ionian cities understandably grew closer, which brought an injection of the vigorous intellectualism of Asia Minor into Athenian life. The stimulus was significant.

The greatest of Athenian leaders, Pericles (495–429 BCE), lavished money on building temples, theatres, schools, and public meeting houses. He held the office of strategos ("general") from 462 to 429 BCE. This was an elected office with a one-year term, but the Athenian constitution placed no limit on the number of terms a strategos could serve; Pericles won reelection thirty-two times. Although he himself had a high aristocratic lineage, he was an ardent populist who broadened the scope of Athenian democracy. Poor Athenians could not vote on legislation but could attend the assembly. He made it easier for them to participate in civic life by offering to reimburse their lost day wages if they wished to attend the municipal council meeting.[1] Athens's gain was the rest of Greece's loss—for no other city had anything like the cultural flowering of Periclean Greece. But even with all its advantages, the flowering of life in Athens was possible only because Athens controlled the treasury of the whole Delian League and appropriated its funds.

Though prosperous, Greek life in the Hellenic era was surprisingly modest. Most homes were comfortable but simple; no palaces were built, not even by those

---

[1] Pericles' generosity attracted the best architects, sculptors, playwrights, scholars, scientists, and poets to Athens.

ca. 260 BCE
Hebrew Bible
translated into Greek
(Septuagint)

431 BCE
Peloponnesian
War begins

432 BCE
Parthenon
completed

331 BCE
Alexander crushes
Persians at
Gaugamela

167–142 BCE
Maccabean Revolt

Pericles   Bust of the statesman and general (strategos) "Pericles the Athenian, son of Xanthippos"—as the inscription reads. 5th century BCE.

few who did achieve great wealth. Personal luxuries were spurned. Instead, prosperous Greeks spent their money on commercial investment, public building projects, and supporting arts and education. Temples, public halls, amphitheaters, baths, and athletic fields all benefited from private largess.

WOMEN, CHILDREN, AND SLAVES

Women were strictly segregated from public life, and girls remained at home until the day of their marriage, when they moved into the home of their husbands. Apart from trips to the market and occasional attendance at religious ceremonies, Greek women lived utterly enclosed lives. Every home had a specially designated "woman's zone" (**gynaeceum**), in which women passed the time with their children and servants. A woman never entered the public area of her house, where visitors might appear, without the permission of her husband. Children started their education at home, learning their letters and numbers and some music from their mothers. Boys usually began attending schools at age seven. These were private institutions that included rigorous physical education, since at age eighteen all boys began military service in the hoplite infantry.

Girls began another kind of service even earlier. From the time of her first menstruation a girl was considered marriageable; this frequently happened as early as age fourteen, the idea being to take maximum advantage of her fertile years. "We have prostitutes for pleasure," wrote one Athenian, "concubines for company, and wives for producing heirs and maintaining the household." Affectionate marriages certainly existed, but few Greeks wed for love. Take two representative gravestone inscriptions:

> Here by this busy road lies Aspasia, a worthy wife now dead. Her husband Euopides put up this monument for her in memory of her good disposition; she was his consort. *(Chios, 5th century BCE)*

> The woman buried here cared neither for clothes nor money in her lifetime, but only for her husband and for maintaining an upright reputation. Dionysia, your husband Antiphilus inscribes your tomb in return for the youthful years you shared with him. *(Athens, 4th century BCE)*

From the time of her wedding, a woman all but disappeared into her husband's house, seldom going into public, and devoting her days to childrearing and weaving. Greek culture abhorred idleness, and since most households—even relatively poor ones—had slaves to do the bulk of domestic labor, married women traditionally kept busy at the loom.[2] A healthy wife might expect to have ten pregnancies in her lifetime, although it remains unclear how many miscarriages she might suffer or how many of her children might die in infancy.

Decorative Painting on a Case from the 5th Century BCE In this scene a woman examines a sample of cloth being shown to her by a weaver.

Wives governed their households—watching over their children, planning menus, caring for household items—but slaves performed most of the domestic chores. Classical Greece lived off slave labor, but slave populations in the ancient world were not self-perpetuating. The conditions of their lives were so harsh that their mortality rates exceeded their birth rates. The Greeks thus constantly needed fresh supplies of slaves in order to continue their lives of democratic freedom. Apart from domestic work, most slaves were used in farm labor and menial shopwork. The least fortunate of the male slaves were put to work in mining or as oarsmen in Greek ships; the least fortunate of the females were the forced sexual partners of their male owners.

> Classical Greece lived off slave labor, but slave populations in the ancient world were not self-perpetuating. The conditions of their lives were so harsh that their mortality rates exceeded their birth rates.

THE POLIS: RITUAL AND RESTRAINT

Each polis administered its major religious celebrations, which naturally differed from one another depending on the particular deities associated with each city. In Athens itself, the two most significant festivals were the Panathenaia, a celebration held every May in honor of the goddess Athena, and the Great Dionysia, a festival honoring Dionysius. (The Panathenaia is the scene famously depicted on the frieze of the Parthenon, now in the British Museum.) Religion was ritualistic, and

---

[2]   Odysseus's wife, Penelope, who spent twenty years at her loom while patiently waiting for her husband to return from his wanderings, was an iconic image.

The Panathenaia   The Panathenaia was the great religious festival held every four years in Athens, in honor of the city's patron goddess. This scene depicts the preparations for the opening ceremony, the high point of which was the solemn procession of Athena's sacred robes to the Acropolis.

it neither asserted a creed nor promoted an ethical code.[3] People presented offerings, performed their prayers, and honored the gods in song. But apart from insisting on observing the required rituals, the religion taught little. No uniformity of opinion existed regarding the afterlife, although the great majority of Greeks believed in **Hades**, a shadowy afterworld to which all who received funeral rites went, regardless of the morality or immorality of their earthly lives. Those who did not receive a proper funeral were thought to wander the world as ghosts.

The Greeks disdained the luxurious diets of the Persians, which they considered a sign of their supposed decadence, and most ate simple meals. Herodotus (1.133) is bemused by Persian eating and drinking habits:

> The day they value most of all is a birthday; on one of those they think it right to set up a greater banquet than usual—for wealthier Persians will arrange to have an ox, horse, camel, or ass roasted whole and set out before them (the less well-to-do use smaller beasts). They eat only a little of their main course but an abundance of desserts; moreover, they never use salt. This is why the Persians say that we Greeks are still hungry when we finish eating, for there is nothing worth having after we finish our main course—but if some delicacies were given us, we would eat our fill. The Persians are very devoted to wine (but they never vomit or piss in front of one another). Such are their customs.

---

[3]   The ancient Greek language had no word corresponding to the English words "belief" or "beliefs" in their religious sense.

They will get drunk even when discussing the most important matters. The following day the host of the house they are in will ask them— now that they are sober—to reconsider their decisions of the night before. If they are still so inclined, the matter is settled; if not, not. If it happens that they deliberate an issue when sober, they reconsider it later when they are drunk.

For the Greeks, grains, olive oil, and wine formed the basis of all meals. Breakfast commonly consisted of barley bread dipped in wine. Lunch was usually a form of soup or stew (made chiefly of lentils, onions, and beans, since fresh vegetables were hard to come by in the cities), accompanied by cheese and honey. Dinner was eaten at nightfall and was the largest meal of the day. For most people this was the only meal at which meat was served. Pork was the cheapest meat, and each city had its own favorite preparation.[4] Fish was relatively rare inland; the coastal cities and the Aegean islanders had little success transporting it inland without spoiling. Men and women always ate separately; in a small house the men ate first, then the women, then the male servants, and finally the female servants. Most Greek houses did not have stone ovens; instead, women cooked by heaping red-hot coals on a flat stone and setting an inverted clay bowl over the pile. Once the stone was hot, they scraped away the coals, placed the food on the heated stone, covered it with the hot bowl, and surrounded the bowl with the coals again. Having such little regard for artful food preparation, however, the Greeks tended to devalue the role that women played in it. Food was fuel, not pleasure.

Drinking, however, was another matter. The Greeks developed the first vintage wines, and among the many civic officials in local government was the person responsible for affixing the municipal seal to wines for export. By reputation, the best wines came from three Aegean islands: Chios, Lesbos, and Thasos; the wine produced in Achaea, the mainland district surrounding Athens, was among the worst. Claudius Aelianus (d. 235 CE), a Roman historian who wrote in Greek, records that Achaean wine was reputed to induce miscarriages in pregnant women.

Wine was drunk throughout the day, always cut (diluted) with water. Drinking uncut wine was considered barbarous, as was the drinking of wine by women, except in Sparta, where moderate wine drinking was thought to increase a woman's fertility. Drinking to excess was also looked down upon, except at **symposia**, the all-male drinking parties where getting drunk was the whole point. Plato's dialogue

---

[4]   The Spartans' signature dish was melas zomos, a dark, thick stew made of pork, vinegar, and pigs' blood. In Aristophanes' play Peace (1.374), a small piglet is said to cost three days' wages for a civil servant.

Divine Wine   A drinking cup depicting the goddess Athena pouring wine for the famous hero Herakles, 5th century BCE.

The Symposium is the most famous depiction of one of these parties, although it is not characteristic. Few people can drink that much and still engage in such intelligent discussion. Still, some Greeks, like the philosopher Socrates, earned renown for their ability to imbibe.[5]

CIVILIZED PURSUITS: EPIC AND LYRIC POETRY

Others gained renown for more civilized pursuits like poetry, at which the ancient Greeks excelled. Epic poetry was still composed in the classical period, but shorter poetic forms like lyric and elegy—the first sung to accompaniment on a lyre, the second to the music of a flute—gained in popularity. The two greatest lyric poets were Pindar (522–443 BCE) and Sappho (ca. 620–570 BCE). Pindar made his name by composing odes for special occasions. Among his most popular verses were a series of odes in honor of victors in athletic contests like the Olympic Games. His poetry is notoriously difficult to translate since he delights in sophisticated meters and rhetorical flourishes.

---

[5]   Socrates never went drink-for-drink against Milo of Croton, a 6th-century BCE Olympic athlete who reportedly ate twenty pounds of meat daily—which he washed down with two gallons of wine.

Sappho, however, invites translation. Her poetry (or what survives of it, anyway) depends less on technical tricks, more on acute observation and emotional directness. According to tradition she wrote some nine volumes of poetry, although only one poem survives in its entirety, a hymn to Aphrodite. Many of the surviving fragments express homoerotic love, and Sappho's island home of Lesbos has given its name to lesbianism. Here she describes her envy of a man who is enjoying her beloved's company at table:

> That man seems to me equal to the gods,
> the one who sits opposite you
> and listens so closely
> to your sweet voice
>
> and your beguiling laughter—
> oh, how the heart in my chest is stirred!
> For whenever I look at you, even for a moment,
> to speak is beyond me—not one single word;
>
> my tongue freezes in silence;
> a lick of flame runs beneath my skin;
> my eyes can see nothing;
> my ears hear only a din;
>
> a cold sweat covers me;
> my body trembles—and I sigh
> and turn greener than grass
> and think I might die.

THE BIRTH OF TRAGEDY

It may seem ironic that the greatest artistic expression of the age was tragedy, but it is not. What epic and lyric poetry were to the Archaic Age, poetic stage tragedy was to the Classical—its characteristic and most powerful expression. Tragedy was more than an art form; it was a public rite and a civic obligation. Athens led the way, although the other major cities soon staged tragedy festivals as well.

The first tragedies we know of were staged in the time of Cleisthenes in the 6th century BCE—indeed, it is possible that the development of tragedy was one of the civic reforms he inaugurated—but the genre possibly dates even earlier.

The earliest complete plays that have come down to us are seven dramas by Aeschylus (525–456 BCE), who introduced nonchorus characters on the stage, which made dialogue possible. Tragedy's origins are uncertain, but it likely originated with the choral odes sung by crowds to the god Dionysius at the spring festival held in his honor in Athens. Dionysius was famously the god of wine, of passionate feeling, of life force. A latecomer to the Greek pantheon, he was a potent but disruptive force, one who promised his followers transformative experience, a sense of moving out of oneself (ecstasy—from Greek ek stasis, meaning "out of nonmovement").

This was an unnerving development. Greek religion had always been passionately adhered to without ever being essentially emotive. Gods and goddesses often had, and played, individual favorites among human beings. Athena's protection of Odysseus comes to mind, as does Hera's guardianship over women in childbirth. Yet they seldom felt or showed any actual emotion toward humans except for episodic wrath. People offered prayers and sacrifices to the Olympian deities, but the relationship between the faithful and the deities was more contractual than intimate. Wanting a good grain crop, they prayed to Demeter, who granted the wish or not depending on whether she liked their offerings. The cult of Dionysius was different. People turned to him not for favors but for spiritual elation and passionate release.

The German philosopher Friedrich Nietzsche (1844–1900) famously attributed tragedy to the Greek world's efforts to rein in the raw emotional power of the Dionysian cult. By subsuming these choral celebrations into a carefully managed public theatrical rite, he argued, the leaders of Athens created tragedy, a genre that provides a cathartic release of elemental passions within a strictly controlled setting. Nietzsche got many details wrong in his analysis, but his *Birth of Tragedy out of the Spirit of Music* (originally published in 1872 and revised in 1886) remains one of the most stimulating books ever written about ancient Greece.

Certain norms governed the practice, one of the most important being that tragic playwrights were expected not to compose original stories but to draw from the store of well-established popular legends and folktales. Sophocles (496–406 BCE) was not the only playwright to write a tragedy about Oedipus; his is simply the best-known version. To the Greeks, it simply required more artistry to captivate an audience with a story they already knew; to rely on an original plot was a cheap stunt—the ancient stage equivalent of a computer-generated special effect in today's movies. One can be startled by such a thing, even impressed, but not emotionally moved. The playwright Euripides (485–406 BCE) was often criticized for his use of innovations—original or little-known stories, unexpected plot twists, surprise endings—although most people granted his

The Amphitheater at Delphi   The amphitheater dates to the 4th century BCE and was renowned for its extraordinary acoustical design, which allowed (and still allows) a whisper to be heard by thousands of people, even in the upper rows.

brilliance with language and characterization. Every major polis staged tragedies as a ritual of religious observance. Athens was the center of theatrical culture with its annual festival called the Dionysia, for which playwrights submitted trilogies of new tragic plays (plus a burlesque piece called a satyr play that served to help the audience recover from the tragic gloom). A civic council selected the most promising plays and produced them for the festival, at which attendance was required of all adult male citizens. At the end of the festival, the audience selected the best trilogy of the year, and its author was granted awards and high honor.

The point of tragedy was to inspire fear and sympathy, which it accomplished by showing the relentless nature of fate and exploiting the paradox that people take pleasure in observing the suffering of others—a paradox made doubly ironic by the world's indifference to human pain. To the Greeks the cardinal sin was **hubris**—the excessive pride that leads people to think that they are in control of their own lives—for the hard reality is that our fates are fixed. Greek morality consisted of recognitions: of our obligations, our limitations, the futility of our aspirations, and our helplessness against the world's indifference. For the Greeks, we cannot alter what the world does to us, but we can control how we respond and adapt to our fates.

In the tales of the Theban ruler Oedipus, the hero begins the play believing he has escaped the fate decreed for him at birth—namely, that he would kill his father and marry his own mother. He discovers that he has done precisely that. Horrified by the revelation, he blinds himself and spends the rest of his life as a wandering beggar. In *Oedipus at Colonnus* the playwright Sophocles has the chorus sing a sorrowful ode as the blind beggar sits in despair:

> What foolishness it is to desire more life, after one has tasted
> A bit of it and seen the world; for each day, after each endless day,
> Piles up ever more misery into a mound. As for pleasures: once we
> Have passed youth they vanish away, never again to be seen.
>
> Death is the end of all.
> Never to be born is the best thing. To have seen the daylight
> And be swept instantly back into dark oblivion comes second.
>   *(lines 1211–1238)*

Other plays tell equally disheartening stories and fill the stages with tears, blood, and crushing misery. The point of this was to drive home a crucial point: there is no reason to expect life to be happy. We are not owed comfort or contentment, and it is wrong to believe we have a right to either or both. To believe that such a right exists is in fact the surest way of achieving neither and ending tragically. Such misery is not a matter of life being fair or unfair; life is simply life, and we ought not to resist or bemoan it.[6] Life thus has no metaphysical meaning, is ennobled by no cosmic purpose—after all, we all spend eternity as mere shadows in a dark and dank afterworld, regardless of the moral quality of our earthly existence. Happiness in life is possible, but it is not a birthright, and the only control we can exert over our existence is to accept what comes. A gloomy outlook but a necessary one, to the Greeks: only by facing this hard reality can we truly have courage, and only thus can we accept both the good that happens and the evil that comes to us. Tragedy humbles us and reminds us to be thankful for small blessings.

> Happiness in life is possible, but it is not a birthright, and the only control we can exert over our existence is to accept what comes. A gloomy outlook but a necessary one, to the Greeks: only by facing this hard reality can we truly have courage, and only thus can we accept both the good that happens and the evil that comes to us.

---

[6] "Let weeping cease, then," sings the chorus in *Oedipus at Colonnus*'s last lines, "and let there be no mourning. These things are in the hands of the gods."

THE PELOPONNESIAN DISASTER

Named for the Peloponnese, the peninsula on which Sparta and Corinth stood, the **Peloponnesian War** (431–404 BCE) lasted for twenty-seven years, although there were periods of truce. The result would be the ruin of Greece. Trying to make sense of it all, in turn, would motivate Athenian contributions to history, medicine, mathematics, and philosophy.

Athens had learned neither humility nor gratitude after the Persian War. Heady with pride and headstrong with determination to retain leadership in Greece, the Athenians spent most of the 5th century BCE bullying the city-states they had helped to defend against Darius and Xerxes. At first, no one dared to question them. When the Athenians began to withdraw funds from the Delian treasury to build up and beautify their own city, only Sparta (and its closest ally, Corinth) sniffed about Athenian hypocrisy. Through the 470s and 460s, however, several cities grumbled openly about Athens treating them like colonies—to which Athens responded by attacking and colonizing them outright (see Map 5.1).

Athenian garrisons were established across Greece, and corps of Athenian officials was set in charge of polis after polis. If they ever questioned their

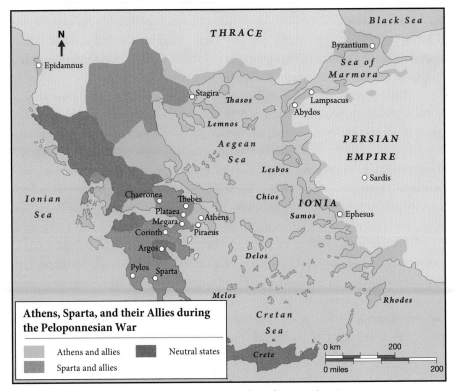

MAP 5.1   **Athens, Sparta, and Their Allies during the Peloponnesian War**

entitlement to an empire, no evidence of it survives. By 440 Pericles had established a peace treaty with Persia so that he could set his sights on Sparta and Corinth, the last barriers to Athenian control of all of Greece. After several more years of provocations and last-minute resolutions, open war between Athens and Sparta erupted in 431 BCE.

Sparta's army was superior to that of Athens, but the Athenian navy ruled the sea—so there were few pitched battles. Instead, the Spartans laid a protracted siege of Athens by land, while the Athenian ships established a blockade that kept food and goods from reaching Sparta by sea. The stalemate favored Athens, until an epidemic of typhus struck the city in 429 BCE and killed roughly one-third of the population, including Pericles. Factionalism then broke out, and Athens began to collapse.

Meanwhile the Spartans struck their own deal with the Persians, who agreed to provide them with a fleet of their own triremes. The Spartans themselves knew little of sailing, but there were enough enemies of Athens around by now to fit out a navy, and by 407 BCE the new naval force challenged Athenian invincibility, which effectively assured a Spartan victory. In 404 the Spartan army entered Athens itself, and the war was over. Corinth and Thebes both demanded the destruction of the city, but Sparta demurred. Instead, they pulled down Athens's fortifications, scuttled its fleet, installed a committee of thirty Athenians, the **Thirty Tyrants**, to govern the defeated city, and returned to Sparta as fast as they could.[7] The Spartan king Pausanias (r. 409–395 BCE) finally intervened and helped to restore democracy in 401 BCE.

Athens never recovered from its defeat, nor did Greece from the general ruin. A pallid democracy was restored in 401, but with its imperial revenues lost and most of its territories scorched, the Athenian economy remained constricted. Sparta shied away from playing any larger role in Greek affairs and focused on suppressing any helots who may have been encouraged by the disaster to attempt rebellion. This made Greece a tempting target for a resurgent Persia, which soon began to ponder another invasion. As it happened, someone else beat them to the punch.

Catastrophes can have beneficial effects. By their very completeness, catastrophes can sweep away cultural clutter, show the failure of institutions, expose social fault lines, and inspire a willingness to rethink old assumptions. The collapse of Greece in the Peloponnesian War led to at least a few positive developments. Politically, the poleis were too weakened to cause further trouble. They spent most of their time bickering internally, trying to find whom

---

[7]   The Thirty Tyrants murdered some fifteen hundred of their political rivals and confiscated their money and property.

or what to blame for the Hellenic downfall, but not all this search for explanations involved snide finger-pointing. A number of brave individuals made deep and serious inquiries into the nature of politics, the weakness of human will, the causes of greed, the quest for justice, and the desire to believe that the world makes sense. These issues had long been essential concerns of Greek cultural and intellectual life but had been examined and explored more in artistic genres such as poetry and tragedy. The intellectual life of post–Peloponnesian War Greece had a more analytical and scientific quality.

Herodotus (484–425 BCE), we saw earlier, had given an exciting new direction to this inquiry when he all but invented historical writing with his *History of the Persian Wars*. Previous historical writing—with the partial exception of the historical books in the Hebrew Bible—had consisted largely of propagandistic narratives, lists of deeds, blow-hard memorials, and the occasional funerary inscription. Herodotus was the first to gather information firsthand, to organize it systematically, and to present it critically—some say not critically enough, but that is for each reader to decide. His successor Thucydides (460–395 BCE) extended Herodotus's methods and created something entirely original.

His *History of the Peloponnesian War* is an astonishing achievement in many ways. Recognizing, as he writes in the book's stately preface, that "the war, when it began, would be great and important beyond any previous war," Thucydides dedicates himself to following it in detail. Before writing, he conducted interviews, reviewed documents, and checked contradictory accounts, paying attention to technological and logistical details with the thoroughness of a general preparing for battle. For Thucydides, the Peloponnesian War was the first ideological war in Western history—a conflict not merely between political states but between states of being. Athenian greed and hubris, and Spartan envy and suspicion, tell only part of the tale. Thucydides digs deeper and presents both sides acting out of different conceptions of freedom.

> For Thucydides, the Peloponnesian War was the first ideological war in Western history—a conflict not merely between political states but between states-of-being.

Freedom, of course, is a relative quality; one often defines freedom in terms of what one is free *from*. To militaristic Sparta, freedom meant freedom from chaos and unpredictability; to hyperambitious Athens it meant freedom from restraint in the pursuit of its desires and perceived rights. Thucydides sees a measure of truth in each point of view but is too committed to political realism to cast his vote entirely for one side or the other. In fact, the casting of votes is itself something Thucydides believes little in. Rather, he identifies as Athens's greatest weakness not its selfishness and hypocrisy but its commitment to democracy. Thucydides argues that democracy, despite its theoretical appeal, is doomed to fail because it is based upon a

TABLE 5.1   **Athens in the 5th Century**

DATE		DATE	
499	Ionian Revolt	430	Birth of Xenophon; Euripides, *Heracleidae*
496	Birth of Sophocles		
494	Phrynicus, *Capture of Miletus*	429	Death of Pericles
490	Darius invades Greece; Battle of Marathon	428	Birth of Plato; Euripides, *Hippolytus*
		427	Sophocles, *Oedipus Rex*
484	Birth of Herodotus	425	Death of Herodotus; Aristophanes, *Acharnians*; Euripides, *Andromache*
480	Birth of Euripides; Battle of Thermopylae		
		424	Aristophanes, *The Knights*; Euripides, *Hecuba*
479	Battles of Salamis, Plataea; Persian War ends		
		423	Aristophanes, *The Clouds* Euripides, *The Suppliants*
478	Delian League established		
477	Athens assumes control of Delian League	422	Aristophanes, *The Wasps*
		421	Aristophanes, *Peace*; Peace of Nicias
472	Aeschylus, *The Persians*	420	Euripides, *Electra*
470	Birth of Socrates; death of Xenophanes	416	Euripides, *Heracles*
468	Sophocles' first victory	415	Euripides, *The Trojan Women*; Sicilian Expedition; herms mutilated
463	Aeschylus, *The Suppliants*		
460	Birth of Thucydides and Hippocrates; Pericles rises to power in Athens	414	Aristophanes, *The Birds*; Euripides, *Ion, Iphigeneia in Tauris*
		412	Euripides, *Helen*
458	Aeschylus, *Oresteia*	411	Aristophanes, *Lysistrata, Thesmophoriazusae*
456	Death of Aeschylus; birth of Aristophanes		
		410	Euripides, *Phoenician Women*
455	Euripides, *Peliades*	409	Sophocles, *Philoctetes*
454	Athens confiscates Delian League treasury	408	Euripides, *Orestes*
		407	Sophocles, *Oedipus at Colonus*
451	Pericles' citizenship law enacted	406	Death of Sophocles and Euripides; Euripides, *Bacchae, Iphigeneia in Aulis*
447	Construction of Parthenon begun		
446	Death of Pindar	405	Aristophanes, *The Frogs*
442	Sophocles, *Antigone*	404	Peloponnesian War ends Regime of the Thirty Tyrants
438	Euripides, *Alcestis*		
432	Parthenon completed	403	Democracy restored to Athens
431	Euripides, *Medea*; Herodotus begins *Persian Wars*; Peloponnesian War begins	399	Death of Socrates

lie—namely, the notion of human equality. To drive his point home, Thucydides composes a handful of brilliant set pieces, either wholly fictitious events or highly imaginative reconstructions of speeches, dialogues, and debates. (The best known of these are "Pericles' Funeral Oration" of 429 [2:34–46], the "Mytilenian Debate" [3.37–50], and the "Melian Dialogue" [5.85–113].) They give Athens's commitment to its democratic ideal elaborate expression, but also subtly expose it as nearsighted, contradictory, and ultimately hopeless.

Thucydides' history breaks off suddenly, in Book 8, with the battle of Cynossema in 411 (a minor victory for Athens over the new Spartan naval force). He leaves the last seven years of the war untreated. The work is clearly unfinished, although historians disagree why the book was never completed. It seems certain that a ninth book was intended, to reflect the nine-book structure of Herodotus's *Persian Wars*; but Thucydides completed enough of his masterpiece to leave the Greek tragedy dissected and exposed with unmatched and gimlet-eyed skill. He leaves the reader with little to hope for in human nature, but wishing for more and more of his extraordinary and dispassionate insight.

MEDICINE AS NATURAL LAW: HIPPOCRATES

Just as Thucydides had given clear-eyed diagnoses of Greek political decline, Hippocrates of Kos (460–370 BCE) divorced illness and disease from superstitions and religious beliefs. In the process, he made human suffering—or, at least, one type of human suffering—a feature of the natural world. His separation of physical health from religious issues also makes him the founder of Western medicine.

Earlier traditions, as in Egypt and Babylon, had built up an understanding of how to treat various maladies, but knowledge of how the body works, how diseases function, and why any given remedy works (or does not) remained mysteries. Such things were attributed to astral influences, spells cast by demons, and the whims of the gods. Hippocrates was the first to study medicine systematically, in order to work out the processes by which herbs and treatments produced their effects. He and his successors compiled the *Hippocratic Corpus*, seventy volumes that discuss maladies (such as epilepsy, the "sacred disease") as natural phenomena rather than divine curses. He was the first to categorize diseases and therefore to produce a preliminary sketch of a natural structure. Acute, chronic, endemic, and epidemic were the first categories, followed by subcategories according to organs and bodily systems.

Hippocrates famously composed an oath to be sworn by all physicians, marking the official start of their careers. The original form of the Hippocratic oath goes as follows:

> I swear by Apollo, Asclepius, Hygeia, and Panacea, and do bear witness before all gods and goddesses that I will remain true to the following oath, to the best of my ability and judgment:
>
> that I will hold as dear to me as my own parents the man who taught me this art [of medicine], will live with him, and if necessary will share my possessions with him;

that I will regard his children as my own brothers, and will teach them this same art;

that I will prescribe health regimens for the good of my patients to the very best of my ability and will never intentionally do harm to anyone;

that I will give no poison to anyone, not even if asked to do so, nor will I advise anyone [to take poison]; neither will I give any woman a pessary to induce abortion;

that I will preserve the purity of my life and my practice;

that I will not perform surgery for gallstones, not even for patients suffering terribly, and that I will instead leave this for those who specialize in this task;

that I will enter homes only to serve the good of my patients, and avoid causing any kind of harm—especially any kind of seduction to engage in sex with any woman or man, free or enslaved, in the home;

and that I will always preserve the confidentiality of anything I learn about my patients and their households in the practice of my profession, not permitting anything to be spread about.

To the extent that I faithfully keep this oath, may I live my life and practice my art enjoying always the respect of all men; but if I fail to do so, and if I violate this oath, may the opposite be the case.

The Oath sworn by new physicians today is considerably different.

But the significance of Hippocrates' work lay not only in its contributions to medical science: he also regarded mankind as part of the natural landscape—capable of, and responsive to, rational analysis. He severed medicine from religion and allied it with philosophy.

MATHEMATICAL ORDERING AND SOPHISTRY

Philosophy, of course, was the area of the Greeks' greatest and most enduring achievement. Much had happened in this field since the Milesians. A group of philosophers known as the **Pythagoreans**—named after Pythagoras (570–495 BCE), who had developed the famous theorem about right triangles—had directed philosophy away from the Milesian focus on primal essences. The Pythagoreans sought instead to identify the rational ordering of those essences, the laws that governed their interaction; hence their focus on mathematics. Heraclitus of Ephesus (mid-5th century BCE), for example, tried to explain the world's obvious

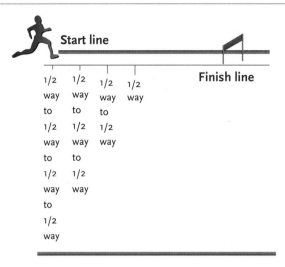

FIGURE 5.1   **A Paradox of Zeno. Like the arrow, the runner will never reach his destination.**

diversity and changeability as a rational patterning and repatterning of opposing forces (hot/cold, light/dark, wet/dry, etc.). If closely observed, even the infinite progressions of a child's kaleidoscope follows a rational pattern. Hence the almost Daoist tone in some of his sayings: "We step and yet we do not step into the same river twice; we are and we are not." "A road goes uphill and downhill at once—it is the same road."[8]

Zeno of Elea (ca. 490–420 BCE) introduced a number of mathematical paradoxes that seem to presage Einstein's theories about time-space continuums. Imagine, for one, that an archer unleashes an arrow at a target. After a certain interval of time the arrow will traverse half the distance; after another, although briefer, interval of time the arrow will traverse half of the shorter distance that remains; after a third interval the arrow will reach the midpoint of the now even shorter remaining distance (see Figure 5.1). The paradox is that the arrow, in crossing an infinite number of midway points en route to the target, will in fact never reach the target. Another Pythagorean, Empedocles of Acragas (ca. 450–390 BCE), undercut Heraclitus's argument about the interplay of opposing forces. Empedocles observed that such coming into existence and passing from existence of new substances makes no sense, since it would necessarily mean the coming into existence and passing from existence of nonexistence itself. Empedocles committed suicide by hurling himself into a live volcano shortly thereafter, thus putting an end to his logical misery.

---

8   "No god or man made the world," wrote Heraclitus. "It is the same for all, always was, is, and will be, an eternal fire eternally kindled and extinguished in equal measures."

A second group of thinkers called the **Sophists** also had their day. Few of their names have come down to us, but in any case the Sophists specialized in packaging ideas rather than in producing anything original. Their emphasis lay in rhetorical skill rather than in genuine investigation: in the bustling economic scene of classical Athens, they aimed to help enterprising people to prosper. The Sophists' closest modern-day analog would be motivational speakers, investment gurus, self-help guides, and leadership coaches of cable-television specials and expensive weekend seminars. They traveled from city to city, offering tuition in everything from public speaking and career guidance to introductory surveys of exciting "useful knowledge" from around the world. These activities are easily mocked as derivative and shallow, and the Sophists have come in for more than their fair share of criticism over the centuries. But to audiences in Periclean Athens, stuffed like game hens with a comfortless religion and the crushing gloom of tragedy, lighter fare like this must have been a welcome respite.

SOCRATES AND THE MEANINGFUL LIFE

The Peloponnesian War crushed the optimism offered by the Sophists. In their place arose a trio of the most influential and impressive philosophers in history, whose lives, written works, and the schools they established changed Western intellectual culture forever. These three individuals—Socrates (469–399 BCE), Plato (427–347 BCE), and Aristotle (384–322 BCE)—permanently altered the direction and scope of philosophy. For the subsequent fifteen hundred years Western science, religion, and politics, as well as philosophy itself, followed the intellectual trajectories they established.

Socrates is the most enigmatic of the three. At least partially trained in the Sophist tradition, he pulled philosophical inspection away from the theoreti-

cal model making of the Milesians and Pythagoreans and insisted that it pursue questions that actually matter to any thinking individual who wants to live meaningfully. Geometrical schema are fine, Socrates felt—but what good are they for answering questions like *What is the right way to live? How can one know anything for certain? What is love?* or *What is justice?* Socrates' signal achievement was to make philosophy a practical urgency—"to pull philosophy back down from the sky," as the Roman writer Cicero put it. Ethics and politics (by which he meant communal ethics), not cosmology and natural science,

Socrates He was reputedly the ugliest but wisest man in Greece during the Classical Age. 4th century BCE.

were the essential concerns of philosophical enquiry, he insisted, or else why bother?

Since he left no writing of his own, we know little about his life. Reputedly the ugliest but most charming man in Athens, he married a woman named Xanthippe, had a family, worked as a stonemason, fought in the Athenian army, participated in municipal government, and had a variety of homosexual lovers. At the age of seventy he was arrested on charges of impiety and corrupting the youth of the city; after an eventful trial he was convicted and sentenced to death by poison—a fate he reportedly accepted with calmness and grace. The charges against him may well have been politically motivated, or at least partly so. Socrates criticized democracy as an irrational political system and had close friends among leading antidemocratic figures in Athens—most notoriously, a sexual relationship with Alcibiades. The charge of impiety rested on his claim to be inspired by a "divine spirit" (daimonion). The corruption charge asserted that he intentionally urged his pupils to question the values handed to them by society.

Socrates founded no formal school but inspired so many later thinkers that he may be the single most influential figure in Western philosophy. Certainly he set the terms of debate, for from his own time until the 19th century ethics and politics remained the central topics of inquiry. Only with the work of Karl Marx and Georg Friedrich Hegel—both mid-19th-century writers— did philosophy turn from these concerns toward the kind of philosophy dominant today. They helped make philosophy the study of the systems (economic, ideological, and linguistic) which restrain, shape, and perhaps control our thinking and lives.

Almost all that we know of Socrates' life and thought comes from four sources: the dialogues of his greatest pupil, Plato; the essays of another pupil, Xenophon; a few scraps of commentary by Aristotle (Plato's student); and a hilarious caricature of him in the comedy *The Clouds* by Aristophanes (446–386 BCE). Together, they present a coherent though not conclusive portrait—of the man whose misfortune was to reach his greatest fame when a sore and humiliated Athens was least inclined to tolerate criticism of its democratic greatness.

Socrates is associated more with a method than a set of ideas. That method consisted of patient and thorough questioning, rather than the assertion of observations or deductions. A consistent pattern emerges in all his appearances in his pupils' dialogues. When asked, for example, to describe the best political system, he begins by asking what we mean by Justice—the quality that all political life aims to supply. Only by understanding the terms we use, Socrates insists, can we begin a proper inquiry. Nothing can be assumed if we wish to seek true understanding. Usually his interlocutors, turned in every direction by his clever questioning, end up admitting that they have no idea how to define anything, and Socrates declares that true philosophical inquiry can therefore at last begin. What the prosecutors at his trial failed to grasp was that Socrates did not doubt that Justice (or Love, or Being, or Truth, or Goodness) exists. He was merely willing to entertain such a doubt as a stimulus to thinking about it.

Despite his charisma and brilliance, or perhaps because of them, he was a terribly annoying man. Think of a conversational bully who delightedly dismantles the ideas of others but never fully offers ideas of his own to replace them. In *The Republic*, Plato's longest and most intricate dialogue, Plato presents Socrates tearing to shreds the ideas of four different characters regarding the nature of Justice. Then, when asked to offer his own definition, Socrates spends the next six books of the dialogue discussing the ideal form of government—but without ever offering his own definition of what Justice actually is. In the end he wins by exhausting his opponents, not by defeating them. Nevertheless, by exposing so brilliantly the human capacity to speak without thinking, Socrates set philosophy on a new course, one pursued avidly by his most brilliant student, Plato.

PLATO AND IDEAL FORMS

Plato came from a wealthy, aristocratic family. Brothers, half-brothers, and cousins populate many of his dialogues—presumably an indication of his pride in his kin. He received an excellent education in mathematics, music, literature, gymnastics, and philosophy, all of which are discussed and cited extensively in his writings. He seems, unlike his teacher, never to have had a profession apart from teaching in the **Academy**, the school he founded when he reached the age of forty. He never married and was wholly homoerotic. As the Peloponnesian War drew to its close, he thought of taking an active role in politics, but he was enraged at the ham-fisted rule of the Thirty Tyrants. When the restored but nearly impotent democracy sentenced Socrates to death, he all but washed his hands of active public life. He took refuge at Megara for a while and possibly traveled to Sicily and southern Italy. Returning to Athens around 385 BCE, he established the Academy, took on pupils, and began to lecture and compose dialogues.

The period from 385 to 360 BCE were the years of his greatest productivity and originality. He peopled his dialogues with artists, politicians, poets, sophists, and orators from the Athenian scene. References to poets and playwrights, often including quotations, appear in almost every dialogue, as do many of the writers themselves. In the last dozen years of his life, 360–347 BCE, perhaps tiring after long labor, he began to outline and dictate in rough form his dialogues to his students, who then fleshed them out in a more turgid, "academic" style. The extraordinary literary polish of the middle years gradually disappeared, although his mind remained as sharp as ever. He became increasingly conservative as he

Plato's Academy   A Roman reimagining of a Greek scene. This mosaic (ca. 100 BCE) shows a half dozen philosophers gathered, presumably, around Plato. Unlike his student Aristotle, who famously paced constantly while lecturing, Plato, a high aristocrat, enjoyed his leisure. Here he rests against a tree while examining a scroll.

aged, though, and by the time he wrote *The Laws*, one of his last works, he was deeply embittered by the world's foolishness.

Most of the dialogues repeat a pattern. Socrates encounters a group somewhere in or near Athens and joins their conversation. It might be at an evening entertainment, along a road to a temple, sitting in a town square, or chatting in a portico. Picking up on an apparently offhand comment by one of the group, Socrates begins to probe his fellows' attitudes, language, convictions, and assumptions until they admit hopeless befuddlement and beg Socrates to set them aright. Socrates sometimes obliges but just as often demurs: the dialogue functions not as a means to a dogmatic conclusion but as an invitation to the reader to continue the discussion. Plato's earliest dialogues, most historians agree, present a historically accurate portrait of Socrates' own philosophy. As the years went on, though, he increasingly used Socrates as a literary device, a mouthpiece for his own ideas.

Plato begins with an observation: the world we observe with our senses is pale and imperfect—defective, jumbled, and filled with apparent contradictions.

And yet we intuit order within it. We see parts of things; we intuit whole things. We observe, for example, two chairs. They may be of different sizes and shapes, made of different materials, weigh different amounts, exhibit different colors, have different combustion points if we apply a flame to them, or even (for the brave) may smell and taste different. And yet we know that they are both indeed chairs. They possess some quality—"chairness"—that perhaps we cannot define, but, like the famous example of the U.S. Supreme Court judge discussing pornography: we know it when we see it.

Plato's philosophy argues that "chairness" really and truly exists; it is an example of what he terms the **Ideal Forms**. Where does it exist? Perhaps in a parallel universe, or as an idea in the mind of God. Who can say? The point is that it does exist, and that everything we perceive as a chair possesses it. Thus to Plato our world should be thought of as a pallid reflection of the world of Ideal Forms, a corrupt descendant filled with flawed and partial representations of the Forms. The Ideal Forms constitute ultimate reality, while our physical world is a cheap knockoff. Plato's dialogues can be thought of as a series of discussions, each about a particular abstract Form—Love, Beauty, Goodness, Art, or Justice— for we can only understand our world in relation to the Forms it so imperfectly represents.

> The Ideal Forms constitute ultimate reality, while our physical world is a cheap knockoff. Plato's dialogues can be thought of as a series of discussions, each about a particular abstract Form—love, beauty, goodness, art, or justice—for we can only understand our world in relation to the Forms it so imperfectly represents.

Plato insists that we can in fact understand the Ideal Forms because of the dual nature of human beings: we are not merely animated flesh but eternal souls temporarily housed in physical bodies. Each soul carries deep within itself an instinctive knowledge of the Ideal Forms, a memory of ultimate reality as yet lacking a clear shape. That is why we feel we know what "chairness" is even though we struggle to express it in words. Plato's philosophy is essentially romantic and mystical. It yearns for and aspires to an ineluctable perfect state of existence that seems as though it should be within our grasp. If only we can keep talking, if only we can remain willing to strip away untested assumptions, if only we can help one another along the way, we will eventually attain the true meaning of Love, Beauty, Goodness, Truth, and Happiness.

No other writer comes close to Plato's skill at portraying philosophy as a kind of pilgrimage, a journey toward a salvation that can be attained only with other people. There are no solitary revelers in Plato's world. Each of his dialogues ends differently, in terms of whether or not a true understanding of any particular Form is attained. Yet they all end with a warm feeling of community, of

Two 4th-Century BCE Busts, Portraying Plato and Aristotle   By tradition, Aristotle is always shown with a shorter beard than his teacher's.

something special having been shared. It is the process of philosophy as much as the ideas attained by it that Plato portrays so lovingly and unforgettably.

ARISTOTLE AND THE PURSUIT OF HAPPINESS

Aristotle was Plato's most distinguished pupil and has a good claim to be among the three or four most influential thinkers in Western history. A tireless worker, he threw himself into the study of everything from ethics and metaphysics to botany and poetics. Ancient sources credit him with as many as two hundred separate treatises, some of very great length. Roughly thirty treatises survive, perhaps more and perhaps fewer, depending on the debated authenticity of a handful of texts.

Despite their unflagging brilliance, though, most of the texts consist not of Aristotle's own writing but of lecture notes later collated and stitched together (according to tradition, by his son, Nicomachus). The books as we have them are leaden, cramped, repetitive, and graceless. If his lectures were in fact like these composite transcripts, Aristotle was a brilliant but dull teacher. The contrast with Plato could hardly be any stronger. Plato was an artist of the highest order; his dialogues have polish, wit, sharp characterization, and narrative drive. They manage the neat trick of expressing complex ideas with such clarity that anyone can grasp them. Aristotle, by contrast, comes across as an astonishing but long-winded polymath struggling to control a buggy Power-Point presentation.

The ideas that come through are vital, even though his range makes it difficult to present them in a systematic way. The key to Aristotle lay in his method: unlike his teacher (but very much like his own father, a physician) Aristotle began not with the theoretical examination of the Ideal Forms but with intense scrutiny of the tangible natural world. He accepted the notion of the Ideal Forms, or claimed to, but he believed that their essential elements appear physically within each object. Existence consists of the continual interplay of Ideal Form and earthly matter—rather like the way our genetic coding continues to affect our physical development throughout our lives. Aristotle, then, offers a compromise between Plato's Idealism and the rough materialism of the Milesians.

Moreover, Aristotle asserts that the continuous nature of the interplay of forces drives the universe forward toward a goal. Everything is in a state of becoming. A seed is on its way to becoming a seedling, then a plant in full flower, then a withering husk, then a decayed nutrient for another seed. Each existing thing, whether animate or not, plays a role in the unstoppable push forward to new life. Since we ourselves are part of this impetus of birth, life, and decay, we can take solace in knowing that our existence is ennobled with purpose. Every existing thing, he says, has a **telos**—an intrinsic purpose, a necessary role in the cosmic drama. The telos of an animal embryo is to become that animal; that of teeth is chew food. For Aristotle's great teacher, the physical world is a flaw and a hindrance to our understanding. Aristotle instead sees the world as a process—a march forward into ever new being (and hopefully, but not necessarily, ever better being).

But do human beings have a telos? If so, is it a general telos applicable to the whole species, or is it unique to each nation or even each individual? I know of a philosophy professor (an Aristotelian, no less) who preyed on female students. When his university learned of it and fired him, he argued that sexual craving for young women was, however unfortunately, his telos and that he therefore had no choice but to pursue them. He consequently sued the university for discrimination against a person with a handicap. He lost.

Aristotle wrestled with these questions over and over. If human life is teleological, is that not the same as saying it is fated or even predetermined? Are we in control of our own destinies, and if not, then what sound basis can there be for morality? Aristotle's answer is characteristically complex. He begins with the observation that ethics is a practical science, not a theoretical one. The point of it is to learn how to act and live a well-ordered life, not to gain some abstract knowledge about the nature of Goodness for its own sake.

Most people, he says, would agree on most ethical propositions: that happiness is better than sadness, that pleasure is preferable to pain, or that courage is superior to fearfulness. We all might disagree on specifics regarding those virtues. Some, for example, might take greater pleasure in being renowned for beauty than for intelligence. But everyone would agree that to have a good reputation for something is a positive ethical value. What interests Aristotle is the relationship between these values. Is courage of greater or lesser value than loyalty? Is it more important to be temperate in one's desires or to be well-liked? Whatever their relative standings, he insists that happiness (*eudaimonia* in Greek—meaning "being in accordance with the spirits," literally, or "living well," colloquially) is the supreme virtue, toward which all other virtues point. To Aristotle happiness must entail something intrinsic to human beings as a species. It is something we possess or experience that no other creatures can; and this, he says, is our capacity for rational thought. If we follow the use of reason, if we cultivate it as a means of life, we can and will attain happiness. Whether or not we are happy has little to do with the contingency of world events and is the product of our own choices—choices in our actions and in how we react to the world. In this way, individual free will is preserved, as is the notion of a human telos. In other words, our telos is to pursue happiness; but whether or not we achieve it, or the way in which we achieve it, is up to us.

> To Aristotle happiness must entail something intrinsic to human beings as a species. It is something we possess or do that no other creatures can; and this, he says, is our capacity for rational thought. If we follow the use of reason, if we cultivate it as a means of life, we can and will attain happiness.

Plato and Aristotle were both interested in politics, though only at a distance. Two of Plato's last dialogues—*The Republic* and *The Laws*—describe a vision of an ideal society, one in which an oligarchy of philosopher-kings would oversee the day-to-day governance of society. A group of Guardians would in turn direct the education, training, and administration of everyday life. The bulk of common humanity is neither able to nor cares to govern its own affairs and is happy to leave the work of running the world to its superiors. It is not clear how Plato intends us to read this treatise. Socrates' arguments never appear so weak reasoned and faulty anywhere else in Plato's writings. He even interrupts the text with allegorical tales that highlight the futility of drawing clear conclusions about anything.

Aristotle, on the other hand, took a genuine interest in politics—even to the point of writing constitutions for various poleis—although he had no direct involvement in political life that we know of. After Plato's death in 347 BCE, Aristotle left Greece altogether and lived in Asia Minor for four years. In 343 BCE King Philip of Macedon (r. 359–336 BCE) invited Aristotle to come to Pella, the capital of Macedon, and tutor his teenage son. Aristotle took the job, in a kingdom to the north of Greece inhabited by a tribe that spoke a language of disputed relation to Greek. There he spent eight years teaching the lad, and then in 335 BCE he finally returned to Athens and established his own school, the **Lyceum**, where he spent the rest of his life giving his interminable lectures.

The lad he tutored in Pella, however, most definitely took an interest in politics. His name was Alexander.

ALEXANDER THE GREAT

Alexander the Great (r. 336–323 BCE) was the greatest conqueror of the ancient world. He took over from his father the realm of Macedon, a semi-Greek kingdom with an inferiority complex, and much of Greece proper, which his father had briefly subdued. By 334 BCE Alexander was firmly in control of all of Greece and had already determined to advance eastward against the Persian Empire. And that was just the start.

In its bloody, insurrection-filled past, Macedon also had suffered in the invasions by Darius and Xerxes. The Greeks themselves regarded the Macedonians as barbarians—or at the very best as poor backward cousins. While Greece prospered during the Periclean age, Macedon remained ignored and reviled. But the self-destruction of Greece during the Peloponnesian War gave Philip, and then his son, dreams of glory. With the discovery of vast gold mines in the southern Balkans, Philip became wealthier than the Delian League had been at its height.

Alexander succeeded to the Macedonian throne in 336 BCE, and within two years he had swooped down on all of Greece. No one could stand in his way, since all the poleis were in such weak condition. In turning his sights to Persia, his thinking was sound. The conflict between Greece and Persia had never been settled definitively. Internal discord and political strife had followed the defeat of Xerxes' forces in 479 BCE, but by the time of the Peloponnesian conflict Persia was already trying to manipulate the outcome in Greece in order to prepare the way for another attempt. Alexander simply recognized, correctly, that Greece would never be free of the Persian threat. He decided to settle the matter once and for all by reversing the scales and sending his Greek army to topple the throne in faraway Persepolis.

Alexander the Great   A Roman copy (1st century BCE) of a Greek original bust.

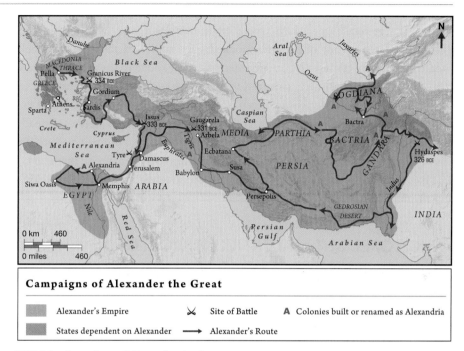

MAP 5.2   Campaigns of Alexander the Great

The narrative of Alexander's campaigns is well known. In 334 BCE he took Asia Minor; within two more years he had conquered the Holy Land and Egypt. By 331 BCE he had advanced through Syria and met the main Persian army at Gaugamela, not far from the ancient Assyrian city of Nineveh along the upper Tigris, and slaughtered it.[9] He then marched to Persepolis, deep into today's Iran, and in 330 BCE he destroyed the capital. Determined to press on until every last vestige of Persian power was defeated, Alexander spent five more years on campaign through the territories of Parthia and Bactria (today's eastern Iran and Afghanistan), then down the Indus River valley, where his astonished men encountered Indian war elephants. Alexander still wanted to press on and take India, but his exhausted men threatened to mutiny, and so in 325–324 BCE he reluctantly led his forces back west to the city of Babylon. It was the most stunning military adventure of the ancient world, an unparalleled feat (see Map 5.2).

But it is one thing to conquer vast territory, and quite another to create an empire. Alexander's long-term plans are unknown, for in 323 BCE he took ill and died, aged thirty-three. He had taken care to establish in his wake a sprawl of Greek-styled cities. Some were newly built from nothing (like Alexandria, in

---

[9]   After the battle of Gaugamela, the Persian emperor Darius III fled into the nearby hills, where he was murdered by a local tribal chieftain. This ended the Achaemenid dynasty.

Egypt), others refashioned with Greek institutions and laws. Within them he placed a loose network of libraries stocked with copies of the best of Greek literature, science, philosophy, and mathematics. He added to these the gathered manuscripts of Persian high culture too—many translated into Greek for the widest dissemination. He also arranged (in fact, ordered on penalty of death) for his leading officers to divorce their Greek wives and to take Persian ones instead. It is unclear whether Alexander intended by this to create a utopian postethnic society. Perhaps he intended simply to develop a new aristocracy, one that identified itself with a new race of his own manufacture. In either case, he was developing an amalgam.

A MONGREL BUT MAGNIFICENT WORLD

The eastern Mediterranean traditions had included the Greek, Egyptian, and Hebrew. The Persian and Babylonian traditions had included the Mesopotamian valley and the eastern lands that had absorbed and assimilated them. As Alexander's vast battlefield settled into relative peace, a single Hellenistic civilization embraced and absorbed both. This mongrel but magnificent world was the **Hellenistic Age** (327–30 BCE), and it lasted until the Romans finally came in the 1st century BCE and instigated a new era.

The political narrative of the time is not particularly interesting. Many wars and palace coups came and went, but none in service of a significant new idea. In general terms, Alexander's enormous war zone split quickly into a quartet of separate states, each governed originally by one of his leading generals: Ptolemaic Egypt, Seleucid Asia, Attalid Anatolia, and Antigonid Greece.[10] Because the new rulers and settlers came from throughout Greece, and not simply from a single city like Athens, the Hellenistic world had a broader degree of cultural cohesion. A single dialect of Greek developed and came into general usage throughout the territories—this was the "common" (*koine*) Greek in which, ultimately, most of the Christian New Testament was written. In all four kingdoms the governments were tightly centralized, and efficient tax collection led to the building up of vast treasuries (see Map 5.3).

Apart from supporting their armies, the main expenditure of the governments was the construction of more and more cities. Manufacturing and

> It is unclear whether Alexander intended to create a utopian postethnic society. Perhaps he intended simply to develop a new aristocracy, one that identified itself with a new race of his own manufacture. In either case, he was developing an amalgam.

---

[10]   Take the -ic and -id endings off the dynastic adjectives, add -us (or -os, if you're a Hellenic purist), and you'll have the names of the first succeeding generals.

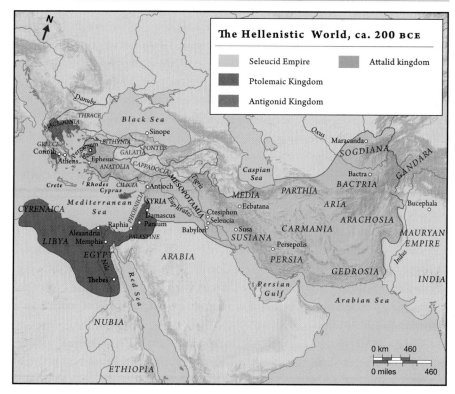

MAP 5.3   The Hellenistic World, ca. 200 BCE

commerce were the hallmarks of Hellenistic life, and these required a solid and expansive urban base. At least three hundred new cities were founded in this era, and hundreds more received huge injections of money to improve their infrastructures. Within a century of its construction, Alexandria had a half million inhabitants; Seleucia had a quarter million.[11] The Seleucids poured money into refurbishing their Mediterranean and Black Sea harbors and extended their roadways into India. The Ptolemies in Egypt hired geographers and cartographers to search out and map new overland trade routes into Arabia, Ethiopia, and Nubia. The Antigonids invested in canals and a vastly increased fleet of ships that was able to trade with Spain and Britain (important sources of silver and tin, respectively).

Not everyone prospered. Farming was still the occupation of the great bulk of the population, and farmers generally lived in poverty throughout the Hellenistic years. Poor crop yields were not the cause. Farmers steadily produced abundant quantities of foodstuffs, and the proliferation of cities meant the increased,

---

[11]   Pergamon, the cultural capital of the Attalid kingdom, had an amphitheater that could seat ten thousand and a library that contained two hundred thousand scrolls.

and increasingly easy, availability of markets. Rather, intentionally harsh tax policies in all the kingdoms kept small farmers poor. Two motives prompted such exploitation: a desire not to impede the development of the urban economies, and a perverse belief that abject poverty would keep the agrarian population incapable of rebellion. Hellenistic splendor thus resulted less from a general prosperity than from the intentionally inequitable redistribution of wealth.

Hellenistic literature, art, and intellectual life were generally not as dramatic, innovative, and profound as in the Classical period. Then again, the autocratic nature of Hellenistic government may not have permitted as creative a spirit to flourish. Cultural life seldom thrives in police states. The fortunes acquired by those in trade and industry, as well as in government, meant a widespread demand for decorative arts—statuary, jewelry, frescos and mosaics, tapestries—to adorn the homes and villas of the well-to-do. The preferred styles were more ornate, as with the elaborate Corinthian style of columns or the exaggerated naturalism of statues like the famous Laocoön. In literature, historical writing and pastoral poetry were the most popular genres (the best writers were Polybius and Theocritus, respectively).

But it was in the sciences especially that Hellenistic intellectual life really shone. Scholars were able to bring together the Greek, Egyptian, and Persian traditions in everything from astronomy and geometry to mathematics, medicine, and physics. The wide availability of libraries and laboratories—both of which were considered "must-have" accessories of the well-to-do—sparked many new abstract and practical advances, word of which spread rapidly. Aristarchus of Samos (310–230 BCE) and Eratosthenes of Cyrene (285–194 BCE) were the preeminent astronomers.

Three Examples of Hellenistic Sculpture, Showing a New Emphasis on Movement and Gesture   The first shows a gladiator or other competitive fighter (identifiable by his lack of armor—or of anything else). The second depicts the goddess Venus in a surprisingly modest pose. The third, which is a Roman copy of a lost Greek original, depicts the legendary figure of Laocoön as he is beset by sea-serpents.

Between them, they proved that the earth and other planets revolved around the sun and determined the circumference of the earth.

In geometry, Euclid (330–270 BCE) led the way. *The Elements of Geometry* became the basic textbook for teaching the subject for fifteen hundred years. In medicine, figures like Herophilus of Chalcedon (335–280 BCE) introduced (briefly, and on the sly) the practice of human dissection, from which he determined the role of the heart in transmitting blood through the arteries—a bit of knowledge quickly lost until it was rediscovered by the English physician William Harvey in the 17th century. Archimedes of Syracuse (287–212 BCE)—the physicist famous for shouting "eureka" ("I've got it!") and running naked through the street—determined the law of specific gravity, devised the first compound pulley, and invented the hydraulic screw propeller.

SECOND TEMPLE JEWS AND JUDAISM

Freed from Babylonian bondage by Cyrus the Great in 539 BCE, the exiled Jews returned to Jerusalem and set to rebuilding their Temple, which they completed roughly twenty years later. The delay resulted from and illustrates some of the tensions that roiled the Jewish world. The Jews who had gone into captivity (the "Children of the Exile") and those who had remained behind (the "People of the Land") regarded one another with deep suspicion and hostility, and their descendants continued the conflict for at least two generations. Who were the "true Jews"—those who had endured foreign enslavement or those who had stayed behind in the Holy Land at great risk to their own safety?

Who were the "true Jews"—those who had endured foreign enslavement or those who had stayed behind in the Holy Land at great risk to their own safety?

To make matters even more complicated, both groups had developed new devotional and legal traditions. Both communities had turned for guidance to networks of rabbis, or legal scholars. For the "Children of the Exile," return to Jerusalem meant the restoration to power of the high priestly family, along with the primacy of Temple worship. The "People of the Land" dismissed the priestly family as mere pawns of the Persian Empire.[12] (The "People of the Land" faction has been edited out of the Jewish canon, for the most part, although it is possible that Isaiah 55–56 carries echoes of their position.) Accusations of treason, corruption, and apostasy flew back and forth. Moreover, many Jewish men in each camp had married non-Jewish women, given the relative shortage of females during the long years of hardship, and the resulting offspring became the

---

[12]   The prophet Ezra was a partisan of the "Children of the Exile."

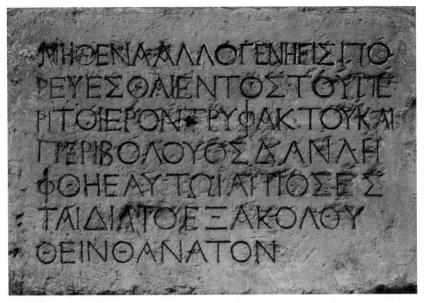

Plaster Cast of an Inscription from the Ruins of the Second Temple   Written in Greek, the inscription stood outside the outermost wall of the Temple grounds; it states that only Jews may enter the Temple precinct itself. Non-Jews found within the walls potentially faced the penalty of death.

objects of much debate on the authenticity of their Jewishness. (Ezra casts the inter-Jewish conflict in economic terms.) Such conflicts continued for another two or three centuries, which resulted in the remarkable amount of legal and literary activity discussed earlier. Most notably, earlier religious texts were revised and new ones produced, down to the revisionist history of 1–2 Chronicles (with which the Jewish canon now ends), which was penned around 350 BCE.

Thus the Jews entered the Hellenistic period engaged in intense debate about their communal identity. The two principal factions soon divided into a multiplicity of sects, distinguished by doctrinal divisions, tribal and political loyalties, class distinctions, and linguistic identities. Opposing notions of political overlordship played a role, too. Both Ptolemaic Egypt and Seleucid Asia claimed jurisdiction over Judea until 198 BCE, forcing the multiple Jewish factions to perform a careful balancing act between the two foreign powers. Judea held no interest for either power, so long as the Jews paid the taxes levied upon them. Yet the rival imperial claims on the land led to the development of large Jewish communities within both Egypt and Asia Minor.

In Alexandria alone, as many as fifty thousand Jews resided, a figure that had quadrupled by the time the Romans replaced the Ptolemies. These Jews retained their religious identity but became so Hellenized that by around 260 BCE they needed to have the Bible translated into Greek, since they no longer understood Hebrew. According to a text known as the *Letter of Aristeas*, a group of seventy-two

Biblical scholars gathered in Alexandria and carried out the task, thus producing the version of Scripture called the **Septuagint** (that being the Latin word for "seventy"). The *Letter of Aristeas* further reports, delightfully, that the seventy-two translators miraculously *spoke as one throughout the entire project, agreeing on each and every word of the translation. Aristeas was a Greek-speaking Jewish historian who lived roughly one hundred years after the Septuagint was completed.*

The Jews in Seleucid Asia likewise Hellenized to a considerable extent, and many rose to positions of social and even political power.[13] Jewish Hellenization involved more than adoption of the Greek language. A partial religious **syncretism**, or union of doctrines, occurred as well, as Judaism made contact with and adopted certain characteristics of the dominant Zoroastrian faith. This is most apparent in the development of an apocalyptic tradition within mainstream Judaism (with its tenets regarding the approach of a messiah) and among some lesser strands such as the Gnostic sects. YHWH's justice shall come upon earth, scatter and destroy His enemies, and reward faithful Israel:

> Behold the LORD Himself
> Comes from afar
> In blazing wrath,
> With a heavy burden—
> His lips full of fury,
> His tongue like devouring fire,
> And His breath like a raging torrent
> Reaching halfway up the neck—
> To set a misguiding yoke upon nations
> And make a misleading bridle upon the jaws of peoples,
>
> For you, there shall be singing
> As on a night when a festival is hallowed;
> There shall be rejoicing as when they march
> With flute, with timbrels, and with lyres
> To the Rock of Israel on the Mount of the LORD.
>
> For the LORD will make His majestic voice heard
> And display the sweep of His arm
> In raging wrath,
> In a devouring blaze of fire,
> In tempest, and rainstorm, and hailstones. *(Isaiah 30.27–30)*

---

[13]   The stories of Tobit, who gained high status in the old Assyrian Empire, and of Daniel, who became advisor to the king of Babylon, were written in the Seleucid era and depict that era's outlook.

The feverish moralism of Zoroastrianism can be detected in a passage like this, showing the two faiths as complementary. Still, apocalyptic belief among most Jews did not develop until after the defeat of the Maccabean Revolt.

THE MACCABEAN REVOLT

The Revolt of the Maccabees (167–142 BCE) originated with a contested succession to the Jerusalem high priesthood during the reign of the Seleucid king Antiochus IV Epiphanes (r. 175–164 BCE). Two main contestants emerged: Jason and Menelaus. Their very names suggest the degree of Hellenization that took place even in the Holy City. Neither was a paragon of virtue.

Jason paid Antiochus a large bribe to win the post, which left Menelaus with no choice but to offer an even larger one; but unfortunately Menelaus did not have enough cash on hand, so he broke into the Temple treasury and stole some golden vessels. The theft outraged the people, and the city erupted in riot. Antiochus invaded the city and established a garrison of his Syrian soldiers on the Temple Mount. These soldiers, consisting of followers of both the Greek and Zoroastrian religions, demanded some sort of accommodation for their religious rites—and Antiochus (with Menelaus's consent as high priest) allowed pagan altars to be set up within the Temple.

This profanation triggered a full-scale Jewish rebellion against Seleucid rule. The leaders of the rebellion were a family called the Hasmoneans—Mattathias and his five sons—but the rebellion itself took its name from that of the eldest Hasmonean son, Judas Maccabeus. The revolt is a great heroic episode in the history of the Jews and, ironically, their last military victory until the establishment of the modern state of Israel in 1948.

The odds were certainly against them, given the size and strength of the Seleucid forces, but the Jewish rebels showed remarkable tenacity. (A story from their retaking of the Temple itself, in 164 BCE, is the origin of the celebration of Hanukkah.) The surprised and exhausted Seleucids gave up the fight in 142 BCE and granted Judea independence. Their new dynasty, the Hasmoneans, would remain in power until they were ultimately brought down by the Romans in 70 CE.

Despite the heroic nature of the revolt, however, the main Jewish texts that record its history, the books known as 1–2 Maccabees, were not admitted into the Biblical canon. The ostensible reason for this—that they may have been written directly in Greek and hence lack a Hebrew source/counterpart—only partially explains their omission. The Septuagint Bible, including 1–2 Maccabees, remained in widespread use in the Jewish world for three hundred years; communities from North Africa to Mesopotamia used it, as did numerous communities within

Palestine itself. The great Jewish philosopher Philo of Alexandria (d. 50 CE) used it. Rabbinical scholars drew upon it in establishing new legislation. Syrian Jews used it to prepare their own translation of the Bible into vernacular Syriac (the Peshitta).[14] For the rest of the Hellenistic period, and for at least two hundred years beyond, the Greek Septuagint was widely accepted canon in the Jewish world. The spread of Christianity in the first two centuries CE, however, altered Jewish attitudes toward their Greek Bible. Because Christians also used the Septuagint, it became tainted in their eyes.

Returning to the Hebrew canon was a way of asserting their difference from the Christians, indeed their independence from them. Hence they began to reconstitute the Hebrew text. The process of producing this version—by compiling old manuscripts, collating excerpts from older liturgical material, and at times even reconstructing the text from memory—resulted in the Masoretic text, the definitive Hebrew-language canon still in use today. (It was codified in the middle of the 3rd century CE.) 1–2 Maccabees, while still revered as part of the Jewish literary tradition, lost its canonical status. In order to disassociate themselves from the upstart new sect, the Jews cut themselves off from the Biblical version that most of them used. In the process, they decanonized the books that record the last great triumph of their ancient era.

---

[14] The Peshitta presents a host of linguistic and interpretive difficulties. The Jewish Scriptures were translated into Syriac from the Septaguint by Jewish scholars (although many passages suggest that they were based on the Hebrew text), but later Christians seem to have rendered a separate Syriac version, which they supplemented with a Syriac version of the New Testament texts. An altogether separated textual tradition is the Targumin—which consists of an Aramaic version of the Scriptures. The Targumin reflect a closer reliance on the Hebrew Bible than on the Septuagint.

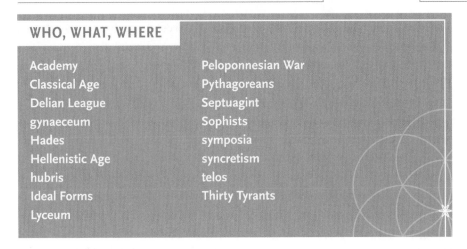

WHO, WHAT, WHERE

Academy	Peloponnesian War
Classical Age	Pythagoreans
Delian League	Septuagint
gynaeceum	Sophists
Hades	symposia
Hellenistic Age	syncretism
hubris	telos
Ideal Forms	Thirty Tyrants
Lyceum	

SUGGESTED READINGS

Primary Sources

Herodotus. *The Persian War.*

Thucydides. *The Peloponnesian War.*

Xenophon. *Hellenica.*

Anthologies

Cohen, S. Marc, Patricia Curd, and C. D. C. Reeve. *Readings in Greek Philosophy: From Thales to Aristotle* (2011).

Irby-Massie, Georgia, and Paul T. Keyser. *Greek Science of the Hellenistic Era: A Sourcebook* (2002).

Lefkowitz, Mary R., and Maureen B. Fant. *Women's Life in Greece and Rome: A Source Book in Translation* (2005).

Tracy, Stephen V. *Pericles: A Sourcebook and Reader* (2009).

Studies

Bagnall, Nigel. *The Peloponnesian War: Athens, Sparta, and the Struggle for Greece* (2006).

Bosworth, A. B. *The Legacy of Alexander: Politics, Warfare, and Propaganda under the Successors* (2005).

Briant, Pierre. *Alexander the Great and His Empire: A Short Introduction* (2010).

———. *From Cyrus to Alexander: A History of the Persian Empire* (2002).

Burn, Lucilla. *Hellenistic Art from Alexander the Great to Augustus* (2005).

Connelly, Joan Breton. *Portrait of a Priestess: Women and Ritual in Ancient Greece* (2009).

De Ste. Croix, G. E. M. *Athenian Democratic Origins, and Other Essays* (2005).

———. *The Origins of the Peloponnesian War* (2002).

Dillon, Matthew. *Girls and Women in Classical Greek Religion* (2002).

Grabbe, Lester L. *A History of the Jews and Judaism in the Second Temple Period* (2006–2008).

Hölbl, Günther. *A History of the Ptolemaic Empire* (2001).

Humphreys, S. C. *The Strangeness of Gods: Historical Perspectives on the Interpretation of Athenian Religion* (2004).

Jonker, Louis. *Historiography and Identity (Re) Formulation in Second Temple Historiographical Literature* (2010).

Kagan, Donald. *The Peloponnesian War* (2003).

Navia, Luis E. *Socrates: A Life Examined* (2007).

Neils, Jenifer, and John H. Oakley. *Coming of Age in Ancient Greece: Images of Childhood from the Classical Past* (2003).

Reeve, C. D. C. *Philosopher-Kings: The Argument of Plato's "Republic"* (2006).

Romm, James. *Ghost on the Throne: The Death of Alexander the Great and the War for Crown and Empire* (2011).

Roochnik, David. *Beautiful City: The Dialectical Character of Plato's "Republic"* (2008).

———. *Retrieving the Ancients: An Introduction to Greek Philosophy* (2004).

Saxonhouse, Arlene W. *Free Speech and Democracy in Ancient Athens* (2008).

Shanske, Darien. *Thucydides and the Philosophical Origins of History* (2009).

Sourvinou-Inwood, Christiane. *Tragedy and Athenian Religion* (2003).

Thomas, Carol G. *Alexander the Great in His World* (2007).

Warren, James. *Presocratics: Natural Philosophers before Socrates* (2007).

Weinfeld, Moshe. *Normative and Sectarian Judaism in the Second Temple Period* (2005).

———. *The Place of the Law in the Religion of Ancient Israel* (2004).

———. *Social Justice in Ancient Israel and in the Ancient Near East* (2000).

Zuckert, Catherine H. *Plato's Philosophers: The Coherence of the Dialogues* (2009).

For additional resources, including maps, primary sources, visuals, web links, and quizzes, please go to **www.oup.com/us/backman.**

CHAPTER 6

The Empire of the Sea: Rome

753 BCE–180 CE

ROME AND THE MEDITERRANEAN

The Romans believed themselves descended from the noble Trojans who had lost their city to Homer's Greeks. They may not have known their own true origin, or they may simply have desired a better one. According to their legend Aphrodite, the Greek goddess of love, fell head over heels for Anchises, a member of the younger branch of the Trojan royal family. Two things resulted from their tryst: a son named Aeneas and the infliction of blindness on Anchises when he was caught boasting of his sexual escapade to some other soldiers.[1] Aeneas played no very great role in the Trojan War, although he famously helped his father escape to safety. After the Greeks had set Troy ablaze, he carried the blind old man on his back through crumbling ruins of flaming timbers. His postwar travels took him into the central Mediterranean, where he learned of a prophecy that he would found a great new nation in central Italy, at a place called Latium.

After a series of adventures Aeneas did indeed reach Latium and brought the region under his control. But he did not found the city of Rome itself. That was the work of two much later descendants of Aeneas, the twin brothers Romulus and Remus, who, also according to the legend, laid the city's foundations in 753 BCE and established a dynasty. Its kings ruled until a rebellion in 509 BCE overthrew the monarchy and established a republic.

From this early date, level-headed pragmatism drove Roman political policies; but even pragmatists like to fantasize about noble ancestors and destined greatness. These spoke, too, to their image as a republic of virtue, even as internal struggles put in doubt the republic's very survival. And indeed Rome achieved its golden age under an emperor, Augustus, and as an empire linked by the Mediterranean Sea.

◀ **Roman Women** Wallpainting from Herculaneum, near Rome, 1st century CE, depicting a set of ladies being groomed by a servant hair-dresser.

CHAPTER OUTLINE

LINKS TO A HEROIC AGE

Their imagined link with Greece's heroic age mattered much to the Romans. On the practical level, an illustrious genealogy and a prophetic fate helped to legitimate, in their own eyes at least, the Romans' lording it over the other tribal and ethnic groups of central Italy. Surrounded by aggressive societies (like the Etruscans and Sabines to the north and east and the Aurunces, Hernici, Marses, and Vosici to the south), the Romans sought safety by conquering those peoples but being careful to incorporate them into their body politic. Although a monarchy, early Rome nevertheless had a brace of advisory and legislative councils (called the Senate and the *comitia curiata*, respectively) that admitted representatives of the other tribes.

On a deeper level, the Romans craved a linkage with ancient heroes because it had none of its own. Mythical tradition told of seven monarchs who began Rome's rise in the world. These legendary kings, who supposedly ruled from the founding of the city to the founding of the republic (753–509 BCE), were for the most part a competent bunch, but none of them would have made a suitable hero in an epic poem. (The regnal dates given here and in Table 6.1 are traditional. Since the existence of the kings themselves is doubtful, the dates of their reigns should not be regarded as factual.)

Not exactly a rogues' gallery, especially when compared to some of the emperors who followed them half a millennium later, but nothing really to boast about, either.

The Romans wanted legitimacy and grandeur, and forging a link with the Homeric heroes provided both.[2] Moreover, by emphasizing their supposed Hellenic roots, the Romans hoped to position themselves as the natural successors to Alexander's empire. Since the Carthaginians had also targeted that particular role, the Romans' claim to Homeric lineage can be seen as a propaganda

---

[1] Zeus, Aphrodite's father, blinded Anchises by hurling down a lightning bolt from Mount Olympus that struck him in the eyes.

[2] Our knowledge of early Rome derives from archeological remains and sources centuries later. In 387 BCE a Gaulish army invaded and (unintentionally, one assumes) burned down the municipal archives.

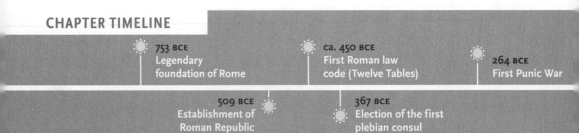

CHAPTER TIMELINE

753 BCE
Legendary
foundation of Rome

ca. 450 BCE
First Roman law
code (Twelve Tables)

264 BCE
First Punic War

509 BCE
Establishment of
Roman Republic

367 BCE
Election of the first
plebian consul

TABLE 6.1   **Rome's Kings**

Romulus (r. 753–715 BCE)	Formed the Roman army into its distinctive shape of individual legions, each composed of six thousand infantry and six hundred cavalry. But he is best remembered for the mass kidnapping of thousands of Sabine women to provide wives for his troops.
Numa Pompilius (r. 715–673 BCE)	Established the priesthood of the Vestal Virgins and abandoned the old lunar calendar for a solar one.
Tullius Hostilius (r. 673–642 BCE)	Was a bloodthirsty warrior who so neglected the gods that on his deathbed, when he cried out to be saved, Zeus blasted him with a thunderbolt that turned his palace and his body instantly to ashes.
Ancus Marcius (r. 640–616 BCE)	Built the first bridge across the Tiber river and founded the port at Ostia, thus connecting Rome to the sea. Otherwise he did nothing more noteworthy than establishing Rome first's saltworks.
Tarquinius Priscus (r. 616–579 BCE)	An Etruscan, doubled Rome's size by conquering the Etruscans, and used the booty he won to finance the construction of the Roman Forum and the Circus Maximus. He also built Rome's sewer system.[1]
Servius Tullius (r. 579–535 BCE)	Revised the constitution, made socioeconomic status the determinant for voting rights, built the great Temple to Diana, and was murdered by his daughter and her husband, Tarquinius Superbus.
Tarquinius Superbus (r. 539–509 BCE)	A violent, loutish, sensualist whose excesses led to his expulsion and the permanent overthrow of monarchy in 509 BCE.

[1] Showing their practical side, the Romans called their sewer the Cloaca Maxima—"the Giant Shithole."

ploy against their main Mediterranean rival. That state's ancestry led back not to Greece but to the Semitic-speaking Phoenicians.

The early Greeks had the stimulus of continual contact with the other peoples of the eastern Mediterranean, but the Romans were in a different situation altogether: Italy, geographically speaking, faces westward. The Apennine mountain chain runs down the eastern edge of the peninsula, forming an imperfect but still significant natural barrier to approach from the Adriatic Sea. Moreover, most of Italy's abundant and fertile agricultural plains, as well as most of her natural harbors, stretch down the western coast. And apart from the great Po River complex that runs eastward across the northernmost part of the peninsula, almost

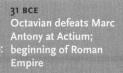

31 BCE
Octavian defeats Marc Antony at Actium; beginning of Roman Empire

212 CE
Roman citizenship extended to all free peoples living in the empire

146 BCE
Rome undisputed master of the Mediterranean

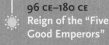
96 CE–180 CE
Reign of the "Five Good Emperors"

all of Italy's rivers flow westward. The only parts of Italy easily accessible to the Greeks were the southern third of the peninsula and the island of Sicily, where we find Greek settlements established as early as the mid-8th century BCE—the time of Homer. For these reasons the earliest **Latins** (the name given to the people who settled the region of Latium) had the greatest degree of commercial and cultural contact not with Greece but with the Etruscans, an advanced society to the north with whom they had close but uneasy relations (see Map 6.1).

The **Etruscans** were a literate people who left behind a considerable body of writing (especially inscriptions). However, since their language is poorly understood, all that we know of them derives from archeological remains plus whatever the Romans and others wrote about them. They were excellent metalsmiths and builders; the Romans appear to have learned the techniques of arch building from them. The Etruscans also introduced the Romans to the blood sport of gladiatorial contests. Such contests originated as an aspect of funeral observances, an offering made in honor of the deceased, and was extremely popular. The historian Livy (Titus Livius [59 BCE–17 CE]) describes a plethora of such games in 174 BCE:

> Many gladiatorial games were held in that year; most of them were unremarkable, but one really stood out from the rest—namely, the games

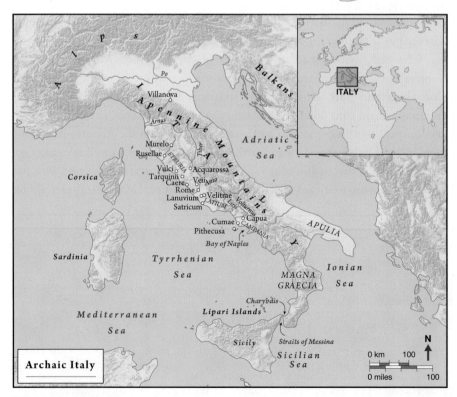

MAP 6.1   Archaic Italy

staged by Titus Flaminius to commemorate the death of his father. These games lasted four days, including the public food distribution, the general banquet, and the handful of theatrical performances that accompanied them. The high point of the festivity, of course, was the three-day contest in which seventy-four gladiators (a high number, in those times) fought.

Titus Flaminius here was a Roman general who later played a big role in the conquest of Greece.

Apart from providing Rome with two of its seven kings, the Etruscans influenced the Latins in two profound ways: morals and religion. If we can credit the stories told about them by the Romans and Greeks, the Etruscans were prosperous and enjoyed their prosperity to the hilt. They held sumptuous feasts twice daily—with both male and female guests reclining on pillowed couches, richly decorated homes, and flowing rivers of wine. Descriptions fill many disapproving Latin and Greek pages—for the Romans, making a virtue of their own relative want, largely disdained luxury as nothing more than self-indulgence. They never aspired to Spartan levels of austerity, but they placed a high value on frugality and self-discipline. Moral strength demanded sacrifice, as they saw it, and the placing of the common good before individual desire. In this way, the Etruscans taught the Romans by negative example.

In religion, however, their influence was direct and positive. The Etruscans practiced divination, or the reading of prophetic signs in certain natural phenomena—the shape of a slaughtered animal's liver, the blood spatter of a beheaded chicken,

Wrestling Match   In this fresco from around 500 BCE from the "Tomb of the Augurs" at Tarquinii, two men wrestle over three metal cauldrons, which are probably the prizes of their contest. The cloaked figure to the left carries a curved staff known as a *lituus*, which was a sign of kingship and, at Rome, a mark of the priests known as augurs, who had charge of the "auspices." One of the chief ways to take the auspices was by defining a field of vision with a *lituus*, and then observing within it the behavior of birds. Here, the cloaked figure seems to be supervising the contest, while the *lituus* and the birds flying over the combatants may indicate that he was seeking to foretell the result.

the rumbling sound of thunder or the groaning of a volcano, or the flight pattern of a group of birds. Divination was common throughout early Italy, but the Etruscan diviners were considered the best.[3] The Romans adopted their practice and remained dedicated believers in it for many centuries. The individuals trained to read signs were called haruspices (singular haruspex), and while the Roman religion never fully recognized them as priests, Roman society turned to them before any undertaking and took their warnings with the utmost seriousness.

REPUBLIC, PROPERTY, AND FAMILY

In place of the overthrown monarchy, the Senate in 509 BCE established a **res publica**, a republic, or commonwealth. Its constitution—mostly unwritten—changed numerous times over the centuries but remained based on the crucial idea of the separation of powers. An elaborate system of checks and balances prevented any individual or group from amassing too much power. The Senate was the dominant body, composed of members of Rome's leading noble families, but its work was complemented by a number of legislative assemblies and executive magistracies. Most magistrates served one-year terms, so campaigning and deal making were more or less constant. Since different social groups were involved in the different offices, prudence dictated that families and classes would form alliances that would compete for choice political positions and passing legislation.

In all, the Republic functioned very much in the spirit of Aristotle's ideal city-state, a smallish, organic society whose government involved all the leading figures of the city in a constantly changing network of mutually dependent relationships. Initially, the class of patricians held the upper hand, but within two generations the struggle between social orders had progressed to the extent that the Republic promulgated—sometime around 450 BCE—its first written law code. Known as the **Twelve Tables** (the name derives from the original dozen wooden slabs on which the code was written and set in public), it formed the basis for all subsequent Roman jurisprudence. It survives only in fragments, but the outline of its contents provides a good sense of its scope.

To judge from their remains, the Tables regarded property rights as the paramount concern of society. Indeed, the internal struggles of the first hundred years of the Republic centered on opening more avenues of government to the enterprising nonpatrician classes, whose strength came from their prosperity rather than noble lineage. In part, property issues featured so prominently in the laws because a debtor's creditor could legally sell him into slavery, if the circumstances warranted it. The Tables, therefore, defined those circumstances. Although the official census

---

3   Livy wrote: "When it came to signs and omens regarding public life, Roman custom was to consult nobody except Etruscan haruspices" (*History* 1.56).

TABLE 6.2 **The Twelve Tables**

Table 1	Laws Regarding Pretrial Preliminaries
Table 2	Laws Regarding Trials
Table 3	Laws Regarding the Execution of Judgments
Table 4	Laws Regarding *Patria Potestas*
Table 5	Laws Regarding Inheritances
Table 6	Laws Regarding Property
Table 7	Laws Regarding Real Property
Table 8	Laws Regarding Torts
Table 9	Laws Regarding the Rights of the Public
Table 10	Laws Regarding Religion
Table 11	Supplementary Laws
Table 12	Supplementary Laws

recognized a hierarchy of six classes, Roman social tradition divided the populace into two groups: patricians could trace their lineage to the members of the first Senate in 509 BCE, while everyone else was plebian. Since the census originated as a means of determining the army service owed by each citizen, military needs, not economic roles, determined social structure.

The essential social unit was the **familia**, a broader institution than "family." A familia consisted of an entire household and included the various aunts, uncles, nephews, nieces, cousins, close friends, clients, concubines, attendants, and house servants who lived under the same roof. It was firmly patriarchal, like the society as a whole. The head of the household (the **pater familias**) held complete authority over the entire familia and was, legally speaking, the sole possessor of its property. Moreover, the pater familias possessed a legal right known as ***patria potestas*** ("paternal power," the subject of the fourth of the Twelve Tables), which gave him the right of life and death over his family. Several passages in the Twelve Tables limn the extent of paternal power:

Pater Familias   An upper-class Roman, identifiable by the robe he wears, is shown holding the busts of his ancestors, probably his father and grandfather. Deceased parents became the household gods of Roman families, and processions with these busts were a common ritual at festivals.

> To any father is given the power of life and death over his children. . . . A father has the power to sell any child of his into slavery, but if a child is sold three times by his

father, he shall be free of his father after the third time. . . . In order to repudiate a wife, a husband shall simply say to her "Manage your [dowry] property for yourself," take away her keys to the house, and expel her.

The father's authority was absolute and not to be questioned. The Romans saw justice in this arrangement, since it was the father's responsibility, ultimately, to preserve the honor of the familia. Without it, a family could not hold its place in society.

THE REPUBLIC OF VIRTUE

Honor means different things to different people. Etymologically, it derives from the Latin word for burden (*onus, oneris*), reflecting the toil and struggle one must maintain to achieve it. To the Romans, honor consisted of playing one's appointed role in the familia and in the Republic. A father's honor lay in preserving his family's economic, social, and moral well-being. The Republic helped by implementing the office of censor, one that quickly became the most prestigious and feared of all the Roman magistracies.

From Plutarch's *Life of Cato the Elder* (ch. 16):

> The office of censor, one might say, towered above every other civic honor and was in fact a perfect climax to a political career. Its powers were many and widespread, and included the authority to inspect the lives and morals of the citizens. The people who created the censorship believed it right not to leave people free to act as they wished without others' seeing and judging them—not in marriage, the begetting of children, the workings of everyday life, or socializing with one's friends. In fact, they deemed these to be the very aspects of a man's life where he shows his truest character.

Plutarch then goes on to describe Cato's most famous exercise of censorial power. A prominent senator named Lucius Quintius had conducted an unseemly relationship with a handsome young lad. Once, when the two were reclining together after a dinner that included too much wine, the young lad declared that he loved Lucius so much that he had run to his house when summoned, even though he had been watching his first gladiatorial combat ever and had been looking forward to seeing a man slaughtered. Lucius, ever the attentive lover, then ordered a convicted criminal beheaded in front of his beloved, to make up for what the lad had missed. Cato, horrified, stripped Lucius of his senatorial rank.

The censor had three specific duties: to maintain the **census** (the official list of all citizens of Rome, their property, and legal class), to administer the finances of the state for all public works, and, most ominously, to preserve public morals.

The first two duties are self-explanatory, but the third deserves comment.[4] The censors could reward or punish an individual, and by extension his entire familia, by entering notations in the official census about the person's moral health. A black mark in the census imposed a moral stain called infamy (*infamia*), which meant the loss of the right to vote or participate in public life, the loss of admission into proper society, the ruin of any hopes to establish suitable marriages for one's children, and a permanent demotion in social status. Hence Romans considered it essential to observe, and to be seen to observe, the moral standards demanded by society.

What ethical crimes earned the censor's black mark? Most had to do with a failure to exercise proper leadership of the familia: living amid excessive luxury; neglecting one's crop fields; overindulgence of one's spouse and children; failure to observe norms regarding marriage, inheritance, or divorce; cruelty to slaves; failure to take care of one's clients; commercial fraud; or participating in disreputable trades like acting or prostitution.

The Romans valued simplicity. Clothing, though coded to distinguish social classes, was unelaborate. Diets consisted of bread, simple vegetable dishes, fruits, and roasted meat, plus wine, which they invariably cut with water. Education in the early Republic was minimal except for those of senatorial or equestrian rank, and it took place entirely in the home: boys received the basics of literacy and numeracy, were stuffed with moral tales of figures from Roman history, and began physical training as a preparation for military service; girls, on the other hand, were instructed in homecrafts like spinning, weaving, and sewing. Economic life centered on farming and local handcrafts, and much of the trade was by barter; in fact, the Republic did not even have a standard coinage until 289 BCE. Houses were simple low structures turned inward to face a central open courtyard; poorer families resided in multiunit apartments that were based on the same design. The images in modern popular culture of the egregious luxury, feasting, and sensual

Customers at a Breadmaker's Stall   Pompeii, 1st century CE.

---

4   To the Romans, certain moral duties were so significant that they deemed it necessary to certify a person's proper observance.

indulgence of the Roman elites are mostly exaggerations. Just as important, when excesses really did exist, most Romans disapproved.

Their religion was polytheistic and animistic, focusing on a multitude of gods and spirits. The well-known deities of Jupiter, Venus, Mars, and the rest bore close resemblance to the Olympian gods and goddesses of the Greeks, and in later centuries the Romans emphasized the union of their mythologies. But for most Romans the smaller local divinities took precedence, especially the family deities known as the "**household gods**" (*lares familiares*), the daily worship of whom was the responsibility of the pater familias. These spirits watched over the family farmland, the household, and possessions. Family ancestors continued to care for their descendants, and so prayers of dedication, thanksgiving, and respect were given to them always.

Religious life demanded constant, dutiful observance, following precise formulas of wording, gesture, and offering. Any mistake or omission rendered the ritual null and void. Since the Romans believed their well-being depended on the care of their spirit gods, observation of proper ritual was a matter of crucial significance. Religion was not a source of joy or spiritual exaltation but rather a moral responsibility. It is not accidental that the characteristic descriptor of Rome's legendary founder, Aeneas, was the Latin adjective *pius*—not pious, but dutiful.

> Since the Romans believed their well-being depended on the care of their spirit gods, observation of proper ritual was a matter of crucial significance. Religion was not a source of joy or spiritual exaltation but rather a moral responsibility.

SIZE MATTERS

The institutions, practices, and civic values established by the early Republic faced a dramatic challenge when the Republic began to expand. By 387 BCE the Roman Republic might had extended only through a sweep of territory roughly thirty miles (fifty kilometers) from the city. The increased area brought with it an increased population, which Rome incorporated under its constitution. Conquered landowners and shopkeepers kept their property and legal rights, but now, as Roman plebeians, they paid taxes to the Republic. The Republic in turn used the additional revenues to connect towns with networks of roads and to bring fresh water into them with systems of aqueducts.

The larger the Republic grew, however, the more concessions it had to make to the **plebeians** who made up the bulk of the population. As early as 400 BCE plebeians had won the right of eligibility to the lower magistracies, and in 367 BCE the Republic elected its first plebeian **consul**—the executive office in charge of the government.[5] Soon the plebeians demanded a voice of their own in government, and the Republic responded by creating a plebeian council (*concilium plebis*)

---

5   Two consuls served each year, sharing executive power.

that played an advisory role. After the next wave of conquests, however, which extended the Republic's power through all of central Italy, the decisions of the plebeian council were made binding even if disapproved by the Senate.

The rise in power of the lower orders appeared to increase the democratic nature of the Republic, but the aristocracy offset this by strengthening their ties with individual clients among the plebeian leaders. Moreover, the complex series of checks and balances between the various assemblies and magistracies prevented any single group from monopolizing power (see Figure 6.1). The Greek historian Polybius (200–117 BCE) was a great admirer of the Republic and was among the first to champion Rome as the natural successor to the Hellenistic world. He wrote: "The result of this ability the various classes have to help or hinder each other mutually is to create in effect a unified government that can respond to any emergency; it is impossible to find a constitution better than this" (*Histories* 6.18).

The conquest of territory gained momentum throughout the 3rd century BCE. It is not clear how much of this resulted from intentional expansionism and how much from successful defensive strategies. However it occurred, by 265 BCE the Romans were in control of nearly the whole of the Italian peninsula and with their command of the westward-facing harbors were poised to move out into the sea-lanes. But there was a problem, because most of the western Mediterranean then lay under the control of Carthage. This wealthy North African city had been founded as a Phoenician colony in the 9th century BCE and came to oversee a vast commercial empire. Carthage had more money, more military power, and more naval experience than the Romans. Carthage was also closer to the island of Sicily than Rome was, and Sicily mattered enormously: it was one of the three greatest grain-producing regions in the ancient world, the other two being Egypt and Asia

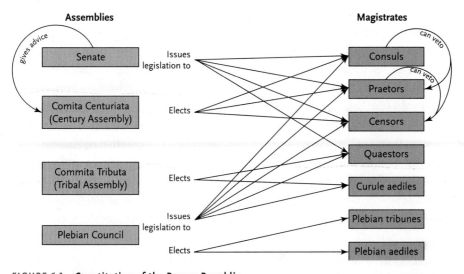

FIGURE 6.1   **Constitution of the Roman Republic**

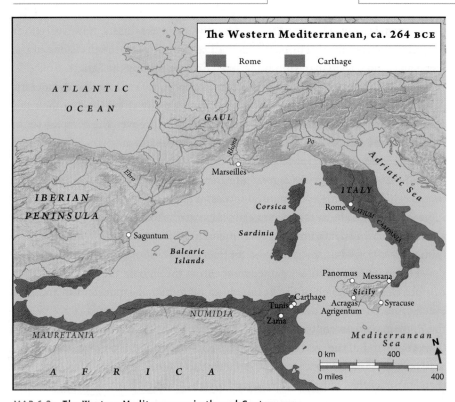

The Western Mediterranean, ca. 264 BCE

Rome   Carthage

ATLANTIC
OCEAN

GAUL

Po

Rhône

Marseilles

Adriatic Sea

ITALY

IBERIAN
PENINSULA

Corsica   Rome
LATIUM

Ebro

Sardinia   CAMPANIA

Saguntum

*Balearic
Islands*

Panormus   Messana

Sicily

Carthage   Acragas   Syracuse
Tunis   Agrigentum
Zama

NUMIDIA

MAURETANIA   *Mediterranean
Sea*

0 km   400   N

A   F   R   I   C   A   0 miles   400

MAP 6.2   The Western Mediterranean in the 3rd Century BCE

Minor. If Sicily fell into Carthaginian hands, Roman Italy would be hard-pressed to feed itself (see Map 6.2).

Neither Rome nor Carthage saw any workable way for them to share control of the Mediterranean, and consequently they never really tried. Rome had two factors in its favor: the solid loyalty of the peoples they had incorporated into the Republic and its mastery of a new technique of naval warfare. By dropping a series of large spiked planks onto the deck of an opposing ship, they could affix it to the Roman vessel, which allowed their soldiers to cross over and fight an infantry battle on the high seas. Between 264 and 146 BCE Rome fought three bloody, ruinous wars with Carthage, won each time, and ended up as the master of the entire western Mediterranean basin. These became known as the **Punic Wars** (the name coming from the Latin word for the Carthaginians—Poeni—that is, Phoenicians), the first being a war for Sicily (264–241 BCE); the second being a war for control of Spain (218–201 BCE); and the last being an assault directly on north Africa (149–146 BCE), which ended with the complete destruction of Carthage and the sale into slavery of every Carthaginian who survived the carnage.[6]

---

6   The oft-told tale of the Romans' plowing the Carthaginian fields with salt to ruin the soil and prevent anyone from resurrecting the city is untrue.

But that hardly ended matters. Off in the east, King Philip V of Macedonia (r. 221–179 BCE) had supported Carthage in its second war with Rome, which prompted the Republic to declare war on him in 200 BCE. Philip surrendered in 197 BCE and Rome freed the Greek poleis that had been under Philip's control, then pulled back. But when the Seleucid emperor Antiochus III (r. 223–187 BCE) moved his army into newly liberated Greece, the Romans returned (191 BCE), drove him out, and pursued him across Asia Minor. Ironically, the Romans' decisive victory over Antiochus took place at Thermopylae, the site of the heroic stand of the Spartan forces against the army of Darius. According to the Greek historian Appian (95–165 CE), the Romans lost only two hundred men at Thermopylae, compared to the Seleucids, who lost ten thousand. (See his *Roman History* 4.20.) So began Rome's expansion into the eastern Mediterranean. By the end of the third Punic War Rome had seized all of Greece and most of Asia Minor. In 146 BCE Rome stood as the undisputed master of the whole sea (see Map 6.3).

The problem was that the Romans had not exactly planned for their success. Their political system, designed to govern a compact land-based republic, unexpectedly found itself in awkward possession of a vast, scattered, sea-based empire. What to do? In the absence of an imperial plan, the Republic simply handed over the

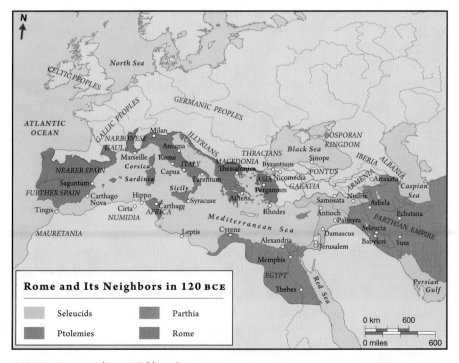

MAP 6.3   Rome and Its Neighbors in 120 BCE

conquered lands to the generals who had taken them, thus outsourcing the expense of maintaining the armies and running the provinces. These generals were thus able to amass vast personal fortunes, and they promptly used these to fund further campaigns and to buy influence with the various councils, assemblies, and magistrates back in Rome. To prevent civil servants from being corrupted by bribes, the Republic developed the tradition of assigning the leading magistrates, after their term of office was complete, to provincial governorships. This got them out of the city and away from the avenues of power, but it also gave them the means to raise fortunes of their own so that they could reenter Republican politics with full coffers.

In other words, the Republic tried to combat corruption by spreading the corruption around. This revolving-door movement from central government to provincial leadership and back again proved immensely profitable to the forty or fifty families who monopolized the process. It also caused terrible hardship and turmoil for the bulk of the people.

The 3rd century's wars had left many of Italy's farms physically and financially ruined, the victims of rampaging soldiers, neglect, or cheap imports of grain that knocked Italy's farmers out of the market. Many thousands of small landholders therefore sold their lands to the rich, who established vast plantations (called **latifundia** in Latin) that specialized in commercial crops like olives and grapes.

Roman Aqueduct   A Roman aqueduct, from Pont du Gard, near Nimes, in France. Built in 19 BCE. The water ran through a channel at the top.

With so many slaves available because of the wars, there were few employment opportunities for the displaced rural classes, who simply flooded into the cities instead, transforming these early manufacturing and commercial centers into centers of consumption.

The population of Rome itself increased to unheard-of levels: from somewhere around one hundred thousand before the First Punic War (264 BCE) to easily five times that figure a little over a century later. By the beginning of the Common Era, the city held well more than a million people within its borders. The government distributed "bread and circuses"—that is, food and entertainment—in order to keep the crowds quiet, but clearly something needed to be done. By the middle of the 2nd century BCE, voices in government were crying out for dramatic reform of the constitution as the only way to prevent the Republic from collapse. But what form would such reforms take?

CAN THE REPUBLIC BE SAVED?

From 133 to 27 BCE the Roman world suffered through a brutal series of internal wars and political struggles. While the names kept changing, the issues at stake and the remedies proposed for them did not. The fundamental issue was whether or not the Republic could, or even should, be saved. Did an empire require a different form of government altogether, and if so, then what form should that government take? Conservative politicians wanted to preserve the constitution at any cost; they believed that traditional Roman values and virtues, if earnestly retained, could make the republican framework work for the whole Mediterranean sprawl. Reformers, on the other hand, were convinced that the Republic was dead, or dying, and that hard-headed realism demanded sweeping change—although not increasing democracy. The battles were fought in stages: between the Gracchi brothers and the Senate (133–122 BCE), between Marius and Sulla (86–82 BCE), between Pompey and Julius Caesar (52–44 BCE), and finally between Marc Antony and Octavian (42–27 BCE).

With the Gracchi, the specific issue had been economic: what should be done about the displaced poor farmers? The Gracchi brothers, Tiberius and Gaius, championed a land redistribution plan that most in the Senate thought too radical; the brothers were assassinated (Tiberius in 133, Gaius in 122 BCE). Marius, a war hero who had served several terms as consul, altered a long-standing policy regarding military recruitment. Admission to the army had earlier required the ownership of land—the idea being that those with a vested interest in the Republic would make the most loyal and effective fighters. But Marius saw how the vast numbers of displaced farmers, and their replacement with large slave-driven latifundia, meant that there were fewer landholders from whom to draw the number of soldiers needed to defend the state. After all, Rome now controlled an empire three thousand miles from end to end. So he dropped the land-ownership requirement altogether. Those opposed to him, led by Sulla, feared that admitting the lowest orders in society would weaken the Republican spirit of the army. After Marius's death, Sulla spent three years undoing Marius's reforms and annihilating those who had supported him. The Republic lurched from one political extreme to another.

Julius Caesar and Pompey the Great (Gnaeus Pompeius Magnus) were both headstrong, powerful egoists, and each regarded himself as Rome's only hope for the future. Ostensibly, Caesar was the radical reformer, while Pompey was supported by the conservatives in the Senate. In reality they both probably wanted the same thing—namely, to run the empire as an empire. The centuries-old system of endless checks and balances between governmental assemblies and offices made efficient administration impossible. And Caesar and Pompey (whose backgrounds were as decidedly undemocratic military commanders) each wanted to institute a streamlined single-command administration. Caesar's power base was in the west; he had conquered Gaul. Pompey had made his name and fortune fighting in the east. Matters came to a head in 52 BCE when the Senate appointed Pompey as sole consul and declared Caesar an enemy of the state. War ensued.

In 49 BCE Caesar drove Pompey from Rome; Pompey fled east to raise more troops. Caesar caught up with him in Greece the following year and in a battle at Pharsalus defeated him. (Pompey escaped from the battle, but was later captured and assassinated.) Caesar returned to Rome and became sole ruler. In 46 BCE he took the title of *dictator*, a constitutional position that gave absolute executive power to a figure selected by the Senate for a set term in emergency situations. Two years later, after he had declared himself dictator for life, he was murdered by a group of nobles who feared that he was going to institute a monarchy.

Dreams of keeping a workable Republic died hard. When the civil struggle entered its final phase, between Marc Antony and Octavian, many still thought the old constitution could be restored. Antony soon left for Egypt to get support from the last ruler of the Ptolemaic dynasty, Cleopatra, with whom he was in love. When Octavian finally defeated Marc Antony at the battle of Actium in 31 BCE, Octavian not only put an end to the strife but added Egypt to the empire as well. Taking the title **Princeps Augustus** (meaning "first in honor"—his name being the first one on the list of Roman citizens kept by the censors), he instituted a new chapter in

> Augustus made a cult of playing by the old rules and upholding traditional values even while reinventing the political system. His reign was unusually successful. The Roman Empire had begun.

Rome's history and inadvertently gave himself a new name: Augustus. Recognizing the utility of maintaining a democratic image, Augustus ruled the empire as an emperor but steadfastly maintained the fiction of the Republic, portraying himself merely as the person who put into action the decrees made by the Senate. Augustus made a cult of playing by the old rules and upholding traditional values even while reinventing the political system. His reign was unusually successful. The Roman Empire had begun.

THE GOLDEN AGE: THE AUGUSTAN ERA

Augustus and all his successors as rulers of Rome held the title of **imperator**, usually translated as "emperor" but which in Republican times was the word for a victorious general, especially one granted the right to a triumph. This was an official recognition of exceptional military achievement, in which the triumphant general was allowed to parade his troops within the city limits amid songs, prayers, speeches, and festivities. At all other times the army was forbidden to cross the city limits (a line called the pomerium) and enter Rome itself. The only organized fighting force permitted within the pomerium was the imperator's personal bodyguard corps—the Praetorian Guards, who also functioned as a police force.

The emperors (the early ones, anyway) scrupulously avoided anything that smacked of monarchy: their homes were comfortable but not palatial; they wore simple dress; they walked the streets of Rome, took part in public debates, and attended religious services. Even their constitutional and honorific titles had Republican roots. The early emperors—not counting the aberrant moral monsters like Caligula (r. 37–41 CE) and Nero (r. 54–68 CE)—cultivated auras of humility, honoring Republican traditions even while exercising central command.[7] Caligula and Nero have been accused of nearly every imaginable vice: incest, theft, graft, torture, murder, prostitution. Nero famously allowed the Great Fire of Rome to blaze for days without doing anything about it, then blamed the Christians for it and staged a bloody persecution of them that resulted in thousands more deaths. After nearly two hundred years of civil strife, most Romans were willing to accept autocracy so long as the autocrats kept the peace, promoted prosperity, and did not flaunt their power.

To accomplish those goals the emperors needed to control the army, facilitate urban growth, and help to integrate the hundreds of ethnic groups that lived within the empire. First of all, the army needed to be professionalized. In Republic times, soldiers had been essentially the paid employees of the generals who commanded them. Caesar had conquered Gaul, for example, largely in

---

[7] Caligula reportedly had his favorite horse ordained as a priest and tried to appoint it to a consulship.

order to acquire a fortune with which he could recruit even more soldiers, in preparation for his struggles with Pompey. Following custom, as many of Pompey's defeated soldiers as Caesar could afford to pay joined his army; and when Octavian/Augustus defeated Marc Antony at Actium, the same held true for him. Augustus's immediate concern upon starting his reign as imperator was to shrink the gargantuan army he had inherited. Hence he commandeered all of Egypt as his personal domain and used the money available through it to offer pensions and award estates to over a quarter million soldiers. This action reduced the army to a manageable twenty-eight legions. Soldiers henceforth received their pay, according to a set scale, directly from Rome itself instead of from the generals.

Given the size of the empire, most government had to be local—which meant that western Europe had to be urbanized. Municipal traditions in the east were widespread and strong, but the west (meaning North Africa, the Spanish peninsula, and virtually all of Europe north of the Alps) remained overwhelmingly rural. Most of Europe itself, moreover, consisted of a vast, dense forest in which the tribal inhabitants had established a sprawl of occasional clearings. To bring order to this world, the emperors began to build cities and a network of roads to connect them. Most inland cities began as military encampments that settlers refilled after the soldiers had moved on. The officials placed over these new settlements administered their surrounding districts, maintained the roads, and established all the public buildings needed to foster Roman civilization: temples, theaters, bathhouses, market squares, courts. So long as they maintained order, kept the population reasonably happy, and avoided blatant corruption, most municipal leaders, and later the provincial governors who represented the next higher stage of the imperial bureaucracy, enjoyed considerable freedom of action. In this way the empire operated more as a confederation of semi-independent city-states and provinces than as a monolithic empire taking orders from an absolutist central regime (see Map 6.4).

Many elements of Roman life contributed to social integration. The twin religious policies of toleration and syncretism played particularly important roles. Polytheisms, generally speaking, accommodate one another easily. My belief in one river god does not necessarily undermine or threaten your belief in another: two different rivers, two different deities—and hence no need for one religion to challenge or usurp the other. And of course it is even possible that the two are the same god manifested and understood differently in different places. When the Romans absorbed first Greece and then the rest of the Hellenistic lands, they recognized the similarities between their faiths. The Greek thunder god Zeus approximated the Roman sky god Jupiter; Aphrodite paired with Venus; Athena resembled Artemis. Such parallels were not coincidental. Polytheisms originate as attempts to explain natural phenomena: storms at sea happen because the sea god is angry about something, for example. And since Mediterranean societies confronted the same major phenomena, the divine powers they used to explain them bore certain

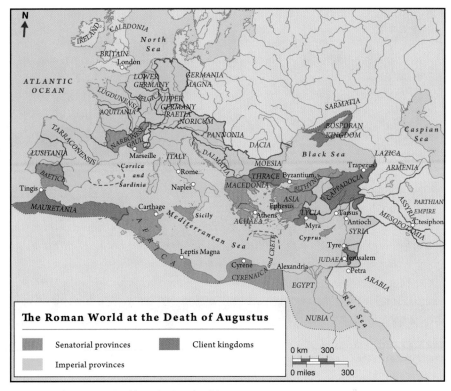

MAP 6.4   The Roman World at the Death of Augustus

similarities. By encouraging the Mediterranean peoples to recognize the same gods and goddesses, the Romans fostered a single, multiethnic civilization.

However, only the higher divinities were merged in this way—the gods and goddesses of Mount Olympus. Daily religious observances for most people still focused on local deities and ancestral worship. This led the emperors to inaugurate communal ruler worship. The custom began as a civil recognition of the deification of late rulers; thus Augustus promoted the deification of the assassinated Julius Caesar, while Tiberius (r. 14–37 CE) championed the postmortem deification of Augustus. Late rulers were to be regarded as universal "household gods"—symbolically, a pater familias to the entire empire; only much later, beginning with the mad Caligula, did the notion arise of recognizing the divinity of the living emperor. By encouraging, and then by requiring, subjects to worship emperors (past or present) as divinities, the Romans tried to keep a degree of common religious practice among the people, so as to counteract the forces that pulled them apart. It did not matter whether or not anyone actually believed in the emperor-god. It mattered only that they were willing to participate in a public, communal ritual once a year in which thanks were given to the divine ruler for his guidance. Dutiful observance, not sincere conviction, was both the goal and the spirit of the requirement; a cohesive civil society, not spiritual enlightenment, was the aim.

The Ara Pacis   Procession of senators and high priests, from a sidewall of the Ara Pacis, the "Altar of Peace," completed in 9 CE.

THE SEA, THE SEA

The Mediterranean Sea—"Our Sea" (**Mare nostrum**) to the Romans—was the essential infrastructure holding the empire together. Geographically, the sea consists of two deep basins separated by an underwater ridge between Sicily and Tunisia, with narrow straits at either end. (The Strait of Gibraltar connects it with the Atlantic Ocean to the west, and the Dardanelles links it to the Sea of Marmara, the Bosporus, and the Black Sea to the northeast.) With a surface area of nearly a million square miles (2.5 million square kilometers), it stretches 2,200 miles from west to east and nearly 1,000 miles at its greatest north-south expanse. Water enters the sea through the two straits and from a handful of rivers—the Nile in Egypt, the Ebro in Spain, the Rhône in France, the Po in Italy. However, the warm climate causes faster than usual evaporation, which in turn causes the Mediterranean's higher than usual salinity—hence the proliferation of salt pans around the coastline.

Despite those million square miles of surface area, though, the Mediterranean is not large enough to have a significant tide. Ships can thus set sail at almost any hour of any day, a significant advantage for the trading cities that surround it. The dominant surface currents circle counterclockwise in both basins, with separate counterclockwise epicycles on either side of the Italian peninsula—that is, in the Tyrrhenian and Adriatic Seas. The Mediterranean's temperate climate results from its fortunate geography, and its smooth waters are a consequence of the relative narrowness of the Strait of Gibraltar: most north Atlantic storms cannot pass through the Strait and instead are diverted up the western coastline of Europe. (This is one reason why it rains so much in England.)

Given these inviting conditions, ancient sailors had an easy time crossing the Mediterranean. Moreover, the many islands and jutting promontories like the Italian and Greek peninsulas meant that sailors could ply the sea-lanes without ever losing sight of land, which made it easy to reach faraway ports without getting lost. The ancients steered by landmarks rather than by the stars. Peoples as far apart as eastern Spain and the Holy Land could be in regular and reliable contact with one another, buying and selling wares, sharing ideas, and establishing permanent relationships. And in fact they needed such contact, because none of the coastal societies were economically self-sufficient. Mountains ring most of the basin, while the Sahara Desert stretches along its southern expanse, which meant that most Mediterranean cities were cut off from their hinterland. In many places the mountains reach almost to the coast. Hence coastal societies could not produce all the foodstuffs and material goods they needed to survive, and therefore they needed to trade with one another in order to stay alive. The natural qualities of the sea made this trade possible virtually year-round—even for bulky, heavy commodities.

The Romans recognized that their central position in the Mediterranean was an ideal site from which to create a network of links between all the peoples of the sea. With Carthage in ruins, no rival stood in Rome's way. But lust for power was not the only motive behind Rome's expansion—and may not even have been the most prominent one. The Mediterranean linked hundreds of coastal societies; a ship sent out from Rome could reach Barcelona in only three days, Alexandria in ten. And these societies shared similar agricultural methods (terracing arid hinterlands, widespread use of irrigation systems), similar diets (grains, fish, olive oil, and wine), and similar social organizations (tradesmen and merchants playing the lead, rather than large landholders). If we think of the Mediterranean as a single entity, then the attractiveness of uniting them under a single administration becomes clear: with a single

> If we think of the Mediterranean as a single entity, then the attractiveness of uniting them under a single administration becomes clear: with a single currency, single law, single tariff code, and single system of weights and measures in place, goods, capital, and services will move with optimal efficiency, raising everyone's standard of living.

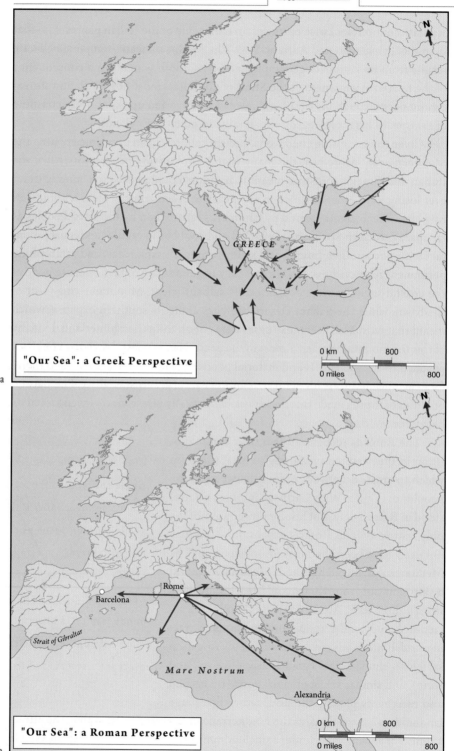

MAP 6.5a,b   **The Mediterranean: Greek and Roman Perspectives Compared**

*Adapted from Malkin, Irad. *A Small Greek World: Networks in the Ancient Mediterranean* (2011).

currency, single law, single tariff code, and single system of weights and measures in place, goods, capital, and services will move with optimal efficiency, raising everyone's standard of living (see Map 6.5a,b).

Experience within Italy had convinced the Romans that people will put up with the loss of political freedom if they can still prosper economically, while policies of inclusion of subjected peoples within the dominant society will go far to relieve civil unrest. When attempting to secure a new territory, the regime begun by Augustus therefore took care to "Romanize" its institutions and trade, reinstall local rulers as representatives of the empire, and then withdraw. Since travel by sea was so quick, the Romans seldom had to occupy the lands they conquered. Word of any rebellion would reach the imperial court quickly, and a fleet could be dispatched long before the rebellion had a chance to take root. In other words, a town or district newly added to the Roman Empire could conceivably never see a Roman soldier again, as long as the laws were obeyed, the taxes paid, and things kept quiet.

Rome's army added territories to the empire, of course, but also provided a tool for social engineering. Taking further Alexander the Great's policy of cultural integration, the Romans opened the army to recruits from every part of the empire—enrolling Celts, Dacians, Illyrians, Libyans, Phoenicians, and Syrians alike, plus many others. In turn, their combined military experience helped bring Roman culture to the provinces. Recruits received three meals a day and a regular salary, traveled from one end of the empire to another, and helped to keep the peace and serve the common cause. Along the way they learned Latin, acquired the basics of Roman law and morals, and practiced Roman civic religion. The goal was to break down each soldier's sense of particular ethnic nationality and replace it with a new identity, based on membership in a larger, interconnected

Loading Grain in a Transport Ship   A worker here pours grain into a barrel; once full, the barrel would be rolled into the cargo area below deck. The name of the ship—*Isis Giminiana*—is given at the far left. The ship's master (*magister*) is Faurales, and the merchant is Abscanius. Two other workers haul sacks of grain up the gangplank, at the right. This fresco comes from Ostia, a port city at the mouth of the Tiber, ca. 200 CE.

Tombstone of a Roman Soldier   Marcus Valerius Celerinus, a citizen of Agrippina in southern Spain and a veteran of the Tenth Legion, had this tombstone prepared "on his own behalf and for the sake of his wife, Marcia." The tomb is in Cologne, Germany, where the pair settled after his retirement from the military. ca. 100 CE. The carving presumably portrays Marcus Valerius at a meal (the Romans ate lying down) surrounded by friends.

society. After twenty years of service, each soldier received either a cash pension or the grant of an estate and could enjoy all the fruits of citizenship.[8] The estates awarded were large, prosperous, and never in the individual soldier's original homeland. Having created a "Roman"—that is, someone whose self-identity and personal allegiance went beyond mere ethnicity, someone who participated in an idea of human unity—the last thing the government wanted was to restore him to his place of birth. In this way, the army used to fullest effect the ability of the Mediterranean, Mare Nostrum, to integrate the peoples of the empire, redistribute them, and cement the idea of "Romanness."

The emperor was the commander in chief of all the legions. In practice, however, the regular command of each legion was given to an imperial representative known as a legate (**legatus**), whom the emperor selected from the members in the Senate. In smaller provinces that required the presence of only a single legion; the legate also served as the provincial governor. In larger provinces, two or more legions were assigned; a separate legate was assigned to each legion, but the autonomous provincial governor served as a superior commander to each legate. In this way, senators endorsed imperial power, while the throne made a point of recognizing senatorial privilege. Even more important, Rome placed senators in positions in which their status was publicly seen. The fiction of republicanism was thus given continual attention, even as true control of the army remained centralized in the emperor's hands.

ROMAN LIVES AND VALUES

The first two centuries CE are known as the era of the Roman Peace, or **Pax Romana**. Like all historical labels it represents only a partial truth, and while most of the empire experienced a sustained if sometimes strained tranquility,

---

[8]   Citizenship was a prerequisite for joining the army. But noncitizens could enlist in the auxiliary forces and earn citizenship after retirement—to be passed on to their sons.

there was more than enough discontent around to keep the soldiers busy. Consider the rebellion in England in 60 CE led by Boudicca, the widow of a Briton tribal king. Some Roman soldiers had plundered the dead king's home, tied up and flogged Boudicca, and made her watch as they raped her daughters. After the attack, Boudicca rallied the Britons to drive the Romans from England. As Tacitus (*Annals*, 14.32–35, 37) narrates it:

> Then a horde of Britons surrounded [the Roman garrison at Camulodunum—modern Colchester] and ransacked and set the town all ablaze, forcing the garrison to take refuge in the temple [to the divine emperor Claudius]; this temple was stormed after a two days' siege. Rome's ninth legion, under the command of Quintus Petulius Cerialis Caesius Rufus, tried to relieve the town but was first stopped, then routed, by the victorious Britons, who massacred the entire infantry.... [Boudicca's troops] delighted in plunder and scarcely gave a thought to anything else, for they continually passed right by Roman encampments and garrisons and headed straight for whatever targets had the most loot and the least protection. The Roman and provincial dead in those places is reckoned at seventy thousand, for the Britons had no interest in taking or ransoming prisoners or exchanging prisoners. All they wanted was to slit Roman throats or put nooses around them, to put Romans to the torch or to crucify them.... Boudicca circled her soldiers in a chariot in which her daughters rode with her, and cried out: "Britons! You are accustomed to female commanders in war time. I am the daughter of accomplished warriors, but I am not now fighting for wealth or for a realm. Rather, I fight simply as an ordinary woman who has lost her freedom; I fight for the wounds done to my body and for the outrage done to my daughters. Roman malice knows no bounds—they murder old men and rape young girls. May our gods grant us the revenge we deserve!'"

In a subsequent battle outside London, in 61 CE:

> The Roman regular troops, keeping near to a gorge that offered a measure of natural defense, held their ground and hurled their javelins with deadly effect at the approaching Briton army and then rushed suddenly forward in wedge formation together with the auxiliary troops. Then our cavalry units, lances in forward position, broke whatever was left of Briton resistance. Their fleeing soldiers could not escape, since their own circle of wagons blocked off any retreat. Our troops spared no one, not even the women or beasts of burden; all, pierced by our weapons, were added to the heaps of the dead. What a glorious victory this

was, one to be compared with our most legendary triumphs. By one report nearly eighty thousand Britons were killed, while we suffered only four hundred dead and slightly more wounded. As for Boudicca, she poisoned herself in the aftermath.

Even so, for all the signs of discontent, no ancient society experienced anything close to the prosperity and social stability of the empire during these two centuries. Cities multiplied and grew, rights of citizenship were continually extended to more and more people, and piracy in the Mediterranean came to an end. Literacy spread, and something close to a regular system of justice ordered everyone's lives, and in 212 CE every person in the empire who was not a slave was declared a citizen (see Map 6.6). The elaborate commercial networks allowed each region of the empire to specialize in producing what it did best.

Two significant economic weaknesses remained, however. First was reliance upon slave labor. Slaves comprised as many as 20 percent of the empire's population, which meant that certain labor-intensive activities—agriculture and mining in particular—were vulnerable to labor shortages. In the ancient world, the mortality rates of slave populations usually exceeded their birth rates, which meant that societies dependent on slave labor continually needed to add new

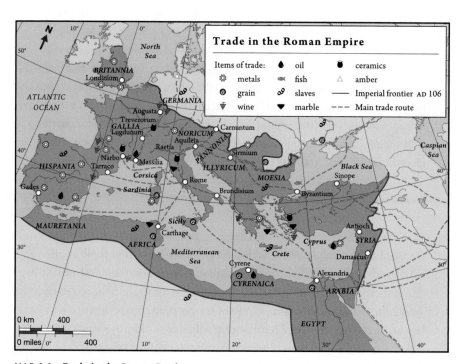

MAP 6.6   Trade in the Roman Empire

Thamagudi, Modern Timgad, Algeria   Founded by the emperor Trajan in 100 ce, Thamagudi boasted a theater, a forum, and paved streets aligned in a checkerboard pattern.

slaves to the mix just to stay even. As long as the empire kept conquering new territories—and thus acquiring new slaves—the problem was held at bay, but only temporarily. The second weakness was Roman fondness for Asian luxury goods like silk and spices, which they purchased in large quantities. This passion drained gold and silver reserves from the western economy. Until the end of the 2nd century CE, western mines were able to keep up, but productivity declined quickly thereafter, which raised the danger of currency devaluation. But during the Pax Romana years these were only potential weaknesses; for the time being, abundance and comfort were the hallmarks of Roman economic life.

The Romans adopted many of the great Greek intellectual and artistic achievements, but popular prejudice of the time regarded Greek culture as effete. They saw it as too inclined to luxury, idleness, and pleasure, especially when compared to the manly self-discipline and pragmatism that they liked to think was the essence of Romanness. Some of this is simply the swagger of the victor, but it would be a mistake to dismiss it outright. Roman culture valued a sense of duty—to the familia, to the household gods, to one's city, and finally to the empire. A good life was a life of virtue, of owed service duly performed. These were the values the Romans brought with them into the eastern Mediterranean, where they encountered the two dominant philosophies of the Hellenistic era: **Epicureanism** and **Stoicism**.

Of the two, Stoicism appealed more to the Romans. Among philosophers the most prominent Roman Stoics were the tragedian, essayist, and statesman Seneca (4 BCE–65 CE) and the former slave turned moralist and teacher Epictetus (55–135 CE). Seneca dedicated many years of his life to serving the empire, even taking on the thankless task of tutoring the teenaged Nero. Even so, he was reputedly epicurean in certain ways—including the bad habits of seducing married women and taking bribes—but these reports may be mere rumors put about by jealous rivals. In the year 65 CE Nero accused Seneca of complicity in an attempt to murder him and ordered his former teacher to commit suicide. Seneca complied by slitting his wrists, only his blood flowed so slowly that he never lost consciousness; he drank poison next, but it too failed to kill him. Finally Seneca immersed his slashed arms in a hot bath. The warmth opened his veins, the blood ran out, and he finally died. Amid reams of bad writing, he left a few pearls: "Act toward men as though God were always watching; speak to God as though men were always listening." "You can tell a man's character by how he receives praise" (*Epistles* 2.2 and 52.12, respectively).

> Roman culture valued a sense of duty—to the familia, to the household gods, to one's city, and finally to the empire. A good life was a life of virtue, of owed service duly performed.

Epictetus, by contrast, lived a life of poverty and austerity. Born lame and into slavery, he nevertheless learned some philosophy from a local teacher after his owner moved to Rome; after gaining his freedom, he went on to teach philosophy himself. In 93 CE he moved back to Greece and set up a school. He remained poor and lived alone until he took in a homeless boy whom he raised. He died in 135. His most memorable passage comes from his *Encheiridion* (*Handbook*):

> In life, you ought always to behave as you would at a formal banquet. A dish is being passed around and it comes to you—so reach out your hand politely and take a modest helping, and then pass the dish along without delay. If a dish does not come your way, don't act out your longing for it by stretching out your hand for it. Just wait until it comes to you. This is how you should act regarding everything in life—including children, wife, career, and wealth. (ch. 15)

Stoic ethics conformed to Roman morals in the broadest sense—with their emphasis on duty, forbearance, self-discipline, and concern for others.[9] Above all,

---

[9]   Stoics believed one should pursue virtue for its own sake, seek tranquility rather than renown, and value wisdom and calm over ambition and glory.

one ought to serve Rome, praise Rome, live for Rome—for only in the empire
and its vision of the unification of all societies in a single working whole can
the harmony of the world be attained. Here is how the first-century poet Virgil
(70 BCE–19 CE) described the empire's destined mission:

> Others shall cast their bronze to breathe
> with softer features, I well know, and draw
> living lines from the marble, and plead
> better causes, and with pen shall better trace the paths
> of the heavens and proclaim the stars in their rising;
> but it shall be your charge, O Roman, to rule
> the nations in your empire. This shall be your art:
> to lay down the laws of peace, to show mercy
> to the conquered, and to beat the haughty down.   *(Aeneid 6.1012–1028)*

For at least 150 years after Augustus, they did this rather well. Dividing society between **honestiores** ("the better people") and **humiliores** ("the lesser
people"), they provided a reliable infrastructure for urban life and a consistent
form of justice for each. The honestiores consisted of the senatorial and equestrian classes, municipal officials, and army veterans, and their status entitled
them to immunity from torture, lesser criminal fines, and, in capital crimes, exemption from crucifixion. (Like Seneca, honestiores condemned to death were
allowed to commit an honorable suicide rather than face the intentionally humiliating and agonizing death by crucifixion.) The humiliores consisted of everyone
else in the empire apart from the slaves—who, in terms of the law, were counted
as property rather than people. People were expected to obey the law, pay their
taxes, participate in public religious rites, and hold to the ethical duties of family
care and public service; if they did so, the empire largely left them alone. Even in
the prosecution of crime, Roman tradition was to allow matters to be resolved
with as little state involvement as possible.

Most civil cases were tried without any public officials whatsoever. A plaintiff filed a complaint with a local magistrate called an aedile who maintained a list
of individuals in the vicinity who held Roman citizenship. Any citizen accepted
by the plaintiff and defendant could serve as judge. The aedile's role was limited
to making sure the temporary judge understood the basics of the law as it per-
tained to the type of case he was judging. The judge's decision was then entered
in the municipal records, and the matter was closed.

Taxes were collected by a tax-farming system. The imperial court determined its budgetary needs for the year and then apportioned the revenues owed
by each province, district, and city in order to meet that need. Local officials,
who presumably understood the economic realities of their own territories

better than administrators back in Rome did, then collected taxes accordingly as they thought most fair and effective given local conditions. If they gathered more than they were required to send to Rome, they kept the surplus (public officials did not receive salaries); if they failed to meet their tax obligation, they were expected to make up the deficit out of their personal funds. Personal profit from public taxation was not frowned upon. In fact, some profit was necessary if the official was to be held liable for years of deficit. What sounds like an invitation to abuse actually worked fairly well. If an official collected so much tax that the people began to grumble, Rome would hear of it quickly enough and deal with the overaggressive governor.

The system was sufficiently effective to survive even disastrous reigns like those of Caligula (r. 37–41 CE) and Nero (r. 54–68 CE), whose well-known personal licentiousness went down poorly with most Romans precisely because such indecency was so very un-Roman. Domitian (r. 81–96 CE), an obsessively controlling personality, left most of the Senate disaffected with his failure to maintain the Augustan fiction of Republican rule, but he did leave the treasury with a surplus in spite of an ambitious building campaign and several expensive military ventures.

THE "FIVE GOOD EMPERORS"

The high point of the Pax Romana came during the reigns of the so-called Five Good Emperors: Nerva (r. 96–98 CE), Trajan (r. 98–117 CE), Hadrian (r. 117–138 CE), Antoninus Pius (r. 138–161 CE), and Marcus Aurelius (r. 161–180 CE). This was the time of the empire's greatest physical expanse and its greatest prosperity, but what really made these emperors so "good" was that they returned to the Republican fiction, giving the Senate its due respect while exercising autocratic control. Moreover, each of the five had the decency not to have a surviving heir, which allowed the Senate to appear to be the deliberative body for the selection of the next emperor. In reality, each of the five adopted his most capable general, who then became his successor after carefully going through the motions of a supposed senatorial election.

The rulers appointed the provincial governors, district officials, and municipal chiefs who then administered the empire locally. Most came from the class of urban elites known as the **curiales**. Their chief duties were to provide justice, collect taxes, maintain roads and waterways, and keep the cities and harbors in good repair. Given the Roman means of tax gathering, these civil servants could acquire great wealth; but their sense of civic-mindedness obliged them to make up for public deficits personally. They were expected to use their own funds to provide public entertainments, food distributions, and religious ceremonies in honor of the emperors. That so many curiales did so provides an index of the strength of Roman public spirit.

During the Pax Romana, in sum, the Stoic and dutiful ethos cultivated by the Romans helped them to create a remarkably stable and proud society. They saw themselves as the heirs to the Greek and eastern worlds, and they eagerly absorbed whatever in those traditions had practical value. Yet they also regarded themselves as morally superior, less inclined to luxury and ease, and dedicated to strong virtues and a hardheaded sense of pragmatic living. Those given to other values were the objects of scorn. For example, the Jews, who refused to Romanize or to serve in the army, were reviled even though the Romans respected the antiquity of their traditions. Marcus Aurelius, author of the popular work known as the *Meditations*, described the secret of the Stoical Roman soul and its superiority to a weak, showy spirit that had appeared on the scene:

A beautiful soul is one that is equally ready at any given moment to relinquish the body and give itself over to extinction and annihilation, or to continue living. Such preparedness must be the result of conscious judgment reached through reason and with dignity if it is to persuade anyone else; it must never result from obstinacy or with soul-killing display—as it does with the people called Christians. *[Meditations 11.3]*

Roman Public Spirit   Tombstone of the mid-second century from Gorsium, Pannonia (Hungary). This monolithic tombstone combines decoration in the Greco-Roman style—such as the grape-vine spiraled columnettes—with local elements. The two women portrayed are wearing "native" dress, with heavy turbans, prominent pendant necklaces, and large pins on their shoulders. At the foot of the stone, two servants are shown frontally under a curved border characteristic of art from the region. The beautifully cut Latin inscription translates, "To the spirits of the dead. Publius Aelius Respectus, city councilor of the municipality, while alive made this for himself and for Ulpia Amasia, his wife. Aelia Materio, their daughter aged ten, is placed here. The parents put up this monument for her memory." The names indicate that the family are all Roman citizens, and the father specifies that he is a city councilor in his community, although without naming it.

WHO, WHAT, WHERE

censor	Latins
census	legatus
consul	Mare nostrum
curiales	pater familias
Epicureanism	patria potestas
Etruscans	Pax Romana
familia	plebeians
honestiores	Princeps Augustus
household gods	Punic Wars
humiliores	res publica
imperator	Stoicism
latifundia	Twelve Tables

SUGGESTED READINGS

Primary Sources

Epictetus. *The Handbook.*

Livy. *History of Rome.*

Marcus Aurelius. *Meditations.*

Plutarch. *Parallel Lives.*

Polybius. *The Histories.*

Seneca. *Epistles.*

Suetonius. *The Twelve Caesars.*

Tacitus. *Annals.*

———. *The Histories.*

Source Anthologies

Beard, Mary, John North, and Simon Price. *Religions of Rome* (2005).

Cherry, David, ed. *The Roman World: A Sourcebook* (2001).

Kraemer, Ross Shepard, ed. *Women's Religions in the Greco-Roman World: A Sourcebook* (2004).

Lefkowitz, Mary R., and Maureen B. Fant, comps. *Women's Life in Greece and Rome: A Source Book in Translation* (2005).

Mellor, Ronald, ed. *The Historians of Ancient Rome: An Anthology of the Major Writings* (2004).

Warrior, Valerie M. *Roman Religion: A Sourcebook* (2001).

Studies

Beard, Mary. *The Roman Triumph* (2009).

Beard, Mary, John North, and Simon Price. *Religions of Rome* (2005).

Boatwright, Mary T. *Hadrian and the Cities of the Roman Empire* (2002).

Carcopino, Jérôme. *Daily Life in Ancient Rome: The People and the City at the Height of the Empire* (2008).

Eck, Werner. *The Age of Augustus* (2007).

Everitt, Anthony. *Augustus: The Life of Rome's First Emperor* (2007).

Fraschetti, Augusto. *The Foundation of Rome* (2005).

Goldsworthy, Adrian. *Caesar: Life of a Colossus* (2008).

———. *The Complete Roman Army* (2011).

————. *The Punic Wars* (2000).

Grubbs, Judith Evans. *Women and the Law in the Roman Empire: A Sourcebook on Marriage, Divorce, and Widowhood* (2002).

Haynes, Sybille. *Etruscan Civilization: A Cultural History* (2000).

Holland, Tom. *Rubicon: The Last Years of the Roman Republic* (2005).

Horden, Peregrine, and Nicholas Purcell. *The Corrupting Sea: A Study of Mediterranean History* (2000).

Lendon, J. E. *Empire of Honour: The Art of Government in the Roman World* (2001).

Milnor, Kristina. *Gender, Domesticity, and the Age of Augustus: Inventing Private Life* (2005).

Mouritsen, Henrik. *Plebs and Politics in the Late Roman Republic* (2001).

Reydams-Schils, Gretchen. *The Roman Stoics: Self, Responsibility, and Affection* (2005).

Rives, James B. *Religion in the Roman Empire* (2007).

Schultz, Celia E. *Women's Religious Activity in the Roman Republic* (2006).

Seager, Robin. *Pompey the Great: A Political Biography* (2002).

————. *Tiberius* (2005).

Southern, Pat. *The Roman Army: A Social and Institutional History* (2007).

Speller, Elizabeth. *Following Hadrian: A Second-Century Journey through the Roman Empire* (2004).

Williamson, Callie. *The Laws of the Roman People: Public Law in the Expansion and Decline of the Roman Republic* (2005).

For additional resources, including maps, primary sources, visuals, web links, and quizzes, please go to **www.oup.com/us/backman.**

CHAPTER 7

Paganisms and Christianities

40 BCE–305 CE

The establishment and spread of Christianity may be the central fact of Western history. Few other phenomena have affected so many people in so many ways. Few have so shaped cultural values, have comforted or tormented so many individuals, have had such influence on intellectual life, or have worked their way into the very fiber of Western identity. Without Christianity, there would be no cathedrals at Chartres, Ely, Milan, Notre Dame de Paris, or Seville. There would be no monasteries of Monte Cassino or Mont Saint-Michel; no Hagia Sophia in Istanbul; and no universities. There would also be no music of Johann Sebastian Bach, Giovanni Pierluigi da Palestrina, Henry Purcell, or Arvo Pärt; no poetry of Dante Alighieri, John Milton, Anna Akhmatova, Czeslaw Milosz, or Geoffrey Hill; no paintings by Michelangelo Buonarroti or Michelangelo Caravaggio; no novels by Fyodor Dostoevsky, James Joyce, François Mauriac, Flannery O'Connor, or Annie Dillard; no philosophy by Saint Augustine, Saint Thomas Aquinas, Immanuel Kant, Søren Kierkegaard, Bernard Lonergan, or Karl Barth. It is even arguable that without Christianity there would have been no Islam, and hence the historical success of Christianity would be the single most influential development in all of Greater Western history.

On the other hand, without Christianity there would have been no Crusades, no Inquisition, no blood libel against the Jews, no forced baptisms of the Native Americans or sub-Saharan Africans, no Wars of Religion in the 16th and 17th centuries, and no Holocaust

THE EARLY CHRISTIAN WORLD

◀ **The Good Shepherd**
This wall painting, ca. 100–200 CE, depicts Jesus as the Good Shepherd. Note the heavily Romanized style: Jesus is beardless and wears a Roman tunic. The fresco is in the Catacombs of Saint Priscilla, under the city of Rome. Early Christians used these catacombs as a burial site and for worship. It was much more common among the early Christian generations to portray Jesus as the Good Shepherd than to depict a crucifixion scene.

in the 20th. No persecutions of Galileo Galilei or Charles Darwin. No agonized debates over abortion, contraception, or homosexuality—or at least, not the same debates that we currently have.

Both lists could be extended easily and infinitely. The history of Christianity in the Greater West is complex, as is its legacy. One would be hard put to identify another idea, invention, school of thought, technology, or value system that has penetrated so far into the DNA of Western culture—and shaped so much of what is both good and bad in it. In this chapter we will see how Christianity arose, how it became a Roman religion, and how it absorbed such intellectual currents of the classical world as Stoicism and Plato.

THE JESUS MYSTERY

The story fascinates, thrills, comforts, angers, and embarrasses at every turn, often all at once. It has touched everything from Western political ideas to sexual mores. Christianity began as an obscure reformist sect within Palestinian Judaism, at one time numbering no more than fifty or so believers. It went on, after three centuries of persecution by the Roman state, to become the dominant faith on our planet.

Approximately 2 billion people today identify themselves as Christian; given a current world population of roughly 5.6 billion, Christians therefore comprise 35 percent of the total. Islam comes in second place, with 1.2 billion faithful (21 percent). Hinduism, with nearly 800 million adherents, ranks third (14 percent). Judaism, by contrast, makes up only 0.27 percent of the world population, numbering a mere 15 million. Jews, indeed, are almost statistically insignificant—an irony, given the hate-filled perceptions of them by anti-Semites (see Figure 7.1).

That development was neither rapid nor assured, however. Instead, Christianity spread with almost painful slowness and suffered repeated and severe setbacks along the way.[1] As late as 300 CE, if one could have surveyed the whole of

---

[1] As many as eight hundred years after the death of Jesus of Nazareth, the religion was still at risk of being wiped out.

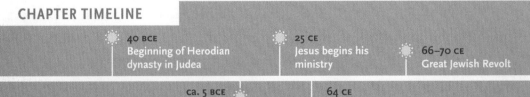

CHAPTER TIMELINE

40 BCE
Beginning of Herodian dynasty in Judea

25 CE
Jesus begins his ministry

66–70 CE
Great Jewish Revolt

ca. 5 BCE
Birth of Jesus

64 CE
Christians persecuted under Nero; death of Peter

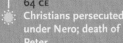

- Christian, 1,965,993,000
- Muslim, 1,179,326,000
- Hindu, 767,424,000
- Non-religious, 766,672,000
- Buddhist, 356,875,000
- Tribal religion, 244,164,000
- Atheist, 146,406,000
- New religions, 99,191,000
- Sikh, 22,874,000
- Daoist, 20,050,000
- Jewish, 15,050,000
- Baha'I, 6,251,000
- Confucian, 5,067,000
- Jain, 4,152,000
- Shinto, 3,571,000
- Parsi (Zoroastrian), 479,000

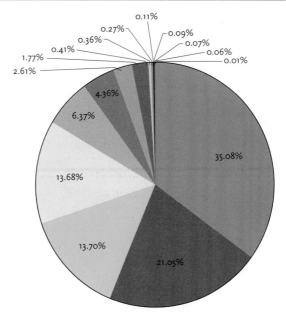

0.11%
0.27%
0.36%
0.41%
1.77%
2.61%
4.36%
6.37%
13.68%
13.70%
21.05%
35.08%
0.09%
0.07%
0.06%
0.01%

FIGURE 7.1   **The World's Religions**

the Roman Empire and then placed a bet on which religion in it was most likely to become the dominant religious force in the Western world, hardly anyone would have picked Christianity. By that date, even after three hundred years of ardent evangelizing, teaching, bearing witness, and, as Christian tradition asserts, the performing of countless miracles by missionaries, Christians made up no more than 2–3 percent of the empire's population and possibly as little as 1 percent.

Moreover, biology, not conversion, accounts for the lion's share of whatever growth did occur in those years. Christians married other Christians and raised their children in the faith. Conversions certainly did take place, and those who brought the gospel of Jesus to the pagans did so at the risk of their lives, a fact later Christians pointed to with pride. But conversions occurred in far smaller

ca. 126 CE
Pantheon built
in Rome

161–180 CE
Reign of Roman
emperor Marcus
Aurelius

355–430 CE
Life of Augustine of Hippo

ca. 140 CE
Last books of the
New Testament
composed

284–305 CE
Reign of Roman
emperor Diocletian

TABLE 7.1   **The Books of the New Testament in the Order of Their Composition**

YEAR (CE)	TEXT	AUTHOR
50	1 Thessalonians	Paul
54–55	Galatians	Paul
55	Philemon	Paul
56	Philippians	Paul
56	1 Corinthians	Paul
57	2 Corinthians	Paul
57–58	Romans	Paul
	(66–73: Jewish Revolt and Rome's Subsequent Destruction of the Temple)	
68–73	Gospel of Mark	Mark
70–90	1 Peter	?
80–85	Gospel of Luke	Luke
80–85	Acts of the Apostles	Luke
80–90	Colossians	? (attributed to Paul)
80–100	James	? (attributed to James, brother of Jesus)
85–90	Gospel of Matthew	Matthew
85–90	Hebrews	? (attributed to Paul)
90–95	Gospel of John	? (attributed to the Beloved Disciple)
90–100	Ephesians	? (attributed to Paul)
90–100	2 Thessalonians	? (attributed to Paul)
90–100	1–2 Timothy, Titus	? (attributed to Paul)
90–100	Jude	? (attributed to Jude, brother of Jesus)
92–96	Revelation	John
95–100	1–2 John	?
120–130	3 John	?
130–140	2 Peter	?

Authors of the Gospels and the Book of Revelation

Matthew	Matthew, a tax collector, was one of the original twelve apostles. By textual evidence, the author was a Jewish Christian who spoke Greek, Hebrew, and Aramaic, who drew on Mark's Gospel and was also not an eyewitness to Jesus's life.
Mark	Mark is attributed by tradition. This is the "John Mark" mentioned in the Acts of the Apostles, who helped Paul on his first missionary tour. Textual evidence suggests the author was a Greek speaker, not an eyewitness to Jesus's ministry, and is addressing an audience that has already experienced persecution.
Luke	Luke was a physician and fellow missionary with Saint Paul. Textual evidence reveals a Greek speaker who knew the Jewish Bible only in its Greek (Septuagint) version and was also not an eyewitness to Jesus's career. Drew on Mark's Gospel. Author was not from Palestine and was almost certainly not born Jewish; hence possibly a Greek who converted to Judaism before subsequently converting to Christianity.
John	Tradition attributes this gospel to John, the son of Zebedee and one of the original twelve apostles. Textual evidence suggests the author was actually a redactor—a disciple of John who later gathered his teacher's sayings. It is possible that the redactor's work was itself later edited, ca. 100–110, by another disciple contemporaneous with the author of 3 John. And the author of Revelation is not the same John.

numbers than many like to think. Christians had a significantly higher profile in the cities of the eastern Mediterranean by the end of the 3rd century CE. Still, through vast stretches of the empire the very name of Jesus had yet to be heard, much less adored.

How a tiny sect thus grew to dominate Western culture is not easy to explain. Even after two thousand years, scholars are still as busy as ever trying to figure it out. Two problems stand in the way and probably always will. First, *Sect* no one approaches the issue of historical Christianity with absolute objectivity. Try as they might to remain detached, scholars are influenced by their personal convictions—even if the conviction is an intentional denial of belief. Second, our principle source for the history of Jesus's life and the careers of his early followers is the **New Testament**, which is a compilation of notoriously difficult texts written over a period of nearly a century. Many other texts— gospels, epistles, miracle narratives, collections of sayings—written in the 2nd and 3rd centuries CE were considered "biblical" in their time but are largely unheard of today. Even as authoritative a figure in Christian teaching as Saint Augustine (354–430) used a New Testament that few people would now recognize.

The canon of the New Testament as the modern world knows it did not become settled until the late 4th century. And its specific wording—reconciling variant readings and filling gaps—was not set until the early 5th, a long time after the events it purports to relate. Twenty-seven texts comprise the New Testament:

- four gospels (Matthew, Mark, Luke, and John)
- a narrative of the apostles' activities immediately after Jesus's death
- seven authentic epistles by Saint Paul
- seven more epistles that tradition attributes to Paul but that he almost certainly did not write
- seven more epistles falsely accredited to four of the original twelve apostles
- a densely symbolic dream vision of the end of the world

None of these twenty-seven works were written in Jesus's lifetime. Jesus himself wrote nothing and is never reported to have ordered his followers to write his teachings down. Hence the lateness of our closest written evidence of Jesus and his ministry. This lateness, combined with the many flaws in the texts, leaves any effort to understand the rise of Christianity facing enormous challenges.

What are some of those flaws? Many are simple discrepancies in chronology. Matthew, Mark, and Luke, for example, all state that the Last Supper took place on Passover, while John records that it occurred sometime before it. Others are flat-out errors—such as Luke's famous setting of the scene in his Infancy narrative, at the start of his second chapter:

> In those days a decree went out from Emperor Augustus that all the world should be registered. This was the first registration and was taken while Quirinius was governor of Syria. All went to their own towns to be registered. *(Luke 2.1–2)*

There was no census of the entire empire under Augustus, however, only a handful of provincial censuses. Moreover, the only census of Judea that Luke could possibly refer to (when Quirinius was the governor of Syria) took place in either 6 or 7 CE, which is at least a decade too late for Jesus's birth. Jesus was actually born between the years 7 and 3 BCE. The modern calendar, based on the number of years since the birth of Jesus, was invented in the 6th century by a Syriac monk who worked backward from his own time, based on the reigns of Roman emperors. But in the process he made an arithmetical mistake—something easily done when working with Roman numerals—which explains how Jesus was actually born several years "before Christ."

Other flaws (if they are flaws) are occasional tensions between the portrayals of Jesus's character in the gospels. Luke's Jesus, for example, shows a particular sensitivity toward women, whereas Matthew depicts a Jesus who shows hardly any interest in them at all—not even in his own mother. Mark's Jesus is a terse miracle worker who, apart from calling people to repent their sins, speaks mostly in parables; John's Jesus, by contrast, is loquacious to an extreme and capable of both precise common-sense speech and sophisticated philosophical language. These aspects of the New Testament texts add to their fascination for the faithful, and to the frustration of nonbelieving readers.

A CRISIS IN TRADITION

The basic outlines of Christian growth are fairly well known, but the precise knowledge of how, when, and where the faith spread, what the specific mechanisms for development were, even the exact content of what people actually believed at any particular time, remain unclear and hotly debated. One rare point of agreement among scholars today is that the history of Jesus of Nazareth and the movement he founded must be understood in the context of Jewish tradition. Jesus was a Jew, as were all of his original followers, none of whom regarded their commitment to Jesus and his teachings as an abrogation of their Jewish identities.

Indeed, they saw Jesus rather as the fulfillment of Jewish prophecy. In his own words, as recorded by Matthew:

> Do not think that I have come to abolish the law or the prophets. I have come not to abolish but to fulfill. For truly I tell you, until heaven and earth pass away, not one letter, not one stroke of a letter, will pass from the law until all is accomplished. Therefore, whoever breaks one of the least of these commandments, and teaches others to do the same, will be called least in the kingdom of heaven; but whoever does them and teaches them will be called great in the kingdom of heaven. (5.17–19)

These assurances might have quieted more Jewish concerns, however, if Jesus himself had been more strictly observant of Torah. Instead, he provoked widespread ire by performing work on the Sabbath, allowing his followers to call him the **messiah**, speaking scornfully of the Temple, and, most boldly of all, referring to himself as the Son of God. By Jesus's lifetime several Jewish traditions were in existence and in uneasy dialogue with one another, but none of them was quite prepared for this.

One rare point of agreement among scholars today is that the history of Jesus of Nazareth and the movement he founded must be understood in the context of Jewish tradition.

The Hellenistic era had resulted in many Jewish factions, divided primarily by two factors: their relative commitments to Temple observance and the authority of the priests, on the one hand, and the new focus on rabbinical leadership and the "oral Torah," on the other. Added to this mix was a potent new element: the belief in a coming apocalypse. This moralism resulted from the rising trend of exogamous marriage (or marriage outside of Judaism) and the exiled Jews' close contact with Zoroastrianism. The political scene contributed a number of factors as well. After the Maccabean revolt against the Seleucids had succeeded, Judea was ruled by the Hasmonean dynasty for a century, the last independent Jewish state until the 20th century (see Map 7.1). While the era had helped foster a Jewish national spirit, however, the Jews were sharply divided toward the dynasty itself. By long tradition Jewish kingship belonged solely to the lineage of the ancient ruler David, which made the Hasmoneans usurpers in the eyes of many. Struggles within later generations of the dynasty only confirmed their critics' opinion of them as imposters. Thoroughly Hellenized, the Hasmonean kings even bore Greek names rather than Hebrew ones.

The kings tried to gain legitimacy by associating themselves closely with the Temple priests and their most important political allies, a party known as the **Sadducees**. These were one of three "philosophical sects" (hairesis) into which

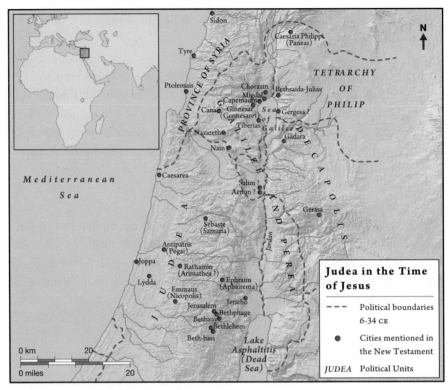

MAP 7.1   Judea in the Time of Jesus

Judea was divided, according to the Jewish historian Josephus (37–100 CE); the other two were called the **Pharisees** and the **Essenes**. The Sadducees were an aristocratic party, the ideological descendants of the "Children of the Exile." They were reputedly strict upholders of Temple ritual, dedicated to the literal reading of Scripture and the rejection of the Oral Torah—"reputedly" because much of what is known of the Sadducees' thought comes from the testimony of writers hostile to them—including the authors of the four Christian gospels, as well as Josephus.

Opposing them were the Pharisees, the party more closely associated with the "People of the Land" and the rabbinical tradition. The Pharisees generally came from the common stock (although, being urbanites, they regarded themselves as superior to the outlying rustics) and resisted Hellenization. They also held a number of religious beliefs that set them apart from other Jews—most notably, a belief in the immortality of the soul and the resurrection of the dead.[2] They took the lead in advocating the arrival of a messiah, a savior of the Jewish

---

[2]   The most renowned figure, believed to have been a Pharisee, was the Babylonian scholar Hillel (110 BCE–10 CE, according to tradition), who is considered the central figure in establishing the core of the rabbinical law and its commentaries—the oral tradition that would later be codified in the Talmud.

people who would return them to freedom and safety. The Essenes, the third Palestinian sect mentioned by Josephus, are more difficult to identify. It is even possible that the word is a catchall term used by writers like Josephus to describe a host of minor Jewish sects that shared certain views. An ascetic community, they lived in isolated congregations and dedicated themselves to repentance and prayer in the hope of achieving mystical union with YHWH. The Essenes were the most eschatological sect within Judaism, meaning they were characterized by expectations of an imminent apocalyptic end of the world, although it is difficult to generalize how widely believed such ideas were.[3]

Jesus of Nazareth thus entered a Jewish world in high-voltage turmoil. When the Romans, led by Pompey the Great, conquered Judea in 63 BCE, they dismissed and jailed the Hasmonean king and ruled in his name for twenty-five years, while Pompey and then Marcus Crassus plundered the province mercilessly. In 40 BCE they installed a new dynasty, the Herodians. The Jews had mostly disdained the Hasmoneans, but they ardently hated the Herodians, and for good reason. Herod the Great, named "king of Judea" in 40 BCE but not actually in power until three years later, was a venal, dissolute, and brutal figure (r. 37–4 BCE). He murdered anyone who stood in the way of his authority—which included two high priests,

his brother-in-law, his mother-in-law, and even his wife. A lover of massive, soulless architecture, Herod built and rebuilt palaces, Roman temples, gardens, amphitheaters, hippodromes, baths, and fountains across Judea—including an ambitious restoration of the Jerusalem Temple itself. And he paid for it all with heavy taxation. Perversely, he ordered a golden imperial eagle to be installed over the gate into the restored Temple. When two rabbis complained of the blasphemy, Herod had them burned alive. Herod died in 4 BCE, after which the emperor Augustus divided Judea into three provinces, one of which was administered by a Roman procurator; the other two went to Herod's sons, Herod Antipas and Philip.[4] By the time Jesus

Jerusalem in the Time of King Herod   A modern model of Jerusalem at the time of the Herodian Temple (ca. 50 BCE).

---

[3]   The Essenes were probably the group whose collected writings, the Dead Sea Scrolls, were discovered at Qumran in 1946.

[4]   Pontius Pilate was the most famous of the Roman procurators in Judea; he held the post for a decade (26–36 CE).

began his ministry, sometime around 25 or 26 CE, Judea was crackling with religious rivalries and social-political tensions.

MINISTRY AND MOVEMENT

The gospels of Matthew and Luke relate a handful of episodes from Jesus's childhood and youth, but only become detailed when Jesus begins his ministry, around the age of thirty. An early follower of John the Baptist, a Jewish revivalist preacher who prophesied the arrival of the messiah and urged his listeners to penance and passionate commitment to God, Jesus took up John's cause after his own baptism. The gospels then relate how Jesus traveled throughout Judea, performing miraculous healings, driving out demon spirits, calling people to a revivified faith and universal love, and especially teaching them about the approach of "the kingdom of God." What he meant by this last point is by no means clear. Some of his followers (and his critics) understood him to be talking about Heaven itself, God's own dwelling place; others regarded the "kingdom" as a state of spiritual grace, a soulful enlightenment. To still others the "kingdom" was this world, the world we inhabit, but made just and perfect by a heavenly appointed ruler, a new King David—earthly life as it should be, in other words.

The differences matter. If the kingdom Jesus spoke of was indeed a paradise and an afterlife, then he was speaking the language of the Pharisees. If he meant a spiritual state of utopian soulfulness, then he was appealing to the Essenes. If he intended an earthly kingdom marked by justice and order, then the Sadducees might have been the intended audience. And still other possibilities existed. As it happened, Jesus's oblique language could have appealed to everyone, which meant that it displeased and offended far more people than it attracted. In the life-and-death struggle of 1st-century Palestine, Jewish scholars on all sides were still fighting over the exact lettering of sacred texts, their meaning, and the purposes to which they were put. For them, Jesus's words often sounded so confusing as to be provocative:

> Then the disciples came and asked him, "Why do you speak to [the crowds] in parables?"
>
> He answered, "To you it has been given to know the secrets of the kingdom of heaven, but to them it has not been given. For to those who have, more will be given, and they will have an abundance; but from those who have nothing, even what they have will be taken away. The reason I speak to them in parables is that 'seeing they do not perceive, and hearing they do not listen, nor do they understand.'" *(Matthew 13.10–13)*

At the same time, he also taught:

> Blessed are the poor in spirit, for theirs is the kingdom of heaven
> *(Matthew 5.3)*

and:

> But many who are first will be last, and the last will be first   *(Mark 10.31)*

which seemed to want it both ways. How can those with an abundance of spiritual enlightenment deserve an increase, while those without will lose what little they have? How can Jesus then turn around and promise that the spiritually poor will be the ones to enter the kingdom while the others will languish? Were these the teachings of a holy man or of a con man?

Jesus was not a solo act. His public ministry began with his joining a movement already in existence—the penitential and revivalist sect of John the Baptist:

> In those days John the Baptist appeared in the wilderness of Judea, proclaiming, "Repent, for the kingdom of heaven has come near!". . . Then the people of Jerusalem and all of Judea were going out to him, and all the region along the Jordan, and they were baptized by him in the river Jordan, confessing their sins. *(Matthew 3.1–2, 5–6)*

The word baptize comes from the Greek *baptizein*, a transitive verb meaning "to dunk" or "to plunge." Jewish tradition had long involved people giving themselves ritual baths of purification; John's innovation was to actively plunge the faithful into the water. He therefore could be referred to as "John the Plunger."

Jesus himself did not begin to preach and to baptize until after learning that Herod Agrippa had arrested John. Jesus thus assumed leadership of a preexisting popular movement, but he quickly put his own stamp on it by summoning a corps of personal disciples, the Twelve Apostles, who then broadcast the idea that Jesus himself was the long-promised messiah. John's more general revivalist movement thus became specifically a Jesus movement, a sect dedicated to his unique ministry. He traveled throughout Galilee, Samaria, and Judea proper—an area roughly forty miles from east to west and roughly eighty miles from north to south—and preached the primacy of a passionate love of God over a formal observance of rituals. The desire and intent behind our actions, he seemed to say, matter more than the actions themselves. When criticized for his inexact observance of Torah, he replied that YHWH cares more for the sincerity in our hearts than for the mechanical precision of our rites (Jesus here quotes two Torah verses: Deuteronomy 6.5 and Leviticus 19.18):

> When the Pharisees heard that [Jesus] had silenced the Sadducees, they gathered together, and one of them, a lawyer, asked him a question to test him.
>
> "Teacher, which commandment in the Law is the greatest?"
>
> [Jesus] said to him, "'You shall love the Lord your God with all your heart, and with all your soul, and with all your mind.' This is the greatest and first commandment. And a second is like it: 'You shall love your neighbor as yourself.' On these two commandments hang all the Law and the Prophets." *(Matthew 22.34–40)*

Jesus's own criticisms of the Pharisees and Sadducees display flashes of temper and a sharp tongue. It is small wonder that the leaders of the two groups grew irritated with him, locked as they were in a bitter struggle to lead the Jewish people and indeed to define the faith itself. They showed little patience for a quick-witted upstart who evinced little respect for either of them.

WHAT HAPPENED TO HIS DISCIPLES?

Jesus's popularity with the Jewish crowds is uncertain. Large numbers of people, perhaps even thousands at a time, regularly turned out to see him and listen to his teaching. However, many of those were undoubtedly mere curiosity seekers, wanting to see him perform one of his famous miracles, rather than true followers of his movement. To many Jews, and perhaps to most of them, he was an item in the short-term news cycle, the subject of gossip and debate, and nothing more; the evidence clearly suggests that he received only the passing attention of most Jews. Even his most loyal disciples had moments of confusion about his mission. After Jesus's arrest by the Romans, many of those followers melted away with extraordinary speed.

When the gospels describe Jesus's final entry into Jerusalem for the Passover holiday, the streets of the city are packed with crowds wanting to get a look at him. The texts present the episode, in fact, as a triumphal messianic march, which may well be how his truest followers perceived it. Yet it was probably the result of the high spirits of thousands of pilgrims visiting the Holy City. The gospels describe thousands of people waving palm fronds at Jesus and strewing them upon the path he took through the city. If this description is accurate, one can just as easily see a knowing playfulness or mock enthusiasm in their gestures, rather than evidence of mass ecstatic religious deliverance. The burden of proof is on those who assert the gospels' historical accuracy.

What tipped the scales against Jesus, ultimately, was the zeal of his disciples to have him recognized as the long-prophesied messiah. This, indeed, is the principal function of Matthew's gospel. Alone of the four gospel writers, Matthew aims specifically at a Jewish audience and focuses on describing those ideas and actions of Jesus that proved he was the long-promised savior. Echoes of the prophets can be heard everywhere. But there was a problem. Jewish tradition anticipated the arrival of an earthly savior, one who would create a safe, unified state for the Jews—in which justice will flourish and YHWH will be praised. Even as messiah, Jesus appeared otherwise; he was a savior of eternal souls, not the leader of a political revival. He did things no messiah was ever expected to do (such as to violate the Sabbath and speak disrespectfully of the Temple), and did *not* do the things that were expected of the savior.

> Jewish tradition anticipated the arrival of an earthly savior, one who would create a safe, unified state for the Jews—in which justice will flourish and YHWH will be praised. Even as messiah, Jesus appeared otherwise; he was a savior of eternal souls, not the leader of a political revival.

This combination made it all but impossible for most Jews to accept him in that role. And in fact the overwhelming majority of Jews did not accept him. The passion narratives in the New Testament are highly dramatic set pieces filled with betrayals, storm clouds, grim-faced soldiers, wailing crowds, moments of tender intimacy, fear and confusion, last-minute conversions, heart-rending questions, and finally stoic acceptance of God's merciful plan to save all mankind. But despite the extraordinary goings on, so compelling and moving to the faithful, the Jews as a whole rejected Jesus's claims to be the messiah.

It is unclear whether this simple claim sufficed to warrant an accusation of blasphemy—the official complaint levied at Jesus by the Jewish head council. Nonetheless, by the time of Jesus's arrest, he had sufficiently alienated enough members of the community to turn them against him. More important to the Roman prefect, Pontius Pilate, was the popular talk among Jesus's supporters that he was the "King of the Jews." This smacked of treason against the Roman state, for only the emperor had the right to designate a client king within the confines of the empire. When Pilate ordered Jesus to be crucified, a sign bearing the words "Jesus of Nazareth, King of the Jews" was placed on the cross above his head.[5] It was Roman practice, when crucifying criminals, to identify their crime in this way.

Pontius Pilate's career as a Roman official is well-known, and so was his taste for rough politics. Philo of Alexandria (20 BCE–50 CE) described him as a "rigid, stubborn, and cruel [administrator] who was known to execute lawbreakers even without a trial. . . . [He was] venal and violent, and he committed innumerable thefts, assaults, persecutions, and executions of the most extraordinary ferocity" (*Embassy of Gaius* 38.299–305). Josephus describes an incident when Pilate confiscated funds from the Temple and used them to fund the construction of an aqueduct; when the Jews predictably gathered outside his court to complain,

---

[5] In Latin, the inscription on the cross reads Iesus Nazarenus Rex Iudaeorum—hence the acronym INRI that appears frequently in images of the crucifixion.

Pilate had secretly scattered dozens of armed soldiers, dressed as Jews, among the crowd. At his signal, the soldiers drew their swords and began attacking the Jews indiscriminately, killing several dozen protestors (*Antiquities* 18.3.2). One inscription survives that attests to him; it was discovered in 1962 in the ruins of a Roman theater at Caesarea Maritima and is now on view in the Israel Museum in Jerusalem. It is a dedicatory inscription, whose Latin reads: [DIS AUGUSTI]S TIBEREUM [PO]NTIUS PILATUS [PRAEF]ECTUS JUDAE [FECIT D] E[DICAVIT] ("Pontius Pilate, the prefect of Judea, had the Temple to Tiberius built and dedicated it to the august gods").

After Jesus's death, the small cohort of people still faithful ran immediately into hiding, since the Romans were determined to stamp the sect out. Soldiers searched for them from street to street. Then something extraordinary happened. Three days after Jesus was buried, groups of believers began to appear in the streets of Jerusalem proclaiming joyously that they had seen Jesus resurrected from the dead. In three days they had transformed, apparently as a group, from terrified fugitives hoping to escape capture into a company of bold, confident witnesses. They not only acknowledged their belief in Jesus but broadcast it at every turn, even at the risk of death.

Faithful Christians then and now have no doubt what caused the extraordinary transformation of that small group of disciples during those three days of hiding in Jerusalem; nonbelievers can only wonder. But one thing is clear: something dramatic happened to those people.

For the next few decades, until they themselves began to die in the 50s, 60s, and possibly 70s CE, those early disciples traversed the eastern half of the empire telling anyone who would listen about the transformative saving power of Jesus "the Christ" (the Anointed One, literally). Threats of popular violence or of state persecution posed no barrier to them. They faced execution with stoic calm, according to both Christian and pagan reports, happy to embrace the death that would reunite them with their savior. Faithful Christians then and now have no doubt what caused the extraordinary transformation of that small group of disciples during those three days of hiding in Jerusalem; nonbelievers can only wonder. But one thing is clear: something dramatic happened to those people.

CHRISTIANITIES EVERYWHERE

Whatever happened in Jerusalem to those first disciples, afterward they went out into the eastern Mediterranean determined to spread the message of Jesus. The problem, of course, was in agreeing upon what that message actually was—and for whom it was intended. Was the Christian message intended for the Jews? For the Jews alone? For all people everywhere? There were factions in the early Christian movement supporting each of those views, plus others. Since Jesus and his initial disciples were all Jews, could non-Jews become his followers? And if they did, did they have to observe Jewish teaching and tradition, as the apostles themselves continued to do? If a non-Jew wanted to become a Christian, in other words, did he or she have to convert to Judaism first?

Problems like these abounded, causing many rifts to break out in the Christian movement; and the problems were exacerbated by the fact that no one had the universally recognized authority to settle such disputes as they arose. Saint Peter undoubtedly was the leader of the original twelve, but who should lead the movement after Peter's death in Rome in 64 CE? Peter's line of successors as bishop ("overseer") of the Christian community in Rome insisted that they were the heirs of Peter's own spiritual authority and hence were to be accepted as the supreme leaders of all Christians everywhere. But hardly anyone agreed with them. Why shouldn't the bishop of Jerusalem, the site of Jesus's Passion, take precedence? Others argued for the primacy of Antioch, the home of the first major Christian community outside of Jerusalem. Some insisted that Jesus's brother James (one of Jesus's four siblings—three brothers and a sister—mentioned in the gospels) had a hereditary right to lead the community. Still others insisted that there should be no single leader at all and that guidance of the church should be left to a council of all the bishops together.

Until such matters could be resolved the early Christians had no way to reconcile the differences in their beliefs—of which there were many. The apostles and early missionaries, after all, preached their messages in synagogues and market squares throughout the eastern Mediterranean, hoping to win as many converts as possible as quickly as possible; but these were the centers of ancient cultures that reached back two thousand years and more (see Map 7.2).[6] The missionaries, predictably, faced flurries of questions. Even those whose hearts were inclined to accept the new faith may have required some intellectual satisfaction before they were willing to commit:

- How can the One True God, Jesus, and the Holy Spirit be three separate beings and one indivisible being at the same time?
- If Jesus was "coeternal" with God, why is there no mention of him in the two-thousand-year tradition of Hebrew writings?
- If Jesus was God in human form, wasn't the fact that he felt temptation, fear, and loneliness (things to which God is presumably immune) evidence that Jesus was at best a lesser version of God?
- How could Jesus's mother, Mary, still be a virgin after the conception and birth of a child?

---

[6] Literacy was high: most of the people who heard Christian testimonies were fairly well versed in Hellenistic traditions.

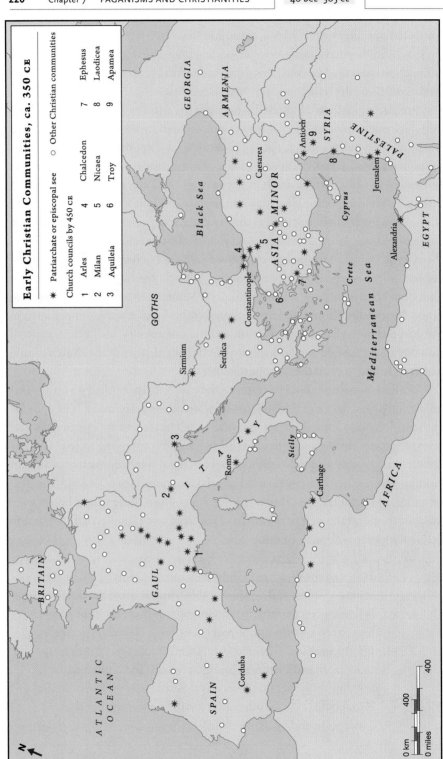

Early Christian Communities, ca. 350 CE

✳ Patriarchate or episcopal see   ○ Other Christian communities

Church councils by 450 CE

1	Arles	4	Chalcedon
2	Milan	5	Nicaea
3	Aquileia	6	Troy

7	Ephesus
8	Laodicea
9	Apamea

MAP 7.2   Early Christian Communities, ca. 350 CE

To crowds familiar with Greek philosophy and the Hebrew Scriptures, not to mention Greek, Persian, or Egyptian medicine, such questions were not easily dismissed.

Answers to such questions are possible; but the apostles and other missionaries were not in regular contact with one another, and they seldom agreed with one another when they were. The communities of converts they established therefore believed starkly different things. For the first three centuries after Jesus's death, in fact, it is inaccurate to speak of Christianity existing at all. What existed instead were many dozens of **christianities** (with a lower-case "c"), each with its own beliefs, liturgical traditions, and customs. There were communities of Christians that denied Jesus's divinity and believed good works were necessary for the salvation of some Christians but not for all. Others believed that Jesus had never in fact died at all but instead had gone into hiding. Some maintained that Jesus passed along some body of

The Gospel of Thomas   Opening page of the Gospel of Thomas, one of many gospels that circulated among early Christians. Most of these apocryphal gospels date well into the 3rd century, but Thomas's is much closer in date to the four canonical Gospels of the New Testament. This papyrus manuscript is in the Coptic Museum in Cairo.

secret knowledge, given only to a few initiates, that gave them the key to understanding that reconciled Christian revelation with Greek philosophy. Still others insisted that baptism was all that was needed to achieve salvation—and that God, Jesus, and the Holy Spirit existed as three separate deities. Some communities believed in the immediate immanence of the Second Coming. They took Jesus at his literal word when he declared that "this present generation shall not pass before the kingdom of God appears." Others counseled a more patient attitude, thinking that the End might not come for a long time. Some believed in bodily resurrection; others found the idea horrifying and ridiculous. Some practiced strict sexual asceticism; others were widely accused of extremes of licentiousness that even included incest.

ROMANS IN PURSUIT

Most Christians practiced their faith in secret, gathering in homes, in remote spots outside the city, in caves, or in warehouses—wherever they might escape notice. They needed to do so because Roman authorities were still in active

Masada Ruins of the Jewish fortress at Masada, where rebel Jews pursued by the Roman army made their last stand. The Dead Sea can be glimpsed in the background. Masada is today the site where Israeli recruits take their oaths of military service.

pursuit of them, for two good reasons. To the Romans religion was a public affair, a means of uniting society in the observance of shared rituals. In contrast, Christians largely withdrew from society and taught, as far as the Romans understood it, that the affairs of this world are meaningless, the only meaningful reality being one's existence in the heavenly kingdom yet to come. To the Romans, this notion was both insipid and criminally aberrant. Christians seldom served in the army and refused to perform sacrifices to the emperor, which called into question their political loyalty. To the stoic Roman mind, engagement in the affairs of the world was a duty and a sign of virtue; to devalue the affairs of the world seemed not ascetic but immoral. Moreover, Christians still spoke of their departed Jesus as a king, and as far as the Romans saw it, loyalty to a dead traitor was as bad as loyalty to a live one. Worse still, the Christians were said to practice ritual cannibalism. Indeed, the central purpose of their gathering together was to eat the physical remains of their god Jesus.[7]

The second thing that condemned Christians in Roman eyes was their relationship with Judaism. The Romans had no love for the Jews, who were arguably the most volatile and troublesome people in the empire, but grudgingly respected the antiquity of their religion. When the great Jewish Revolt of 66–70 CE erupted,

---

[7] Even if the Christians ate the body of Jesus only symbolically, in bread and wine, the idea was repulsive to Roman sensibilities.

Rome responded with heavy force, crushed the rebels, destroyed the Temple, killed untold thousands of Jews, and dispersed the rest once and for all. The slaughter was memorably fierce, and was meant to be. In only a few years the Jews had passed from being, to Roman eyes, the denizens of a hard-to-handle province to a despised race of stiff-necked ingrates. As the troops marched through Palestine in search of more Jews to kill or exile, they inevitably encountered groups of Christians who were eager to disassociate themselves from the Jewish majority. It is not a coincidence that the Christian Gospels began to be written at this time, with large servings of anti-Jewish language.

By the 70s and 80s CE the number of Christians who were not ethnically Jewish finally overtook the number who were. That itself required some redefinition of the relationship between the two faiths; but when the Jews became the leading active enemy of the Pax Romana, there was additional reason for the Christians to emphasize that they were not Jewish. The gospels make the case with unnerving thoroughness.

> But when [John the Baptist] saw many Pharisees and Sadducees coming for baptism, he said to them, "You brood of vipers! Who warned you to flee from the wrath to come? Bear fruit worthy of repentance. Do not presume to say to yourselves, 'We have Abraham as our ancestor'; for I tell you, God is able from these stones to raise up children to Abraham." *(Matthew 3.7–9)*

> After this Jesus went about in Galilee. He did not wish to go about in Judea because the Jews were looking for an opportunity to kill him. Now the Jewish Festival of Booths was near. . . . The Jews were looking for him at the festival and saying, "Where is he?" And there was considerable complaining about him among the crowds. While some were saying, "He is a good man," others were saying, "No, he is deceiving the crowd." Yet no one would speak openly about him for fear of the Jews. *(John 7.1–2, 10–13)*

> Jesus said to [the Jewish leaders], "If God were your Father, you would love me, for I came from God and now I am here. I did not come on my own, but he sent me. Why do you not understand what I say? It is because you cannot accept my word. You are from your father the devil, and you choose to do your father's desires. He was a murderer from the beginning and does not stand in the truth, because there is no truth in him." *(John 8.42–44)*

Of course, to argue that one is not Jewish is not necessarily the same thing as to be an anti-Semite, but such an emphasis, made over a sufficiently long time span, certainly opens the door to the evolution of a type of Jew hatred. And as the christianities slowly spread around the Mediterranean, they continually had to repeat and refine their non-Jewishness: the diaspora of the Jews meant the side-by-side establishment of new Jewish communities in the cities as well. Wherever Christian communities took root, in other words, so too did new Jewish ones, and the efforts to explain themselves to the pagans began over and over again.

Persecution by the Romans was intermittent but brutal. Under certain emperors—Nero (r. 54–68 CE), Domitian (r. 81–96 CE), Maximinus (r. 235–238 CE), Decius (r. 249–251 CE), and Diocletian (r. 284–305 CE) being the most notorious— many tens of thousands of Christians were arrested and killed. The lucky ones were quickly executed; the others faced torture and humiliation before vast crowds in Roman forums. Popular resistance to Christians was ubiquitous and took many forms, from angry words to social ostracism to rough street violence, but persecution itself began in Rome as a deliberate policy before spreading, in the 2nd and 3rd centuries CE, into the provinces.

The first persecution occurred under Nero, during whose reign the first Christian communities were established in Rome under Saints Peter and Paul. When the city experienced a catastrophic fire in 64 CE, Nero found the newcomer Christians to be a convenient scapegoat and contrived for them a gruesome means of execution: he ordered hundreds of Christians to be covered in bloody animal skins, which made them the prey of packs of wild dogs; others were crucified; still others he had coated in paraffin and set alight as human torches. When the provincial governors took up the cause, they attempted to balance viciousness with some sense of fairness: Christians who relapsed into paganism were forgiven, while those who held Roman citizenship were remanded to imprisonment in the capital. Only noncitizens who remained obstinate in refusing to renounce their Christian faith received the death sentence.

The christianities deserved hateful treatment in Roman eyes for any number of reasons. The tendency of monotheisms to deny the reality of all other divinities is partially to blame, but the empire did not find any deviation from standard pagan practices absolutely unendurable. (They did not, after all, always crush the Jews.) Moreover, it was not at all clear to the Romans—or indeed even to many of the Christians themselves—that Christianity was a strictly monotheistic faith. Later, most Christians believed in the mystery of the **Trinity** (that is, the existence of a single God in a union of three separate and divine "Persons"). For the first three centuries CE, though, this was simply a high-intensity muddle that set Christians against Christians with much of the same ferocity that the Romans reserved for all of them.

More to the point was the secrecy with which Christians practiced their faith. Religion was a public activity in the Pax Romana period, a necessary means by which people developed a communal identity and a sense of shared destiny. Romanness was more than a matter of citizenship; it comprised an ethical vision of human unity, a vision whose living symbol was the emperor. To reject the imperial cult and the universal Olympian gods, in Roman eyes, was to reject this foundational vision and to sow discord. The refusal of most Christians to serve in the army—the principle instrument for constructing Romanness—

Catacombs   Early Christian burial niches in the catacomb of Saint Callisto, in Rome.

only added to their ignominy. And of course the common Christian teachings that the affairs of this world do not matter and that one ought to worry only about the life in the world to come struck most Romans as simply but profoundly weird. The christianities therefore tore at the social fabric, and their followers therefore richly deserved to be torn to shreds by yapping packs of wild dogs. The punishment was not cruel but fitting and even mimetic.

PAGAN VITALITY

The fact that Christianity ultimately rose to dominate Western culture can blind us to the residual strength of the pagan cults. Roman religions continued to thrive for centuries, attracting new adherents and shaping both civic and personal lives by the millions. If anything, the empire's portfolio of *religiones licitae* ("legally approved religions") grew faster and stirred hearts deeper than Christianity could even hope to do. Moreover, pagan religion did not remain static but rather continued to develop new ritual traditions, emotional resonances, and intellectual sophistication. Rome embraced new deities by the score (including, of course, the deified emperors themselves) and built thousands of new temples across the empire. Paganism must be seen, in other words, as a vital, thriving, expansive, and energetic network of cults, not as a dusty relic patiently awaiting Christian conversion and enlightenment.

The expanding cult of the emperors is the most visible development in religious life. From the moment that Augustus dedicated the first temple to the deified Julius Caesar in 29 BCE, the veneration of Rome's supreme leaders became one of the most important public rituals. The practice was intended to unite the people in an act of thanksgiving for the blessings of the Pax Romana.[8] Augustus's own deification followed immediately upon his death in 14 CE, and after this the pattern was set for the regular, though not absolutely consistent, elevation of emperors to divine status after their deaths. The political motive behind emperor worship is obvious, but that does not necessarily mean emperor worship was insincere. Most ancient pagan religions did not divide the physical world and the heavenly world as absolutely as the Jewish and Christian monotheisms did. Divine forces permeated the physical world and caused or affected most natural phenomena, and the gods themselves wandered through our world at will and spoke to people through signs and oracles. Pagan folklore and literature was full of tales of humans venturing into the afterworld, too: Odysseus, Orpheus, and Aeneas are the best-known examples. So the idea that a living human ruler could be imbued with divine qualities was not out of the question, no matter how transparently self-serving such a notion might be.

In the first three centuries CE, nearly half of all state temples erected were dedicated to deified emperors living or dead. Statues of them were frequently added throughout the empire to temples that were already dedicated to another god or goddess. Emperors also imported into the capital city gods from regions around the empire that were associated in some way with the personal history of the ruler. Septimius Severus (r. 193–211 CE), for example, built a massive new temple of 140,000 square feet (13,000 square meters) in the heart of Rome in honor of Bacchus and Hercules. Neither was unfamiliar, but their unique pairing was the cultic practice of Septimius's hometown in North Africa. It highlighted the emperor as the living embodiment of cultic and civic unity—the linchpin holding together the whole fabric of the Pax Romana.[9]

The **Pantheon**, built by the emperor Hadrian (r. 117–138 CE), was an all-purpose temple dedicated, as its name suggests, to the whole roster of major deities within the empire. Consisting of a portico (or porch) with a colonnade of three ranks of granite columns, behind which emerged a vast rotunda covered with a splendid

---

8   The temple, on the south side of the Forum, formed the most regularly used backdrop for public speeches by later emperors.

9   The Pantheon dome, which weighs five thousand tons (4,500 metric tons) is the largest unreinforced concrete dome ever constructed.

concrete dome, it was—and remains—a stunning site. Bright shafts of sunlight shoot through a circular opening at the top of the dome and move through the area of the temple as the sun courses through the sky. The Pantheon was consecrated as a Catholic church in the seventh century, named in honor of Santa Maria dei Martiri.

The state cult took great pains to absorb and authorize new cults in the provinces, so that religious life not only took on a unifying structure but grew more varied while doing so. New cults arrived with every generation and every territorial expansion of the empire. The best known were the cults of Cybele (or Magna Mater—the "Great Mother"), Isis, Mithras, and Sol Invictus (the "Unconquered Sun"), but there were countless others. These cults had diverse and often obscure origins. The Mithras cult, for example, originated in

The Pantheon   Interior of the Roman Pantheon, whose construction was finished around 126 CE. The dome consists of reinforced concrete and is by far the largest concrete dome ever constructed. A circular opening at the top lets in (apart from rain) a dazzling beam of light that moves around the walls, illuminating the shrines of the various Olympian deities.

Asia Minor but claimed descent from the ancient Persian religious figure of Zoroaster, whereas the cult of Isis—which had certainly begun in very ancient Egyptian times—took on its Roman shape in Hellenistic Greece. In other words, what many of the provincial cults had in common was a fictional ancient and eastern ancestry, and this convenient invention lent spiritual weight to the cult's claims.

Historians often refer to these new cults collectively as "Eastern mystery religions," but they shouldn't. The term implies a set of energetic new faiths sharing oriental origins and a common practice—ritually initiating worshippers into a set of secret mysteries. Such teachings are said to have imbued the new devotee with spiritual knowledge and direct contact with the divine. A Belgian historian, Franz Cumont (1868–1947), put forth this notion in 1906. The vast bulk of evidence discovered since then, however, refutes Cumont's chronology, his suggested provenance of the cults, and the interpretive role they play in explaining the rise of Christianity.

Were these new religions a reaction against the centralizing efforts of the emperors? If so, they failed. The embrace of the new practices by Rome revitalized pagan religion in the first three centuries CE. It encouraged believers to participate in civic rituals and filled their hearts and minds with hope and comfort. In 110 CE the governor of Bithynia wrote admiringly to the emperor Trajan (r. 98–117) about the resurgence in traditional religion:

> It is now indisputable that temples long abandoned are being used frequently and that sacred rituals long forgotten are being observed again. The meat of sacrificial animals can be purchased anywhere one goes, too, whereas so long ago buyers of it could hardly be found. Judge from this how many peoples' lives can be reformed; all they need is a chance at repentance. *(Pliny the Younger, Letters 10.96–97)*

Pliny's closing line suggests a new development in religious thought—the belief in, and the desire for, forgiveness of sins. The idea was not altogether new. Ancient paganism stressed community with others in the present world more than the attainment of another, better life in a world yet to come. It privileged the ideas of civic virtue and ritual exactitude over ethical improvement, and it emphasized *doing* good instead of *being* good. In other words, instead of earning forgiveness of one's sins and whatever reward such forgiveness would entail, it stressed acting to unite the community.

Dead Man Walking   The 2nd-century BCE painting on linen depicts the goddess Isis as she leads the newly deceased, who carries the peacock feather that signifies his purification at the examination by Osiris, to the underworld god Anubis.

Some of the provincial cults, like those of Isis and Mithras, did posit an afterlife to which repentant believers went. (The afterlives of the unrepentant or the unbelievers were less clear.) Those who died in the cults' good graces could look forward to an eternal reward of some sort. A 3rd-century CE epitaph erected on the tomb of Aurelia Prosodos, an Isis worshipper, by her husband, Dioskourides, reads: "To the gods of the underworld, Dioskourides, husband of Aurelia Prosodos, the best and sweetest of companions, erects this memorial. Farewell my lady! May Osiris grant you a draught of cool water." In the Isis cult, Osiris revived the worthy deceased with a drink from an underworld spring, which began their enjoyment of eternal peace and pleasure.

In another innovation, several of the new cults were text-oriented. Religious writings are as old as the dirt in Egypt, of course, but earlier examples (with the exception of the Jewish scriptures) were by and large mere collections of set prayers and ritual formulas. Influenced by the Hellenistic spread of philosophical and literary inquiry and the textual frenzy of Second Temple Judaism, however, the new religions of the first centuries CE produced a new type of religious literature. These speculative, interpretive texts explored ideas about the relationship between the mundane and divine worlds, the nature of human life, and the purpose of human suffering. The gods of the provincial cults were not simply divine potentates demanding rote prayers and well-practiced rituals. Instead, they were benevolent beings who understood human difficulties and desired that we live upright and ethical lives—in some cases (Isis, Mithras, the christianities) in order to attain an otherworldly salvation, but in others (some strains of Judaism, for instance) simply in order to pursue justice and morality for their own sakes. The new texts were not scriptures—that is, they did not have the canonical status of the Jewish and Christian writings; nor did they fill the same sort of liturgical function. Instead, they explored the intellectual ramifications of their central conceits.

Good examples are the "Attis" poem by the 1st-century CE poet Catullus (84–54 BCE), the long essay "On Isis and Osiris" by Plutarch (46–120 CE), and the philosophical verse treatise *On the Nature of Things* by Lucretius (99–55 BCE). Works like these dissociate philosophy from religion, a development that enriched both traditions. Philosophy received a new stimulus, by focusing less on the nature of the universe and more on the human lives within it. In turn, religion became increasingly a thing to think about and not simply to perform. As the ancient Greek thinker Epicurus (341–270 BCE) had famously put it: "Any philosopher's words that do not aim to relieve human suffering are meaningless." The new provincial cults increasingly sought more than universal order and the submission to fate or divine desire. Instead, their followers desired solace, forgiveness, and the promise of a personal contentment. The Greater Western world entered the Common Era with a new attitude of spiritual and intellectual questing—an attitude that would shape the civilization of the next thousand years.

> The Greater Western world entered the Common Era with a new attitude of spiritual and intellectual questing—an attitude that would shape the civilization of the next thousand years.

STOICISM AND NEOPLATONISM

Two philosophical schools offered alternatives to all the pagan and Christian faiths, even while contributing to their intellectual development: Stoicism and Neoplatonism. The first, Stoicism, in fact dated back to Hellenistic times, well into

Marcus Aurelius Equestrian statue of the great emperor and Stoic philosopher. His reign, which ended in 180 CE, marks the highpoint of the Pax Romana.

the 3rd century BCE, but it received new life from Roman writers like Seneca and Cicero. They saw in it the perfect expression of Roman virtues such as self-discipline, service to community, and calm acceptance of divine law. Another burst of Stoic philosophy—a widespread and influential one, considering its source—came from Marcus Aurelius, who ruled the Roman Empire from 161 to 180 CE. His aphorisms, compiled in a book that he called "Notes to Myself" but is now known as the *Meditations*, appealed to many Imperial Age pagans and early Christians. (It helped that Aurelius wrote his book in Koine Greek, the same dialect used by the New Testament authors, which made his teachings more readily accessible to the adherent of the early christianities.) In line with earlier Stoic tradition, he believed the world is governed by an overarching sense of order and purpose, in service to which human lives play out. The only true happiness results from accepting one's limitations, keeping one's disappointments and frustrations in perspective, and performing one's duties to one's family, society, and the gods.

Aurelius's term for "order and purpose" is the Greek **Logos**, which resonated with anyone familiar with the Gospel of Saint John, where the word had much the same meaning.[10] The Logos, in the Stoic sense, gives not only a sense of the cosmos's purposefulness but also a measure of solace. It addresses the individual seeking both a place in the transient world and a permanent one in the divine world to come:

> The handiwork of the gods is replete with Providence, and the hand of Fate is not detached from nature. Rather, Fate spins and weaves the threads that Providence ordains. Everything flows from the home of the gods; more than that, a sense of needful purpose and well-being pervades the whole creation of which you are a part. Every part of the natural world contains and preserves an element of goodness that is given to it by the very nature of the world as a whole. . . . Take comfort in this thought, and live always by these doctrines. If you wish to face death with something other than mumbling confusion, give up your fascination with study, and let your heart be at rest and express simple gratitude to the gods for what they have done. (*Meditations 2.3*)

---

10   Meaning "word," literally, logos can also be seen in the suffix "-ology" that denotes so many English terms for science—like biology, geology, and meteorology.

Stoicism offered more than a set of rules to follow or a group of ideas to adhere to. Some examples: "No action is good if performing it causes you to violate a trust or behave shamelessly" (3.7). "Do not act as though you will live ten thousand years, for death is the fate that awaits you. Therefore, while you're alive and able, seek the Good" (4.17). "Do not hold life itself to be the only thing of value. Consider the infinite measures of time and space that lie behind you and before you; in the face of these eternities, what difference does it make whether you live for three days or three generations?" (4.50). "If a cucumber is bitter, throw it away; and if your path is full of briars, change direction. That is all you need to do. It is not for you to ask, 'Why do such things exist?'" (8.50). Stoicism cultivated the soul and urged people to perform spiritual exercises through daily reflection, prayer, and contemplation of the fact of mortality. The Stoics called these practices the discipline of **askesis**—meaning "peace of mind"—from which English word *asceticism* derives. Many early Christian leaders saw the compatibility between their religious beliefs and Stoic ethics and used the pagan notions to explain their faith.

The Platonic tradition also kept its appeal with pagans and, increasingly, Christians, in an amalgam known as **Neoplatonism**. A series of Plato's disciples continued teaching at the Academy long after his death in 347 BCE, most of them engaged in collecting, editing, codifying, and commenting Plato's vast writings. A loose network of Platonist schools also spread across the Hellenistic lands, which ensured that Plato's philosophy and his way of doing philosophy would have the most wide-reaching influence in the centuries following his death. Plato taught the existence of an Ideal Universe, from which our muddled and benighted cosmos derives. This harmonized with many of the new provincial cults and provided them with intellectual support. Most of the later Platonists were equally passionate in observing their pagan convictions. In Plato they thus found an intellectualized version of their cults.[11]

Plutarch (46–120 CE), a wealthy Greek who was an enthusiastic supporter of the empire, dedicated his life as a priest of the Oracle of Apollo at Delphi. He also composed a shelf of stylized biographies, moral essays, literary criticism, and Platonic commentaries. His best-known and best-loved work is the series of *Parallel Lives*, in which he pairs eminent statesmen from Greek and Roman history. In these lively, intimate portraits of their respective virtues (or lack thereof), his concern is not with the details of political history but with the moral character of his subjects.[12]

---

[11] Saint Ambrose of Milan (340–397) and Saint Augustine of Hippo (354–430) are among the Church Fathers. Boethius (480–524), the greatest Christian philosopher of the early Middle Ages, is another.

[12] William Shakespeare used North's Plutarch when composing *Julius Caesar, Antony and Cleopatra*, and *Coriolanus*.

As he himself put it, he was interested in "the offhand occasion, word, or anecdote ... that brings to light men's true tempers more than the story of any of their great battles, even those in which ten thousand men may have died." Nevertheless, Plutarch knew how to tell a good story. His narratives of the disastrous Athenian campaign to Syracuse, of Pompey's defeat at Pharsalus and subsequent death, and of the suicide of emperor Otho, for example, are gripping set pieces. The *Parallel Lives* have been popular ever since Plutarch's own time. Roman society read them avidly, as did most Christian scholars at least until the 4th century. In the Renaissance, Sir Thomas North (1535–1604) produced the first version in English in 1597—although he cribbed it from a French translation since he knew no Greek.

Plutarch's essays, by contrast, which medieval commentators grouped under the catchall title of *Moralia* ("Ethical Matters"), have never been as popular but give an indication of the breadth of his interests. They move from "Consolation to My Wife," written after the death of their infant daughter, to the profound "On the Delay of Divine Justice," which tackles the problem of why evildoers prosper. Yet another, the speculative "On the Face of the Man in the Moon," attempts a cosmology—a system for explaining the origins and structure of the entire universe. In all, the *Moralia* unite a committed Neoplatonic philosophy with a commonsense search for the alleviation of suffering. Pagan religion received a jolt of intellectual rigor in the works of writers like Plutarch, which helps to account for its continued vitality even after Rome reached the peak of its power.

Many early Christians felt the attraction of that rigor as well. Saint Augustine of Hippo embraced Neoplatonic tenets in his attempt to explain the existence of evil in a universe created by a good and loving God. (The explanation: evil is a void, not a presence; it comprises simply an absence of good.) Another leading writer, the Alexandrian theologian and Biblical exegete Origen (185–254), used the Neoplatonic notion of *emanation*—the idea that the created world results from the outward-flowing essence of life from the eternal center of the Logos. In this way he explained the migration of souls from the Heavenly Divine and out into the created world. Origen supplemented this notion with the idea of spiritual return, a kind of undertow of purified souls flowing back toward the creating center. This idea did not originate with him; his younger contemporary Neoplatonic philosopher Plotinus (204–270; a pagan) had been elaborating the concepts of spiritual resurrection and return, as handed on to him by his own teachers, for years. But Origen was the first Christian thinker of note to explicate salvation in intellectual terms derived from a philosophical tradition.

Also Neoplatonic, but ultimately unorthodox from the Christian perspective, was Origen's denial of bodily resurrection. Origen is a unique figure in Christian history: he is regarded as one of the great church fathers, the first Christian philosopher of any note, yet most of his published ideas were formally condemned by later councils. He left behind an enormous body of writing; Saint Jerome credited him with nearly two thousand separate works. That is clearly an exaggeration, but nevertheless, the enormity of his production is one reason why there has never been a satisfying biography made of him.

A later writer (ca. 500), known as Pseudo-Dionysius the Areopagite, went even further. He distinguished between the return of all living creatures to their source (a pagan notion) and a uniquely Christianized version of the idea, in which souls were not subsumed into the Divine Identity but instead had the Likeness of God restored to them by divine grace. This may seem too subtle a distinction, but Pseudo-Dionysius deemed it necessary in order to avoid pantheism. His identity remains a mystery. Until the 12th century his works were believed to have been written by Dionysius the Areopagite—the Christian convert mentioned in Acts 13.17 and whom popular tradition long conflated with Saint Denis, the patron saint of France (d. 250). In the 12th century the scholar Peter Abelard proved the impossibility of Dionysius being the author, a discovery for which he was nearly killed by angry monks. Hence the awkward attribution to "Pseudo-Dionysius." Revered throughout the Christian world, Pseudo-Dionysius is a saint in the Orthodox Churches; his idea of theosis (the taking on of the Likeness of God by the saved soul) is a central aspect of the Orthodox theology of salvation.

Aspects of Neoplatonism can be found in many other early theologians, including Saint Jerome (ca. 347–420 CE), who produced the definitive Latin version of the Bible—called the Vulgate—for western Christianity. Still another, John Scotus Eriugena (815–877), was a 9th-century Irish scholar prominent in the court of Charles the Bald (r. 843–877) in France and of Alfred the Great (r. 871–899) in England.[13]

> Like the pagan cults, early Christianity received high-octane intellectual fuel injections from Stoicism and Neoplatonism. Both enriched it enormously by adding to its intrinsic emotional appeal a degree of sophistication that it had previously lacked.

Eriugena was the most brilliant scholar of his age. Most his works, being so heavily influenced by Neoplatonism, were later condemned by the church. One pope (Honorius III, r. 1216–1227) even described them as "crawling with worms of heretical perversion." Among those perversions was Eriugena's claim that hell does not exist as a place but only as a condition, and that its punishments were purifying rather than punitive.

Like the pagan cults, early Christianity received high-octane intellectual fuel injections from Stoicism and Neoplatonism. Both enriched it enormously by adding to its intrinsic emotional appeal a degree of sophistication that it had previously lacked. For the next fifteen hundred years Christian philosophers, scientists, mathematicians, and logicians were among the leading scholars in Western civilization

---

[13] Eriugena was known to be a quick wit. When Charles the Bald, goading him, asked what was the difference between a drunkard and an Irishman, Eriugena replied, "Only a table."

and usually made up the majority of them. This was not necessarily because of the cultural hegemony of the Latin and Greek churches, but simply because the Christian faith itself invited, prompted, and demanded intense intellectual effort. It inspired the fascination of what is difficult, and required its followers to acknowledge complex ideas about the nature of world, human freedom, the meaning of suffering, and the purpose of existence.

Most notably, these early centuries of the Common Era introduced an emphasis on self-awareness, self-examination, and self-criticism. They urged the development of personal conscience and the constant striving for meaning and improvement, ideas that would mark Western culture indelibly. Such concerns had existed before, of course, but never with the same degree of emotional urgency and intellectual resolve. Western culture became marked by a kind of intellectual and spiritual restlessness, convinced that life has genuine meaning and purpose but never quite certain that it had discovered them. All the same, it was confident that the effort to find them was necessary and ennobling.

WHO, WHAT, WHERE

askesis
christianities
Essenes
Logos
messiah
Neoplatonism

New Testament
Pantheon
Pharisees
Sadducees
Trinity

SUGGESTED READINGS

Primary Sources

Eusebius of Caesarea. *The History of the Church.*
Josephus. *The Antiquities of the Jews.*
———. *The Jewish War.*
Marcus Aurelius. *Meditations.*
Philo of Alexandria.

The Dead Sea Scrolls.
The Gnostic Gospels.
The Nag Hammadi Library.
The New Jerusalem Bible.

Anthologies

Elliott, Neil, and Mark Reasoner, eds. *Documents and Images for the Study of Paul* (2010).
Ehrman, Bart D. *The New Testament and Other Early Christian Writings: A Reader* (2003).

Warrior, Valerie M. *Roman Religion: A Sourcebook* (2001).

Studies

Brakke, David. *The Gnostics: Myth, Ritual, and Diversity in Early Christianity* (2011).

Brennan, Tad. *The Stoic Life: Emotions, Duties, and Fate* (2005).

Brown, Peter. *The Body and Society: Men, Women, and Sexual Renunciation in Early Christianity* (2008).

———. *The Rise of Western Christendom: Triumph and Diversity, AD 200–1000* (2003).

Denzey, Nicola. *The Bone Gatherers: The Lost Worlds of Early Christian Women* (2008).

Ehrman, Bart D. *Lost Christianities: The Battles for Scripture and the Faiths We Never Knew* (2005).

Engberg-Pedersen, Troels. *Cosmology and the Self in the Apostle Paul: The Material Self* (2011).

Ferguson, Everett. *Backgrounds of Early Christianity* (2003).

Fredriksen, Paula. *Augustine and the Jews: A Christian Defense of Jews and Judaism* (2008).

———. *From Jesus to Christ: The Origins of the New Testament Images of Jesus* (2000).

———. *Jesus of Nazareth, King of the Jews: A Jewish Life and the Emergence of Christianity* (2000).

González, Justo L. *The Story of Christianity.* Vol. 1, *The Early Church to the Dawn of the Reformation* (2010).

Jacobs, Irving. *The Midrashic Process: Tradition and Interpretation in Rabbinic Judaism* (2008).

Johnson, Luke Timothy. *Among the Gentiles: Greco-Roman Religion and Christianity* (2010).

———. *The Writings of the New Testament: An Interpretation* (2010).

Lampe, Peter. *From Paul to Valentinus: Christians at Rome in the First Two Centuries* (2003).

Lieu, Judith M. *Christian Identity in the Jewish and Graeco-Roman World* (2004).

Luijendijk, AnneMarie. *Greetings in the Lord: Early Christians and the Oxyrhynchus Papyri* (2009).

MacMullen, Ramsay. *Romanization in the Time of Augustus* (2008).

Meier, John P. *The Vision of Matthew: Christ, Church, and Morality in the First Gospel* (2004).

Rasimus, Tuomas, Troels Engberg-Pedersen, and Ismo Dunderberg, eds. *Stoicism in Early Christianity* (2010).

Stark, Rodney. *Cities of God: The Real Story of How Christianity Became an Urban Movement and Conquered Rome* (2007).

Wilken, Robert Louis. *The Christians as the Romans Saw Them* (2003).

———. *The Spirit of Early Christian Thought: Seeking the Face of God* (2005).

For additional resources, including maps, primary sources, visuals, web links, and quizzes, please go to **www.oup.com/us/backman.**

CHAPTER 8

The Early Middle Ages

306–750 CE

THE EARLY MIDDLE AGES

The Greater Western world underwent a series of shocks from the 4th to the 8th centuries that gave a radically new direction to its development. Roman might had peaked in the late 2nd century, after which imperial control entered a holding pattern while internal squabbles dominated the political scene. Those squabbles centered on a constitutional problem: the empire had never established an orderly process for succession to the throne, which meant that the death of each emperor triggered some sort of contest for power. It led to a period of Roman decline, but also to the rise of a "new Rome" in the east—in Byzantium. Christianity, too, met a new development in a new revelation, the rise of Islam. And Christianity, in turn, changed in character, turning inward amid a Europe of warring rulers and scholar monks.

These four centuries are known as the **Dark Ages** in western Europe and as the Age of Ignorance (*al-Jahiliyyah*, in Arabic—also translatable as the "Age of Barbarism") in the Islamic world; for the Greek-speaking lands of the eastern Mediterranean, however, this was a heroic age when the achievements of the ancient world were fortified by the rapid development of Christianity. From their magnificent new capital city of Constantinople on the Bosporus—the strait separating the Black

◀ **Crown of King Recesvinth**
The Visigoths were justly famous for their metalwork, and this crown (worn only in formal ceremonies) is one of their best-known pieces. It is made of gold encrusted with rock crystals, pearls, and sapphires.

Commodus as Hercules
The emperor Commodus (r. 180–192) loved to portray himself as a manly man, and, rather like Vladimir Putin today, he regularly staged rigged athletic contests in which he always emerged victorious. Here he has had himself sculpted as Hercules.

Sea and the Mediterranean—the people of this new Byzantine Empire achieved a level of wealth, power, and cultural glory that were never seen again. They also witnessed the spread of a great new religion in Islam.

THE IMPERIAL CRISIS

Trouble emerged for the first time, in a major way, with the death of Marcus Aurelius in 180. Aurelius had designated his son Commodus (r. 180–192) to succeed him, but Commodus was a poor ruler, a snarky, ill-mannered lout who threw tantrums when he did not get his way. He thought of himself as a great athlete, dressed in lion skins, carried a club, and wanted everyone to call him Hercules. And in fact his petulance led more than once to his ordering the execution of senators and officials who had opposed his wishes. The political atmosphere grew rancid in a way it had not been in a hundred years. Commodus's death set off a civil war between a host of civil and military officials, and this became the unfortunate pattern for nearly every imperial succession throughout the 3rd century. The army accordingly grew in prominence as the sole bulwark against social decay, which meant that power passed almost exclusively to a series of generals; but since each successive general's claim to legitimacy came only from having seized power by brute force, ambitious rivals in the military in turn killed each one. In the sixty-seven years from 218 to 285 there were as many as eighty-three claimants to the throne—only a handful of whom died of natural causes.

CHAPTER TIMELINE

284–305 CE
Reign of Roman emperor Diocletian

313 CE
Edict of Milan

330 CE
Founding of Constantinople

480–547 CE
Life of Benedict of Nursia

312 CE
Battle of the Milvian Bridge

323–325 CE
Council of Nicea

391 CE
Christianity becomes official religion of Roman Empire

Nonstop war undermined the economy by disrupting farming and commerce, and the warmongering generals made matters worse by intermittently devaluing the currency so they would have more coinage on hand with which to pay their troops. But this triggered runaway inflation and drove hordes of laborers into the cities in search of employment or alms, causing the urban centers to become choked with homeless and desperately poor people. The smallpox virus then did the rest. By the end of the 3rd century the empire was reeling from disaster to disaster, the army was divided, decimated, and demoralized, and the economy sputtered and wheezed like a dying engine.

> By the end of the 3rd century the empire was reeling from disaster to disaster, the army was divided, decimated, and demoralized, and the economy sputtered and wheezed like a dying engine.

IMPERIAL DECLINE: ROME'S OVERREACH

By cruel coincidence, this was when the imperial borders suddenly faced their most severe challenge with the inrush of the Germanic peoples along the Rhine-Danube frontier and the renewed attack of the Persian Empire, which was then under the Sassanid dynasty, in the east. The earliest Germans to arrive in large numbers, the Ostrogoths and Visigoths, were bribed with money and promises of assistance. They were asked only to spare the cities of the eastern Mediterranean and move instead into the underpopulated rural west, but the Persians could not be so easily disposed of. The lure of controlling the Holy Land and the Hellespont—the linchpins between the European and Asian economies—proved too great, causing the Persians to determine on outright conquest.

The Romans fought back valiantly but with little luck. The low point for them came in 260, when the Persians captured the emperor Valerian (r. 253–260) in battle. They held him as a slave, forcing him to kneel on all fours as a stepping stool for the Sassanid ruler when he mounted his horse. The mad succession

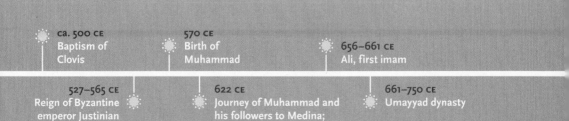

ca. 500 CE
Baptism of
Clovis

570 CE
Birth of
Muhammad

656–661 CE
Ali, first imam

527–565 CE
Reign of Byzantine
emperor Justinian

622 CE
Journey of Muhammad and
his followers to Medina;
beginning of Islamic calendar

661–750 CE
Umayyad dynasty

of emperors continued unchecked, the western provinces of the empire became overrun with invading Germanic groups, and effective government from the center all but disappeared.

A respite appeared with the long reign of a stern, no-nonsense emperor named Diocletian (r. 284–305). He came from a long line of Dalmatian peasant farmers, had received only an elementary education but was raised with a deep belief in the rightness of the empire, and had sought a career in the army. A talented soldier, he rose quickly through the ranks and was popular with the soldiers he commanded. When the briefly serving emperors Carus (r. 282–283) and Numerianus (r. 283–284) died—according to several ancient sources, Carus being struck by lightning and Numerianus of a mysterious eye inflammation—the army overwhelmingly threw its support behind Diocletian, who faced enormous problems. They included a wrecked economy, a restive army, Germanic and Persian invasions, and a bloated, inefficient administration. His solutions were as blunt as his personality.

Persian Ascendancy   This is the most famous of the Sassanid rock reliefs, not only because of its workmanship but because of the scene it portrays: the great victory of Shapur I (r. 241–272) over the Roman emperors Valerian and Philip the Arab. Valerian was captured, executed, then stuffed and mounted on the wall at Shapur's palace.

The worthless currency that had triggered the inflation could hardly be helped: Europe's known gold and silver mines were largely tapped out by Diocletian's time, and without an influx of precious metals the fiscal crisis would continue. Diocletian addressed the problem by essentially withdrawing Rome's currency from circulation and returning the empire to a barter economy. Taxes were collected in kind (clothing, food, tools, manufactured goods, or whatever), and imperial soldiers were paid in the same. The debased coinage—once recaptured, melted, and recast—eventually regained some of its value in Mediterranean trade, but a true money economy would not return to continental Europe until the 10th century. He similarly recast the imperial army into separate civil and military divisions, with one force of "border troops" manning the Rhine-Danube frontier. This long line of fortified stations, together with a separate force of "palace troops," served as a roving field army that was under direct imperial command. Diocletian's border troops were essentially a form of civil militia made up of deputized residents, both Roman and German, of the frontier areas.

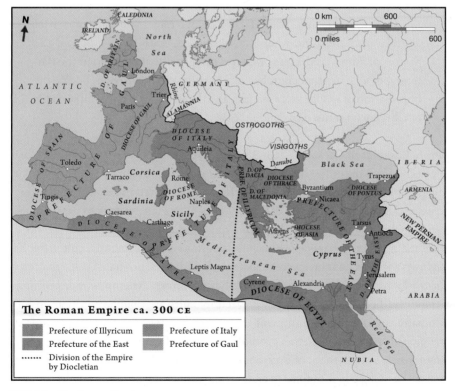

MAP 8.1   **The Roman Empire, ca. 300 CE**

The palace troops, the more professional fighting force, who were paid with real cash, were thus freed to concentrate on the struggle against the Persians to the east, with good results.

Last, Diocletian chose not to streamline the administration, but to cut it into separate units, instituting the **Tetrarchy**—a new system whereby the empire was formally divided into two halves, east and west, with a separate emperor (*augustus* in Latin) for each (see Map 8.1). Moreover, each augustus was assisted by a **caesar**, or junior emperor, who succeeded to the position of his augustus upon that person's death or retirement and who then appointed a new caesar to assist him. At a stroke, Diocletian eased the bureaucratic burden on the central administration and resolved the constitutional crisis by providing a regular means for the selection of new augusti.

MARTYRDOM AND EMPIRE

Diocletian is best remembered for instituting the longest and most vicious of the state attacks upon Christians.

> In the nineteenth year of Diocletian's reign ... in the month of April ... near the time when Christians celebrate the Passion of the Savior ... [imperial decrees] were promulgated that demanded the flattening of all Christian churches, the burning of all Christian books, the humiliation of all Christian leaders, and the imprisonment of all servants of Christ who refused to denounce their faith,

wrote Eusebius of Caesarea (263–339), the most reliable chronicler of the Great Persecution, at the outset of his *History of the Church*. He then went on to describe, chapter by bloody chapter, the beating, flaying, decapitation, drowning, burning, rape, and mauling by animals of thousands of Christian martyrs.

Diocletian was less interested in wiping out the Christians than he was in persuading them to participate in civic celebrations of the imperial cult. After all, his own wife and daughter were reported to have been Christians. What mattered instead was the unraveling of social cohesion across the empire. For centuries Rome had been held together by a carefully cultivated public spirit, a sense of Romanness, and the commitment to an ideal greater than parochial ethnic or religious concerns. Diocletian promoted the cult of emperor worship as a unifying force, a living symbol of everyone's participation in a world larger than themselves. The Christians' refusal to endorse the official cult, or even to give it empty lip service, seemed to strike at the very heart of the empire, and he therefore concluded that they had to be crushed into submission.

But that is not what happened, at least not with the majority of them. Many of the thousands whom Diocletian sent to their death accepted their fate with quiet resolve and even, if we can trust our sources, with some measure of happiness. Martyrdom, they felt, was a prize to be embraced. Reunion after death with the Christ whom they had served in secret all their lives seemed too great a blessing to merit dreading the temporary unpleasantness that preceded it. Crowds eager for blood and tears certainly saw all the blood they could possibly want but, instead of tears and wailing, too often had to put up with hymns, prayers, and laughter.

Medallion of Saint Mamai   Saint Mamai, an early martyr popular with the Georgian people in the Caucasus, was thrown to the lions by the Romans in 275 CE. This 11th-century medallion depicts Mamai fearlessly astride a lion while brandishing a cross, symbolizing the victory over death won by Mamai and by all believers in Christ.

Martyrologies—the narrative records of martyrs' sufferings—can seldom be taken literally. Their whole purpose is to glorify God by testifying to both the unimaginable sufferings endured by his saints and the stoic calm and joyful spirit expressed by those saints even when caught in the lion's maw or pierced by the executioner's blade. The more gore, the better, and the more superhuman the acceptance of brutal death, the better still. Few writers could resist the implicit invitation to exercise their imaginative and descriptive powers, and fewer still even attempted to resist. Hence, when a Christian writer like Lactantius (240–320) penned his vivid chronicle *On the Deaths of Those Persecuted for Christ*, he found it easy to identify plenty of victims of Roman cruelty; the challenge lay in maintaining the fever pitch of his descriptions of the horrors they suffered. As with the history of Eusebius of Caesarea, after thirty pages of Lactantius's nonstop beheadings, eviscerations, poisonings, burnings, beatings, and beast manglings, one can sense the writer's rhetorical exhaustion—and there are still three hundred pages to go.

Nevertheless, even allowing for exaggeration in the sources, enough Christians accepted their martyrdom with such grace that the Romans who witnessed it were astonished and befuddled. What was it about this religion that could enable someone to accept death happily, even eagerly? Was this something to envy or was it simply insane? It is unclear how many Romans, if any, were sufficiently moved by the martyrs' behavior to convert to the faith. Yet it is certain that the Great Persecution got more people thinking about Christianity, and perhaps talking about it, than had been before. If Diocletian had intended to annihilate the faith, his plan backfired.

It is unclear how many Romans, if any, were sufficiently moved by the martyrs' behavior to convert to the faith. Yet it is certain that the Great Persecution got more people thinking about Christianity, and perhaps talking about it, than had been before. If Diocletian had intended to annihilate the faith, his plan backfired.

A CHRISTIAN EMPEROR AND A CHRISTIAN CHURCH

In 305, having done all that he could to save the empire, an exhausted Diocletian resigned from the imperial office (the only person to do so in Roman history) and returned to his homeland farm, dedicating his last years to his private passion: growing cabbages. His mechanism for the orderly transfer of power failed in its first attempt, however, and another civil war quickly engulfed the empire. When the smoke finally cleared a new emperor sat in the throne: Constantine the Great (r. 306–337), whose eventful reign changed everything—for he was the first Roman emperor to be a Christian.

According to the source most contemporary with the event, Constantine's conversion had occurred on the eve of the battle that would decide the civil war. A rival named Maxentius had also claimed the imperial title in 306; attempts to negotiate a power-sharing arrangement continually failed, and in 312 the two sides broke into open warfare. The conclusive battle took place a few miles north of Rome, at the Milvian Bridge. Reportedly, a heavenly voice spoke to Constantine in a dream and told him to embrace Christianity and to paint the cross on his soldiers' shields before the next day's battle. He did so, won the battle, became sole emperor, and committed himself to Christianity on the spot. The story seems too contrived to be true. It suggests, none too subtly, that the religion itself caused the military victory, even though the soldiers can hardly have been believers. From this point on, it implies, imperial success could only come so long as the empire served the Christian God.

However the conversion occurred, it did in fact occur. Constantine's conversion must have been sincere since there was no conceivable political advantage to gain from it. Christians, by the year 312, made up no more than 2 or 3 percent of the Roman population and may have constituted as little as 1 percent. Even if one considers only the urban population of the eastern half of the empire—that is, the geographic area and demographic group with the highest proportion of Christians—the new faith made up no more than 10 percent of the populace.

The impact of his conversion was immediate and dramatic. In 313 he issued the **Edict of Milan**, which legalized Christianity and guaranteed religious freedom for all faiths within the empire:

> It pleases us to remove altogether the legal restraints issued heretofore regarding the Christians, any one of whom may henceforth practice the Christian faith, if he wishes, freely, openly, without molestation . . . and in free and unrestricted liberty of religious worship. . . . And moreover, in order to promote peace in our time, we grant to all religions [within the Empire] the right of free and open observance of their faith.

Constantine did more than legalize Christianity, though; he opened the imperial coffers in support of it. He ordered that public funds be made available to compensate individuals whose property and cash deposits had been confiscated for religious reasons. He poured money into building churches, training priests,

Dear Prudence   Mosaic of Christ in his heavenly throne, surrounded by his apostles and Saints Prudence and Praxedis. From the 4th century on, the Good Shepherd iconography of Christ gave way to images of Jesus as the mighty king of heaven or the stern judge of the Last Day. The kinder, gentler Jesus did not become the norm again until the 12th century.

promoting evangelical missions, copying sacred writings, and setting up Christian charitable houses. He granted Christians special tax privileges and showed personal preference for selecting Christians to serve in government offices. Not surprisingly, Christianity began to spread among the people of the east at a rate never before experienced.

Paganism remained legal for several more decades but the momentum was now decidedly in Christianity's direction. The years of struggle and persecution were over. By the end of the 4th century the majority of the eastern Roman population had embraced the new faith, and it became the official religion of the Roman Empire in 391, thanks to the emperor Theodosius I (r. 379–395).

Freed from persecution and permitted at last to practice their faith openly, Christians now poured into the town squares to preach—and this is when the long-simmering problems of the "christianities" came into focus. To his horror, Constantine found that no two Christian groups believed the same things, embraced the same values, worshipped in the same way, read the same canon, or recognized the same authority. Most accepted Jesus of Nazareth as the biblical messiah and Son of God, but many did not. Most believed that he had died on the Cross and rose from the dead, but many did not. Most believed that he was physically present in the consecrated bread and wine of the Eucharist, but many did not. Most believed that he was in some way coeternal with God the Father and the Holy Spirit, but many did not. Constantine recognized that the christianities risked continued fracturing and internal fighting unless something was done. Accordingly, he summoned an ecumenical council to meet at the eastern city of Nicaea, ordering the leaders of every Christian community in the empire to come. With one notable exception, the bishops all came. The council lasted for two years (323–325), passed dozens of resolutions, and symbolically capped their activity by issuing the **Nicene Creed**, which has stood ever since as the universal standard, the statement *par excellence* of fundamental Christian belief.

Constantine regarded the newly standardized Christian Church as his own dominion. He had tradition behind him: in pagan Rome the emperor had held the title of **pontifex maximus** ("chief priest"), which made him the leader of the entire cult. The empire did not distinguish between political authority and religious authority, and Constantine saw no reason to alter the arrangement simply because the religion itself had changed. Taking the formal title of "thirteenth apostle," Constantine insisted that the emperor, so long as he himself was a Christian, was by that fact alone the supreme authority over the Christian church.

This brought him into conflict with the pope, Sylvester I (r. 314–335)—the one and only bishop who refused to attend the Council of Nicaea, since doing so would have implied a recognition of the emperor's authority over the church. (The pope did send a representative, though, to keep an eye on things.) Papal claims to power rested on Saint Peter. Since he had undeniably been the leader of the original group of Apostles, and since he had ended his days as the bishop of the Christian community of Rome, his successors as bishop of Rome therefore inherited the leadership of the church. The problem for those successors was that few Christians outside of Rome accepted their logic. Peter's original authority was beyond question, but after Peter's death (in 64 CE) the leadership of the community of bishops was an open question. Why should the bishop of Jerusalem not take precedence? Or the bishop of Antioch (the first city outside of Jerusalem to have a formally organized community)? Why should leadership not be left to a free election among all bishops? As it happened, most of the popes for the first thousand years of Christian history had little authority outside of their own city of Rome. Many were respected and even granted special honors, but few were obeyed. Starting with Constantine, the holders of the imperial title assumed their own supremacy over the church and exercised it.[1]

THE RISE OF "NEW ROME"

Constantine arrived at one additional epoch-making decision: in 324, in the midst of preparations for the Council of Nicaea, he decided to abandon Italy and build a new capital city in the east. He chose the site known to the ancient Greeks as *Byzantion* (in Latin, *Byzantium*), on the promontory between the Sea of Marmara and the Black Sea. This was where Europe and Asia met, the nexus of east-west trade, and the strategic node for overseeing the administration of the eastern empire. By the 4th century it seemed clear that the western half of the Roman Empire was in severe decline. And while most hoped for its survival, Constantine and his successors recognized that the eastern half of the empire was the more important half, being the virtual cradle of Western civilization. It was an urban, commercial, literate, and sophisticated world, newly given an additional sense of unity and purpose by

Constantine and his successors recognized that the eastern half of the empire was the most important half, being the virtual cradle of Western civilization. It was an urban, commercial, literate, and sophisticated world, newly given an additional sense of unity and purpose by its now-rapid assumption of a Christian character.

---

[1]   Pope Sylvester did the best he could, under the circumstances. He approved the legislation of the Council of Nicaea, including the Creed, and simply reissued it under his own name.

its now-rapid assumption of a Christian character. The western half of the empire, in contrast, was weaker, poorer, ruder, agrarian, and expendable.

From the new capital built on the site of Byzantium, now renamed Constantinople, the rulers of the **Byzantine Empire** kept their eyes trained eastward, vaguely acknowledging their links to the backward west but putting little effort into propping up the crumbling administration there. The Byzantines regarded their eastern empire as a "new Rome" purged of its pagan past and explicitly dedicated to creating a Christian realm. The new capital was formally dedicated on May 11, 330.

The Byzantine Empire of the 4th and 5th centuries wrapped around the eastern edges of the Mediterranean like a giant reversed letter C. It included all of today's countries of Libya, Egypt, Israel, Jordan, Lebanon, Syria, Turkey, and most of the Balkan states (see Map 8.2). Hundreds of ethnic groups resided within this zone, chiefly in the cities or within a day's journey of them. Since travel and communication were so easy, thanks to the long-familiar sea-lanes and coastal roads, the government in Constantinople was able to retain centralized rule. The heart of the empire was the great Asia Minor landmass, the center of grain production. Within a few generations, Byzantine society sloughed off its use of Latin and reverted to the Greek that had been the norm there until the arrival of the Romans.

The territory of Greece itself held a sentimental place in Byzantine hearts but was a relatively minor province in terms of economic and cultural life. The real nodes of energy apart from Constantinople itself were the coastal

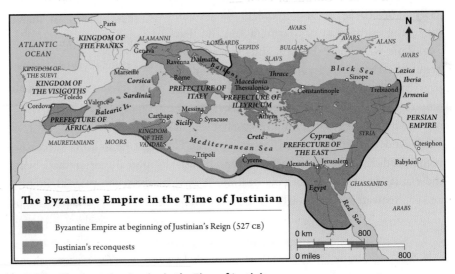

MAP 8.2   **The Byzantine Empire in the Time of Justinian**

cities—Thessalonika, Ephesus, Antioch, Caesarea, Tripoli, and Alexandria—and a handful of inland cities like Jerusalem, Damascus, and Chalcedon. Manufacturing, trade, shipping, and finance were their lifeblood, but they also maintained hundreds of schools, academies, libraries, salons, and theaters that kept alive the classical traditions of literature, philosophy, and to a lesser degree science. In addition, the 4th and 5th centuries saw a frenzy of church building as Christianity at last sank its roots deeply into the culture.

The Byzantines did not give up entirely on the west, but their readoption of the Greek language represented a practical, not merely a symbolic, turning away from the Latin-speaking west. Trade between east and west declined precipitously, since the west produced little that the east needed, apart from slaves. The western empire continued to hobble along with its own augustus (who was decidedly subordinate to the augustus in Constantinople). But in 476 a German general named Odoacer put an end to the sham: he deposed the weakling ruler and declared the western empire dead.

The Byzantine emperors occasionally showed some interest in influencing western matters by forming ties with several of the Germanic warlords who thenceforth dominated Europe. Justinian I (r. 527–565) actually reconquered much of southern Italy and the central part of the North African coast, in a quixotic effort to reconstitute the old empire. His efforts failed in the end, though, since the economic gains from the conquests never came close to offsetting the expense of the military effort. He scored more lasting achievements with his vast construction projects within the city of Constantinople, including his completion of the magnificent Church of Hagia Sophia, and his compilation of the *Corpus iuris civilis* ("Corpus of Civil Law"). The *Corpus* formed the basis of all jurisprudence in Byzantium until the 15th century and provided a model for the development of the canon law of the Catholic Church.

A SPLENDID, BELEAGUERED CAPITAL

The stalling out of Justinian's military efforts turned into actual losses of territory by his immediate successors. Under emperors Maurice (r. 582–602) and Phocas (r. 602–610) Byzantium lost Egypt, Palestine, Syria, and parts of Asia Minor itself to the Persians, who made another of their periodic efforts to control the western reaches of the Fertile Crescent. These were hard-fought campaigns that nearly brought Byzantium to its knees. Heraclius (r. 610–641) spent his entire reign in a life-or-death struggle to put the empire back on solid footing. But so much territory had been lost that he lacked the funds to pay his soldiers, a weakness that also allowed groups of Avars, Bulgars, and Slavs to encroach on imperial lands in the Balkan region.

Heraclius reorganized the army into a new system of **themes** (Greek *thema*, meaning "regiment" or "division"), which apportioned the lands of the empire to the military officers and gave them civil and economic jurisdiction over them. The commanders then subdivided their zones into individual landholdings for each soldier serving under them. In this way, Heraclius stripped away the bloated, centralized imperial administration and replaced it with the army itself—which now, instead of receiving salaries from Constantinople, derived its own revenue from its landholdings and the fees it collected in return for its civic functions. It was a radical move, but one that dramatically improved military morale and effectiveness, since the soldiers henceforth had reliable sources of income and a personal stake in defending the empire from further attack.

Thus restructured, the Byzantine world achieved high degrees of prosperity and stability. Constantinople acted as the economic hub of the empire: all commerce passed through it. The city fiercely guarded its monopolies on coinage, interest rates, weights and measures, and manufacturing standards, through which it exercised direct control of trade. In Justinian's time the Byzantines had learned how to cultivate silkworms and to spin the silk they produced, which allowed them to begin their own manufacturing of high-value silk cloth. The loss of market share felt by the silk traders from the Near East helped trigger a wave of wars against the Byzantines throughout the 7th and 8th centuries.

The splendor of the city was extraordinary, with hundreds of churches, fine palaces, theaters, baths, and bazaars (see Map 8.3). Most of the empire's cities suffered from Constantinople's dominance, since the capital drained commercial life from the provinces. Provincial cities continued, of course, but they became more political and religious administrative centers than sites of industry and trade. This change had important social and cultural consequences for the old class of urban elites. The descendants of the Roman curiales, they had previously formed the backbone of intellectual and cultural life, but they gradually disappeared from the 7th century on. Those curiales had been chiefly responsible for cultivating and preserving classical learning, everything from Homeric epics to Athenian stage tragedies and the works of the great philosophers. But the narrowing provincial character of the cities resulted in a narrowing of urban education as well. Primary schooling remained available in most cities, but beyond this level the only education consistently available was religious—devotional writings, hagiographies (or lives of the saints), ecclesiastical chronicles, and the like. In other words, what the provinces gained in piety they lost in general intellectual sophistication. High culture throve only in the capital.

The Persians unleashed a new campaign into the Holy Land in 612 and two years later took Jerusalem. A rebellion against the Persians by the city's Christian inhabitants led to a brutal crackdown. For three days the Persian

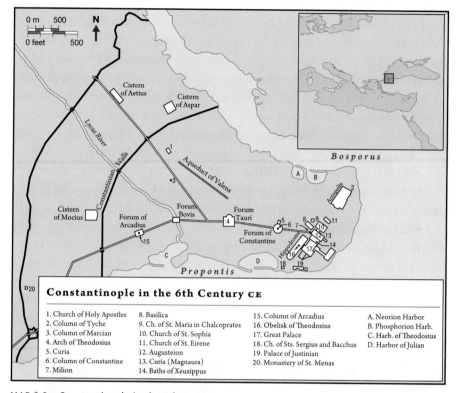

MAP 8.3   **Constantinople in the 6th Century CE**

soldiers smashed Christian shops, homes, and churches until hardly a single Christian building was left standing by 614. A late Byzantine chronicler named Theophanes described it:

> In this year, the Persians conquered all of Jordan and Palestine, including the Holy City, and with the help of the Jews they killed a multitude of Christians—some say as many as ninety thousand of them. The Jews [from the countryside], for their part, purchased many of the surviving Christians, whom the Persians were leading away as slaves, and put them to death too. The Persians moreover captured and led away not only the Patriarch of Jerusalem, Zechariah, and many prisoners, but also the most precious and life-giving Cross.

Theophanes' account is not entirely reliable in its specifics, but it seems clear that a bloodbath occurred, and it was a harbinger of things to come. From the 7th century onward, a new tone of open hostility toward non-Christians entered much Christian writing, and military conflicts in the east took on qualities of religious revenge seeking. Up to this time, Christians generally had shown much more hostility to other Christians—the old problem of the many christianities—than they had shown to non-Christians. The 7th century marks a dark turning point in Christian relations with the world. The Byzantines, reformed and re-energized, launched a counteroffensive in 622. Heraclius chose a symbolic spot for his attack: he and the army set sail from Constantinople, sailed around Asia Minor, and landed at the Bay of Issus—the exact location from which Alexander the Great had launched his conquest of the ancient Persian Empire. From there, like Alexander, Heraclius scored victory after victory until he had regained virtually all of Syria, Jordan, and Palestine.

In that same year of 622, far to the south, a charismatic and ambitious figure led his small sect of persecuted followers from the city of Mecca, deep in the Arabian Peninsula, to the city of Medina, where they received a friendlier welcome. This journey came to be commemorated by those followers as the *Hijrah* ("journey," literally, but "exodus" symbolically) and the dawn of a new age. They carried with them a sense of divine mission—to bring their new faith, Islam, to all the Arab peoples. Their leader was Muhammad, the Prophet of Allah (570–632).

Hagia Sophia   Three views of the Hagia Sophia, constructed during the reign of Justinian (527–541) in Constantinople: external view (the minarets were added under the Ottomans, who converted the church into a mosque); two internal views that give a sense of the massive interior and its brilliant play with sunlight.

"THE AGE OF IGNORANCE"

The Arabs had inhabited the peninsula that bears their name for many centuries. It is a forbidding place, roughly one million square miles (2.6 million square kilometers), consisting of an arid central plateau that slopes from west to east and is surrounded by several deserts. Most notable are the rocky Nefud (or Syrian) Desert in the north and the Great Arabian Desert (Arabic *Rub' al-Khali*, or "Empty Quarter"), which alone makes up a quarter of the entire peninsula.[2] Two mountain ranges exist, one running parallel to the Red Sea coast on the southwest and the other stretching along the peninsula's southeastern coast, the site of today's country of Oman. Some water is available: several stretches of marshland dot the Red Sea coastline, and large aquifers run beneath much of the peninsula, but usually at depths too great to reach. Where the levels of sand and rock are not too extreme, some natural oases and wadis—seasonal riverbeds—occur, and it is possible to dig wells (see Map 8.4).

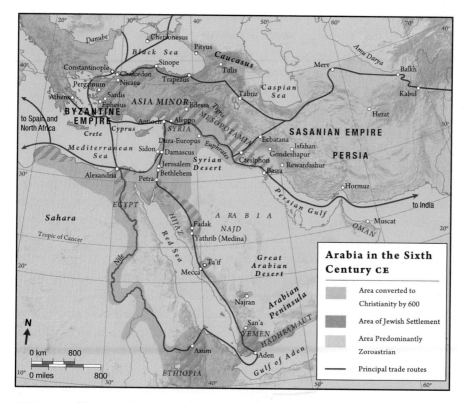

MAP 8.4   Arabia in the 6th Century CE

---

[2]   The sands of the Great Arabian Desert reach depths, in spots, of more than one thousand feet (three hundred meters). Daytime temperatures, moreover, can reach 130°F (55°C) in the summer.

But the essential geographical fact of premodern Arabia is that only 1 percent of the land could support agriculture and permanent human settlement. Division of the Arab peoples is thus a natural consequence of geography. The highland plateau accommodates grazing of sheep and goats and is the traditional home of the nomadic Bedouin tribes; the fertile southwestern coastal zone is the abode of the Yemeni Arabs. Between those extremes, pre-Islamic tradition claimed that most of the peninsula's people are descended from two legendary ancestors: Qahtan and Adnan. Qahtan, according to the tradition, was the progenitor of the "pure Arab" people (al-Arab al-aribah) in the southern part of the peninsula, while Adnan fathered the "Arabized Arabs" (al-Arab al-musta'ribah) of the north. By the start of Islam in the 7th century, Qahtan and Adnan were reinterpreted as the offspring of Ishmael, the son of the Biblical patriarch Abram/Abraham through his concubine Hagar.

Whatever their origins, many Arab tribes were united by their language, of which each group possessed its own distinct dialect. Arabic is a Semitic language, related to the tongues of the ancient Akkadians, Assyrians, Babylonians, and Hebrews; and indeed the Arabian Peninsula is thought by many to be the point of origin of all the Semitic peoples. Clan and tribal identities ran deep, and everything from the dialect one spoke to the head-dress one wore and to the lengthy chains of patronyms that comprised one's name marked one as the member of a particular group, with particular social standing.[3]

Such markers mattered, for the peoples of Arabia lived by trade, and long-established traditions existed that gave each group specific rights and privileges. Distributors rather than producers, the Arabs produced few commercial goods that interested the non-Arab world, but made their living largely by bringing luxury goods from China, India, and sub-Saharan Africa into the eastern Mediterranean. The silk route across Asia carried silks, spices, and perfumes overland from China, through India and Persia, and into Byzantium, and provided opportunity for the northern Bedouin tribes; but other routes existed as well. The Yemenite tribes of the southern peninsula brought goods by ship out of India, then up the Persian Gulf, where they were handed off to the tribes of the Najd plateau. Sabaean tribes along the Red Sea coastline carried gold and gemstones from Ethiopia northward to Syria and Palestine. The Arabs, acculturated to the harshness of the terrain and mounted on their camels, made ideal long-distance carriers. Their caravans stretched across the endless miles linking east and west, north and south.

Arab historians termed the period before the advent of Islam the "Age of Ignorance" or "Age of Barbarism" (al-Jahiliyya). The simple absence of Islam

---

[3]   The dialects spoken by many of the southern-most tribes have more elements in common with the Semitic languages in Ethiopia than with the Arabic dialects found elsewhere throughout the peninsula.

suffices to merit the name. Indeed, some writers used the term to embrace all of human history, but most Arabs defined **al-Jahiliyya** more precisely as the period from the death of Jesus to the birth of Muhammad in the year 570 CE. Many of those intervening years were in fact particularly chaotic. Clashes arose between the Roman and Persian Empires, between the Byzantines and the Persians, and between Christian sects, all to the north, and to the south between the Yemenites of Arabia and the Abyssinians of Ethiopia. These struggles caused occasional but severe disruptions of the Arab trading networks, disruptions that often boiled over into violence between tribes and clans.

Muhammad belonged to the Hashim clan within the Quraysh tribe, a group that had long been associated with administering the great pagan shrine in the commercial city of Mecca. This shrine, called the **Ka'ba**, was a kind of Arab pantheon, an ecumenical temple to all the pagan deities of all the Arab peoples. Pilgrims from all over the peninsula came to Mecca to pray at the shrine and

An Oasis in the Desert   This is the Khaybar oasis north of Medina. Khaybar was home to the largest Jewish community in Arabia. After the Prophet Muhammad led his community on the Hijrah from Mecca to Medina, in 622, he attempted to convert the Jews there, many of whom were members of a tribe known as the Banu Nadir. Jewish resistance to conversion led to tense relations with the Muslims, who were in possession of an army once Muhammad became the governor of the city. In 625 the Banu Nadir were expelled from Medina and made their way north to Khaybar. In 628 Muhammad attacked Khaybar and killed most of the Jewish population. The episode lives on in both Jewish and Islamic life. Palestinians today often shout "Khaybar! Khaybar!" when demonstrating against the Israelis. A rocket popular with Hezbollah terrorists has been dubbed Khaybar II.

present offerings to the gods. These pilgrims, together with the merchants who frequented the city, made Mecca a particularly vibrant city with more cross-cultural contact than most Arab sites. A sizeable Jewish community existed too, although there is no evidence of any meaningful Christian presence until the early 6th century. Abyssinian warlords in Ethiopia, who had recently converted to Christianity, then crossed the Red Sea and seized parts of the southern Arabian coast.

Such back-and-forth attacks were commonplace in ancient times, with Arab chieftains often in control of coastal Ethiopia and Ethiopian chieftains often in control of coastal Arabia. In the 6th century, however, with Byzantium and Persia at war to the north and with African tribesmen gaining power in the south, an urge to promote pan-Arab cohesion took root and fostered a militaristic streak in Arab society that regarded the entire non-Arab world as a threat to its existence. The problem was: What could unite so disparate a sprawl of tribes and clans? The answer came in the form of a divine mission and the identification of the Arabs as a new Chosen People.

THE ISLAMIC REVELATION

This was the context in which the Prophet Muhammad received his revelations and in which his followers received his teachings. Muhammad had been born into poverty and began his rise in the world when he went to work for a wealthy widow named Khadija and began to handle her commercial interests. After several years, he and Khadija married. Muhammad's trading activities brought him out of Arabia and as far north as Syria, long solitary journeys that suited his meditative temperament. At some point Muhammad made contact with Judaism and Christianity, although we do not know the specifics of what he learned or how.

In the year 610, at the age of forty, Muhammad received the first of a series of dazzling visions that continued for the rest of his life. They summoned him to a unique role—as the final prophet of the One True God—and they called upon the Arab people to unite and bring God's message, as delivered through Muhammad, to all the nations on earth. This message was the **Qur'an**, a divine text inscribed on a golden tablet in heaven by God Himself. In his mystical transports, Muhammad saw the heavenly text and read it aloud to his followers. (In Arabic, the book's title means "recital.")

The core message of the Qur'an is that all religions are false except for belief in the One True God, called Allah in Arabic, who created all things and has ennobled human life with a divine purpose, which is to serve and worship him through a regimen of daily prayers and adherence to his laws. To those who do so, the merciful and compassionate Allah will grant the reward of eternal bliss in a paradisiacal garden; the remainder of sinful mankind, by Allah's stern but just judgment, will enter eternal torment in a fiery hell.

> Praise be to Allah, Who hath sent His Servant the Book, and hath allowed therein no crookedness. (He hath made it) straight (and clear) in order that He may warn (the godless) of a terrible punishment from Him, and that He may give glad tidings to the believers who work righteous deeds, that they shall have a goodly reward, wherein they shall remain for ever; further that He may warn those (also) who say, "Allah hath begotten a son": No knowledge have they of such a thing, nor had their fathers. It is a grievous thing that issues from their mouths as a saying. What they say is nothing but falsehood! *(Qur'an 18.1–5)*

The Qur'an identifies Christians and Jews as the "People of the Book," who deserve a measure of respect but who also have a special obligation to recognize the completion of their revelational history in Allah's Prophet. Pagan polytheisms, however, deserve little patience:

> Those who disbelieve, among the People of the Book and among the polytheists, were not going to depart (from their ways) until there should come to them clear evidence—the Messenger from Allah, rehearsing scriptures kept pure and holy: wherein are books right and straight. Nor did the People of the Book make schisms, until after there came to them clear evidence. And they have been commanded no more than this: to worship Allah, offering Him sincere devotion, being true (in faith); to establish regular prayers; and to give zakat [a special tax for charity]; and that is the religion right and straight. Those who disbelieve, among the People of the Book and among the polytheists, will be in hell-fire, to dwell therein (for aye). They are the worst of creatures. Those who have faith and do righteous deeds—they are the best of creatures. Their reward is with Allah: Gardens of Eternity, beneath which rivers flow; they will dwell therein for ever; Allah well pleased with them, and they with Him: All this for such as fear their Lord and Cherisher. *(Qur'an 98.1–8)*

Mankind's chief responsibility is therefore submission (*islam* in Arabic) to Allah's absolute authority—and that duty gave its name to the religion, **Islam**. Among the virtues that Allah commands are modesty, charity, and sobriety. Moreover, He requires tolerance of Judaism and Christianity, Islam's revelational predecessors, but directs his faithful to eradicate stiff-necked pagans who reject Islam.

Muhammad preached to the crowds in Mecca soon after his first revelation, and as the revelations continued his message became more refined. He came to describe Islam as the final and perfect phase of the relationship established by God in his covenant with the patriarch Abram/Abraham. The Arabs themselves, he preached, are descended from Abraham's liaison with his concubine Hagar, which produced their son, Ismail. Islam thus stands in an evolutionary relationship with Judaism and Christianity. Jesus, the Qur'an proclaimed, was in the line of prophets that began with Moses. The role of the prophets was to elaborate a better understanding of God's desires, and as the Jews continued to disobey and misunderstand, God continued to send prophets—including Jesus. The Christians, though, had also failed—in failing to live up to what God expected of them and in their shocking mistake of thinking Jesus was actually God. All this had inspired Allah to make one last, full, and perfect revelation through Muhammad and the revealing of the Qur'an.

FROM PREACHER TO CONQUEROR

Muhammad preached that Allah had chosen the Arab people to bring this message to the world, and that this mission was therefore intended to bring an end to tribal strife. The people of Mecca, and especially the Quraysh leaders who owed their status to their role in Arab paganism, did not take kindly to Muhammad's call to end the pagan cults. In 622, after twelve years of tense conflict, the Meccans drove him and his small company of believers from the city.[4] Muhammad then journeyed northward to Medina. This journey (the Hijrah) is commemorated by Muslims as the beginning of Islam's expansion and marks year one of the Islamic calendar. Medina, a commercial and cultic rival of Mecca, proved more receptive to Muhammad's teaching, and within two years Muhammad was in fact in command of the city.

Success in Medina inaugurated a discernible tonal shift in the spreading of the Islamic message, since from 624 on the Prophet was in possession of an army. The Qur'anic passages revealed in Medina have a more activist and determined tone than the earlier Meccan revelations, and later Islamic texts depict the Prophet from this point on as a conqueror as much as a preacher. Ibn Ishaq (704–768), Muhammad's first biographer, proudly relates how the Prophet, after defeating the Jewish community at Medina, which had allegedly plotted against

---

4   The ninth surah (chapter) of the Qur'an expresses Allah's anger at the pagan leaders in Mecca who had sometimes befriended the Prophet and turned against him, as the local power struggle worked itself out.

him, beheaded between seven hundred and nine hundred of the Jewish leaders. Buoyed by his success, Muhammad then began a series of rapid military ventures to defeat the Meccans and seize control of the peninsula. In 629, after five years of fighting, Muhammad was victorious. Once both Mecca and Medina were in his hands, Muhammad was able to bring most of the Arabian Peninsula under his command before his death in 632. Given the sparse settlement of Arabia, the strategic key was to gain control of the handful of trade routes connecting the peninsula with the outer world. Muhammad understood this from his commercial travels. Once his Muslim forces were in a position to cut off the supply routes, the rest of the Arab tribes had no alternative but to surrender.

Before he died, Muhammad purified the Ka'ba of its pagan trappings and rededicated it to Allah with a newly revealed truth: the large Black Stone encased within the shrine had been sent to earth from heaven in order to show Adam and Eve where to build their first altar. Displaced by the Great Flood described in the Hebrew Bible, the long-forgotten stone was found by Abraham and his son Ishmael, who identified it and built a temple to house it, the very first temple to Allah. The Ka'ba is that temple—and although what stands there now is a later, rebuilt temple, it still occupies the original site established by Abraham. It is thus the holiest site on earth to Muslims, who pray five times daily while kneeling in

Completing the Hajj   Pilgrimage (*hajj*) to Mecca is an obligation of every able-bodied Muslim. The endpoint of the pilgrimage is the sacred Ka'ba, the holiest site in Islam. Pilgrims perform a circular march (*tawaf* in Arabic) around the temple. Those who cannot enter the precinct may perform the tawaf on the roof.

the direction of it. Muslims who make the required ritual pilgrimage (hajj) to Mecca walk in procession seven times around the Ka'ba. Those lucky enough to get next to the "House of Allah" (*Bayt Allah*, as it is known) will kiss the stone, which has the wondrous ability to absorb the believer's sins and render him pure.[5] The mosques built for communal worship by Muslims contain an inset wall notch that points in the direction of the Ka'ba and provides the visual focal point for group prayers.

From the Prophet's death in 632, Muslim leaders also kept an eye on the international scene, to prepare for the military expansion of Islam; Muhammad himself had clearly intended to advance northward into Palestine and Syria and was making plans to do so when he caught a sudden fever and died. The long wars between Byzantium and Persia had exhausted both empires, and the time was right for the Arab advance. Muhammad had died without naming a successor, however. Most of the leading figures, known as the "Companions of the Prophet," threw their support around Muhammad's father-in-law Abu Bakr, who took the title of **caliph** (*khalifah al-rasul Allah*, meaning "deputy of the Prophet of God").

Abu Bakr (r. 632–634) spent two years completing the conquest of Arabia and subduing Muslim groups who had rejected his succession. Upon his death, the Companions chose Umar (r. 634–644), an early convert, to succeed Abu Bakr. Umar directed his army northward, and within two years the Arabs had conquered Jerusalem, Antioch, and Damascus. Only one year later, in 637, Muslim forces took the Persian capital of Ctesiphon. According to Persian sources, the Arab soldiers were dazzled by the opulence of the capital and went on a looting spree. Taking care to send the required one-fifth of the booty to caliph Umar, back in Medina, the army still netted enough for each soldier (reputedly eighteen thousand of them) to receive twelve thousand gold coins. Moreover, forty thousand Persian nobles were brought back to Medina as slaves.

The rest of the Persian Empire surrendered to the Muslims by 651. Egypt fell to the Arabs in 646—a crucial development that deprived Byzantium of a most important food source. It also triggered a quantum leap for the Muslims in developing as a naval power: when the Muslims took Alexandria, Egypt's major port, two-thirds of the Byzantine imperial fleet happened to be tied up in the harbor. For a desert-dwelling people, the Arabs took to the sea very quickly; this is why.

By 677 Muslim forces had reached the walls of Constantinople itself.[6] By 711 the Arabs had extended their conquests all along the coast of North Africa, had

---

[5]   According to Qur'anic tradition, the stone was originally a brilliant white color but has absorbed so many sins over the centuries that it has turned black.

[6]   The Byzantines drove the invaders off by using a weapon called Greek fire—a naphtha-based compound that burst into flame when it came in contact with water.

Dome of the Rock   Exterior view of the Dome of the Rock mosque in Jerusalem. Completed in 691, the mosque is built upon the site, according to tradition, from which the Prophet pushed off from Earth during his mystical Night Journey through the heavens. Apart from this tradition—which for Muslim faithful has Qur'anic authority behind it—there is no evidence that Muhammad ever visited Jerusalem.

taken Sicily and the Balearic Islands, and had crossed the Strait of Gibraltar and seized Visigothic Spain. The Western world had never seen a military juggernaut like this: in 622 Muhammad and his small group of followers had been forced from their home in Mecca, yet within a hundred years those followers had conquered an empire that stretched from Spain to India, an area twice the size of that conquered by Alexander the Great (see Map 8.5).

> The Western world had never seen a military juggernaut like this: in 622 Muhammad and his small group of followers had been forced from their home in Mecca, yet within a hundred years those followers had conquered an empire that stretched from Spain to India, an area twice the size of that conquered by Alexander the Great.

COMPULSION OR CONVERSION?

With their stunning victory over a much-weakened Persia and with their containment of a much-weakened Byzantium, there was no power on the scene capable of halting or even slowing the Arab advance. Moreover,

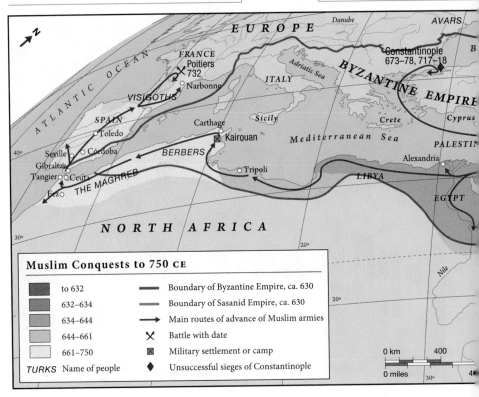

MAP 8.5   Muslim Conquests to 750 CE

many people welcomed the Muslims for the relief they brought from the ever-increasing taxes levied upon them by the Greeks and Persians to finance their wars with one another. Muslim attitudes to their new subjects took some time to work out. The fraternal and quasi-evolutionary relationship between Judaism, Christianity, and Islam prevented the Muslims from persecuting Jews and Christians. The Qur'an itself insists that "there is no compulsion in religion"—meaning that Jews and Christians cannot be forced to accept Islam—since Allah's desire is for genuine conversion, not a terrified acceptance of new faith to avoid execution. Caliph Umar, in return for the surrender of the inhabitants of Jerusalem, guaranteed the religious freedom of the Jews and Christians residing there and laid out the terms by which the communities would live. This text, known widely as the Pact of Umar, formed the model for the Muslim legal doctrine of the **dhimmi**, the "protected minorities" living under Islamic authority. The Jews and Christians, as People of the Book, deserved such treatment, in the hope that respectful handling by their Muslim rulers would help them to see the superiority of Islam and thereby win their conversion.

The Persians fared less well. Though regarded by some early Muslim leaders as another People of the Book and therefore deserving of legal protection,

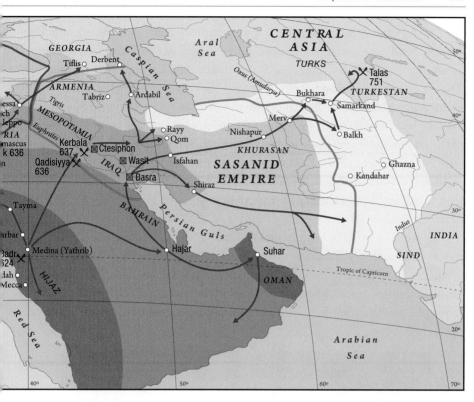

the Zoroastrian Persians were widely regarded as mere pagans. And most of the Arab soldiers and clerics, citing Qur'anic authority, claimed the right to compel the conversion of pagans, to destroy their temples and idolatrous art, and to set fire to their sacred writings after a four-month grace period:

> But when the forbidden months are past, then fight and slay the pagans wherever ye find them, and seize them, beleaguer them, and lie in wait for them in every stratagem (of war): but if they repent and establish regular prayers and pay zakat, then open the way for them, for Allah is Oft-Forgiving, Most Merciful. *(Qur'an 9.5)*

Arab chronicles assert that the victorious Muslims never faltered in observing the dhimmi status of law-abiding Persians; Persian sources, on the other hand, document widespread atrocities at the local level. Surviving legal records contain no reference to a single Muslim being prosecuted for violating the rights of a Zoroastrian. That may indeed mean that no such violations took place, but it is more likely that such violations were never prosecuted.

By the early 8th century the Islamic empire was an unqualified military success, but it consisted of a microscopically thin grid of ethnically Arab Muslims governing an overwhelmingly non-Arab and non-Muslim population. From the Atlantic coasts of Spain and Morocco to the Indus River valley in India, the Arabs ruled a polyglot mix of Romano-Hibernians, Visigoths, Berbers, Egyptians, Syrians, Jews, and Persians (to name only the most prominent groups). In much of the empire the Arabs made up less than 1 percent of the population. Subjects were encouraged to convert to Islam through positive appeals and by imposing restrictions on non-Muslim activities. The most important restriction, rigorously monitored, was a complete ban on any public expression of a non-Islamic faith or of any criticism of Islam.

Conversion brought with it membership in the governing society, immunity from most non-zakat taxes, military and political preferment, and economic privileges, in addition to the innate spiritual blessings of the faith. Non-Muslims possessing dhimmi status had to pay a heavy poll tax (*jizya*). They were also forbidden to practice their faith or discuss it in public, could not testify against a

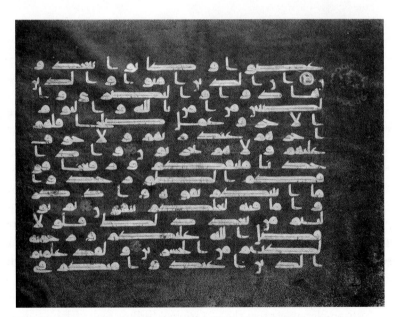

An Early Qur'an   The Qur'an is, to all Muslims, the Holy Book of God, written by him in heaven on tablets of gold. The text came to Earth by means of the Prophet's revelations. God allowed Muhammad to see the holy text and recite passages aloud to his followers. These passages were saved and memorized by the community, and after the Prophet's death in 632 they were compiled and transcribed. But there is no human agency in the production of the text itself, which makes the Qur'an unique among the scriptures of the three Greater Western monotheisms. Pictured here is a fragment from an early North African Qur'an, written in Kufic script.

Muslim in a court of law, and had to wear special items of clothing that identified their inferior status—usually a wide belt called a *zunnar*. Although Muslims could take dhimmi-status wives, their offspring were automatically regarded as Muslim. Islamic law forbade dhimmis to construct new houses of worship for themselves, and strict jurists denied them the right to fix older houses falling into disrepair, since such construction work would effectively constitute a public expression of their faith. As a result churches, synagogues, and Zoroastrian temples everywhere decayed until they were no longer safe for use, and the communities that had used them effectively ceased to worship as communities.

Given this combination of positive enticements to convert and restrictive discouragements to continue in their own faith, the subjects of the Arab empire gradually began to embrace Islam. Nevertheless, the process was slow, and it was not until the 10th century that Islam became the majority religion in the empire, a point at which Muslim popular attitudes toward their dhimmi neighbors changed dramatically for the worse.

SUNNIS AND SHI'A

Caliph Umar died in 644, stabbed by a Persian slave who resented the Arab take-over. When the Muslim leaders met to select the next caliph, two main contenders vied for the position: Uthman ibn Affar, an early convert from among the Quraysh tribe, and Ali ibn Abi Talib, the Prophet Muhammad's nephew and son-in-law (Ali had married Muhammad's daughter Fatima). Most of the community preferred Uthman, who subsequently became the third caliph (r. 644–656). The disgruntled Ali did not have to wait long for his turn, however, since Uthman was murdered by a party of Egyptian rebels who saw no reason why Egypt's acceptance of the Islamic faith had to entail the country's political subjection to the culturally inferior Arabs.

Ali was elected to succeed Uthman, becoming the fourth caliph (r. 656–661), and he quickly established his capital at the fortified eastern city of Kufa, on the banks of the Euphrates River about one hundred miles south of Baghdad. The move disappointed many Arab leaders, who felt it as an insult to their homeland and therefore transferred their allegiance to a kinsman of the slain Uthman, a figure named Mu'awiya who had served as the provincial governor of Syria and resided in Damascus, a heavily Arabized city. Tensions between Mu'awiya and Ali rose with each passing year and could well have broken out into full-scale civil war, except that Ali was murdered in Kufa in the year 661 by a local rebel.

This series of elections, rebellions, and murders triggered the fundamental schism of the Muslim world into the Sunnis and Shi'a. (In Arabic *Shi'a* is the plural noun, *Shi'i* is the plural adjective.) The rift is both political and religious. **Sunni** Muslims regarded selection by the community as the sole legitimate means to leadership of the Islamic world. The **Shi'a**, on the other hand, insisted that political and religious legitimacy could pass only to members of the Prophet's hereditary line. For them, Ali and his descendants via Fatima were thus forever the true successors to Muhammad. The Sunnis take their name from the *sunan* ("principles" in Arabic), the written and oral legacy of the Prophet's teachings and personal actions. The Shi'a (whose name derives from *shi'at Ali*, "the party of Ali") stress the divine appointment of the **imams**, the heavenly appointed heirs of Muhammad, whose words and judgments they regard as infallible. The Shi'a regard Ali as the first imam and the first true caliph, and consequently they reject most of the religious customs established under caliphs Abu Bakr, Umar, and Uthman.[7]

The antagonism between Sunnis and Shi'a grew sharper as their traditions developed. The Shi'a comprised roughly a tenth of the Islamic world, and while Shi'i dynasties rose to power in Egypt and parts of North Africa, Persia quickly became and remained the heartland of Shi'ism.

CLASSICAL TRADITIONS AND WESTERN EXPANSION

The Arabs' conquests exposed them to the Greater West's centuries-long intellectual, scientific, and artistic traditions, but they disdained any aspect of Zoroastrian learning and resented the Persians' embrace of Shi'ism. This made the Arabs much more open to the Greco-Roman and Judeo-Christian intellectual legacy. But the Arabs were new to literacy and could not access the texts available to them. Starting in the 8th century, groups of Syrian Christians—mostly scholar-monks—began to translate the writings of the ancient Greeks and Romans into Arabic for the benefit of their new rulers. Their activity was prodigious: within two or three generations the whole corpus of Western thought lay available for Arab scholars to read. It included the mathematical and geometrical works of Euclid and Archimedes, the medical knowledge of Hippocrates and Galen, the historical texts of Herodotus and Thucydides, the books of the Hebrew Bible and the New Testament, and works of geography, astronomy, poetry, and law. Roman histories, legal texts, Stoic meditations, and technical treatises were available too. The leading Muslim scholars absorbed most of this knowledge eagerly, finding in it much that was of immediate practical value.

---

[7]   Several denominations of Shi'ism developed in the early centuries, differing from one another primarily in the individuals each recognized as a true imam.

As a rule, any text or genre of inquiry that could be reconciled with Islamic doctrine received a warm welcome. It made the Muslim world for several centuries considerably more knowledgeable about the classical tradition than Latin Europe. But the Greek philosophical tradition was another matter. Under the first caliphs, and then under the Umayyad dynasty, which ruled the empire from 661 to 750, however, the study of Greek philosophy was regarded as dangerous and possibly blasphemous. Why would anyone look to pagans like Plato and Aristotle for answers to questions about the purpose of human life, the nature of truth, the definition of justice, or the understanding of morality? After all, all those answers were available in the Qur'an and the sunnah.

> Starting in the 8th century, groups of Syrian Christians—mostly scholar-monks—began to translate the writings of the ancient Greeks and Romans into Arabic for the benefit of their new rulers. Their activity was prodigious: within two or three generations the whole corpus of Western thought lay available for Arab scholars to read.

Numerous Islamic philosophers did indeed read Greek philosophy (especially Aristotle). Al-Kindi (d. 870), al-Farabi (d. 951), Ibn Sina (d. 1037), al-Ghazali (d. 1111), and Ibn Rushd (d. 1198) all wrote brilliant commentaries upon it. But in the medieval era most of these figures were despised by other Muslims and had to live in nearly perpetual exile, traveling from city to city and court to court, offering their skills in medicine to Arab nobles in return for temporary safe haven. To the great bulk of Islamic society, philosophy was not necessarily evil but merely irrelevant, a brain-churning waste of time when one could be pondering the Qur'an and the judgments of Islamic legal scholars. Greek tragedy also fell on deaf ears among the Muslims, for the idea of an inexorable fate other than the determination of the all-knowing Allah was anathema to them. Consequently, the great plays were neglected absolutely—never performed, never recopied, never commented upon.

The Umayyad dynasty moved the empire's capital from Mecca to Damascus, a more central location for overseeing such a vast empire and for pursuing the ultimate goal of conquering Constantinople. The dynasty was not at all popular and even today is widely regarded with disdain by Muslim scholars. Several reasons existed for their lack of popular support. First, the dynasty's clear bias to promote ethnically Arab military and civil officers, preferably from prominent old Arab families, earned the ire of groups newly converted to Islam. The Muslim principle of the "brotherhood of all believers" seemed to get mere lip service in the actual empire. Second, the Umayyads all too quickly assumed the attitude of a divinely appointed monarchical family, whose personal wishes were all too often presented as Allah's will. Despite the military victories of the era and their construction of important edifices like the Dome of the Rock mosque in

Jerusalem or the Great Mosque in Damascus, the Umayyads were widely viewed as self-aggrandizers who turned the cause of **jihad** to personal gain.

Expansion in the west culminated in 711 with the conquest of Spain. A Muslim army crossed the Pyrenees in 732 with an eye to winning Gaul, but was repulsed by an upstart Frankish warlord named Charles Martel. The Muslims retreated behind the Pyrenees and devoted their energies to furthering the spread of Islam among its subjects. Western Europe remained a confusing sprawl of Germanic warlords and shaky kingdoms, illiterate and only nominally Christian, distrustful of their aloof Byzantine cousins. It was also the poorest place on earth—surrounded, dwarfed, and threatened by an aggressive, energetic, and determined Islamic empire larger than anything they had ever heard of.

BARBARIAN KINGS AND SCHOLAR-MONKS

Medieval historians call the period in western Europe from the 4th to the 8th centuries the **Dark Ages**; to ancient historians it is **Late Antiquity**. Both groups are right. Or perhaps it is better to say that neither group is altogether wrong. For much of the period from 300 to 800 CE western Europe was a god-awful bloody mess of a place, filled to the rafters with poverty, famine and disease, nearly constant warfare, almost universal illiteracy, and a material standard of living that is horrifying to consider. And yet many of the institutional practices and cultural values of the earlier age were still alive, if in beleaguered and benighted form.

After the Western Roman Empire collapsed, its place was taken by a wild parade of warlord semi-states ruled by thuggish clan leaders. Some of these warlords offered a modicum of administration and security. Most, though, dedicated themselves to pillaging whatever food and material wealth they could find—or to retributive attacks on rivals who had already stolen what they themselves had been plotting at.

A 6th-century monk in Celtic England named Gildas described village life in the aftermath of Saxon raids this way:

> Sadly, the streets of our villages are filled with the ruins of once-high towers that have been pulled to the ground, with stones pried from fences or left over from the smashing of sacred altars, with dismembered pieces of human bodies that are so covered with lurid clots of blood that they look as though the people had been run through a press, and whose only chance for any kind of burial is to rot in the ruins of collapsed homes; all the rest will simply fill the stomachs of

ravenous beasts and birds. . . . To this very day not one of our villages is what it used to be. Instead, all lie desolate, routed, and ruined. *(On the Destruction of England, ch. 24, 26)*

Most of the people of western Europe, at least 90 percent of them, were re-duced to subsistence farming. Probably one-half of all children born died before reaching the age of five, and one-half of all females who made it to marriageable age died before reaching the age of twenty-five, usually in child-birth. Tens of thousands of homeless refugees, and perhaps even more, roamed through the countryside at any given time, either having been driven from their homes by new waves of settlers, in flight from marauders, or in search of new territories where they could start afresh without rivals on the land. Meanwhile, the Medi-terranean cities contracted into tiny hamlets—sometimes a mere 10 percent of their former populations—and into corners of the settled urban area, leaving the emptied quarters to decay into ghost towns. Manufacture and trade beyond the immediate region became all but extinct. The sole exception was the thriving commerce in slaves (see Figure 8.1).

Despite the miseries of the time, important aspects of Roman antiquity sur-vived. Roman law remained in effect—inconsistently, to be sure, but not alto-gether forgotten. The Latin language remained the dominant tongue in the west, and the barbarian kings did what they could to emulate and continue those el-ements of Roman tradition that they found useful. Intellectual life in the west was limited to the Christian monasteries that dotted the landscape from the 4th century on, but displayed real zest and ingenuity. Thus while it was an age of poverty and chaos, it was a creative chaos. Ultimately it saw the amalgamation of the Roman, Germanic, and Christian cultures into the fascinating hybrid called **medieval** society.

One of the first chroniclers of the medieval era, Bishop Gregory of Tours (538–594), described the contemporary atmosphere memorably in the opening prologue to his *History of the Franks*:

A great number of things keep happening—some good, some bad. The people of the various petty princedoms keep quarreling with each other in the fiercest way imaginable, while our rulers' tempers keep bursting into violence. Our churches are assailed by heretics, then retaken in force by our Catholics; and whereas Christian faith burns hot in the hearts of many, it is no more than lukewarm in those of others. Church buildings are pillaged by faithless pagans as soon as they are gifted by faithful Christians. But no one has yet emerged who is a sufficiently skilled writer that he can record these events in a

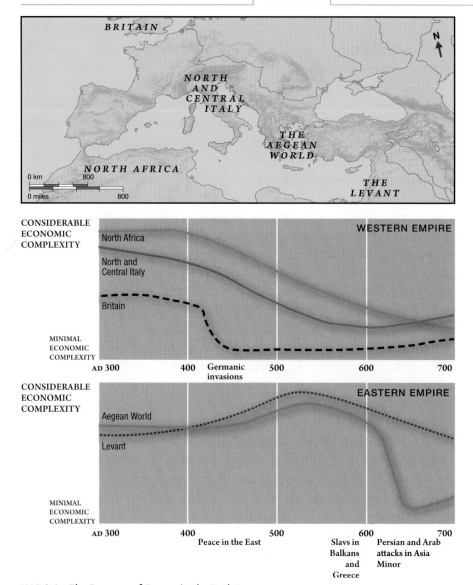

MAP 8.6   The Economy of Europe in the Dark Ages
* Adapted from Ward-Perkins, Bryan. *The Fall of Rome* (2006).

straightforward way, whether in prose or in verse. In fact, throughout the towns of Gaul the knowledge of writing has declined to such an extent that it has virtually disappeared.... [And so] I have undertaken this present work in an effort to preserve the memory of the dead and bring them to the attention of those yet to come; but my style lacks all polish, and I have had to devote too much of my attention to the clashes between the good and the wicked.

This period from the 4th to 8th centuries was one of the longest and most dire and challenging eras in Western history. Our sources for it are few—as books seldom get written in active war zones—but enough evidence survives to provide a basic outline of what occurred. The picture is not pretty.

DIVIDED ESTATES AND KINGDOMS

The Germanic peoples who streamed into western Europe confronted innumerable challenges, not the least of which was the terrain. Most of the European continent north of the Mediterranean coastline consisted of dense forest. Newcomers faced bitter resistance from the people who had already settled open areas, and so were forced to keep moving or to clear their own lands and begin farming from nothing. Moreover, various cultural traditions that had served the Germans well in the east served them ill in the more sedentary west.

One example is the early nomadic custom of dividing a man's estate equally between his surviving sons. This practice had provided for each new generation, because herds of animals could replenish their own numbers—but a western farm could not survive such division quite so easily. By the end of the second generation, if not earlier, the distributed lands were not sufficient to support a family. The most promising options, in such a case, were either to expand one's holding by clearing more forest at the perimeter (which worked in some cases, but in others seemed only to defer the problem) or to abandon the land altogether in search of new territory elsewhere. That move, however, exposed them to more hostilities, whether from previously settled peoples, other migrating bands, or warrior thugs. And once they found new places to settle, they faced the difficulty of clearing forests, digging wells, building homes, and beginning to farm, with only the tools they had managed to bring with them.[8] Under such conditions, most of continental Europe remained stubbornly mired in poverty until the 9th century.

The same problem of subdivision hobbled any sort of political development after 476: a warrior might turn himself into a king by forcing his will upon terrorized farmers, but he usually ended his life by dividing his kingdom among his heirs. One example will suffice. A brutal warlord named Clovis, a member of the Germanic group known as the Franks, carved out a sizeable kingdom for himself around the year 500 and made himself, briefly, the most powerful ruler in western Europe (see Map 8.6). When he died in 511 his realm was parceled out to each of his four sons: Theuderic, Chlodomer, Childebert, and Lothar. Theuderic,

---

[8]   Until the 9th century, most northern farmers still relied on wooden implements, such as wooden shovels, wooden plow blades, and wooden pitchforks.

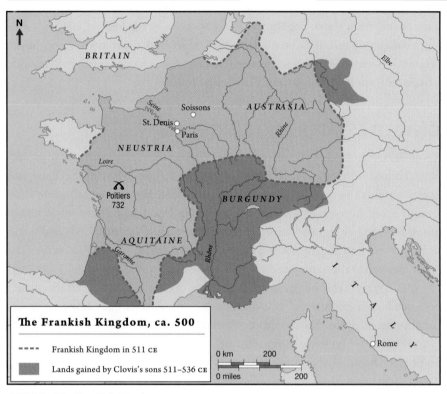

MAP 8.7   The Frankish Kingdom, ca. 500

however, went on to have two sons of his own; Chlodomer had three. And while Childebert had only daughters (who could not inherit, according to Frankish custom), his younger brother Lothar made up for him by producing seven boys. In only two generations, therefore, a single kingdom had split into twelve autonomous principalities, each with its own officials, tax system, laws, courts, weights, and measures. Any chance of stable governance quickly died out in such circumstances, but there is little evidence that many of the warlords were interested in even trying to provide it.

Gregory of Tours fills the four hundred pages of his *History* with tale after tale of savagery:

> This Rauching [a Frankish warlord] was extraordinarily vain—a man filled to bursting with pride, arrogance, and impertinence. He treated his servants as though he denied they were human beings at all.... For example, whenever a servant stood before him, as was usual, with a lighted candle while Rauching ate his meals, he would force the poor fellow to bare his legs and hold the lit candle between his knees

until it burned down to a stub. He would then demand that a new candle be lit, again and again, until the servant's legs were entirely scorched. If the servant cried out or tried to run, a drawn sword quickly stopped him, and Rauching himself would convulse with laughter as he watched the man weep. *(History of the Franks 5.3)*

Gregory relates another tale about Rauching. Two of his servants fell in love and, knowing that he would forbid their union, ran to a local priest for protection. The priest negotiated on their behalf and extracted a promise from the warlord that "he would allow the couple to stay united forever." Once the pair were back at his stronghold, Rauching ordered a massive tree to be felled and its trunk split in two lengthwise, with each half hollowed out, as one would do in making a pair of canoes. Rauching then bound the servants together, encased them in the rejoined hollow tree trunk, and buried them alive in a deep trench, saying with a roaring laugh, "See? I haven't broken my promise. I haven't 'split them up'!" (5.3).

An 8th century writer, Paul the Deacon, in his *History of the Lombards*, vividly described a different kind of horror—the prevalence of rape, and the efforts some women made to avoid it:

> [Lombard women] used to put the flesh of raw chickens under the band that held up their breasts; and this, once the summer heat had spoiled and putrefied it, gave off a horribly foul odor. Thus when the Avars [another invading tribe] tried to rape them they found that they could not bear the stench—and thinking that the smell was natural to these women, they ran away, cursing loudly that all Lombard women stink.

Until a means was found to pass on undivided realms, little significant advance in government was possible. Most early Germanic kings and princes were itinerant; they traveled constantly, bringing whatever instruments of governance they had (records, copies of laws, accounts) with them. As often as not, individuals petitioning a ruler for justice had first to overcome a basic logistical problem: finding out where the king was, and then going to him.

THE BODY AS MONEY AND WOMEN AS PROPERTY

Given these difficulties, little lasting political development took place. Rule was personal, not institutional. Customs varied enormously from "kingdom" to "kingdom," from tribe to tribe, and even from clan to clan. As the Germans gradually settled the land and interacted with the old Roman populace, though, a degree of cultural assimilation occurred. Although easily 90 percent of the population remained illiterate, the old tribal customs that had been passed down orally for generations began to be written down in the 5th, 6th, and 7th centuries. These records provide our first nonliterary glimpses of Germanic values and practices.

Germanic law, such as it was, was constructed from the ground up, much like our modern system of torts. Individual conflicts were dealt with as they arose and were judged by some sort of group consensus, and each case, once settled, provided a precedent for similar cases in the future. This ad hoc construction explains the somewhat random nature of the earliest written codes; they were the result of compiled specifics, not of ideological blueprints put into action. Nevertheless, some sense of consistent values emerges from the codes. In most of the codes the issues of property, inheritance, marriage, and taxation are preeminent, which is to be expected.

The most striking feature of criminal law is the apportioning of compensatory payments for the physical injury of another, a system called **wergeld**. In these brutal times, to harm or kill another man was quite literally to threaten the existence of his entire family, which depended on his labor for food production and on his strength for physical protection. Murder or assault thus threatened the family, which all too often responded to this sort of crime by declaring a blood feud. Wergeld provided an alternative to endless vendettas. The system varied in its details from tribe to tribe, but the central idea remained the same: to compensate a victim, or his or her clan, by paying for the loss of a life, or for an injury to a vital or nonvital body part. Every part of the body was assigned a monetary value—so much for an arm, an eye, a foot, and so on, right down to the fifth toe on either foot.[9]

Germanic law regarded women not as property but as legal minors regardless of their age, under the more or less permanent guardianship of their fathers and husbands. Among the Salian Franks, for example, a group who ultimately settled in northern France in the 5th and 6th centuries, a woman who married against her father's will forfeited her rights to any family property and could be put to death by any family member. Among the Burgundians, who settled in eastern France at about the same time, a man could divorce his wife at any time and for any reason, so long as he returned her dowry and paid an additional sum as interest. Any woman who tried to leave her husband was to be drowned in a swamp. One exception to this Germanic rule was the Visigoths, who settled in Spain in the 6th century. Visigothic custom allowed an unmarried woman over the age of twenty to be a free adult, legally responsible for herself.

---

[12]   Wergeld may sound comical or horrifying, but also familiar; after all, our own personal-injury insurance policies follow the same general idea.

A girl was considered marriageable when she began to menstruate and was able, in theory at least, to produce children; this usually happened around the age of fifteen. Within marriage, strict division of labor between the sexes was the norm. While men did the plowing—an arduous task that generally required a man's physical strength—women performed most of the daily agricultural work from that point on: planting, weeding, fertilizing, and so on. Men focused on hunting, building, blacksmithing, felling trees, and clearing swamps. Men and women worked together to bring in the harvest, however.

A generation or two after settling in their respective parts of western Europe, most of the Germanic groups experienced a severe shortage of women. This happened for two reasons. First, relentless famine had forced the settlers to practice infanticide. In times of failed crops, which were many, this was an easy, if horrible, means of preserving the food supply. And since boys did the heavy labor, infant girls were the most frequent victims of infanticide. Second, many of those girls who survived childhood subsequently died in childbirth, as the strains of pregnancy and delivery on malnourished teenagers living in squalor commonly resulted in their death.

The shortage of women ironically caused an increase in their relative social "value," according to a crude formula of supply and demand, which the law codes came to reflect. By the 8th century, Germanic women had many more legal protections and freedoms than before. In marriage, men began to owe dowries to their brides, not the other way around, in order to secure a mate; this dowry became in many cases the bride's own property that she controlled directly and in her own name. The custom also arose whereby a husband owed his bride a **Morgengab**, or "morning gift," after their wedding night, to compensate her for her lost virginity. These developments hardly made Dark Age life significantly brighter, but they do illustrate some of the ways that Germanic culture adapted to its new circumstances.

CHRISTIAN PAGANISM

The most visible of the new circumstances was the Germans' gradual acceptance of Christianity. The traditional religion they had brought with them into the west was polytheistic and animistic: by offering prayers and gifts to the deities, they hoped to influence the workings of nature. Wotan and Thor were two of the most significant pagan gods, and they figured large in the tales of Germanic mythology. Wotan represented the forces of the Sun, Thor of Thunder and Lightning, Many of the German tribes encountered Christianity as early as the 4th century, as missionaries rushed westward to evangelize them. But the conditions of western Europe required missionaries to follow a different strategy than they had used in the cities of the eastern and central Mediterranean. Since continental Europe had no cities where the missionaries could address the hearts and minds of the multitude, they focused instead on the smallish number of Germanic rulers, princelings, and tribal warlords.

Aided (the sources assure us) by stupendous miracles, the missionaries converted this upper echelon of leaders and urged them to order the conversion of their clans and tribes. Dark Age writers like Gregory of Tours, Paul the Deacon, and Jordanes all relate fantastic tales of dramatic conversions of German rulers who then directed their victorious soldiers to receive baptism and join the cause of Christ. Of course, all that really happened in these forced baptisms—if anything happened at all—is that the rulers' subjects simply added Jesus to the long list of deities they continued to worship. Sincere in its way, no doubt, but hardly reason to regard them as Christian. Models of conversion from the top of society downward to the masses, usually either forced or enticed, can work, but they work slowly.

The Jelling Stone   This 10th-century Danish runestone is one of a series erected by King Harald Bluetooth (r. 958–986), who is traditionally regarded as the first of his people to convert to Christianity. The stones commemorate that conversion and offer atonement for his parents' pagan hostility to the faith. "Bluetooth" wireless technology is named after Harald, for the simple reason that one of its founders was reading a novel about the king at the time. The company's logo consists of the runic version of the letters H and B.

For many years and generations, and possibly for centuries, such Dark Age society was characterized by a curious, muddy amalgam of the two religions. When King Clovis of the Salian Franks ordered his followers to adopt Christianity by accepting mass baptism around the year 500, the Franks' conversion was real but incomplete. Jesus became for them a true deity but one of no more significance than the local forest god or one of their divine ancestors. Under these conditions, Dark Age Europe gradually produced a Christian religious culture that retained significant elements of pagan practice within it.

Christmas trees, for example, have nothing essential to do with the story of Jesus's birth. But the pagan Germans had a tradition of honoring the tallest tree in each forest as the unique domicile of the forest's ruling deity, and so they would honor the god by offering it gifts, decorations, and songs of praise. This pagan ritual slowly acquired a Christian gloss until, by the 9th century, the popular incorporation of tree worship into Christian practice was complete.[10] Another example is the popular celebration of bunnies and decorated eggs at Easter—neither of which appears in any Gospel version of Christ's Resurrection. Germanic peasant farmers owed a special tax to their tribal leaders at the onset of spring as an expression of gratitude for having helped the people to survive the perils of winter. Since theirs was a moneyless economy, they paid this tax with what they had at their disposal: baskets of eggs and springtime litters of bunnies. Residual pagan practices feature considerably less in most Eastern Orthodox forms of Christianity.

The long grip of hybrid versions of "Christian paganism" was indirectly abetted by the extraordinary popularity of monastic life. Many religions have ascetic and contemplative elements in them, and Second Temple Judaism fairly bristled with them. For their first three hundred years Christian missionaries were too busy in the streets and marketplaces of the eastern Mediterranean, spreading the Word (usually just ahead of the Roman police) to bother with the retired life of ascetic spirituality. Theirs was a calling to action, not meditation. But a Christian form of monasticism began in earnest in the 4th century. **Monasticism** rejected normal family and social life, along with the concern for wealth, status, and power. In their place, it favored a harsh life of solitude and spiritual discipline. What inspired this principled withdrawal from the world was, ironically, the gradual success of the Christian message itself.

By the 4th century Christianity had come a long way in the east. Although technically illegal and subject to periodic persecution until 313, Christianity had spread sufficiently that most easterners, especially those who lived in cities, were at least passingly familiar with it. The persecution under Diocletian had taken tens of thousands of lives, but it had highlighted both the number and the resolve of the Christians then alive. In turn, it earned them the grudging respect of many pagans. When Constantine I announced his own conversion and issued the **Edict of Toleration**, Christianity's hour had finally arrived.

POCKETS OF INTELLECTUAL LIFE

And this was precisely the problem for many Christians. How could they prove to God, and to themselves, that they had the same heroic commitment to him that their ancestors had possessed, ancestors who had quite literally risked their lives every day for Christ? To be a Christian after 313 involved none of the risk, the danger, and the suffering that it had carried before. After the Edict of Toleration, in fact, to be a Christian was easy, even fashionable.

---

[13]   As Christianity became more prominent in religious lives, its message of life renewed through the sacrifice and resurrection of Jesus harmonized with earlier pagan tradition and absorbed it.

For many faithful this proved intolerable, and so they intentionally sought out the loneliest, most rigorous, and most difficult way they could devise to love God—not out of spiritual masochism, but rather like an athlete who pushes herself to the limits of her ability in the pursuit of excellence. Individuals experiencing such desires went out into the deserts and forests, living in caves or on wind-blasted hilltops, exposed to the elements and wild beasts, scavenging for their food or begging it from passersby. Eventually, these ascetics began to live together in isolated communities where they tried to pattern their lives on those of the Twelve Apostles, as a sacred community united in their dedication to live as an idealized Christian mini-society unto itself.

Monasticism was extraordinarily popular in the 5th through 9th centuries, with hundreds of monastic houses established throughout the eastern and central Mediterranean, and it added a rich new element to a fast-Christianizing society. But when the movement came into western Europe it had rather a different impact. There the trickle-down model of evangelization had created a religiously hybrid world in which Christianity was poorly understood and haphazardly practiced. But when those individuals with deep, resonant, and knowledgeable commitments to the faith entered monastic life, they exacerbated the problem of popular religious ignorance, by removing from society the very individuals most capable of correcting and deepening the Christian life of the masses.

Hundreds of monasteries and convents were established in the early medieval era, from Ireland to Hungary, from Spain to Poland, from Sicily to Sweden (see Map 8.7). Many represented isolated pockets of intellectual and artistic life amid the general gloom of illiteracy and poverty. Perhaps 90 percent of these houses organized their daily lives according to the **Rule of Saint Benedict**, a communal handbook written by Saint Benedict of Nursia (480–547) to guide the monastery he had established at Monte Cassino in southern Italy. Benedict's Rule attracted so many adherents because it required relatively moderate discipline. It also had a balanced focus on the monks' physical and intellectual, as well as their spiritual, well-being. Benedictine monks were required to spend several hours each day in physical labor and in study as necessary adjuncts to their central function of worship. The physical labor, which primarily involved some sort of farmwork, helped to make each monastery self-sufficient. How else could a community cut itself off from the world if it could not feed itself and produce its own tools, clothing, and shelter?

But Benedict's insistence on study had the most important consequences for medieval Europe, for monasteries virtually monopolized book production. Novice monks received a carefully designed education that taught them to speak, read, and write Latin, as well as the basic elements of arithmetic, geometry, astronomy, and music. This training required the borrowing, copying, and commenting upon of the books of the western world's religious and secular learning. A constant stream of books thus flowed from monastery to

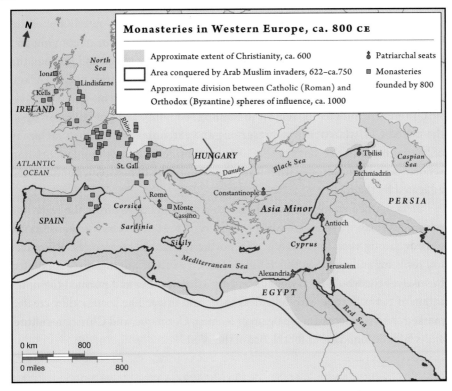

Monasteries in Western Europe, ca. 800 CE

- Approximate extent of Christianity, ca. 600
- Area conquered by Arab Muslim invaders, 622–ca.750
- Approximate division between Catholic (Roman) and Orthodox (Byzantine) spheres of influence, ca. 1000
- Patriarchal seats
- Monasteries founded by 800

MAP 8.8   Monasteries in Western Europe, ca. 800 CE

Lindisfarne   The ruins of Lindisfarne Monastery and the opening-page of the Gospel of Matthew in the Lindisfarne Gospels, ca. 700.

monastery, creating western Europe's first libraries. We owe nearly the entire surviving corpus of classical Latin literature to the busy labor of copying and recopying by these monks. They preserved the poems of Virgil and Juvenal; the histories of Tacitus, Livy, and Suetonius; the speeches and letters of Cicero; and the plays of Seneca and Terence, among others. Once they had mastered the classical literature, monks moved on to reading, copying, and commenting upon the sacred Christian writings, preserving and extending the intellectual legacy of the faith. Until the start of the 12th century, nearly every single Christian scholar in western Europe either was a member of the Benedictines or had been educated by them.

In fact, when western Europe began to emerge politically from the Dark Age ruin, monks played a central role in the recovery. In the 8th century a new aristocratic warrior family rose to power in the northern Frankish territories. Resourceful, resilient, and ruthless, this family—known as the Carolingians—appointed themselves the would-be saviors of western Christendom and pursued the unification of Latin Europe with relentless focus and drive. The society they created marked the first successful amalgam of Roman, Germanic, and Christian culture, and it laid the foundations for the rise of the West.

WHO, WHAT, WHERE

al-Jahiliyya
Byzantine Empire
caesar
caliph
Dark Ages
dhimmi
Edict of Milan (also known
    as Edict of Toleration)
imams
Islam
jihad
Ka'ba
Late Antiquity

medieval
Monasticism
Morgengab
Nicene Creed
pontifex maximus
Qur'an
Rule of Saint Benedict
Shi'a
Sunni
Tetrarchy
themes
wergeld

SUGGESTED READINGS

Primary Sources

Benedict of Nursia. *The Benedictine Rule.*
Boethius. *The Consolation of Philosophy.*
Gregory of Tours. *History of the Franks.*
Ibn Ishaq. *Life of the Prophet.*

Paul the Deacon. *History of the Lombards.*
Procopius. *The Secret History.*
The Qur'an.

Source Anthologies

Gregory of Tours. *The Merovingians* (2005). Edited and translated by Alexander Callander Murray.

Head, Thomas, ed. *Medieval Hagiography: An Anthology* (2001).

Smail, Daniel Lord, and Kelly Gibson, eds. *Vengeance in Medieval Europe: A Reader* (2009).

Swan, Laura. *The Forgotten Desert Mothers: Sayings, Lives and Stories of Early Christian Women* (2001).

Studies

Cook, Michael. *Commanding Right and Forbidding Wrong in Islamic Thought* (2001).

Crone, Patricia. *God's Rule: Government and Islam; Six Centuries of Medieval Islamic Political Thought* (2005).

———. *Meccan Trade and the Rise of Islam* (2004).

Donner, Fred McGraw. *Muhammad and the Believers: At the Origins of Islam* (2010).

Dunn, Marilyn. *Emergence of Monasticism: From the Desert Fathers to the Early Middle Ages* (2003).

Evans, J. A. S. *The Age of Justinian: The Circumstances of Imperial Power* (2001).

Geary, Patrick. *The Myth of Nations: The Medieval Origins of Europe* (2002).

Goldenberg, David M. *The Curse of Ham: Race and Slavery in Early Judaism, Christianity, and Islam* (2005).

Harmless, William. *Desert Christians: An Introduction to the Literature of Early Monasticism* (2004).

Hawting, G. R. *The First Dynasty of Islam: The Umayyad Caliphate, AD 661–750* (2000).

Heather, Peter. *Empires and Barbarians: The Fall of Rome and the Birth of Europe* (2010).

Kennedy, Hugh. *The Prophet and the Age of the Caliphates: The Islamic Near East from the Sixth to the Eleventh Century* (2004).

Khalek, Nancy. *Damascus after the Muslim Conquest: Text and Image in Early Islam* (2011).

Lawrence, C. H. *Medieval Monasticism: Forms of Religious Life in Western Europe in the Middle Ages* (2001).

Levy-Rubin, Milka. *Non-Muslims in the Early Islamic Empire: From Surrender to Coexistence* (2011).

MacLeod, Roy. *The Library of Alexandria: Rediscovering the Cradle of Western Culture* (2000).

Mottahedeh, Roy P. *Loyalty and Leadership in an Early Islamic Society* (2001).

Smith, Julia M. H. *Europe After Rome: A New Cultural History, 500–1000* (2005).

Wickham, Chris. *Framing the Early Middle Ages: Europe and the Mediterranean, 400–800* (2005).

———. *The Inheritance of Rome: Illuminating the Dark Ages, 400–1000* (2010).

Wood, Ian. *The Missionary Life: Saints and the Evangelisation of Europe, 400–1050* (2001).

For additional resources, including maps, primary sources, visuals, web links, and quizzes, please go to **www.oup.com/us/backman.**

CHAPTER 9

Reform and Renewal

750–1258

In middle of the 8th century, separated only by a few years, two palace coups took place two thousand miles from each other. Such events were commonplace in both realms and often involved blindings, beheadings, and poisonings—with at least one monarch ripped apart by having her limbs tied to four horses driven in four directions. At first, perhaps, these two seizures of power did not seem remarkable. But each set its society on a new course of development and brought their worlds into direct and lasting conflict. One brought the reign of Charlemagne, the other the golden age of Islam.

THE GREATER WEST, ca. 1200 CE

The centuries that followed witnessed much of the best and the worst of their societies' medieval era. They included unimagined prosperity, intellectual advance, artistic flourishing, religious revival, and political development—but also fiery hatred, social oppression, academic censorship, and xenophobia. They defined the broad division in Islam between Sunnis and Shi'a, still evident today, and the reinvention of Europe, with feudal society and medieval cities. Perhaps most notoriously they included the Crusades in the Holy Land, and also a new chapter in Jewish history.

◀ **Astrolabe** A 12th-century astrolabe from Muslim Spain. The increase in maritime trade across the Mediterranean by 1000 owed a lot to technical innovations introduced by Muslim and Jewish scientists, many of whom worked in Spain.

TWO PALACE COUPS

The first coup took place in Damascus in 750, when a family known as the **Abbasids**, members of the Banu Hashim clan, which traced its ancestry back to the great-grandfather of the Prophet, rebelled against the Umayyad rulers of the Islamic empire. The Umayyad dynasty had never been popular. Despite building the shrine of the Dome of the Rock in Jerusalem and the Great Mosque in Damascus, they were seen (probably correctly) as more interested in power than in the faith. They only made things worse by reserving all positions of leadership in the empire for ethnic Arabs. Their prejudice led to severe economic and social trouble, as large numbers of Egyptians and Persians converted to Islam, abandoned their farms, and migrated to the cities, where they expected to receive preferment. The subsequent decline in agricultural production caused food prices to spike and imperial revenues to fall. The empire's cities swelled with disaffected populations, who found out the hard reality that membership in the **ummah**, or Islamic community, depended very much on the color of one's skin.

As unrest gained pace in the 8th century, the Abbasid clan in Khurasan, in northeastern Iran, began laying the groundwork for regime change. Although themselves Arab, the Abbasids championed a pluriethnic vision of Islam. They cagily sought support among the Shi'a who had taken refuge in Iran with false promises of elevating their choice to the caliphal throne after the coup. Finally, in 750, they struck. Led by clan patriarch al-Saffah ("the Slaughterer"), they routed the Umayyads on the battlefield, took control of the state, and promptly moved the capital eastward to their newly established city of Baghdad.[1] The Abbasids presided over the opening of the Islamic world to non-Arabs. Persians especially rose to prominence under the new regime, winning positions at court, in the provincial government, and in

---

[1]   Al-Saffah invited the remaining Umayyads to dinner. Just as the first course was being served, his agents sprang from their hiding places, knives flashing. Only one Umayyad family member escaped.

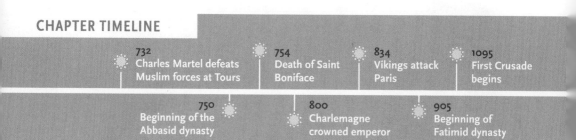

CHAPTER TIMELINE

732 Charles Martel defeats Muslim forces at Tours

754 Death of Saint Boniface

834 Vikings attack Paris

1095 First Crusade begins

750 Beginning of the Abbasid dynasty

800 Charlemagne crowned emperor

905 Beginning of Fatimid dynasty in Egypt

the Islamic schools. This began a sweeping process of cultural change, sometimes known as the "Persianization" of Islamic culture.

The second coup was much less bloody but no less epoch-making. The Frankish warlord-kings who had held sway over Gaul since Clovis's acceptance of Christianity around 500 were on the whole a sorry lot. These were the **Merovingians**. Impious, lecherous, suspicious, mostly illiterate, and generally hot-headed, they fought incessantly, plotted even more, and showed no persuasive interest in doing more with rulership than acquiring wealth and rooting out real or suspected rivals. From the mid-7th century on, they are known as the "do-nothing kings," whose ineffectiveness enabled local warlords and officials to usurp power for themselves.

The most successful of the usurpers was a family from northeastern Gaul known as the **Carolingians**. By the early 700s the founder of the dynasty, Pepin of Heristal, was serving as a regional Merovingian official but was in reality an all-but-autonomous ruler. He passed his position on to his illegitimate, though only, son, Charles Martel (d. 741), who added much of northwestern Gaul to the family domain. The secret to the Carolingians' effectiveness was a combination of vision, ruthlessness, and luck. The family early on developed a view of themselves as the self-appointed saviors of Christian Gaul and eventually of western Europe, destined like the biblical David to replace the rejected king Saul (that is, the Merovingian house), and establish a righteous and lasting realm.

For the next four or five generations the family advanced their dedication to uniting and strengthening western Christendom. One of the most dramatic events in this pursuit was Charles Martel's victory in 732 over Spanish Muslim forces that effectively stopped the Islamic advance into Europe. In 754 Charles Martel's son Pepin the Short completed the takeover of the Merovingian throne by persuading the papacy to recognize him as the true legitimate king of the Franks. The last Merovingian was deposed and the first Carolingian king enthroned.

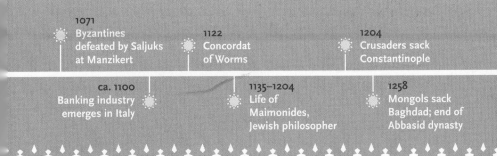

1071
Byzantines
defeated by Saljuks
at Manzikert

1122
Concordat
of Worms

1204
Crusaders sack
Constantinople

ca. 1100
Banking industry
emerges in Italy

1135–1204
Life of
Maimonides,
Jewish philosopher

1258
Mongols sack
Baghdad; end of
Abbasid dynasty

THE CAROLINGIAN ASCENT

Pepin the Short (r. 754–768) became the king of the Franks by the acclaim of his people and the recognition of his title by Pope Stephen II (r. 752–757). He and his successors, Charles Martel and Charlemagne, stressed practical needs of connecting their realm and building an independent empire. The pope, for his trouble, gained in Pepin a military ally against the newest Germanic group to rip through Italy (the Lombards) and a tacit recognition that the Holy See was the arbiter of political legitimacy in Europe. Pepin accommodated Stephen by recognizing the pontiff's position as the secular ruler of the so-called Papal State, a wide swath of land across the middle of the Italian peninsula. With a strong ally and steady source of income, the papacy was able at last to exercise some genuine authority in the world, although the precise nature and extent of that authority remained uncertain for many years. Pepin energetically promoted his family's importance to championing the cause of Christianity.

There is something of a conundrum to Pepin's rise. The Carolingians were genuinely pious and dedicated to promoting the evangelization of barbarian Europe. Yet they owed their rise to power to their oppression of local churches. As early as Pepin of Heristal in the 720s, the Carolingians had ransacked the monasteries in their domains in order to raise the revenues they needed to pay their soldiers. Monasteries, after all, were the wealthiest institutions in western Europe, possessors of large estates well run with collective labor forces. Their sacristies were often filled with valuable items bequeathed by pious neighbors. Some of them also held deposits of cash or valuables from nervous owners who feared leaving them in their own homes.

The Carolingians presented their monasteries with a simple choice: These are barbarous times, and you can either give us your valuables to pay for our soldiers or you can be left alone to face certain annihilation by barbarian hordes or, even worse, the advancing Muslims. With their purses thus filled, the Carolingians' army swelled in size, enabling them to bring more and more of France under their authority. Charles Martel's great victory over the Muslims in 732, on the plain between Tours and Poitiers, solidified the family's heroic status and justified (in their own minds, at least) their manhandling of the monks. As the semiofficial *Chronicle of Saint-Denis* put it:

> The Muslims were marching to the city of Tours in order to destroy it, the Church of Saint Martin, and all the surrounding countryside, when Charles—that illustrious prince—opposed them at the head of his whole army. He set his soldiers in formation and fell upon

the enemy as ferociously as a hungry wolf falls upon a stag, until, by the grace of Our Lord, he had slaughtered on the field three hundred thousand of the enemies of Christianity, including their king Abd ar-Rahman. This was how he came to be called Martel ["hammer"], for he struck down his foes on the field as though he were a hammer made of iron, or steel, or any other type of metal. And the most amazing thing of all was the fact that he lost only fifteen hundred of his own men that day.

Success followed success, and by the end of Pepin the Short's reign almost all of modern France lay under Carolingian control.

What distinguished the Carolingians from other warlord families was their genuine dedication to transforming the societies they ruled. Pepin the Short built nearly as many monasteries as he ransacked and established churches and schools. He supported missionary work among the barbarians and at least attempted to develop an infrastructure of roads and bridges that would connect villages and towns. The Carolingians were also distinguished by their good luck: for five generations in a row they produced a single heir who inherited the family domain entire, without dividing it among siblings.[2] The greatest missionary of the age was Saint Boniface (680–754), an Anglo-Saxon monk who spent forty years preaching to the barbarians of the north, founding monasteries, churches, and schools with undiminished zeal (see Map 9.1). He had the ardent backing of the Carolingian court, "without which," Boniface wrote in a letter to a friend, "I could neither administer my churches and defend my clergy nor continue the fight against idolatry." Charles Martel, in fact, created four dioceses in southern Germany in his honor (at Salzburg, Regensburg, Freising, and Passau) and appointed him metropolitan, or supreme administrative officer among a group of bishops, over all German lands east of the Rhine River. In return for this support, Boniface made sure that all the bishops he appointed, from the Low Countries to Saxony, declared loyalty jointly to the papacy and the Carolingian ruler. The relationship between Rome and the Carolingians can be thought of as a partnership, although one in which the Carolingians had the dominant role.

---

[2] The Carolingians did not rely on luck alone. They kept scores of mistresses and limited intimacy with their wives to the minimum needed to produce a male heir. Their method was not foolproof; in fact, several of the Carolingians did produce multiple legitimate heirs. Disease and warfare carried off most of them before political division occurred. In a few cases, a sudden assassination or imprisonment sufficed.

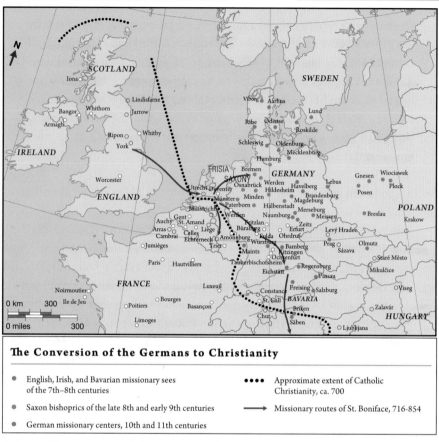

The Conversion of the Germans to Christianity

- ● English, Irish, and Bavarian missionary sees of the 7th–8th centuries
- ● Saxon bishoprics of the late 8th and early 9th centuries
- ● German missionary centers, 10th and 11th centuries
- ●●●● Approximate extent of Catholic Christianity, ca. 700
- ⟶ Missionary routes of St. Boniface, 716-854

MAP 9.1   The Conversion of the Germans to Christianity

CHARLEMAGNE

Pepin the Short died in 768, leaving two legitimate sons: Charles and Carloman. Carloman very conveniently died, however, leaving Charles (r. 768–814) as sole ruler of an undivided kingdom. Charles, known as Charlemagne ("Charles the Great"), spent the next forty years campaigning across Europe, expanding his realm into northeastern Spain, eastern Germany, Italy, Bohemia (part of today's Czech Republic), the Hungarian plain, and the northern reaches of the Balkans (today's Slovenia, Croatia and Bosnia and Herzegovina). His great goal was to unite Latin Europe under a single government with a comprehensive legal system, a network of churches and schools, a reliable basic infrastructure, and a regularized system of weights and measures (see Map 9.2).

Charlemagne's energy was prodigious. He also suffered from lifelong insomnia, which he inflicted on his courtiers:

> He habitually awoke and rose from his bed four or five times a night.
> He would hold audience with his retinue even while getting dressed or

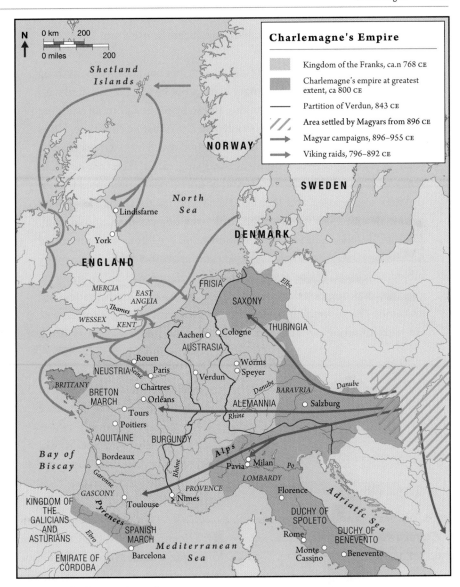

Charlemagne's Empire

Kingdom of the Franks, ca.n 768 CE

Charlemagne's empire at greatest extent, ca 800 CE

——— Partition of Verdun, 843 CE

Area settled by Magyars from 896 CE

Magyar campaigns, 896–955 CE

Viking raids, 796–892 CE

MAP 9.2 Charlemagne's Empire

putting on his boots; if the palace chancellor told him of any legal matter for which his judgment was needed, he had the parties brought before him then and there. He would hear the case and render his decision just as though he was sitting on the bench of justice. And this was not the only type of business he would carry on at these hours, for he regularly performed any one of his daily duties, whether it was a matter for his personal attention or something that he could allocate to his officials. (Einhard, *Life of Charlemagne, ch. 24*)

A promoter of education, he worked hard to educate himself too:

> He had the gift of easy and fluid speech and could express anything he wanted to say with extraordinary clarity. But he was not satisfied with the mastery of just his native tongue, and so he made a point of studying foreign ones as well; he became so adept at Latin that he could speak it as easily as his native tongue, and he understood much more Greek than he could actually speak. His eloquence was so great, in fact, that he could very well have taught the subject. And he energetically promoted the liberal arts, and praised and honored those who taught them. He studied grammar with Peter the Deacon, of Pisa, who was then an old man. Another deacon, a Saxon from Britain named Albinus and surnamed Alcuin, was the greatest scholar of his time and tutored the king in many subjects. King Charles spent many long hours with him studying rhetoric, dialectic, and astronomy; he also learned mathematics and examined the movement of heavenly bodies with particular attention. He tried to write too and had the habit of keeping tablets and blank pages under his pillow in bed, so that in his quiet hours he could get his hand used to forming the letters—but since he did not begin his efforts as a young man, but instead rather late in life, they met with little success. *(Life of Charlemagne, ch. 25)*

The Sword of Charlemagne   Known as the Sword of Charlemagne—even though it is at least one hundred years too old to have been his—the sword was used at the coronation ceremonies of all the kings of France throughout the Middle Ages. Long held in the treasury of the church of Saint-Denis, it is now housed in the Louvre.

A pragmatic streak led the Carolingians to pursue a limited form of meritocracy; perhaps they had no real alternative. Anyone with a useful skill could find service somewhere in the regime. After all, the relentless traveling of the royal court exposed them to a parade of ineptitude. Everything from illiterate priests to judges with no knowledge of the law made the need for reform clear. To the palace-capital at Aachen (Aix-la-Chapelle, on today's French-German borderlands), the court brought poets and theologians from Spain, historians and legal scholars from Italy, grammarians from Ireland, and Biblical exegetes from England. But they also scouted out skilled stonemasons, carpenters, metal smiths, scribes, weavers, tanners, musicians, coopers, and herbalists. Social background usually took a back seat to the more important issue of ability.

Charlemagne viewed power and status as commodities that he alone possessed and could parcel out at will. He governed his vast realm by delegating local, provincial authority to a caste of counts (*comites* in Latin) who represented the king and exerted power in his name; but these were not hereditary positions. The title of count was a job description, not a designation of social class. Charlemagne could appoint the lowest-born peasant as count, if he wished, and that count's position of honor would be equal to that of any count who claimed an aristocratic background. Ability and loyalty to the throne were what mattered most. The court held several assemblies each year, to which various counts and other officials were summoned. A typical summons read like this:

> In the name of the Father, and of the Son, and of the Holy Spirit. Charles, the most serene, august, heavenly crowned, magnificent, and peaceful emperor, and also, by God's mercy, the King of the Franks and of the Lombards, to Abbot Fulrad.
>
> You are hereby informed that I have decided to convene my General Assembly this year in eastern Saxony at the place called Stassfurt, on the Bode River. I therefore command you to come to this place on the fifteenth day before the calends of July—that is, seven days before the Feast of Saint John the Baptist—with all your men suitably armed and at the ready, so that you will be prepared to head out from that place in any direction I choose. In other words, come with arms, gear, and all the food and clothing you will need for war. Let every horseman bring a shield, lance, sword, knife, bow, and supply of arrows. Let your carriage train bring tools of every kind: axes, planes, augurs, lumber, shovels, spades, and anything else an army might need. Bring also enough food to last three months beyond the date of the assembly, and arms and clothing to last six.
>
> I command, more generally, that you should see to it that you travel peacefully to the aforesaid place, and that as your journey takes you through any of the lands of my realm you should presume to take nothing but fodder for your animals, wood, and water. Let the servants belonging to each of your loyal men march alongside the carts and horsemen, and let their masters be always with them until they reach the aforesaid place, lest a lord's absence be the cause of his servants' evildoing.

Send your tribute—which you are to present to me at the assembly by the middle of May—to the appointed place, where I shall already be. If it should happen that your travels go so well that you can present your tribute to me in person, I shall be greatly pleased. Do not disappoint me now or in the future, if you hope to remain in my favor.

Palatine Chapel   Interior of the Palatine Chapel at Charlemagne's imperial capital at Aachen.

Clearly, the counts were kept aware that they owed their status entirely to the king's favor, not to any birthright of their own. Moreover, the king trained and sent out teams of *missi dominici* (literally, "dispatched royal agents" or "traveling lords"), who moved in regular circuits throughout the realm, reviewing comital records, holding open courts, and inviting the local populace to come forth with complaints about the job performance of the counts.

It was a primitive system of government but one that was meant to evoke the ruling style of the ancient Roman emperors, seeking a balance of centralized aims and local needs. The Carolingians admired the Roman idea of getting their subjects to see themselves as part of a larger civilization, although in the Carolingians' case the larger civilization was Latin Christianity, not Roman paganism. When building his palace complex at Aachen, Charlemagne ordered its chapel to be modeled on the Byzantine church of San Vitale that Justinian had built in Ravenna. And he had nearly identical marble pillars, stone columns, and glittering wall mosaics (and the appropriate skilled workmen) hauled north from Italy to do it.

IMPERIAL CORONATION

On Christmas Day in the year 800, Charlemagne was crowned augustus by Pope Leo III (r. 795–816). The significance of this was symbolic and also more than symbolic. The symbolic significance had to do with the date. The now-standard **anno Domini** system of dating—that is, reckoning the years from the purported time of Jesus's birth—was still a novelty. It had been created by a Syrian monk in the 6th century but had only become used in the west after the English scholar-monk Bede (d. 735) had promoted its use. By the time of Charlemagne's coronation, most literate people in Europe used the new system. Still, the bulk of the population probably still thought in terms of the old system (called annus mundi II) they had inherited from earlier times; and according to the old system the year 800 was actually the year 6000.

According to Einhard's *Life of Charlemagne*, which was written to order during the reign of Charlemagne's heir, Louis the Pious (r. 814–840), Charlemagne was surprised and incensed by the coronation. He would not have attended Mass even on Christmas if he had known what Leo what planning to do. But Charlemagne had been in Rome since early November, and the man who never slept would never have been caught in an unplanned coronation. More likely, some mishandled detail in the crowning ceremony caused his angry outburst. Regardless, Charlemagne probably took advantage of the calendrical quirk of the year 800/6000 to make his coronation signal the start of a bright new age in history.[3]

However, the significance of his coronation was far more than symbolic: it sent a political message to Byzantium. Seeking support for their claims to political legitimacy, Dark Age rulers like Clovis had frequently turned to the Greeks. The Byzantines, for their part, regarded the Latin westerners as ill-mannered and backward poor cousins, nominally members of the Christian family but hardly the sort of relatives one boasts about. Most Byzantines, in fact, regarded the loss of western Europe as a blessing in disguise. Charlemagne's coronation, however, changed everything. By assuming the imperial title, he effectively declared the Carolingian court independent of and equal to the Greek east. Moreover, by receiving the crown from the pope, the Carolingians established a way to pass on the imperial title in which the Byzantines had no role.

> By assuming the imperial title, Charlemagne effectively declared the Carolingian court independent of and equal to the Greek east. Moreover, by receiving the crown from the pope, the Carolingians established a way to pass on the imperial title in which the Byzantines had no role.

Constantinople was not pleased with this declaration of independence but was powerless to do anything about it. Compounding matters, the throne in Constantinople was occupied at the time by a headstrong woman named Irene (r. 797–802), who had seized power by organizing a coup against her ineffectual

---

[3] Think of Charlemagne at his coronation as almost like a modern politician who coordinates speeches and ribbon-cutting ceremonies to coincide with significant anniversaries.

son Constantine VI. Charlemagne sent her an embassy and proposed marriage. If the marriage happened, his ambassadors urged, the eastern and western empires would unite, the growing rift between the Latin and Greek Churches would heal, and the Christian world could mount a powerful joint offensive against Islam. Irene was inclined to accept but she fell from power before she could give her answer.

Irene had been empress during the reign of her husband Leo IV (r. 775–780) and ruled as empress-regent while their infant son grew up. In 797, however, she had ordered her son to be blinded and left to die. She then assumed the gender-bending title of "emperor" (*basileos* in Greek), not "empress" (*basilea*). She was already unpopular, and her interest in marrying Charlemagne was the last straw and led to her overthrow. Several horrified Byzantine high officials plotted the coup. They seized Irene, cut off her hair, and forced her into a convent, never to emerge. Once in the convent, she seems to have accepted her fate with grace, seeing her life as a nun as a penance for her cruelty to her son. She died in 805.

Charlemagne, we are told, was so furious at this spoiling of his grand plan that he even formed a brief alliance with the Abbasid caliph in Baghdad, Harun al-Rashid (r. 786–809), to mount a two-pronged invasion of Byzantium. Nothing came of it. In the end, Charlemagne married twice. His first wife, Ermengarde, bore him six children; his second, Judith, produced two more.

CAROLINGIAN COLLAPSE

Carolingian luck ran out after Charlemagne's death in 814. At his death, Charlemagne's crown passed to his sole surviving heir, Louis the Pious (r. 814–840), but Louis had few of his father's gifts. Studious and well-meaning, he nevertheless lacked charisma and quick wit. He was also intensely straitlaced and moralistic— hence his nickname—and banished from the court all the dancing girls and mistresses who had made his father's sleepless nights less lonely. Instead of feasts, music, and gaiety in the imperial swimming pool, Louis enjoyed poring over plans to reform monastic life.[4] Even worse, Louis was determined to make up for his father's sexual libertinism by remaining staunchly faithful to his wife. As a result Louis was survived by three sons, all of whom hated him; after his death they divided up the kingdom and quickly went to war with one another.

The delicate sense of cultural unity across Latin Europe fostered by the earlier Carolingians now dissolved almost immediately into factionalism. The splintering of the empire could not be stopped, and within one hundred years of Charlemagne's death his empire had devolved into dozens of petty principalities.

---

4   Aachen is the site of a natural hot spring, over which Charlemagne had ordered his palace built.

The nicknames given to the late Carolingian princelings illustrate the decline. In no particular order: Charles the Bald, Louis the Stammerer, Charles the Simple, Louis the Blind, Charles the Fat, Louis the Child.[5] Civil war became incessant. The dozens of principalities soon shattered into hundreds of them, and Europe seemed likely to slip into another Dark Age.

Exacerbating the internal rot, new waves of invaders attacked Europe. Another nomadic group emerged from the central Asian steppe and marched into the plains of eastern Europe below the Danube River. These were the Magyars, the ancestors of today's Hungarian nation. They were a localized threat, however, encroaching only on the easternmost former members of the Carolingian state, although the people of northern Italy also had some reason to fear them. A much greater threat came from the north—the Vikings. Their hordes had begun to beset Latin Europe as early as Charlemagne's time; as the Carolingian state fractured, the invasions gained pace. What made the Viking threat so severe was the unpredictable nature of their attacks. Unlike the Magyars—a large, slow-moving land force—the Vikings raided in smallish groups of perhaps two dozen fighters per warship. Those ships, moreover, were designed to sail in as little as three or four feet of water, which meant that the Vikings could move upriver. Most of Europe's rivers flow northward and westward—opening directly on the Atlantic, the North Sea, and the Baltic Sea—in other words, directly in front of the Vikings' approach. The attackers were thus able to move with terrific speed and attack far inland. Viking warships attacked Paris in 834, during the reign of Louis the Pious, and even sacked Seville, the capital of Muslim Spain, about a decade later. There was no advance warning for these raids. The Vikings simply appeared all of a sudden, attacked and pillaged, and disappeared before any kind of defense could be mounted. And of course the incessant internal squabbling of the late mini-Carolingians only made the problem worse. Here is how a church council lamented the suffering of the time:

> Our cities are depopulated, our monasteries wrecked and put to the torch, our countryside left uninhabited. . . . Indeed, just as the first humans lived without law or the fear of God and according only to their dumb instincts, so too now does everyone do whatever seems good in his eyes only, despising all human and divine laws and ignoring even the commands of the Church. The strong oppress the weak, and the world is wracked with violence against the poor and the plunder of ecclesiastical lands. . . . Men everywhere devour each other like the fishes of the sea.

---

[5]   There was even a princeling named Bozo (although he was more capable than most of his peers).

In the words of the Old Norse poet Snori Sturluson (1179–1241), the Vikings "were like mad dogs or wolves, biting the edges of their shields, / and were as strong as bears or bulls. They killed men everywhere / and nothing could stop them—not fire, not steel." No wonder that scattered figures across Europe, gathering crowds of frightened followers around them, began to proclaim the end of the world.

And then the Muslims came again.

THE ISLAMIC EMPIRE

The Abbasid era (750–1258) is generally regarded as medieval Islam's Golden Age. From their magnificent new capital at Baghdad the caliphs transformed Islam's original Arab culture. The transformation also unleashed new problems, as that culture encountered western philosophy. With the inevitable backlash and the breakup of the empire, relations with western Europe were transformed as well. At the heart of Abbasid policy was the earnest, though cautious, welcoming of the involvement and traditions of the **malawi** ("clients," literally), the non-Arab Muslims. This new, open attitude was driven in part by simple pragmatism: by the mid-8th century, ethnic Arabs were no longer the numerical majority of Muslims. Taken together, Berbers, Egyptians, Kurds, Persians, and Syrians greatly outnumbered the relatively small nation of Arabs who still monopolized all positions of political, military, and religious authority.

Among the malawi, the largest single group by far were the Persians. The first wave of transformation under the Abbasids, therefore, was the intentional spread and promotion of Persian culture. Administrative integration came first. Persia, of course, had had long experience with administering a vast empire, going back to Cyrus the Great. Their tactic then had been a carefully controlled system of provincial governors called satraps; this same idea reemerged under the Abbasids as the network of new officials called **viziers**. A vizier (from Arabic *wazir*, meaning "helper" or "assistant") was the governor of a district and the personal representative of the caliph, a combination of administrator and ambassador.

To offset the inevitable danger of decentralizing imperial power, the Abbasids increased the number and extent of the state-owned estates (*sawafi*) within each province. They also increased the fiscal contributions owed by each province to Baghdad. With the new income, the Abbasids developed the city of Baghdad itself, improved the pay of the army, and continued developing the infrastructure that held the Islamic world together. Moreover, they withdrew from the viziers the authority to appoint local religious judges, or **qadis**, and monopolized control of all judicial appointments. Still, some loss of authority was inevitable. The viziers in Syria and Asia Minor bore the brunt of continuing the offensive against

Byzantium throughout the 9th and 10th centuries, a war they largely financed by themselves, which resulted in their increased autonomy from Baghdad.

SUNNIS AND SHI'A

The caliphs themselves remained more directly concerned, diplomatically and politically, with events in the east where restive groups of Shi'i Muslims began to rebel. The Shi'a had originally supported the Abbasids since they were in accord with the Abbasids' general call for the return of caliphal authority to members of Muhammad's family; but when the Shi'a found out that their particular line of that family would not be succeeding, they withdrew their support.

The rift between Sunni and Shi'i Muslims widened and grew more bitter with every generation. The dispute involved more than simply the Alids' claim to inherit the Prophet's mantle as leader of the Islamic community—a view that essentially defined Shi'ism during the Arab hegemony. Rather, an explicitly religious element entered the tradition. The death of the beloved Shi'ite leader Husayn ibn Ali al-Shahid, Ali's son, in battle against the Umayyad forces in 680, had inspired the creation of a passion narrative. Popular belief expected Husayn's return as the **Mahdi**—the "Guided One" who will emerge at the end of time and secure Islam's ultimate victory on earth. This belief now evolved into the Shi'ite doctrine of the "hidden imam," an imam, for the Shi'a, being the divinely appointed successor to Ali's line.

What differentiated the various sects of Shi'ism that emerged in Abbasid times was the number of true imams each group recognized, before the final imam went into hiding to await the moment of messianic return. The Shi'a, bound by their allegiance to Ali's descendants, thus incorporated the religious teachings and legal judgments rendered by those imams. In this way, their varying political programs transmuted into a web of traditions very much at odds with the Sunni majority.

The Abbasids were in a bind. In order to retain the support of the Islamic majority they had to champion Sunni orthodoxy, yet they owed the success of their coup against the Umayyads to the backing they had received from the Shi'a. Moreover, the open bias they showed for promoting Persians at court led to demands by other malawi groups for similar treatment. The rulers embraced as many aspects of the various malawi cultural traditions as could harmonize with Islamic teaching, whether Sunni or Shi'ite. The Persians, for example, had an ancient custom of veiling of their women whenever they appeared in public. This was done not to denigrate women but to express ethnic pride: inferior non-Persian men had no right to look upon a Persian woman. And since it seemed impractical to blind the empire's entire population of subject males, they veiled

Veiled Women   A late rendering of an early episode in Islamic history.
This 17th-century fresco, from Safavid Iran, shows a scene of women
mourning the dead, during one of the *riddah* wars of the first Islamic
century (650–750 CE). The veiling of women, practiced by most Near
Eastern peoples to some degree, was particularly associated with
Persian culture, and it came to be the enforced norm within Islam after
the Abbasid dynasty relinquished Arab Damascus and moved the
capital east to Baghdad. The so-called Persianization of Islam then
commenced. The Abbasids remained in power until the Mongols
destroyed Baghdad in 1258.

their Persian women instead. It was a badge of honor, an expression of superiority. This practice harmonized well, however, with the Qur'anic demand for sexual
modesty, and so became generally Islamized.

THE QUR'AN AND THE PHILOSOPHERS

A thornier problem arose from the very nature of the Qur'an. Many malawi
had adhered to ancient Zoroastrian and Gnostic traditions, which found secret
knowledge and multiple meanings in holy texts. The Qur'an's essence as the
literal word of Allah seemed to operate against those traditions. Abbasid-
supported jurists like Abu Hanifa [P] (d. 767), however, resolved this tension by
reinterpreting the verse "Whether ye hide what is in your hearts or reveal it, Allah
knows all" (3.29). This became a justification for **takiyya**—the intentional
dissimulation of what one believes—since the Qur'an itself had both a literal
meaning and also a number of hidden meanings, open only to interpretation by
an initiated few. For Shi'i Muslims takiyya grew in importance from a bitter

necessity during times of Sunni persecution to a fundamental and obligatory duty, the denial of one's faith as an expression of it. Another Zoroastrian idea absorbed into Islam was the notion of God as the Primeval Fire or Primordial Light, which then emanated out into the universe. By the middle of the 9th century the Shi'a had transformed this notion into their conception of the imam as the human epiphany of this Light.

On the Sunni side, some Yemeni and Bedouin tribes had long practiced a legalized form of concubinage. In *mut'a* (literally "pleasure" or "enjoyment"), a man married a woman for a prearranged period of time—a year, a month, a week, or even a single day—and paid her a prorated dowry in return for his "enjoyment" of her.[6] It is unclear how widespread the practice was in pre-Islamic times, but some evidence dates it as early as the 4th century among the Bedouin and possibly even earlier among some groups of Egyptian traders. Some later writers claimed that the Prophet himself had practiced it (al-Tabari, *Chronicle* 1.1775–1776). Sunni jurists rejected mut'a and the claim that the Prophet had ever been involved in it. But from the time of the legal scholar al-Shafi'i [A] (d. 819), a compromise allowed it, provided that the term of the marriage not appear in the written marriage contract. The Shi'a, in contrast, championed mut'a from the start (and still practice it widely today).

When Islam spread northward into the Levant and westward across North Africa, it encountered not only Judaism and Christianity but also the classical traditions of Greece and Rome. In an effort to curry favor with the new governors, groups of Christian scholar-monks in Syria began to translate works from the classical age into Arabic: Euclid's treatises on geometry, Plato's dialogues, the histories of Xenophon, the scientific and logical treatises of Aristotle were all translated. Intrigued by what they read or heard about, the caliphs maintained two principal centers for this translation in the late 8th and throughout the 9th century, both located in Baghdad. One was led by an Arab scholar named Yaqub al-Kindi [A] (d. 870) and the other by the Syrian Christian physician Hunayn ibn Ishaq [S] (d. 873). Hunayn ibn Ishaq also made the first translation of the Septuagint version of the Hebrew Bible into Arabic.[7]

The al-Kindi school focused on philosophical, literary, and logical texts, whereas the ibn Ishaq school tended to emphasize the Greek scientific and medical writings. Muslim scholars showed little interest in the Romans, whose intellectual works they regarded as derivative of the Greeks, although they did admire the Romans' adeptness with technology. But for every eager scholar wanting to

---

6   For a marriage of only one day, the marriage price could be as low as a handful of grain or dates.

7   By the time of the Abbasid takeover in 750 fully 50 percent of all Christians lived under Islamic rule. As they became Arabized, it became necessary to translate the Scriptures into Arabic.

pursue Greek knowledge, dozens of suspicious clergy cautioned against the ideas of unbelievers. The early Christian communities had exhibited a similar hesitation toward pagan Greek learning, until figures like Saint Augustine of Hippo and Boethius showed that classical learning posed no inherent threat to Christian orthodoxy. It could in fact help to clarify Christian ideas and beliefs. Resistance to the Greek tradition was as tenacious and passionate as the support expressed for it by scholars like al-Kindi.

Few of the great Muslim philosophers could read Greek; most depended on the translations made for the caliphal court. And like academics everywhere, some of them claimed more expertise than they actually had. Here is al-Kindi's thumbnail synopsis of Aristotle's *Metaphysics*:

> In the work called *Metaphysics* Aristotle sought to explain those things that exist yet do not possess matter; and how these things may co-exist with things that do have matter—and yet remain unconnected to matter and separate from it. He sought also to affirm the Oneness of God (the Great and Almighty), to explain God's many beautiful names, and to explicate how God is the causal agent of everything in the universe, making everything perfect—for God is the God of the universe, governing everything in His complete and perfect wisdom.

But Aristotle never said anything remotely like this. Was al-Kindi a charlatan? Certainly not. More likely, he wished to deflate clerical concerns about the dangers in seeking knowledge from non-Islamic traditions. He therefore tried to deflect criticism by making Aristotle sound like someone who would surely have been a Muslim if only he had been lucky enough to live in Islamic times.

This was cheating, of course, but at other times al-Kindi took brave stands:

> There is nothing shameful in admiring, and even in acquiring, the Truth, no matter where It comes from. To the student of Truth there is nothing that matters except Truth, and Truth is never cheapened or lessened by the person who states it, not even if he comes from a distant land and belongs to a backward nation. Indeed, Truth belittles no one and ennobles all.

Those interested in Greek philosophy thus faced a twofold problem: to show how a pagan discipline could explicate Islamic truth while preserving the authority of revelation. Does revealed truth need logical explication? Does offering one undermine the authority of the revelation?

Islamic thinkers had started to wrestle with these questions even before their discovery of the Greek tradition. From the Prophet's death in 632, Muslims and would-be Muslims had tried to answer a number of fundamental questions about the faith—the kinds of questions that anyone intrigued by the faith might raise. Was the Holy Qur'an created, or had it existed in heaven from all eternity? If it was present from the Creation, then why did Allah bother with the partial and imperfect Jewish and Christian revelations? And why does the Qur'an's message appear to change? How can it call first for Arabs to embrace Islam for repentance of their sins and to foster Arab brotherhood and unity, when later it calls Arabs to bring the message of Allah to the entire world?

Those interested in Greek philosophy thus faced a twofold problem: to show how a pagan discipline could explicate Islamic truth while preserving the authority of revelation. Does revealed truth need logical explication? Does offering one undermine the authority of the revelation?

Another group of questions centered on Allah's attributes. In stating that Allah sees everything, hears our prayers, speaks, has knowledge, exerts will, and wields power, does the Qur'an imply that Allah is anthropomorphic—a kind of eternal man? And a third set of questions asked whether Allah's omniscience implies that every human's destiny is predetermined. Do we have free will, or has Allah, in knowing our ultimate fates, effectively set our ultimate fates?

The practical and immediate need to confront these matters resulted in a body of ideas and disciplines known as **kalam** (literally "speech" or "word," but

Truth Attainable by Rational Argument   In this scientific manuscript from 13th-century Persia, two great rationalists, Aristotle and his pupil Alexander the Great, lead a discussion of the medicinal properties of certain animal organs and secretions.

usually translated as "theology"). Kalam was not philosophy and did not pretend to be. Instead, it was a method of inquiry into a limited number of specific issues that needed resolution, and its goal was to ease Islam's acceptance by cultures with long-established traditions that privileged rational thought. Reason, of course, is a universal trait. But the value placed upon reason, to the detriment of other ways of knowing, is a cultural one. As Islam spread, and as questions about the fundamental nature of Allah, his Qur'an, and man's free will were articulated, Sunni leaders resolved them by seeking a consensus among the community of scholars. This was the tradition known as **ijma'** ("consensus"), a principle that embraced the use of reason to resolve a religious question. But ijma' was not open-ended. Once the community's answer on any given questioned had been authoritatively expressed, the question was considered closed for all time. Tradition trumped any rethinking of any issue.

But the Christian-initiated translations of the Greeks posed another problem: as a result of their work, Muslim scholars encountered real philosophy (*falsafah* in Arabic), or open-ended rational inquiry. In philosophy, the answer given to any question does not close the matter; rather, it invites continual reappraisal. Philosophy is therefore as much an attitude of mind as it is any particular body of ideas, and it is not (ideally) an attempt to produce a desired goal. The liberal atmosphere of the early Abbasid years allowed philosophy to bloom, as the caliphs al-Ma'mun [A] (r. 813–833), al-Mu'tasim [A] (r. 833–842), and al-Wathik [A] (r. 842–847) encouraged new translations of and commentaries on the Western philosophical canon. They promoted as well the study of the philosophical and scientific traditions of Zoroastrian Persia and Buddhist India. In addition to the schools at Baghdad, these caliphs also opened a second center for liberal studies at Basra, in Iraq.

Opinions varied on the acceptability of the new cultural injections, but for the moment the inclusionists won. Prominent among these was a group of scholars known as the **Mu'tazilites** ("the Dissenters"). The Mu'tazilites had widely varying views but they shared a belief, or an inclination to believe, that whenever tradition and reason were in conflict, the scale tipped in reason's favor. Another way to describe the Mu'tazilites is as the party inclined to prevent ijma' from sealing off intellectual inquiry. For this reason alone, they were generally disliked and distrusted by most Sunnis; but what earned the Sunni's real ire was the Mu'tazilite position on the "createdness" of the Qur'an. The caliph al-Ma'mun, a strong Mu'tazilite sympathizer, even proclaimed this position the official doctrine of the state and required appointees to public office to swear allegiance to it. He triggered a violent revolt and died soon thereafter under suspicious circumstances.[8]

---

[8]   One tradition asserts that al-Ma'mun was resting by a river and asked some courtiers what he should eat. They just happened to have some dates at hand. He died on the spot, presumably poisoned.

THE SPLINTERING OF THE CALIPHATE

The cultural proliferation and ethnic egalitarianism of the Abbasids outraged many and inspired a predictable backlash. "O Lord," cried one offended Arab elitist, "the sons of whores have multiplied so much—please guide me to another land where I need not deal with bastards!" And as it happened, many were guided away from the cosmopolitan empire. The last Umayyads had fled as far as Spain, where they officially seceded from the empire and declared an independent kingdom of their own in 756. Other regions soon followed suit: Algeria broke away in 779; Morocco in 789; Tunisia in 800; Khurasan (northeastern Iran and part of Afghanistan) in 819; Sind (roughly the territory of today's Pakistan) in 867; and Egypt, too, in 868, only to have its rebels overthrown and succeeded by a new dynasty called the Fatimids in 905. So too did numerous smaller princedoms. Thus the cultural glories of the Abbasid Golden Age came at the cost of the political shattering of the empire (see Map 9.3).

Many issues played into the disintegration, only starting with concern about heretical ideas. Other issues were ethnic pride and racial bias, a sense of unfair commercial and tax policies, and frustration over the stalling out of strong jihad in favor of soft intellectualism. It is no coincidence that the splinter states became seedbeds for strict reform movements, such as the Almoravids and the Almohads. These sects, and others like them, called for halting what they regarded as the cosmopolitan rot that had beset Islam. They demanded a return to the militarism, discipline, and order of the great conquering age of the Prophet and his Companions. Only by restoring the active spirit of jihad, the reformists asserted, could the great cause of bringing Islam to the world be fulfilled.

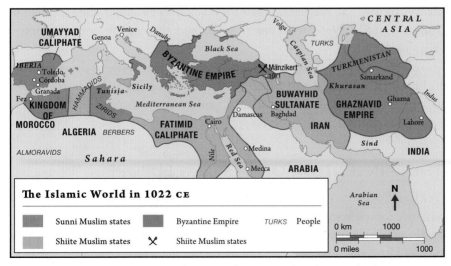

MAP 9.3   The Islamic World in 1022 CE

Two important developments coincided with the break-up of the Islamic empire. First, internally, Muslims had become the majority in two or three generations. Conversion, coercion, and emigration had caused the Jewish and Christian populations to shrink. Most Muslims states still recognized the legal rights of their non-Muslim subjects as dhimmis. But it is one thing to live in tolerance with foreign communities that vastly outnumber one's own, and it is quite another when one's own community has become the majority and the other groups suddenly appear as out-of-place foreigners. Acts of anti-Jewish and anti-Christian hostility became increasingly common through the 9th and 10th centuries, especially in areas experiencing temporary economic troubles. They became common features, too, of the reformist movements of the age. This was popular violence rather than state-run persecution in most cases, although the victims may not have appreciated the difference.

Second, this fracturing of the great Islamic empire coincided with the breaking up of the Carolingian empire in Europe. With western Europe entering another dark period, many of the splinter states saw an opportunity to expand commerce. After all, whether for dynastic, ethnic, or religious reasons, many of the splinter states disliked each other intensely and preferred to trade with Christian Europe than with their Islamic neighbors. Hence the new wave of Islamic attacks on Europe in the 9th and 10th centuries, coinciding roughly with the Magyar and Viking invasions. By 850 Muslim forces had conquered Sicily, parts of southern Italy, and the Balearic Islands, and they had made successful raids on Sardinia, Corsica, and the cities of Marseilles and Rome. But the Islamic attacks were not campaigns of conquest. Rather, they were attempts to carve out zones of interest, economic trading posts, and certain resources. And, as often as not, they were competing with one another to create these zones. For example, the Aghlabids of Tunisia seized Sicily in part in order to make sure that the Rustamids of Algeria did not get it.

All these developments transformed European and Muslim relations, which had been characterized by violence, distrust, and suffering. When the smoke cleared, Latin Europe and the Islamic world were each profoundly different places than they had been before.

THE REINVENTION OF WESTERN EUROPE

The Carolingian collapse was so spectacular and complete that it allowed Europe to reinvent itself in the 9th and 10th centuries—in the north via a new network of lords and vassals, bound by feudal bonds, and in the south by the growth of cities, powered by trade. The church, beset by corruption of astonishing proportions, responded with a reform movement of its own that remade the entire institution and put Christian life on a wholly new trajectory. The combination of these reinventions—social, civic, and spiritual—led directly to some of the greatest achievements of the medieval era. They also paved the way for the Crusades.

In France itself, the heartland of Carolingian power, the decay of the state and the pressure of foreign invasion caused farmers and their families to abandon their scattered homesteads and to take shelter in groups, under the protection of whatever strongman might exist in the district. Having little or nothing else to give in return for protection, they offered their labor. By this simple demographic shift, a society of individual farmers evolved into a new society based on **manors**—collective farms under the authority of lords. The lords owned the land and the major share of its annual yield, though the work was done by dependent farmers called **serfs**. Serfs were not slaves, although their daily lives differed little from slavery; lords could not buy and sell serfs as though they were mere property. Rather, serfs and lords were tied together by complex networks of mutual duties and rights. Serfs could not leave the manor, for example, or marry their offspring to someone from another manor, without their lords' permission. Lords were required to resolve disputes between serfs. The services owed back and forth made medieval manors like miniature communities, like agrarian states unto themselves.

The peasants brought varied backgrounds to their collective work, including knowledge of techniques like crop rotation, the use of wheeled plows, and the invention of horseshoes (which allowed quicker and more agile horses to replace lumbering teams of oxen as draught animals). Crop yields nearly doubled as a result. By living and working collectively, sharing labor, skills, and resources, farming on manors became much more productive. Crop surpluses became the norm, and western Europe became a food exporter for the first time in its history. It was largely to secure access to this food supply that the rump states of the broken Islamic empire began to compete for trading zones along the Mediterranean coast. And this trade allowed the new class of manorial lords to become rich—rich enough eventually to give up wooden manorial houses for stone castles (see Figure 9.1).

But the manorial lords lacked any real political legitimacy. They were, in many cases, of questionable ancestry and social status, men to whom war refugees had fled in desperation. These warlords (the Latin term is *milites*) used a variety of strategies to legitimate themselves. One popular option was simply to invent aristocratic genealogies for themselves, claiming descent from the Carolingians or some other early elite family. Another method was to form ties with other milites—a medieval equivalent of the modern practice of governments recognizing one another. By securing the support of other milites in the region, a warlord acquired at least a veneer of political authenticity.

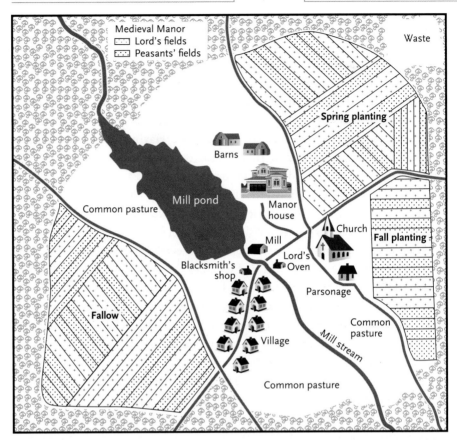

FIGURE 9.1   **A Medieval Manor**

These relationships between warlords had substance: some forms of military service, counsel, and economic assistance were invariably involved. Since each warlord differed in the amount of land or social recognition he commanded, these relationship slowly took on a hierarchical form, with a senior partner and a subordinate one—hence the terms **lord** and **vassal**, respectively. In forming a tie, a lord bestowed on the vassal dominion over the latter's allotted manor or manors, and the vassal in turn pledged to serve the lord loyally. In a public ceremony, the lord handed over a symbolic clod of earth, to represent the manors being bestowed. Since the Latin word for this land was *feudum*, these relationships were generally known as **feudal bonds**.

By the start of the 11th century, these connections had spread like a neural network across much of northern Europe; by the start of the 12th century they dominated it. Along with manors and feudal relations, they helped create a new society based on land tenure and ties of personal loyalty. Serfs worked for a landlord in return for the security and primitive justice he provided, while milites were bound to one another as lords and vassals. The system varied quite a bit from territory to territory. The feudal networks in France, for example, were significantly more elaborate, hierarchical, and complicated than those in England. When William the Conqueror (r. 1066–1089) seized the island in 1066 and parceled out the lands, he made it all but impossible for his vassals to redistribute the land to vassals of their own. Germany added its own twist, as great lords created feudal relations with high-ranking churchmen—abbots and bishops. Since these men would presumably not be producing heirs, there was little danger of the feudal lands becoming hereditary holdings.

MEDITERRANEAN CITIES

Mediterranean Europe followed a different trajectory. By long-standing custom, social position here had depended less on controlling land than on participating in the public life of the community: merchants, financiers, civic officials, and professionals formed the backbone of southern European life. Urban life had declined during the long centuries of the Dark Ages—some cities had collapsed to the point where they had only one-tenth of the ancient population levels—but revived under the short-lived stability of the Carolingians. Food surpluses from the new manors gradually made their way into urban markets. The Muslim attacks of the 9th and 10th centuries forcibly (and probably unnecessarily) opened those markets to trade with North Africa; cities like Barcelona, Genoa, Marseilles, Montpellier, Pisa, and Venice were the first to establish permanent commercial relations with the Muslim countries, and as a result they witnessed a dramatic rise in their wealth and power (see Map 9.4).

The Mediterranean accordingly roared back to life, much as the ancient Romans had first imagined, and from the 11th to the 15th century these cities were the economic powerhouses of Europe.[9] At the same time, the Byzantines' ground losses to the Muslims forced them to reorient their military and commercial attention northward, into the Slavic Balkan lands and the territories around the Black Sea. And as the Greeks gradually relinquished their control of the sea-lanes in the eastern Mediterranean, the Latin cities moved in aggressively. More cities joined in—Amalfi, Gaeta, Naples, Tarragona—and soon Latin Europe's commercial network, having expanded throughout the Mediterranean, spread around Spain, through the Gulf of Biscay, and into the North Sea. They brought lumber, minerals, wool, and metal ores to the manufacturing centers along the coast, transporting eastern silks, spices, metalwork, and dyed cloth back to the

---

[9] In the middle of the 12th century, the annual commercial tax revenue from the city of Palermo alone was four times that from the entire kingdom of England.

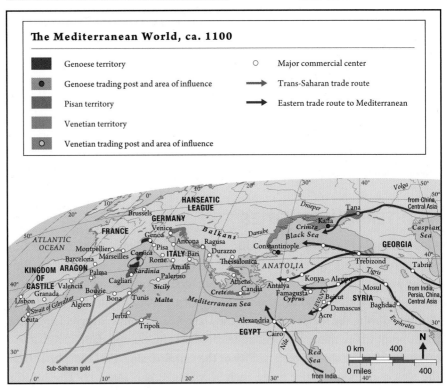

MAP 9.4 The Mediterranean World, ca. 1100

west. Developments in ship design led to larger and swifter commercial vessels, capable of delivering larger cargoes at less cost. Meanwhile the growing use of financial instruments like letters of credit reduced the danger of carrying large amounts of cash. By the late 11th century, an embryonic banking industry had already emerged in Italy.

Mediterranean cities quickly became multiethnic polyglot emporia, much as they had been during the Pax Romana. A visitor to 12th-century Barcelona or Pisa, for example, would find the streets and markets crowded with merchants. They came from Alexandria, Athens, Brussels, Famagusta, Lisbon, Palermo, and Tunis, and a dozen other places—with more than a sprinkling of Jews from all round the Mediterranean. The interaction between groups was regulated by complex systems of municipal and religious laws, ethnic customs, class privileges, and commercial traditions. Merchants of different ethnicities, cities, or particular social strata each had specific rights and privileges, negotiated between communal governments. In order to keep straight who was who, Mediterranean cities began to use dress codes to identify people. These **sumptuary codes** elaborately regulated styles of dress, types of fabrics, headgear, footwear, numbers of buttons,

Amalfi   A panoramic photograph of Amalfi, a small town on the southern Italian coast that rose to great wealth and power in the 10th–12th centuries. This photo, from the late 19th century, shows how wealth and power did not always depend on or result in the physical growth of the city.

and the sorts of decorative badges, pins, and scarves each person could wear. The idea was not to shame groups but to establish the rules of their engagement.

The communicative calculus could be elaborate: a Muslim cloth merchant from Famagusta (in Cyprus), for example, conducting business in Montpellier with a Christian member of the jewelers' guild from Marseilles was entitled to a specific set of legal rights. One had to know who one was dealing with, or there was no deal. Moreover, since different groups often had different housing and dietary requirements, the custom quickly arose of segregating the cities: merchants from cities that did a lot of business with one another were awarded buildings, streets, or even whole neighborhoods to themselves. There they had special houses, butcher shops, alehouses, worship sites, so that each could live according to their own customs.

Most cities were governed by municipal councils and various administrative executives, most of whom in turn were drawn from the urban elites. This group consisted of local rural aristocrats, well-to-do merchants, the professional classes (bankers and lawyers, chiefly), and representatives of the leading artisanal and commercial guilds.

THE REINVENTION OF THE CHURCH

The Catholic Church also reinvented itself in the post-Carolingian centuries. It needed reform badly, for many forms of corruption had taken hold by the 9th and 10th centuries. The problem with the church, though, was not that it had "become corrupt." Rather, it had been corrupted by the milites, the secular war-lords in Latin Europe. Simply put, the warlords, to raise funds for their armies, revived the old Carolingian practice of ransacking their own churches and mon-asteries. Many simply plundered and ran off with the spoils, but others conceived of a longer-term strategy for tapping into ecclesiastical wealth: they expelled the clerical leaders (often by killing them) and sold their positions to their military and political underlings and supporters. By placing their clients in ecclesiastical positions, the warlords secured a set percentage of the churches' annual revenues. In turn, they rewarded their followers with fancy titles, accoutrements, salaries, and prestige. This abuse was called **simony** and it was rampant, from village churches and small monasteries to large episcopacies and even the papacy. Few religious houses avoided the onslaught.

The chronicles of the 10th and 11th centuries abound with abominable be-havior by warlord lackeys in Church position. The nadir was reached in Rome. During a period remembered as the "Pornocracy" (904–984), the Holy See was bought and sold numerous times among the leading families in Roman politics. Pope John XII (r. 956–963) was reported to have sold the bishopric of one town to a ten-year-old boy, as a birthday present from the boy's father.[10] The tradition of state control of the church dated back to the emperor Constantine and the Council of Nicaea. The more recent tyranny of the Carolingians had been stark, but they never abused the Church in the same way that the warlords now did. The fundamental reform required was to insist on the church's freedom from secular control. **Libertas ecclesie!** ("Freedom for the church!") became the demand of the reformers.

The reform movement began at the grassroots level, on the new manors, where the problem of simony was felt most acutely. To the peasants, simony not only looked bad but created a profound spiritual crisis. The Carolingians, after all, had struggled mightily to promote Christian education and to improve the quality of parish church life. As a result, by the mid- to late 10th century probably a clear majority of western peasants were meaningfully, knowledgeably Chris-tian. And the one teaching they all knew was that they needed the sacraments in order to achieve salvation, especially baptism.

---

[10]   John's favorite mistress, it was said, wore a papal crown, sat on a throne, and turned one wing of the palace into a whorehouse. He died in bed with a married woman.

But does a "priest" who got his job only by buying the title from a warlord actually have sacramental authority? Even if the "priest" does perform a Eucharist, are the bread and wine of that ceremony truly turned into the Body and Blood of Christ? And if not, is the ceremony of any value at all? If a peasant couple has a sickly infant whom they want to have baptized, is the baby truly baptized if the "priest" is a simoniac? The question was not theoretical: probably one-half of all children born in Europe at this time died before the age of five. Since Catholic doctrine maintained that only baptized Christians can be saved, the couple's baby would presumably suffer eternal damnation because of the illegitimacy of the "priest's" action. It gets more complicated, too: What if the priest in question had been properly trained for his vocation, but his ordination to the priesthood had been performed by a simoniac bishop? Or if that bishop's elevation to the episcopacy had been performed by a simoniac archbishop—perhaps by that ten-year-old boy appointed by John XII?

Outraged peasants understood one thing quite well: this problem existed because the milites had taken over the churches. Warlords no longer merely controlled the peasants' lives on the manors; their greed for church revenue now placed even the peasants' eternal souls in jeopardy. Demands for freeing the churches from the warlords' clutches therefore began on the manors, where the population could express collective complaint. These rallies for reform, called **Peace of God** assemblies, began as individual demonstrations. However, they multiplied in number, since peasants everywhere had essentially the same complaint and the same sole method of protest available to them. They thus took on the appearance of a movement—indeed, the first mass movement in Western history.

Movements need leadership. That leadership came from Europe's bishops. The reawakening of Europe's cities had revived the episcopacies as well. Although defined as the spiritual descendants of the Twelve Apostles, bishops had always been second-tier figures in the Latin Church. When over 90 percent of the population lived in the countryside, churchmen in cities lacked prestige—especially since hardly any cities in continental Europe were of any real size. In Charlemagne's time, for example, the city of Paris was only 7.5 acres (3 hectares) in area. By comparison, the university campus at which I teach is 75 acres (30 hectares) in area.

Monasteries had always been the real centers of power in Latin Christianity, going back to Saint Benedict in the 6th century. Most of the scholars drawn into the Carolingian court had been monks and abbots, and monastic wealth (when it was not plundered) was the largest accumulated treasure in most districts. As cities grew in size and number, the relative importance of bishops did too. And they seized on the Peace of God assemblies as a means to place themselves at the forefront of church reform. Bishops began to convene regional councils, scheduled and organized assemblies, arranged for large-scale public Masses, commissioned speakers, issued calls for specific *milites* to relinquish their strangleholds over their churches, and above all promoted themselves as the leaders of the reformed church. The more success they had in winning churches' freedom, the faster they rose in popular estimation.

By the time the reform reached the papacy (the last part of the church to be reformed) the bishops were clearly the dominant power brokers. But as the bishops took center stage, so too did the pope—who was, after all, the bishop of Rome.[11] The Church in the world had become the center, and the church removed from the world had moved to the margins. Europe's leading kings, however, were not enthusiastic about having an independent papacy. The second half of the 11th century was thus filled with diplomatic, rhetorical, and military wrangling between Rome and her rivals. Important turning points were the pontificates of Leo IX (r. 1049–1054) and Nicholas II (r. 1059–1061). Leo spent much of his time as pope on the road, bringing the majesty of the office to the eyes of Europe's commoners for the first time, and Nicholas created the **College of Cardinals**—which subsequently acquired sole power to elect the next successor to Saint Peter. These two pontificates were, each in its own way, declarations of papal independence. By the time of Gregory VII (r. 1073–1085), military forces under the German ruler Henry IV (r. 1056–1106) invaded Italy and imprisoned the pope. When papal defenders from southern Italy raced to his rescue, they found that Henry had fled north. They sacked the city mercilessly, which forced Gregory to sneak out of Rome in disguise lest the outraged populace murder him.

Papal-reform Conflict   The German emperor Henry IV, facing rebellion from his nobles, pleads with Countess Matilda of Tuscany to help persuade Pope Gregory VII to end the rebellion. This image appears in an 11th-century manuscript of *The Life of Matilda, Countess of Tuscany.*

---

[11]   At first the overwhelming majority of popes came from monastic backgrounds. In the second thousand years of Christianity, more than 90 percent of popes were bishops before rising to the Holy See.

This was the tipping point in the papal-reform conflict, and all sides recognized a need to find a compromise. In 1122 it was reached: the **Concordat of Worms**, signed in that year, affirmed the papacy's independence. They recognized that only a free election by the College of Cardinals could legitimately select the pontiff. On the secular side, lay rulers vowed to accept the church's own appointees to clerical positions, but retained the right to bestow all the lands and revenues associated with those appointments. The great reform, everyone hoped, was finished.

THE CRUSADES

Between 1095 and 1291 Latin Europe fought a series of large-scale military campaigns to win back the Holy Land, which had been under Muslim control since 639. Numerous small-scale efforts continued after that but amounted to little. Nonetheless, the Crusades changed societies and regimes throughout the Mediterranean.

The Crusades are unique in Western history, for they are the only wars that were formally sanctioned and blessed by the church. To take part in them was considered not only morally justifiable but a positive spiritual action. These wars, the church proclaimed, pleased God and made one a better Christian—to the point that if a soldier died on crusade, he was assured forgiveness of all his sins and eternal salvation. (Assuming that he had had a penitent heart and pure motives.) The church called for crusades, preached them from the pulpit, formally inducted their leading fighters, and helped arrange their financing. As enthusiasm for crusades to the Holy Land waned in the 13th century, the crusades' mechanism of preaching and finance were brought to bear on conflicts elsewhere in Europe.

While a new phenomenon, the crusades were nevertheless a product of the centuries that had preceded them. If one disregards the religious motive that lay behind them, the crusades appear as simply the newest chapter in the centuries-old struggle for control of the eastern Mediterranean shore. These lands offered access to both the European economy, centered on the sea, and the overland Asian economy composed of the great silk and spice routes. Its geographical location made the Holy Land valuable long before it became holy. The Phoenicians and the Hittites fought over it. So did the Egyptians and the Sea

While a new phenomenon, the Crusades were nevertheless a product of the centuries that had preceded them. If one disregards the religious motive that lay behind them, the Crusades appear as simply the newest chapter in the centuries-old struggle for control of the eastern Mediterranean shore.

Peoples, the Hebrews and the Canaanites, and then the Persians and the Greeks, followed by the Greeks (under Alexander) and the Persians. The Romans came next, then the Persians again, the Byzantines after that, and then finally the Arabs under the Prophet Muhammad. And the litany of conflicts continues after the Crusades ended. In short, the Crusades had a larger context of East-West struggle that involved many more factors than religion alone. But the religious factor is what makes the Crusades unique. To find ways to justify warfare is one thing, but how did the Latin West ever develop the idea that Jesus wanted them to kill Muslims?

> In short, the Crusades had a larger context of East-West struggle that involved many more factors than religion alone. But the religious factor is what makes the Crusades unique. To find ways to justify warfare is one thing, but how did the Latin West ever develop the idea that Jesus wanted them to kill Muslims?

Part of the answer lies in the great reform effort, where intellectual reform was as important as institutional renewal. At the many councils convened during the 10th and 11th centuries, the church debated, among many other things, the theology of warfare. Under what conditions, if any, may a Christian legitimately use physical violence? Jesus had preached "Blessed are the peacemakers" and had accepted his own torture and death, but did that necessarily imply that Christians must never use any kind of force? Did the bravery of the martyrs of the first Christian centuries require all Christians to deny a right of self-defense when attacked? If one sees a criminal brutally assaulting a woman, is one committing an un-Christian act by pulling him off and beating him into submission?

Such questions were not just hypothetical. Latin Europe was overwhelmingly Christian by the late 11th century, but it was also a society organized for warfare—a secular hierarchy of warlords in the north and a congeries of maritime communes, each with its own militia, in the south. The reformed church needed to find ways to manage and restrain conflicts. One method it employed was the **Truce of God**, a solemn ban on warfare on holy days and on assaulting pilgrims. Those who violated the truce were excommunicated. Christian warfare was acceptable, the church decreed, only if it met three criteria: it must have a just cause, it must be fought in a just way, and it must be declared by a just authority.

By the end of the 11th century, many Europeans believed that warfare against Islam was indeed a just cause. After enduring centuries of persecution under the Romans, Christians in the Holy Land, across North Africa, and throughout the Mediterranean faced conquest by the followers of Muhammad. In creating the great Islamic empire, after all, Muslim armies had killed tens of thousands (and possibly hundreds of thousands) of Christians and Jews. Islamic law formally protected the rights of their subject Christians and Jews, but reality on the ground was often quite different. This is not altogether surprising. Under the early caliphs there had been a concerted effort to protect the empire's dhimmis, but as the years went by, churches and synagogues fell into disrepair as Muslims gradually became the majority group within the overall population. As Islamic unity then shattered into a maze of ethnic, sectarian, and dynastic rivalries, popular willingness to tolerate the non-Muslims in their midst only declined. The 10th and 11th centuries saw repeated popular attacks on Christians and Jews and sporadic state-run persecutions.

The popularity of pilgrimage as a Christian devotion complicated matters. For centuries waves of pilgrims had ventured from Europe to the Holy Land— with Muslim blessing—to worship at the sites associated with Christ. Pilgrimage, however, is by its very nature a public display of faith and therefore at odds with dhimmi law. Muslim ire focused on the European pilgrims traveling through their lands, less so on their own Christian subjects, and those pilgrims began to experience bitter street-level harassment and violence. Soon enough, though, intolerance of the dhimmis themselves took root in many places. Islamic reform groups like the Almohads and Almoravids in Spain and North Africa made no secret of their determination to crush the Christians and Jews living among them. In 1009 the Egyptian ruler al-Hakim (r. 996–1021) demolished the Church of the Holy Sepulcher in Jerusalem (the church built over what is believed to have been Jesus's actual tomb) and ordered every church and synagogue in his realm similarly destroyed. Christians across Europe were horrified but not altogether surprised. To take arms against such attacks therefore seemed to satisfy the requirement of a just cause.

Church of the Holy Sepulcher   What the crusaders were after: the tomb of Christ at the Church of the Holy Sepulcher in Jerusalem. The present chapel structure was built in the 13th century. Earlier buildings were damaged or destroyed by various attackers, the most notable being the Egyptian caliph al-Hakim in the early 11th century.

BUT NOT A WAR AGAINST ISLAM

There were eight major Crusades, all except the First Crusade ending in failure. The soldiers of the first campaign conquered the Holy Land in 1099 and carved four separate states out of it (see Map 9.5). These became nominally Christian states, although the overwhelming bulk of their populations were Muslims, Jews, and non-Latin Christians. Despite their violent creation, however, the states quickly developed internal policies that granted as much autonomy as possible to the native groups. The crusaders turned into surprisingly lenient rulers, as evidenced by the fact that thousands of Muslims and Jews migrated to the crusader states before they were crushed in 1291. While the Crusades aimed to wrest the Holy Land from Muslim control, they were not a general war on Islam itself. Christian trade with Muslims continued in the Mediterranean cities throughout the Crusades—and in fact increased steadily. Muslim sources of the age never present the struggles for the Holy Land in religious terms, and the Christian conquest of Jerusalem in 1099 triggered no groundswell of outrage outside of Palestine itself.

Nor were the Crusades a fight against Arabs. If the Crusades began with any specific enemy in mind, it was the Seljuk Turks whose arrival near the holy sites in the 1060s and 1070s did the most to interrupt the passage of pilgrims. The Abbasids had long courted the Turks, whose military might was considerable, and hoped to use them against Shi'i princes in Syria, Palestine, and Egypt who refused to obey Baghdad. The Turks were new to Islam, but they burned with the zeal often found among recent converts. With the caliphs' blessing they marched westward, defeated the Byzantine army at Manzikert in 1071, and spread throughout Anatolia, setting up an independent state. But many of the nomadic warriors refused to settle down and raided the Arab-led states to their south. The threat to the splinter states inspired them to crack down on their dhimmis in a show of force. The age demanded an expression of rigorous jihad, and it got it.

Caught between Crusaders from the west and Turks from the east, the Byzantines survived by playing one side off the other. They no longer had the military might to assert themselves and became adept at diplomatic manipulation, acquiring for themselves a reputation for trickery and unreliability. The Crusaders came to despise the Byzantines as much as the Muslims, which explains the wild violence unleashed when the soldiers of the Fourth Crusade (1202–1204) sacked Constantinople.

The Siege of Antioch (1098)
William of Tyre's *Histoire d'Outremer* ("History of Events across the Sea") is one of our best sources for the first two crusades and the internal life of the crusader states between wars. Here the siege of Antioch—the most strategically important battle of the First Crusade—is depicted.

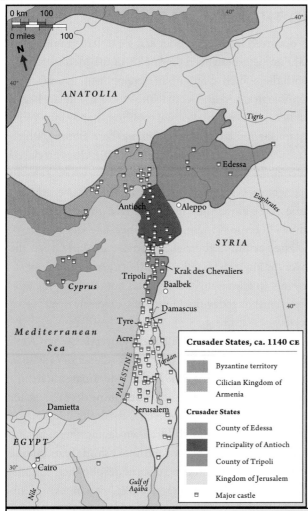

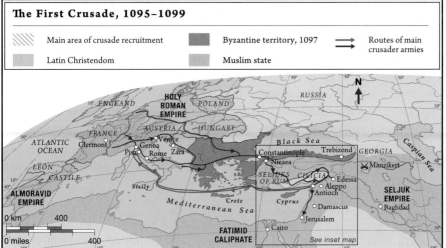

MAP 9.5   The First Crusade and the Crusader States

PARLIAMENTS AND THE MAMLUK EMPIRE

Several important changes occurred in the Crusader era. First, large numbers of Latin Christians from feudal Europe experienced the vitality of the Mediterranean. They brought back north with them ideas about urban development, manufacture and commerce, schools, technologies, and intellectual life. Western scholars began to learn Greek and Arabic and to use both intellectual traditions to advance Western thought. Cities were established in large numbers in northern Europe, which catalyzed economic growth. By the end of the Crusader era, in 1291, cities produced well more than half of the economic output of northern countries, which helps to account for the rise of parliamentary systems of government. As cities became the main providers of tax revenue to the kings, they also demanded a voice in the government. In the course of the 13th century in England, France, and Germany, representatives of the urban classes acquired the right to advise the king, then the power to initiate legislation for the king, and finally the authority to veto the king by controlling his purse. (They met in a separate "house" so as not to offend the aristocracy by their mere presence, just as today the House of Commons meets separately from the House of Lords.)

Second, the arrival of the Turks upset and ultimately overthrew the Arab rulers of the Middle East. In their place, the Turks created an independent state in Anatolia, called the Sultanate of Rum, and a second Turkish-dominated state in a reunited Egypt and Syria, called the Mamluk Empire. The **Mamluks** (Arabic for "slave") originated as an elite bodyguard unit for the Abbasid caliphs. Their name derives from the practice of seizing Christian children, enslaving them, raising them as Muslims, and putting them through an extraordinary military discipline and training. These slave-soldiers were culturally Turkish, despite their origins, and were independent of the tribal loyalties of the regular Muslim armies.[12] Nominally subject to the caliphs in Baghdad, these two states comprised the center of Islamic power (see Map 9.6). In 1258 Abbasid power disappeared entirely when the Mongols destroyed Baghdad; the Mongols' self-proclaimed drive for world domination ended when they were decisively defeated themselves by the Mamluks only two years later. Turkish hegemony over the Islamic world lasted in one form or another until the early 20th century.

Third, the Byzantine Empire effectively ceased to exist as a world power. When the Crusaders wrecked Constantinople in 1204, they held on to the empire for seventy years, parceling it out to themselves as fiefdoms. For three generations the mainly French usurpers plundered Greece and all her holdings, determined

---

[12]   The Mamluks were highly respected for their abilities—to the point that freemen were known to offer themselves as slaves in order to become eligible for service.

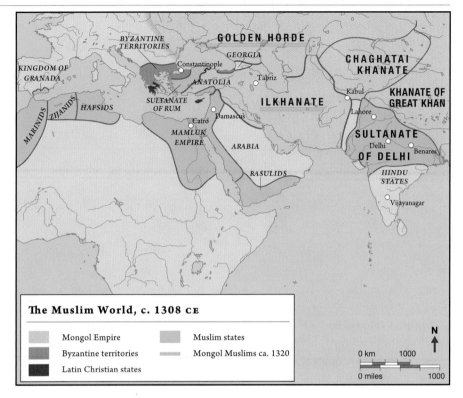

MAP 9.6   The Muslim World, ca. 1308 CE

to crush the Orthodox Church and replace it with Roman Catholicism. By the time they were driven out, in 1278, the empire was in tatters and continued to live only as a weak confederation of four minor states. Using their diplomatic acumen, it managed to survive until its final defeat by the Ottoman Turks in 1453, but for much of its last two centuries the Byzantine Empire consisted of little more than the city of Constantinople itself.

JUDAISM REFORMED, RENEWED, AND REVILED

Scattered by the Romans in 70 CE, the nation of the Jews disappeared from history as a political entity. They were left stateless, exiled from their homeland, hounded by Christian evangelists, and still subject to persecution by the Romans. Yet the Jews survived—by adapting imaginatively to the societies where they lived, while clinging to the core of their traditions.

As a Mediterranean people, they scattered, predictably enough, around the sea basin (see Map 9.7). In most places local laws forbade them to own farmland, and hence the Jews of the Diaspora became even more heavily urbanized than

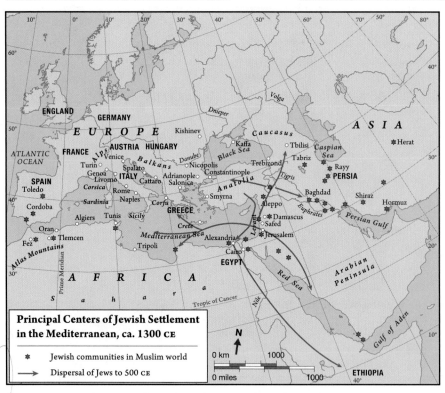

Principal Centers of Jewish Settlement in the Mediterranean, ca. 1300 CE

✳　Jewish communities in Muslim world

→　Dispersal of Jews to 500 CE

0 km　1000
0 miles　1000

MAP 9.7　**Principal Centers of Jewish Settlement in the Mediterranean, ca. 1300 CE**

they had been before. Life in cities, moreover, offered them a modicum of safety, since they tended to live as discrete communities. In their own designated neighborhoods, they could have at least limited autonomy.

The class and sectarian rifts that had characterized life in Judea in Christ's time ceased to have meaning. They were all exiles now and the Temple was no more. The rabbinical strain of Judaism that traced its roots to the Babylonian Captivity hence became the norm for Jewish life. In city after city, Jews established their synagogues and schools, their butcher shops and eateries, and settled into lives as merchants and professionals.

As during their first exile in Iraq, the Jews quickly found that life as a religious minority presented challenges not addressed in the Torah. How should one live a Jewish life in a non-Jewish world? The rabbis therefore set to work to gathering, sifting, organizing, and commenting on the decisions handed down by earlier religious judges. At the same time new judgments were being rendered from one end of the Mediterranean to the other. These judgments and the precedents on which they rested were studied at the great rabbinical academies and eventually were codified in the **Talmud**. It had two parts—the Mishnah (the collected rabbinical laws, compiled around 200 CE by R. Judah ha-Nasi) and the Gemara (commentaries on the laws compiled around three hundred years later). Together, they formed the central pillar of medieval Jewish life. There were competing versions—one produced by scholars in Babylon (where the rabbinical tradition dated to the 6th century BCE) and another in Jerusalem.[13] Although both are considered valid, when the word Talmud is used, it generally refers to the Babylonian version.

Throughout the Middle Ages, most rabbis in Europe received their training at the academies in the Levant, either in Jerusalem or in Baghdad. An important new chapter of Jewish history began with the Carolingian collapse in the late 9th century. A number of late Carolingian princes, hoping to ignite some local manufacturing and commercial activity, invited Jewish communities to relocate from the Mediterranean and to settle permanently in northern Europe. They offered various enticements—legal autonomy under Carolingian protection, advantageous tax schedules, housing allowances, and so on. Once such guarantees were in place, scores of Jewish families, companies, and social networks migrated to the north and settled in the small towns that dotted the Rhine river valley and along the Seine.

For example, in 1084, shortly after arranging the legal founding of Speyer as a municipality, its lord, Bishop Rudiger, issued the following charter:

> In the name of the Holy and Indivisible Trinity, I, Rudiger, by the grace of God bishop of Speyer, having completed the task of establishing Speyer as a legally recognized city, determined to increase the city's honor a thousand-fold by bringing a community of Jews to live permanently within it; and so I invited in Jews from abroad and from Jewish communities in other towns. Moreover, I enclosed them within a fortified wall, lest they be too easily harmed by the rioting common people. . . . I gave them license and privilege to work at money changing according to their desire . . . and I bestowed upon them, from the church's holdings, a burial ground for their own possession and use. . . . As much as I am the ruler of Speyer's [Christian] residents, so is the archisynagogos for the Jews [therein]: he has power to judge all disputes and petitions brought before him. . . . In general, I have granted to the Jews of Speyer— as a crowning grace to my benevolence—statutes of such benefit to them as to be unequalled anywhere in Germany.

As decades passed, these small communities prospered and grew.

Although they remained in more or less continuous contact with the Mediterranean communities, northern Jews soon began to follow a different path of development from southern Jews. These different paths ultimately resulted in the

---

[13] Although called the Jerusalem Talmud, it was actually compiled by scholars in and around the city of Tiberias, along the western shore of the Sea of Galilee.

formation of two distinct Jewish cultural traditions—that of the **Ashkenazim** in the north and the **Sephardim** in the south. The Ashkenazim were the most geographically remote from their homeland, surrounded by a society that did not welcome their arrival. They therefore turned inward, developing a brilliant culture that focused on preserving Talmudic tradition at all cost. The Sephardim, comfortably Mediterranean, were in constant contact with Arab, Greek, and Latin cultural developments, and they participated more directly in intellectual exchange and changes in cultural norms. The stark contrast between Ashkenazic and Sephardic Judaism became apparent when groups from both traditions migrated back to the Holy Land when it was under Crusader control. They wore different styles of clothing, followed different liturgies and rituals, and spoke different vernaculars.[14] Providing separate synagogues, butcher shops, markets,

Jewish Synagogue and Christian Church   During the long Reconquista of Spain from Muslim control, many towns and villages changed hands numerous times. Mosques were turned into churches, then back into mosques, then again into churches, over and over. Synagogues were also built, taken over, handed back, reclaimed for another repeatedly. This 13th-century building in Toledo, in central Spain, was a mosque that was eventually converted into the church of Santa Maria la Blanca. Skilled craftsmen of all faiths found work in the near-constant renovation. In a handful of Christian churches in Spain, the vine-tracery patterns carved on arches by Muslim stonemasons turn into Arabic lettering and spell out the *shahadah*: "There is no god but Allah, and Muhammad is his prophet."

---

[14]   The southerners spoke early forms of Ladino, related to Old Spanish. The northerners spoke early forms of Yiddish.

and housing for both communities challenged the ingenuity of the Crusader-state regimes and led to near-constant low-grade social friction.

North or south, east or west, medieval Jews lived in their separate districts in the cities. And these districts were frequently encircled by protective walls both to mark the territory of Jewish autonomy and to protect the Jews from angry Christian mobs. (The local rabbi possessed the key to the gate.) The church insisted that the only proper Christian response to the Jews was tolerance and coexistence—and that it was the church's special responsibility to protect the Jews. As Pope Innocent III (r. 1198–1216) put it in 1199:

> No Christian may use violence in order to force a Jew to receive baptism . . . for no one who has not willingly sought baptism can be a true Christian. Therefore let no Christian do a Jew any personal injury—except in the case of carrying out the just sentence of a judge—or deprive him of his property, or transgress the rights and privileges traditionally awarded to them. Let no one disturb the celebration of their festivals by beating them with clubs and hurling stones at them; let no one force from them any services which they are not traditionally bound to render; and we expressly forbid anyone . . . to deface or violate their cemeteries or to extort money from them by threatening to do so.

But a declaration like this is usually a recognition that such crimes did occur—which they did, frequently. Popular violence against Jews was a constant element of medieval life. Almost without exception, a papal call for a Crusade to the Holy Land triggered a popular uprising against the Jews. Most infamously, in 1096 rabid crowds murdered hundreds of Jews in Cologne, Mainz, and Worms. In the aftermath of these slaughters, the church took measures to prevent anti-Jewish violence whenever it summoned a Crusade, but those measures usually failed. Official forms of persecution existed too. In the city of Toulouse, for example, a representative of the Jewish community was required to stand on the steps of the Christian cathedral every year on Good Friday and be publicly slapped in the face by the bishop.

Despite the harsh circumstances confronting them, the Jews of the 9th to 12th centuries flourished. Their communities benefited from the economic growth of the era, which they had helped to produce. Their synagogues and schools brimmed with life, and many Jews played important roles in Christian society as advisers, teachers, translators, and intermediaries. Two of the greatest Jewish thinkers of all time emerged at this time too: Rashi (1040–1105) and Maimonides (1135–1204). Rashi lived in northern France and is regarded as the supreme commentator on the Talmud. To the present day, printed editions of the Talmud always include Rashi's line-by-line commentary on each page. Rashi's commentaries on the Bible were important not only to Jewish scholars but to certain Christian ones as well. Later Franciscan scholars like Saint Nicholas of Myra had a special affinity for his writings. Maimonides, by contrast, was Sephardic, growing up in Seville. The arrival in Spain of the Almohads, one of the brutal Sunni reformist sects, made life there untenable, so Maimonides traveled throughout the Mediterranean. He settled at last in Cairo, where he worked as a physician during the day and spent his nights writing legal texts, medical treatises, Biblical commentaries, and philosophy. His two major works were the *Mishneh Torah*—an enormous compilation of Jewish law, with commentary—and the *Guide for the Perplexed*, a brilliant but difficult analysis of the relationship between reason and faith.

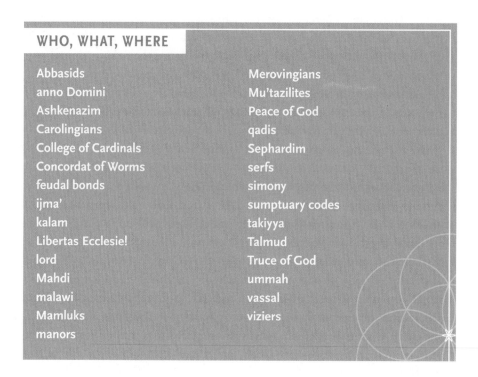

WHO, WHAT, WHERE

Abbasids	Merovingians
anno Domini	Mu'tazilites
Ashkenazim	Peace of God
Carolingians	qadis
College of Cardinals	Sephardim
Concordat of Worms	serfs
feudal bonds	simony
ijma'	sumptuary codes
kalam	takiyya
Libertas Ecclesie!	Talmud
lord	Truce of God
Mahdi	ummah
malawi	vassal
Mamluks	viziers
manors	

SUGGESTED READINGS

Primary Sources

al-Baladhuri. *The Origins of the Islamic State.*
Benjamin of Tudela. *Itinerary.*
Einhard. *The Life of Charlemagne.*
Ibn al-Haytham. *The Advent of the Fatimids.*
Ibn Ishaq. *The Life of Muhammad.*

Maimonides. *The Guide for the Perplexed.*
Rashi. *Commentary on the Torah.*
al-Tabari. *The History of al-Tabari.*
Theophanes. *The Chronicle of Theophanes the Confessor.*

Anthologies

Allen, S. J., and Emilie Amt, eds. *The Crusades: A Reader* (2003).

Constable, Olivia Remie, ed. *Medieval Iberia: Readings from Muslim, Christian, and Jewish Sources* (2011).

Dutton, Paul Edward, ed. *Carolingian Civilization: A Reader* (2004).

Lopez, Robert S., and Irving W. Raymond, trans. *Medieval Trade in the Mediterranean World: Illustrative Documents* (2001).

Shinners, John, ed. *Medieval Popular Religion, 1000–1500: A Reader* (2006).

Studies

Bachrach, Bernard S. *Early Carolingian Warfare: Prelude to Empire* (2000).

Beckwith, Christopher I. *Empires of the Silk Road: A History of Central Eurasia from the Bronze Age to the Present* (2009).

Chazan, Robert. *God, Humanity, and History: The Hebrew First Crusade Narratives* (2000).

———. *The Jews of Medieval Western Christendom: 1000–1500* (2007).

Constable, Olivia Remie. *Housing the Stranger in the Mediterranean World: Lodging, Trade, and Travel in Late Antiquity and the Middle Ages* (2003).

Cook, Michael. *Commanding Right and Forbidding Wrong in Islamic Thought* (2007).

Crone, Patricia. *Meccan Trade and the Rise of Islam* (2004).

Crone, Patricia, and Martin Hinds. *God's Caliph: Religious Authority in the First Centuries of Islam* (2003).

Davidson, Herbert A. *Moses Maimonides: The Man and His Works* (2004).

Friedmann, Yohanan. *Tolerance and Coercion in Islam: Interfaith Relations in the Muslim Tradition* (2003).

Griffith, Sidney H. *The Church in the Shadow of the Mosque: Christians and Muslims in the World of Islam* (2008).

Heather, Peter. *Empires and Barbarians: Migration, Development, and the Birth of Europe* (2009).

Hillenbrand, Carole. *The Crusades: Islamic Perspectives* (2008).

Jotischky, Andrew. *Crusading and the Crusader States* (2004).

Kennedy, Hugh. *The Prophet and the Age of the Caliphates: The Islamic Near East from the Sixth to the Eleventh Century* (2004).

McCormick, Michael. *Origins of the European Economy: Communications and Commerce, AD 300–900* (2002).

Moore, R. I. *The First European Revolution, c. 970–1215* (2000).

Peri, 'Oded. *Christianity under Islam in Jerusalem: The Question of the Holy Sites in Early Ottoman Times* (2001).

Ray, Jonathan. *The Sephardic Frontier: The Reconquista and the Jewish Community in Medieval Iberia* (2008).

Tolan, John V. *Saracens: Islam in the Medieval European Imagination* (2002).

Tyerman, Christopher. *God's War: A New History of the Crusades* (2009).

Wickham, Chris. *Framing the Early Middle Ages: Europe and the Mediterranean, 400–800* (2007).

———. *The Inheritance of Rome: Illuminating the Dark Ages, 400–1000* (2009).

For additional resources, including maps, primary sources, visuals, web links, and quizzes, please go to **www.oup.com/us/backman.**

CHAPTER 10

Worlds Brought Down

1258–1453

The 13th and 14th centuries were an age of unparalleled achievement and trauma. The earliest signs of a recognizably modern European world appeared—parliamentary government, an embryonic form of capitalism, universities, the emerging primacy of science, and the spread of literacy and vernacular culture. Modern technologies like mechanical clocks, eyeglasses, magnetic compasses, paper mills, and portolan charts came into use. So too, however, did "medieval" practices like the inquisition against heretics and the blood libel against the Jews. The Catholic Church assumed the basic institutional form it has today, but it also witnessed an extraordinary wave of popular mysticism and lay evangelism. Some even feared that lay revelation would displace the church as the mediator between God and man. Interest in science surged, in the confident belief that the cosmos was a rational structure whose deepest secrets could be discovered. At the same time, the greatest scientific mind of the age wrote to the pope to warn that the Antichrist, fast approaching, would appear in the guise of a scientist. Economically, Europe

THE GREATER WEST, ca. 1453

◀ **The Triumph of Death**
Painted ca. 1562 by Pieter Bruegel the Elder (1525–1569), this picture represents the horrors of the warfare then starting to reengulf western Europe—the Wars of Religion. The "Triumph of Death" motif dates to the 14th century, when the Black Death poured over the entire Greater West. Bruegel gave it new and horrible life in this painting. "About suffering they were never wrong / the Old Masters," wrote W. H. Auden in his great poem "Musée des Beaux Arts."

finally overtook the Islamic world in wealth and ingenuity. Yet its very success carried within it the seeds of catastrophe. It also contributed to a growing willingness of society to ignore the teachings of the church.

The Islamic world similarly shone, even as it split permanently into three distinct civilizations. The Mongols brought the caliphate to a sudden and savage end, but their equally sudden withdrawal from the scene opened the door to new Muslim conquests, eastward into India and across the Red Sea into sub-Saharan Africa. Three new powerful states emerged—the Mamluks in Egypt and Palestine, the Ottoman Turks in Asia Minor and Syria, and the Safavids in Persia. Meanwhile Muslim Spain fell into a slow, painful decline. Sectarian differences continued, but the urgency of the conflicts between them abated. However, the Sufi movement, which the advance of the Turks westward had accelerated, remained a challenge for Islamic society.

The creative achievements of the age were extraordinary. This should come as no surprise: periods of tremendous affluence and power, and periods of horrific suffering, often inspire great imaginative leaps. The great figures of the late Middle Ages included poets and writers like Rumi [P] (1207–1273), Dante Alighieri (1265–1321), Hafez [P] (1315–1390), Yunus Emre [T] (1240–1321), Geoffrey Chaucer (1343–1400), and the anonymous compiler of the *Arabian Nights*; philosophers like Ibn Arabi [A] (1165–1240), Albertus Magnus (1193–1280), Saint Thomas Aquinas (1225–1274), Gersonides (1288–1345), William of Ockham (1288–1348), Ibn Khaldun [A] (1332–1406), and Hasdai Crescas (1340–1410); scientists like Thomas Bradwardine (1290–1349), and Nicole Oresme (1320–1382); artists like Giotto di Bodone (1267–1337); composers like Guillaume de Machaut (1300–1377); and political thinkers like Marsiglio di Padova (1275–1342). An age that produced these has a claim on anyone's interest. It is important to consider these two centuries together, for the ways in which societies responded to the shared horrors of the 14th century were largely shaped by what had happened in the 13th.

CHAPTER TIMELINE

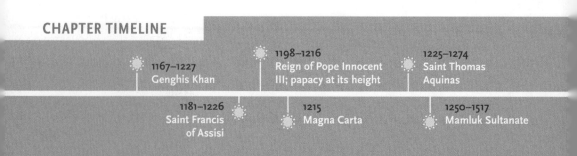

1167–1227
Genghis Khan

1198–1216
Reign of Pope Innocent
III; papacy at its height

1225–1274
Saint Thomas
Aquinas

1181–1226
Saint Francis
of Assisi

1215
Magna Carta

1250–1517
Mamluk Sultanate

LATE MEDIEVAL EUROPE

Latin Europe's history had been shaped by two opposed waves of development. The dual economic and cultural engine of the Mediterranean region spread its influence northward, bringing elements of cosmopolitan urban life, intellectual innovation, and cultural vibrancy into the European heartlands. Political leadership, however, came from the north, as the great monarchies of England, France, and Germany pushed their boundaries southward, drawn by Mediterranean commerce and the gravitational pull of the papal court. The cross-fertilization of north and south benefited each and fostered Europe's ability to reform and revitalize itself. In the contemporary Muslim world, by contrast, innovation came largely from outside, in the dominance of newly Islamicized new foreign rulers—the Ottoman Turks and their ethnic cousins, the Mongols and Tatars.

Feudal England, France, and Germany were the leading powers of the age. Their kings and princes dominated the political scene, and their soldiers provided the overwhelming bulk of the Crusaders. From the 11th to 13th centuries, they continually extended their power southward to reach the Mediterranean. Germany's emperors from the time of Otto I (r. 962–973) claimed sovereignty over northern Italy, and they showed themselves willing to compromise their authority over the German nobles in order to achieve it. France's Capetian dynasty, which came to power in 987 with little more than the city of Paris to its credit, engaged in five generations of aggressive diplomacy: through marriage, it brought more and more of central and southern France into the family domain. By the reign of Louis VII (r. 1137–1180), it reached as far south as the Pyrenees, though it still lacked a Mediterranean outlet—which finally came with Philip IV's (r. 1180–1223) Crusade against the Cathars in southern France and Louis IX's (r. 1226–1270) marriage to Margaret of Provence.

England's monarchs had pursued similar aims. At its zenith in the reign of Henry II (r. 1154–1189), the royal domain included England, Normandy, Brittany, Maine, Anjou, Gascony, and Aquitaine. As Henry's successors gradually

 1258
Mongols annihilate
Baghdad

1347
Black Death arrives
in Western Europe

1453
Ottomans capture
Constantinople

1337–1453
Hundred Years' War

1370–1405
Reign
of Tamerlane

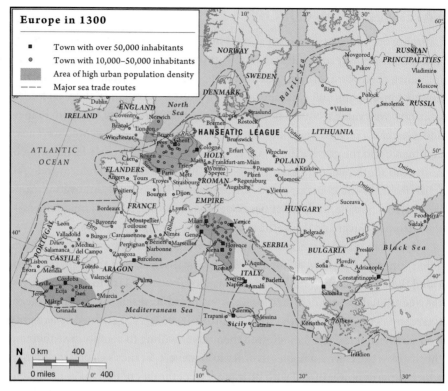

MAP 10.1   Europe in 1300

lost control of the French territories, they compensated by opening a strategic offensive in the Mediterranean marriage market. The countervailing wave was the northward spread of Mediterranean urban institutions and commercial techniques. Cities proliferated in the 12th and 13th centuries across feudal Europe. And they brought with them Roman law, notions of municipal citizenship, commercial and artisanal guilds, schools and universities, and even Mediterranean dress codes. These eased the interactions of the increasingly polyglot and ethnically varied cities (see Map 10.1).

The church, too, reached the zenith of its worldly power. The great Gregorian Reform had resulted in a sturdy, hierarchical organization—of priests, bishops, archbishops, and, at the summit, the Holy Pontiff. Popes like Innocent III (r. 1198–1216) and Gregory IX (r. 1227–1241) exercised a degree of power that no earlier popes had ever had. The new papacy based its authority on a principle called **plenitudo potestatis**—literally "fullness of power" but better translated as "ultimate jurisdiction"—which stressed the church's responsibility toward the world. On the Day of Judgment, it argued, every person must stand before God and be held responsible for his or her sins, but the members of the church must also be held accountable. Did your priest teach you the doctrines of the church?

Did he help guide you through life's challenges and temptations? Did he nourish you with the sacraments? Since the clergy bear some responsibility for every person's ultimate fate, the church must have a right to pronounce on the doings of our lives, particularly any aspect of life that carried a substantial moral component (admittedly a wide catchment area). Plenitudo potestatis did not assert the church's right to control individual lives, only its right to be heard.

SCHOLASTICISM

Through its bishops, the church oversaw the universities of Europe (see Map 10.2). This was the great age of **scholasticism**—really a curriculum rather than a philosophy. Scholastic learning was based on the conviction that the whole of the cosmos was rationally ordered: God, having created Man as a rational creature, has given him the ability, but also the responsibility, to determine the universe's operation. Not surprisingly, the rediscovered works of Aristotle took center stage. Scholastic writers specialized in a type of encyclopedia called a **summa**, which attempted to summarize all existing knowledge on a given topic. Scholastic

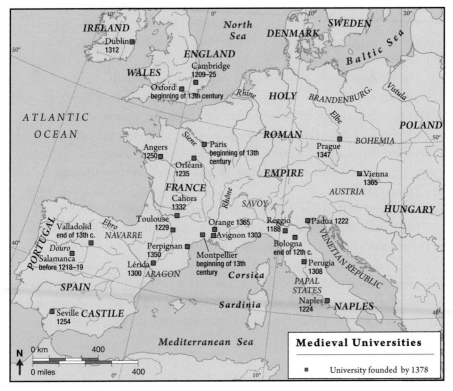

MAP 10.2   Medieval Universities

scholars believed in the unity of truth in all areas of human experience. Apparent inconsistencies in human knowledge are merely imperfections in our own understanding, not flaws in nature.

No one will ever award Albertus Magnus (1193–1280)—or his brilliant pupil Saint Thomas Aquinas (1225–1274)—prizes for prose style. They wrote in an annotated outline form: lists of questions followed by lists of answers, with subsections, objections, and counterassertions inserted wherever deemed appropriate. One might be reading lines of code for a computer program. For them, elegance lay in the thought behind the words, not the words themselves. Indeed, any stylistic flourishes that drew attention away from the ideas undermined the force of the argument. True beauty lay in the perfect rational ordering of God's Creation and in the perfectly rational representation of it in words. Here, for example, Aquinas argues that the soul does not die when the body does:

> Nothing in nature is destroyed by that which brings its existence to a perfected state. Now the perfection of the human soul consists in its acquisition of total knowledge and virtue—things attained by the withdrawal from the body. For knowledge is made perfect when it apprehends Ideas, Goals, Purposes, which are immaterial things; and virtue is made perfect when one does not give in to bodily passions but tempers and restrains them by reason....
>
> Natural desires do not exist in vain. Humans naturally crave eternal existence; and while it is true that all creatures desire to keep living, only human beings rationally apprehend existence. To apprehend existence absolutely, as man does, is not the same thing as to desire to continue in the present moment, as dumb animals do. Therefore man seeks permanent existence for his soul simply because he apprehends absolute and eternal existence....
>
> If the destruction of the body means the destruction of the soul, then it must follow that any weakening of the body entails a weakening of the soul. But in reality, if the soul is weakened in any way by a weakening of the body, that is only coincidental ... and if our understanding flags or falters because of fatigue, injury, or weakness in the body—this is not necessarily fatigue, injury, or weakness in the understanding itself but only in those bodily faculties that the understanding utilizes. (*Summa contra Gentiles* 2.79)

The prose is bloodless (even more so in the original Latin). The point of it is to strip away rhetorical effect so that the beauty of God's Truth—in this case, the eternality of the human soul—can shine through, like sunlight through a windowpane.

Scholasticism represents a powerful moment in the history of Western culture, when it seemed possible to understand everything. The cosmos appeared to work with a formal perfection, and the limits of the human intellect seemed boundless.[1] But unlike the distant and indifferent Creator of the deists of a later time, the God of the scholastics was present, active, brilliant, and benign—an artist and scientist. The rational mind, Aquinas and others insisted, is not a tool but a beautiful gift through which we can perceive all the divine and hidden harmonies of life. This confidence overflowed into other areas of medieval life, like the construction of vast cathedrals and literary masterpieces like Dante's *Divine Comedy*. It would be a long time before the Western world was again so self-confident.

> Scholasticism represents a powerful moment in the history of Western culture, when it seemed possible to understand everything. The cosmos appeared to work with a formal perfection, and the limits of the human intellect seemed boundless.

The monastic wing of the church, for its part, remained wealthy and influential at the local level. Abbots, however, no longer numbered large among the power brokers in Rome, just as monastic schools had given way to the universities. Popes from the late 11th century on were almost always drawn from the pool of bishops—a trend that continues today. But monastic life underwent several reform efforts that brought new life to the calling. New orders—notably the Cistercians and the Carthusians—gained renown for sanctity and discipline, though they did not place much emphasis on scholarship as the Benedictines

Interior of Sainte-Chapelle, Paris   The stained glass windows of Sainte-Chapelle (1246–1248) are a fine example of the vibrancy of Gothic Art. The pointed arches and ribbed vaulting of the Gothic style can be seen clearly.

---

[1]   Scholasticism's confidence in the human intellect did not appear again in the West until the Enlightenment of the 18th century.

had done. Contemplative by design, these new orders were also sites of intense mystical experience.

MYSTICISM

Mysticism, or direct contact with God, was indeed among the most striking elements of the age. It was hardly a new phenomenon. The voices that had sent Abraham on his first wanderings in the Holy Land, the burning bush on Mount Sinai through which Moses heard God's commands, the warnings of the Biblical prophets—all these were God's piercing of the veil between the divine world and our own. In the Christian era, figures like Saint Jerome and Saint Augustine had had mystical revelations. God spoke to the masses countless times through the miracles of the saints. What was unique about the mystical experiences of the late Middle Ages was their sheer number. Many hundreds—even thousands—of people claimed to have had an irruptive experience of God, either in the form of visions or otherworldly voices. They included austere Carthusian monks and courtly poets, but also everyday peasants and town dwellers. At times, it seemed almost an epidemic, and historians have in fact looked for a clinical cause—such as prolonged famine, tainted food or water, or bacterial infection. But since claims of mystical experience stretched from Scotland to Portugal, from Majorca to Denmark, and from Belgium to Poland, a natural cause seems unlikely. None, at any rate, has ever been found.

Gero Cross   A fine example of Gothic art. This crucifixion scene, carved in wood, was donated to the cathedral at Cologne by Archbishop Gero in the 14th century.

These revelations centered on Christ. People heard Christ, saw Christ, spoke with Christ, embraced Christ, and kissed Christ. Moreover, the Christ whom they encountered was not the stern, lordly King of Heaven and Judge of the Last Day (the most common images of Christ in early medieval art). Rather, he was the gentle, loving, tender-hearted Christ who suffered and died out of his love for all mankind. One mystic, an Englishwoman named Margery Kempe (1373–1438), speaking in the third person, describes how on a pilgrimage to Jerusalem

[she] wept and sobbed as plenteously as though she had seen Our Lord with her bodily eye, suffering His Passion at that time. Before her in her soul she saw Him verily by contemplation, and that caused her to have compassion. And when they came up on to Mount Calvary, she fell down because she could not stand or kneel, and rolled and wrestled with her body, spreading her arms abroad, and cried with a loud voice as though her heart would burst asunder; for, in the city of her soul, she saw verily and clearly how Our Lord was crucified.

After she returned to England, the sightings continue.

When she came home to England, [the visions] came seldom at first, as it were once a month, then once a week, and afterwards daily; and once she had fourteen [visions] in one day, and another day she had seven, and so on, as God would visit her, sometimes in church, sometimes in the street, sometimes in her chambers, sometime in the fields, whenever God would send them, and she never knew the time nor the hour when they would come.

Two aspects of the mystical epidemic stand out. First, people experiencing contact with God did not come away with new insights into theological mysteries or dramatic new interpretations of Scripture. They did not know how to live better, make the world a safer and more prosperous place, or unlock the secret meanings of life. Time after time, they described their experiences simply as intense waves of emotion. They felt an overwhelming sensation of God's love—as though God wanted only to remind people that he hadn't forgotten them. He sees their suffering and wants to reassure them that they are loved. Here is another Englishwoman, Julian of Norwich (1342–1416):

I have begged repeatedly to understand what God meant by these visions ever since I had them. Finally, after more than fifteen years, I received the answer, for I heard in my soul the following words: "Would you like to know the Lord's message in all this? Then learn this well: Love was His message. Who showed this message to you? Love did. What did He show you? Love. Why did He show it to you? Out of Love. Hold on to this idea and you will forever grow in your knowledge and understanding of Love; otherwise you will never know or learn anything."

And this is how I learned that Love was Our Lord's message. I saw with certainty that even before God created us He loved us, and that His Love has never slackened, and that His Love shall endure forever. All the works He has done have been done out of this Love; in this Love He has created all things for our good use; and in this Love our lives are everlasting. We began to exist at the moment of our creation, but the Love that made us was in God from the beginning of time. Our truest beginning is therefore in His Love, and all of this we shall see in God, without end.

Second, mysticism privileged women. Vastly greater numbers of women reported experiencing this sort of contact than men did, and it seems likely that even greater numbers of women experienced the visions without reporting them. Hildegard of Bingen (1098–1179) was a noble-born German abbess who dramatically described her visions in prose, painting, and in music. Hadewijch of Flanders (d. ca. 1245) composed a long sequence of poems and letters that described her own "mystical marriage" to Christ in the vocabulary of courtly love. Julian of Norwich, quoted above, was an educated commoner who at the age of thirty had sixteen separate visions. As a result, she became a recluse and devoted the rest of her life to puzzling out what had happened to her. Her *Revelations of Divine Love* is one the most moving of all mystical books.

Hildegard of Bingen   Hildegard was a famous and beloved abbess, a renowned mystic, and perhaps the first multimedia artist. She had mystical visions from the age of eight, although she never told anyone for more than thirty years. She became a nun and was eventually made abbess of her community of Bingen. When, in her late thirties, she admitted to her brother (who was a priest) that she had started having visions as a child and in fact still had them, he urged her to write. She wrote several books in which she tried to put into words what her experiences felt like and meant to her. When she decided that she could not describe her experiences in words, she put down the pen and took up a paint brush, composing dozens of ecstatic, expressive paintings. When that too proved insufficient, she composed music in the hopes that here at last she could describe what it feels like to be in God's intimate presence. Much of her music survives and is available on recordings. In the image presented here, she begins to write. The manuscript from which this image was photographed was destroyed in World War II.

While many mystics criticized contemporary problems in the church, none saw themselves as rebels against it. In fact, most took special care to champion orthodox doctrine. But while they spoke of their visions and their faith with a passionate intensity, it is possible to detect a grave dissatisfaction with the church and the world.

THE GUILD SYSTEM

The mystical exaltations may have had something to do with the economic vibrancy of the late Middle Ages. The medieval economy had grown at an impressive steady rate since the late 11th century. Fueled by agricultural surplus and the reopening of commercial ties with the Islamic world, it saw advances in financing, manufacturing, and shipping. But not everyone was pleased with this embryonic form of capitalism. The church, itself among the wealthiest of institutions, had a conflicted relationship with it, for capitalism functioned on the use of credit. Credit—that is, the loaning of money at interest—was morally suspect to many churchmen, since it entailed profiting from someone else's need. The very success of the economy raised the potential danger of materialism. The more money, possessions, property, and investments people had, the church feared, the more time they would devote to their management. God does not care about the value of our possessions, the church counseled, but about the value of our lives. Wealth is indeed better than poverty, but it is not intrinsically good.

> The very success of the economy raised the potential danger of materialism. The more money, possessions, property, and investments people had, the church feared, the more time they would devote to their management. God does not care about the value of our possessions, the church counseled, but about the value of our lives.

That did not stop people from pursuing wealth by an impressive array of new techniques. Among the most important innovations was the **guild** system. A medieval guild was not unlike a modern trade association or cartel: it set prices, quality standards, methods and volume of production, and wages paid to workers. It also assigned market shares to individual artisans or merchants. Each city had its own guilds, usually one for each artisanal industry (brewing, weaving and dyeing, metalwork), and another set for the commercial companies (finance, trading, shipping) that brought the goods to market. Guilds played important roles in urban life, funding charities, schools, and hospitals. Among the bylaws of the wine and beer merchants' guild at Southampton in the 13th century, for example, was this provision:

> Whenever the guild is in session the lepers at [the hospital of] La Madeleine shall receive in alms from

Two Master Craftsmen   Nanni di Banco (1383–1430) carved this relief of a stonemason and a woodcarver in honor of their guild.

the guild eight gallons of ale, as shall the sick in [the hospitals of] God's House and Saint Julian's. The Franciscans shall receive eight gallons of ale and four gallons of wine; and sixteen gallons of ale shall be distributed to the poor from whatever spot the guild meets at. . . . If any guild member should fall into poverty and cannot pay his debts, and if he is unable to work and provide for himself, then he shall receive from the guild one mark [of silver] every time the guild meets in session, in order to relieve his suffering.

Guilds not only complemented but at times nearly replaced the charitable functions of the church, which many feared had become too *plenitudo* of its own *potestatis*. The reach of the church in the late Middle Ages was extensive. It orchestrated Crusades, ran and policed the universities and cathedral schools, oversaw the workings of the marketplace, judged the activities of Europe's bedrooms, excommunicated kings and princes, warred with them on occasion, and staged councils to determine ever finer details of canon law. Many feared it had lost sight of its central mission of ministering to the people. This was the impetus behind the founding of the **mendicant orders**, groups dedicated to assisting the clergy in the performance of their evangelical mission. These orders grew rapidly in number, size, and popularity, and their astonishing success can be attributed to two principle factors—their unique dedication to serving the common people and the fact that they, unlike the clergy they assisted, opened their membership to women.

THE MENDICANT ORDERS

The two leading mendicant groups were the **Franciscans** and the **Dominicans**. The Franciscans, established by Saint Francis of Assisi (1181–1226) and approved by Pope Innocent III, dedicated themselves to preaching and service to the urban poor. They begged for alms and food and donated whatever they collected to the destitute. They preached a simple message of love, forgiveness, and charity. People flocked to them wherever they went. The Dominicans, on the other hand, aided the church's teaching mission. Too many faithful, especially in the countryside, still lacked proper religious instruction and so drifted into heresy. Heresies, in fact, enjoyed something of a golden age in the 13th and 14th centuries. Saint Dominic de Guzmán (1171–1221), an earnest Spanish cleric, established the order named after him (officially known as the Order of Preachers) in 1216 in the hopes of bringing the heretical back into the Catholic fold. He recognized that heresy was not the product of human evil or of Satanic mischief but was simply a consequence of the church's failure to provide appropriate religious education. In response, the Dominicans established schools across Europe, debated heretical ideas, and preached tirelessly.

The two most prominent heresies were Catharism and Lollardy, and both of them were profoundly critical of the church (see Map 10.3). The **Cathars**, the more eccentric of the two, posited two separate and equal gods, one absolutely good and the other absolutely evil. Trapped in the cosmic war between them, humans were condemned to a miserable cycle of reincarnation. To the Cathars the physical universe was the creation of the evil deity; our souls, by contrast, were created by the good god. We therefore participate in the cosmic struggle by overcoming our own physicality, the demands of the flesh, and the human concern for material wealth. Once we have achieved the appropriate spiritual state, we break the cycle of reincarnation and our souls are released from our bodies in a spiritual exaltation that tips the cosmic scale in favor of the universal good. The Lollards were almost dull in comparison.

Lollards condemned church corruption and worldliness. They believed in the right of nonpriests to preach, and they taught that to live according to the spirit of Christ was more important than to follow the many letters of the church's

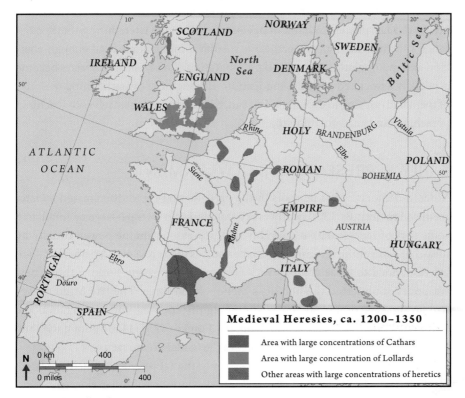

Medieval Heresies, ca. 1200–1350

- Area with large concentrations of Cathars
- Area with large concentration of Lollards
- Other areas with large concentrations of heretics

MAP 10.3   **Medieval Heresies, ca. 1200–1350**

laws. The Lollards had no common body of doctrines; they shared instead a general anticlericalism toward Rome, whose obvious wealth and involvement with earthly matters vitiated its spiritual authority in their eyes.

The Dominicans confronted these and other groups with relentless preaching and arguing. Dominicans were confident that the errant had only to hear Christian truth properly presented, and they would return to the church's embrace confidently and with gratitude. Of course, it did not always work out that way, which led to the development of a sterner educational tool—the inquisition. The **inquisition** began as a pedagogical program to counter heresy: determine what an individual or group actually believed, and then demonstrate its errors. Its origin lay in a principle of ancient Roman law analogous to our modern "probable cause" hearings. According to this principle, certain crimes are so detrimental to society that the state has a right, and indeed a responsibility, to investigate preemptively if there is a reasonable likelihood that the crime might be in the offing. Heresy fell into this category, because it imperiled the soul not only of the heretic; any innocent bystander might succumb.

Like other interrogation methods used in medieval times, inquisition did not shy away from using physical force, but it did not rely on force exclusively. The Inquisition of popular legend and Hollywood films, with black-hooded sadists plying red-hot pincers in dank dungeons, largely came later, during the Renaissance and Reformation. Nevertheless, medieval inquisitions used enough coercion and manipulation to earn a dark reputation. The Dominican friars became especially associated with the inquisition, although the overwhelming majority of them had nothing to do with it. Instead, they dedicated themselves to teaching, preaching, and peaceful ministry.

EARLY REPRESENTATIVE GOVERNMENT

Modern democracy has its roots in the parliamentary tradition created by late-medieval society. By 1300 nearly every state in Latin Europe, large or small, had some sort of representative assembly that possessed genuine power, usually by means of controlling the king's or prince's access to tax revenue. Aristocratic society responded to these changes with changes of their own. For one thing, new weaponry soon tested the nobility's monopoly on force. The late Middle Ages had no shortage of warfare, but the most significant of all the conflicts was the Hundred Years' War between England and France (1337–1453). Along with the Black Death, it sounded the death knell of the feudal aristocracy.

Noble courts were nothing new. As early as the 1st century CE Tacitus related, somewhat fancifully, how ancient Germanic warriors met with clan elders in a regular council he called a **comitatus** ("assembly"). But the late-medieval addition of representatives of the common people signified the real breakthrough. The governments' need for revenue drove the issue, but does not explain it entirely. Since Europe's nobles and churches remained exempt from taxation, the king's only recourse was to tax the free commoners in the cities. The urban classes responded positively, for the most part, provided that the king granted them in return a voice in the formation of government policy. By the 12th century such commoners' council held an advisory role in government, but by the 13th, when the urban manufacturing and commercial sectors represented the bulk of their realms' collective economic output, the cities' advisory role grew and became actual power to control the royal purse.

Mayor Taking the Oath of Office In the mid-12th century norms surrounding the selection of mayors, and the powers they possessed, stabilized. Called by different names in different regions—*mayor* (England), *potestaat* (Flanders), *Burgomeister* (Germany), *podestà* (Italy)—they were elected officials with terms of office ranging from one year to life. Here the mayor of Bristol, England takes the oath of office, ca. 1479.

The transition was not always smooth. Constraints on royalty in England included the signing of **Magna Carta** in 1215 and the Provisions of Oxford in 1258, and both came about after high drama and much strong-arm maneuvering. In France, the Capetian kings from Louis VIII (r. 1223–1226) on were hobbled not only by their feudal obligations to the nobles but also by their practice of awarding land grants called "apanages" to the younger sons of each Capetian generation. As consolation prizes for not inheriting the crown, apanages were independent provinces that required their holder to perform no service to the throne. The Capetians therefore had even greater need to seek the financial assistance of the urban populace, which they did by developing the French parliament—the **Estates General**.

The German case was more complicated. The emperor Frederick II (r. 1215–1250) had inherited the German Empire from his father and the Kingdom of Sicily (which included southern Italy) from his mother, and frankly had little interest in Germany at all. His southern realm was wealthier and more cosmopolitan. Frederick encouraged urban growth within Germany but also issued, in 1231, the Constitutions in Favor of the Princes of Germany, which severely curtailed the power of those cities and indeed of his own feudal claims to privilege. He gave up a strong German monarchy in return for the German princes' leaving him alone to pursue his own goals in the Mediterranean. Nevertheless, his actions helped solidify the gains made in establishing the German parliament—known as the **Diet**.

By 1250 or thereabouts, the balance between the authority and status of the commoners and the nobles was changing dramatically. The milites ("warlords") had easily justified their emergence in the 11th century, with their monopoly on political power and privileged status. After all, they generated through their manors the largest portion of economic production in the realm. They alone could perform government service since they had a virtual monopoly, among the laity, on literacy; and they provided the dominant and most effective military service. But the rise of the urban economy had shifted economic dominance within Europe to manufacturing and commerce instead of agriculture, and the spread of literacy among city dwellers had opened up civil service to commoners. Government became professionalized, in other words, and men of noble birth began to shun the lesser offices of civil administration. That left room for commoners to enter and replace them. As two of the three struts that legitimated noble privilege gradually disappeared, voices began to murmur darkly about unjustified privilege.

CHIVALRY

The word *chivalry* derives from the French word for horsemanship and originally denoted skill at mounted shock combat: heavily armored knights astride thundering warhorses, bearing swords, lances, maces, and flails. Knights proved their worth at tournaments, fighting other knights in all-too-real contests in which many were killed. They sought not merely renown but position as a vassal to higher lords in search of loyal underlings. An 11th century text like the popular *Song of Roland* depicted its hero as the very summit of knightly perfection—an unsurpassed warrior loyal to his lord but to very little else. The fictional Roland exhibits no qualities other than his usefulness on a battlefield. By the 12th century, however, a significant change had occurred, and the ideal knight portrayed in literature was more a figure like Sir Lancelot, Sir Galahad, or Saint Perceval of the Arthurian tales. All were still champion fighters, but also models of **chivalry** in a new sense—comportment, noble demeanor, learning, and piety.

> The noble class felt the need to emphasize at every turn the chasm that separated it from commoners: the nobles were not different because privileged, they seemed to say, but were privileged because different.

They were sensitive to music and art, and above all chivalric lovers of virtuous noblewomen.[2]

As the 13th and 14th centuries came, and the aristocratic leadership of society began to give way to a new set of values, chivalry took on newer and more symbolic roles. Coats of arms, for instance, which had originally served the practical purpose of identifying battlefield participants, began to adorn everything a nobleman owned, from tableware and fireplace masonry to goblets, gloves, and stationery. Aristocrats not only patronized musicians and poets; they now endowed colleges, scholarships, chapels, and hospitals, and emblazoned them all with their names and heraldic signs. Genealogy became a passion of the elite, and its results (often fanciful) were published in books and embroidered on tapestries. Songs, tales, and histories enumerated their elevated sensibilities. Commerce and trade were denigrated as beneath the dignity of a lord. The noble class felt the need to emphasize at every turn the chasm that separated it from commoners: the nobles were not different because privileged, they seemed to say, but were privileged because different. And the difference was essential, not functional.

But the military role of the knightly class remained and sufficed to maintain the hierarchy. So long as mounted shock cavalry remained the premier fighting force, commoners might complain about abuses of privilege, but not about the very idea of privilege. In contrast, popular rebellions of the late Middle Ages—the three best known are the **Jacquerie** uprising in France (1358), the **Ciompi Rebellion** in Italy (1378), and the **Peasants' Revolt** in England (1381)—shared a common

Noble Warrior   Illuminated initial from English copy of the Letters of Pope Gregory I, 12th century. English scribes in the Middle Ages were particularly well known for the vitality and fluidity of the draftsmanship. This example, from a 12th-century copy of the Letters of Gregory I, shows a noble warrior—identifiable from his stance on top of a common foot-soldier, plus his brandishing of a fine sword—fighting a two-headed dragon. It is a brightly colored image, filled with hues of airy blue, green, gold, light copper, and red.

---

[2]   Lancelot's mistake was not in loving Lady Guinevere but in loving her with the wrong kind of love, adultery.

element: they questioned the very order of medieval society, not merely the abusive actions of a few elites within it.

> When Adam delved and Eve span,
> Who was then the gentleman?

asked an anonymous poet of the time. Though simply phrased, it was a radical question: When God created the world in all its original perfection, were there any "gentlemen"? Any privileged few who lived off the labor of the many? If not, then the existence of them now must be a distortion of God's original intent, which could be no other than a radical equality of all mankind.

The couplet was referred to in a sermon delivered by one of the leaders of the Peasant's Revolt, a priest named John Ball (1338–1381). The story is retold in the Historia Anglicana of Thomas Walsingham (d. 1422), with a fiery commentary:

> "When Adam dalf, and Eve span, who was thanne a gentilman?:
> From the beginning all men were created equal by nature, and that servitude had been introduced by the unjust and evil oppression of men, against the will of God, who, if it had pleased Him to create serfs, surely in the beginning of the world would have appointed who should be a serf and who a lord.

Ball ended by recommending

> uprooting the tares that are accustomed to destroy the grain; first killing the great lords of the realm, then slaying the lawyers, justices, and jurors, and finally rooting out everyone whom they knew to be harmful to the community in future.

In the 14th century several simple, inexpensive technologies developed in weaponry, which knocked the third and final strut out from under aristocratic claims to justified privilege. The two most significant weapons were the longbow and the crossbow, which appeared first in Wales and Scotland, where they were used to repulse the English armies of King Edward I (r. 1272–1307), and possibly even before that. Of course, the **longbow** is familiar today simply as the "bow and arrow," but prior to this century, bows were largely used by noble cavalry. The physical challenge of sitting astride a broad warhorse while fully armored, though, meant that knights' bows were relatively short in length and hence of limited power and range. The Welsh and the Scots, however, hit upon the idea of turning bows into infantry weapons instead, which allowed them to increase the length of the bow significantly. Longbows were often a full six feet (1.8 meters) long, and their arrows could pierce a suit of armor at a distance of two hundred yards (180 meters).

The **crossbow** was the medieval equivalent of a sawed-off shotgun, and it shot thick metal darts called *quarrels*. A ratcheted steel gear, turned by a steel crank, drew the bowstring; once released, the quarrel likewise could pierce plate armor and even shatter the bones it protected.[3] Crossbows date back to Alexander the

A World Turned Upside Down   The battle of Poitiers (1346), the first great battle in the Hundred Years' War. The English are on the left, with infantry longbowmen shown—inaccurately—in the front lines. Confronting them are the mounted knights of France. Much bloodshed ensued, ending in a surprise English victory. Similar slaughter occurred at Crécy (1356) and Agincourt (1415), although the war ended, in 1453, with a French victory.

---

[3]   In Spain, the crossbow may have been used as a surgical tool. A quarrel embedded in a soldier's bone could be removed by tying it to a quarrel shot by a crossbow in the opposite direction.

Great. The late medieval weapon, however, used a steel, not wooden, bow piece, which gave it tremendous force and required the crank to arm it. The crossbow was designed for close-range killing and holds the distinction of being the first weapon ever banned by the Catholic Church—not for its deadly force per se but because it allowed the unthinkable: with it, commoners could kill noblemen almost at will. This was more than social inversion, the church declared; it was an intrinsically immoral attack on God's ordering of society.

> The crossbow was designed for close-range killing and holds the distinction of being the first weapon ever banned by the Catholic Church—not for its deadly force per se but because it allowed the unthinkable: with it, commoners could kill noblemen almost at will. This was more than social inversion, the church declared; it was an intrinsically immoral attack on God's ordering of society.

THE HUNDRED YEARS' WAR

The **Hundred Years' War** (1337–1453) was the longest (although not continuous) war in Western history—and almost the longest in preparation. England and France had experienced fierce tensions and rivalries since 1066, when William the Conqueror crossed the English Channel with his army and conquered England. From this time on the English kings, as kings, were autonomous sovereigns but, as dukes of Normandy, also vassals of the throne in Paris. French kings were thwarted whenever they tried to curb the ambitions of their Norman vassals, however. And when the Norman kings managed to acquire even more French territories through strategic marriages—such as the marriage of Henry II (r. 1154–1189) to Eleanor of Aquitaine—the vassals stood more powerful and respected than the lords.

Matters came to a head when England's king Edward III (r. 1327–1377) claimed the French throne for himself. Legally, his claim was correct, as he was married to the last remaining heir of France's king Philip IV (r. 1286–1314). However, the French court would have none of it, found an alternative (a man named Philip of Valois), and the war began. On again, off again, the Hundred Years' War left the French countryside ravaged and her people dispirited (see Map 10.4). The English, who were vastly outnumbered, avoided pitched battles and instead sent innumerable small raiding forces, armed with longbows and crossbows. Their mission was to vandalize as much French territory as possible, terrorize the people, then return before the French could muster their enormous feudal army. The war matters primarily for the way in which it was fought, since the English weapons could pierce the French suits of armor and render mounted knights ineffective.

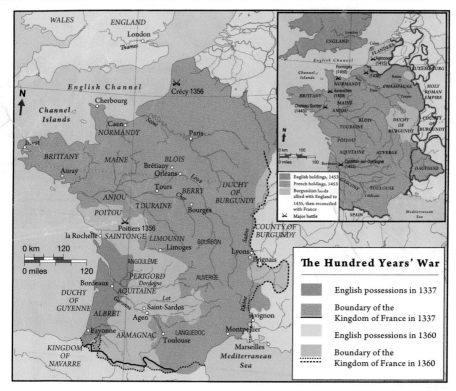

MAP 10.4   **The Hundred Years' War**

At stake was not simply dynastic territorial rights but an entire way of life. As one chronicler described an early English victory, at the battle of Crécy in 1356:

> The English [longbow] archers stepped forward and shot their arrows with great might—and so rapidly that it seemed a snow-blizzard of arrows. When these arrows fell on the Genoese [one of France's allies at the time] and pierced their armor, they cut the strings of their own weapons, threw them to the ground, and ran. When the king of the French, who had arrayed a large company of mounted knights to support the Genoese, saw them in flight he cried out, "Kill those blackguards! They're blocking our advance!" But the English kept on firing, landing their arrows among the French horsemen. This drove the charging French into the Genoese, until the scene was so confused that they could never regroup again.... [When the slaughter ended,] it became clear that the French dead numbered eighty banners, eleven princes of the realm, twelve hundred knights, and thirty thousand commoners.

Joan of Arc   An early image of Joan of Arc, showing her in armor but without her hair cropped.

The war ended with an improbable French victory, led by a charismatic peasant girl named Joan of Arc, who claimed to have received messages from Heaven telling her to drive the English from France. The French army briefly rallied under her leadership and scored several victories, until Joan was captured in battle and executed by the English in 1431. Shortly thereafter the Burgundians, who had been allied with England against the French, reversed course and sided with the French. With their newly combined forces, the French and Burgundians drove the English from the land, and in 1453 a permanent peace was settled. The first death knell of the feudal aristocracy had been sounded, however, despite the victory.

THE PLAGUE

Another, even direr death knell sounded across the Western world in late 1347, when a fleet of Genoese merchant ships returning from the Black Sea arrived in the harbor at Messina, Sicily. Aboard the vessels was a pack of rats carrying the bubonic plague. This disease originated in eastern Asia and had worked its way westward along the trade routes; the violent advance of the Mongol army under Genghis Khan (1167–1227) probably sped matters up considerably. Since the disease had never existed before in western Europe, the people had no biological means of fighting it off, and it took several centuries for the necessary antibodies to develop among the populations at large. Waves of the plague—known popularly as the **Black Death**—therefore returned to Europe until well into the 18th century.

This was the single worst natural disaster in Greater Western history, killing has many as fifty million people in less than three years—roughly one-third of the European and Muslim populations (see Map 10.5). The results were horrific. A Sicilian eyewitness recorded:

> At the start of November [in 1347] twelve Genoese galleys . . . entered the port at Messina. They carried with them a disease so deadly that any person who happened merely to speak with any one of the ships' members

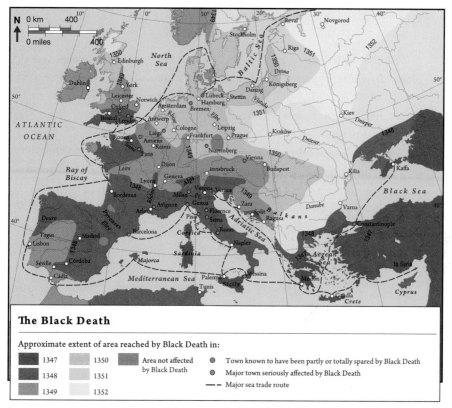

The Black Death

Approximate extent of area reached by Black Death in:

1347	1350	Area not affected by Black Death	● Town known to have been partly or totally spared by Black Death
1348	1351		● Major town seriously affected by Black Death
1349	1352		– – Major sea trade route

MAP 10.5   **The Black Death**

was seized by a mortal illness; death was inevitable. It spread to everyone who had any interaction with the infected. Those who contracted the disease felt their whole bodies pierced through with pain, and they quickly developed boils about the size of lentils on their thighs and upper arms. These boils then spread the disease throughout the rest of the body and made its victims vomit blood. The vomiting of blood normally continued for three days until the person died, since there was no way to stop it. Not only did everyone who had contact with the sick become sick themselves, but also those who had contact only with their possessions.... People soon began to hate one another so much that parents would not even tend to their own sick children.... As the deaths mounted, crowds of people sought to confess their sins to priests and to draft their wills, ... but clergy, lawyers, and notaries refused to enter the homes of the ill.... Franciscans, Dominicans, and other mendicants who went to hear the confessions of the dying fell to the disease—many of them not even making it alive out of the ill persons' homes. *(Michele da Piazza, History of Sicily)*

In England:

> At the same time sheep began to die everywhere throughout the
> realm. In a single pasture one could find as many as five thousand car-
> casses, all so putrefied that no animal or bird would go near them.....
> Sheep and cattle wandered aimlessly through meadows and crop fields,
> for there was no one to go after them and herd them. As a result, they
> died in countless numbers everywhere, in ditches and hedges.... More-
> over, buildings both large and small began to collapse in all cities, towns,
> and villages, for want of anyone to inhabit them and maintain them. In
> fact, many whole villages became deserted; everyone who lived in them
> died and not a single house was left standing. It is likely that many of
> these sites were never inhabited again.   *(Henry Knighton, Chronicle)*

In Paris, another writer described a popular reaction to the crisis:

> Some said that the pestilence was the result of infected air and
> water,... and as a result of this idea many people began suddenly and pas-
> sionately to accuse the Jews of infecting the wells, fouling the air, and
> generally being the source of the plague. Everyone rose up against them
> most cruelly. In Germany and elsewhere—wherever Jews lived—they
> were massacred and slaughtered by Christian crowds, and many
> thousands were burned indiscriminately. The steadfast, though foolish,
> bravery of the Jewish men and women was remarkable. Many mothers
> hurled their own children into the flames and then leapt in after them,
> along with their husbands, in order that they might avoid being forcibly
> baptized.   *(Jean de Venette, Chronicle)*

The Spanish Muslim writer Ibn Khaldun [A] (1332–1406) summarized the ruin
this way:

> It was as though humanity's own living voice had called out for
> oblivion and desolation—and the world responded to the call. Truly
> Allah inherits the earth and all things upon it.   *(Ibn Khaldun, Muqaddimah)*

People tried every medicine, folk cure, and prayer they knew, all to no effect.
In several instances townsfolk, who knew that the disease had something to do
with rats, intentionally burned their entire towns to the ground in order to drive
the rats away, but this of course only accelerated the spread of the contagion. By
the time the plague had spread its way through nearly every corner of Europe,

Burying Plague Victims   A page from the Annals of Gilles de Muisit, late 14th century, in Tournai, showing crowds struggling to bury all the dead left in the in Black Death's wake.

it left behind piles of corpses so massive that people hardly knew what to do with them. Scores of "death ships" bobbed directionless on the seas, every person on board dead, with the victorious rats silently gnawing on their remains.

The consequences of such a catastrophe are almost unimaginable. The fatalities, coupled with the fear of interpersonal contact, halted agricultural and industrial production and severed all commercial ties. The death of so many farm animals had equally long-term effects: wool and dairy production all but ceased, and the loss of oxen and horses as draught animals meant that farming would be slow to restart. Once the immediate crisis passed, however, twin spirals of inflation and recession followed. Urban workers who had survived could demand higher wages for their labor, and this, combined with the general scarcity of goods, triggered rapid increases in prices. Rural workers faced a different problem. So many people had died that even decreased food production met local needs—and hence food prices dropped precipitously. When rural workers demanded lower rents for their work on the land, the landlords could therefore refuse. And the low crop prices hurt the farmers more than the decreased rents had helped them.

Each return of the Black Death over the centuries left new iterations of the same miseries in its wake. No epidemic ever reached the hopeless severity of the first wave, since the gradual development of antibodies among the Europeans meant that fewer people died. But fear of the plague haunted the West for many generations.

So in general terms, urban workers who survived the Black Death profited from the decimation while rural workers were driven even deeper into poverty.

Each return of the Black Death over the centuries left new iterations of the same miseries in its wake. No epidemic ever reached the hopeless severity of the first wave, since the gradual development of antibodies among the Europeans meant that fewer people died. But fear of the plague haunted the West for many generations.

CONQUEST OF THE ISLAMIC WORLD

The 13th and 14th centuries witnessed the near-complete takeover of the Islamic world by a new wave of foreign conquerors, who dominated Muslim life for the next three hundred years, reconfiguring its map and introducing new cultural and social elements into Islamic identity. Leadership of Islam had long been monopolized by two groups, the Arabs and the Persians. While often in tension with one another, they had nevertheless worked out some sort of creative and nutritive cultural compromise. As the Abbasid state crumbled, however, ethnic and doctrinal conflicts arose between the populations of each rump state and its Arab or Persian rulers. The arrival of the newcomers, moreover, created at times cutthroat competition between the Muslim states. Neither of the groups of newcomers was monolithic: instead, each was a mongrel assemblage made up of numerous tribes and clans linked by language: the Mongols and the Turks.

The more destructive of the invaders were the **Mongols**, who began moving westward in the 12th century. No one knows the precise origin of the Mongols, or even if they have one. Ancient Chinese records trace them back to a group they called the Donghu (3rd century BCE), which was actually a confederation of various peoples speaking related dialects of an early version of the Mongolian language. But some scholars claim to see elements of early Turkish dialects in the Donghu as well. Certainly the Mongols, as they spread across Asia, maintained continuous contact with Turkish-speaking groups and absorbed elements of Turkish culture. (As the two groups gradually merged, they became known in the west as the Tatars.[4])

Nomadic peoples of the steppes found it natural to form occasional alliances and confederations—and to disband them just as casually. When gathered, these armies were often of considerable size. Fighting on horseback, they moved quickly and specialized in lightning strikes on other nomadic groups and small population centers. Siege machinery was largely unknown to them, which allowed fortified cities to withstand their assaults. The Mongols were a diverse group of tribes along the northern and northwestern borders of China, and the Chinese themselves had

---

[4]   The name Tatars derives from Latin *Tartarus,* "hell."

been traditionally among the Mongols' favorite targets for raiding. Centuries of such attacks had prompted the Chinese to build the Great Wall. While not impregnable, the wall repulsed attackers and migrants alike with sufficient success that it was a major reason for the seemingly endless waves of invaders and nomads who moved westward across Asia and into the Western world.

Under their brilliant but brutal commander Temüjin (ca. 1167–1227), the Mongols forged another of their periodic confederations. Better known by his title of Chinggis (Genghis) Khan, or "Universal Ruler," he broke through the wall in 1207 and subdued the northern half of China. The Chin emperor surrendered in 1214 and awarded Genghis Khan an enormous tribute payment of gold and silver coins. Sources say that it required three thousand horses to carry. At this point Genghis might have stopped his conquests, for in diplomatic records he referred to himself as the "supreme emperor of the east" and wrote to the Persian ruler in Khwarezmi (modern day) as the "supreme emperor of the west." The hapless Persian, however, rejected Genghis's peace offering and slaughtered all 450 members of the diplomatic embassy Genghis had sent. This called for revenge, and in 1219 Genghis Khan moved westward and quickly crushed what was left of the Persian state.

Khan left local rulers in place, so long as they swore unquestioning obedience to him, and he installed Mongol tax collectors in each region, to ensure a flow of revenue into his coffers. Some towns rebelled and slew these Mongol officials as soon as Genghis had moved on, which prompted the great Khan to return in wrath and annihilate entire populations. Once he was even reported to have ordered the killing of every living creature in a city, including its domesticated animals. Ali ibn Athir [K] (1160–1233), the great Kurdish historian, described the Mongols memorably in his *Universal History*:

> Even Antichrist, though He strike down all those who oppose him, will spare those who follow Him—but these Mongols spared no one, not even men, children, or women; they even ripped open the stomachs of women who were pregnant and killed their unborn children. . . . These people came out of the lands of China and attacked cities . . . in Turkestan . . . and advanced on Samarkand, Bukhara, and other sites in Transoxiana. One of their armies made it as far as Khurasan and continued their campaign of conquering, pillaging, and ruining until they reached . . . the borders of Persia, Azerbaijan, and Iraq, . . . all of which they destroyed and wholly depopulated, except for a small remnant, in less than a year's time.

Coming as it does near the end of the *History*, ibn Athir's passage denotes the apocalyptic role he saw the Mongols to be playing. Surely the end of the world was nigh, if such malevolent power as the Mongols possessed could roll over the

The Siege of Baghdad   The conquest of Baghdad in 1258 by Genghis Khan's successor Hulagu, from a Persian manuscript of the 15th century.

world at will. Had he lived another quarter century, ibn Athir would have seen his worst imaginings realized.

The Mongol conquests were far greater than those achieved by any earlier people, or by any people since, but to call it an empire is inaccurate. The Mongols never achieved any sort of governance over the areas they laid waste and showed little interest in doing so. Genghis Khan died in 1227, and was succeeded by his third son, Ögedai (r. 1227–1241), who continued to push the borders of the Mongol-dominated realm further west until they reached Anatolia. Another branch of his army, moving north of the Black Sea, threatened Hungary, and even reached northward to the Baltic Sea and southward to the Balkans. Under Hulagu (r. 1217–1265), Ogedai's son and successor, the Mongols annihilated Baghdad in 1258. According to Muslim sources, as many as two hundred thousand people were killed in a week-long orgy of slaughter. The Mongols destroyed the royal library (one chronicle reports that the Tigris River ran black from the ink of all the books hurled into it) and burned dozens of mosques, schools, and hospitals. At the end, Hulagu had the Abbasid caliph, al-Musta'sim [A] (r. 1242–1258), rolled up in a Persian carpet and then trampled by Mongol horsemen. A contingent of Mongol soldiers then pressed further westward as far as Damascus, but were finally repulsed in 1260 at 'Ayn Jalut, near Nazareth, by a Mamluk army coming out of Egypt. At its height in 1279, the Mongol Empire covered some twelve million square miles (thirty-one million square kilometers) of land, nearly one-quarter of the Earth's land surface (see Map 10.6a,b).

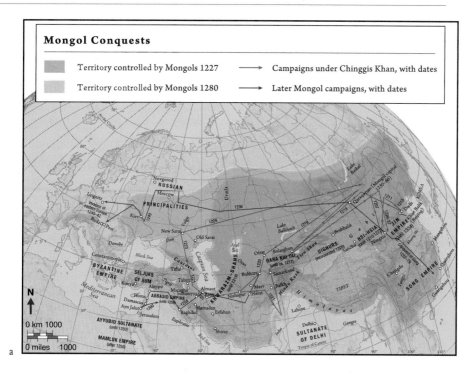

a

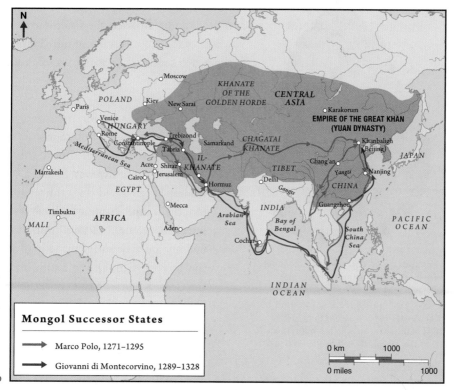

b

MAP 10.6a,b   **Mongol Conquests and Successor States**

IN THE WAKE OF THE MONGOLS

The Mongols began to fight among themselves after the death of Genghis' grandson Kublai Khan (r. 1260–1294), and the enormous territory they held broke into a number of smaller though still considerable states. The most important of these were the Golden Horde, which dominated the southern Russian steppe; the Il-Khans, who held power over most of the previously Persian-controlled part of the Islamic empire; the Chagetai Khans, who controlled central Asia; and the Yuan dynasty, which held titular leadership over all the Mongol realms from their capital in Beijing.

Numerous Western states and individual rulers attempted to forge some sort of peaceful relations with the Mongols. Louis IX of France famously sent an emissary to Batu Khan (r. 1227–1255), the khan of the Golden Horde, congratulating him on his conquests and offering to bestow those lands on him officially in return for Batu's conversion to Christianity, becoming Louis's vassal, and paying him an annual tribute.[5] The church sent out teams of Franciscan missionaries with the unenviable charge of converting the Great Khans to Christianity. One of these was Fr. Giovanni di Montecorvino (1247–1328), who established a church at Beijing, built a Christian school for 150 slave children he had purchased and manumitted, and translated the Psalms and the whole of the New Testament into Tatar for them. He sent back to Rome an extraordinary letter:

A Mongol Passport   An engraved safe-conduct pass issued from the court of the Mongol ruler Kublai Khan (1215–1294). Its bearer was guaranteed safety while traveling through the Mongol lands. The inscription reads: "By the strength of Eternal Heaven, an edict of the khan. He who has not respect [for the bearer of the passport] shall be guilty."

> I, Fr. Giovanni di Montecorvino, set out from the city of Tauris, in Persia, in the year of Our Lord 1291 and made my way to India, where I remained for thirteen months ... and baptized about a hundred people. ... I then continued my journey until I made it all the way to [China], the realm of the Great Khan who rules over the Tartars and to whom I presented the letter of our Holy Father the Pope, inviting him to adopt

---

5   Batu responded that he would teach Louis a lesson by burning Paris down around his ears.

the Catholic faith of Our Lord Jesus Christ. The Khan is too set in his idolatrous ways to change, although I must record that he has extended great friendship to us Christians in the years I have been living here in his realm. . . . I have built a church in [Beijing], where the Khan has his chief residence, . . . and in this church I have baptized some six thousand people, as near as I can reckon. . . . I believe it is possible that, if I had had two or three comrades to aid me, the Khan himself might have been baptized by now, and for this reason I beg that if any friars are willing to come this far and dedicate themselves to so great a task. . . then they will come. . . .

It has been twelve years since I had any news of the papal court, our Franciscan order, or the general goings-on in Europe. Two years ago a fellow from Lombardy came here—a surgeon—and spread the most vicious rumors about the papal court and other matters, but since these blasphemies are too horrible to be true I beg to hear the truth and pray that my fellow Franciscans, to whom I address this letter, do all they can to bring my request to Our Holy Father the Pontiff. . . . As for myself, I have grown old and gray; even though I am only fifty-eight, toil and trouble have aged me. I have acquired a working knowledge of the language and script used by the Tartars, and have already translated the New Testament and the Psalter for them. . . . To the best of my knowledge there is no king or prince anywhere in the world who can compare to the Great Khan in terms of the vastness of his realm, the number of his subjects, or his wealth. But here I must now stop.

[Beijing], the eighth of January, in the year of Our Lord 1305.

The Great Khan referred to by Friar Giovanni was Temür Khan (r. 1294–1307), the son of Kublai Khan. Kublai, the grandson of Genghis Khan, had been the ruler of the Mongol Empire at the time of Marco Polo's supposed stay in China—"supposed" because not all scholars agree that Marco Polo actually made it to China. Temür Khan is not to be confused with Timur (r. 1370–1405), the Turkish founder of the Timurid dynasty, better known in English as Tamerlane. Two years later, Pope Clement V (r. 1305–1317) appointed Giovanni the archbishop of Beijing and sent him the assistants he had requested.

The "vicious rumors about the papal court" put about by the visitor from Lombardy, however, were not in fact too horrible to be true. Pope Boniface VIII (r. 1294–1303) had begun his pontificate with a splendid jubilee that brought as many as a million pilgrims into Rome; but papal stature had declined precipitously since then. Boniface, a rock-ribbed papal triumphalist, had provoked widespread ire by his insistence that "it is absolutely necessary to every single

Papal Gift   This is a copy of a now-lost original painting by Zhou Lang in 1342, depicting the arrival of a gift horse from Pope Benedict XII to the last Mongol ruler of China, Shundi. The gift was brought to the Chinese court by a Franciscan emissary named Fra Giovanni di Marignolli.

human being's salvation that he be subject to the Roman pontiff"—a declaration that he meant most literally. The claim was not new, but Christians across Europe chafed at the tone. Philip IV of France, who understood Boniface's claim to undermine his own desire to tax the French clergy, responded by issuing an arrest warrant for the pope, accusing him of everything from murder and bribery to devil worship and sodomy. When Philip's soldiers encountered Boniface at his vacation residence in Anagni, they slapped and beat the old man (Boniface was then nearly seventy) mercilessly; he died three days later of traumatic shock. Small wonder that Friar Giovanni, in Beijing, could hardly believe what his Lombard visitor had told him.

At the height of their power the Mongols controlled an almost unimaginably vast empire, from Beijing to the Euphrates River, and from Moscow to the Arabian Sea. In their wake, they left behind vast numbers of dead. In China alone, census records show that the population in 1200, before Genghis Khan's invasion, stood around 120 million people; in 1300 it figured only 60 million. Ibn Battuta [A] (d. 1378), the famous Spanish Muslim traveler, reported that Persia's population fell from 2.5 million in 1220 to a mere 250,000 in 1260. Some estimate that fully half of Russia's population died as a result of the Mongol conquests; one eyewitness to the destruction of the city of Kiev (the Russian capital at the time) described it this way:

> When the Mongols launched their next attack, upon Russia, they
> caused enormous destruction, leveling many cities and fortresses and

butchering countless men. They besieged Kiev, the capital, for a long time—and when they finally took it they put to death nearly everyone living in it. When my companions and I traveled through that area, we saw the skulls and bones of innumerable corpses lying everywhere on the ground. Kiev at one time had been a large and densely populated city, but now it hardly exists at all—a mere two hundred homes still stand, and every one of their inhabitants has been reduced to slavery. *(Giovanni di piano Carpini, 000, History of the Mongols)*

The Mongols had little interest in actual governance; they left most of the peoples under their control free to live according to their traditional laws and customs, provided that they sent taxes and tribute whenever asked and obeyed without question any new law that the khans decreed. The Mongols understood the significance of trade and were scrupulous about awarding and enforcing safe-passage guarantees to merchants (who paid handsomely for them). Beyond this, however, they showed no real concern for administration, relying simply on massive violent retribution against any group who resisted Mongol authority, to keep peace and order. Time and again, they slaughtered entire towns and villages, punishing collectively any infraction committed by anyone. Merchants and travelers moving across Asia commented repeatedly on the tranquility and order they saw everywhere throughout the Mongol-controlled continent, but as

Europe largely escaped the Mongols' wrath; the Islamic and Chinese worlds took the full brunt of it. The shock was sufficient to set Islamic history on an entirely new path.

Fr. Giovanni recognized in the ruins of Kiev, the tranquility was really the paralysis of brutalized people.

Europe largely escaped the Mongols' wrath; the Islamic and Chinese worlds took the full brunt of it. The shock was sufficient to set Islamic history on an entirely new path.

A NEW CENTER FOR ISLAM

The Turkish-led Mamluk Sultanate, consisting of Egypt and the Holy Land as far as the length of the Euphrates River, largely escaped the catastrophic violence of the Mongols. And so it became, for 250 years, the strong center of western Islamic civilization. The **Ottoman Turks** (tribal cousins of the Seljuk Turks of two centuries earlier) had arrived in force in the latter part of the 13th century, under their charismatic leader Osman (r. 1281–1324). They brought with them a new stability—and a new civilization facing both east and west. Centered upon Asia Minor, the Ottoman Empire was really a confederation of more or less independent realms, united in their recognition of the overlordship of the family of Osman. Among the most significant of these constituent realms was the Mamluk Sultanate.

Stretching from modern-day Libya on the African coast to northern Syria, the Mamluk Sultanate centered on the great cities of Alexandria, Cairo, Jerusalem, Damascus, Antioch, and Aleppo (see Map 10.7). It also lasted through two distinct periods that are sometimes, though incorrectly, called dynasties: the Bahri (1250–1382) and the Burji (1382–1517).

A **sultan** was a military officer, a general-in-chief, and the position was therefore open to advancement from within the army. Most sultans in fact gained office by selection from the leading generals. A few sultans did attempt to pass their position on to their sons, but usually the heirs were ousted by rival generals. The Bahri and the Burji were both foreigners to the region. The Bahri sultans were Kipchak Turks, an ancient people who had originated in Siberia and slowly migrated westward, reaching the Middle East around the middle of the 11th century, where they found employment in the highly disciplined ranks of the Mamluk soldiery. The Burji, by contrast, were ethnic Circassians, an obscure group from the Caucasus Mountain region who spoke Turkish in addition to their ancestral Adyghe language. (The name Circassian comes from the Turkish for "people from the Caucasus.") Both periods were characterized by short-lived sultanates: twenty-seven reigns in the Bahri era (an average of four years apiece) and twenty-six in the Burji (an average of 5.2 years apiece).

Islam had been an international multiethnic religion since the late 7th century, but political, religious, and social authority had been monopolized for

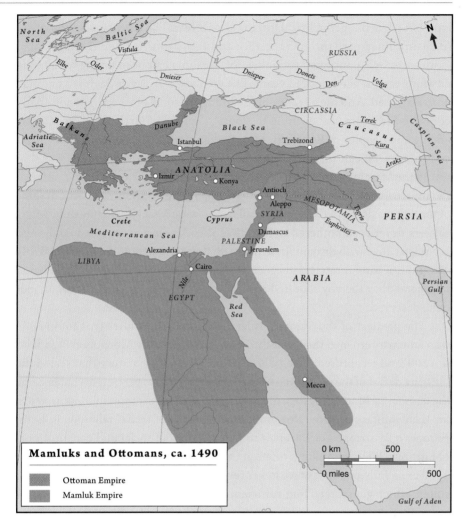

Map showing:

Mamluks and Ottomans, ca. 1490

- Ottoman Empire
- Mamluk Empire

0 km   500

0 miles   500

Labels on map: North Sea, Baltic Sea, Vistula, Elbe, Oder, Dnieser, Dnieper, Donets, Don, Volga, RUSSIA, CIRCASSIA, Terek, Caucasus, Kura, Caspian Sea, Araks, Balkans, Danube, Black Sea, Trebizond, Istanbul, Adriatic Sea, ANATOLIA, Izmir, Konya, Antioch, Aleppo, MESOPOTAMIA, Tigris, PERSIA, Crete, Cyprus, SYRIA, Euphrates, Mediterranean Sea, Damascus, PALESTINE, Jerusalem, Alexandria, LIBYA, Cairo, Nile, ARABIA, Persian Gulf, EGYPT, Red Sea, Mecca, Gulf of Aden

MAP 10.7   **Mamluks and Ottomans, ca. 1490**

over six hundred years by just two groups, Arabs and Persians. The rise of the Mongols and Turks not only shattered those monopolies but drove the long-ruling societies into secondary status in their own homelands. They would not fully emerge from the political shadows until the 20th century. Moreover, Mamluk rule, occasioned as it was by military force, relied on force to sustain itself.[6] The atmosphere of violence both colored and contributed to a sense of failed jihad. The Crusaders had been driven from the Holy Land in 1291, it is

[6]   More than half the Mamluk rulers were assassinated or executed after mostly sham trials. More than half the remainder were forcibly deposed or resigned under threat of deposition.

true, but Islam as a geopolitical force was in retreat. The Christian Reconquista in Spain gained pace through the 13th and 14th centuries, and the survival of Constantinople continued to rankle, for Muslims had been trying to take the city for nearly seven hundred years. The great capital city of Baghdad had also been flattened. And the advance of the Mongols, some of whom had nominally converted to Islam, did nothing to slow the spread of Orthodox Christianity among the peoples of Russia and the Balkans, whom they dominated politically for several centuries.

In the Mamluk state, therefore, a concerted effort to restore a strong, authoritarian Islam continued. This was ironic, since many of the Mamluks—from some of the sultans down to the common soldiers—were Muslim in name only. Many soldiers never even bothered to learn to speak Arabic and regarded Arabs and Egyptians alike with disdain. In this regard, they were not unlike the supposedly Muslim Il-Khan ruling class in Persia, and, being largely uncommitted to religion in general, they thereby acquired reputations for religious tolerance that are not quite deserved.

The greatest of the Mamluk rulers was the first: Baibars (r. 1260–1277), who famously crushed the Seventh Crusade, defeated the Mongols at 'Ayn Jalut in 1260, and recaptured the city of Antioch in 1268—a victory that sealed the ultimate defeat of the remaining Crusader states. He also perfected what became the distinctive Mamluk system of granting lands to officers and soldiers in return for their military service. Not unlike the network of feudal relations in Latin Europe, only stripped of Europe's complex system of social and constitutional obligations, it left common farmers at the mercy of their Mamluk overlords. By 1300 or so fully one-half of whatever revenues each lord raised was owed to the sultan, which guaranteed him sufficient funds to keep adding new slaves to the army. Fortunately for the sultan, much of the spice trade from east Asia had been rerouted to avoid the Mongols and came instead by ship around the Arabian peninsula and up through the Red Sea, thus entering Egyptian markets directly. Until its collapse in 1517, therefore, Mamluk society remained extraordinarily wealthy, although the bulk of the wealth was monopolized by the ruling elite. In turn, the populace grew ever more dissatisfied with Mamluk governance as the decades passed.

CONSERVATISM AND REACTION

With so much wealth at their disposal, the Bahri and Burji did more than expand their armies: they also patronized art in rather showy but often brilliant ways. Sumptuously woven textiles and carpets became a hallmark of their courts (and highly prized commodities among the European well-to-do). Their palaces were showcases for decorative glass, enameled lamps and statuary, exquisite ironwork, and libraries filled with books of fabulously ornate calligraphy and jeweled bindings. Moreover, the Mamluks built scores of new mosques and religious schools (madrasas) and bestowed lavish endowments upon them. The Mamluks had a particular enthusiasm for Sufism, which the bulk of Sunnis had difficulty reconciling themselves to, and brought hundreds of Sufi masters and thousands of Sufi texts into their realm.

In a reaction against what they regarded as the gaudiness of Mamluk culture, much of the most vigorous intellectual life under the Mamluks was reactive and conservative and was found among the Arabs, Egyptians, Kurds, and Syrians, who smarted under the new regimes. The greatest figure of the era was Ibn Taymiyyah [K] (1263–1328), a prolific legal scholar whose works urged a return to the stripped-down essentials of Islam, insisted on conservative readings of the Qur'an and hadith, and raged against the dangerous influence of Sufism. (One of his favorite words is *bid'a*—"reckless innovation" or even "newfangled nonsense.") Taymiyyah insisted on the Qur'an's absolute authority and rejected any efforts to

interpret its meanings apart from the most literal and exact. Although trained in kalam and philosophy, he rejected speculative thought as fundamentally un-Islamic and called for all Muslims to adhere to jihad against all the enemies of the faith—among whom he included the Mongols and the Shi'a. He also called on Muslims to reject the cult of Islamic saints, which he regarded as an impious absorption of Christian practice.[7] And perhaps most significantly for later centuries, he ardently championed the restoration of ethnic Arab leadership over international Islam.

The Black Death decimated the Islamic world just as it did the European, and the Mamluk Sultanate never fully recovered from the blow. In Cairo alone, as many as forty thousand people perished.

A Mosque Lamp A lovely oil-burning lamp made of enameled glass. Dating to the late 14th century, the lamp is Egyptian or Syrian in make.

7　"Many of these saints' venerators do not even know that this is a practice derived from the Christians. May Christianity and its followers be accursed!" (*Kitab Iqitada*).

When the Burji dynasty replaced the Bahri in 1382 they made factionalism even worse by purging the Turkish elite and installing their Circassian fellows, through whom they ordered even heavier taxation of the common populace. The Burji likewise earned well-deserved reputations for graft and corruption that further alienated them from their subjects in Egypt and Syria. But so long as the Mamluk military machine stood supreme, there was little anyone could do about them.

By 1500, however, two things had occurred that brought Mamluk power to an end. First, the Portuguese had rounded the African continent and interjected themselves into the spice and silk trade coming out of India, thus depriving the Mamluks of desperately needed revenue. Second, the Ottoman Turks, whose enthusiastic embrace of gunpowder and cannons gave them a clear tactical advantage over all rivals, challenged Mamluk control of Syria and Palestine with an assault on Aleppo. This gained, the Turks pressed further southward, taking all of Syria in less than a year, and in early 1517 capturing Cairo itself, putting an end to the Mamluk era. The establishment of Ottoman power inaugurates Islam's modern era.

THE OTTOMAN TURKS

No one would have predicted it, but the Ottoman regime gave the Islamic world its lengthiest, stablest, and most prosperous rule. To a certain extent, they had the Mongols to thank for that. The Mongol devastation was so vast, and their extortion of wealth afterwards so extensive, that Iraq and Iran required at least a century to recover. Meanwhile the realm of the Seljuk Turks, who had dominated most of Anatolia since their victory over the Byzantines at Manzikert in 1071, had broken up into a sprawl of warring principalities, which the Ottomans were then able to pick off one at a time. The turning point was a severe defeat inflicted on the Seljuks by the Mongols in 1243 at Köse Dağ in northeastern Anatolia.

In 1453 the Ottomans under their leader Mehmed II [T] (r. 1451–1481) achieved what Muslim armies had dreamt of since the 7th century—the conquest of Constantinople, which they made their own capital. Only the Mamluks, far to the south, rivaled the might of the Ottomans. By 1500 even the Mamluks were in retreat, leaving the Ottomans as undisputed leaders of the Islamic world, a position they held until they finally fell from power in the aftermath of World War I. Through most of its long history, the Ottoman Empire comprised most of North Africa, the Hijaz (that is, the western coastal strip of Arabia including the holy cities of Mecca and Madina), Palestine, Mesopotamia, Syria, Anatolia, the Balkans, Hungary, and the Crimea. This was an area larger than the Byzantine Empire had ever been.

They had the advantage of arriving on the scene when everyone else (Mamluks excluded) was weakening. Under the Seljuks, much of the Greek Orthodox and Armenian Christian populations had been driven off the land by the Turkish leaders' need to award land parcels to their soldiers. Unattached Turkish frontier warriors and mercenaries (called *ghazis*, in Turkish) made things worse, massacring and enslaving Christians in roughly equal numbers in the 12th and early 13th centuries. Famines and disease took care of much of the rest.[8] By the time the Ottomans came to power, the Turks' scorched-earth policies had emptied most of the Anatolian countryside. Many of the displaced Christians relocated to the Balkan and Black Sea territories, where the Byzantines still exercised some control, while town dwellers preferred to emigrate into Latin Europe, especially Italy. Changes in the place-names of Asia Minor tell the story: Byzantine Sinope became Turkish Sinop; Trebizond was renamed Trabzon; Adrianople reemerged as Edirne; Pergamon became Bergama; Germanicopolis acquired the name Çankırı; Nicaea became known as İznik; and so on (see Map 10.8). Those Christians who remained faced punitive taxation and various forms of social discrimination, and occasionally some entire villages converted in order to gain a sounder footing under the new regime. By 1300 Asia Minor was overwhelmingly Muslim, and the Ottomans responded by building hundreds of new mosques, madrasas, hospitals—even temporary housing for new converts, as a means of instructing them in Islamic customs.

The Ottomans had an even stronger enthusiasm for Sufism than the Seljuks had, and they consequently brought in Sufi preachers in huge numbers. The Sufis

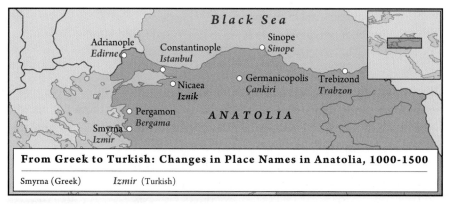

From Greek to Turkish: Changes in Place Names in Anatolia, 1000-1500

Smyrna (Greek)   *Izmir* (Turkish)

MAP 10.8   From Greek to Turkish: Changes in Place Names in Anatolia, 1000–1500

---

[8]   Warriors for hire flocked to 13th-century Anatolia from all around Europe and the Middle East.

bore special responsibility for converting the remaining Christians, which they did by emphasizing a kind of religious syncretism not seen since Roman times. Sermons drew direct parallels between the Twelve Apostles and the twelve Shi'a imams; others presented Allah, Muhammad, and Ali as an Islamic Trinity. The way had been prepared for these preachers by earlier figures like the great Sufi poet Jalal ad-Din Muhammad Balkhi [P] (1207–1273), better known in the West as **Rumi**, who penned thousands of verses, a number of sermons, and a famous collection of letters. Although he was a strict Muslim, Rumi's poetry frequently aimed at an ecumenical appeal:

> In search of Allah I ventured among the Christians and looked upon the Cross,
> But I did not find Him there;
> I entered pagan temples and looked upon the idols,
> But I did not find Him there.
> I explored the mountain cave at Hira [the site of Muhammad's first Qur'anic revelation]
> And even went as far as Kandahar, but I did not find Him there.
> So I made up my mind to climb to the top of Mount Caucasus,
> But there I found only a phoenix's nest.
> Turning around, I set out for the holy Ka'ba, the refuge of young and old,
> But I did not find Him even there.
> Trying philosophy next, I looked for insight in the writings of Ibn Sina,
> But I did not find Him there. . . .
> Finally, at last, I looked in my own heart, and found Him;
> He had been there all along. *(Quatrain 1173)*

His writings champion Islam but without disparaging other faiths. His approach seemed too gentle to many of his contemporaries, especially those Sunnis who were ill at ease with Sufi emotionalism. Yet the beauty of his poetry secured him an avid readership that lasts to the present day.

The unsettled nature of much Muslim life, as the Il-Khans plundered Iraq and Iran and as the Muslims in Spain continued to collapse in the face of the Reconquista, meant a continuous flow of immigrants into the Ottoman lands, which brought skilled labor and administrative talent to where they were needed. Judges, theologians, engineers, and civil bureaucrats, as well as farmers and artisans, poured into the region in large numbers. This enabled Ottoman society to stabilize quickly as a developed economic and political entity. And the Byzantine disappearing act opened Thrace, Macedonia, and the Balkans to Turkish expansion too. Under Murad I [T] (r. 1359–1389) the Turkish army added most of Bulgaria to the Ottoman domain as well, although Murad himself died shortly thereafter in battle against the Serbs at Kosovo.[9] In formalizing the peace accord after the fray, a prominent Serb princess married Murad's son and heir, Bayezid I; the union was reportedly an unusually happy one. Even more significantly, Serbian forces promptly joined up with Bayezid and helped him to attack Bosnia, Herzegovina, and parts of Hungary.

The stronger the Ottomans became, however, the more suspicious of them the Mongol Il-Khans in Persia and the Mamluks in Egypt grew. The popularity of Sufism among the Turks, and its sometimes troubling ecumenical traces, added to the popular hostility toward them. Bayezid I [T] (r. 1389–1403) went so far as to name his first three sons Musa [Moses], Issa [Jesus], and Mehmed [Muhammad], which was beyond the pale in most Sunni eyes. When the Ottoman rulers, mimicking the Mamluks, formed their own personal bodyguard of slave-soldiers (called janissaries, after the Turkish *yeniçeri*—meaning "new soldier"), many of whom were Greek Christians, they gave the appearance of being weak in their commitment to Islam; this rumor justified the attacks made on the Ottomans by the Mongols and Mamluks.

Despite those attacks, the Turks entered the 15th century as the clear leaders of international Islam. Turkish replaced Arabic and Persian as the language of diplomacy, and ethnic Turks filled the upper ranks of the civil and military hierarchies. When Constantinople was finally taken in 1453, it was renamed Istanbul and established as the new capital of the Turkish state. The move was doubly symbolic: not only did the Islamic world itself now stand triumphant over the Byzantines, but the Ottomans, unlike all earlier Muslim leaders, took up residence in the very city that straddled Asia and Europe. Islam would henceforth be a civilization on two fronts, facing both east and west, rooted in the faith that arose from Arabia but as much involved in Western ways as in Eastern. It was no coincidence that what enabled the great sultan Mehmed II (r. 1444–1446, 1451–1481) to finally achieve the conquest of Constantinople was his use of massive cannons that had been forged for him by engineers in Hungary. It was an eastern army with western technology.

> Islam would henceforth be a civilization on two fronts, facing both east and west, rooted in the faith that arose from Arabia but as much involved in Western ways as in eastern.

---

[9] The battle of Kosovo only later became enshrined as a moment when Serbs heroically gave their lives against the Muslim infidel.

The Conquest of Constantinople   A fresco on the outer wall of a Byzantine church depicting the siege of the city by Suleiman the Magnificent. The massive cannons used by the Ottomans to break the defenses had been forged in Hungary by the ironworkers' guild, in hopes that Suleiman would settle for Constantinople and leave the Hungarians alone. They were wrong.

PERSIA UNDER THE IL-KHANS

The Mongols were themselves shamanistic, meaning that they followed tribal spiritual leaders who were in contact with the spirit world and worked as miracle healers. They were generally tolerant of other religions and did little to hinder the development of Christianity or Islam. There were, of course, exceptions. One early emir of Il-Khan Persia, Nawruz, issued a decree:

> All [Christian] churches shall be torn down, their altars destroyed, and all celebrations of the Eucharist shall cease; moreover all hymns of praise and ringing of bells to call Christians to prayer shall be abolished. I decree too that the leaders of all Christian and Jewish congregations shall be killed.

But although several prominent Mongols did convert to Christianity, Islam was far more successful in spreading its message among not only the Mongols themselves but their tributary peoples as well. Since the arrival of the Seljuk Turks in the 11th century, a significant number of Muslims were Turkish-speaking. This gave the Muslims a considerable advantage in proselytizing, for the long history of interaction between the Turks and Mongols had fostered widespread understanding of their respective languages. Moreover, groups of Turks had traditionally been among the Mongols' chief steppe allies in the occasional confederations of tribes that formed and dissolved over the centuries. Mahmoud Ghazan (r. 1295–1304), the ruler of the Il-Khan kingdom in Persia, converted to Shi'a Islam—probably as a political move. (Rumors had it that he continued to practice shamanism privately.) He now declared Islam the official religion of the Il-Khanate. Turkish gradually replaced Mongolian as the language of the Il-Khan state, and Turks and Mongols held the supreme political and fiscal offices. Ethnic Persians, however, continued to make up the bulk of the civil administration throughout Iraq and Iran.

A few cultural and intellectual highlights stand out in the Il-Khan period. Rashid ad-Din Hamadani [P] (1247–1318) was a physician and historian; his encyclopedic *Jami al-Tawarikh* ("Compendium of Chronicles") is one of the greatest of medieval world histories. Sa'di [P] (1184–1291) was a Sufi poet of considerable talent in both Persian and Arabic, although much of his fictional writing (for which he was widely admired) is marred by a surprisingly callous spirit. In one story from his book *The Rose Garden* (1.40), for example, he tells of a Chinese slave girl who rejects a Muslim prince's advances and is sent off, as a punishment, to be raped by a black slave "whose upper lip stood higher than his nostrils, whose lower lip hung down to his neck…and whose armpit stench smelled like pitch." Sa'di evidently intended this story, and others like it, to be humorous, but it is a humor based on cruelty. Hafez Shirazi [P] (1315–1390) is perhaps the best loved of all Persian poets down to the present day; his lyrical verses praised the beauty of the human form in language reminiscent of religious mysticism.[10]

The Tatars never enjoyed much popularity with the peoples of Iraq and Iran. Turkish managed to replace Mongolian as the official court language, and ethnic Persians still dominated the higher echelons of civil affairs. Too much of Il-Khan policy had been aimed at diverting wealth into Mongol hands, though, for there to be any popular base to their power. After 1335 there were no more Mongols in charge, since the Il-Khan line died out; this triggered a long series of civil wars between petty emirs. Adding to Persia's troubles, a new dynasty in China—the Ming—came to power, conquered Mongolia, and cut off the silk routes across central Asia. Persia's economy consequently went into a tailspin.

Another Tatar warlord, around 1400, named Timur the Lame, or Tamerlane (r. 1380–1405), briefly terrorized Iraq and Iran while trying to reestablish Tatar

---

[10] Scholars in Il-Khan Persia also translated Chinese medical texts and perfected blue-and-white ornamental tile work.

Tamerlane on the Move   This scene shows his invasion of India, ca. 1590.

supremacy. He cut a huge swath of destruction: Baghdad, Delhi, Isfahan (where he notoriously ordered forty thousand citizens beheaded and, feeling whimsical, had a pyramid made of their skulls), Aleppo, Damascus, and Iznik. He burned mosques, schools, and libraries everywhere he went, ordered all Christian churches torn down, and rounded up all the most skilled artisans and deported them to his own capital at Samarkand, where they were forced to finish their lives constructing palaces and monuments in his honor. No one mourned his passing, and it would take many generations for Iraq and Iran, already smarting from earlier Mongol atrocities, to recover from the damage he had inflicted on them.

WHO, WHAT, WHERE

Black Death	Jacquerie
Cathars	Lollards
chivalry	longbow
Ciompi Rebellion	Magna Carta
comitatus	mendicant orders
crossbow	Mongols
Diet	Ottoman Turks
Dominicans	Peasants' Revolt
Estates General	plenitudo potestatis
Franciscans	Rumi
guild	scholasticism
Hundred Years' War	sultan
inquisition	summa

SUGGESTED READINGS

Primary Sources

Anonymous. *The Secret History of the Mongols.*
Anonymous. *The Arabian Nights.*
Alighieri, Dante. *The Divine Comedy.*

Chaucer, Geoffrey. *The Canterbury Tales.*
Froissart, Jean. *Chronicles.*
Ibn Battuta. *Travels.*

Ibn Khaldun. *The Muqaddimah.*

Ibn Taymiyya.

Kempe, Margery. *The Book of Margery Kempe.*

Rumi.

Anthologies

Aberth, John. *The Black Death: The Great Mortality of 1348–1350; A Brief History with Documents* (2005).

Dean, Trevor, trans. *The Towns of Italy in the Later Middle Ages* (2000).

Doss-Quinby, Eglal, Joan Tasker Grimbert, Wendy Pfeffer, and Elizabeth Aubrey, eds and trans. *Songs of the Women Trouvères* (2001).

Massoud, Sami G. *The Chronicles and Annalistic Sources of the Early Mamluk Circassian Period* (2007).

Murray, Jacqueline, ed. *Love, Marriage, and the Family in the Middle Ages: A Reader* (2001).

Studies

Aberth, John. *From the Brink of the Apocalypse: Confronting Famine, War, Plague, and Death in the Later Middle Ages* (2001).

Allsen, Thomas T. *Culture and Conquest in Mongol Eurasia* (2001).

Amitai-Preiss, Reuven. *Mongols and Mamluks: The Mamluk-Īlkhānid War of 1260–1281* (2005).

Arnold, John. *Inquisition and Power: Catharism and the Confessing Subject in Medieval Languedoc* (2001).

Beckwith, Christopher I. *Empires of the Silk Road: A History of Central Eurasia from the Bronze Age to the Present* (2010).

Blumenfeld-Kosinski, Renate. *Poets, Saints, and Visionaries of the Great Schism, 1378–1417* (2006).

Cahen, Claude. *The Formation of Turkey: The Seljukid Sultanate of Rūm; 11th to 14th Century* (2001).

Cohn, Samuel K., Jr. *Lust for Liberty: The Politics of Social Revolt in Medieval Europe, 1200–1425; Italy, France, and Flanders* (2006).

Dunn, Alastair. *The Peasants' Revolt: England's Failed Revolution of 1381* (2004).

Dyer, Christopher. *Making a Living in the Middle Ages: The People of Britain, 850–1520* (2003).

Goffman, Daniel. *The Ottoman Empire and Early Modern Europe* (2002).

Inalcik, Halil. *The Ottoman Empire: The Classical Age, 1300–1600* (2001).

Inalcik, Halil, and Donald Quataert, eds. *An Economic and Social History of the Ottoman Empire* (2005).

Leopold, Antony. *How to Recover the Holy Land: Crusading Proposals of the Late Thirteenth and Early Fourteenth Centuries* (2000).

Liu, Xinru. *The Silk Road in World History* (2010).

Pegg, Mark Gregory. *The Corruption of Angels: The Great Inquisition of 1245–1246* (2001).

Rouighi, Ramzi. *The Making of a Mediterranean Emirate: Ifrīqiyā and Its Andalusis, 1200–1400* (2011).

Rubin, Miri. *Gentile Tales: The Narrative Assault on Late Medieval Jews* (2004).

Sumption, Jonathan. *The Hundred Years War* (2000–2011).

For additional resources, including maps, primary sources, visuals, web links, and quizzes, please go to **www.oup.com/us/backman.**

TEMPLA DOMVM EXPOSITIS VICOS FORA MOENIA PONTES:
VIRGINEAM TRIVII QVOD REPARARIS AQVAM.
PRISCA LICET NAVTIS STATVAS DARE COMMODA PORTVS:
ET VATICANVM CINGERE SIXTE IVGVM:
PLVS TAMEN VRBS DEBET: NAM QVAE SQVALORE LATEBAT:
CERNITVR IN CELEBRI BIBLIOTHECA LOCO.

CHAPTER 11

Renaissances and Reformations

1350–1550

The Renaissance, the period in Europe roughly from 1350 to 1550, is one of the few eras in Western history that named itself. The cultural elite of the time believed they were living in an age of self-conscious revival. They were bringing back to life the ideas, moral values, art, and civic mindedness that characterized, they believed, the two high points of Western culture: Periclean Athens and Republican Rome. One of the first to use the term was the Italian writer, painter, and architect Giorgio Vasari (1511–1574), who celebrated a new epoch of civilized life. After a thousand years of medieval brutality and barbarism, Vasari claimed, Italian artists and thinkers

THE GREATER WEST, ca. 1550

◀ **Pope Sixtus IV** Sixtus IV (r. 1471–1484) is remembered for building the Sistine Chapel, establishing the Spanish Inquisition, and developing the Vatican Library. Record collection had long since become professionalized in the papal court; in fact, references to standing administrative offices with bureaucratic support date back to the 6th century, but a formal library was another matter. Sixtus saw the need for a centralized permanent collection of the church's manuscripts. Pope Nicholas V (r. 1447–1455) was the library's actual founder, but Sixtus greatly expanded and reorganized it and also made it available to scholars. Sixtus was a Franciscan, one of the last of his order to hold the papacy, but quickly became enamored of the pomp and splendor of the Renaissance court. He appointed a half dozen of his nephews to the College of Cardinals, including Giuliano della Rovere—the tall figure in the center—who later became Pope Julius II (r. 1503–1513), the target of Erasmus's great satire *Julius Excluded from Heaven*.

had bravely restored the lost perfection of art and philosophy as known to the ancients. An earlier Renaissance writer on education, Pier Paolo Vergerio (1370–1444), insisted that only the study of the classical liberal arts can lift society from the moral and spiritual decay of the medieval era. "Only those liberal arts," he proclaimed, "are worthy of free men; they alone can help us to attain virtue and wisdom . . . [and fill in the gaps in our moral knowledge] which the ignorance of the past centuries has intentionally created."

Una rinascità—a "rebirth" of classical values that gave fresh hope and creative energy to Europe. It also led to the greatest eruption in Greater Western religion since the birth of Islam—the Protestant Reformation.

"I FIXED UPON ANTIQUITY"

Not everyone in the Renaissance shared Vasari's and Vergerio's sense of the near mythic magnificence of antiquity, and it took some time for the English version of the word *rinascità* to catch on. It did not acquire positive connotations in English until John Ruskin (1819–1900) used it in his famous study of architecture *The Stones of Venice* (1851): "This rationalistic art is the art called Renaissance, marked by a return to pagan systems" (1.1.23). Most of Vergerio's and Vasari's contemporaries were simply grateful to have been born after the filthy muddle of the Middle Ages. Francesco Petrarca (1304–1374), usually regarded as the first Renaissance man, expressed this nostalgia for the deep past of Rome and Athens. In an open letter written toward the end of his life, called the *Letter to Posterity*, he recalls his youthful studies:

> I had more of a well-rounded mind than a keen intellect, and was naturally inclined to every type of virtuous and honorable study but especially to moral philosophy and poetry. After a while, it is true, I began to neglect poetry in favor of sacred literature, in which I soon found a buried sweetness that I had previously acknowledged to be there but only in a perfunctory way; now however I found its sweetness so great

CHAPTER TIMELINE

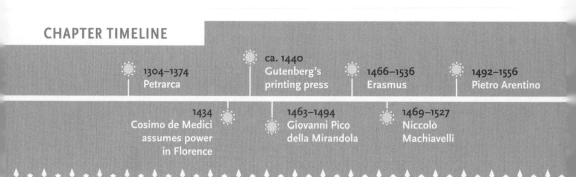

1304–1374 Petrarca	ca. 1440 Gutenberg's printing press	1466–1536 Erasmus	1492–1556 Pietro Arentino

1434 Cosimo de Medici assumes power in Florence

1463–1494 Giovanni Pico della Mirandola

1469–1527 Niccolò Machiavelli

that poetry became a mere afterthought for me. Out of all the subjects that intrigued me, I fixed especially upon antiquity—for the truth is that our own age repels me and has always done so. Indeed, were it not for the love of those I hold dear, I would rather have been born in any age but our own. I have spent most of my life thinking about other eras, in fact, as a way of ignoring my own, and that is why I have always loved the study of history.

However, the Renaissance—or the early part of it, anyway—shared more with its preceding age than it wanted to admit. The three ideas most characteristically associated with the Renaissance—classicism, humanism, and modern statecraft—represent no essential break with medieval life at all. They may in fact be thought of as the culmination of medieval strivings.

> The three ideas most characteristically associated with the Renaissance—classicism, humanism, and modern statecraft—represent no essential break with medieval life at all. They may in fact be thought of as the culmination of medieval strivings.

CLASSICISM, HUMANISM, AND STATECRAFT

The cult of classical learning and literature had its origins in early Western monastic life. Novice monks had long been directed to study the Roman poets Virgil and Horace, the historians Suetonius and Sallust, and the playwrights Terence and Seneca. It was their means to learn Latin before being granted access to the Scriptures and the patristic literature. The works of Aristotle, Ptolemy, Galen, and Euclid, moreover, had dominated university education from the start. But the great scholars of the Renaissance broadened this core canon by seeking out long-lost manuscripts; virtually anything by a classical author was of interest. Petrarca himself unearthed Cicero's *Letters to Atticus*, lying unused and unknown on a dusty library shelf in Verona for centuries, and brought out a new edition of it.

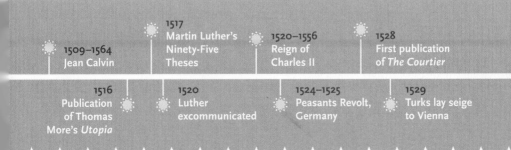

1509–1564
Jean Calvin

1517
Martin Luther's
Ninety-Five
Theses

1520–1556
Reign of
Charles II

1528
First publication
of *The Courtier*

1516
Publication
of Thomas
More's *Utopia*

1520
Luther
excommunicated

1524–1525
Peasants Revolt,
Germany

1529
Turks lay seige
to Vienna

What distinguished the Renaissance approach to the classics was a passionate conviction that they contained all that humans have best thought and best expressed. It was simply impossible not merely to be educated but to be a complete, satisfied, and accomplished human being without knowing the wisdom of the ancients. Pier Paolo Vergerio described the classical canon as "the only literature whose study helps us in the pursuit of virtue and wisdom, and brings forth in us those most sublime gifts of body and mind that ennoble men's spirit and that are properly regarded as second only to virtue itself as our most dignified attainment." This was more than mere affectation. Poseurs seldom engage in such intense archival and philological work. Renaissance scholars traveled through scores of libraries and archives, sifted through piles of manuscripts, corrected the minutest scribal errors, and commented prolifically on the cultural context and multiple meanings of a writer's text. Moreover, these scholars put their learning to use in works of their own, in every genre from poetry to stage drama, epistles to essays, histories to philosophical treatises.

The concern in this period to develop human potential, to value the particular, and to assert the inherent dignity of each person is called **Renaissance humanism**. The idea itself was not new, but the degree of emphasis placed on it was. The catastrophes of the 14th century, after all, had inspired many to doubt the values and assumptions of the high medieval era—the belief in a rationally ordered cosmos, a benevolent deity, the naturalness of a hierarchically structured society, the conviction that good will triumph over evil. The Black Death, after all, had shown no apparent concern to kill only the wicked, and the other calamities of the time had made people grow suspicious of systems of thought or social organization. What does one do, when everything a society takes for granted has been shown to be a sham? The world is a perilous place, a mad, painful jumble of impressions, sensations, thoughts, desires, fears, and inchoate longings. One struggles

The Cult of the Classics   Renaissance artists and writers regularly turned to classical Rome, and to a lesser extent to Periclean Athens, for inspiration, finding in these worlds the best models for the conduct of individual life and civil society. There was of course an element of affectation in this, but more generally it derived from a sincere conviction that the most practical guides to good living came from the pre-Christian world. This page from a new translation of Pliny's *Natural History* printed for a Florentine banker—Filippo Strozzi (1428–1491)—is a case in point. More than four years were spent on its production, and the costs involved totaled over 125 gold florins.

in vain to create anything like order or meaning. The best one can do is to find comfort, beauty, or value in the broken shards of the world scattered at one's feet. Humanism celebrated such simple pleasures: the precise arch of an eyebrow or the drape of a garment in a painting, the warm hue of sunlight entering a window, the sense of balance within an enclosure created by the artful placement of objects, the beautiful potential energy in a tensed coil of muscle. A focus on the particular called for a representational art, one attuned to the hard but transitory reality of objects in time. Medieval art had more widely used symbolic and allegorical representations.

Scholars in the Renaissance still wrote in Latin, but most of the creative literature of the age was in the vernacular. This too mimicked medieval practice, but reflected a different reason. In the Middle Ages, scholarship was written in Latin because it was the common tongue of the learned. Physicians in Spain could communicate with physicians in Hungary or Denmark; mathematicians in England could be read in Portugal or Poland. In the Renaissance, however, scholars wrote in Latin (or sometimes in Greek) out of a conviction in the intrinsic superiority of the classical languages. Latin and Greek, in the "pure" forms used in ancient times, were seen as uniquely capable of expressing complex thought. Imagine a demand today to make Shakespearean English the only form of English worthy of public discourse. Anyone who could read a computer manual in that language would be a rare person indeed—and not necessarily a better person because of it.[1]

The most famous of Renaissance descriptions of humanism came from Giovanni Pico della Mirandola (1463–1494), a brilliant polymath. His "Oration on the Dignity of Man" lays out the fundamental elements of the movement in elegant language:

> I read somewhere of a Muslim writer named Abdullah who, when asked to identify the most wondrous and awe-inspiring thing to appear on the world's stage, answered, "There exists nothing more wondrous than Man." Hermes Trismegistus expressed the same view when he wrote, "What a great miracle is Man, Asclepius!"
>
> But when I began to consider the reasons behind these opinions, every particular of their arguments for the magnificence of human nature failed to persuade me.

[1] Scholars sought to take the living Latin and Greek they had inherited and purge them of what they considered barbarisms and corrupt usages.

The unconvincing arguments include man's existence as a rational creature or as master of the physical world.

What strikes Pico della Mirandola as the essential and glorious point about humans is rather something else: to us alone has God given the freedom and ability to be whatever we want, to become whatever we desire, and to achieve whatever we wish. A flower has no choice but to bloom, wither, and die; a stone may serve as a building block, a projectile, or a hindrance in the road, but it has no destiny of its own, no yearning to become something. Humans alone, he insists, are free to be whatever we wish to be.

> You alone, being altogether without limits and in possession of your own free will, ... have it within you to establish the limits of your own nature.... Alone at the dark center of his own existence, yet united with God, Who is Himself beyond all created things, Man too exists beyond every created thing—and who can help but stand in awe of this great Fate forger? Even more: How is it possible for anyone to marvel at anything else?

To describe Man as, essentially, his own Creator was to flirt with heresy—and Mirandola did in fact run afoul of the church. To his credit, he admitted that he had overreached on several matters, issued a number of corrections and retractions, and announced his interest in becoming an obedient monk. He died suddenly at age thirty-one, however. Someone had slipped arsenic into his wine. His fate should not distract us, though, from recognizing the fundamentally religious nature of humanism. Humanism was not a secular philosophy. It sought to define the place of humanity in God's divine plan, to parse the relationship between Man and God, and so to glorify both.

Humanism was not a secular philosophy. It sought to define the place of humanity in God's divine plan, to parse the relationship between Man and God, and so to glorify both.

The third major element of the Renaissance was statecraft. The concept of a state is a relatively modern one—and a legal fiction. A state as a thing in itself, independent of the people who comprise it and following its own norms and rules, requires a degree of abstraction. Simply to gather a number of people to live in the same space, after all, does not make a city. A city, by definition, is a legal entity, with power—the power to tax, for example, or to administer justice, to legislate, or to police miscreants. It exists on paper and in law, and it makes its powers available to those who dwell within it. Earlier notions of government had regarded the state as a network of personal relationships, but not necessarily as a distinct object. It had the king at the center, with his web of obligations and privileges to his nobles, his commoners, and the church. Exceptions to this model existed, of course, but until the 13th century they were in the minority.

Renaissance theorists and power brokers, taking their cue from late medieval writers like Brunetto Latini (1220–1294) and Marsiglio di Padova (1275–1342), thought of the state in a new way. The political state was a thing, a part of the natural world, and it functioned according to rules. Political leaders who understood this governed most effectively, because they could direct the state by means of its own internal logic. Statecraft therefore involved understanding systems of law, taxation, and economy. It involved the intricacies of diplomacy and negotiation, the mechanisms of crowd control, the manipulation of public opinion, and the knowledge of when to deceive or to exert force. Idealism had no part in it, and politics became a hard science rather than an expression of personal desire. For that very reason, however, it offered the perfect site for educated men of the

The Ambassadors   A powerful but somber piece by Holbein the Younger. Called *The Ambassadors*, it depicts a French nobleman dispatched to London on a diplomatic errand, together with his friend, a French bishop. Together they represent the active and the contemplative modes of life, with objects representing knowledge, power, and art in the background. The diagonally oriented object in the foreground, when looked at obliquely, is a skull representing Death.

Renaissance. Conscious of their abilities, and dedicated to the ancient Roman virtue of civic-mindedness, they could take their proper place within the world by mastering its rules and methods.

THE POLITICAL AND ECONOMIC MATRIX

Europe needed men of ability, Italy especially. Italy was by far the most developed urban society in Europe, followed closely by southern France and eastern Spain. Yet its political scene was a mess. The northern city-states, where the Renaissance began, had long been under the leadership of the German emperor, at least in name. His titular sovereignty dated to the 10th century, when Otto I subdued the region and gained the imperial crown. In the intervening three hundred years, emperors had brought armies over or around the Alps, intermittently but repeatedly, to assert their claims. And most of Italy's city-states opened their gates, bowed deeply, and paid their ritual and financial tribute. But once the armies were safely back in Germany, the Italians instantly returned to their independent republican ways.

The rise of the Hohenstaufen dynasty, however, had altered the rules of the game dramatically. Its joint rule over northern Italy and the Kingdom of Sicily (the result of a marriage alliance) included the southern third of the peninsula. That made urgent the need felt by many northerners to end permanently the imperial claims over their territories. Others, however, saw some utility in the on-again, off-again imperial connection, and so opposed autonomy. This scenario, in which the papacy became deeply involved, led to strife between and within each of the city-states. The Papal State, caught as it was between Hohenstaufen power bases to the north and the south, spent nearly the entire 13th century in diplomatic and military stratagems to break the power of the German/Italian/Sicilian connection. By the time of the 14th century's disasters, northern Italy was a mercenary's dreamscape. Wars large and small, palace coups, assassinations, plots, pillagings, enforced exiles, and institutional corruption had spread everywhere (see Map 11.1).

A unique feature of the Italian scene, however, helped pave the way for the Renaissance. Italian nobles tended to live within the cities, even though their rural estates were distant, and hence they played an active role in urban culture that nobles in Continental Europe did not. That included both ancient lineages and wealthy commoners whose riches had helped them purchase aristocratic titles. Moreover, the elitist bias against trade and commerce that characterized northern aristocratic society was much less virulent in Italy. Hence, by the start of the 15th century, an alliance had developed between the urban aristocrats and the mercantile and banking families of the bourgeoisie. This allowed them

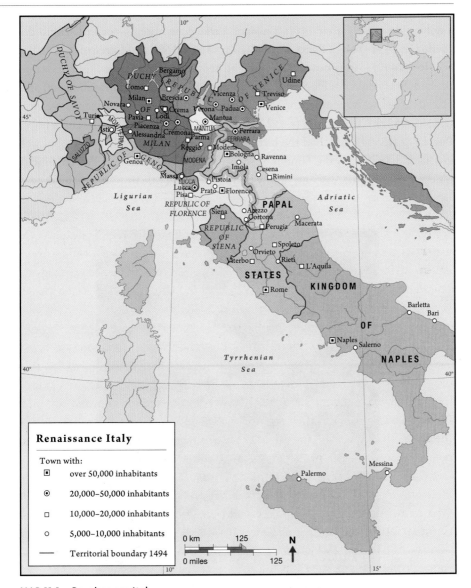

MAP 11.1   Renaissance Italy

to usurp republican government, to institute direct and often tyrannical control over the city-states. Most who did so, mimicking the 1st-century emperor Augustus, maintained the fiction and rituals of republican government while establishing despotic rule.

Most city-states thus had actual, if barely functioning, republican governments between 1350 and 1450 (the first half, roughly, of the Renaissance), but despotic governments from 1450 to 1550 (the second half). In Florence, for example, the Medici family, which had risen through the ranks in banking and textiles, gained a noble title shortly after 1400. Through three generations—under Cosimo de' Medici (r. 1434–1464), Piero de' Medici (r. 1464–1469), and Lorenzo de' Medici (r. 1469–1492)—they governed a pretend republic. In 1531 the family became the hereditary dukes of Florence (later elevated to the status of an archduchy) and placed three family members on the papal throne during the Renaissance—Leo X (r. 1513–1521), Clement VII (r. 1523–1534), and Leo XI (r. 1605). (A fourth pope, Pius IV [r. 1559–1565], had the birth name of Giovanni Angelo Medici but was unrelated.) In Milan, the famous Visconti and Sforza families followed similar trajectories, with the Visconti family taking the ducal title in 1369 and holding it

The Medici as the Magi Wealth has its privileges, among which has been the tradition of artists inserting portraits of their patrons into their religious paintings. Traditionally this was done by placing the patron somewhere within the frame of the original biblical story, but with this painting of the Three Magi coming to worship the child Jesus, the painter has gone one step further by portraying Lorenzo de' Medici and his family members as the Magi themselves. The imposition is apt, since the gifts brought by the Magi (gold, myrrh, and frankincense) were symbolic of the finance and spice trading that brought the Medici their enormous wealth. The painting is by Benozzo Gozzoli (1420–1497).

until the family line died out in 1447. At that point the Sforza family (of peasant origins, with several generations of mercenary soldiers thrown in) took over and governed by fiat until 1535. The d'Este family in Ferrara, who had led local politics since 1264, won a ducal title in 1452 (and another in 1471) and held on to power until 1597. Likewise the Gonzaga family in Mantua, where they ruled without stop from 1328 to 1708.

The concentrations of wealth and power in these city-states, and in others like them, made possible elaborate systems of patronage, which gave a tremendous boost to intellectual and artistic life. Again like Augustus, Renaissance despots put their resources to work in the public sphere. They commissioned scores of palaces, chapels, public fountains and market squares, mausoleums, fortifications, libraries and museums, schools, and hospitals. All were done in the newest styles and were richly decorated with paintings, sculptures, frescos, and tapestries—and they provided hundreds of opportunities for scholars, artists, and architects. Art was not for art's sake alone in the Renaissance. It expressed humanist values and aesthetics while serving to elevate the civic spirit. It also promoted the glory and wisdom of the patron whose support made the art possible.

The depressed economy contributed as well, since labor costs were comparatively low. The building frenzy of the 14th and 15th centuries therefore represented a jobs program: it bolstered support for the regimes by putting people to work. Manufacturing still limped along, since the shrunken population meant a decreased need for most goods; the demographic recovery was slow across Europe. The city of Toulouse, for example, had numbered thirty thousand in the early 14th century, and by the early 15th it had only eight thousand. Within Italy, Genoa had lost more than one-third of its population; Bologna and Milan had each lost half; Florence had lost three-fourths. Many towns did not regain their 13th-century populations until the 20th century. Moreover, the ongoing struggles against the Ottomans, who pressed their frontiers to the gates of Vienna, interrupted trade with Asia. Even with such drastically reduced numbers, the drift of rural poor into the cities ensured a constant labor surplus. Labor costs therefore were cheap, making the vast construction projects of the Renaissance possible.

The rich are with us always. Even in a depressed economy, concentrations of capital exist and often grow, so long as the possessor is lucky or clever (or corrupt) enough to seize the opportunities. In the Renaissance, those opportunities existed, especially in finance and armaments. With so much construction to perform and so much war to wage, those with capital were able to lend it at handsome rates of interest. Meanwhile manufacturers found markets always in search of weaponry and construction equipment. Venice's Arsenal—its shipbuilding factory—employed three thousand laborers at the start of the 15th century. Tax records from that time show that two-thirds of the city's merchants made at least six thousand ducats per year, and one-half of those fortunate merchants actually made well over twelve thousand. Seven merchants actually had annual incomes of over 140,000 ducats.[2] Such severe inequities in the distribution of capital ensured that rents and wages worked in favor of the elite. So did the power of the guild leaders and urban nobles. In Milan and Basel, a mere 5 percent of the population controlled one-half of each city's wealth. No wonder they had the ability to commission palaces, endow museums and libraries, dress in expensive silks and furs, and commission such splendid works of art. The Renaissance, for all its cultural glories, was a miserable time to be a poor farmer or a simple workman— which is precisely what the overwhelming majority of people were.

THE RENAISSANCE ACHIEVEMENT

Art and intellectual life tend to thrive when supported. The cult of patronage— that is, the eager support of painters, sculptors, poets, and scholars as a sign of one's cultivation—and the appreciation of individual talent gave a tremendous impetus to new forms of expression and the pursuit of knowledge. The influx of scholars and artists from the east also contributed, as the Ottomans closed in on the remnants of Byzantium. One Sicilian humanist, Giovanni Aurispa (1376–1459), rushed to Constantinople in the years leading up to the Turkish siege and came back with over two hundred manuscripts that might otherwise have gone up in flames. Copyists were hired by the hundreds in every city to get texts like these reproduced and circulated.[3] The invention of the printing press by Johannes Gutenberg in 1440 allowed books to pour over Europe like a tide. Aldus Manutius (1450–1515) was the most celebrated of humanist publishers; his printing house in Venice produced editions of well over a hundred Latin and Greek texts before his death.

Vernacular literature, or literature in local languages rather than Latin, also began to appear in print. This is important because most of the truly memorable literature produced in the Renaissance was in the common, not the learned, tongues. Petrarca's great sequence of sonnets and love-songs to his beloved Laura (the *Canzoniere*) have proved enduringly popular, while his Latin epic poem about the Roman general Scipio Africanus—called *Africa*—is turgid and lifeless. Much better is Ludovico Ariosto's (1474–1533) immense, and immensely

---

[2]   A Venetian ducat of that time was minted of roughly 3.5 grams of gold (one-eighth of an ounce). Gold, in 2012 U.S. dollars, has hovered around $1610 per ounce. A very rough estimate of the value of 6000 ducats, therefore, would be perhaps $1,200,000. In Shakespeare's play *The Merchant of Venice*, the amount loaned by Shylock to Antonio, on surety of "a pound of flesh," was half that amount.

[3]   By the start of the 15th century, Florence had opened the first lending library in Europe: one could actually borrow the books and take them home rather than having to read them on site, as before.

entertaining, mock-epic *Orlando Furioso* ("Crazed Roland"). It tells of the mad adventures of Charlemagne's knight Roland, who loses his mind when his beloved Angelica falls in love with a Muslim prince and moves to China. Then he turns into a one-man juggernaut, rampaging through Europe, Asia, and Africa and destroying everything in sight.

Not many Renaissance stage plays have lasted; only two are still widely read and produced today. Pietro Aretino (1492–1556), known in his lifetime as the "Scourge of Princes" for his scathing wit and willingness to blackmail the prominent when short of funds, wrote several brilliant bawdy comedies— along with a considerable amount of technically clever pornographic poetry.[4] The best, a comedy called *La cortigiana* ("The Woman Courtier"), tells of an upright wealthy citizen from Siena who receives an appointment as a papal cardinal. Traveling to Rome for his installation, he sees a beautiful young woman sitting at a window and decides he must have her as a mistress. The comedy ensues when a scheming con artist tries to teach the elderly man how to flatter and entice the young beauty—all the while pursuing a plan of his own.

ET DIST. SOL. ET LVNAE. 30

Greek to Me The Romans, being of a pragmatic bent, became expert innovators in engineering but showed relatively little interest in pure science, and hence the science inherited by the scholars of the Middle Ages was based firmly on, and consisted largely of commentary on, the science of the ancient Greeks. The page shown, from a book printed in Pisa, Italy, in 1572, depicts a passage from *On the Distances and Sizes of the Sun and Moon* by Aristarchus (3rd century BCE). The text and drawing examine the ratios of the diameters of the sun, Earth, and moon and calculate how they affect the light and dark portions visible during a lunar eclipse.

The other great Renaissance comedy is *La mandragola* ("The Mandrake Root"), by Niccolò Machiavelli (1469–1527). The play, which appeared in 1518, tells of another upright elderly man, Nicia, newly married to a stunning but sexually shy beauty named Lucrezia. Unable to convince his bride to sleep with him, the foolish husband confides in a dashing young ne'er-do-well named Callimaco who, desiring Lucrezia for himself, hatches a plot. He tells Nicia that he has

---

4   A 2008 performance of Aretino's *Songs of Lust*, set to modern music, was withdrawn in London after complaints about their obscene content.

learned, through careful study of ancient Greek scientific manuscripts, of a potion made from mandrake root. When given to a woman, it instantly enflames her with a lust that cannot be denied. The drug has an unfortunate side effect, however: the first man to have sex with the woman will die immediately afterward. Nicia declares that he wants Lucrezia, but not enough to die for it. Callimaco then announces, tremblingly, unwillingly, that he himself suffers from an unspecified mortal illness and has only a few days to live. So great is his admiration for Nicia and his desire to perform a useful service before he dies that he volunteers for the suicide mission.

La mandragola surprises most people who read or watch it. They usually come to the play knowing Machiavelli from another work of his, a small political treatise called *The Prince*. In 1499 the people of Florence had overthrown the Medici despot and restored republican government. Machiavelli, a Florentine, loved and served its republic with passionate dedication for thirteen years, from 1499 to 1512—as a diplomat, civil servant, and military overseer. Late in 1512, however, a counter plot restored Lorenzo de' Medici to power. Machiavelli was dismissed, arrested for conspiracy, tortured, and ultimately released. In retirement at his country estate, he then gave himself over to study and writing.

The Prince, although he never published it, was the first thing Machiavelli wrote. (He circulated it among a small circle of friends and dedicated it to Lorenzo de' Medici—probably in hopes of winning a position in the new government.) It is a notorious book, praised by some for its clear-eyed realism about how political power actually works and vilified by others as little more than a how-to manual for thugs. To modern readers, inured by long experience of politicians' lies, manipulations, and occasional crimes, the book no longer shocks. Stable society, Machiavelli argues, results more from stable order than from benevolent instability. Therefore a prince's first responsibility is to secure his own power, even if the exercise of that power is unjust. Ruthlessness should not be pursued for its own sake, but a wise prince will never rule it out altogether. A prince ought always to maintain an upright public appearance, but behind the scenes he should use any means at his disposal—including lying, cheating, stealing, or killing—in order to maintain power. Although *The Prince* never uses the phrase, its essential message is that in politics the end justifies the means.

Clear-Eyed Realist Niccolò Machiavelli (1469–1527) and a page from his philosophical masterpiece, *The Discourses on Livy*, in praise of republican forms of government.

Once the book was published, five years after Machiavelli's death, people read it with a shudder of horror. Machiavelli's defenders point to the chaotic state of Italian politics at the time, with French, German, Savoyard, and Spanish invaders at every turn. *The Prince*, they suggest, is simply a plea for a no-nonsense messianic figure who would restore Italian liberty. Perhaps. His letters, though, suggest that Machiavelli was a man of republican Florence, first, last, and always. He would have been delighted to see Ferrara, Mantua, Milan, Pisa, or Venice crushed by a foreign army if that were to Florence's gain. Complicating matters, he dashed off *The Prince* in a few weeks. Machiavelli then spent four years (1513–1517) composing his major work, *Discourses on Livy*, which elaborates a complex and passionate argument on the superiority of republican government over any other type of political organization.[5] "Governments of the people are superior to any government by a prince" (1.58).

Less controversial were Marsilio Ficino (1433–1499) and Baldassare Castiglione (1478–1529). Ficino was a celebrated philosopher who spent his career at the Medici court. He had mastered classical Greek as a young man and became a devout exponent of Neoplatonism. His greatest achievement, in fact, was a translation into Latin of the entire corpus of Plato's writings, which he completed in 1470 but did not publish until 1484 (having taken some time, meanwhile, to prepare for the priesthood). Until then, Plato had hardly been known in Latin Europe, and Western intellectual life had been long dominated by Aristotle. Ficino's other major works include a long treatise, *On Platonic Theology*, which explicates Christian doctrine on the immortality of the soul using Platonic ideas. He argues that the unique, characteristic destiny of the human soul is to investigate its own nature, but such investigation inevitably results (at least temporarily) in confusion and misery. Hence the ultimate goal of the soul is to rise above physicality, to become disembodied, and to achieve union with the divine. As a hybrid philosophical and mystical treatise, it is a stunning exercise. Ficino was the tutor of many Neoplatonists, most famously of Giovanni Pico della Mirandola, the author of the "Oration on the Dignity of Man."

Castiglione came from an ancient noble family near Mantua and spent his entire life in the circle of social and political elites. He served as a personal aide and confidante to the marquis of Mantua and then to the duke of Urbino and spent several years in Rome as an ambassador to the papal court, then several more as papal nuncio to the royal court of Spain in Madrid. He is remembered primarily for *The Courtier*, which is a kind of memoir written in the form of a fictional philosophical

---

[5]   "No properly run republic should ever find it necessary to overlook the crimes of any given citizen because of his supposed excellence" (Machiavelli, *Discourses* 1.24).

dialogue. In it he laments the passing of the Renaissance's golden era, when human-ism was at its height. By the 16th century Italy was overrun by ambitious foreigners, and courtly life as Castiglione had known it (or at least as he chose to remember it) had declined into a tawdry arena of power grabbing, money grubbing, and social climbing. He depicts fictionalized versions of the companions of his youth—elegant, charming, cultivated, effortlessly superior to everyone—who spend four evenings in an extended conversation about the qualities of an ideal courtier.

To Castiglione the courtier is above politics: he graciously advises any figure deemed worthy of attention but does not advocate any particular political phi-losophy. This marks a shift from the original ideal of humanism, which expected a passionate civic spirit from its adherents. Castiglione's figures expound on the need for courtiers to appreciate music and poetry, to excel at dancing, sports, and refined conversation, to understand the importance of fashion as well as affairs of state. In short, courtiers should exist beautifully, all the while exuding an air of nonchalance and unpracticed elegance. *The Courtier* was extraordinarily popu-lar, going through more than one hundred editions between its appearance in 1528 and 1616. Its significance lay in its elegiac mood: at a time when Europe's nobles were being displaced from political life, Castiglione consecrated for them the qualities that lifted them forever above the common rabble.

THE PROTESTANT RENAISSANCE

As the ideas and values of the Renaissance spread northward, they took on new styles, concerns, and emphases. Ultimately, if indirectly, they led to the shattering of the religious unity that had marked Latin Europe since the advent of Christianity.

It took some time for humanism to catch on in the north. The prolonged agony of the Hundred Years' War in England and France certainly impeded the spread of the new learning. So did the resistance of the universities of Paris and Oxford—both strongholds of Aristotelianism. As for Germany, intellectual life there had long been centered in the royal and aristocratic courts. The royal court at Munich, for example, had been a refuge for scholars like Marsiglio di Padova and William of Ockham in the 14th century, when both had fallen out of favor in Paris and Oxford, respectively. Now Germany had fractured into hundreds of principalities (nominally under the authority of the Habsburg dynasty—the weak successors to the crushed Hohenstaufens—but effectively autonomous), and its relatively few universities did not rush to embrace new ideas.[6] When humanism

---

[6]   Munich did not acquire a university until 1472. Even then, the university was at Ingolstadt, several miles away.

did finally begin to take root, around the year 1500, it did so in an altered form known as **Christian humanism**.

Like humanism in Italy, Christian humanism rejected scholastic system building and looked to the past for new models of thinking and behavior. However, Christian humanists showed a strong preference for texts and traditions that contributed directly to religious faith. Their goal was not to become better all-round individuals but better Christians. Consequently, they focused less on the writings of the ancient philosophers and poets and more on the early writings of the Christians—especially the New Testament itself. In the visual arts, the northern Renaissance likewise showed much less interest in depicting classical pagan themes. Rather, painters and sculptors avidly adopted Renaissance techniques to produce striking new presentations of biblical imagery. The Christian humanists were passionate reformers, dedicated to promote Christian education and practical piety through the preparation of newer and better texts. Their often-stated goal was backward looking: to restore Christian faith to its original purity as practiced in the apostolic community.

The Christian humanists were not yet anti-Catholic, only anticlerical. The shortage of priests had always been direr the further north one traveled in Europe, with exceptions in cities like Paris, London, and Mainz, but the problem had been persistently acute since the Black Death. Clergy at the grassroots level were in painfully short supply, and those who were available were often poorly trained. Hence northerners had developed strong traditions of lay piety. They focused less on the church's sacramental life and more on the simple reading of Scripture, the singing of hymns, and communal prayer. Religious fraternities and sororities abounded, offering many a life of organized piety, education, and moral rigor that deemphasized ecclesiastical dogma and ritual. The best

The Four Holy Men "A panel on which I have bestowed more care than on any other painting" is how Albrecht Dürer (1471–1528) described this powerful group portrait, completed in 1526. It depicts, from left to right, Saint John the Evangelist, Saint Peter (holding his ever-present key to paradise), Saint Mark, and Saint Paul the Apostle (who carries a copy of the Bible and a sword, the latter being a reference to his martyrdom). Dürer was a passionate supporter of the Lutheran Reformation, and the bottom portion of each panel (since lost) bore passages from Luther's German translation of the Scriptures. The intensity of the men's expressions and the classical simplicity of their dress testify to the spiritual earnestness of the Protestant Reformers—being awed and humbled by the magnificence of what they regarded as the rediscovered beauty and majesty of the Word.

known of these organizations was the Brethren of the Common Life, estab-
lished in 14th-century Holland and spreading quickly across northern Europe.
Its most famous alumni were Desiderius Erasmus (1466–1536) and Martin
Luther (1483–1546).

ERASMUS: SATIRIST AND ITINERANT SCHOLAR

Erasmus was arguably the greatest of all humanist scholars, admired for the
breadth of his classical learning, his quick wit and generous spirit, and the elegance of his writing. The illegitimate son of a Dutch priest in training and a
physician's daughter, he grew up in Rotterdam and received his primary education at home. In 1483, however, both of his parents died in a new outbreak of
the plague. Supported by the Brethren of the Common Life, Erasmus entered
a series of monastic and lay-fraternal schools, where he was unhappy with the
frequently dour discipline but delighted in their extensive libraries. In 1492,
brilliant but penniless, he took monastic vows, entered an Augustinian house,
and was soon ordained to the priesthood. He hated monastic life, though, and
thought most of his fellow monks to be joyless and haughty automatons. Fortunately, a bishop from Cambrai, not far away in northern France, heard
of Erasmus's brilliance and took him on as a personal secretary in 1495.
The bishop urged Erasmus to pursue more formal study and sent him to the
University of Paris.

Once he had finished his degree, Erasmus set out for England, where he had
been invited to lecture at the University of Cambridge. Freed from the bishop's
service, Erasmus spent the rest of his life as an itinerant scholar, lecturing at
various universities and visiting one noble court after another. Chronically
short of funds, he was offered many lucrative academic posts throughout his life
but declined them all, preferring his freedom. He also rejected several offers to
be appointed a Catholic bishop and two nominations to the College of Cardinals. He studied and wrote constantly, even while traveling. In fact, he claimed
to have written much of his most famous work, *The Praise of Folly* (1509), while
on horseback during a trip to England to visit his friend Thomas More. He died
in Basel in 1536.

Despite such an unsettled life Erasmus produced an astonishing amount of
writing. His letters alone fill eleven fat volumes in their standard edition. He wrote
in three distinct voices. His most popular works were witty satires like *The Praise
of Folly* that aimed to entertain people while nevertheless pointing out society's
flaws and foibles. Folly here delivers a monologue on the crucial but unappreci-
ated role she has played in human history. Everyone from kings and princes to

peasants and peddlers, she claims, owe something to her for the simple reason that humans all prefer foolishness to common sense. Every page of history proves her point. In works like this, or his popular *Colloquies* (1518), Erasmus lampoons pedantic teachers, hypocritical clerics, greedy landlords, shrewish wives, petulant youths, preening nobles, untrustworthy merchants, and others with a wit that is pointed but almost never mean-spirited.

Erasmus's most notorious satire is a prickly piece called *Julius Excluded* (1513), a lengthy sketch depicting a confrontation at the Gates of Heaven between the recently deceased Pope Julius II (r. 1503–1513) and Saint Peter. Julius is drunk when he arrives and tries to unlock the gates with the key to his private money chest. Asked to account for his many sins, ranging from murder to sodomy, Julius replies that his sins were all forgiven "by the pope himself"—meaning, of course, Julius himself. When Saint Peter refuses to admit Julius into heaven on account of his excessive concern for

Erasmus of Rotterdam   Given the fact that he was the most traveled, best connected, and highly regarded religious scholar in Europe, there are surprisingly few contemporary portraits of Erasmus, the man who made a heroic last-ditch effort to reform Catholic Christianity before Martin Luther's break with Rome. This portrait, by fellow Dutchman Quentin Metsys (1466–1530), captures the quiet determination of the man. Despite his gift for satire and enjoyment of good (and sometimes bawdy) humor, Erasmus dedicated long years of work to exposing problems within the Catholic Church and promoting a spiritual rejuvenation that would keep all Christians within the arms of the church. His failure marks an important turning point, since most of the great reforms in the church in earlier centuries had been inspired from without. From Erasmus's time to the present, Catholic reform has been largely driven from within the institutional leadership.

worldly power and war making, the pope throws a fit, threatens to excommunicate Peter, and announces that he will raise an army to burst through the gates and take Paradise by force.[7]

Erasmus also composed a long series of moral polemics, earnest in tone yet intended for a general audience. In these books—like *Handbook of the Christian Soldier* (1503), *Education of a Christian Prince* (1516), and *The Complaint of Peace* (1517)—he condemns empty religious formalism and urges people to seek out the vital spirit of Christ as depicted in the Bible. They should live simply,

---

[7]   At one point the pope complains to Saint Peter, "You would not believe how *seriously* some people take little things like bribery, blasphemy, sodomy, and poisoning!"

honorably, peaceably, and with sincere conviction. These satirical and serious works were immensely popular: it has been estimated that, by Erasmus's death in 1536, some 15 percent of all the printed books purchased in Europe had come from his pen. In his third vein, Erasmus toiled at the most detailed and exacting textual scholarship—revised and annotated editions of the writings of the Latin fathers Saint Ambrose (d. 397), Saint Jerome (d. 420), and Saint Augustine (d. 430). He followed these projects with his masterpiece, a new critical edition of the Greek New Testament (1515), whose fifth and final version appeared in 1535. Known as the Received Version (*Textus receptus*), it was used by most early translators of the New Testament into English and other vernaculars. These works had a much smaller readership, understandably, but he regarded them as his chief legacy to the world.

MARTIN LUTHER: THE GIFT OF SALVATION

Among those who used Erasmus's New Testament as the basis for a vernacular translation was Martin Luther, the German monk whose agonized quest for salvation triggered the break with the church known as the **Protestant Reformation**. Like the humanists who sought to restore ancient morals, Luther sought to re-create what he believed to be Christian belief and practice as they had existed in the apostolic Church. He saw himself as a restorer, not a revolutionary, a liberator rather than an insurrectionist. The distinction is important, for it helped to set the stage for the brutal course the conflict ultimately took. Luther, a brilliant biblical scholar, had the gift of presenting his ideas in clear, forceful language that ranged easily in emotional pitch from exquisite descriptions of God's loving kindness to the coarsest verbal abuse of his foes (who consisted of anyone who disagreed with him). His charisma, energy, and passionate feeling were immense; he needed such powerful drive, for his ultimate goals—once he decided that compromise with the church was impossible—were nothing less than the complete overthrow of Catholic tradition and the resetting of the Christian clock, so to speak, fifteen hundred years back.

Luther was born—proudly—of modest, laboring stock in northern Germany. His hardworking parents instilled piety and order in him from an early age, and when it came time for his education they sent him to a school run by the Brethren of Common

Life, the same group whose austere and rigid discipline had so disillusioned the young Erasmus. Hoping to establish his son in a legal career, Luther's father sent him to the University of Erfurt, but Martin was drawn instead to theology and the classical languages. In 1505, aged twenty-two, he shattered his father's hopes by taking vows as an Augustinian monk. A mere two years later he was ordained a priest.

His vocation brought him no peace, though. Belief in God tormented Luther, for he could see no way to please him. God's majesty was so immense, so vast, and so inconceivably great, that Luther found it impossible to believe that anyone could merit salvation. No one de-

A Restorer, not a Revolutionary   Martin Luther (1483–1546), in a portrait by Lucas Cranach the Elder (1472–1553). Apart from his work as an artist, Cranach was an early enthusiast for the printing press, and in time became one of Martin Luther's publishers. He is revered as a saint in both the Episcopal and Lutheran Churches in the United States.

serves to be saved, he believed, for the simple reason that no one can deserve to spend eternity in God's presence. How can anyone possibly claim to merit that? And yet that was precisely what Christian tradition told him to pursue—a life of prayer, repentance, good works, and devotion that would earn him the salvation Christ had promised to everyone who did so. Luther observed his monastic discipline with fanatical determination, even to the point where his abbot feared for his sanity. And yet the fear that nothing he did could possibly justify his standing before God never left him. So sharp grew his agony, he later wrote, that he began to despise God for having created a game that we cannot win—and then punishing us with eternal torment for losing it:

> Even as a blameless monk I still felt certain that in God's eyes I was a miserable sinner—and one with a very troubled conscience—for I had no reason to believe that God would ever be satisfied by my actions. I could not love a righteous God who punished the unrighteous; rather, I hated Him. I was careful never to blaspheme aloud, but on the inside, in the silence of my heart, I roiled and raged at God, saying, "Is it not enough for You that we, miserable sinners all, are damned for all eternity on account of original sin [the notion that, as a result of Adam and Eve's

misbehavior, all human beings come into the world with a moral stain upon them from birth]? Why do You add to our calamity by imposing the Ten Commandments on us as well? Why add sorrow upon sorrow through the Gospel teachings, and then in that same Gospel threaten us with judgment and wrath?"

But then came the breakthrough. Having been sent by his exhausted abbot to teach theology at the University of Wittenberg, Luther, in 1513, was preparing lecture notes on Saint Paul's Epistle to the Romans, a text he had read countless times before, when suddenly a new insight flashed through his mind:

> I pondered these words night and day until, at last, God had mercy on me and gave me to understand the connection between the phrases "The justice of God is revealed in the Gospel" and "The just will live through faith" [Romans 1.16–17]. I suddenly began to understand that God's justice—that is, the justice by which a just person may live forever—is a gift of God won by faith. . . . All at once I felt reborn, as though I had entered Paradise through gates thrown wide open, and immediately the whole of Scripture took on a new meaning for me.

In other words, *of course* God knows that we do not "deserve" salvation. But salvation is God's gift to us, and he simply wants us to have it anyway.

After this flash of insight, the rest of the Scriptures' meaning lay open, as though Luther was seeing it for the first time. To be righteous in the eyes of God, one did not have confess one's sins to a priest, give alms to the poor, or earn indulgences by ritual devotions like pilgrimages or vigils. One did not have to follow disciplines like praying cycles of the rosary or not eating meat on Fridays. One attains righteousness simply by having faith in Christ; one must accept the salvation he offers as an unmerited gift. This idea became canonized in Luther's understanding as **justification by faith alone** (*sola fide* in Latin). It results not from our merit but from God's grace alone (*sola gratia*), as expressed uniquely through Christ's sacrifice on the Cross (*solo Christo*). Moreover, everything that God requires of us is expressed not through the teaching authority and tradition of the church but through the words of Scripture alone (*sola Scriptura*). Anything beyond biblical teaching is superfluous to salvation at best, and an impediment to it at worst. Few of these ideas were new. In fact, many of them had been enunciated by Saint Augustine (d. 430), the founder of Luther's own monastic order. But Luther carried them to a degree far beyond Augustine or any other theologian.

REBELLION AGAINST THE CHURCH: "NINETY-FIVE THESES"

Luther's theology offended the church because it made the church irrelevant. From the time of the Gregorian Reform in the 11th century, the church had developed its theology of salvation, with itself as intermediary. The church and the believer worked together to effect salvation, through teaching and ministry, the sacraments and pious action. The relationship was not a crude contract, although many saw it that way and had been making similar complaints since at least the second half of the 14th century.

What prompted Luther's rebellion against the church was not merely his new understanding of Scripture—for it was not, after all, new. Rather, it was his ire over the church's practice of selling **indulgences**, a donation to the church as a means of satisfying the requirements for the forgiveness of sin. From the 12th century on, Catholic doctrine had understood penance for sin to have four elements: contrition, confession, absolution, and satisfaction. One first has to repent honestly for what one has done; second, one must confess the sin fully to a priest; then, third, one receives absolution from that priest if the confession is sincere and genuine; and fourth, one must then make some sort of restitution for what one did. An indulgence—earned by some explicit act of charity or devotion— was a way of meeting the fourth demand. A special donation to the church was one way of earning the indulgence. Hence, while it was not an act of "purchasing forgiveness," it certainly could look like one— especially if the process was abused. And it was, egregiously, in Luther's time.

Many people had criticized the practice, including Erasmus. The Renaissance popes, as involved as ever in Italian politics, had waged wars against various despots, had tried to resist the advancing Ottoman Turks, and had expanded the church's network of universities across Europe. As a result, they were in constant and desperate need of funds, and many turned to the offering of indulgences as a reliable means of raising cash. An enormous campaign spread throughout Germany and Italy to raise funds for the construction of the new Saint Peter's Basilica in Rome (designed in part by Michelangelo and Bernini). In 1517 Martin Luther, just recently released from his spiritual tortures, witnessed the abusive and predatory selling of

Anti-Catholic Propaganda   This anonymous woodcut of 1520 by a German satirist depicts the devil (complete with wings and clawed feet) sitting on a letter of indulgence and holding a money collection box. The devil's mouth is filled with sinners who presumably bought letters of indulgence in good faith, thinking they had been absolved from their sins.

indulgences in both places and was outraged. The symbolic starting point of the Protestant Reformation was not his biblical epiphany in 1513 but his Ninety-Five Theses—condemning the theology of indulgences.

The **Ninety-Five Theses** are simply a list of assertions that Luther declares himself prepared to argue—but the arguments themselves are not part of the text. This sort of posting bulletins of ideas was a common practice in universities of the time. Like the modern practice of publishing the prospectus of one's doctoral dissertation, it invited argument and discussion. He got it. Pope Leo X (r. 1513–1521) spent three years examining Luther's position and finally responded with a papal bull on June 15, 1520, called *Exsurge Domine* ("Arise, O Lord"). He condemned forty-one of the theses as heretical, and he gave Luther sixty days to reconsider his position and withdraw the offending statements. Luther answered back by publicly burning his copy of the bull on December 10, exactly sixty days after it was issued. After this, there was only one action Leo could take: On January 3, 1521, the pope excommunicated Luther. From this point on, little effort was made to mend fences. The people of Germany flocked to Luther's message by the thousands, and then by the tens of thousands. Within a few years the religious unity of Christian Europe was permanently sundered.

"The Pope is the Antichrist, and the Catholic Church is the most unruly of all crooks' lairs, the most brazen of all brothels, and the Kingdom itself of Sin, Death, and Hell," Luther wrote in a late book titled *On the Roman Papacy: An Institution of the Devil*. Pope Leo, for his part, dismissed Luther as "a German drunkard who will mend his ways once he sobers up." The language is not edifying. But once the rift between Luther and the church was opened, it developed quickly into an unbridgeable chasm. What began as an in-house theological dispute took on more and more political and social pressures. Two political issues were of special significance: the constitutional arrangement within Germany, and the threat posed by the Turks.

For two centuries the four hundred or so princes of Germany had enjoyed independence from imperial control, while the relatively weak Habsburgs went about adding to their domain in eastern Europe and by marrying available heiresses throughout the Continent. When Charles V (r. 1520–1556) came to the throne, he succeeded, by a genealogical quirk, to several lines of Habsburg-family legacies. These territories, when considered in the aggregate, put him in the unexpected position of having the German princes surrounded (see Map 11.2). His formal title(s), used on all his official records, ran as follows: "Charles, by grace of God the elected Holy Roman Emperor, forever August, King in Germany, King of Italy, Castile, Aragon, León, both Sicilies, Jerusalem, Navarra, Granada, Toledo, Valencia, Galicia, Majorca, Sevilla, Sardinia, Cordova, Corsica, Murcia, Jaen, the Algarves, Algeciras, Gibraltar, the Canary Islands, the Western and

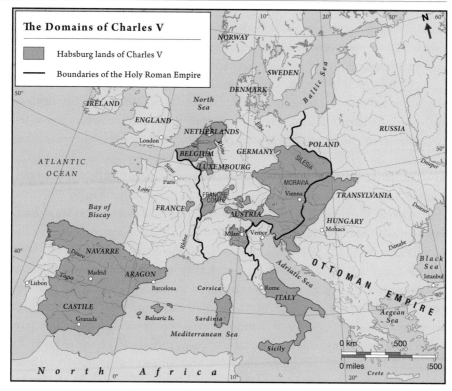

MAP 11.2   **The Domains of Charles V**

Eastern Indies, the Islands and Mainland of the Ocean Sea, etc. etc.; Archduke of Austria, Duke of Burgundy, Brabant, Lorraine, Styria, Carinthia, Carniola, Limburg, Luxembourg, Gelderland, Athens, Neopatria, Württemberg, Landgrave of Alsace, Prince of Swabia, Asturia and Catalonia, Count of Flanders, Habsburg, Tyrol, Gorizia, Barcelona, Artois, Burgundy Palatine, Hainaut, Holland, Seeland, Ferrette, Kyburg, Namur, Roussillon, Cerdagne, Zutphen, Margrave of the Holy Roman Empire, Burgau, Oristano and Gociano, Lord of Frisia, the Wendish March, Pordenone, Biscay, Molin, Salins, Tripoli and Mechelen, etc."

By constitutional tradition, Charles had no cause to take advantage of his position by imposing his rule on the princes. However, since he was, as emperor, the defender of Catholicism, he considered seriously his obligation to combat the Protestant heresy. The princes, for their part, had good reason to support Luther: he had essentially given them control of the new churches.

Luther's *Address to the Christian Nobility of the German Nation* (1520) had laid out his vision for the organization and administration of his reformed church. Since there was no supreme spiritual authority—each believer needing only his Bible and his own conscience—the Protestant Church needed only secular administration and guidance. For that, Luther turned to the princes.

A prince who formally broke with Rome and converted to Lutheranism was entitled, Luther wrote, to confiscate the Catholic ecclesiastical lands, properties, and wealth within his principality and to lead the administration of the new reformed churches. The temptation was great, but most princes feared that seizing the extensive holdings of the churches and monasteries would cause Charles V to rush to Catholicism's defense. Hence, even though most of the nobles converted to Lutheranism, they hesitated to start plundering. But then the second political issue came into play.

The Turkish threat was complicated. Ottoman forces had driven deep into Europe, after taking Constantinople in 1453, in hopes of weakening Christendom. Charles V, naturally, spearheaded the effort to hold them at bay. Many Protestant princes hoped to form an alliance with the Ottoman sultan, Suleiman the Magnificent (r. 1520–1566), who had come to his throne at roughly the same time as Charles V came to his. Such a pact, they hoped, would leave Charles as the surrounded party and thereby neutralize his power. Diplomatic relations between Protestant rulers and Suleiman were extensive. The Turks had large numbers of Jews and Christians living within the European part of their empire, and for the time being, at least, they treated them with the tolerance required by dhimmi law. Dhimmi law did not protect Christian and Jewish buildings, however, and Suleiman advanced steadily. When the Turks overran Buda, the capital of Hungary, they delighted in destroying churches and synagogues throughout the city. Indeed, they set aflame a collection of Renaissance art as rich as anything in Florence or Milan.[8]

Suleiman's advance compelled Charles to mobilize his forces; but since the Turks were not yet threatening Habsburg lands directly, Charles bided his time. The Lutheran princes kept negotiating with Suleiman, to keep the pressure up. An alliance did not happen, but Suleiman concluded that Charles was too weak to offer any real resistance and so launched a fresh attack in 1526, quickly taking most of Hungary. After a brief pause he advanced his army at far as Vienna, to which he laid siege in 1529. At this point even the Protestants were worried. Luther published in that same year the pamphlet *On the War against the Turks*, in which he called for a united European front against the Ottomans yet rejected as un-Christian the notion of a Crusade. Suleiman's siege failed, however, and the Turkish advance was temporarily stopped.

With so much at stake in terms of geopolitics, it is not surprising that the rhetoric of the religious dispute became feverish. Catholics and Protestants at all levels of society hurled abuse at each other. Erasmus and Luther, for a while, maintained a

---

[8]   Buda—supposedly named after Bleda, Attila the Hun's older brother—much later incorporated with the small nearby town of Pest, to become today's Budapest.

civilized debate in print over theological issues like free will, the workings of divine grace, and the interpretation of Scripture. (The two men never met personally.) Other than that, though, most of the religious battle was in poisonous language. When large numbers of German peasants were persuaded by radicals to rise up in arms against their landlords in 1524 and 1525 in a rebellion known as the **Peasants' Revolt**, Luther responded savagely. While the peasants had been stirred by Luther's insistence on the dignity of all believers, he called on the princes to take bold action.

If his aim was to scare the peasants into submission, *On the Thieving, Murderous Hordes of Peasants* was a brilliant success:

> Therefore every one of you who can should act as both judge and executioner.... Strike them down, slay them, and stab them, either in secret or in the light of day ... for you ought always to bear in mind that there is nothing more poisonous, dangerous, or devilish than one of these rebels.... For baptism frees men's souls alone; it does not liberate their bodies and properties, nor does the Gospel call for people to hold all their goods in common.... Fine Christians these peasants are! There can hardly be a single devil left in hell—for I do believe they have all taken possession of these peasants, whose mad ravings are beyond all measure.... What a wonderful time we live in now, when a prince can better merit heaven by bloodshed than by prayer!

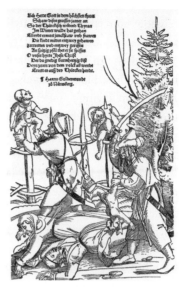

Turkish Atrocities Throughout the 16th and 17th centuries the Ottomans made repeated efforts to expand their control in southeastern Europe, twice getting as far as the gates of Vienna. This woodcut depicts popular fears of Turkish savagery. "Such amusements are common in all wars," warned Erasmus in 1530, when this image was published. The Turks did commit atrocities like those shown here, but no more so than what European Catholics and Protestants inflicted on one another (and what both sometimes inflicted on the Jews) throughout the Wars of Religion.

Most of the rebels, denied Luther's expected support, laid down their weapons at once. The rest were quickly defeated in a battle at Frankenhausen in May 1525, and the revolt ended. The rebel leader, an apocalyptic firebrand named Thomas Müntzer, was executed. The cost of victory was high, however. As many as one hundred thousand people lost their lives.

After this, the "Protestantization" of Germany gained pace, as the princes rushed to support Luther's program and seized church lands and treasuries. Sincere religious conviction undoubtedly motivated them, but political and economic factors obviously were also at play. By formally adopting the Lutheran cause, princes acquired—with Luther's own blessing—the authority to appoint pastors to the new churches. This effectively placed the nobles in charge of the entire institution. Freed from having to meet their former fiscal obligations to Rome or to recognize the authority of ecclesiastical courts, the princes likewise ensured the obedience of the new Lutheran churches to noble demands. The policies they developed came to be summarized by the phrase *Cuius regio, eius religio* ("The religion of the ruler determines the religion of the land"). And most of the princes promoted the new *religio* in order to strengthen their grip on the *regio*.

THE REFORMATION GOES INTERNATIONAL

Like other reformers before him and since, Martin Luther believed that those who joined him in rebellion would agree with him on what to replace tyranny with. But things seldom turn out that way. People, it seems, unite more easily in opposition to a present evil than they rally around a new vision of future good. With its spread beyond Germany, especially in the legacy of Jean Calvin, Protestantism in fact thrived on divisions.

When Luther began his revolt, many among the pope's advisors recommended immediate and dramatic action. Luther, after all, seemed intent on tearing down the entire Catholic tradition. However, just as many others counseled a quietist approach. Once Luther validated the idea that people can interpret the Scriptures for themselves, they pointed out, they would soon disagree with Luther's interpretations as much as they disagree with Rome's. The rebellion would then splinter into countless factions and soon disappear under its own dead, fractured weight.

Each group of advisers was half right. At the start, Luther saw his actions as a much-needed campaign to correct flaws in Catholic belief and practice, not as a drive to destroy the church. He was a reformer, not a revolutionary. Dramatic counter-action was indeed called for, but not in the urgent sense recommended by the alarmists. As for the second group, they saw correctly the coming splintering of the reformers into rival groups, but their assumption that division meant failure was wrong. They had severely underestimated the extent of anticlerical feeling—and the intense resentment of the church's abuses and failings. By the time they realized their mistake, it was too late. Luther and his followers had flooded Germany with polemical pamphlets, sermons, hymnals, catechisms, and above all the Bible itself in translation.[9]

---

[9]   Luther and his followers understood the power of the new technology of printing.

It took a generation, more or less, for Luther's ideas to catch on outside of Germany. His basic ideas were known. How could they not be, considering the enormity of the scandal he had caused? However, Luther wrote most of his works in German—since vernacular Scripture reading and vernacular worship were so central to his theology. And translators did not rush to bring his works into other tongues. Luther had taken care to produce a number of pamphlets and broadsides in Latin, to encourage the spread of the revolt. His ongoing debate in print with Erasmus—the most revered scholar in the Christian world—also kept his program in the spotlight. Still, when Protestantism did start to spread, it did so on the heels of the spread of Christian humanism. Many saw that intellectual effort as preparation for the spiritual regeneration coming out of Germany.

Not all northern humanists were, or became, Protestant. Many of the most famous, in fact, remained staunchly Catholic. What contributed to the spread of Protestantism was not humanism itself but rather the dialogue between Renaissance and Reformation. It was the spirit of questioning, of returning to ancient sources. Many heard that dialogue and clung ever more fiercely to the Catholic tradition. Many others, though, who might otherwise never have thought it possible, heard in the debate a calling to a wholly new, and newly holy, path.

SCHOLARS AND ACTIVISTS

The best of the Christian humanist scholars were all dedicated Catholics: Guillaume Budé (1467–1540), Jacques Lefèvre d'Étaples (1455–1536), Cardinal Francisco Ximénez de Cisneros (1436–1517), and Joan Lluís Vives i March (1493–1540). Other writers—primarily Protestants like Ulrich Zwingli (1484–1531), Jean Calvin (1509–1564), and John Knox (1514–1572)—remain better known and were more historically significant because of their activities in the world. But pure scholars should have their due, too.

Budé was a classical linguist, one of the finest Greek scholars of his generation. Supported by the French royal court, he produced a Greek lexicon that remained the standard for scholars for nearly two hundred years. He was also the founder of the school that later became the Collège de France and of the library that ultimately grew into the Bibliothèque Nationale, both in Paris. Lefèvre, also a royal favorite, was an industrious writer of biblical commentaries as well as editions and translations of patristic texts. In 1530 he published the first ever translation of the entire Bible into French.

De Cisneros held immense power in Spain: he was the archbishop of Toledo, was twice the regent for the crown, and served as grand inquisitor at the high point of that institution's power in Spain. As a statesman Cisneros was blunt and direct even to the point of cruelty. He was not at all averse to ordering the forced baptism

Polyglot Bible   A page from the Complutensian Polyglot Bible (1514–1517) published by Cardinal Francisco Cisneros, one of the great humanistic achievements of the Renaissance. The three main columns present the Biblical text in Hebrew, Latin, and Greek, while underneath are printed passages in Aramaic (Targum), where they survive, and alternative readings. The Complutensian edition was used extensively by the English translators who produced the King James Bible (Authorized Version) in 1611.

of the Moors of southern Spain and the burning of the Arabic manuscripts in the library at Granada. As a scholar, he was patient in the extreme: he spent fifteen years producing the Complutensian Polyglot Bible—an impressive work that reproduced, in parallel columns, the best texts then available of the entire Bible in Aramaic, Greek, Hebrew, and Latin.

Lluís Vives, a much more sympathetic figure, dedicated long years to social reform as well as to reform within the church. He was an earnest champion of education for women and welfare for the poor. The fourth-generation son of a *converso* family—that is, a family that had once been Jewish—he witnessed the Inquisition's execution of his father, grandmother, and great-grandfather.[10] And although he never wavered in his Christian commitment, he left Spain as soon as he could and never returned. After studying in Paris, he became a professor of philosophy at Oxford and spent his time between Oxford and the royal court in London, where he served as private tutor to the Tudor family.

PROTESTANTISM WITHOUT LUTHER

Among the Protestant humanists, the most influential were Ulrich Zwingli and Jean Calvin. Zwingli left behind over twenty volumes of writings—sermons, biblical exegesis, topical essays, some poetry—but little of this is read by anyone other than specialists. His impact was in the world of action rather than thought. He was born to a Swiss farming family and received a good though unremarkable education. In 1498 he enrolled at the University of Vienna, but was expelled for reasons no one has ever discovered. He was ordained a priest and spent several years as a military chaplain. A crisis of conscience, however, led him to withdraw

---

[10]   Scholars use *inquisition*, with a lowercase *i*, to refer to the inquisitorial process in the Middle Ages. Uppercase *Inquisition* is reserved for the Renaissance, when what had been a medieval process turned into a formal institution.

from his post and take up duties as a simple parish priest in a small village in Switzerland. This position gave him ample time for self-education, and in a few years he had mastered Greek and acquired a usable knowledge of Hebrew.

By 1516 personal study of the Scriptures had inspired him to doubt the value of much Catholic doctrine and ritual. But he was too timid to admit his opinions in public until Martin Luther began his public work in 1517 with the Ninety-Five Theses. Zwingli then dedicated himself to the twin goals of supporting Luther's Reformation and securing Switzerland's independence from French, Italian, and imperial meddling. He formally broke with Rome, and by 1522 most of the German-speaking cantons of Switzerland had done the same and had placed themselves under Zwingli's leadership. He moved to Zurich, which became second only to Luther's Wittenberg as the unofficial capital of the Protestant movement.

Zwingli's brand of Christianity differed from Luther's in a number of specifics. In fact, Zwingli, who did not meet Luther personally until 1529, is one of the very first examples of a Protestant who broke away from the movement's founder. He died in battle against armies from the Catholic southern portion of Switzerland, and the embryonic church he had created became subsumed by the new church created by Jean Calvin.

A brief but violent interlude, however, preceded Calvin on the scene. Several dozen radical members of Zwingli's church at Zurich quit Switzerland and took up residence in exile at Münster, in northwestern Germany. Disgusted by what they considered the immoral joining of Protestant religion with secular government (Luther and the German princes, Zwingli and the Swiss town councils), they established themselves as an apocalyptic sect known as the **Anabaptists**.[11] Their name means "rebaptizers," for the group rejected infant baptism as meaningless by itself and called for a second baptism in adulthood. They also embraced a literal reading of Scripture, polygamy (although the extent of this is still debated), and the imminent approach of Christ's Second Coming. The sect came under the charismatic leadership of Jan van Leiden, who proclaimed himself the successor to the King David of Biblical times and his Münster church as the reincarnation of the Jerusalem Temple. Zwingli and Luther both denounced the group, as did all the Catholic rulers of the time. Persecutions followed as Münster was stormed by the Catholic prince (and bishop) of the city, the Anabaptists were tortured and executed, and their sympathizers across Europe were arrested.

---

[11] Crushed by its enemies, the Anabaptist movement disappeared. The Mennonite church, founded by Menno Simons (1496–1561) of Holland, is a late offshoot that still survives.

By the time Jean Calvin established his own Reformed Church in Geneva, the conflict between rival Christianities had moved well beyond a war of words. Most of the Scandinavian territories (Finland was the exception) had declared for Lutheranism by the end of the 1520s. Lutheranism had also sunk deep roots in northern Germany and parts of Poland, Hungary, and the Low Countries. England was, for the time being, still staunchly Catholic, although Henry VIII's (r. 1509–1547) marital woes led him to break with Rome over the course of the 1530s (see Map 11.3).

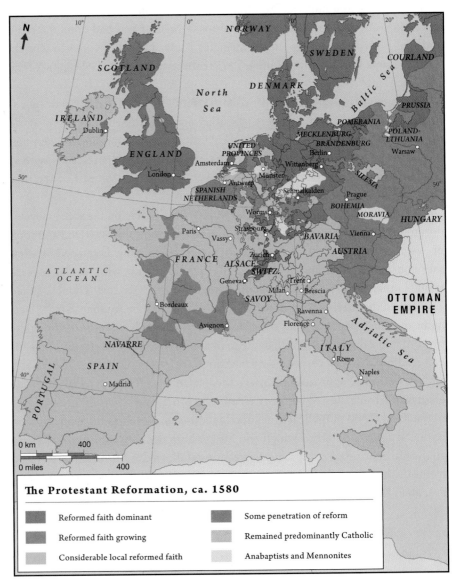

MAP 11.3   The Protestant Reformation, ca. 1580

CALVIN: PROTESTANTISM AS THEOLOGY

At first glance, Calvin seems an unlikely revolutionary. Quiet, reserved, intensely bookish, he studied (under pressure from his father) for a legal career at the University of Bourges, where he fell under the spell of humanist classicism. At about the same time—somewhere around 1530—he had an evangelical conversion that changed his entire life. He described the event in the introduction to his later *Commentary on the Psalms*:

> All at once, God overpowered my mind, which at that point was far more incorrigible in such matters than one might expect in one so young, and opened it [to the Truth]. Having been given this sampling of, this introduction to, true godliness, I instantly burned with such a passion to have better knowledge of it that, even though I never abandoned my other studies entirely, I pursued them with much less drive than before.

If his account is accurate, his was an intellectual rather than mystical conversion, although it was no less passionate for that. True to his bookish nature, he turned almost immediately to writing the first edition (1535) of his main work, *Institutes of Christian Religion*, which he continued to revise until his death. (Its final and definitive editions appeared in 1559 in Latin and in 1560 in French.)

The *Institutes* was the first work to lay out the emerging theology of Protestant Christianity in a systematic, logical, organized way. Here is a representative passage, on how the Reformed Church uses discipline:

> It is necessary, likewise, to distinguish between different kinds of sins, for some are only minor infractions whereas others are enormous and enormously wicked crimes. In order to correct the latter, mere warnings and reproofs do not suffice, and one must resort to sterner measures—as Paul shows [1 Corinthians 5.1–5] when he does not allow himself to rest content after having condemned the man of Corinth who had committed incest, but immediately excommunicates the man after his conviction for the crime. Now we begin to see how the spiritual authority of the Church, which corrects sins according to God's Word, preserves our health, orders our lives, and establishes bonds of unity among us; for whenever the Church banishes from the community those guilty of adultery, fornication, theft, robbery, sedition, false witness, or any other crimes of that sort, or when it banishes those stubborn people who criticize God's Holy Judgment, even after having been admonished for lesser sins, it [the church] exercises no unauthorized rational power but only the jurisdiction that God Himself has given it. In order that no one may refuse to

recognize this judgmental power of the Church, or think that it represents only the opinion of the community of believers, God Himself
bears witness that [the church's judgment] it is nothing less than His judgment of the case, and that what the Church does upon earth is ratified
in Heaven. For the Church has by God's Own Word the authority to
condemn the wicked and to receive the penitent back into the favor of the
Church. Anyone who believes that the Church could even exist without
this power to discipline is sorely mistaken—for how could we do without
the very thing that God saw fit to give us? The reasons why this is necessary
will be made clear in its action. *(Institutes of Christian Religion 4.12.4)*

Martin Luther, like his model Saint Augustine, had been far too impulsive a
writer ever to write anything like this.

Calvin shared Luther's central, defining notion of an infinitely majestic, all-
powerful, and all-knowing God whose transcendent might and will is in absolute control of the entire cosmos. But Luther softened this commanding image
by emphasizing the infinitely merciful, because unmerited, love that God feels
for us. Calvin stressed instead the unfathomable mystery of God's justice. Since
he is all-knowing, argued Calvin, God has known since the moment of Creation
which human beings were to be saved and
which were to be damned—and these
fates are sealed absolutely by the sheer
force of God's will. There is nothing any
human being can do to alter his or her
fate. Does this mean that many apparently "good" people will be punished in
hell while many apparently "bad" people
are rewarded in heaven? Yes, it does; but
this, to Calvin, is simply the consequence
of our complete inability to understand
God's purpose, rather than a sign of God's
supposed hypocrisy. We must remain
faithful to the belief that God's ways are
ultimately and supremely just, even if we
cannot comprehend them. In essence,
what Calvin called for was an attitude of
radical humility before God, an absolute
submission of the soul to the Almighty's
wisdom, power, and righteousness.

Unlikely Revolutionary Sketches of Jean Calvin
(1509–1564), the founder of the Reformed
(Presbyterian) Church, made in a notebook by
one of his university students who preferred
doodling to taking lecture notes.

But this is not an attitude of passivity. It is precisely because we cannot know whether we are among the **Elect** (his term for those predestined for salvation) that Calvin demands of his followers the strictest possible adherence to moral standards. To the Elect, he writes, good ethical behavior will come naturally and be the sign of their chosen status. To those who are not elected, their moral behavior will not affect their ultimate fate in the slightest—but they therefore have all the more reason to live according to a godly standard. The joy of such a life is in fact the only meaningful pleasure they will have before confronting the eternal torments of hell. Membership in good standing in the Reformed Church—Calvin's name for the branch of Christianity he established—is a likely indicator that one is among the Elect. Membership in the despised Roman Catholic Church or the Orthodox Churches is as likely an indicator as a life of gruesome sinfulness that one is not. But while being a Calvinist immeasurably improved one's odds of salvation, it alone determined nothing. The central concern of life therefore should not be the destiny of our individual souls but the fulfillment of God's purpose on the entire earth.

Calvin's teachings found receptive audiences all around Europe. Apart from its success in Switzerland, Calvinism became the dominant creed in Holland (where it became known as the Dutch Reformed Church), in Scotland (where it was called the Presbyterian Church), in parts of France (where Calvinists were called Huguenots), and in parts of England (where they were ultimately called Puritans). The theocratic state he established in Geneva earned a well-deserved reputation for severity, but Geneva also earned a reputation for modest, honest, and godly behavior. Calvinist communities emphasized simplicity and austerity in worship. Anything that smacked of Catholic ritual or hierarchical structure was eschewed. Instead, churches were communities of equals—joined together in prayer, Scriptural reading, hymn singing, and listening to sermons. How can there be a pecking order among the Elect? Sermons indeed form the centerpiece of Calvinist worship, since they are by nature ruminations on Scripture. Calvin himself was too gifted a scholar to insist on only literal readings of the Bible, although he tended to seek out symbolic or other interpretations only after considering the literal first.

Still other reformers and groups branched off to form new denominations, but these were considerably smaller in size and tinged with elements of ethnic or national rebellion. Lutheranism and Calvinism were the two with the greatest international appeal, and by the middle of the 16th century they had torn the religious fabric of Europe asunder. Only in the late 20th century, in the aftermath of two World Wars and the Holocaust, would there arise serious efforts to reconcile the fissures in Christianity.

THE REBIRTH OF SATIRE

Religious upheavals reflected developments in other aspects of cultural life. The conjunction of increasing literacy rates and the mass availability of printed texts generated a demand for literary entertainment unlike anything the Western world had experienced before. Not that the love of literature was itself new, but oral tradition could now give way to print on paper. Reading became a common pleasure of everyday life, no longer the reserve of scholars and monks. Printing houses across Europe poured out a steady stream of poetry, histories, stage dramas and comedies, travelogues, essays, memoirs, popular science tracts, and collections of letters and speeches.

Not everyone in Europe was reading Erasmus, Luther, and Calvin constantly—which is probably a good thing. In addition to Machiavelli and Aretino, three European writers stand out in the first half of the 16th century: Thomas More (1478–1535), Ulrich von Hutten (1488–1523), and François Rabelais (1493–1553). They could hardly have been more different in their personalities and life stories, but the most famous works of all three were satires.

Satire had been one of the most popular literary genres among the Romans. The English word satire, which appeared for the first time in 1509, in fact derives from Latin *satura* (denoting a witty poem that ridicules vice), not from Greek *satyricos* (which refers to the lewd stage comedies that accompanied tragedic festivals). A few Greek writers had practiced satire—Menippus (3rd century BCE) is the best example—but the Romans excelled at it. "Satire is all ours," once bragged Quintilian (36–96 CE), Rome's greatest literary scholar. But satire had all but disappeared during the Middle Ages. Levity about the world's idiosyncrasies and human foibles did not appeal very much to the monks who established the classical canon in their scriptoria. With the rise of classical humanism, however, satire came back to life. There were, after all, plenty of people to satirize: warmongering popes, fey aristocrats, affected scholars, grasping financiers, humanistic despots, self-absorbed artists.

UTOPIAS AND BOOK BURNINGS

Erasmus helped to revive prose satire with his *Praise of Folly*, and satire in prose, in fact, became the preferred style in the 16th century. His close friend Thomas More penned a popular though curiously dour *Utopia* (1516).[12] It consists of two parts, the first being an imaginary discussion between More and a traveler-adventurer named Raphael Hythlodaeus on the various ills then besetting Europe. High on the list are the enclosure movement, poverty, religious intolerance, the failure of

---

[12]   More is best known as the royal chancellor who refused to recognize Henry VIII's divorce and paid for it with his head.

systems of justice, and the propensity to war. In the second part, Hythlodaeus describes for More his travels to a "perfect society"—a far-distant island in the Atlantic named Utopia (which is an Anglicized version of the Greek phrase "no place").

Utopia is a crescent-shaped island, two hundred miles across, in which the population lives in scattered communities of about seventy-five thousand each. All goods are held in common; citizens take turns, in two-year shifts, farming the land and working at artisanal crafts; medical care and primary education are free and available to all. There are no lawyers; all wives are subservient to their husbands, to whom they must confess their sins once every month; and the penalty for pre- or extramarital sex is enslavement. There are a lot of slaves, consequently, who do most of the hard labor. Although meant as a satire, there is

Utopia This woodcut by Ambrosius Holbein (1494–1519)—older brother of the famous artist Hans Holbein (1497–1543)—was the frontispiece for a 1518 edition of *Utopia*. Against a backdrop of the fictional island, Raphael Hythlodaeus describes the Utopian way of life to More.

nothing in *Utopia* to make a modern reader laugh, for More was largely humorless. (According to a family memoir he laughed at court jesters when they made pratfalls, but at little else.) He tried and failed on that score. *Utopia* remains a valuable book, though, not least for the insight it provides into its author's mind.

Far more successful as satire is the fictitious *Letters of Obscure Men* (1517) by Ulrich von Hutten, a swashbuckling imperial knight and occasional humanist writer. Born to a noble family in northern Germany, he grew up in a castle near the ancient settlement of Fulda. His parents dispatched him to a monastery when he was eleven, apparently to insure against his elder brother's claim upon the family estate. Six years later, in 1505, Ulrich escaped and wandered from city to city, leading a roguish life as an occasional student (he attended four universities in Germany), a poet, an amateur humanist scholar, and a willing sword for hire. Around 1509 he appeared in northern Italy, working as a mercenary soldier between stints at the universities of Pavia and Bologna. But by 1512 he was back in Germany serving as a Free Imperial Knight.

In 1515 the Duke of Württemberg killed a beloved cousin of his whose wife he had designs on. Ulrich responded by publishing blistering Latin poems that ruined the Duke's reputation and led ultimately to his overthrow. They made Ulrich famous, and in 1517 Maximilian I (r. 1493–1519) appointed him the poet laureate of the German Empire. In that same year, Ulrich became a passionate supporter of

Martin Luther and coauthored, with his humanist friend Johann Jäger (who used the pseudonym Crotus Rubeanus), the *Letters of Obscure Men*.

Filled with clever wit and broad, coarse humor, the *Letters* purport to be addressed to a prominent nobleman by fanatical Catholic monks and friars regarding why it is necessary to burn Jewish books like the Talmud and anti-Christian polemical literature. The diatribe is in reference to a real event: the debate, several years earlier, between the famed humanist scholar Johann Reuchlin and a group of zealous Catholic inquisitors who had argued for the same cause. (The title echoes the *Letters of Notable Men* that had passed between Reuchlin and his adversaries.) The *Letters* were written in intentionally bad Latin, making much of their humor impossible to convey in English. Reading them, it is clear that Ulrich never lost his hatred of Catholic monks, who might well respond to Protestantism and satire with book burnings, and this book is a settling of old debts. He gives his monks outrageous names like Brother Goatmilker and Brother Shitshoveller, attributes all sorts of lechery to them, and describes them nervously defecating under their robes during public debates. Ulrich's aim is less to defend the Jews (even though he was indeed an opponent of the book burnings) than to ridicule the pretensions and hypocrisy of the Catholics. The aristocrat who receives the letters—a real figure in Ulrich's time—also comes in for a lambasting. The monks sordidly declare their passionate relations with his wife.

A summary cannot relate the brilliant wordplay, sharp character depiction, and intellectual cleverness of the *Letters*. The book deserves to be better known and someday may find the translator it deserves. It was published anonymously, though its authorship was never in doubt. Ulrich spent his last years trying unsuccessfully to urge the independence of the German Empire from papal involvement. He contracted syphilis, and when the disease became acute he took refuge in Switzerland, near Lake Zurich, where he died in 1523.

RABELAIS: THE IN-HOUSE CATHOLIC ATTACK

The best-known of the three satirists was François Rabelais. Little is known for certain about his life. Born to a wealthy country lawyer, he received a sound education. A devout Christian, he entered the Franciscan order sometime around 1510 and about a decade later was ordained a priest. He traveled to libraries around France and earned a reputation as a first-rate classical scholar, but in 1524 he suffered the indignity of having his Greek books confiscated by one of his superiors, who thought they might lead to heresy. Rabelais successfully petitioned Pope Clement VII (r. 1523–34) in 1524 for release from his Franciscan order and to be allowed to join the Benedictines. Through his new order he studied medicine in Paris. However, since he disliked Benedictine life too, he broke his vows and moved to the University of Montpellier to continue his medical training. He finished in record time, quickly sired two children with a local widow, and then moved on to practice medicine in Narbonne and Lyons.

In 1532 Rabelais published a brief satirical novel, *The Horrible and Terrifying Words and Deeds of the Renowned Pantagruel, King of the Dipsodes*. When this proved unexpectedly popular, he followed it with three more volumes that continue Pantagruel's adventures while also providing, in another volume, the backstory of Pantagruel's father, Gargantua. The five books are now published together as a single work, *Gargantua and Pantagruel*. (A supposed sixth book, written by an opportunistic forger, appeared in 1564, eleven years after Rabelais's death.) Gargantua and Pantagruel are giants—enormous, misshapen, driven by inexhaustible appetites of body and mind, and delighting in broad scatological humor—and the same can be said of *Gargantua and Pantagruel* the novel. It is a **picaresque**, a vast sequence of discrete episodes. The closest it comes to offering a coherent story is a lengthy but loose narrative in Books 3 and 4 about their efforts to help a friend. (Another giant, named Panurge, wishes to locate an oracle known as the Sacred Bottle for help deciding whether to marry a girl whose fidelity is uncertain.) Though lively, the novel is shapeless, repetitive, and long.

What was its purpose? Rabelais certainly wanted to entertain his readers and make them laugh.[13] *Gargantua and Pantagruel* and the *Letters of Obscure Men* are the only truly funny books written in that unfunny century. Being satire, the laughs they raise come at someone's expense; we laugh because someone is being ridiculed. Both books have numerous targets, but they share one in particular, the Catholic clergy. If von Hutten attacks them from the Protestant side, Rabelais offers a Catholic in-house attack.

The wounds he inflicts, however, result not from rapier wit but a heavy two-handed broadsword. Much of Rabelais's humor is the clowning of a teenager who thinks he is clever when he is being gross. He mocks dry-as-dust scholastic theologians and pompous overfed monks by exaggerating their flaws a hundredfold. He lambasts puritanical morality by having his heroes indulge in orgies of food, sex, and drink that would make a Roman emperor blush. Bodily functions stain every page. In one early passage (1.17), Gargantua caps off a drinking binge by untying his codpiece and peeing so much he floods the entire city of Paris, "drowning 260,418 people, plus women and children." Two other entire chapters (3.26, 3.28) consist of nothing more than a list of improvised nicknames for a character, all of them employing a variant of the word "scrotum."

---

[13] "Mirth is my theme, and tears are not; / For laughter is man's proper lot" is the famous ending couplet of Rabelais' verse preface.

Still, the verbal energy is extraordinary. Rejoicing in his freedom from Church Latin, Rabelais pours words onto the page in a kind of vernacular euphoria. The novel is a hymn to the French language and a celebration of human freedom: freedom to think, to scoff, to lust, to indulge in manic excess, to coin words, to imagine outrageous scenes, to offend, to risk boredom, and to delight in whimsy. Ultimately, it is about the freedom to hope for a better world than the one we live in. As a work of art it has failings, but as the expression of an irrepressible spirit it can never cease to fascinate. And that spirit is humanism.

WHO, WHAT, WHERE

Anabaptists	picaresque
Christian humanism	Peasants' Revolt
Elect	Protestant Reformation
indulgences	Renaissance
justification by faith alone	Renaissance humanism
Ninety-Five Theses	Satire

SUGGESTED READINGS

Primary Sources

Calvin, Jean. *Institutes of Christian Religion.*

Erasmus of Rotterdam. *Julius Excluded.*

———. *The Praise of Folly.*

Hutton, Ulrich von. *Letters of Obscure Men.*

Luther, Martin. *Address to the Christian Nobility of the German Nation.*

———. *The Freedom of a Christian.*

———. *Table Talk.*

Machiavelli, Niccolò. *Discourses on Livy.*

———. *The Mandrake Root.*

———. *The Prince.*

Rabelais, François. *Gargantua and Pantagruel.*

Vasari, Giorgio. *Lives of the Artists.*

Anthologies

Black, Robert, ed. *Renaissance Thought: A Reader* (2001).

Janz, Denis R., ed. *A Reformation Reader: Primary Texts with Introductions* (2008).

King, John N., ed. *Voices of the English Reformation: A Sourcebook* (2004).

Wiesner-Hanks, Merry. *The Renaissance and Reformation: A History in Documents* (2011).

Studies

Baylor, Michael G. *The German Reformation and the Peasants' War: A Brief History with Documents* (2012).

Benedict, Philip. *Christ's Churches Purely Reformed: A Social History of Calvinism* (2002).

Bolzoni, Lina. *The Gallery of Memory: Literary and Iconographic Models in the Age of the Printing Press* (2001).

Caffiero, Marina. *Forced Baptisms: Histories of Jews, Christians, and Converts in Papal Rome* (2011).

Diefendorf, Barbara B. *From Penitence to Charity: Pious Women and the Catholic Reformation in Paris* (2006).

Eisenstein, Elizabeth. *The Printing Revolution in Early Modern Europe* (2005).

King, Ross. *Machiavelli: Philosopher of Power* (2009).

Levi, Anthony. *Renaissance and Reformation: The Intellectual Genesis* (2004).

MacCulloch, Diarmaid. *The Reformation: A History* (2005).

Martines, Lauro. *Strong Words: Writing and Social Strain in the Italian Renaissance* (2001).

Mazzotta, Giuseppe. *Cosmopoiesis: The Renaissance Experiment* (2001).

McGrath, Alister E. *Reformation Thought: An Introduction* (2001).

Nauert, Charles G., Jr. *Humanism and the Culture of Renaissance Europe* (2006).

Oberman, Heiko A. *Luther: Man between God and the Devil* (2006).

O'Malley, John W. *Trent and All That: Renaming Catholicism in the Early Modern Era* (2000).

Ozment, Steven. *The Serpent and the Lamb: Cranach, Luther, and the Making of the Reformation* (2012).

Parks, Tim. *Medici Money: Banking, Metaphysics, and Art in Fifteenth-Century Florence* (2006).

Pettegree, Andrew. *The Book in the Renaissance* (2011).

———. *Reformation and the Culture of Persuasion* (2005).

Randall, Michael. *The Gargantuan Polity: On the Individual and the Community in the French Renaissance* (2008).

Stjerna, Kirsi. *Women and the Reformation* (2008).

Taylor, Barry, and Alejandro Coroleu. *Humanism and Christian Letters in Early Modern Iberia, 1480–1630* (2010).

Wiesner-Hanks, Merry E. *Women and Gender in Early Modern Europe* (2008).

For additional resources, including maps, primary sources, visuals, web links, and quizzes, please go to **www.oup.com/us/backman.**

CHAPTER 12

The Last Crusades

1492–1648

A ll wars are religious wars in one sense. "There are no atheists in foxholes," asserted a phrase popular in World War II. Even if untrue, it expresses a truism: for many people, the hard fact of death elicits something like religious dread.

THE AMERICAS IN 1600

ATLANTIC OCEAN

PACIFIC OCEAN

■ Spanish
■ Portuguese

Soldiers often take refuge in faith to survive war's horror. But are they drawn to fight in defense of their belief? As part of the religious realignment in Europe, wars left millions dead and much of Western society both economically and morally exhausted. The philosopher Thomas Hobbes (1588–1679) described life itself at this time as a tragic "war of all against all," in which existence was "solitary, poor, nasty, brutish, and short."

◀ **Passage to India**   In 1497 the Portuguese explorer Vasco da Gama (1469–1524) rounded the southern tip of Africa and initiated Europe's first direct contact with the peoples of the eastern African coast; with the help of an Indian ship's pilot he met in the port city of Mombasa (in today's Kenya) the following year, he sailed directly across the Arabian Sea and landed in India. The Arab merchants who then dominated the region gave him a cold welcome, and three years later (1501) da Gama returned at the head of a fleet of warships and seized control of the city of Calcutta. This image from ca. 1558 shows the type of trade ship used by the Portuguese at this stage in their rise to global power. This was a carrack, recognizable by its three (sometimes four) masts, rounded stern, raised fore- and aftcastles, and most especially by its absence of heavy guns. Galleons were the premier warships by the middle of the century; carracks (some of which weighed more than a thousand tons, unloaded) were for transporting vast cargoes.

Moreover, Europe's religious realignments took place within the exciting, yet terrifying, context of an immensely broadened world. The first encounters with the New World brought epidemics that killed as much as 99.9 percent of indigenous Americans. At the same time, it brought demographic and moral changes to Europe, including population growth and a new idea of order rooted in the family. The "war of all against all" also became more specifically a war against others, including witches, Jews, and the East—where the tensions between Sunnis and Shi'a intensified as well. It also led to shifts of power between European nations, including England, the Dutch, and Spain.

THE NEW WORLD

For over four thousand years the entire known world had consisted of three continents: Europe, Africa, and Asia. From the start, the peoples of the Greater West had shown more restlessness and curiosity about the world than any other ancient culture. Phoenician travelers, beginning around 1200 BCE, had journeyed a bit beyond the Straits of Gibraltar and into the Atlantic. The Greeks had circumnavigated the British Isles by 300 BCE, and by the end of the 1st century CE the Romans had made contact with merchant-explorers from China. The latter ventured as far as the Euphrates River shortly after the time of Constantine the Great, around 360 CE, although much later the Ming dynasty closed China off from the outside world.[1] The first Christian missionaries had reached China well before the western Roman Empire fell in 476. Viking raiders had spread out through the Baltic, North, and Mediterranean Seas and had reached a corner of North America by the 10th century. The Muslim Arabs, followed by the Persians and Turks, had carved out vast realms on all three continents and developed techniques to map the

---

[1]   Under their great admiral Zheng He (1371–1433), Chinese fleets made it as far as the mouth of the Persian Gulf, to the Horn of Africa, and probably even up the Red Sea to Jiddah, not far from Mecca.

CHAPTER TIMELINE

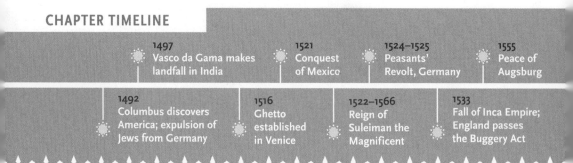

1497 Vasco da Gama makes landfall in India	1521 Conquest of Mexico	1524–1525 Peasants' Revolt, Germany	1555 Peace of Augsburg

1492 Columbus discovers America; expulsion of Jews from Germany	1516 Ghetto established in Venice	1522–1566 Reign of Suleiman the Magnificent	1533 Fall of Inca Empire; England passes the Buggery Act

new territories. European stirrings in the Atlantic were thus only the latest phase in a centuries-long tradition of restlessness.

The Portuguese led the way. As early as 1415 their ships began to make contact with the coast of western Africa, down the expanse of what is today the country of Morocco. With the enthusiastic support of the royal Prince Henrique the Navigator (1394–1460), Portuguese fleets sailed next to the Azores and the Canary Islands. By 1445 they had reached the westernmost tip of the continent, at today's neighboring states of Senegal and Gambia. In the 1460s they began to curve eastward under the massive overhanging bulk of the Saharan expanse. Their ships crossed the equator in 1474, and in 1488 they reached the Cape of Good Hope at the southern tip of Africa. Only nine years later, in 1497, under the command of Vasco da Gama (1460–1524), the first European fleet made landfall in India (see Map 12.1). These were journeys of exploration and trade, not of conquest. Da Gama told the local ruler in Calcutta that he was

> the ambassador of the king of Portugal—the ruler of many lands and a man of such wealth that no one in this part of the world can compare; and that for sixty years this king's predecessors had dispatched ships to explore the seas in the direction of India, where they had heard that Christian kings like themselves lived. To connect with these Christian monarchs was the sole aim of their explorations, not to seek silver and gold—for the kings of Portugal possessed such tremendous wealth in these metals as to make them uninterested in whatever gold or silver was to be found in India or any other place.

Da Gama meant hardly a word of this, and it is doubtful his Indian host believed any of it. A genuine spirit of exploration for its own sake motivated those who put to sea and those who financed them. So, however, did an expectation of profit.

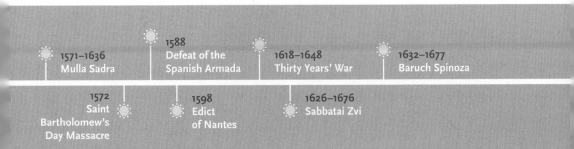

1571–1636
Mulla Sadra

1572
Saint Bartholomew's Day Massacre

1588
Defeat of the Spanish Armada

1598
Edict of Nantes

1618–1648
Thirty Years' War

1626–1676
Sabbatai Zvi

1632–1677
Baruch Spinoza

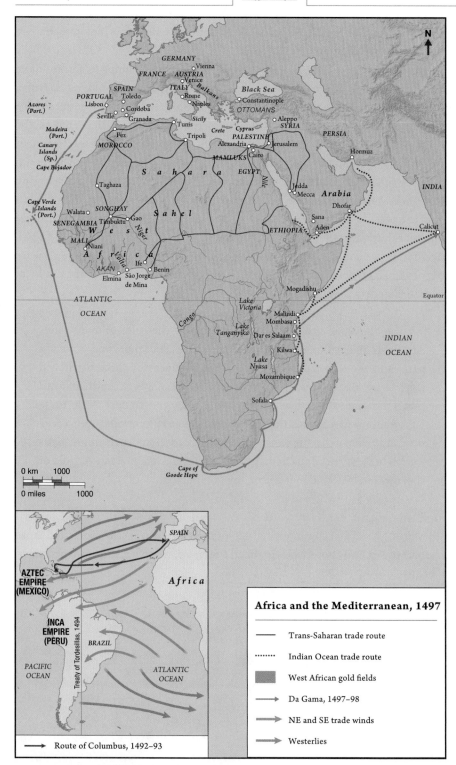

N

GERMANY
○Vienna
FRANCE AUSTRIA
○Venice
SPAIN   ITALY   Balkans
PORTUGAL Toledo   ○Rome   Black Sea
Azores   Lisbon○   ○Naples   ○Constantinople
(Port.)   ○Cordoba   OTTOMANS
Seville○   ○Granada   Sicily   Cyprus   ○Aleppo
Madeira   Tunis○   Crete   SYRIA
(Port.)   ○Fez   ○Tripoli   PALESTINE   PERSIA
Canary   MOROCCO   Alexandria   Jerusalem   ○Hormuz
Islands   MAMLUKS○Cairo
(Sp.)   EGYPT
Cape Bojador   S a h a r a
○Taghaza   Jedda○   Arabia   INDIA
Cape Verde   ○Mecca   Dhofar○
Islands   Walata○   SONGHAY   S a h e l   Sana○
(Port.)   SENEGAMBIA Timbuktu○ ○Gao   Aden○   Calicut
W e s t   ETHIOPIA
MALI   ○Niani   Mogadishu○
A f r i c a
AKAN   ○Ife   ○Benin
Elmina   São Jorge
de Mina

ATLANTIC   Lake   Equator
OCEAN   Victoria   Malindi○
Congo   Mombasa○
Lake   Dar es Salaam○
Tanganyika   INDIAN
Kilwa○   OCEAN
Lake
Nyasa
Mozambique○

Sofala○

Nile
Niger
Volta

0 km   1000   Cape of
Goode Hope
0 miles   1000

SPAIN

AZTEC
EMPIRE   A f r i c a
(MEXICO)

INCA
EMPIRE   BRAZIL
(PERU)

PACIFIC   ATLANTIC
OCEAN   OCEAN

Treaty of Tordesillas, 1494

→ Route of Columbus, 1492–93

Africa and the Mediterranean, 1497

——— Trans-Saharan trade route

·········· Indian Ocean trade route

▢ West African gold fields

——→ Da Gama, 1497–98

——→ NE and SE trade winds

——→ Westerlies

MAP 12.1   Africa and the Mediterranean, 1497

NEW CONTINENTS AND PROFITS

From the early 9th century sub-Saharan gold, spices, slaves, and ivory had been prized commodities in Mediterranean trade. Muslim merchants in Spain and Morocco had first brought these items to Europe, which accounts for the tremendous wealth of cities like Granada and Cordoba. (Tax records show that the Muslim inhabitants of Toledo alone held six thousand black slaves in the 10th century.) These were luxury goods enjoyed by the elites. When Christian forces drove the last Muslim rulers from Iberia in the 15th century, they took over control of this trade and determined to expand it. The commodities exchanged for these luxury items were predominantly textiles, metalwares, glazed pottery, glass, and paper. Not surprisingly, some of the coastal African peoples had embraced Islam in the intervening centuries, but this posed no bar to trade. Money mattered, not faith. When Vasco da Gama reached India in 1497, he mistook Hinduism for a quaint Eastern version of Christianity but identified precisely every precious stone and spice in the markets. Once in Calcutta, the Portuguese quickly established trading posts along the south-western Malabar Coast of India. Within twenty years they had spread their commercial network to the Malay Peninsula, the Indonesian archipelago, and the Moluccas Islands; within another two decades, by 1542, they had reached Japan. Their first permanent trading post in China, at Macao, was established in 1555 (see Map 12.2).

> Money mattered, not faith. When Vasco da Gama reached India in 1497, he mistook Hinduism for a quaint Eastern version of Christianity but identified precisely every precious stone and spice in the markets.

Cristoforo Colombo's (1451–1506) innovation in 1492 was to propose reaching Asia by sailing directly westward rather than circumnavigating Africa to the south. Colombo was an Italian from Genoa, but he sailed under the Spanish flag of Ferdinand and Isabella. Such international arrangements were common, so no wonder just about every state ever associated with Colombo claims him as a native: to the Spanish he is Cristóbal Colón; streets and squares in Barcelona commemorate Cristòfor Colom; and the Portuguese proudly recall Cristóvão Colombo.[2] A few writers have argued that he was a Jew by ethnicity, but the evidence for this is extremely weak. Still, there is no reason, apart from lazy habit, to call him Christopher Columbus.

Every educated European since the 12th century had known that the world was round. Colombo was unprepared for the size of the globe, and so the length of his historic journey, but not the fact of it. And then he ran into an unexpected speed bump, the New World. Colombo never realized that the Caribbean islands

---

2   The English explorer John Cabot, who carried the Tudor flag as far as Newfoundland in 1497, was actually another Italian—Giovanni Caboto (1450–1508), from Venice.

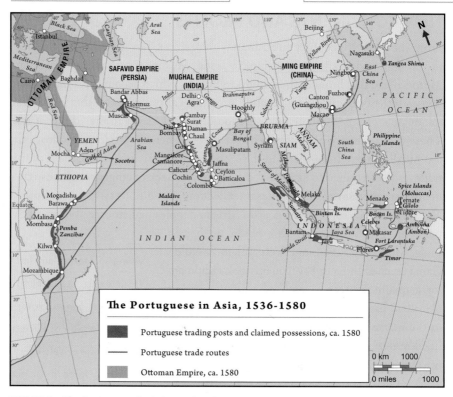

MAP 12.2   The Portuguese in Asia, 1536–1580

he had landed at were in fact the outer islands of two vast new continents. Despite four voyages to the New World, he believed to his dying day that he had sailed to islands just off the coast of Asia (see Figure 12.1). Such misjudgments do not lessen his achievement, however. The Atlantic passage was one of the greatest technical and human-adventure feats in Western history, and it had earth-changing consequences.

In his ship's log, Colombo duly recorded his first encounter with the indigenous people of the islands:

When it became clear that they welcomed us, I saw that it would be easier to convert them to Our Holy Faith by peaceful means than by force, and so I offered them some simple gifts—red-dyed caps, necklaces of strung beads, and so on—which they received with great pleasure. So enthusiastic were they, in fact, that they began to swim out to our ships, carrying parrots, balls of cotton thread, spears, and other items to trade.... Still, they struck me as an exceptionally poor people, for all of them were naked—even the women, although I saw only one girl among them at the time. Every one of them I perceived to be young (that is, under

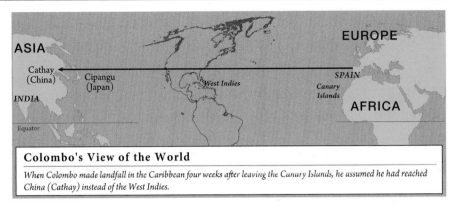

Colombo's View of the World

When Colombo made landfall in the Caribbean four weeks after leaving the Canary Islands, he assumed he had reached China (Cathay) instead of the West Indies.

FIGURE 12.1   **Colombo's View of the World**

the age of thirty), finely shaped and with handsome faces. . . . They appear to own no weapons and to have no knowledge of such, for when I showed them our swords they reached out and grabbed them by the blades, cutting themselves unexpectedly. . . . When I inquired, by pointing, about the scars visible on some of their bodies, they made me to understand, also by pointing, that people from another island had attacked them and tried to carry them off as slaves, but they resisted. . . . Overall they struck me as being clever, and I believe they would make good servants and could easily become Christian, since they have no religion of their own. They learned quickly to repeat the handful of words we taught them. If it please God, I intend to bring six of them home to Your Majesties, so that they might be taught to speak our language. Apart from the parrots, I saw no animals of any kind on the island.

Colombo's curiously unenthusiastic tone probably reflects his disappointment in the poverty of the people. Expecting the vast riches of China's silk and spice trade, he found instead naked islanders with nothing but ready smiles and a number of parrots. On subsequent journeys he discovered more of the natural wealth available, and his enthusiasm recovered noticeably. Within a few years other adventurers had reached both the North American and South American mainlands, and mapmakers began to appreciate that two entirely new continents had been found.

News of the discovery spread quickly across Europe, and soon wave after wave of explorers and adventurers set sail. In 1513 the Spanish admiral Vasco Núñez de Balboa (1475–1519), standing atop a hill in what is today's nation of Panama, became the first European to see the Pacific Ocean. Only six years later Fernão de Magalhães (Ferdinand Magellan, 1480–1521) set out to circumnavigate the entire globe, an astonishing feat that took three years and claimed the lives of 262 of his

The First Published Image of the New World
Cristoforo Colombo's first report to the Spanish kings of his discovery was published in Basel in early 1494; printed here is one of the illustrations that accompanied the Latin text. It shows Colombo arriving on the shore of "the island of Hispania" in a small landing craft. He offers a goblet as a peace offering to the inhabitants, who appear to be uniformly naked, male, and beardless, gathered at the shore to meet him.

initial crew of 280, including his own. Tales of the wealth available in the New World and in Asia set off a fiercely competitive wave of explorers, soldiers, and government representatives eager to stake out their claims (see Map 12.3).

Geographic location gave an immense advantage to the Atlantic seaboard nations of Europe: Portugal, Spain, France, the Low Countries, and England. The Mediterranean states, which had lived by maritime trade since 3000 BCE, were shut off from the New World bonanza since they could not pass the Straits of Gibraltar—which the Atlantic states had quickly sealed off like a cork in a bottle. Left to trade with Asia only through the Ottoman-controlled land routes, they began a long and slow commercial decline. This resulted in a fundamental change in the structure of the European economy, and by the end of the 16th century economic dominance had shifted away from the Mediterranean. The Atlantic states entered the 17th century as the economic and political powerhouses of Europe.

> The Mediterranean states, which had lived by maritime trade since 3000 BCE, were shut off from the New World bonanza since they could not pass the Straits of Gibraltar—which the Atlantic states had quickly sealed off like a cork in a bottle.

The sudden and massive influx of gold from the New World triggered the rise of the Atlantic commercial economies. This gold was seized chiefly from the Aztecs and Mayans of Central America and the Incas of what eventually became Peru and Bolivia. Credit for these seizures belongs above all to the army of **conquistadores** ("conquerors") led by Hernán Cortés (1485–1547), who subdued Mexico in 1521, and Francisco Pizarro (1471–1541), who vanquished the Incas in 1533. The conquerors' forces were astonishingly few in number: Cortés commanded an army of no more than six hundred conquistadores, and Pizarro had only 180. The Europeans' technological advantage is obvious: supplied with firearms, they could mow down the spear-carrying natives with considerable ease. But their victory had been made incalculably easier by an inadvertent biological warfare that preceded them on the scene.

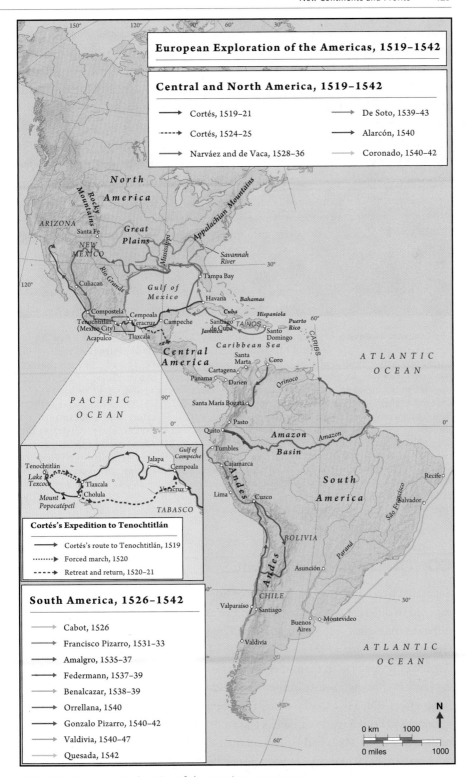

European Exploration of the Americas, 1519–1542

Central and North America, 1519–1542

⟶ Cortés, 1519–21
⤏ Cortés, 1524–25
⟶ Narváez and de Vaca, 1528–36
⟶ De Soto, 1539–43
⟶ Alarcón, 1540
⟶ Coronado, 1540–42

Cortés's Expedition to Tenochtitlán

⟶ Cortés's route to Tenochtitlán, 1519
⤏ Forced march, 1520
⤏ Retreat and return, 1520–21

South America, 1526–1542

⟶ Cabot, 1526
⟶ Francisco Pizarro, 1531–33
⟶ Amalgro, 1535–37
⟶ Federmann, 1537–39
⟶ Benalcazar, 1538–39
⟶ Orrellana, 1540
⟶ Gonzalo Pizarro, 1540–42
⟶ Valdivia, 1540–47
⟶ Quesada, 1542

MAP 12.3 **European Exploration of the Americas, 1519–1542**

The Conquest of Mexico   For a quarter century after Colombo's discovery of the New World, Spanish explorers and traders had established settlements only in the islands of the Caribbean; only a handful of expeditions had visited the mainland, to trade. Enough contact was made, however, for the transmission of European diseases like smallpox, influenza, and measles to the indigenous peoples of Central and South America, who, never having been exposed to them before, had no natural resistance to them. In many places throughout the New World as much as 90 percent of the population was killed before any European appeared directly on the scene. This painting, from the second half of the 17th century, illustrates the dramatic conquest of the Aztecs by Hernán Cortés in 1519. The Aztec empire had long been the most powerful (and violent) of the New World kingdoms. Cortés began his campaign with only six hundred soldiers—although he picked up many conscripts on his way to the Aztec capital of Tenochtitlan, shown here in the background—which was a sufficient number to bring down the once-great empire.

CONQUEST AND EPIDEMICS

Separated by a vast ocean, the peoples of Europe and of the New World had been exposed to different types of bacteria and viruses and had consequently developed different biological responses to them. The sailors who landed with Cristoforo Colombo on the island they called Hispaniola (today's Haiti and the Dominican Republic) brought with them the viruses for smallpox and measles. Neither disease had ever existed before in the New World, so they ran unchecked with horrifying effect. On Hispaniola alone, the population, which an early Dominican missionary (Friar Bartolomé de Las Casas, 1484–1566) had estimated to be three million strong in 1492, had fallen to a mere five hundred by 1538. That is a loss greater than 99.99 percent. In the opposite direction, some Europeans contracted a form of syphilis in the New World that seems never to have been present before in Europe. Within a few years, five million Europeans had died of it. Yet the impact on the New World was far greater.[3]

A Franciscan missionary, Friar Toribio de Benavente Motolinia (1484–1568), described how the natives "did not know how to treat the disease ... and consequently died in whole piles, like bedbugs. In many places, in fact, entire households died all at once, and since it proved impossible to bury so great a number of corpses, our

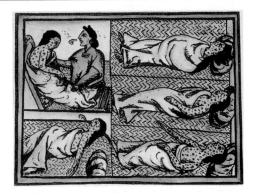

Smallpox Victims The protracted isolation of the peoples of the Americas from the rest of the world made them vulnerable to a battery of diseases European colonists brought with them: the breath of a Spaniard was said to be sufficient enough to kill. These 16th-century illustrations, drawn by a native Mexican artist, depict smallpox victims. In the upper left panel a doctor attempts to treat his patient—undoubtedly he failed.

soldiers simply pulled down the houses over these people, letting their own homes serve as their tombs." Pizarro found similar circumstances favoring him when he stormed through Peru and Bolivia. Even a century later, in far-off Massachusetts Bay, smallpox and measles erased nine-tenths of the Native American population between 1617 and 1619. Such numbers are horrifying to imagine. Motolinia wrote that when Cortés led his men in triumph through the Aztec capital of Tenochtitlan—on the site of today's Mexico City—the soldiers could traverse the entire city stepping only on the corpses of smallpox victims, without ever once setting foot on the ground.

Such unintended suffering does not excuse the outright brutishness of the Europeans. In sailing to Africa, India, and China, the Europeans had shown no interest in conquest and colonization since they were able to acquire what they wanted—nonperishable luxury goods—by simple trade. Their technological advantage, in military hardware, over the sub-Saharan Africans was as great as it was over the indigenous New World peoples, but it did not prompt them to slaughter millions and seize their lands. The smallpox epidemic changed everything, and as a consequence the Europeans instantly developed a different attitude toward the land: here lay two vast and supremely wealthy continents that were, in effect, uninhabited—or near enough to uninhabited to persuade the conquistadores to finish the job. Moreover, the Protestant Reformation accelerated European interest in the New World. They saw not only an opportunity for evangelization,

---

[3] Cortés was able to conquer Mexico in 1521 with only six hundred men-at-arms because 90 percent of the Aztecs had already been obliterated by smallpox by 1520.

but also a means to finance their struggles back home. The coincidence of the discovery of the New World's gold and silver deposits, and the bubbling over of the Catholic-Protestant rift into outright war in the 1540s, was too great to be entirely coincidental.

Once they had seized control of the gold and silver mines, the Europeans set to the large-scale production of cash crops like cotton, sugar cane, and tobacco. These commodities fetched high prices, retained consistent demand, and traveled well across the long distance from New World to Old. The annihilation of the local populace presented a problem, though, since all three crops were exceptionally labor intensive in their production. Without a large infusion of people to work the land, producing them was out of the question. There were only two ways to put people on the land in the numbers needed: settlement and slavery.

NEW CROPS AND THE ENCLOSURE MOVEMENT

It is one thing to explore and trade and another to settle. Europe's expansion could not have become the permanent development it did without demographic changes, including growing populations with reduced access to land ownership. These fundamental changes made it possible, and desirable, to export people—which is another way of describing overseas expansion.

After severe contraction in the late Middle Ages, Europe's population began to grow around 1500 and did so steadily for the next three hundred years (see Figure 12.2). A gradual decline in outbreaks of plague accounts for much of this, but so does improvement in the food supply. Famine has always been nature's principal method of population control. For the premodern world, steady growth in demographic numbers is a sure indicator of steady growth in the availability of food. Europe saw just such a steady growth from the 16th to 18th centuries, for two reasons. First, food exports to the Ottoman-controlled east declined. And second, Europe was introduced to new crops from North and South America—the most important being corn (maize), beans, tomatoes, and potatoes. It is unlikely that these were brought back with the intention of introducing new foodstuffs. Rather, they were probably loaded on ships as victuals for those making the journey back to Europe (see Map 12.4). Most Europeans disdained corn (maize), which they thought inedible for humans; they prized it instead as animal fodder. Tomatoes made exotic sauces and side dishes. Beans and potatoes, though, were radical innovations. By long-standing feudal customs, Europe's

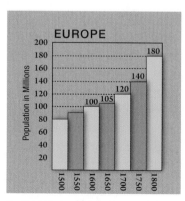

FIGURE 12.2   **Population Growth in Europe, 1500–1800**

manors remained dedicated to grain production, but beans and potatoes quickly dominated the peasants' individual garden plots. Gradually, fields normally left fallow were also given over to the new crops, which helped replenish the soil. Their high yields made them popular, not as market crops but as staples of the peasants' own diets. By the 17th century farmers on the Continent were eating as many as one to two dozen potatoes a day. Not the most satisfying of diets, but infinitely preferable to famine. Potatoes could also be distilled to produce vodka. Other grains that formerly went to peasant diets became available for distilling too.[4]

Increasing food supplies, however, meant declining agricultural prices. Small landholders who could not keep up with their rents therefore risked sliding back in debt bondage, and the manorial lords who lived off those rents faced severe potential drops in their own incomes as well. For many aristocrats, an answer to their trouble lay in the **enclosure movement**: By enclosing farmland—that is, by constructing a border of fences or thick hedgerows around it—landlords could evict their tenants, convert crop fields to meadows, and raise sheep or other herd animals instead. Their labor costs thus declined sharply, and the wool

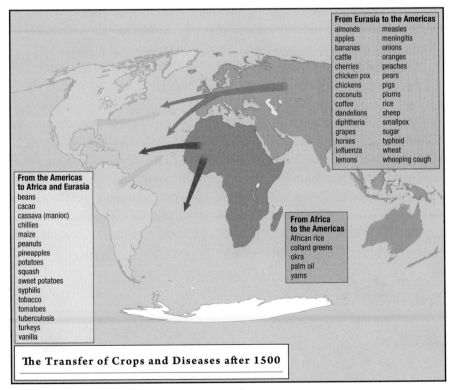

The Transfer of Crops and Diseases after 1500

MAP 12.4   The Transfer of Crops and Diseases after 1500

---

[4] The large-scale production of gin and whisky began—and so did greater alcoholism among the common people, with the usual social ills that accompany it.

generated by their sheep was self-renewing. Moreover, the steady rise in human population meant a steadily growing demand for textiles. In this way landed nobles improved their incomes significantly, but at the expense of the evicted farmers. Lacking the funds to purchase new lands of their own, rural workers had difficulty supporting themselves.

Thomas More had described the problem as early as 1516 in his *Utopia*, in which his narrator explains the rise of crime:

> It's because of sheep. These animals, so naturally mild and so easy to tend, can now be said to have become uncontrollable devourers, consuming even the people themselves; they empty homes, devastate crop fields, and turn whole villages into ghost towns. Anyplace where sheep can be raised to produce fine and rich wool, the nobles, gentry, and even the abbots (those supposed "holy men"!), not content with their rents and yearly fees, and feeling that it is not enough to live in luxurious laziness and do no actual good in the world, but choosing instead to bring actual harm into it, enclose all the land for pasture and put an end to farming. They demolish homes and level villages. The churches they allow to remain, of course, but only so they can use them as sheepfolds. As though they did not waste enough [land] already on coverts and private parks, these fine people are now destroying every human dwelling and letting every scrap of usable farmland run wild. *(Book 1)*

Evicted farm families had few options. The younger men could enter the military or merchant marine, and the females could seek positions as domestic servants, but for many the solution lay in seeking new fortunes abroad. The New World needed settlers in large numbers. It was a difficult decision, to travel thousands of miles from home, take up residence on a foreign continent, and begin the work of clearing the land afresh. But many chose to do so, because of population rise and land hunger. The feverish religious hostilities of the time, too, provided ample reason to quit the Old World for the New.

THE PATRIARCHAL FAMILY

Along with the Protestant reforms, these developments also led to a greater emphasis on the traditional family, with the husband firmly established at its head. But threats to family and state abounded, or were believed to abound, throughout the 16th and 17th centuries. And these threats, popularly believed to come primarily from witches and Jews, were considered so dire that society justified the most extraordinary measures to root them out.

Luther, Calvin, and the other Protestant leaders did not think of themselves as social reformers. When radicals like Thomas Müntzer (1488–1525) interpreted Luther's theology as a call to social rebellion, resulting in the Peasants' Revolt, Luther responded with characteristic vigor and called for the rebels' extermination. The Reformers, in fact, relied on existing social and political structures for their vision of a new Christendom: from feudal princes in Germany to urban elites in Switzerland, the existing social models provided the backbone of the Protestant campaigns.

And a strong backbone was needed, according to Luther, Calvin, and others. Human nature was too depraved, too ensnared in its own sinfulness, to be trusted. Figures of authority were needed to provide discipline. Protestant theology championed the notion of the "priesthood of all believers"—meaning that each individual could discern the teachings of the Bible for him- or herself. But only strong and demanding leaders could make sure that people lived according to the truths they read in Scripture. Hence Luther granted power to the German princes to enforce the teaching of the new Lutheran churches within their domains. Calvin established the town councils of the Elect to supervise, judge, and punish the Reformed citizens of Geneva and elsewhere.

Both men wrote extensive commentaries on the following passage from the New Testament:

> Let every person be subject to the governing authorities, for there is no authority except from God, and those authorities that exist have been instituted by God. Therefore whoever resists authority resists what God has appointed, and those who resist will incur judgment. For rulers are not a terror to good conduct, but to bad. Do you wish to have no fear of the authority? Then do what is good, and you will receive its approval; for it is God's servant for your good. But if you do what is wrong, you should be afraid, for the authority does not bear the sword in vain! It is the servant of God to execute wrath on the wrongdoer. Therefore one must be subject, not only because of wrath but also because of conscience. *(Romans 13.1–5)*

Since sinfulness is present in us from birth, disciplined authority needed to be as much a cornerstone of parenting as was love itself. Hence Protestant social ideology called for the patriarchal family as the fundamental unit of godly society. In that family, the man stood as the undoubted leader, charged with the protection and care of the whole household. The mother was subject to her husband's authority and given the special task of beginning the moral and spiritual education of their children. Luther and Calvin here drew on Saint Paul's Epistles: "Wives, be subject to your husbands as you are to the Lord. For the husband is the head of the wife just as Christ is the head of the church, the body of which He is the Savior. Just as the church is subject to Christ, so also wives ought to be, in everything, to their husbands" (Ephesians 5.22–24).

The Scottish Reformer and founder of the Presbyterian tradition, John Knox (1510–1572), wrote an infamous treatise called *First Blast of the Trumpet against the Monstrous Regiment of Women* (1558).

> To promote a woman to bear rule, superiority, dominion, or empire above any realm, nation, or city, is repugnant to nature; contumely [an insult] to God, a thing most contrary to His revealed will and approved ordinance; and finally, it is the subversion of good order, of all equity and justice. In the probation of this proposition, I will not be so curious as to gather whatsoever may amplify, set forth, or decor the same; but I am purposed, even as I have spoken my conscience in most plain and few words,

The Patriarchal Family Cornelius Johnson (1593–1661) was a popular portraitist among the English aristocracy of the 17th century. This 1640 painting shows Arthur, 1st Baron Capell (1604–1649), together with his family. Capell was a staunch Royalist in England's Civil War, who personally escorted Queen Henrietta Maria to safety in France in 1646. Captured by Cromwell's forces in 1648, Capell was briefly imprisoned in the Tower of London before being executed. His eldest son, Arthur, shown at the far left here, joined what was left of the Royalist army even though he was only twelve years old at the time. This portrait shows the family posing before their formal garden. Note that of the three females in the picture, one (his wife, Lady Elizabeth Capell) is looking respectfully at her husband, the second daughter (Mary) is gazing at her baby brother, and the eldest daughter (Elizabeth) is looking slyly away to the right; only the males in the picture look directly at the viewer. Is it a coincidence that in this image, completed just before the outbreak of the Civil War, the Capell's garden is empty and storm clouds appear to be gathering over it?

so to stand content with a simple proof of every member, bringing in for my witness God's ordinance in nature, His plain will revealed in His word, and by the minds of such as be most ancient amongst godly writers. And first, where I affirm the empire of a woman to be a thing repugnant to nature, I mean not only that God, by the order of His creation, has spoiled [deprived] woman of authority and dominion, but also that man has seen, proved, and pronounced just causes why it should be. Man, I say, in many other cases, does in this behalf see very clearly. For the causes are so manifest, that they cannot be hid. For who can deny but it is repugnant to nature, that the blind shall be appointed to lead and conduct such as do see? That the weak, the sick, and impotent persons shall nourish and keep the whole and strong? And finally, that the foolish, mad, and frenetic shall govern the discreet, and give counsel to such as be sober of mind? And such be all women, compared unto man in bearing of authority. For their sight in civil regiment is but blindness; their strength, weakness; their counsel, foolishness; and judgment, frenzy, if it be rightly considered.

Husbands and fathers exercised their authority in a variety of ways. Physical discipline was permitted within certain limits, but men were expected above all to lead by setting examples of rigorous and godly behavior. To help them, most Protestant denominations offered some form of personal and family counseling. They also emphasized Bible reading within all family devotions. But since the godly family was the basic unit of godly society, the society itself had an intrinsic right to step in and exert authority when a parent failed. Public shaming, social ostracism, banishment from church life, and imprisonment were widely practiced.

SEXUAL MORALITY

At least in their first two or three generations, Protestant Christians placed a significantly sharper and more constant focus on sexual morality than their Catholic peers. Chastity before marriage and fidelity within it remained the moral ideal for all Christians, but Catholic Europe had long allowed a certain liberality in sexual matters, especially for men. Prostitution, while regulated, had been legal throughout Europe for centuries, for example, and no social stigma fell on the men who frequented prostitutes.[5] One way that Protestants sought to curb prostitution—apart from simply closing down the brothels—was through early marriage. With access to legitimate sexual release, they believed, men would not

---

5   Men had tended to put marriage off until they were established in a trade, which could take until their thirties.

be tempted to resort to illegitimate means. These earlier marriages helped account for the population increase that marked the century.

The era also witnessed new efforts to combat homosexuality. Same-sex eroticism had been regarded as a sign of weakness since Roman times. Christianity added the notion that the activity was immoral since it denied the procreative function that was sexuality's whole intent and purpose. Until the 13th century, however, homosexuality was not a criminal offense. By 1260 in France, homosexual acts became punishable by death. Comparable measures were instituted across Europe, at both the national and local levels, although it remains unclear how often such laws were enforced. Hostility to homosexuality increased with the need to rebuild the population after the Black Death as well. While Renaissance classicism brought more liberal attitudes, in Florence alone over 15,000 people were arrested for sodomy between 1432 and 1502 (though not all were convicted). The Spanish Inquisition arrested over 1,500 people on charges on homosexual acts between 1540 and 1700.

Protestantism's emphasis on Biblical truth (*sola Scriptura*) sharpened antihomosexual sentiments significantly, although formal condemnations came mostly at the local levels of government.[6] One notable exception was the Buggery Act passed by England's King Henry VIII (r. 1509–1547) in 1533, which remained in force until 1861, when the death penalty it called for was replaced by a sentence of life imprisonment.

> Forasmuch as there is not yet sufficient and condign punishment appointed and limited by the due course of the Laws of this Realm for the detestable and abominable Vice of Buggery, [whether] committed with mankind or beast: May it therefore please the King's Highness, with the assent of the Lords Spiritual and the Commons of this present parliament assembled, that it may be enacted by the authority of the same, that the same offence be from henceforth adjudged a felony, and that such an order and form of process therein to be used against the offenders as in cases of felony at the Common Law; and that the offenders being hereof convicted—by verdict, confession, or outlawry—shall suffer such pains of death, and losses and penalties of their goods, chattels, debts, lands, tenements, and [inherited properties], as felons do according to the Common Laws of this Realm; and that no person offending in any such offence shall be admitted to [the king's] clergy; and that Justices

---

6   Just six passages from the Bible explicitly condemn homosexuality, and two are simply New Testament restatements of Old Testament proscriptions. The Scriptures record no direct teaching from Jesus.

of the Peace shall have power and authority within the limits of their commissions and jurisdictions to hear and determine the said offence, as they do in the cases of other felonies.

What makes any type of sexual activity a crime against the state instead of a matter of personal morality? In Protestant Europe, where the state had become the administrative head of the religious community, a sin against public morals was also a crime against civil society. Hence homosexuality—along with adultery, masturbation, foul language, gambling, and drunkenness—required a civil response. Protestants read the Bible as mandating the two-parent, heterosexual,

"A Jan Steen Household"   Jan Havickszoon Steen (1626–1679) was a prolific and popular genre painter of the Dutch Golden Age, who made a handsome living from his scenes of everyday life among common town and country dwellers. Sometimes comic, sometimes tragic, and sometimes a mixture of the two, his paintings were known for their attention to the crowdedness and chaos of domestic living—to such a point that even today a common Dutch colloquialism describes a messy, squalid space as "a Jan Steen household" (*een huishouden van Jan Steen*)—a phrase roughly comparable to the American expression "a pigsty." This painting is one of his moralistic images, showing the dangers of drunkenness. (Steen grew up in a family of tavern keepers, and knew what he was talking about—or rather painting.) Apart from the unbecoming postures of the two figures in the foreground and the uninviting physical scene, a woman and two companions (musicians?) are stealing the drunken pair's cloaks in the background.

married nuclear family. Any sexual activity outside that norm was in essence a threat to the godly state.

ENEMIES WITHIN: WITCHES AND JEWS

Popular belief in witchcraft had roots in pre-Christian classical, Germanic, and Celtic culture. Ancient and medieval beliefs differed from those of the early modern era, however. Earlier Europeans had held that some individuals (thankfully, not many) are simply born with an intrinsic ability to summon supernatural forces at will, which they used for good or ill. In contrast, people of the 16th and 17th centuries developed the belief that magical powers resulted from an explicit and conscious contract made between the witch (who could be male or female) and Satan. Witchcraft was now believed to be intentional—a power that an individual chose to acquire—rather than an innate, though freakish, ability possessed from birth. And that made popular fear of it all the stronger, especially given the era's particular emphasis on human weakness and sinfulness. If people could be so easily coaxed into a pact with Satan, then witchcraft could conceivably take over our world and bring about its ruin. A witch was not merely someone "possessed of powers" but someone actively engaged in evil, and the danger he or she represented required immediate action.

That action consisted of mania, arrest, trial, torture, and execution on a scale that is difficult to comprehend. Campaigns against witches began to increase markedly toward the end of the 15th century but became frenzied after 1560, once Europe's religious disputes turned violent. From 1560 to 1670, nearly two hundred thousand people across Europe were accused of witchcraft and subjected to judicial persecution or mob violence (see Figure 12.3). Roughly one quarter of them were executed. Those who confessed and repented—which required identifying other witches and agreeing to testify against them—were briefly imprisoned, frequently marked by a tattoo, fined, and released. Yet they were socially shunned for the rest of their lives. Germany, Switzerland, and eastern France had the most witchcraft trials per capita. And while there seems to be no substantial difference between the frequency of Protestant and Catholic prosecutions of witchcraft, it does appear that the Protestant-Catholic divide played a role: witchcraft mania struck most ferociously where Protestants and Catholics were most even in number. The witches who appeared in stage dramas like William Shakespeare's *Macbeth* were realistic characters to audiences, in addition to whatever symbolic role they played in the text. In the end, however, no country was immune to witchcraft.

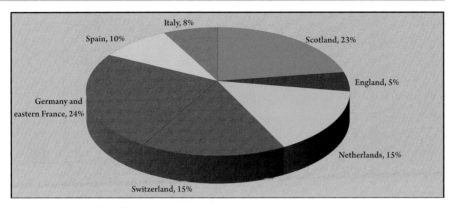

FIGURE 12.3   **Witchcraft Trials, 1450–1750**

Neither was any sex. Both men and women were believed capable of sell-ing their souls to Satan, although at least three-quarters of those arrested for witchcraft, and nearly 90 percent of those executed for it, were women. (Ire-land was the sole exception: roughly 90 percent of its prosecuted witches were male.) Popular assumptions about women's nature—as emotional, impulsive, passionate, demanding creatures—fueled the phenomenon. Women were re-garded as generally weaker than men, but especially in regard to sex. Ideas about sexuality, derived from ancient Greek medicine, held that female lust, once aroused, was insatiable.[7] Only a demonic lover like Satan, it was assumed, could satisfy a woman's sexual longing—and that was precisely the appeal used by the devil to ensnare his victims. Men who became witches were gener-ally assumed to have been enticed into it by women who had already given themselves over to satanic lust.

In this way, the witchcraft craze accords with the period's concern with sexuality in general. Ironi-cally, the era's emphasis on early marriage was directly related to its fear of unchecked sexuality. It demanded being the "godly wife and mother" responsible for her children's moral education, the subjection of wives to their husbands, and the sacralization of domestic life. A force as powerful and unpre-dictable as a woman's body needed to be firmly controlled—or else all hell, literally, could break loose.

> A force as powerful and unpredictable as a woman's body needed to be firmly controlled—or else all hell, literally, could break loose.

---

[7]   Many of the constraints placed on women—such as limiting their appearance in public or regulating their dress—were justified as protecting them from their own inability to control their passions.

Anne Hendriks, brulée à Amsterdam, A° 1571. | *Anne Heinruchs zu Amsterdam verbrent, A° 1571.*

Burning the Enemy Within   A convicted witch being executed in
Amsterdam in 1571.

THE JEWS OF THE EAST AND WEST

The era was cruel to Jews as well. Late medieval hostility to Jews had resulted in
a series of expulsion orders, first from England (1290), then from France (1306)
and Germany (numerous times), and finally from Spain (1492) and Portugal
(1497). Forced from one territory to the next, the Jews gradually concentrated
in the Low Countries, Italy, North Africa, and the Ottoman Empire, where the
Ashkenazic and **Sephardic** traditions of Judaism once again confronted one
another (see Map 12.5).

   For the host countries, the sudden increase in the Jewish populations aggravated social tensions and led many to segregate the Jews into **ghettos**. Regulations
like these had been common since the 12th century. The surge in Jewish numbers
within those districts, however, frequently led to new legislation limiting the Jews'
freedom to move and act within the larger community. Venice established the first
modern ghetto in 1516, but other cities were quick to follow.[8] Life in these communities was often difficult, since Jews from many backgrounds were thrust shoulder
to shoulder, within a larger social context of economic decline and Christian hostility. The economic decline occurred largely because of the shift of economic power
from the Mediterranean—where the Jews had taken refuge—to the Atlantic seaboard, which happened at the same time. Only those Jews who had migrated to the
Low Countries moved into a society of economic growth.

---

[8]   The word *ghetto* likely derives from the Italian *borghetto*, meaning a "small borough" or "precinct."

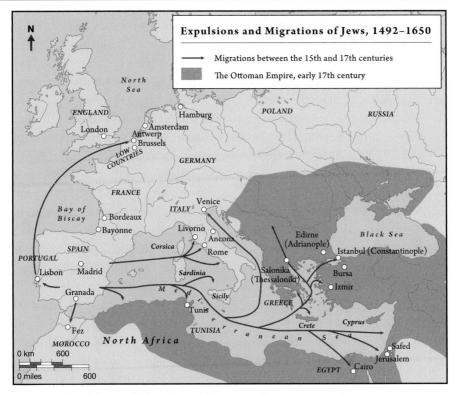

Expulsions and Migrations of Jews, 1492–1650

⟶ Migrations between the 15th and 17th centuries

⬛ The Ottoman Empire, early 17th century

MAP 12.5   Expulsions and Migrations of Jews 1492–1650

Not surprisingly, as most Jews' social and economic lives grew shaky in the 16th and 17th centuries, many found solace in new messianic movements, especially in the Ottoman state, which, after 1515, included the Holy Land. Jewish refugees from Europe generally received a cordial welcome from the Ottoman rulers Bayezid II [T] (r. 1484–1512) and Selim I [T] (r. 1512–1520), who encouraged Jews to settle in the Holy Land.[9] Many Jews, upon arriving in the Holy Land, expressed surprise at the squalor into which the cities had fallen. An Italian refugee, R. Obadiah of Bertinoro, sent a letter back to friend in which he estimates there being "only about seventy [Jewish] households in all of Gaza," while in Hebron he found "only twenty households, . . . half of them coming from Spain and just recently arrived." In Jerusalem itself he found "only seventy households left, all of them poverty-stricken and with no means of support. . . . Anyone who has food to last a year, or the means to procure it, is considered wealthy here."

In Italy, led by charismatic adventurers like Solomon Molcho (1500–1532) and David Reubeni (1490–1541), and in the Ottoman Empire, inspired by R. Isaac Luria (1534–1572) and R. Hayyim Vital (1543–1620), thousands of Jews believed in the

---

[9]   Spanish Jews set up the first printing press in the Ottoman state. Two Sephardic Jews, Joseph Hamon and his son Moses Hamon, served for a total of thirty years as personal physicians to the sultans.

imminent arrival of the long-promised messiah. These four figures, and others like them, preached a message of intense spiritual and social reform to prepare for the restoration of the Davidic Kingdom. These movements involved a minority of the Jews, but they were popular enough to make the rulers of their host countries concerned about the potential for social unrest.

Reubeni was an especially enigmatic figure, known today primarily through his diary. A curly haired and heavily bearded dwarf, he had a striking appearance. He probably came from the large Jewish community at Cranganore in India, but at some point he traveled to Khaybar, in today's Afghanistan. In 1522 he appeared in Sudan, speaking to crowds about a large Jewish kingdom in the east, supposedly ruled by his brother Joseph. For some reason, Reubeni also claimed to be a direct descendant of the Prophet Muhammad. His life's aim was to create a military alliance between European royalty and his supposed royal brother to open a two-front war upon the Ottoman Empire. In 1524 he went to Rome, entering the city while riding a white horse, and was received by Pope Clement VII (r. 1523–1534). With Clement's recommendation in hand, he approached the Portuguese king João III (r. 1521–1557), the rulers of Milan and of Venice, and finally the Habsburg emperor Charles V, each of whom promised some form of aid. (In Italy he made friends with Solomon Molcho, the son of Jewish parents who had converted to Christianity. Solomon reconverted to Judaism and, at Reubeni's encouragement, circumcised himself.) Reubeni's habit of complaining to these rulers about their treatment of native Jews, however, turned them against him. Sometime around 1531 he was arrested in Italy and sent to Spain, where he was tried by the Inquisition. No official record of his trial or execution survives, but a later chronicle records that in 1541 "a Jew from India who had come to Portugal" was put to death by the Inquisition at Llerana in southern Spain. His diary survives in the Bodleian Library in Oxford and was published in 1895.

When Sabbatai Zvi (1626–1676) came along and preached his own version of messianic deliverance, he found an enormously receptive audience. He was from Smyrna (modern Izmir, Turkey). **Kabbala**, a mystical interpretation of scripture developed by rabbis, had originated centuries before. In 1648, however, in fulfillment of a kabbalistic prophecy, Zvi declared himself the Messiah and ultimately moved to Istanbul, where he converted a Jewish scribe who promptly forged an ancient-looking revelation document from the patriarch Abraham.

> I, Abraham, confined for forty years to life in a cave, spent a long time in pondering when the miraculous time of deliverance might come, when suddenly, a heavenly voice cried out: "A son named Sabbatai will be born to Mordechai Zvi in the year 5386 [1626]. He, the great Messiah, will humble the Serpent and take his seat upon my throne."

Armed with this, Zvi preached to Jews throughout the Ottoman lands—Istanbul, Athens, Alexandria, Cairo, Gaza, Jerusalem, Aleppo—and gained followers everywhere. Jews as far away as Italy, France, Germany, and the Netherlands joined the movement. At least one entire community, at Avignon, made preparations to quit the city and move with all their belongings to Jerusalem, to join the anticipated new kingdom.

Zvi went so far as to issue a universal proclamation to all Jews:

> Sabbatai Zvi, the first-born son of YHWH, and the Messiah and Redeemer of all the people of Israel, to all the sons of Israel, sends Peace. Since you have been thought worthy to behold the great Day of Fulfillment promised by YHWH through His prophets, all your sorrows and lamentations must end and be turned to celebrations, your fasts be turned into feasts, and your tears must cease. Rejoice, instead, with psalms and hymns! Let your days of sadness and despair become days of jubilation! For I have appeared!

As unlikely as it sounds, the proclamation generated enormous excitement throughout the international Jewish world. Zvi's portrait began to be printed in Jewish prayer books (frequently appearing next to images of King David). His initials were carved on synagogue walls and embroidered onto flags, and prayers for him were inserted into Jewish liturgies.

A Messiah on His Throne
Sabbatai Zvi (1626–1676) was a Sephardic Jew who grew up in Smyrna (modern Izmir) in western Anatolia. A sensitive lad, troubled by violent mood swings, he began to experience mystical revelations in 1648 that intimated he was the long-expected messiah of the Jewish people. It is unclear how much he believed these revelations at first, and how many followers he acquired, but in 1665, after receiving a number of confirming signs that dispelled all doubt, he and his followers publicly proclaimed his messianic mission. This page from a prayer book, published in Amsterdam in 1666, shows him enthroned, with angels bringing him a heavenly crown. Note the lower image, which has him presiding over a table at which are gathered the representatives, presumably, of the Twelve Tribes of Israel. The Hebrew word *tikkun* in large print in the center of the image means the "restored harmony" expected to be provided by the messiah.

The speed of the Sabbatean cult's rise reflects the misery and difficulty of Jewish lives. Persecutions of the Jews grew in number and ferocity throughout the era, leading many to find hope only in a miraculous deliverance. Even a number of Christian groups enthused over the supposed Messiah's arrival, although they were probably more excited by the idea of the Jews leaving Europe than they were about their liberation. But the Ottoman ruler Mehmed IV (r. 1648–1687) grew concerned about

Zvi's popularity. Afraid that large numbers of Jews migrating to Israel would push for its independence, he began to pressure Zvi to stop his activity. Zvi responded, on September 16, 1666, by suddenly announcing his conversion to Islam—for which Mehmed rewarded him with great wealth, a prominent position at court, and several new wives. To Jews everywhere, the blow was devastating, and the Sabbatean movement fell apart instantaneously.

Most of the founders of Protestantism were surprised by the refusal of the Jews to convert to Christianity. For centuries, figures like Martin Luther believed, the Jews had bravely and correctly held out against the false teachings of the Catholics. "If I had been born a Jew," he wrote in *On Jesus Christ Having Been Born a Jew* (1523), "and if I had witnessed such idiots and buffoons [as the Catholics] trying to teach and administer Christian truth, I would as soon have turned myself into a pig as into a Christian." But surely, most Reformers confidently felt, once the beautiful Gospel truth was restored by the Protestants, the Jews would rush to accept it. Conversion would be their reward for enduring centuries of Catholic idiocy and persecution. "We will receive them with open arms, permit them to trade with us, to work with us, live among us, hear our Christian preaching, and witness our Christian way of life." When that failed to happen, the reaction was severe.

Luther himself penned many private letters to friends in which he railed against Jewish perfidy. He also released his wrath publicly in several viciously anti-Semitic tracts, the most notorious being *On the Jews and Their Lies* (1543):

> What ever shall Christians do with the damned, rejected Jews? We can hardly tolerate having them live among us as they do—for if we do, now that we know of their lies, hatred, and blasphemy, we will be complicit in their evil. We are powerless to convert them, but powerless too to put out the unquenchable fire of God's wrath, of which the prophets wrote. . . . Here is what I recommend. First, we ought to burn down their synagogues and schools, and bury underground whatever is immune to fire, so that no one ever again needs to see a single stone or cinder of them. . . . Their homes too should be set ablaze and destroyed. . . . Let all their prayer books and copies of the Talmud be taken from them, for it is by means of these that they propagate their idolatry, their lies, their foul cursing, and their blasphemies.

The tract goes on like this for two hundred pages. Luther was arguably no more anti-Semitic than many of his peers, but he was among the most influential and outspoken. His works may not have persuaded tolerant Christians to become otherwise—and it deserves pointing out that many individuals disagreed with Luther, in print. Yet his uniquely authoritative position among Protestants probably encouraged and confirmed many anti-Semites in the bigotry they already had.

The early modern era, in sum, was marked by harsh religious tensions compounded by severe economic dislocations. Small wonder, then, that so many dispossessed Christians fled to the New World. Small wonder, too, that so many dispossessed Jews fled to the Old.

WARS OF RELIGION

When societies employ force, they often justify their action by recourse to the divine. The ancient Hebrews, for example, considered some wars ethically justifiable as self-defense (*milhemet hovah*). Other wars, however, such as their conquest of the Promised Land from the Canaanites, they deemed to be a religious obligation (*milhemet mitzvah*), a manifestation of YHWH's victory over the false gods of the peoples of the Palestinian plain. The Greeks never entered battle, when they could help it, without first making offerings to the gods and looking for signs of heavenly favor or disfavor. They found divine revelation in everything from cloud patterns in the sky to the spray of blood in the sacrifice of an animal. In ancient Rome the constitutional authority to declare war laid not with the emperor, the consul, or the Senate but with the *fetiales*—the college of priests.

Christianity posed a problem to medieval warriors (if they bothered to think about it), since Jesus's message had focused so intently on peace. He offered no resistance to those who sought to do him harm and forgave those who had already done it. Fortunately for the warlords, though, Dark Age–era Christianity emphasized Jesus as the stern Lord of Heaven, the All-Powerful Judge of Last Days, rather than the Prince of Peace. Still, the church struggled for centuries to determine a Christian ethic for war. How can one justify even a war of self-defense when the greatest heroes of the church were martyrs? Can one be a soldier and a Christian at the same time?

> Still, the church struggled for centuries to determine a Christian ethic for war. How can one justify even a war of self-defense when the greatest heroes of the church were martyrs? Can one be a soldier and a Christian at the same time?

Medieval Muslims had less trouble with the matter: the Prophet himself had been an avid soldier, and the Holy Qur'an enjoined all believers, under certain circumstances, to take up arms for the faith. The Islamic empire had been achieved by the sword first and proselytizing later. The pious names (*laqab*) adopted by the early caliphs illustrate this attitude: al-Saffah ("the Slaughterer"), al-Mansur ("the Conqueror"), al-Muntasir ("the Victorious").

For Protestant Christians the moral sovereignty of the Bible posed no absolute bar to violence. They could point to Old Testament precedents, and the New Testament, too, opened the door to force. "Do not think that I have come to bring peace to the earth," warned Jesus. "I have not come to bring peace, but a sword.

For I have come to set a man against his father, and a daughter against her mother, and a daughter-in-law against her mother-in-law; and one's foes will be members of one's own household" *(Matthew 10.34–36).*

Most Christians do not read this passage as inciting conflict. It simply recognizes that commitment to the new faith can introduce dissension even within a family. But others noted that Jesus himself used violence on at least one occasion, described in all four gospels, when he encountered the money changers in the Temple: "Making a whip of cords, he drove all of them out of the temple ... [and] poured out the coins of the money changers and overturned their tables" (John 2.13–15). Moreover, the Gospel writers passed up the perfect opportunity to condemn all military activity—when crowds came to John the Baptist, asking what they needed to do in order to be saved. John replied not that soldiers needed to renounce the army but only that they should "not extort money from anyone by threats or false accusation, and be satisfied with [their] wages" (Luke 3.14).

Stories like this may not have been on everyone's mind in the 16th and early 17th centuries. Yet wars raged widely (see Map 12.6). The brief but bloody Peasants' Revolt in Germany in 1525 served as a kind of prologue to the other conflicts of the age, since it involved the four chief elements—religious conflict, economic conflict, social conflict, political conflict—characteristic of the era. The blows to Christian unity quickly reached France, but in England the adoption of Protestantism in fact signaled the end of a long civil war and the start of a new golden age. It took the Thirty Years' War in Germany, however, to embroil all of Europe.

THE PEACE OF AUGSBURG AND THE EDICT OF NANTES

The Protestant movement was only eight years old when the Peasants' Revolt erupted, but it had already progressed far enough to shred permanently any sense of Christian unity. Encouraged by Luther's open approval, the Protestant nobles responded in force and crushed the rebellion. The experience sharpened more antagonisms than it resolved, however, and set the stage for the coming battle with the emperor Charles V. The Catholic nobles in southern Germany—none of whom had stood up to support the peasants—feared the aroused might of their Protestant peers and looked to Charles to restore order.

But while they hoped for Protestantism's defeat, the Catholic princes were chary of Charles's ending up with more power in Germany as a result. When Charles finally began military action in the 1540s, support from the Catholic princes was at best occasional and at worst verged on treason. For this reason, the war quickly degraded into an inconclusive series of advances and defeats. Finally, when it appeared certain that neither side could gain a clear victory, Charles and

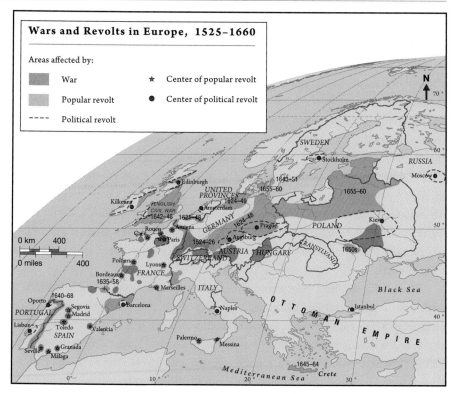

MAP 12.6   **Wars and Revolts in Europe, 1525–1660**

the Lutheran princes agreed to a compromise settlement. Known as the **Peace of Augsburg** (1555), it granted Lutheranism legal recognition and established *cuius regio, eius religio*, already encountered in chapter 11. With this policy, the religion of the local ruler determined the state religion of the principality, with certain guarantees offered to the rights of the religious minority.

Any hopes that the Augsburg compromise might serve as a model for other countries failed the first test, and in 1562 France became embroiled in a religiously charged civil war that raged for over three decades. The problem was that the Augsburg treaty had recognized the legal validity of Lutheranism but had not done so for Calvinism (since Calvin's version of Christianity had a negligible presence in Germany). And Calvin, who now lived across the Swiss border, in Geneva, longed to secure legitimacy for his followers back home.[10]

His chance came in 1562, when control of the French monarchy came up for grabs. The young King Francis II had died in 1560 after only one year on the throne, leaving his even younger brother, Charles IX (r. 1560–1574), to succeed

---

[10]   By 1562 nearly one-fifth of the French population was Calvinist—primarily in the southern and eastern parts of the realm.

him. The question of the regency—that is, of someone appointed to run the government on Charles's behalf until he came of age—exposed political rivalries and religious antagonism as well. Each of the two leading noble families had ties to royalty, but one was Catholic and the other Calvinist. The Catholic faction was led by the duke of Guise, while the prince of Condé and Henri de Navarre led the Calvinists—who were called **Huguenots** in France. The queen mother, Catherine de' Medici, formed yet another faction of her own. Although essentially a court conflict between aristocratic rivals, the war quickly engulfed the whole population. The leaders of each faction appealed to the masses and turned a dispute over the *roi et loi* ("king and law") into a fight over *foi* ("faith"). Mob violence determined the course of the war almost as much as the actual armies did, for Catholics and Calvinists everywhere attacked each other. They ransacked each other's churches and plundered each other's shops and households. Clergy on both sides urged the fight onward.

The war's grimmest episode was the **Saint Bartholomew's Day Massacre**, a week-long orgy of violence that began as an assassination plot and turned into a mass riot (August 23–29, 1572). The Huguenot leaders had come to Paris to celebrate the wedding of Henri de Navarre, the Huguenot leader, to Marguerite de Valois, the sister of French king, Charles IX (r. 1560–1574). The marriage was intended to ease relations between Catholics and Protestants by uniting their causes in the royal family, but Catherine de' Medici hoped to put a decisive end to the fighting by plotting their murder. The murders spurred mobs to action, and soon crowds in other cities had joined in. When the killing finally ended, thousands of Protestants lay dead, the victims of shooting, strangling, knifing, and drowning. In addition to Paris, massacres took place in Angers, Bordeaux, Bourges, Gaillac, La Charité, Lyons, Meaux, Orléans, Rouen, Saumur, Toulouse, and Troyes—all cities that had reverted to Catholic rule. The riots sparked Protestant fury, predictably, and the Huguenots redoubled their efforts to bring down the royal house, aided now by sympathetic Protestants from Germany and the Netherlands. Catholic Spain responded in turn by sending its troops into southern France. France's civil war threatened to engulf all of Latin Europe.

The whole miserable struggle ended when the next French king, Henri III (r. 1574–1589), was murdered at more or less the same time as the Huguenot leader, the Duke of Guise. Henri de Navarre, married to Princess Marguerite, acceded to the throne. Although the Protestant champion, he made the cool calculation that France, being 80 percent Catholic, had to have a Catholic king. "Paris is worth a Mass," he reportedly declared, then announced his conversion to Catholicism. It took several years to convince the Catholics of his earnestness and to mollify the disappointment of the Protestants. In the end,

No "Restored Harmony" Here   On August 23, 1572, a plot to assassinate leaders of the Huguenot faction in Paris—probably but not certainly instigated by Catherine de' Medici—inspired a terrifying wave of mob violence by thousands of the city's Catholics against their Protestant neighbors. Some estimates put the number of Protestants killed in the riot as high as thirty thousand. The original target of the assassination plot, Gaspard de Coligny, the military leader of the Huguenots, can be seen hanging out of a window to the right. (He was only wounded, but was subsequently executed.) Catherine de' Medici is at the far back, toward the left, emerging from the Louvre and examining a pile of Protestant corpses.

though, he won the support of both and began a long reign that is widely regarded as one of the high points of French history—as Henri IV (r. 1589–1610). In 1598 he promulgated the **Edict of Nantes**, which guaranteed religious freedom, under certain restrictions, throughout the realm. This edict, together with the Peace of Augsburg, established a legal right to believe as one wishes— but in both cases freedom of religion was technically imposed on the people by the king, rather than arising from a demand bubbling up from the populace. In other words, it was a power of the monarch to impose, not a right claimed by the people. For a brief spell the Continent had achieved peace, but it had not attained tolerance.

THE CHURCH OF ENGLAND

Meanwhile, a different sort of religious settlement had evolved in England. There a civil war known as the **War of the Roses** (1455–1485) had erupted soon after England's humiliating defeat in the Hundred Years' War (1337–1453), as various factions fought to shift the blame for England's loss and to win the throne.[11] The War of the Roses never involved large numbers of commoners, but it decimated the English nobility. When the war ended in 1485, a relatively minor aristocrat named Henry Tudor became king, largely by attrition. Ruling as Henry VII (r. 1485–1509), he understood that he could make no elaborate claims of distinguished lineage or heavenly favor—and he did not attempt to do so. He governed modestly and frugally, making sure not to upset the delicate truce. Henry was quick to recognize the potential of the New World discoveries, though, and he invested heavily in developing England's meager maritime capability.

When his son Henry VIII (r. 1509–1547) came to the throne, the kingdom had begun its climb to wealth and power on the international stage. Portraits of Henry VIII convey an aura of manly vitality and newfound wealth altogether absent from portraits of his cautious father. They differed not only in personality but royal self-regard. Henry VIII's portraits exude confidence, swagger, and more than a touch of the gaudiness of the nouveaux riches—for that is precisely what the Tudor monarch was becoming. His marriage in 1509 to Catherine of Aragon, the daughter of the king of Spain, was a corporate merger of the two leading Atlantic seaboard powers. It promised to secure England's new dominant position in Europe for generations to come.

But then came the matter of divorce. Catherine, a pious, loving woman but without a robust physique, had produced several sickly children, and only one—a daughter, Mary—had survived infancy. By 1525, after sixteen years of marriage, it seemed likely that Catherine would not produce the male heir Henry so desperately needed. He decided to divorce her. This move offended Rome (since the marriage had happened only by means of a special papal grant in the first place), the royal house of Spain (since their princess was being publicly humiliated), and the German emperor (since he was Catherine's nephew, and was already smarting from his losses to the Lutherans in his realm). After much dramatic though failed diplomacy, Henry decided in early 1533 to break with the Catholic Church and establish the **Church of England**, or Anglican Church. It was a Protestant church with the monarchy as its supreme head.

Henry famously had six wives before he died. The first had given him Mary, the second produced his only son, Edward, and the third gave birth to another daughter, Elizabeth. Wives four and five gave him nothing but misery, and number six brought genuine affection and comfort to his last years. In creating the Anglican Church, however, Henry did more than establish yet another form

---

[11]   The War of the Roses took its name from the white and red roses on the respective heraldic badges of the noble houses of York and Lancaster.

of Protestantism; he brought England directly into the turmoil raging across Europe. Another version of Christianity was arguably the last thing Western culture needed at the time. Worse, it set the two countries leading the exploration of the New World and the new international economy at odds with one another. England and Spain, briefly united in Henry's marriage to Catherine and on the brink of becoming a joint superpower, instead remained bitter rivals through the rest of the century. Henry's action did result in an enormous increase in royal income, though. He ordered the suppression of every Catholic monastery in the realm and seized all their holdings—which may have amounted to one-fifth of the real estate in England and Wales. The Tudors used this wealth, along with their New World riches, to buy support in both houses of Parliament.

At Henry's death in 1547, the throne passed to his son Edward VI (r. 1547–1553). Only ten at his accession, he never emerged from the shadow of the regency council established for him. The steps made to eradicate Catholicism were undone when Edward fell ill and died, and the throne passed, after some intrigue, to his elder half sister, Mary (r. 1553–1558). Mary, as the daughter of the scorned Catherine of Aragon, was resolutely Catholic and determined to restore Catholicism. Her reign has entered popular memory as a nightmare of religious violence, earning her the nickname of "Bloody Mary." In reality, she was quite popular at first, especially with the many Catholics who still remained in the kingdom. Even many Protestants sympathized with her after her father's break with Rome. But her decision to marry Felipe of Spain in 1554 changed matters and dispelled any hopes that a peaceful religious settlement might be reached. (In Germany, the Peace of Augsburg was still a year away.)

A wave of political purges and religious persecutions marred her last three years on the throne, with roughly three hundred Protestant leaders hunted down as enemies of the crown and killed. Their stories were told—with more love for melodramatic detail than for historical accuracy—by John Foxe in his *Book of Martyrs*, first published in 1563. (Its actual title was *Actes and Monuments of these Latter and Perillous Days, Touching Matters of the Church*). The work is enormous, longer even than the Bible. And for a while it had nearly as much authority over English Protestants; a decree in 1570 ordered that a copy of it be placed in every cathedral church in England.[12]

Mary died childless, and the crown passed to her half sister, Elizabeth I (r. 1558–1603), in whose reign England reached the apogee of international power and prestige. Commonly regarded as England's golden age, this was the era of

---

[12]   Until the start of the 19th century, the three most widely disseminated books in England and America were the Bible (Authorized Version), John Bunyan's *A Pilgrim's Progress*, and Foxe's *Book of Martyrs*.

the poet-playwrights Christopher Marlowe (1564–1593), William Shakespeare (1564–1616), the pirate-adventurers Sir Francis Drake (1540–1596) and Sir Walter Raleigh (1552–1618), and the composers William Byrd (1543–1623) and Thomas Campion (1567–1620). Elizabeth secured a religious settlement that established the Anglican Church as the official faith, with the monarch as its supreme leader. This compromise was a hybrid of Catholic ritual and Protestant theology, and it proved amenable to a majority of her subjects. She placed legal restrictions on Catholic holdouts, but she was even sterner with the more radical wings of the Protestant movement, such as the Puritans, who began to see the New World as more inviting.

"The Only Defense of the Christian Faith"
Engraving dated 1596 of England's Queen Elizabeth I (r. 1558–1603), showing her as erect and unyielding as the marble pillars on either side of her. She holds the usual signs of royal power (orb, scepter) but stands between two unusual other symbols: the falcon atop the left-hand pillar, feeding her young, and the falcon to the right, who rises as a phoenix. The inscription at the bottom (supplemented by a boilerplate poem beneath) lauds her as "the only defense of the Christian faith." The defeat of the Spanish Armada in 1588 had marked the highpoint of her popularity. Owing to economic troubles and a protracted war in Ireland, though, by the late 1590s she was losing control over her privy council and some of her popular regard with the masses, a slow slide that continued until her death. This image seems part of an effort to boost her public image.

Elizabeth increased England's involvement in the new Atlantic economy, which brought her into direct conflict with Spain. She promoted the piracy campaigns of Sir Francis Drake against the Spanish fleets returning from the New World, laden with gold and silver. She also underwrote further exploration of North America. Given the already tense relations between England and Spain, Elizabeth's actions were sure to cause further trouble—which came in 1588 when Felipe II (r. 1554–1598) sent his famous armada to invade England. After the smaller, lighter English fleet defeated these massive warships, England's involvement in the hornets' nest of Continental politics only became more intense.

Spain was also fighting at the time against the Netherlands, which had formed part of the Habsburg Empire. Smarting under Catholic rule, the staunchly Calvinist Dutch revolted against Felipe in 1566. They fought over religion, of course, but even more important was the money to be made in the New World. The Dutch resented having to send a portion of their earnings to Madrid, and they therefore sued for independence. England was happy to see Spain lose to the

Netherlands, and so gave the Dutch whatever overt and covert assistance they could afford.[13] The benefits proved obvious. With Spanish naval might curtailed, England established its East India Company in 1600. The Dutch founded their own East India Company in 1602, leaving them and England as the two most prominent European trading nations in the subcontinent. In North America, England built its first settlement in Virginia in 1607, and the Dutch colonized the southern portion of the island of Manhattan in 1612. Spain thus entered the 17th century in a state of severe economic decline.

THE THIRTY YEARS' WAR

These economic rivalries, political aspirations, and religious conflicts culminated in the last and bloodiest of the Wars of Religion: the **Thirty Years' War** (1618–1648), between Protestants and Catholics in Germany, drew in all of Europe. Like the other wars of the era, this conflict sprang from other motives than religious faith. Nor was the war inevitable, even though, with hindsight, it is easy to see it coming. Most of the European countries became involved in it, in one way or another. The war dragged on for so long in part because the Atlantic states profited from it: so long as the Germans remained mired in civil strife, they could not interfere with or compete against the English, Dutch, French, and Spanish who were busy plundering North and South America. All of the fighting took place in German territories, which makes sense given that the war was as much about Germany's constitutional problem as it was about religion (see Map 12.6).

Its effects were devastating: roughly one-fifth of the entire German population died. France and England both sent assistance to both sides of the conflict. When the Protestants were winning, they aided the Catholics; and when the Catholics were winning, they sent aid to the Protestants. The Dutch helped whichever side promised to help them keep their independence from Spain. Denmark entered the conflict with the aim of seizing northern German territory for itself. The king of Poland joined the fighting in order to defend the Catholic faith. He also claimed the throne of Sweden and hoped for papal and imperial recognition of his claim. The Swedes, for their part, fought to defend Protestantism—and to gain a military alliance with Orthodox Russia against Catholic Poland.

As with the Hundred Years' War between England and France, the significance of the Thirty Years' War lay in how it was fought rather than in the dreary narrative of which side won which battle in any given year. This was the first European-wide war. It was also the first war in which most of the fighting used modern

---

[13] The playwright Christopher Marlowe served briefly as a spy for Elizabeth in Holland.

weapons based on gunpowder. Armed commoners now formed the overwhelming bulk of the armies, marching in formation, with lines of muskets flanked by cumbersome but mobile artillery. Under the command of cavalry officers still drawn from the upper classes, the armies were larger than any that had taken the field before. At the first battle of Nördlingen in 1643, for example, close to 50,000 soldiers took part, and 10,000 lay dead on the field by battle's end. Only two years later a second battle was fought on the same site, with 30,000 soldiers entering the fray and only 20,000 coming out alive. Similar slaughter took place at Breitenfeld in 1631, at Lützen in 1632, at Breda in 1634, at Thionville in 1639, at Jankau in 1635, and at Lens in 1648. Corpses lay rotting by the thousands in fields all across central Europe.

Among the most vivid testimonies to the war's savagery is a remarkable novel by Hans Jakob Christoffel von Grimmelshausen (1621–1676). Kidnapped by Hessian soldiers when he was only ten, he was captured in battle and redrafted into military service by several armies until the war's end in 1648. His novel, *The Adventurous Simpleton,* appeared in 1668 and tells of a young simpleton who, like

Armies before Professionalization   The small northern French town of Aire-sur-la-Lys had the misfortune of being near Calais, England's vital port entrance into France, and hence always fought over. Between the Hundred Years' War (1337–1453) and the Thirty Years' War (1618–1648) it was besieged nearly a dozen times. This painting from the latter conflict shows the crude makeup of mass armies: no longer the aristocratic-led cavalry, and not yet the professionalized infantry of the Age of Absolutism.

von Grimmelshausen, witnesses horrors and is pressed into service. An early scene sets the tone:

> At first I did not intend to force you, gentle reader, to accompany these soldiers to my father's homestead, for I know what evil things are about to happen there; but the nature of my story requires me to leave some record of the brutal acts performed, time and again, by those involved in the war here in our Germany.... After stabling their horses, the soldiers all set about their appointed tasks, the sum of which was the utter ruin and desolation of our farm. Some began to slaughter all of our animals and set them stewing or roasting, so that it appeared as though they were preparing a jolly feast; but others ransacked our house from top to bottom.... Whatever they did not want to cart away they tore to pieces. A few started to thrust their swords into the haystacks and bales of straw, to find any hidden sheep or swine they could add to the slaughter.... Our maid Ursula, shame to tell, was dragged into the stable and so roughed up that afterwards she refused to come out. Then they took one of our hired workmen and stretched him out flat upon the ground, and, prying his mouth open with a bit of old wood, they dumped a slop bucket full of shit and piss down his throat. They called this a "Swedish cocktail."

After rounding up other farmers in the neighborhood, the soldiers began interrogating them.

> First they took the flints out of their pistols, jammed the farmers' thumbs into the opened space, and used the pistols as thumbscrews to torture them as they would witches. One poor fellow, even though he had confessed to no crime at all, they thrust into the oven, and lit it. They wrapped a rope around another fellow's head and twisted it with a piece of wood until blood gushed from his mouth, nose, and ears.... I cannot report much about what happened to the women, young girls, and maidservants of the district, for the soldiers prevented me from seeing it; but I remember hearing pitiful screams coming from each corner of our house. *(1.4)*

Much of the novel's horror comes from Grimmelshausen's identifying the soldiers simply as *soldiers*. He often does not differentiate between Bavarians, Saxons, Austrians, Thuringians, Swedes, Dutch, French, Spaniards, Danes, Poles, Lutherans, Calvinists, or Catholics. They are all simply soldiers, there are no meaningful

Title Page of *The Adventurous Simpleton* (1668)   The first great German-language novel. Its author, Hans Jakob Christoff von Grimmelshausen (1621–1676), like the novel's main character, was abducted as a child and pressed into service in several armies throughout the Thirty Years' War. Unlike the novel's hero, Grimmelshausen never flew to the moon or visited the center of the Earth.

sides to the conflict, and the war is its own repellent cause and justification. But the novel offers more than scenes of savagery. Simpleton runs away from the army and finds his way through a dizzying series of unpredictable adventures. He turns himself into a populist highwayman à la Robin Hood; he impersonates a woman; he takes the place in high society of an aristocrat; he becomes a con artist and a religious pilgrim; he explores a utopian society of mermaids and mermen who live at the bottom of a lake in the Black Forest. At turns hilarious and horrifying, the novel depicts a treacherous world without order. It is a chaotic quest not for a Holy Grail but for simple human decency and the tiniest bit of stability in life.

Grimmelshausen wrote several other novels, each a sequel to his first, usually narrated by a minor character from *Simpleton*. The series recalls Geoffrey Chaucer's *Canterbury Tales* in its shifting kaleidoscope of experiences and views. Though little read today, Simpleton is the greatest German novel before Goethe, and it has never been surpassed as a depiction of war as collective insanity.

WARS OF RELIGION: THE EASTERN FRONT

Christian Europe was not the only theater of conflict. Events in the Middle East, too, turned violent in the 16th and 17th centuries, thanks to a similarly toxic mixture of religious, economic, and ethnic enmity. Three large, multiethnic states dominated the Islamic world around 1500: the Ottoman Empire, the Mamluk Sultanate in Egypt and Syria, and Safavid Persia. Twenty years later only two remained, and they challenged each other for leadership of the Muslim world for the next two hundred years.

Turks and Persians, heading up the Sunnis and Shi'a, respectively, were the standard-bearers of Islam. Ethnic Arabs held decidedly second-class status in both societies, and efforts to alter their position failed before the military might of the dominant regimes. Bayezid II [T] (r. 1481–1512) and his son Selim I [T] (r. 1512–1520) were anxious to continue the policy of aggressive Ottoman expansion and drove the Turkish army northward into the Black Sea, westward into the Balkans, southward toward Egypt, and eastward toward Persia. Bayezid even constructed a large naval fleet that defeated the Venetians in 1503 and left the Turks in command of the eastern Mediterranean sea-lanes. Bayezid had a more peaceful side to his personality, though, and took particular delight in managing the palace schools (sometimes even volunteering to examine students personally) and in fostering trade.

Selim—whose nickname Yavuz ("the Inflexible") describes his personality— began his reign with a near paranoid fear of Persian designs on his realm and spent his first two years in power executing forty thousand suspected Safavid sympathizers in Anatolia. Non-Muslims fared better under these two than did non-Sunni Muslims. Nearly a quarter million Jews emigrated to the Ottoman realm after the European expulsions and settled in Anatolia and Palestine. Like many of their predecessors and courtiers, however, Bayezid and Selim practiced an eclectic form of Islam. It was formally Sunni but tinged with a passionate admiration for **Sufism**.

The Turkish affinity for Sufism may have had its roots in the shamanistic cults of pre-Islamic times. But whatever its origins, it frequently set the Turks at odds with the more staid Sunni and Arabic majority they governed. Urged on by heavyweight scholars like Ibn Taymiyya [K] (1263–1328) after the fall of the Persianized Abbasids, Arab leaders in the 14th century had again placed the 'ulama ("brotherhood," or "community") at the center of Sunni life. In this conservative view, the traditions of the Qur'an, **hadith**, and **sunnah** were paramount, and all forms of speculative theology and metaphysical innovation were denounced.

Ibn Taymiyya's career, together with those of his acolytes, can in fact be thought of as a small-scale Islamic analog to the Protestant Reformation:

- It demanded a strict return to the authority of early texts.
- It called for stripping away every aspect of religious life not specifically called for in those texts.
- It condemned as heretics all who disagreed with them or who used their ideas for other purposes.
- It was openly hostile to all forms of monastic life and to the cults of popular saints.
- It considered the earliest religious community (the Twelve Apostles for Luther, the Companions of the Prophet for Ibn Taymiyya) the most perfect in its observance of confessional life.

All of these traits were shared by the Sunni and Protestant reformers.[14] Ibn Taymiyya's party attacked Sufism as fundamentally un-Islamic, since it emphasized ecstatic union with God over strict observance of his laws. His immediate

---

[14]   In modern times Taymiyya inspired Muhammad ibn Abd al-Wahhab [A] (1703–1792), the founder of Wahhabism, the official doctrine of Saudi Arabia.

acolytes included Ibn Kathir [A] (1301–1372) and Ibn al-Qayyim al-Jawziyya [A] (1292–1350). Little had changed by the 15th century, except for the even deeper entrenchment of the conservative position.

THE WANING OF THE SULTANATE

The Ottoman economy peaked under Selim I's son and heir Suleiman I [T] (r. 1520–1566). Suleiman, the contemporary of Charles V in Europe, is known in Europe as "Suleiman the Magnificent." In the Muslim world, he is called "Suleiman the Lawgiver" in recognition of his work in codifying the great mass of legislation he inherited from his predecessors. He also made the imperial administration more efficient. He was a successful warrior as well, extending Ottoman power to Hungary.[15]

With the opening of the Atlantic trade, however, the Ottoman economy gradually slowed and stagnated. Population increase both fueled the initial growth and brought about the stagnation. When the economy was still expanding, immigration increased significantly. The arrival of the Jews formed only a part of this; a much greater factor was the influx of Muslims from Egypt and Syria and parts of Persia. Cities like Edirne, Trabzon, and Iznik grew by as much as 80 percent, while scores of others grew by 40 to 50 percent. Rural villages increased by 30 to 40 percent over the 16th century. Ultimately, overpopulation set in and was felt first in the countryside. Available farmland grew scarce, and local authorities responded by permitting the clearing of forests. Woodland, never abundant in much of the region, became even scarcer and contributed to a loss of commercial diversity. Adding to the trouble was the influx of gold and silver from the New World, which led to inflation. In 1580, for example, it took sixty silver Turkish coins to equal one gold ducat (then the international standard currency of account), but only ten years later it required 120. By 1640 it took 250. The price of basic commodities like wheat increased by a factor of twenty between 1500 and 1600.

As in Christian Europe, economic misery made religious and ethnic tensions worse. Popular resentment of ethnic and religious foreigners, especially of the relatively newcomer Sufis and Shi'a, increased. Street violence between factions forced local officials to take more direct and heavy-handed actions to keep the peace. But this required money. Over the 16th and 17th centuries, therefore, the power of the Ottoman sultanate waned. Provincial governors and urban or district commanders

---

15   Suleiman ultimately led his armies all the way to the gates of Vienna (which they failed to take).

Now It's Istanbul, Not Constantinople   A painting from 1537 showing a bird's-eye view of the now-Turkish capital of Istanbul. The picture still follows the medieval tradition of orienting maps with east at the top; a modern viewer needs to turn his or her head sideways to the left. The Hippodrome and the former Church of Hagia Sophia (now renamed the Ayasofya Mosque and renovated to include two minarets) are the two largest structures visible. Though subject to brutal pillage after its 1453 fall to the Ottomans, the city recovered quickly and became a welcoming refuge for Jews who fled the rising religious antagonisms of the 16th and 17th centuries.

first demanded the right to collect their own taxes and then used the revenue to finance their new political muscle.

The sultan's loss of fiscal and political power catalyzed the conservative trend in religion. **Madrasas** across the Ottoman state declared their opposition to any sort of speculative thought. Preachers condemned public morals for straying from the early 'ulama.[16] Even the natural sciences, which had been one of the glories of Islam in the medieval period, came under attack. When Murad III [T] (r. 1574–1595) had an astronomical observatory built in 1579, local preachers—mostly

---

[16]   Especially popular targets for preachers were the new enthusiasms for coffee and tobacco, brought over from the New World.

Arabs—condemned it as an offense against Allah to attempt to unravel the secrets of the act of creation and hired mobs to tear it down.

NEW CENTERS OF INTELLECTUAL LIFE

The creative centers of intellectual life thus moved from the Ottoman center to Egypt and Persia. Cairo emerged as the vital site for scientific work. It was also the home of Ibn Khaldun [A] (1132–1406), whose great *Muqaddimah* ("Introduction to History") posited a new philosophy of history, based on materialism—or the pursuit of worldly goods rather than spiritual ends. Safavid Persia, by contrast, became the center for metaphysics. Its great achievement was a philosophical program known as **illuminationism** (*al-hikmat al-ishraq*), starting with a learned Sufi named Shahab al-Din Suhrawardi [P] (1155–1191). Its central figures were al-Amili [P] (1546–1622), Mir Damad [P] (d. 1631), and especially Sadr ad-Din al-Shirazi [P] (1571–1636)—better known in the Islamic world by the name **Mulla Sadra**. The author of *Transcendental Wisdom*, he remains the most influential thinker in the Persian philosophical tradition down to the present. A key feature of illuminationist, or ishraqi, thought is its effort to harmonize Sufism, Shi'ism, and rational philosophy.

Illuminationism was in fact a common feature of Greater Western philosophical thinking of the age, although European and the Middle Eastern thinkers arrived at it by different trajectories. In western Europe it is expressed in the philosophies of Baruch Spinoza (1632–1677) and Gottlieb Leibniz (1646–1716). Spinoza, a heretical Jew excommunicated by his Amsterdam synagogue, was also a heretical illuminationist. He argued for a highly original form of pantheism that asserted that God was Nature Itself (*natura naturans*, in his posthumously published masterpiece—the *Ethics*) and that every facet of and occurrence in nature (*natura naturata*) is a necessary consequence of God's existence. But the identification of God and Nature should not elicit an attitude of wonderment and awe from human beings. To Spinoza, human life has no divinely ordained purpose and the occurrences of nature possess no supernatural meaning; they simply *are*. The rational study of nature leads to no spiritual revelation, only to a rational understanding of God's manifestation within nature—which, Spinoza insists, is illumination enough for anyone.

> To Spinoza, human life has no divinely ordained purpose and the occurrences of nature possess no supernatural meaning; they simply *are*.

Leibniz, by contrast, sees divine emanation everywhere. He rejects pantheism in favor of an idea to which he gave the awkward name of monadology; all forms of natural life are composed of fundamental units he calls monads, which contain within themselves all the qualities of the life-form they make up.

Spinoza   Baruch de Spinoza (1632–1677) was the greatest Jewish philosopher since Maimonides, although his ideas led to his receiving a writ of *herem*—a form of excommunication in Jewish law. The wording of the writ is striking. Its central portion reads as follows: "The leaders of this holy community, long familiar with the evil ideas and actions of Baruch de Spinoza, have tried repeatedly and by numerous stratagems to turn him from his evil ways; but we have failed to make him mend his wicked ways—in fact, we hear fresh reports every day about the abominable heresies he practices and teaches, and the monstrous deeds he continues to perform. . . . And [therefore] we have decided that the said Baruch de Spinoza should be excommunicated and expelled from the people of Israel. . . . [Wherefore], in accordance with the will of the Holy One (may He be ever blessed) and of this Holy Congregation, and in the presence of the holy scrolls of the Torah, with their 613 commandments, we hereby excommunicate, cast out, curse and damn Baruch de Spinoza with the same form of excommunication with which Joshua condemned Jericho, with the curse with which Elisha cursed the boys, and with all the curses which are written in the Book of the Law. Cursed be Baruch de Spinoza by day and cursed be he by night; cursed when he lies down and cursed when he rises up; cursed when he goes out and cursed when he comes in. The Lord will not spare him; His righteous anger and wrath will rage against this man, and bring upon him all the curses written in the Law. May the Lord blot out his name from under heaven, and condemn him to separation separate from all the tribes of Israel with all the curses of the covenant as they are contained the Law."

The concept is difficult to grasp—and Leibniz himself had difficulty in expressing it—but may be thought of, for organic matter at least, as something akin to a particular life-form's unique genetic code. God himself, says Leibniz, is not present in nature, as Spinoza would uneasily have it, but his intent is present in the system of monads. The study of nature does not bring us, therefore, into God's presence, but it does illuminate for us the workings of his mind.

In Persia, illuminationism derived from the attempt to harmonize Islamic doctrine with classical Greek thought and the mystical elements of Zoroastrianism, and hence to give Sufism a measure of intellectual respectability within the larger Muslim world. Elements of illuminationism date to the 12th century but the theory was given its fullest and most brilliant expression in the work of Mulla Sadra, the greatest Muslim philosopher of the modern era. Mulla Sadra's most important book, *The Four Journeys of the Intellect* (1638), maps out four stages in the route to spiritual and philosophical enlightenment. He dissects the cognitive processes that lead from the understanding of the physical world to a consideration of the essence of God and the nature of the relationship of humans to the Creator. Illumination is both a divine blessing and a technique of enlightenment, an aspect of spiritual discipline.

Sadra does not see God in creation like Spinoza; neither does he behold a divine intelligence in it like Leibniz. Rather, he sees a mystical unity in creation that parallels the unity of God himself and draws the enlightened believer into a stronger desire for spiritual ascent, a return to the Oneness at the heart of all things. Sadra thus pulls together and harmonizes Sufi mysticism, Aristotelian rationalism, and Neoplatonic emanationism.

> Philosophy is the process of perfecting the human soul by coming to a true understanding of things-as-they-are, which is achieved—when it is achieved at all—through rational demonstration rather than intuition or appeal to prior authority. By means of philosophy, we come to resemble our Creator, and this allows us to perceive and ascribe a rational order to His creation.

Most of Arab Islam adhered to a staid and increasingly conservative form of Sunni Islam, eschewing scientific and metaphysical innovation in favor of rigid tradition. As early as the late 14th century Ibn Khaldun had observed that most of the creative intellectual energy in the Islamic world came from non-Arabs. From the *Muqaddimah*:

> All the great grammarians have been Persian, . . . all the great legal scholars. . . . Only the Persians still write great books and dedicate themselves to preserving what is known. Thus, a saying attributed to the

Prophet himself rings true: "If Knowledge was suspended from the highest ceiling in heaven, the Persians alone would get it." ... All the intellectual arts, in fact, have long since been abandoned by the Arabs and become the sole preserve of the Persians.

The encouragement given to non-Arab Islamic and pre-Islamic traditions by the Ottomans thus stemmed from a sincere interest in promoting innovation and enquiry, but it also served a political purpose by providing a counterweight to the Arab-centric views holding sway from the Arab Peninsula through Palestine and Syria. It also provides another example of the interconnected nature of the cultural life of the Greater West.

THE OTTOMANS: FROM STRIFE TO WARFARE

Tensions between the Ottomans, their Sunni Arab base, and the Shi'i Safavids grew increasingly bitter. The Ottomans' economic stagnation worsened, while Safavid Persia not only carved out its own Islamic identity, but challenged the very notion that the center of Muslim civilization lay with the Arabs and Turks. The pulse of vital Islamic life, Persians insisted, had moved permanently eastward to Iran. The Persian **shah** (emperor) Ismail (r. 1501–1524), who believed himself divine, ordered the immediate conversion of all Sunnis in Iran to Shi'ism on penalty of death. And he made good on the threat by executing tens of thousands, confiscating their homes and goods, closing their mosques, and absconding with the funds for their schools. He also urged the Turkish people to overthrow the Ottomans. As a colorful warning to the Ottoman ruler (Bayezid II), Ismail had another political rival killed, had the skin removed from his corpse and ordered it stitched around a life-size straw figure of the man, and sent it to Istanbul.[17]

Predictably, wars broke out between the two states (see Map 12.7) and continued through the reign of Ismail's son Tahmasp I [P] (r. 1524–1576). Religious hatred intensified with each new reign. Ismail II (r. 1576–1578) played a role in Persia analogous to that of England's Mary Tudor. He tried to force the realm to reconvert to Sunni Islam, but the purges and persecutions he ordered became so bloody that his closest supporters poisoned him after only two years on the throne. Occasional persecutions of Iran's Jewish and Christian communities broke out in the 16th century, but in the 17th religious relations improved significantly. In general, as the Shi'a became more firmly established and were less involved in strife with Sunni holdouts, they eased up on oppression of Jews and Christians. Moreover, many Jewish immigrants from further west earned the shah's gratitude by

[17] Ismail kept his rival's skull—gold-plated and encrusted with jewels—and used it as a drinking cup.

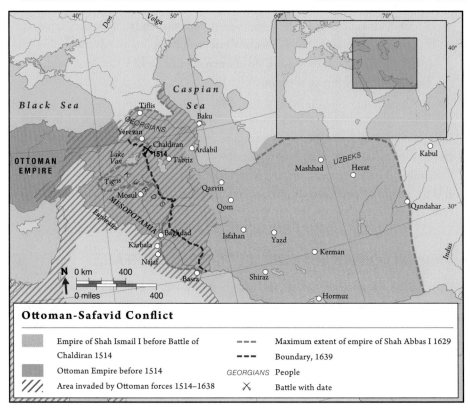

MAP 12.7   Ottoman-Safavid Conflict

introducing him to gunpowder and the casting of heavy artillery. The desire by rulers like Abbas the Great [P] (r. 1588–1629) to increase Iran's export of silk textiles and Persian rugs also opened the way for Armenian Christians, long expert in the crafts, to thrive under Safavid rule.

Ottoman relations with the west remained uneasy, especially with Habsburg Austria and Venice, their neighboring rivals for control of trade routes. The absence of a natural boundary between the Turkish and the Austrian realms kept mutual concerns for safety at a high level. And with the relative decline of Mediterranean trade relative to the Atlantic, control of the sea-lanes in and out of the Levant became all the more important. At the Battle of Lepanto in 1571 an alliance of naval forces led by Venice and King Felipe II of Spain defeated the Turkish fleet and decimated its corps of experienced officers. The so-called Long War (1593–1606) against Austria highlighted the need to modernize the Ottoman army with gunpowder weaponry, but resistance to Western technology among the Arab populace made this an unpopular development.

TABLE 12.1   **Sultanate of Women**

NAME	YEARS IN POWER	MOTHER OF	WIFE OF	ETHNICITY
Ayşe Hafsa	1520–1534	Selim I	Suleiman I	Tatar
Nur-Banu	1574–1483	Selim II	Murad III	Venetian
Safiye	1594–1603	Murad III	Mehmed III	Venetian
Hatice	1617–1621	Ahmed I	Osman II	Serb
Kösem	1623–1648	Ahmed I	Murad IV and Ibrahim I	Greek
Turhan Hatice	1648–1683	Ibrahim I	Mehmed IV	Ukrainian

Just as unpopular and destabilizing was the repeated phenomenon of women running the imperial government. The era of the 16th and 17th centuries in general—but especially the period of the 1640s and 1650s—is referred to as the **Sultanate of Women** (*kadınlar saltanatı* in Turkish; see Table 12.1). During the reigns of several weak-minded rulers, such as Ibrahim I (r. 1640–1648), and several minorities, such as that under Mehmed IV (r. 1648–1687), the leading members of the imperial harem effectively controlled the government. Taking the title of "queen mother" (*valide sultan* in Turkish), these women ran the state, directed foreign policy, and oversaw the fiscal system. What made matters worse, from the point of view of their disgruntled, mainly Arab, subjects, was the fact that most of these women were non-Muslim by birth and their embrace of Islam was therefore suspect. (The Ottomans made a point of marrying as many Christian-born wives as possible, as a nod to their Christian subjects.) In the 16th century the most prominent sultanas were Nur-Banu and Safiya, who either ran or helped to run the Ottoman state in the years 1574–1583 and 1595–1603, respectively. Both of Venetian descent, they restored relations with Venice after the battle of Lepanto and strengthened commercial ties between their empires. Two figures who especially stood out in the 17th century were Kösem, the Greek-born mother of Ibrahim, and her Turkish daughter-in-law Turhan Hatice, whose rivalry was as much personal as political and ended with Kösem's assassination in 1651.

The 16th and 17th centuries, in sum, were not necessarily more religious or more filled with religious hatred than earlier periods in Christian or Islamic history. However, religion became enmeshed in economic and ethnic rivalries of an unusually large scale. Money and the ties of blood intensified religious antagonisms until they reached a degree of fanaticism unlike anything that had existed before, with the possible exception of the medieval crusades. Such antagonisms would not reach this fever pitch again until the 20th century.

WHO, WHAT, WHERE

Ashkenazic	Mulla Sadra
Church of England	Peace of Augsburg
conquistadores	Saint Bartholomew's Day Massacre
Edict of Nantes	Sephardic
enclosure movement	shah
ghettos	Sufism
hadith	Sultanate of Women
Huguenots	sunnah
illuminationism	Thirty Years' War
Kabbala	'ulama
Madrasa	War of the Roses

SUGGESTED READINGS

Primary Sources

Diaz, Bernal. *The Conquest of New Spain.*

Grimmelshausen, Hans Jakob Christoffel von. *The Adventurous Simpleton.*

Las Casas, Bartolomé de. *A Short Account of the Destruction of the Indies.*

Montaigne, Michel de. *Essays.*

Mulla Sadra. *The Four Journeys of the Intellect.*

Anthologies

Diefendorf, Barbara B. *The Saint Bartholomew's Day Massacre: A Brief History with Documents* (2008).

Kors, Alan Charles, and Edward Peters, eds. *Witchcraft in Europe, 400–1700: A Documentary History* (2000).

Pryor, Felix, comp. *Elizabeth I: Her Life in Letters* (2003).

Symcox, Geoffrey, and Blair Sullivan. *Christopher Columbus and the Enterprise of the Indies: A Brief History with Documents* (2005).

Studies

Buisseret, David. *The Mapmaker's Quest: Depicting New Worlds in Renaissance Europe* (2003).

Bonney, Richard. *The Thirty Years' War, 1618–1648* (2002).

Briggs, Robin. *Witches and Neighbors: The Social and Cultural Context of European Witchcraft* (1996).

Clark, Stuart. *Thinking with Demons: The Idea of Witchcraft in Early Modern Europe* (1999).

Dale, Stephen F. *The Muslim Empires of the Ottomans, Safavids, and Mughals* (2010).

Diefendorf, Barbara B. *Beneath the Cross: Catholics and Huguenots in Sixteenth-Century Paris* (1991).

Dursteler, Eric R. *Renegade Women: Gender, Identity, and Boundaries in the Early Modern Mediterranean* (2011).

Fairchilds, Cissie. *Women in Early Modern Europe, 1500–1700* (2007).

Fritze, Ronald. *New Worlds: The Great Voyages of Discovery, 1400–1600* (2005).

Greyerz, Kaspar von. *Religion and Culture in Early Modern Europe, 1500–1800* (2007).

Hartz, Glenn. *Leibniz's Final System: Monads, Matter, and Animals* (2006).

Holt, Mack P. *The French Wars of Religion, 1562–1629* (2005).

Israel, Jonathan I. *European Jewry in the Age of Mercantilism, 1550–1750* (1989).

Kamen, Henry. *Spain, 1469–1714: A Society of Conflict* (2005).

Kaplan, Benjamin J. *Divided by Faith: Religious Conflict and the Practice of Toleration in Early Modern Europe* (2007).

Kleinschmidt, Harald. *Charles V: The World Emperor* (2004).

MacHardy, Karin. *War, Religion, and Court Patronage in Habsburg Austria: The Social and Cultural Dimensions of Political Interaction, 1521–1622* (2003).

Moris, Zailan. *Revelation, Intellectual Intuition, and Reason in the Philosophy of Mulla Sadra: An Analysis of the Al-Hikmah Al-'Arshiyyah* (2003).

Nadler, Steven. *Spinoza's "Ethics": An Introduction* (2006).

———. *Spinoza's Heresy: Immortality and the Jewish Mind* (2002).

Newman, Andrew J. *Safavid Iran: Rebirth of a Persian Empire* (2008).

O'Malley, John W. *Trent and All That: Renaming Catholicism in the Early Modern Era* (2000).

Parrott, David. *Richelieu's Army: War, Government, and Society in France, 1624–1642* (2001).

Peirce, Leslie. *Morality Tales: Law and Gender in the Ottoman Court of Aintab* (2003).

Pursell, Brennan C. *The Winter King: Frederick V of the Palatinate and the Coming of the Thirty Years' War* (2003).

Thomas, Hugh. *Rivers of Gold: The Rise of the Spanish Empire* (2004).

Wiesner-Hanks, Merry E. *Early Modern Europe, 1450–1789* (2006).

Wilson, Peter H. *The Thirty Years War: Europe's Tragedy* (2009).

For additional resources, including maps, primary sources, visuals, web links, and quizzes, please go to **www.oup.com/us/backman.**

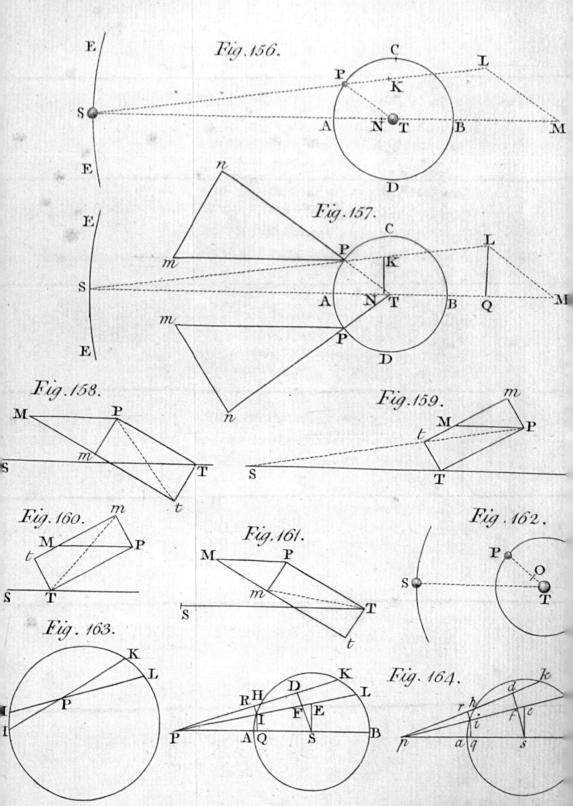

Fig. 156.

Fig. 157.

Fig. 158.

Fig. 159.

Fig. 160.

Fig. 161.

Fig. 162.

Fig. 163.

Fig. 164.

CHAPTER 13

Science Breaks Out and Breaks Through

1500–1700

In the 13th century a Franciscan scholar from England named Roger Bacon (1214–1294) gleefully tore into everyone around him who thought of themselves as scientists. He could, and did, find fault in anyone. Phrases like "damned fools," "ignorant asses," "inept buffoons," and "miserable idiots" pepper his writings in his own colorful Latin. Science, he argued, had been for too long a prisoner to philosophers who never thought to test their abstractions against the evidence of their senses. When a renowned figure like Albertus Magnus (1206–1280) came to lecture at the University of Paris and was received "like a second Aristotle," Bacon reacted bitterly: "Never before in the history of the world has there been committed a[n intellectual] crime as perverse as this."

Ironically, Bacon's assault on scientists marked the beginning of what we call today the Scientific Revolution. Bacon did not oppose grand theories in themselves. Rather, he believed that the only valid way to reach them was through observation. "Experimental science is the Queen of All Sciences, the goal of all

THE GREATER WEST, ca. 1700

◀ **The Geometry of Gravity** Sir Isaac Newton's *Principia* (1687) was the closest thing the world had yet seen to a scientific Theory of Everything and dominated the field of physics until the start of the 20th century. This plate from the original edition illustrates some of Newton's theorems visually. The top image (Figure 156), for example, illustrates his thoughts on the gravitational interaction of three bodies: a central and fixed star, represented by the letter T, and two planets in orbit around it, P and S.

our speculation," he wrote in his *Opus Maius* ("Large Study"). But even that was not sufficient. One had to master all the sciences—including mathematics, optics, astronomy, botany, and physics—before one could even begin to theorize about any one of them. Bacon spent many years achieving just that mastery, as well as learning Greek and Hebrew (and possibly a smattering of Arabic), in order to reach the grand synthesis that he believed only he could achieve. In the end, however, struggles within the Franciscan order forced Bacon into house arrest and silence; he never had the chance to elaborate his grand Theory of Everything.

In the 17th century Sir Francis Bacon (1561–1626) earned fame for his brilliance in law and philosophy, and he cultivated friendships among England's most wealthy and privileged people. Bacon (of no known relation to his medieval namesake) could, and did, flatter anyone. Bacon spent his last five years on the philosophical work that had always fascinated him. He planned a massive, comprehensive work to be called the *Great Instauration*—meaning the great refounding of the entire Western intellectual tradition—but completed only a handful of discrete books that were to form parts of the whole. His *Novum Organum* ("New Instrument") in 1620 reworked Aristotelian logic, while *The New Atlantis* in 1627 was a utopian fantasy. He envisioned, like Roger Bacon had several centuries earlier, a grand masterwork, a complete synthesis of human intellectual understanding. His focus, however, was on the process of analysis rather than on the gathering of data or the testing of hypotheses. Given facts A and B, what conclusions or assumptions can we validly draw from them—and how can we distinguish the valid from the invalid?

Both Bacons addressed the same problem, although from different angles: what are the intrinsic flaws in human thinking? What errors stand between us and Truth, and how can we overcome them? The world overwhelms us with data, impressions, facts, and observations, and our history overwhelms us with ideas, theories, opinions, and conjectures. We need a clear guide to dealing with all this input. How can we know that we are thinking properly?

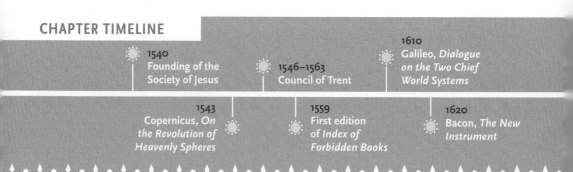

CHAPTER TIMELINE

1540
Founding of the
Society of Jesus

1546–1563
Council of Trent

1610
Galileo, *Dialogue
on the Two Chief
World Systems*

1543
Copernicus, *On
the Revolution of
Heavenly Spheres*

1559
First edition
of *Index of
Forbidden Books*

1620
Bacon, *The New
Instrument*

The **Scientific Revolution** of the 16th and 17th centuries was not a rejection of tradition, unlike Renaissance humanism, but a new phase in its development. The astonishing discoveries of the age placed science at the center of intellectual life in a way that was unique to the West. Fields like mathematics, medicine, and astronomy had always played important roles in intellectual culture. Plato's Academy, remember, expected everyone to master geometry before beginning philosophical study. However, in the 16th and 17th centuries they did more than place the sun at the center of the solar system, discover the universal law of gravitation, and defy the Inquisition and the Islamic retreat from science. They also came to define intellectual life and establish the standards by which it developed and was judged. The story from Bacon to Bacon helps to explain why.

THE COPERNICAN DRAMA

Science interested few people during the Renaissance; at best it formed a minor hobby for some. Like the classical Romans they emulated, Renaissance thinkers showed a keen interest in applied technology but spent little time on pure science. One partial exception was the great artist Leonardo da Vinci (1452–1519), whose curiosity about the natural world and eye for observation inspired him to make intricate drawings of human anatomy, various forms of plant and animal life, and types of machines. He even performed a few human dissections, on the sly. But while such work reflected a strong intuitive grasp of how things in the material world function, they are still not science—which may be one reason why Leonardo left these studies to private journals and notebooks. The only other Renaissance figure who may qualify as a scientist was the Swiss physician Philip von Hohenheim, better known by his nickname of Paracelsus (1493–1541). His understanding and practice of medicine was thoroughly medieval, although he did some pioneering experimentation with various chemicals and minerals in the treatment

1637
Decartes, *Discourse
on Method*

1687
Newton, *Principia
Mathematica*

1660
Royal Society
Founded (London)

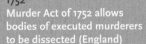
1752
Murder Act of 1752 allows
bodies of executed murderers
to be dissected (England)

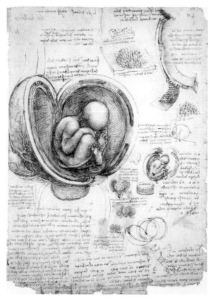

Drawing of a Fetus in a Womb   Leonardo da Vinci (1452–1519) performed as many as three dozen human dissections in his lifetime (he also dissected several cows and monkeys), which gave him unparalleled knowledge of the body. He prepared over two hundred detailed drawings for publication as a book on anatomy. As shown in this drawing of a fetus, he also wrote extensive notes. The book, *A Treatise on Painting*, was never published in his lifetime. This image also shows da Vinci's use of "mirror writing," which he used not for any secret purpose but simply because he was left-handed and found it easier to write this way without smudging the page.

of disease. His most significant discovery was the development of laudanum—a tincture of opium dissolved in alcohol that was used to treat a host of maladies until the early 20th century. Paracelsus is otherwise remembered primarily for the popular legends that arose around his involvement in alchemy.

The revival of pure science began with developments in astronomy. The revival sprang from a new model by Nicolaus Copernicus (1473–1543) of the motion of the planets, confirmed by careful calculations by Tycho Brahe (1546–1601) and Johannes Kepler (1571–1630). And it led Galileo to a direct confrontation between science and the church. Cosmology had formed a key component of Western science and philosophy from the beginning, going back to the ancient Greeks. The geocentric model handed down for two thousand years posited a static earth at the center of the universe, with the sun and other "moveable stars" (the planets) swirling about it in perfect circular orbits. The unmoving "fixed stars" comprised bright points on the ceiling of Creation. The universe was thus a single, finite, enclosed entity with mankind—Nature's masterpiece—at its center. Christians, to the extent they thought about such things at all, saw no reason to challenge the geocentric model, and indeed felt that it contributed to the Christian view of Man as God's supreme creation. Science was religion's handmaiden. God created the universe, in fact, in order to provide humans with a home. To study the workings of the natural world, therefore, was to most Christians a way of praising God and strengthening faith by deepening our appreciation of God's Creation. Throughout the Middle Ages in fact the church was the primary institution, and often the only one, promoting the study of science. When Western science revived in the 16th century, it did so once again hand in hand with Christian faith. It is a modern conceit that science advanced only when it divorced itself from religion; that divorce became finalized only in the 19th century. The Scientific Revolution therefore needs to be understood as an offshoot of religious history.

Flaws in the geocentric model were evident from the start. Even to the naked eye, the movement of the planets across the night sky was irregular: the transit of Venus (a mini-eclipse caused when Venus passes between Earth and the sun) was just one such irregularity. If the planets all move in ever-widening perfect concentric circles around a stationary Earth, how could the orbits of Venus and the sun intersect in this way? Over the centuries astronomers had come up with scores of intricate arguments to explain away the inconsistencies of the geocentric model, but with each new refinement the system seemed less and less viable.

Sometime around 1510 the German-Polish astronomer Nicolaus Copernicus (Mikołaj Kopernik in Polish) began to develop a different model that resolved many of the irregularities. This **heliocentric** model posited that the sun was the fixed center, and Earth was one of the planets in orbit around it. By 1514 he had begun to circulate his findings among a handful of friends. They spent years gathering more precise observational data, and Copernicus continued to refine his hypothesis. His book, *On the Movements of the Heavenly Bodies*, was not published until 1543, the year of his death.

When Western science revived in the 16th century, it did so once again hand-in-hand with Christian faith. It is a modern conceit that science advanced only when it divorced itself from religion; that divorce became finalized only in the 19th century. The Scientific Revolution therefore needs to be understood as an offshoot of religious history.

Copernicus had feared the book would set off a firestorm within the Catholic Church, but it did not. As early as 1536 a scientifically inclined cardinal, Nikolaus von Schönberg, had already written to him, encouraging his work:

> It was several years ago that I first heard of your skills, about which so many people were constantly speaking, and first developed such high regard for you. . . . What I learned was that you had not only mastered the knowledge of the ancient astronomers but had in fact created an entirely new cosmology according to which the Earth moves [in orbit] while the sun actually holds the most fundamental or central place in the universe. . . . At the risk of intruding upon your activities I want to urge you, with the utmost seriousness, to make these discoveries of yours known to scholars, and please to send me (as soon as is feasible) your writings on the workings of the universe, together with your data tables and anything else you may have that pertains to this important matter.

More criticism came from Protestant leaders, for whom the explicit teachings of Scripture carried more weight. Luther himself is often said to have condemned "that damned fool Copernicus" for challenging the authority of Scripture. (In reality, there is little evidence that Luther was fully aware of Copernicus's work.) Church condemnation did come, but not until some six decades later when the debate had shifted to Galileo's elaborations of the heliocentric theory and his claims for the scientific process that propounded it.

Copernicus had prepared for some resistance. In the preface to his book, he directly addressed the reigning pope, Paul III (r. 1534–1549). His book, he said, offered a simple hypothesis, an explanation of planetary movements that accommodated the available data far better than any permutation of the geocentric model. He closed with a dignified appeal to the church's concern for scholarly truth:

> I have no doubt that our most skilled and talented mathematicians will concur with my findings, so long as they are willing to investigate, with all the honest seriousness that scholarship requires, the arguments I have set forth in this book in support of my theories. But still, in order that everyone, both the learned and the nonlearned, may see that I hide from no man's judgment, I have decided to dedicate these findings of mine to Your Holiness, rather than to another, for even in this remote part of the world where I reside Your Holiness is regarded as preeminent in dignity for the position you hold, for your love of learning, and even for your interest in mathematics. . . . And if there should be any amateurs who (not letting their ignorance of mathematics stand in the way of a chance to pass judgment on such matters) presume to attack my theory because it contradicts some passage of Scripture that they misinterpret for their own purposes, I simply do not care; in fact, I dismiss their opinions as mere foolishness. . . . Mathematics is written for mathematicians. . . . I leave it to Your Holiness and all learned mathematicians to judge what I have written.

He defends his method more than his conclusions. What follows, in other words, is a set of mathematical proofs subject only to the critical review of mathematicians. He makes no theological or even astronomical claims, but argues only that his model conforms to the available data more precisely than earlier models.

Word of Copernicus's work spread quickly around Europe, and a number of scholars elaborated on the heliocentric theory. The Danish astronomer Tycho Brahe, for example, devoted his career to making ever more precise chartings of planetary movements and stellar positions. This improved data made possible the next major leap in astronomy, when Brahe's German pupil Johannes Kepler formulated three famous axioms of planetary motion. These axioms hold that the planets move in ellipses around the sun, that they move at nonuniform speeds, and that the

Nicolaus Copernicus A portrait of Mikołaj Kopernik (Nicolaus Copernicus; 1473–1543) emphasizing his Catholic piety, and a page from his book *On the Revolution of the Heavenly Spheres*, which he published just before his death.

velocity of each planet throughout its orbit is in direct proportion to its distance from the sun at any given moment. Kepler had fought a childhood battle with smallpox that had left him very nearsighted. Unable to gather his own observational data, he used the mountain of astronomical tables and star charts left behind by his teacher. With these, he validated his model with a mathematical precision that few of his contemporaries could equal or even understand. Even Galileo initially ignored it.

GALILEO AND THE TRUTH OF NUMBERS

Galileo Galilei (1564–1642) was a genius in astronomy, mathematics, and physics, as famous in his day as Albert Einstein was in the 20th century. His achievements in any one of those fields alone would warrant his being remembered.[1] Trained in mathematics, which he later taught at the University of Padua, he learned astronomy largely on his own and with the use of his telescope. In *The Starry Messenger,* the first report of his astronomical discoveries in March 1610, he describes the most significant of his discoveries: the moons of Venus. The force of this discovery is often difficult for modern readers to appreciate. The geocentric model made no allowance for smaller bodies in orbit around the planets. Everything, in the classical view, orbited the Earth. Yet here was direct evidence against it.

---

[1]   Galileo was a skilled tinkerer too, renowned for his redesign of the telescope (invented by Hans Lippershey, of the Netherlands) and of the geometric compass (used by surveyors and artillerymen).

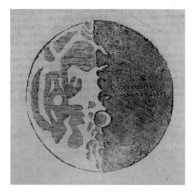

Galileo's Drawing of the Surface of the Moon Galileo Galilei (1564–1642) developed but did not invent the telescope. He was not even the first to write about its uses for astronomy. By the time he published *The Starry Messenger* (1610), in which this sketch of the lunar surface appears, a Jesuit missionary in Beijing had already published a book about the telescope—in Chinese—for Wanli (r. 1572–1620), one of the last of the Ming Dynasty emperors. But Galileo did build the best of the early telescopes, and with it he made the then-astonishing discovery that the moon's surface was rough and pockmarked, as shown above.

The elaborate mathematical arguments of Copernicus and Kepler were easily ignored. By the astronomers' own admission, they were nothing more than conjectures, a way to make the numbers fall into neater computational alignment. Few people then alive even understood them. But Galileo's discovery was as solid and incontrovertible as the New World continents that Cristoforo Colombo had run into in 1492. Anyone with a telescope (and Galileo himself sold them, as a business venture, on the side) could look up in the sky and see Venus's moons for themselves. Galileo's findings were confirmed by none other than Christoph Clavius, the most prominent expert in mathematics and astronomy in the church, and the city of Rome gave Galileo a triumphant welcome in 1611.

Yet years later he was arrested and forced to recant. What had changed? Two factors principally, and Galileo shares in the blame for the first. In 1623 he published a treatise on comets in which he made a crucial mistake: he argued that comets were not physical objects but only optical illusions—tricks of refracted sunlight. Moreover, in putting forth this (wrong) hypothesis, he went out of his way (not unlike Roger Bacon) to insult astronomers who had asserted (correctly) that comets were in fact fiery solid bodies passing through the solar system far beyond the orbit of our moon. Several of those astronomers, however, were highly regarded clerics who taught at the church's college in Rome, and the papal court was in no mood to countenance such outright rudeness. Several years earlier, in 1616, the church had condemned the heliocentric model as contrary to Scripture, and Galileo was given a friendly warning to refrain from promoting or teaching Copernicanism. He complied, for the most part; but the offensive passages in his treatise on comets called for some sort of response.

If Galileo's first problem was scientific and political, his second concerned Scripture. What happens when scientific conclusions and Biblical statements are in conflict? In his letter to the Grand Duchess Christina, published in 1615, he argues that the Bible should be interpreted in a way that makes it compatible with the scientific finding. Here he invited a debate that Copernicus and Kepler had studiously avoided. They had presented heliocentrism as a mathematical theory only. Although aware that it contradicted Scripture, they offered no opinion about which form of truth was preferable. Galileo, however, brought the Copernican claims into direct open conflict with Scripture—and he made it clear that in his mind the Bible had to accommodate science, not vice versa.

That opinion, combined with his offensive mockery of the church's leading astronomers, turned the tide against him. Several clerics denounced him from the pulpit, and the scandal grew until Galileo was finally called before the Inquisition at Rome in 1632. Galileo's crime was not that he accepted the heliocentric theory; it was that he asserted it as incontrovertible truth. Science, Galileo held, was self-confirming. The Bible was not merely wrong, it was irrelevant. "The purpose of the Holy Spirit is to tell us how to get to Heaven," he wrote, "not to tell us how the heavens operate." And that is what brought on his condemnation.

> Galileo, however, brought the Copernican claims into direct open conflict with Scripture—and he made it clear that in his mind the Bible had to accommodate science, not vice versa.

Science and religion in the Greater West had always known tension, but the strain was proof of their close relationship. Apart from Jewish and Muslim scholars, every Western scientist of any note since the fall of the Roman Empire had been a sincere Christian, often at odds with the church but always identifying with it. And every Jewish and Muslim scientist had been a devout, if sometimes unorthodox, believer.[2] The first identifiable atheist—that is, one who expressly denies the existence of any deity whatsoever—in Greater Western history was not a scientist at all but a German seminary dropout. Matthias Knutzen (1646–1675) published three pamphlets in 1674 denying "God, any Authority from On High, and all sects and their ministers." All that is needed to live a moral life, he wrote, is "to harm no one, live honestly, and give each person his due."

Scripture, Galileo implied, allows room to maneuver; science, though, does not. The Church's position—and, to include the Protestants, the churches' position—was that two thousand years of tradition should not be overthrown because of some opaque mathematical formulas that relatively few people understood properly. The problem, essentially, was epistemological rather than theological: What exactly does it mean, "to *know* something"? At what point can mere humans justifiably declare that a given statement is universally true?

---

[2] Copernicus and Galileo were both devout Catholics, and Brahe and Kepler were pious Protestants.

THE OTHER SCIENTIFIC REVOLUTION: THE COUNCIL OF TRENT, 1546–1563

Epistemology, or the study of nature of knowledge itself, implies teaching, which brings us to how Christian society responded to the challenges of the era. The Protestant Reformation is only the most obvious of the problems it confronted. Just as significant were the growth of modern monarchies, the early stages of capitalism, the missionary challenge of the New World, and the development of the new science. But the period's difficulties can be, and often have been, overstated. Seen in terms of the actual changes it prompted, the early modern crisis paled in comparison with the Middle Ages, when the church reinvented itself from top to bottom in order to help Europe emerge from the post-Carolingian ruin. The Roman Catholic Church of 1100, say, was a radically different institution from what it had been in 900, whereas the church in 1700 remained essentially what it had been in 1500; if anything, it was even more conservatively so. The reputed dying words of Pope Paul IV (r. 1555–1559) provide an apt epilogue to the Renaissance-era papacy: "Of all the pontificates since the time of Saint Peter, mine has been the most lamentable. Oh, how I regret everything that has happened. Pray for me!"

And yet they overstate the case. The church in fact responded vigorously, and, perhaps surprisingly, that response did not exclude the growth of science. One might even call it the other scientific revolution.

———————— + ————————

Reform was certainly needed, and figures like Erasmus and More had spent their lives calling for it. Even the most worldly of Renaissance popes recognized that many of the faithful were put off by the church and its cumbersome institutions. The problem was how to find reforms that would please everybody. Through much of the 14th and 15th centuries, when the Holy See was a political football of the Italian nobility, a movement arose to strengthen the role of general councils in ecclesiastical governance. The popes, many of them more concerned with their personal fates than with the office they held, opposed this "conciliarism" vehemently, but the resulting deadlock only aggravated the problems that both sides were supposedly trying to confront. The success of Protestantism produced urgent calls for a general council; papal dithering only made the calls more insistent.[3] But then, surprisingly, the Protestant juggernaut stalled. By 1540 every state in Europe that would become Protestant had done so; no new national-scale conversions were won by any of the major Protestant branches.

---

[3]   Pope Leo X (r. 1513–1521) famously dismissed Martin Luther at first as "some drunken German who will repent once he sobers up."

Beginning with Pope Paul III (r. 1534–1549), the court in Rome finally took the lead in bringing on reform. He appointed a commission of high-ranking clerics to investigate church abuses, whose final report, published in 1536, laid bare scores of problems in the administration of the church, the actions of the episcopacies, and shortcomings in parish life. In 1537 he issued a bull condemning the enslavement of the indigenous peoples of the New World; in 1540 he confirmed the formation of the Jesuits, a teaching and missionary order; and in 1542 he authorized the creation of the Holy Office—the Roman Inquisition. Last, after securing guarantees that its proceedings would be subject to papal approval, he called for a full ecumenical council to study and propose solutions to the general reform of Catholic life (which has come to be known as the **Counter-Reformation**). This **Council of Trent**, which convened (with a few intermissions) from 1546 to 1563, was the most important assembly of its kind until the Second Vatican Council of 1963–1965.

Although the religious revolt in northern Europe was obviously its trigger, the Council of Trent was more than a response to Protestantism; efforts at reform had begun long before Luther appeared on the scene. Nevertheless, the council's initial actions offered no hint of compromise but rather highlighted the differences between what it regarded as Catholic truth and Protestant lies. If anything, they asserted the Catholic position with even more force than before. The problem confronting the church, they believed, was not with doctrine itself but with the ways in which doctrine was taught to the people. The changes most needed were therefore in leadership and organization.

After Paul III, Pope Julius III (r. 1550–1555) devoted himself to personal pleasure—in particular, his infatuation with an illiterate, fourteen-year-old street beggar named Innocenzo. Julius moved Innocenzo into the Vatican palace (and the papal bedroom), awarded him several wealthy benefices, appointed him the abbot of the monastery of Mont Saint-Michel, and made him a cardinal. But the popes

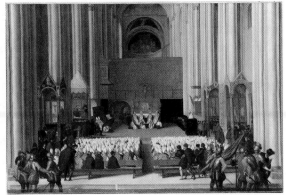

Catholic Reform   Pope Paul III (r. 1534–1549), in an oil portrait by Titian (Tiziano Vecellio; 1490–1576) and the high pomp of the Council of Trent (1545–1563), which laid out the plan for the Catholic Counter-Reformation.

who succeeded him pressed the council to reach even farther in its ambition: Paul IV (r. 1555–1559) and Pius IV (1559–1565).[4] The Council ordered a streamlining of the church bureaucracy, outlawed ecclesiastical pluralism (the practice of a single individual holding appointments to serve in multiple parishes of dioceses), and heightened the responsibility of bishops to oversee the life of their provinces. Most important of all, it charged them with improving the education of their clergy and of the flocks they served. To assist them, the church helped to build hundreds of new parish schools to train teachers for them. At the higher levels, the church increased the funding for universities and reorganized curricula.

THE SOCIETY OF JESUS

Several new ecclesiastical orders joined the campaign and dedicated themselves specifically to education: the Ursulines ("Company of Saint Ursula"), founded in 1535 and papally approved in 1544, created a network of schools for girls across Europe and soon in the New World. More famous still was the Society of Jesus, commonly called the **Jesuits**, found by Saint Ignacio de Loyola (1491–1556) in 1540. "A Society founded for a single, central purpose—namely, to strive for the defense and propagation of the Faith, and for the progress of souls in Christian life and doctrine," the Jesuits dedicated themselves to preaching and teaching at all educational levels, although historically they have tended toward higher education. Founded as they were by a former soldier—Loyola, a Spanish noble and career military man, experienced a conversion while recuperating from severe battle wounds received in 1521—the Jesuits formed a compact and highly centralized organization. They took vows of poverty, chastity, and absolute obedience to their superiors, especially to the pope, and became the church's most successful tool in bringing Christianity to the outside world.

Within ten years of their founding, the Jesuits had established mission schools in India and Japan, and by 1600 they had extended their reach into South and North America and into sub-Saharan Africa. And since the Council of Trent particularly emphasized the doctrinal point that for Catholics, unlike Protestants, doing "good works" was an essential requirement of Christian living, the reformed church stepped up its involvement in charitable work among the world's poorest peoples. The combined efforts of these new orders, especially in their conflation of schoolroom teaching and service, helped gain many converts in the New World. They even returned many Protestant believers in southern Germany, parts of Bohemia, and throughout Poland-Lithuania to Catholicism.

---

[4]   Julius is the last pope known to have been sexually active and the last pope to have been explicitly homosexual.

Education requires books, however, and education in the Catholic faith faced a further obstacle: non-Catholic books were easily available too. The post-Trent church confronted the problem—or thought they had done so—by producing an **Index of Forbidden Books**. The first version of the *Index,* promulgated in 1559, was regarded as too severe in its strictures, and a revised and slightly moderated version appeared in 1564. The *Index* was continually updated over the centuries, with over forty editions published between 1564 and its suppression in 1966, making it the longest institutionalized censorship in Western history. It was also, arguably, the least effective, since few of the condemned books ever went out of print. In fact, the *Index* represented a perfect shopping list for individuals who wanted to read materials

Jesuit Missionaries   The Jesuits were pivotal in revitalizing the Catholic Church's evangelical and educational missions. In this 18th-century painting from Lima, Peru, the order's founder, St. Ignatius Loyola, appears in the center, flanked by two loyal followers, St. Francis Borja and St. Francis Xavier. At the bottom, figures representing Africa, Asia, North America, and South America bear witness to the extent of Jesuit missionary activity.

officially denied them. True, 90 percent of the books ever placed on the list were dense theological treatises that non-Catholics or lay Catholics were unlikely ever to read in the first place. Even so, the 1564 *Index* singles out quite an impressive list of writers. It condemned the works of Pietro Aretino, Sir Francis Bacon, Jean Calvin, Nicolaus Copernicus, Desiderius Erasmus, Henry VIII of England, Martin Luther, Niccolò Machiavelli, François Rabelais, and William Tyndale (an early translator of the Bible into English). Also forbidden were the Qur'an and the Talmud. Later editions added the *Essays* of Michel de Montaigne and the scientific writings of Johannes Kepler and Galileo Galilei.

Jesuit training emphasized all-round education, so that society members would be prepared for any educational or missionary challenge the papacy might throw their way. Even today, the training of a Jesuit takes up to thirteen years. Though grounded in classical humanism, Jesuit education branched off into mathematics and astronomy. Several of the leading scholars of the age were Jesuits. Fr. Christoph Scheiner (1573–1650) was a German astronomer who discovered sunspots independently of Galileo; he also wrote one of the first treatises on the physiology of the human eye. Fr. Alexius Sylvius Polonus (1593–1653) was a Polish astronomer like Copernicus and specialized in the design of ever more refined telescopes. Although primarily an engineer, he nevertheless used his instruments, mastery of mathematics, and Copernican theory to compose a new work on the design of the solar calendar.

Another influential Jesuit, Fr. Carlo Borromeo (1538–1584), was no scholar but dedicated his career to promoting a better-educated clergy. Coming from a wealthy aristocratic family (his mother was a Medici), he used his personal fortune and the large income from his position as archbishop of Milan to found numerous colleges and seminaries. He also established the Academy of the Vatican Nights, an informal symposium to keep church leaders informed of the newest learning.

Most Jesuit astronomers accepted Galileo's work up through *The Starry Messenger*. Fr. Roberto Bellarmine (1542–1621) did, even after he was made a cardinal and placed in charge of the Inquisition. A theologian by training, Bellarmine first attracted attention as a professor at the Roman College, where, in addition to teaching priests-in-training, he wrote the four-volume *Disputation Regarding the Controversies in the Christian Faith* (1593), in which he systematically confronted the theological positions of the leading strains of Protestantism. The English and German governments in fact endowed several university professorships whose specific mission was to devise counterarguments against Bellarmine's book.

When Galileo's work was investigated by the tribunal in 1610, Bellarmine understood the science well enough to accept his discoveries—and arranged for the dropping of charges against him. He added a private warning not to proclaim Copernicanism publicly. Galileo followed the advice and pursued other research until 1623, when a cardinal who was friendly to him and supported his research—Maffeo Barberini, another Jesuit—was elected as Pope Urban VIII (r. 1623–1644). Galileo took this as a sign that the heliocentric theory was finally going to win public acceptance, and so he turned again from his work in physics to astronomy. By 1632 he had written his treatise *The Two Chief World Systems*, but he blundered. The new treatise was written in the form of a dialogue between geocentric and heliocentric astronomers, and even though Galileo was careful to make the heliocentrists capitulate at the end, he nevertheless made the old-style astronomers look foolish. Even worse, he named the spokesman for the traditionalists Simplicio ("Simpleton"). He should have known better. When Inquisitors petitioned to place Galileo on trial, an irritated Urban allowed them to proceed.

As Galileo learned, tone matters. The church had promoted scientific work for centuries and had a tradition of accepting ideas and discoveries not immediately reconcilable with doctrine. It understood that knowledge proceeds by probing, doubting, and testing. What matters is patience and humility. Galileo had sufficient patience but lacked modesty when it came to his work. Other Catholic scientists of the era presented new findings every bit as jarring to traditional sensibilities as

Galileo Galilei, by an Unknown Painter   To the right is a depiction of his trial by the Inquisition.

Galileo's, but presented them as discoveries in progress rather than indisputable truths. A German named Athanasius Kircher (1601–1680) was a pioneer of microbiology and linguistics.[5] An Italian physicist named Francesco Maria Grimaldi (1618–1663) made the first observations that led to the wave theory of light; he also compiled the first map of the lunar surface that described its geological features in detail. These men understood scientific research as a never-ending process, a slow groping toward truth, but one that can never declare final success. The infinite complexity of the universe precludes such hubris. But Galileo effectively altered the rules, or at least claimed that the rules were alterable and that pure truth—final and complete—was attainable. His revolutionary breakthrough was not heliocentrism in itself but the argument that the scientific method justifies itself, ratifies itself. Biblical authority and intellectual tradition mean nothing in the face of empirical data and rigorous mathematical logic. The separation of science from religion, in other words, was not a divorce. It was an annulment.

> Biblical authority and intellectual tradition mean nothing in the face of empirical data and rigorous mathematical logic. The separation of science from religion, in other words, was not a divorce. It was an annulment.

INQUISITION AND INQUIRY

Inquisition is a historical term, a word denoting a specific phenomenon of the past. One could even call it a technical term since it describes a precisely defined and regulated judicial process established by the Catholic Church in 1184. That process

---

[5]   Kircher was the first to describe microbes, and he correctly identified ancient Egyptian hieroglyphics with the Coptic language. He also wrote an entire encyclopedia of the Chinese language.

evolved over time, naturally, but even into the 19th century the word referred to a special type of investigation, conducted by ecclesiastical or secular authority, for the sake of public safety. To this extent, it is like the word "fascism"—a multifaceted but technically precise historical referent. But Inquisition, like fascism, is also a popular term, loosely used to describe almost any investigative process or institution that one deems profoundly unfair.

The Inquisition of the early modern era differed significantly from its medieval forebear. Pope Lucius III (r. 1181–1185) had established the Inquisition as a way of stopping the unjust execution of people for dissident religious beliefs. False beliefs within Christianity—heresy—was a sin against the church but was also a crime against the secular medieval state, and in the 12th and 13th centuries the aristocratic courts of Europe were quick to act against heretics—convicting them, killing them, and confiscating their property. The church took a dim view of heresy but championed the idea of intellectual free inquiry. Lucius's decree of 1184 helped to codify a strict, narrow definition of actionable heresy and brought state exercise of authority over heretics under the church's jurisdiction. As brutal and backward as the medieval Inquisition is to modern sensibilities, it is important to note that the number of people killed for dissident Christian beliefs across Europe declined sharply after the Inquisition's establishment.

Even so, ugly is ugly; and even without the use of physical torture (and most inquisitions never resorted to it) the threatening nature of the inquiry, its potential for unspeakable cruelty, was obvious and coercive. That ugliness grew, and the cruelty became a standard operating procedure, in the early modern era when the Inquisition was officially taken over as an institution of the governments. In the 16th and 17th centuries the monarchical states in France, Portugal, and Spain assumed control of it—as did the lesser princes in Germany, Italy, and the Low Countries—and used it to terrorize dissidents and control political opponents. Churchmen actively colluded in the process, certainly, but the notorious Inquisition of the time was as much an indicator of the loss of church power as it was an index of religious and intellectual intolerance.

Although some supported the idea, the Inquisition was not the weapon of choice for dealing with the Protestant Reformation. The Protestants, after all, declared their own separation from Rome and hence no longer came under the church's jurisdiction; later, the policy of *cuius regio, eius religio* granted a certain degree of toleration across the Catholic-Protestant divide. The Inquisition instead focused on three principal targets: witches, false converts from Judaism and Islam, and scientists. The witchcraft craze has been discussed. The issue of false converts was a complex one, arising from financial envy, racial prejudice, and unease about aristocratic stature. The conversion of nonbelievers to Christianity was a desire central to Christian aspirations since the dawn of the religion, but fanatical worries arose from the 15th century onward that many of Europe's converts were converts in name only—people who publicly proclaimed their Christianity but privately retained their Jewish or Muslim practice. Such suspects were referred to as crypto-Jews and crypto-Muslims.

The concern was not merely that they were religious frauds but that there was something intrinsic to their makeup. Some element in their collective blood-lines, it was feared, permanently tainted their Christianity and kept them from a genuine and full commitment. That would have been bad enough, for most of the bigots of the time; but what made matters even worse was the upward social mobility of the professional classes of the Renaissance and after. Noble families in economic decline often married wealthy, ambitious urbanites from the rising merchant economy. For them, the danger of exposing their pure noble blood to the inferior and possibly diseased elements in Jewish or Muslim blood set off a clamor of concern. Crypto-Jews and crypto-Muslims, in other words, were perceived as a threat to noble security and privilege as much as a threat to faith.

The last class of Inquisitorial victims, the proponents of the new science, are the most difficult to generalize about. Their names have become causes célèbres over the centuries. Giordano Bruno (1548–1600), a Dominican friar, mathematician, and cosmologist, provides the most dramatic example. Bruno had little training in science but much amateur enthusiasm for it. Seizing eagerly upon Copernican

Expulsion of the Moriscos from Spain   This painting by Pere Oromig depicts the expulsion of the Moriscos (suspected pseudo-converts from Islam) from the coastal town of Vinaròs, in eastern Spain, in 1609. Moriscos comprised nearly one-third of the population of this part of Spain at the time.

heliocentrism, he soon went further—without any good scientific reason for doing so. He argued that the universe is infinitely large, that the fixed stars were suns like ours that have planets of their own in orbit around them, and that the existence of life on these planets is a likelihood. He consequently denied the special nature of human beings as part of God's Creation, which was tantamount to denying the special role of Christ as the savior of humankind. His admirers over time have given him too much credit: he spun out so many ideas about science that the chance of at least some of them turning out to be true was high. He was an intelligent man, but it is a mistake to consider him a scientist in the sense that Galileo was. Nevertheless, he fell victim to the Inquisition. The court followed its usual tactic of delay, negotiation, and appeal; if Bruno would have only agreed to keep a low profile for a few years, he might well have been given his freedom. But he refused and was executed in a public square in Rome, with his ashes dumped into the Tiber River.

The most famous case of all is that of Galileo. Two inquiries into his science occurred, one in 1616 and another in 1633. The 1616 tribunal, led by Cardinal Bellarmine, reiterated the church's partial condemnation of heliocentrism and let Galileo go with a warning. Copernican theory could continue to be discussed and investigated, so long as it was presented only as a mathematical hypothesis instead of incontrovertible truth. Sixteen years later, having won further fame with his discoveries in optics, physics, and the study of tides, as well as his mathematical theory of infinite sets, Galileo breached his 1616 agreement. In his *Dialogue on the Two Chief World Systems*, he argued openly for the heliocentric model as the indisputable truth. Hence the Inquisition's action against him arose from the complaint that he had broken a contract with the church as much as from his scientific views. The formal judgment rendered by the tribunal reads as follows.

> Seeing that you, Galileo, ... were denounced by this Holy Office in 1615 for asserting the truth of the false doctrine, maintained by some, that the sun is the unmoving center of the universe and that the Earth moves in orbit around it ...
>
> And seeing that ... it was agreed that if you refused to stop [proclaiming this theory as decided truth] this Holy Office could order you to abandon the teaching altogether ... and that you could therefore be subject to imprisonment ...
>
> And seeing that ... your *Dialogue on the Two Chief World Systems* has recently been published ... in which you try to give the impression that the matter is still undecided, calling it only "probable" ... and that you confess that numerous passages of the book are written in such a way that a reader could in fact draw the conclusion that the arguments for [heliocentrism] are irrefutable ...

We conclude, proclaim, sentence, and pronounce that . . . you have made yourself strongly suspected of heresy.

His punishment was house arrest and penance, and the Inquisition ordered his *Dialogue* to be burned. Galileo agreed and spent his last years in quiet work.[6] In 1638 he published his last major work, the *Discourses on Two New Sciences*, which treats problems of motion, acceleration, and mathematical theory. His trouble with the Inquisition was clearly related to, but not solely composed of, his belief in heliocentrism itself; rather, the immediate issue was his breaking of a sacred vow.

The more general and important issue, though, was in the debate about truth itself. Discussing Copernican theory was something the church's own astronomers did with enthusiasm. But to leap from enthusiasm to dogmatic certainty was

Measuring Acceleration   This model reproduces Galileo's experiment for measuring the acceleration of falling bodies. By placing bells at various places along the inclined plane and measuring time via the small pendulum at the plane's top, Galileo was able to show that the distance traveled by a ball rolled down the plane was always proportional to the square of the time elapsed. (A medieval scholar, Nicholas Oresme (1320–1382), had already determined that, but his discovery had been forgotten by Galileo's time.) More truly original was Galileo's determination, contrary to Aristotelian physics, that the speed with which objects fall is a vacuum—hence neutralizing the effects of air resistance—is independent of their mass.

---

[6]   The legend that Galileo at his verdict muttered under his breath "Even so, it moves" is most likely false. The first instance of it appears in a fanciful Spanish painting after his death.

something few were prepared to do, and the church believed it had a responsibility to warn people not to rush into making that leap. The case of Galileo and the Inquisition marks an important turning point in intellectual history—the rise of a belief in *quantification.* If the numbers in Theory A work more precisely and consistently than the numbers in Theory B, this belief goes, then Theory A is for that reason alone accepted as true. But is that really the case? By every imaginable quantitative index, the United States won the Vietnam War—but did it? Conversely, all of the numerical data published by Bernard Madoff for twenty years showed that his investment schemes were fraudulent—and yet knowledgeable investors still poured billions of dollars into his criminal business. Anyone who has ever argued that their scores on standardized exams do not reflect the reality of their knowledge and skills is holding to a position consonant with that of the Inquisition. Right or wrong, the Inquisition trusted God's Word more than it trusted mathematical formulas.

> Anyone who has ever argued that their scores on standardized exams do not reflect the reality of their knowledge and skills is holding to a position consonant with that of the Inquisition. Right or wrong, the Inquisition trusted God's Word more than it trusted mathematical formulas.

THE REVOLUTION BROADENS

It is unclear how much all of these discoveries and debates mattered outside the walls of academia and of the church. History books always present intellectual infighting as high drama, but outside the ivory tower academic squabbles often appear squalid or even silly. (Is it a coincidence that novels about life in academia are always comedies?) To a 17th-century peasant shoveling manure out of a cow stall, it probably did not matter whether that manure was at the fixed center of the universe or if it was in orbit around the sun. All he cared about was getting it out of the barn before the landlord came and beat him for not keeping up with his duties. But discoveries in other fields mattered a great deal at the time, because of their immediate practical value. Increasingly, too, they mattered because of ethical tensions as older taboos declined, especially in regard to Islam.

In medicine, William Harvey (1578–1657) identified the circulation of blood in the human body via the intricate system of heart, veins, and arteries. The existence of internal organs and tissues came as no surprise, but physicians had never understood their individual functions or their working together as a system. Harvey's work opened the door to comprehending the human body as an integrated organism. In chemistry, Robert Boyle (1627–1691), extrapolating from the atomic theory inherited from ancient Greece, described the molecular structure of compounds. In physics he both determined the role of air in the propagation of sound and derived **Boyle's law**, which states that the volume and pressure of a gas at constant temperature vary inversely. These discoveries helped in deriving new chemicals and stabilizing air pumps. In biology Robert Hooke (1635–1703) employed a compound microscope to discover the cellular structure of plants, which, when studied over time, gave hints of the actual process of growth. Organic life, Hooke was the first to assert, is an ongoing process of growth and decay according to natural principles. By analyzing fossils he came close to developing a full-blown theory of evolution almost two hundred years before Darwin.

All this points to an important development. If Galileo had effectively removed God from the workings of the physical cosmos, later scientists began to discover the structures that took the place of Providence. However useful these discoveries might have proved, could they compensate for the loss of a divine purpose in life? When one takes away the idea that the universe functions, however mysteriously, according to a heavenly plan, then one risks the fear of a random, meaningless existence. The poet John Donne (1572–1631) described this feeling

TABLE 13.1 **Major Works of the Scientific Revolution, 1500–1700**

1543	*On the Revolutions of the Heavenly Spheres*	Nicolaus Copernicus (1473–1543)
1543	*On the Makeup of the Human Body*	Andreas Vesalius (1514–1564)
1600	*On the Magnet and Magnetic Bodies*	William Gilbert (1544–1603)
1609	*The New Astronomy or Celestial Physics*	Johannes Kepler (1571–1630)
1610	*The Starry Messenger*	Galileo Galilei (1564–1642)
1614	*The Wonderful Law of Logarithms*	John Napier (1550–1617)
1619	*The Harmonies of the World*	Johannes Kepler
1620	*The New Instrument*	Sir Francis Bacon (1561–1626)
1628	*On the Motion of the Heart and the Blood*	William Harvey (1578–1657)
1632	*Dialogue on the Two Chief World Systems*	Galileo Galileo
1635	Academie française founded	
1637	*Discourse on Method*	René Descartes (1596–1650)
1653	*On the Arithmetical Triangle*	Blaise Pascal (1623–1662)
1658	*The Spirit of Geometry*	
1660	Royal Society of London founded	
1660	*New Experiments Physico-Mechanical*	Robert Boyle (1627–1691)
1661	*The Skeptical Chymist*	
1687	*Principia Mathematica*	Sir Isaac Newton (1643–1727)

of loss and confusion in "An Anatomie of the World" (1611), written for an aristocratic patron on the anniversary of the death of his wife:

> Then, as mankind, so is the world's whole frame
> Quite out of joint, almost created lame,
> For, before God had made up all the rest,
> Corruption ent'red, and deprav'd the best;
> It seiz'd the angels, and then first of all
> The world did in her cradle take a fall,
> And turn'd her brains, and took a general maim,
> Wronging each joint of th'universal frame.
> The noblest part, man, felt it first; and then
> Both beasts and plants, curs'd in the curse of man.
> So did the world from the first hour decay,
> That evening was beginning of the day,
> And now the springs and summers which we see,
> Like sons of women after fifty be.
> And new philosophy calls all in doubt,
> The element of fire is quite put out,
> The sun is lost, and th'earth, and no man's wit
> Can well direct him where to look for it.
> And freely men confess that this world's spent,
> When in the planets and the firmament
> They seek so many new; they see that this
> Is crumbled out again to his atomies.
> 'Tis all in pieces, all coherence gone,
> All just supply, and all relation;
> Prince, subject, father, son, are things forgot,
> For every man alone thinks he hath got
> To be a phoenix, and that then can be
> None of that kind, of which he is, but he.
> This is the world's condition now.

The poem expresses above all the pain that follows a great personal loss. Yet it succeeds because the dread of a shapeless and unintelligible universe was felt so widely at the time. "The world's condition now" seemed one of decay and doubt; ordered existence is so jumbled and out of joint that one does not even know "where to look for it." Even God himself, the poem laments, could do nothing to set matters aright, since "corruption ent'red, and deprav'd the best" before a divine order could be introduced.

Sic Transit Gloria Mundi   Done in Spain in 1655, this painting serves as a sly cautionary comment. A sleeping nobleman dreams of wealth, power, knowledge, art, beauty, and military prowess, only to have an angel enter the dream, holding a banner that reminds him that death is the end of all things.

It is a powerful poem that should be read whole; the passage here comprises perhaps one-sixth of it. Not all scientific discoveries, it asserts, are advances, for they come at a cost. Take the discovery of the circulation of blood. This breakthrough occurred not simply because William Harvey happened to come along and figure it out. It became possible only with the dissection of human bodies—corpses, mostly, but some still alive.

THE ETHICAL COSTS OF SCIENCE

Deep cultural taboos against the desecration of the body had forbidden dissections for millennia. These taboos predate Christianity and even Judaism. The elaborate funeral rites of the Egyptians and Mesopotamians, with their careful cleansing and wrapping of the body, the incantation of prayers and hymns, the presentation of offerings, the ceremonial burial or burning of the remains under the guidance of priests—all these document a powerful need to treat the dead with decorum. At the end of Homer's *Iliad*, Achilles drags Hector's dead body behind his chariot as he circles Troy. For Achilles it is a moment of triumph; for the reader or listener, it is a moment of moral horror: How can the great Greek hero behave so monstrously? Does Achilles even deserve our interest? To an ancient audience, the scene cast doubt on all that had gone before. In Sophocles' great tragedy *Antigone*, the drama turns on the treatment of the dead. Before the story begins, Antigone's brother Polyneices had led a rebellion against King Creon, who defeated the rebels on the battlefield and ordered that their corpses be left to rot in the field, "prey to the wild dogs and vultures." Antigone's tragedy is to be caught between the king's command and the laws of her religion, which demand proper burial rites for the dead. At the play's conclusion she chooses to bury her brother and accepts her own inevitable execution for disobeying the king.

William Harvey was able to make his great discovery because, by the 17th century, many Western states had come to believe that certain individuals *deserved* to have their bodies desecrated; it was a final supreme punishment for the worthlessness of their lives. After Harvey's breakthrough, detailed knowledge of the operation of the internal organs followed quickly, but these advances required a new horror: the careful cutting open of victims while they were still alive. Harvey himself participated in some of this. The wretches to whom this was done spent weeks, and sometimes months, in constant agony.[7]

Who were these miserable people? It varied from state to state, but in general the possibility of dissection after death awaited anyone convicted of murder, treason, or counterfeiting. Theft too opened the door to the cutting table, if the person one stole from was well-connected. (Heretics and witches did not need to fear the dissector's knife; they were burned at the stake. Besides, it was assumed that they were unnatural and so would not contribute to the understanding of normal human physiology.) A hardness of heart toward certain sectors of society had to exist before Harvey could make his discovery. Many people felt a concern that scientific knowledge can come at too high a price, ethically speaking, for the benefits it brings. Even today, people today seldom stop to wonder where the thousands of cadavers used each year in our medical schools come from. Individuals who donate their bodies to science make up only a fraction of the bodies used. The rest are the unclaimed remains of America's homeless population, donated by our county morgues. Practices vary from state to state in the United States. Illinois, for example, requires county medical examiners to keep unclaimed bodies for sixty days before releasing them to medical schools; Maryland requires a wait of only fourteen days. Medical examiners in New York, however, are allowed to release unclaimed cadavers within twenty-four hours.

---

[7]   Physicians would make strategically placed incisions, then peel away layers of skin and muscle, in order to observe, for example, the full process of digestion from stomach to bowel.

Two Views of Human Dissection   On the left, Rembrandt van Rijn (1606–1669) shows a dignified exhibition of the start of a lesson on human anatomy; at this time, religious and civil law permitted a handful of dissections to be performed, under strictly regulated conditions. On the right, William Hogarth (1697–1764) shows a considerably more careless and cavalier approach, after Absolutist law permitted the dissection of those convicted of felonies.

But the picture becomes cloudier the more we look at it. Dissections actually were fairly common in the Middle Ages in the Mediterranean regions of Europe and in the Middle East. In Muslim Spain a physician named Ibn Zuhr [A] (1091–1161) performed dissections for research and several autopsies. He was in fact the first physician to deny that the human body was composed of four humors—though he found few people who believed him—and he invented the medical procedure now known as tracheotomy. A physician to Saladin himself, al-Baghdadi [P] (1162–1231), anatomized the corpses of a famine that struck Egypt in 1200, where al-Baghdadi had traveled in order to meet the great Maimonides.

In Christian Europe decrees forbidding the dissection of human remains for the purpose of transporting them to a distant burial site appeared as early as the 1160s, but these were not prohibitions of dissection generally. When in the Third Crusade (1189–1193) the German emperor Frederick Barbarossa (r. 1152–1190) drowned in a river in Asia Minor, his troops, wanting to bury him whole in Jerusalem, tried to preserve his body in vinegar. The human body, it turns out, does not pickle very well, and as Frederick decomposed, the crusaders buried his flesh, organs, and bones in three separate sites. By the late 13th century, in fact, dissections for the teaching of anatomy were standard in the leading medical schools such as the University of Montpellier. At the University of Bologna, another center for medical research and teaching, dissections were performed annually from 1315 on and were made available to the public. It was only in northern Europe that human dissections were both taboo and illegal, and those countries had a less developed scientific tradition. England forbade human dissections until the 16th century, and

Law in the Ottoman Empire A page from a legal handbook, *The Confluence of the Currents (Multaka al-abhur)* by Ibrahim al-Halabi (1459–1549). Al-Halabi was from Aleppo and spent the first half of his long life in Syria and Egypt, studying and then teaching Hanafi law—one of the four main schools of legal thought in Islam. Around 1500 he moved to Istanbul and became the imam at the great mosque built by the sultan Mehmed II (r. 1451–1481). The *Multaka*, published in 1517 and shown here with some of its many annotations by later writers, remained the authoritative Hanafi text for the next three hundred years.

even after authorizing them on criminals, the law permitted a total of only ten per year throughout the kingdom.[8] Thus the acceptance of dissection came specifically in Protestant Europe, where it was reserved for social malefactors.

THE ISLAMIC RETREAT FROM SCIENCE

The ethical cost of science detached from religious faith may not have troubled the Muslim world in the same way as it did in parts, at least, of the Christian West. At least it seems that way, but science had largely disappeared from Muslim intellectual culture, displaced by legal and theological studies, historical writing, and poetry. From the 7th to the 11th centuries the Islamic world had excelled in every science—medicine, physics, astronomy, mathematics—on both the theoretical and practical levels, leaving Latin Europe far behind. By the 13th century, however, the Latin West had taken the lead. Throughout the Renaissance, much of the Islamic world was too engulfed in warfare and internal strife to continue supporting scientific academies and observatories. The arrival of the Ottomans and Mongols, the rise to power of the Safavids in Persia, and the political recalibrations all three caused drove intellectual effort into philosophical and historical pursuits in the effort to redefine the very nature of Islamic identity. The new conservative element in Islam, exemplified by Ibn Taymiyya in Damascus, dominated the curricula in the madrasas from the 14th century onward and kept the schools' focus intently on the Qur'an, hadith, and sunnah. Their goal was to produce pious and obedient Muslims, not to advance learning. Memorization of the traditional canon was the goal, not the pursuit of new knowledge. Except for Mamluk Egypt, science in the Islamic world stagnated in the early modern era.

This decline did not go unnoticed. The great scholar Mustafa Katip Çelebi [T] (1609–1657) famously bemoaned the shortcomings of his age:

> There are so many ignorant people . . . their minds as dead as rocks, paralyzed in thoughtless imitation of the ancients. Rejecting and belittling all

---

8   The Murder Act of 1752 finally allowed the body of executed murderers to be available for dissection. France, Germany, and the Low Countries allowed the anatomization of anyone convicted of gross felonies.

new knowledge without even a pause to give it any consideration, they pass themselves off as learned men but really are just ignoramuses who know nothing about the world or the heavens.... The [Qur'anic] admonition— "Have they not contemplated the kingdom of Heaven and Earth?" [7.184]— means nothing at all to them, and they seem to think that to "contemplate the Earth and sky" means to stare at them like a cow.

He was not alone in his complaint. Even one of the Mughal emperors of Muslim India, Muhi ad-Din Muhammad Aurangzeb [P] (r. 1658–1707), lamented the fall in intellectual stature of Islam. In a diatribe against one of his early tutors, he harshly condemned what passed for education in the Muslim world:

> And what were some of the things you taught me? You taught me that France was a small island whose greatest king had previously been the king of Portugal, then of Holland, and then of England! You taught me that the kings of France and of Spain are just like our own petty provincial princes!... God be praised! What impressive knowledge of geography and history you had! Wasn't it your duty to teach me about the ways of the world's nations—their exports, their military might, their methods of warfare, their customs and religions, their styles of government, their diplomatic aims?... Instead, all you thought I needed to know was Arabic grammar and law, as though I was a judge or jurist.... By the time my education was finished I knew nothing at all of any science or art, except how to toss off some obscure technical terms that no one really understands!

Throughout much of the Ottoman Empire, frustration at the increasingly arid curriculum of the madrasas drove the more creative minds on to new schools known as *khanqas*, where the emphasis was on Sufi mysticism. Poetry, music, and metaphysical writing formed the core of this schooling, much of it powerfully imaginative and emotive. (Graduates from the khanqas frequently celebrated the completion of their studies by hurling the textbooks from their madrasa years into wells.) But science was still ignored. Memorization and transmission trumped exploration at every turn, leaving the European world unchallenged in its pursuit of scientific truth.

THINKING ABOUT TRUTH

Having severed its connection with the religious intellectual tradition, European science needed new standards. That includes standards of practice, criteria for determining the quality of evidence and argument, and principles for defining scientific truth. Without such agreement, scientific progress would be fitful at best, permanently hobbled at worst. Suppose one conducts an experiment several times and always achieves the same result. At what point may one legitimately conclude that this result is *always* the result—the natural and inevitable result of that experiment? Five times? Five hundred times? Five thousand times? When does it cease to be a mere result and become a conclusion? When does a general conclusion become an accepted scientific theory, and when does it finally become—the Holy Grail of research—a law of nature? Starting with Galileo and those who supported him, science had sloughed off its ancient standards and criteria but had yet to agree upon new ones to replace them. Even science, it turned out, needs a philosophy.

The 17th century was replete with efforts to establish this new philosophy, as new findings emerged from laboratories and lecture halls across Europe. Two of the most significant figures in this effort were Sir Francis Bacon (1561–1626) and René Descartes (1596–1650), and Isaac Newton (1642–1727) then made their ideas the foundations for mathematically precise scientific laws.

Francis Bacon we have already introduced. As the son of a career courtier, he grew up in high society, learned its manners, and became accustomed to its privileges. (His father, Sir Nicholas Bacon, had been the lord keeper of the Great Seal to Elizabeth I.) He worked as a lawyer and held a seat in Parliament. In 1589 he finally gained his first position in the royal administration and worked his way up, until, in the reign of James I (r. 1603–1625), he made it to the top of the pile, serving as lord chancellor and—a last plum—his father's old position as keeper of the Great Seal. But Bacon had expensive tastes. Even with all his income, he built up enormous debts, which may or may not have led to his taking bribes. Scandal swirled around him for several years as his enemies and creditors colluded to bring him down. In 1621 he finally fell from power in disgrace. Though he was allowed to keep his properties and aristocratic titles, he was barred from all political life and from most of privileged society.

A profoundly cautious man, except when it came to his spending habits, he advocated an uncompromising empirical approach to all knowledge, the gradual acquisition of discrete fact after fact, observation after observation, all of them subjected to repeated testing to insure their accuracy, until one has finally assembled enough data to hazard a general hypothesis. Mankind is prone to drawing hasty assumptions, he argued in *The New Atlantis*, and the only antidote is the patient accumulation of tested and retested facts.

Francis Bacon   Sir Francis Bacon (1561–1626) in all his finery, before his fall.

Roger Bacon, the medieval Franciscan, had already identified four barriers to intellectual progress, errors so common as to be nearly universal:

There are, in fact, four distinct impediments along the pathway to Truth—stumbling blocks, if you will, that get in the way of every man, no matter how learned he may be, and frustrate anyone who strives to reach the Truth. These impediments are: first, the precedents established by ill-equipped earlier authorities; second, long-established customs; third, the passionate sentiments of the ignorant masses; and fourth, our own habits of hiding our ignorance by the ostentatious display of what we think we do know.

Francis Bacon likewise identified four problems, which he called "illusions" (*idola* in Latin). Here he located the source of error in human nature, our own habits of thinking, the words we use, and tradition. While the correlation is not exact, he clearly had the earlier Bacon in mind:

There are four types of illusions that bedevil the human mind— illusions to which, in order to keep them distinct, I have attached particular names. These are the illusions of the tribe, illusions of the den, illusions of the marketplace, [and] finally illusions of the theater. . . .

The *illusions of the tribe* are the fallacies inherent in human nature, . . . [above all] the human tendency to consider all things in relation to itself, whereas everything that we perceive via our senses and reason is actually just a reflection of ourselves, not of the universe. The human mind resembles nothing so much as a flawed mirror, and like such a mirror it imposes its own characteristics upon whatever it reflects, and distorts and disfigures it accordingly.

The *illusions of the den* are the fallacies inherent in each individual. Every mind possesses—in addition to the fallacies common to all men everywhere—its own individual den or cavern whose qualities intercept and corrupt the light of Nature as it receives it. This may result from each person's individual and unique disposition, from his education, his interaction with others, or his reading. . . .

There are also what I call the *illusions of the marketplace*, the illusions created by the daily interactions and conversations we have with each other—for we speak through language but words have been formed arbitrarily . . . and they throw everything into confusion. . . .

Finally, the fallacies I call the *illusions of the theater*. By this term I mean those mistakes that creep into men's minds from the teachings of different

philosophies and from erroneous arguments. We must regard every philosophical system yet designed or imagined as nothing more than a play that
has been staged and performed—a charade, in other words.

He saw scientific thinking as the careful piling up of individual bricks of
knowledge to create a solid edifice. But Bacon himself never did any actual science; a wealthy aristocrat and career administrator, he was accustomed to telling
other people how to do their jobs. Descartes, on the other hand, practiced what he
preached.

DESCARTES AND THE QUEST FOR TRUTH

René Descartes received a good Jesuit education as a youth, but when he left school
he was, he wrote, "filled with so much doubt and false knowledge that I came to
think that all my efforts to learn had done nothing but increase my ignorance." In
1618 he met a gifted Dutch mathematician named Isaac Beeckman (1588–1637),
and for entertainment they invented mathematical problems for each other. From
this sort of play Descartes came to realize that geometric forms likes lines and
curves, when marked on a graph, could be described by algebraic formulas. Thus
was born **analytical geometry**, a discovery that set the trajectory for Descartes's
intellectual life. As he began to elaborate on his original finding in 1619, he all but
disappeared for nine years—moving from city to city, from France to Italy and the
Netherlands, never telling anyone his addresses (which he changed regularly
anyway), and gradually selling off the properties he had inherited from his parents.
"To live well, live in secret" became a favorite personal motto. He emerged from
self-exile in 1628 in the Netherlands, where he remained for twenty years, though
still moving frequently. He moved to Sweden in 1649 at the request of its queen,
who appointed him her tutor, but caught pneumonia and died in February 1650.
     Descartes's greatest achievements were in mathematics and philosophy.[9] The
invention of analytical geometry, apart from its inherent value, made possible the later
discovery of calculus and mathematical analysis (differential equations and the like).
His best-known work, however, remains the *Discourse on Method* (1637), which he
wrote as an introduction to a volume of several scientific papers. In it he presents not
only his own working method as a scientist but a creed, a set of principles that guide
one to true knowledge, a hybrid of science and philosophy.

---

[9]   Descartes also made numerous advances in optics, meteorology, physics, and even physiology. As a young
      man, he dissected cows.

He vows "never to accept something as true which I did not distinctly know for myself to be true." Rather than encouraging skepticism and doubt, however, Descartes advocates passionately for certainty. Doubt is not a philosophy, but merely a tool—and Descartes detested thinkers like Montaigne who seemed to him to regard skepticism as the end point of human endeavor. For Descartes, it is the point at which one needs to start thinking the hardest. But what does "knowing" consist of? And what, precisely, is truth?

Descartes   René Descartes (1580–1666), the French mathematician and philosopher.

Descartes begins with a distrust of the senses. The data we gather about the world through our senses cannot be fully trusted for the simple reason that our sense perceptions are imperfect. That includes things we observe with our eyes, or the sensations that derive from touch or smell. Optical illusions are common; people often hear sounds or voices that are not actually present, or fail to hear those that are. Individuals who have lost a limb frequently report feeling an itch on a part of their body that is no longer there. Knowledge based on sense data, therefore, can never be entirely trusted, since it depends on a flawed system of observation—a fact that undermines the very foundation of experimental science. One can try to validate one's data by performing an experiment numerous times and gathering the data with scrupulous repetitive care. Nonetheless, logically speaking there is no absolute certainty that an experiment that repeatedly renders one result after five million consecutive attempts may not suddenly give a different result on the five-million-and-first.

True and absolute knowledge, if possible at all, must therefore derive from a different source than empirical observation. For Descartes that source is logic. Logical thought is itself an absolute reality, or, as he famously put it, "I think, therefore I am" (*Cogito ergo sum* in Latin). I can doubt everything I see, everything I hear, everything I touch, smell, or taste. I can even doubt whether I am alive. But even in the absence of all sense data, my thinking mind—all by itself—knows that I am doubting, knows that I am thinking about thinking, and therefore I know absolutely that I exist.

"Congratulations," one might say. "You exist. So what?" But Descartes's insight contains the germ of a revolution in scientific and philosophical thought. Absolute truth, he argues, is theoretical instead of physical, and the theoretical expression of physical reality is ultimately more real than any physical manifestation of it. Consider, for example, a circle. One can express the idea of "circleness" by drawing one on a piece of paper, but also by describing it in words. "A figure in

two dimensions made up of all the points equidistant from a single central point."
The description in words is one level of abstraction above the physical drawing on
paper. But one can move to an even higher level of abstraction by describing a
circle in algebraic notation, as a mathematical formula. This, to Descartes, is an
absolute truth, because this formula will describe
all circles, in every place and throughout all time. If
scientific investigation seeks to understand the
truth about circles, it must work at this abstract
level. Only here can absolute truth exist and be
understood.

> Descartes described an entire
> universe guided by an immense,
> internally consistent, and utterly
> logical set of laws and formulas that
> the human mind can grasp—and
> this way of thinking has dominated
> Western scientific life ever since.

Descartes described an entire universe guided
by an immense, internally consistent, and utterly
logical set of laws and formulas that the human
mind can grasp—and this way of thinking has
dominated Western scientific life ever since. Scien-
tific research of all types—whether in physics, chemistry, microbiology, astronomy, medicine, or any other field—begins with an assumption that everything
operates according to a set of natural laws. The goal of research is to peel back
the covering of the universe and see the logical structure underneath. It may be
a coherent structure of unimaginable complexity, but we do not doubt that it is
there and that it makes rational sense.

Modern physics, for example, includes the laws of quantum mechanics and of
general relativity. Both are universally accepted, and yet they seem to contradict
one another fundamentally. Do physicists therefore give up their research grants
with a shrug? "Physics . . . it was worth a try, but I guess it just doesn't work."
Obviously not. They continue their work on the assumption that still another
paradigm exists, one that we have yet to discover but which is absolutely out
there, that reconciles our two apparently irreconcilable current systems.

John Donne had complained that the universe is "all in pieces, all coherence
gone." Descartes was the first to argue convincingly that another type of system,
based on fixed and unalterable natural laws, can take the place of Biblical and classical authorities—and that humans can figure them out. Just as the human mind exists
within, but also beyond, the body, the abstract laws of nature exist within and beyond
the physical universe. They guide it, shape it, drive it, and ennoble it with purpose.

NEWTON'S MATHEMATICAL PRINCIPLES

The first person to deliver on Descartes's promise was Sir Isaac Newton (1643–1727),
the greatest scientist in Western history before Albert Einstein (1879–1955). He
came from an undistinguished family and received a fairly standard education at a

boarding school. As a boy he enjoyed tinkering with machines, a hobby he continued throughout his life.[10] He earned a bachelor's degree in 1664 from Cambridge
University in classical studies, but by that time he had already started to teach himself mathematics and physics by reading the works of Descartes. When the plague
swept through England, he withdrew to his family's rural home, where he began his
work in optics and in the calculation of infinite series. The first resulted in his discovery that light can be broken into the spectrum of colors and has the properties of
a wave, and the second resulted in his discoveries of integral and differential calculus. Within two years he had become the leading mathematician of his age and
earned a prestigious professorship at Cambridge, where he remained for thirty
years. He spent his last thirty years in London serving as master of the Royal Mint
and president of the Royal Society.

Newton's greatest achievement was his *Philosophiae Naturalis Principia Mathematica* ("Mathematical Principles of Natural Philosophy"), published originally
in 1687. It is not light reading. Newton was a cranky, obsessive loner who loathed
being disturbed in his work, especially by people who could not understand the
complexity of his thinking—which was just about everyone. Only three hundred
copies of the first edition of the *Principia* were printed, which was probably well
more than the number of people capable of making sense of it. Newton insisted on
having empirical data as the basis for his high-flying mathematical formulations,
and hence the *Principia* skips from topic to topic, wherever there is sufficient data
to begin computing. Nevertheless, the variety and number of topics Newton addresses add up to a comprehensive theory about the physical world.

Its fundamental and astonishing idea is the theory of universal gravitation.
The idea that things such as apples fall to the ground was hardly startling news.
What prompted Newton's thinking was the question of why the planets do not
fall to the Earth's surface. Plainly there is evidently nothing holding them in
orbit in the sky. Physical theory had been based for centuries on the belief that
motion was an intrinsic quality of all matter. Water flows because that is what
water does; the atoms that propel our bodies forward are in constant movement
because movement is life itself. Death, in this view, is a cessation of natural movement. Newton argued instead that motion results from the interaction of objects,
and he showed that the interaction can be calculated precisely by taking into account their mass, velocity, and direction of motion. In this way he developed the
physical concept of force. But he then complicated matters by introducing another idea—what he called the "weight" (*gravitas* in Latin) or attraction that all

---

[10]   Newton invented the reflecting telescope—one that uses a curved mirror rather than a second lens to
focus captured beams of light.

physical objects feel toward one another whether they are in a static or dynamic state. Thus was born the idea of gravity.

In his descriptions of gravity, which he further showed to be determined in permanent ratios according to mass, distance, and force, he produced a comprehensive explanation for physical actions as simple as an apple's fall from a tree and as complex as the elliptical orbits of the planets in the solar system. Descartes had shown the logical necessity of a universal set of natural laws governing all matter. Now Newton provided the mathematical formulas that those laws consisted of. The universe was not only internally coherent according to a single, though undeniably massive, set of laws, but those laws were knowable, calculable, and provable. When Newton died in 1727, he was given a hero's funeral and buried in Westminster Abbey.

THE CHOICES FOR WESTERN SOCIETY

The immediate impact of the Scientific Revolution was moderate, but it changed Western culture profoundly. The universe became in the popular mind less of a divine and glorious mystery and more of a fascinating mechanism, with all that is good and bad in that transition. The new tenets included the belief in a rational explanation for everything we experience, the considered reliability of an idea that is based on quantifiable evidence, and the habit of privileging the demonstrably logical over the intuitive. All came increasingly to characterize much of Western thought. Western society, being the most open to the rational exploration of the world and the exploitation of its potentialities, became poised to do just that (see Map 13.1).

> The immediate impact of the Scientific Revolution was moderate, but it changed Western culture profoundly. The universe became in the popular mind less of a divine and glorious mystery and more of a fascinating mechanism, with all that is good and bad in that transition.

Not that there were not sounds of alarm raised. When the Royal Society, England's premier institution for the promotion of science, was established in London in 1660, some warned that it was nothing short of the beginning of a Satanic apocalypse. One prominent Anglican clergyman, Robert South (1634–1716), denounced the members of the society in a sermon in 1667 as

> the profane, atheistical, epicurean rabble . . . who have lived so much in the defiance of God . . . a company of lewd, shallow-brained huffs [blowhards] making atheism and contempt of religion the sole badge of wit, gallantry, and true discretion. . . . The truth is, the persons here reflected upon are of such a peculiar stamp of impiety, that they seem to be

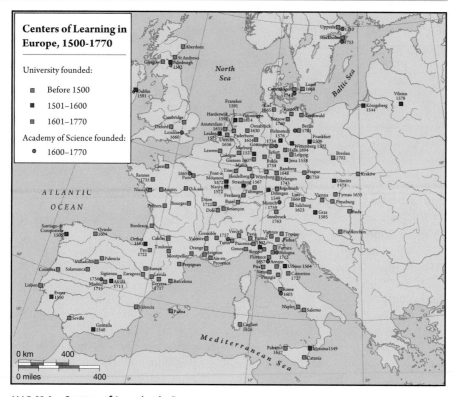

MAP 13.1   Centers of Learning in Europe, 1500–1770

a set of fellows got together, and formed into a diabolical society, for the finding out new experiments in vice.

Developments in the Christian West and the Islamic West now sharply diverged. Europeans came increasingly to view the world as knowable, explorable, and understandable. In fact, it became something that the West could dominate. At the same time, the Islamic world took a pronounced inward turn, eschewing science and exploration in favor of a reexamination of tradition. Neither path was intrinsically right or wrong, but both resulted from conscious cultural choices and as the expressions of value. The consequences of those choices would be felt for centuries to come.

WHO, WHAT, WHERE

analytical geometry	heliocentric
Boyle's law	*Index of Forbidden Books*
Council of Trent	Inquisition
Counter-Reformation	Jesuits
Epistemology	Scientific Revolution

SUGGESTED READINGS

Primary Sources

Bacon, Francis. *Novum Organum.*

Descartes, René. *Discourse on Method.*

Galilei, Galileo. *The Starry Messenger.*

Hobbes, Thomas. *Leviathan.*

Anthologies

Donnelly, John Patrick, ed. and trans. *Jesuit Writings of the Early Modern Period, 1540–1640* (2006).

Finocchiaro, Maurice A., ed. and trans. *The Essential Galileo Galilei* (2008).

Hellyer, Michael. *The Scientific Revolution: The Essential Readings* (2008).

Jacob, Margaret. *The Scientific Revolution: A Brief History with Documents* (2009).

Studies

Biagioli, Mario. *Galileo's Instruments of Credit: Telescopes, Images, Secrecy* (2007).

Bireley, Robert. *Religion and Politics in the Age of the Counterreformation: Emperor Ferdinand II, William Lamormaini, S. J., and the Formation of the Imperial Policy* (2011).

Blackwell, Richard J. *Behind the Scenes at Galileo's Trial* (2006).

Brooke, John, and Ian Maclean, eds. *Heterodoxy in Early Modern Science and Religion* (2006).

Dear, Peter. *Revolutionizing the Sciences: European Knowledge and Its Ambitions, 1500–1700* (2009).

Evans, Robert J. W., and Alexander Marr. *Curiosity and Wonder from the Renaissance to the Enlightenment* (2006).

Feingold, Mordechai. *The Newtonian Moment: Isaac Newton and the Making of Modern Culture* (2004).

Gaukroger, Stephen. *The Collapse of Mechanism and the Rise of Sensibility: Science and the Shaping of Modernity, 1680–1760* (2011).

———. *The Emergence of a Scientific Culture: Science and the Shaping of Modernity, 1210–1685* (2006).

———. *Francis Bacon and the Transformation of Early-Modern Philosophy* (2001).

Godman, Peter. *The Saint as Censor: Robert Bellarmine between Inquisition and Index* (2000).

Henry, John. *Knowledge Is Power: How Magic, the Government, and an Apocalyptic Vision Inspired Francis Bacon to Create Modern Science* (2004).

Jardine, Lisa. *Ingenious Pursuits: Building the Scientific Revolution* (2000).

Lindemann, Mary. *Medicine and Society in Early Modern Europe* (2010).

Park, Katharine. *Secrets of Women: Gender, Generation, and the Origins of Human Dissection* (2010).

Park, Katharine, and Lorraine Daston. *Early Modern Science* (2006).

Shea, William R,. and Mariano Artigas. *Galileo in Rome: The Rise and Fall of a Troublesome Genius* (2003).

Spiller, Elizabeth. *Science, Reading, and Renaissance Literature: The Art of Making Knowledge, 1580–1670* (2004).

Tutino, Stefania. *Empire of Souls: Robert Bellarmine and the Christian Commonwealth* (2010).

For additional resources, including maps, primary sources, visuals, web links, and quizzes, please go to **www.oup.com/us/backman.**

CHAPTER 14

From Westphalia to Paris: Regimes Old and New

1648–1750

"Those who did not live in the 18th century before the [French] Revolution do not know life at its sweetest," declared the French career diplomat Charles de Tallyrand-Périgord (1754–1838). An egoist right to the tips of his fingers, Tallyrand knew what he was talking about. The period of the Ancien Régime ("Old Regime"), from 1648 to 1789, was a time of unparalleled privilege and delight for the European upper aristocracy. Its belief in absolute order spread throughout society as well, inspiring a demand for norms in the arts and even everyday life. While England's civil wars led to a constitutional monarchy, the Islamic world in fact grew more conservative. As international trade grew and a new economic system came into being, however, Europe faced a new round of crises and war. Urban manufacturing and commerce had long since become the main engines of economic life, but the landed

THE GREATER WEST
IN THE AGE OF ABSOLUTISM

Peterhof
Potsdam
Schönbrunn
Versailles

○ Palaces built by
   Absolutist monarchs

◀ **Teaching Manners**
Enlightenment Europe placed profound importance on proper manners, one example being the publication of the first etiquette manuals for "proper" urban families. In this painting by Jean-Baptiste Chardin (1699–1779), a governess upbraids her charge for having dirtied his hat—presumably having dropped it on the ground during a tennis match.

elite still enjoyed various rental incomes, judicial fees, annuities, ecclesiastical and governmental sinecures, and military revenues. That was more than enough for them to live in lavish comfort, especially given their most closely held privilege—exemption from paying taxes. While agreement between states brought peace, it too further concentrated wealth and power, and philosophy rose to the occasion with an argument for tyranny.

This was the **Baroque Age**, when fabulously ornate palaces, churches, summer residences, concert halls, libraries, museums, theaters, pleasure gardens, and private academies sprang up by the hundreds across Europe. Most were filled to bursting with paintings and sculptures and rang with the music written by liveried court composers and played by servant musicians—all for the enjoyment of the wealthy, powdered, perfumed, and brilliantly attired nobles. Their images, coats of arms, and marble-inscribed names bedecked everything in sight. The display sought not merely to impress but to overwhelm the viewer with its expressive power. And that meant the power not of the architect, artist, or composer, but of the nobleman whose authority and station made such glories possible. Europe's elites had always enjoyed their privileges, but seldom on this scale.

The all-encompassing grandeur was designed to stun the people into a state of paralyzed awe. But such a display was possible only by means of a brutal hoarding of wealth. Few periods in Western history ever saw a more intense concentration of power and wealth among the elites—or such widespread penury and suffering by the common people. The German poet Johann Wilhelm von Goethe (1749–1832) described Europe's peasant farmers as "caught between the land and the aristocracy as between an anvil and a hammer." Not a comforting image—especially when one realizes that Goethe did not make the observation out of sympathy for the commoners' plight, but merely as a recognition of what was and needed to be.

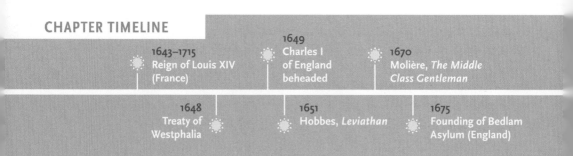

CHAPTER TIMELINE

1643–1715
Reign of Louis XIV
(France)

1649
Charles I
of England
beheaded

1670
Molière, *The Middle
Class Gentleman*

1648
Treaty of
Westphalia

1651
Hobbes, *Leviathan*

1675
Founding of Bedlam
Asylum (England)

THE PEACE OF WESTPHALIA: 1648

By 1648 most of Continental Europe was exhausted by over one hundred years of brutal warfare. Unable or unwilling to continue the carnage, all sides sued for peace. The **Peace of Westphalia** (1648) is an umbrella term for a collection of individual treaties that ended the hostilities. It rearranged political borders, created a framework of mutually agreed upon principles, and established a network of recognized sovereign governments. Over one hundred delegations had participated in the negotiations, which had taken seven years: sixteen nations, sixty-six German imperial principalities, and twenty-seven nongovernmental interest groups (such as churches, corporations, and guilds). This was the first general diplomatic congress in Western history, and it provided a model for subsequent international assemblies.

The peace dramatically revised the political map of Europe by splitting some states, joining others, carving out new independent entities, and moving many traditional boundaries (see Map 14.1). In so doing, it paid little attention to preserving ethnic domains. The goal instead was to produce a balance of power between the states created by the peace. If each new state was roughly equal in power to its neighbor, the thinking went, then wars would be less likely to break out between them. But to create such a balance, sheer acreage was not enough to consider; population density, economic and technological development, access to ports and rivers, and the availability of natural resources all had to be factored in. The resulting map shows several new states (an independent Denmark, Holland, Portugal, and Switzerland, for example) scattered amongst the larger territorial powers (Austria-Hungary, Bavaria, Brandenburg-Prussia, France, Poland-Lithuania, Spain, and Sweden). Moreover, countries now had a mechanism for creating alliances in order to check an ambitious neighbor. This eased tensions by allowing each state to control its own foreign policy in a meaningful way. Even small states like Denmark or Holland had strategic strengths that made them valuable allies. Threatening to withdraw their

1683
Ottoman siege of
Vienna repulsed

1689–1725
Reign of Peter the
Great (Russia)

1736
Fall of Safavid
Dynasty, Persia

1756–1763
Seven Years' War

1688
Glorious
Revolution,
England

1720
South Sea
Bubble

1755
Samuel Johnson,
*Dictionary of the
English Language*

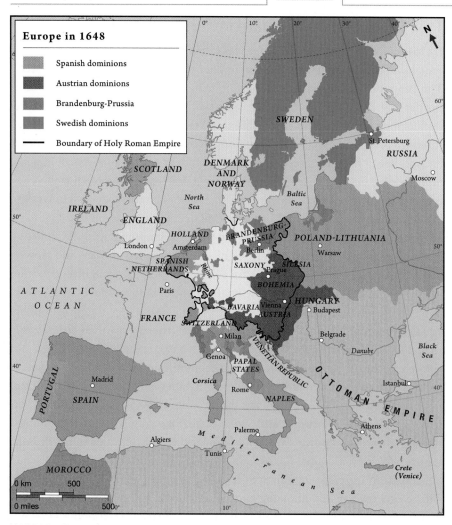

Europe in 1648

- Spanish dominions
- Austrian dominions
- Brandenburg-Prussia
- Swedish dominions
- —— Boundary of Holy Roman Empire

MAP 14.1   Europe in 1648

support from an alliance could make even a large state like France or Spain reconsider their policies.

The Westphalia treaties also reaffirmed the principle of religious establishment—the idea that the ruler of each state could determine its official religion (*cuius regio, eius religio*)—while guaranteeing the freedom of other faiths and denominations within certain prescribed limits. Strictly speaking, religious establishment meant more than a preference for any particular faith or denomination and was distinct from theocracy. Rather, it created a formal relationship between the state and the specific church. Religious establishment in the modern sense, in which the established church serves as an organ of the state, was a product of the Protestant Reformation: England established the (Anglican) Church of England

The Landed Gentry   Thomas Gainesborough (1727–1788) was the premier portraitist of 18th-century England, which was ironic since he had a profound dislike for the upper classes. His speed was admired as much as his skill, which kept a constant stream of commissions coming his way. In this dual portrait (1750) of Robert and Frances Andrews, a wealthy gentry couple, Gainesborough slyly lets some of his disdain for his subjects show. The couple looks distinctly out of place in the tranquil setting, like foreign objects imposed on the countryside. Mrs. Andrews, then only eighteen, sits stiffly on an elaborate wooden bench. The area of her lap was left deliberately unfinished, perhaps to allow for the inclusion of a baby in the future. Mr. Andrews, aged twenty-four, has a look of forced nonchalance. Gainesborough has pushed the couple to the side in order to spend more time painting the landscape (his real artistic love). No workers, implements, or farm animals are on the scene, except for a small herd of sheep far in the distance, which gives the land an eerily lifeless look.

in 1533, and the (Lutheran) Church of Sweden came into formal existence in 1536. Most of the states carved out by the Peace of Westphalia had in practice established churches, although few had the formal legal structures uniting church and state as did England and Sweden.

This sprawl of new or heavily revised territorial states left most monarchs without serious rivals for power. Where councils and parliaments had provided a limited check on royal ambitions, few of these customs survived intact. The aristocracy remained wealthy, privileged, and secure in their control of the agrarian countryside, but also unable to unite in opposition to royal aims. The new states were professional bureaucracies—uninviting to most nobles, who found it more to their liking to remain in their baroque palaces and chateaux than to crowd into expensive cramped quarters in the busy capital cities. Moreover, individual rulers could now consolidate extensive, centralized authority over their common subjects, so long as they avoided using that power to threaten their neighbors. In other words, the alliances and guarantees that aimed to prevent a king from intimidating his neighbors actually helped him to tighten his grip on his own subjects. In this way the peace helped to trigger the rise of royal **absolutism**, or a king's absolute power—not as a consciously deliberated policy, but rather as the unintended consequence of the quest for a balance of power.

THE ARGUMENT FOR TYRANNY

The argument for tyranny is a simple one, to its enthusiasts: it provides freedom. That may seem contrary to common sense, but the argument is sound. We define freedom by what we are free *from*. Many people, quite understandably, think of freedom as independence, or not being subject to control. To others, however, true freedom consists of freedom from chaos. The restoration of order after a long period of anarchy can thrill people with a sense of regained liberty—the liberty of a reliable, well-regulated tranquility.

The argument is an old one. The Archaic- and Classical Age Greeks celebrated their tyrants (*tyrannoi*, like Solon and Psistratus) and wrote them into their constitutions, as necessary correctives to democracy's occasional tendency to drive the cart into a ditch. The Roman Republic too allowed for constitutional dictatorship, a temporary though renewable grant of unlimited authority to revise the laws, reform government, and command the military. Julius Caesar had been a dictator—and a popular one at that until he appointed himself dictator for life, which made him effectively a king and all but assured his own assassination. In times of crisis, as when an airplane is spinning out of control or a ship is foundering in a storm, the rights to individual self-expression and self-determination do not further the cause of rescue. There is no time to hold elections, seek consensus, and let everyone on board freely express views about what to do. Instead, the argument goes, salvation requires a single firm hand on the controls and a single strong voice barking orders to an obedient crowd. Tyrants can make mistakes, of course, but they at least have the potential of saving the ship. Noisy, messy democracy and respect for independence of thought and action in such a plight only guarantees a crash.

The catastrophic wars of religion and civil wars before them, many now argued, were the result of liberalizing, mass-driven politics. In retreating from traditional authority since the 12th century, Europe had nearly committed suicide and had all but lost its collective mind in the crazed pursuit of witches. Only a restoration of patriarchal society, headed by noble male authority, could save the West from ruin. But this could not be done quietly or subtly. The aristocracy needed to parade its power, boast of it, and glorify it in everything it did. And the higher the aristocrat, the greater the need for spectacle. Kings, of course, needed to

> The aristocracy needed to parade its power, boast of it, and glorify it in everything it did. And the higher the aristocrat, the greater the need for spectacle.

parade their glorious position more than anyone else.[1] Jean Domat (1625–1696), a prominent jurist and royal favorite, justified the ostentation:

> Law grants the sovereign many rights, one of which must be the right to public display of anything that gives evidence of the grandeur and majesty needed to express the authority and dignity of his high and wide-ranging office. . . . God Himself [after all] wants monarchs to augment the authority He has shared with them, in ways that promote the awed respect of the people, and this can be achieved only by the grandeur conveyed by the brilliance of their palaces.

The Peace of Westphalia did not institute absolute monarchy in any formal sense, but it did establish the conditions that made its rise likely. Some early indicators of royal dictatorship had emerged even before the peace. In France the rapid concentration of power by the monarchy had begun under King Louis XIII (r. 1610–1643), whose chief minister— (Armand-Jean du Plessis) Cardinal de Richelieu (1585–1642)—summed up the problems confronting the throne when he first came to power in 1624:

> The Protestants acted as though they shared the state with you, the nobles, as if they were your equals rather than your subjects, and the governors of the provinces as though they were monarchs of their own offices. These scenarios set a bad example, one so harmful to the kingdom that even Your most loyal courts were influenced

Richelieu Armand-Jean du Plessis, Cardinal-Duc de Richelieu (1585–1642), was the sickly younger son of a low-ranking noble family, who grew to become the most powerful figure in the kingdom of France after the king himself. Richelieu believed firmly in the necessity of an absolutist monarchy; only a strong central monarch, ably guided and determined to exert his authority energetically, could maintain civil order. His rapid rise in the church and the French government went hand in hand. Consecrated a bishop in 1608, he became France's secretary of state in 1616; in 1622 he was made cardinal, and two years later he was Louis XIII's chief minister—a post he held until his death.

---

[1] Privilege, in the Age of Absolutism, was not a consequence of power but the very essence of it.

by it and were driven—unreasonably—to build up their authority to the detriment of Your Own. Might I add that every individual seemed to measure
his worth by the boldness of his presumption, ... each one deeming the
privileges he held from You valuable only to the extent that they satisfied his
greedy fantasies. ...

Sure in the knowledge of how much good a king can accomplish when he
puts his power to proper use, I, in my confidence, dared to promise Your
Majesty that You would soon regain control of Your state and that before
much time elapsed Your wisdom and courage, together with God's blessing,
would put the realm on a new path. I swore to Your Majesty that I would
spare no effort and would use whatever power it pleased You to grant me to
ruin the Protestants, to break the stiff-necked pride of the aristocracy, to return
all Your subjects to Your dutiful service, and to restore Your name to the high
position it deserves in foreign lands. *(Political Testament, ch. 1)*

Richelieu accomplished all this and more with a mix of careful negotiation and
heavy-handed intimidation. He neutralized most of Louis XIII's foes thanks to his
network of domestic and international spies, his ability to charm, and his willingness to bribe, and above all his ruthless conviction that only an all-powerful throne
could keep France safe and strong. Richelieu's passion for order and security is as
evident in his personal life as in his public policies, and in this he represents many
of the qualities of the Age of Absolutism.

THE SOCIAL CONTRACT

Richelieu's dedication to a supremely powerful monarchy was instinctive, but more
than one philosopher of the time reached a similar position. None of these thinkers
directly created absolutism as a political force, but they help explain the sentiments
that gave rise to it. The philosopher most closely associated with the theory of
absolutism is Thomas Hobbes (1588–1679). Hobbes was not England's first philosopher, nor even her first political philosopher; he was, however, the first to write
philosophy in English. A contemporary of René Descartes, with whom he corre-
sponded, and Sir Francis Bacon, Hobbes spent most of his adult life as a tutor and
secretary to William Cavendish, the second Earl of Devonshire, which left him
ample time to take advantage of the earl's magnificent library. He had broad interests that included history, law, mathematics, and physics, as well as philosophy.
Forced to spend time in exile in Paris after the arrest and subsequent execution of
King Charles I in 1649 because of his strong royalist views, Hobbes returned in
1651 with the completed manuscript of his best-known work, *Leviathan*.

Although his own life was comfortable, Hobbes's philosophy owed much to the violence and misery of his age. He emphasizes the instincts for self-preservation and self-regard that are natural to all people. Our polite, civilized behavior toward one another is an acquired attribute, one that masks and hopefully controls our baser passions for food, wealth, power, pleasure, and status. The problem, he argues, lies in the finite nature of the things we desire. Seeking always to satisfy ourselves, we unavoidably live in a state of constant competition with one another. "The war of all against all," as he memorably put, corrodes our civilized veneer and leads us into periodic anarchies like the one Europe suffered after 1500. Moreover, people are unequal in abilities—some being stronger, others faster, still others more cunning, or more agile. The war of all against all therefore becomes a permanent state, with

> no place for industry, because the fruit thereof is uncertain; and consequently no culture of the earth; no navigation or use of the commodities that may be imported by sea; no commodious building; no instruments of moving and removing such things as require much force; no knowledge of the face of the Earth; no account of time; no arts; no letters; and which is worst of all, continual fear and danger of violent death; and the life of man solitary, poor, nasty, brutish, and short.

It is a pessimistic view of life. (A long-ago student of mine once submitted an essay on the horrors of the early modern era "in which life was, in Hobbes's view, 'solitary, poor, nasty, British, and short.'") But it is not altogether surprising, given the agonies Europe had experienced since the discovery of the New World, the Protestant Reformation, the Wars of Religion, civil wars, Inquisitions, and witchcraft mania.

Hobbes sees only one way out of the misery of the state of nature: limitless sovereign authority. Only by transferring our innate rights of self-determination to a governing authority entrusted with absolute power over the people can we hope to free ourselves from chaos. Interestingly, Hobbes does not much care whether the absolutist government is a monarchy, an oligarchy, or a democracy. All that matters is that the government, whatever its form, has unquestioned power to compel obedience. Unlimited and indivisible power to legislate, adjudicate, execute, and enforce, in a single sovereign entity, is the only way to live an ordered, peaceful, and prosperous life. Of course it also fails to prevent the abuse of that power; but Hobbes counters this charge with two assertions. First, no absolute tyranny can ever be worse than absolute chaos. And second, when people recognize their complete obedience to the Sovereign Authority, a stable and peaceful enjoyment of life really does result. Their total submission

The Social Contract Title page of the first edition (1651) of *Leviathan* by Thomas Hobbes (1588–1679), the first work of political science in English.

> Government, which bears responsibility for preserving social stability, may therefore legitimately assert its will on the community whenever it deems it necessary to do so. Renunciation of personal liberty, in other words, is the price of peace; but the truest form of freedom, Hobbes insists, lies in that very renunciation.

to the Sovereign Authority will temper any possible inclination that authority might have to abuse its power.

Leviathan is a difficult book to read. Its archaic English—all four hundred pages of it—defeats all but the most determined readers. (I have modernized its spelling and punctuation.) But it deserves attention. A darker yet more substantial work than Machiavelli's *Prince*, *Leviathan* elaborates what later became known as **social contract** theory. This theory holds that when people decide to live in community they enter a covenant with each other, compromising their individual free wills in return for the benefits of society. Government, which bears responsibility for preserving social stability, may therefore legitimately assert its will on the community whenever it deems it necessary to do so. Renunciation of personal liberty, in other words, is the price of peace; but the truest form of freedom, Hobbes insists, lies in that very renunciation.

Richelieu and Hobbes were not the only 17th-century figures to argue for absolutism, but they are the most interesting. Both men were brilliant, moody, and pessimistic about human nature, and each worked diligently to bring their ideas to fruition—Richelieu in deed, Hobbes on the page. Had they met, they might have recognized one another as kindred spirits despite their religious differences. For all his worldliness, Richelieu was a devout Catholic, and scholars still debate whether Hobbes was an atheist.[2] Each also had humane pursuits. Richelieu collected classical manuscripts (later donated to the Sorbonne, of which he was the

---

[2]   Can one be committed to Christianity while endorsing secular absolutism? Hobbes says yes, but was he just trying to avoid inflaming the still-smoldering religious antagonisms of his age?

chief executive), founded the Academie française (the premiere literary society in France), patronized painters and sculptors, and ardently promoted theatre. Hobbes dabbled in mathematics and physics, published his own translations of Thucydides and Homer, and wrote a vivid history of the English Civil War. Still, both men shared unsettling and ominous views about human nature and the hard realities of life. Their influence was profound, and the fears they articulated were shared by many—fears that allowed absolutism to take root and flourish. For a while on the Continent, it could enjoy even popular support.

ABSOLUTE POLITICS

The dominant dynasties, and the most representative, of the Old Regime were the Bourbons in France, the Habsburgs in Austria and (a separate branch of the family) in Spain, the Hohenzollerns in Brandenburg-Prussia, and the Romanovs in Russia. A web of intermarriages that in some cases went back generations or even centuries connected the royal families to one another. Even so, ties of affection were minimal and always gave way to politics. Standing armies became arms of the state, as royal families undertook vast building projects to display their rule. Mercantilism, the economic system to support their disastrous self-indulgence, also devastated much of the population.

Despite the supposed "balance of power" established at Westphalia, France was the dominant Continental state in every way. With somewhere between 15 and 18 million people, France around 1648 had twice the population of Spain and three times that of England. With its superior resources concentrated among the upper orders, all of whom lavished funds on the arts, French culture flowered. This was the age of the playwright Molière (1622–1673), the painter Nicolas Poussin (1594–1665), and the composer Jean-Baptiste de Lully (1632–1687). Young King Louis XIV set immediately to increasing the size of his army, in the hope of matching France's cultural clout with its military muscle.

Brandenburg-Prussia, by contrast, was a surviving remnant of the old Holy Roman Empire, steeped in tradition and pride but for the moment a poor, defenseless, war-shocked ruin. Much of the worst fighting of the Thirty Years' War had taken place here, leaving large stretches of the countryside desolate and many towns depopulated. Economic development came slowly, and most commercial, technological, and institutional innovations appeared here one or two generations after they had taken root in England, France, or Holland.

Habsburg Austria had a long genealogy going back to the Middle Ages, but the traumas of the 17th century had left much of its land depleted and demoralized. The Ottoman Turks advanced upon Austria almost as soon as the

Another Siege of Vienna   In 1683 the Ottomans again marched against the Habsburg Empire (their first effort having been in 1529). The Turks had an army of nearly one hundred thousand soldiers. The Habsburgs called on their Polish and Lithuanian allies to join in the defense and carried the day. In this painting by the Flemish artist Frans Geffels (1624–1694), the Turks have launched their assault on the city. The Poles and Lithuanians have not yet appeared on the scene. According to legend, as part of the celebration over their defeat of the Turks the Viennese bakers' guild created a new pastry: the croissant, which was designed to mimic the Islamic crescent, visible on the Turks' flag above the tent on the left. The idea is that every time one tears open a croissant, one is in effect calling the Turks a rabble of puff pastries.

Westphalia agreements were signed; by 1683 they had reached Vienna, which they besieged for two months before giving up.[3] (Forces from Poland, Russia, Venice, and the papacy joined the subsequent Austrian counteroffensive.) The Turkish defeat reenergized Austrian pride, an emotional swell that led to a sharp improvement in economic and social stability. This was the era of Austria's climb as a cultural capital, especially the cities of Salzburg and Vienna; the first Austrian composer of note, Heinrich Ignaz Franz Biber (1644–1704), almost single-handedly turned Salzburg into a pilgrimage site for music lovers. The background to the Romanov dynasty lay in a decade-plus of famines, civil wars, and foreign invasions known as the Time of Troubles (1601–1613).

Mikhail I Romanov (r.1613–1645) came to power just before the Thirty Years' War engulfed Europe and died before it ended, but he took advantage of Europe's deadly self-absorption to drive out the (Polish-Lithuanian) invaders besetting his country and solidified his control over all of Russia. When Piotr I (Peter the Great) came to power in 1689, he brought with him the style and techniques of autocratic rule that he had learned earlier when traveling in the west. Together they laid the foundation for a czarist state that would last until 1917.

---

[3]   The Turks used the ancient temple of the Parthenon in Athens as their main munitions storehouse. When Venetian artillery units took aim on it, the temple was blasted into the ruin it is today.

TABLE 14.1 **The Age of Absolutism**

AUSTRIA (HABSBURG)	BRANDENBURG-PRUSSIA (HOHENZOLLERN)	FRANCE (BOURBON)	RUSSIA (ROMANOV)	SPAIN (BOURBON)
Leopold I 1658–1705	Friedrich Wilhelm 1640–1688	Louis XIII 1610–1643	Mikhail I 1613–1645	Felipe I* 1621–1665
Josef I 1705–1711	Friedrich III 1688–1713	Louis XIV 1643–1715	Alexei 1645–1676	Carlos II* 1665–1700
Karl VI 1711–1740	Friedrich Wilhelm I 1713–1740	Louis XV 1715–1774	Theodore II 1676–1682	Felipe V 1700–1746
Maria Theresa 1740–1780	Friedrich II the Great 1740–1786	Louis XVI 1774–1792	Ivan V 1682–1689	Ferdinando VI 1746–1759
Josef II 1780–1790	Friedrich Wilhelm II 1786–1797		Peter I the Great 1689–1725	Carlos III 1759–1788
Leopold II 1790–1792	Friedrich Wilhelm III 1797–1840		Katerina I 1725–1727	Carlos IV 1788–1808
Franz II 1792–1835			Peter II 1727–1730	
			Anna 1730–1740	
			Ivan VI 1740–1741	
			Lizaveta 1741–1762	
			Peter III 1762	
			Katerina II the Great 1762–1796	
			Pavel 1796–1801	
			Aleksandr I 1801–1825	

* The last two Habsburg kings of Spain

POLICE STATES

Autocracy is not conceptually difficult to grasp, since dictatorships follow a few set patterns of development. The regimes of the 17th and 18th centuries were above all police states. Raw military muscle and the willingness to use it both secured and expressed their power. The king's army in France mustered merely 20,000 soldiers in 1661; by 1700 it numbered 400,000. The Prussian army in the Thirty Years' War had consisted mostly of unreliable mercenaries, with the result that Swedish forces had ravaged the countryside almost at will. After 1648 the Prussian monarch began to assemble a professional standing army of his own. It began small: between five and six thousand men. But by 1750 it had ballooned to 180,000. Control of the Austrian army was given to a professional military officer from France, Prince François-Eugène of Savoy (1663–1736), who oversaw its transformation from a ragtag mixture of old feudal forces and mercenaries into a national institution with modern methods of supply, training, and command. After only a few years' work, he had increased the size and quality of the Austrian forces to such an extent that they drove one hundred thousand Ottoman Turks eastward from Austrian lands by 1687, after which he turned the army around and expelled a French force from the west. Austria thus entered the 18th century with a professionalized army of nearly one hundred thousand men.

The transformation of the Russian military was even more dramatic. Long consisting of an informal conglomeration of semifeudalized noble cavalrymen known as **streltsi**, the army was disbanded and brutally purged of political rivals by Tsar Piotr I in 1698. Piotr was determined to bring Russia in line with Europe, in terms of economic and political development, and resolved not only to catch up with Europe but to do so by emulating it. He modeled his new army along French and Prussian lines, put his soldiers in Western-style uniforms, gave them Western weapons (muskets and artillery), and hired Western officers to train them.

These massive new armies drew from the lower orders of their respective societies for the rank and file; men from the urban and professional classes or the lower nobility dominated midlevel officer ranks. The highest ranks were still primarily the purview of the high nobility, but tended to include only those for whom the military was a lifelong career. Only Prussia used a military draft; in every other country, volunteers served. And there was no shortage of volunteers. The king's army offered commoners three meals a day, a salary, solid training, and the possibility of a pension after a certain number of years in service—things they had little or no chance of attaining on their own. These were "drum and bugle" armies, divided into companies that fought in formation using long, unbroken lines. Discipline was harsh and frequently brutal: beatings, fines, half rations, and imprisonment were common. The penalty for breaking ranks was flogging. Executions were common too. In Austria, Prince François-Eugène liked to perform them personally on soldiers who failed to obey orders on the battlefield. Piotr I once personally executed five soldiers accused of rebellion, after allowing others to prepare the way by torturing the men first.

The Peace of Westphalia, however, was largely successful in maintaining a relatively peaceful Europe. Conflicts remained, a couple of them even large-scale matters, but Europe between 1648 and the start of the French Revolution in 1789 was a much more peaceful place than it had been in the 140 preceding years. Most of the wars of the era arose from Louis XIV's grandiose plans to create a greater France, or more accurately to secure a number of extranational regions that might buffer France from external attack: the War of Devolution (1667–1668), the

Franco-Dutch War (1672–1678), the War of the League of Augsburg (1688–1697), and the War of the Spanish Succession (1701–1714). Louis came to regret his overreaching, although not until the very end of his life. On his deathbed, Louis is reported to have advised his heir (his great-grandson Louis XV): "Don't follow the bad example I've set."[4]

Why then were such enormous armies created? With fewer foreign and civil wars to fight, the soldiers were put to use policing their own populations. Soldiers marched the streets and plazas, stood in university lecture halls, observed church services, watched crowds entering and leaving theaters, policed the countryside, guarded government buildings, and monitored harbors. They guarded city gates, performed maneuvers in town squares, staffed prisons (one of the new inventions of the age), and inspected printing houses. Without such vast reserves of manpower, royal absolutism was unthinkable. Maintaining the

Prussian Military Discipline   By the middle of the eighteenth century, the Prussian line infantry made full use of flintlock muskets and bayonets, as well as drilling, which involved the rotation of the front and rear lines after each salvo. "If my soldiers were to think, not one of them would remain in the army," Frederick II of Prussia is reputed to have said. The painting above shows Frederick's forces charging directly into the fire of the Austrians at the Battle of Hohenfriedberg in 1745, which the Prussians won.

---

[4]   Louis on his deathbed: " I was too quick to start wars, and I kept them going out of vanity. . . . Be a peaceful ruler, and devote yourself above all to easing the suffering of your subjects."

military—paying salaries, providing weapons and uniforms, serving meals, offering housing, supporting pensioners—remained a central concern of every monarch of the 17th and 18th centuries. The costs even in peacetime were enormous; the occasional conflicts of the age drove the expenditures exponentially higher.

Old Regime monarchs also relied heavily on separate companies of royal commissioners and civil servants—called *intendants* in France, and known collectively as the **Directory** in Prussia—who traveled through the provinces and inspected the handling of royal and administrative affairs. These commissioners held jurisdiction over all matters relating to public finance (whether collecting it or paying it out), public safety, and justice. They also formed part of the kings' extensive networks of intelligence gatherers. Drawn chiefly from the urban professional classes, commissioners served the king personally and did not hold public office, and hence they received their own salaries directly from the royal purse. They were expensive supervisors to maintain, since the kings not only paid their salaries but also equipped them with trappings appropriate to a representative of the king. In Prussia, in fact, all government positions of high and middling rank were reserved for military personnel, which effectively excluded much of the traditional aristocracy from power. It also made the king's position all the more secure, since literally everyone who worked in his government received a salary directly from him. In return for their exclusion from government, the nobles received royal permission to reinstate serfdom on their estates.

SELF-INDULGENCE WITH A PURPOSE

Expensive too were the sometimes grand, sometimes grotesque, building projects of the age. Palaces and churches decorated with baroque profusion arose by the score, year after year, as did lecture and concert halls, libraries and museums, scientific laboratories, and academies. Louis XIV, stung by rebellions and resistance in Paris, moved outside the capital and began construction of the immense palace complex at Versailles, which became the permanent seat of power from 1682 on. And other rulers built their own imposing piles too.[5]

Versailles itself had been a small rural village of only a thousand inhabitants fifty years earlier. Louis's palace—known properly as the Château de Versailles—transformed the simple hunting lodge that had previously existed on the spot into a spectacularly vast edifice that housed the entire royal court. The Château possessed well over a half million square feet of floor

---

[5]   Friedrich II of Prussia built the palace at Potsdam, just outside Berlin; Piotr I of Russia built Peterhof; the Habsburgs in Austria established the palace of Schönbrunn, just outside Vienna.

The Château De Versailles   With 2,300 rooms, a roughly equal number of ornate windows, and over 600,000 square feet (55,000 square meters) of floor space, the Château de Versailles is by far the grandest public structure built in the Age of Absolutism. Intended to showcase royal splendor and the French culture that the king personified, every bit of material used to build, furnish, and decorate Versailles was produced in France. In this painting (1668) one can see the extensive park and gardens as well as the château itself.

space (55,000 square meters) divided among seven hundred rooms, most of them magnificent. Thousands of paintings, drawings, sculptures, tapestries, and precious objects lined the walls and adorned every room. The effect on a first-time visitor is overwhelming—not so much for its beauty (although it is indeed beautiful) as for the audacity of its grandeur.

Louis's decision to build a new home for his court was self-indulgent but with a purpose. By creating a single space for the royal government and by demanding the constant attendance of France's aristocrats, Louis was able to keep an eye on the nobles and keep them under his sway. Louis never forgot that his reign began with an aristocratic rebellion against him. Called the **Fronde**, this rebellion (1648–1653) had not targeted Louis personally; the king was only ten years old when the trouble began.[6] Instead, the Fronde was a reaction against the royal finance minister Cardinal Jules Mazarin (1602–1661), the successor to Cardinal Richelieu, who had imposed a tax on judicial officials and sought to curtail

---

[6]   *Fronde* is the French word for slingshot—a favorite weapon of the Paris rebels, who used them to shatter the upper windows of the royal buildings.

a number of aristocratic privileges. It took five years to quell the rebellion, and Louis resolved to keep a permanent eye on the nobles by requiring their presence under his own ornate new roof. To make his job easier, he had the palace lined with secret passages, one-way mirrors, and peepholes; and he maintained a large private staff to spy on the goings-on in every room. The Duc de Saint-Simon (1675–1755), whose keen-eyed *Memoirs* provides an irreplaceable view of life at court, summarized the key role of Versailles as a means of controlling the nobles:

> [Louis] loved splendor, grandeur, and opulence in everything and inspired similar tastes in everyone in his court, even to the point where the surest way to earn a royal favor—perhaps the honor of receiving a word from him—was to spend extravagantly on something like a horse and carriage.... There was a sly political purpose in this, for by making conspicuously expensive habits the fashion at court (even making them a sort of requirement for people of a certain rank) he forced the members of his court to live beyond their means, which inevitably brought them to depend on royal favors in order to maintain themselves. But this [habit of indebtedness] turned out to be a plague that gradually infected the entire country, for in no time at all it spread to Paris, then to the army, and finally to the provinces, and now a man of any social standing at all is judged solely by the costliness of his daily habits and the extravagance of his luxuries. Such foolhardiness—the result of vanity and ostentation— has brought vast worry in its wake and threatens to result in nothing short of a national disaster and utter collapse.

This was prescient: the story of the French economy in the 18th century is one of constant and compounded indebtedness, a fiscal rot of staggering proportions that ultimately brought down the entire regime. For the present, however, the spending continued at an astonishing pace.

It is doubtful that Saint-Simon ever spoke so boldly to the king himself about the danger. A far braver man was François Fénelon (1651–1715), a Catholic priest appointed in 1689 as tutor to Louis XIV's grandson. As part of his teaching Fénelon composed a novel in 1694, *The Adventures of Telemachus*, which describes the travels and education of the son of the famed Greek king Odysseus. The novel mounts a stinging attack on the ideas of divine-right monarchy and absolutism. "Good kings are quite rare," it says at one point; "in fact, the majority of them are rather poor." It also denounces as evil the pursuit of glory through war and the sickening love of luxury. Fénelon's book became hugely popular across Europe and was translated into a half dozen languages. (It also provided the plot for Mozart's 1781 opera *Idomeneo*.)

Louis XIV hated it but recognized the good effect Fénelon's tutoring had on his grandson, a famously spoiled brat. He was brave enough to speak out in a 1694 letter to the king:

> Sire, for thirty years now Your ministers have broken every ancient law of this state, in order to increase Your power. They have infinitely increased both Your income and Your expenses, but in the process have impoverished all of France and have made Your name hated—all for the sake of the luxury of Your court. For the last twenty years these same ministers have turned France into an intolerable burden to her neighbors through bloody war. Wanting nothing but slaves, we now have no allies. And in the meantime, Your people are starving and rebellion is growing. You are thus left with only two choices: either to let the rebellion spread, or to resort to massacring the very people whom You have driven into desperation.

In 1696 Fénelon was appointed archbishop of Cambrai, but the following year was relieved of his position as tutor.

MERCANTILISM AND ABSOLUTISM

Supporting the absolutist regimes was a varied set of economic policies known collectively as **mercantilism**. For about 250 years, from roughly 1500 to 1750, this was the prevailing model for understanding and managing the economic life of northern Europe: England, France, and the Netherlands were the chief centers of mercantilist thinking, with Austria, Germany, Spain, and Sweden comprising a second tier. The Mediterranean economy also contained mercantilist elements but was less dominated by them overall. Mercantilism, in general, defined economic wealth as tangible assets: the money in circulation, land and mineral resources, the available precious metals, the aggregate of physical goods that can be produced from nature's resources. Global wealth therefore is static. Since the Earth is not increasing in size, the amount of economically valuable material is therefore fixed, and the aim of commerce is thus to maximize the amount of valuable stuff—actual specie and goods—in one's possession. The two most efficient means of doing so are to increase the amount of bullion in one's possession, either through mining precious metals or by appropriating the bullion of others, and to export more commercial goods than one imports.[7] But either way,

---

[7]   In a closed system, one becomes richer than one's rivals by gathering more of the available "pieces" of wealth; the number of "pieces" in the system, however, remains constant.

Mercantilist Center   The town of Bristol was founded shortly before the Norman Conquest of 1066 and for a while was important chiefly at the launching place for English armies on their way to Ireland. The discovery of the New World raised its significance enormously, and by the 17th century Bristol was the second-largest and busiest port in the kingdom. Between 1600 and 1750 Bristol was the principal site from which English slave-traders shipped African slaves to the New World. This painting, ca. 1760, shows the busy quay, where goods were loaded and unloaded.

the world economy is a "zero-sum game"—meaning that growth is reduced to mere hoarding. Wealth is thus a matter of distribution rather than creation.

> Mercantilism, in other words, did not aim at the prosperity of an entire people, nor did it think that possible to achieve. Rather, its purpose was to concentrate wealth among as few individuals as possible.

Mercantilism thus champions **protectionism**—the blocking of imports by tariff barriers, usually, and, if necessary, by law. The system, since it was based on the idea of artificially manipulating the distribution of wealth, also welcomed the awarding of monopolies by government (in return for sizeable bribes and licensing fees), the fixing of prices and wages, the blocking of competition, and the imposition of high domestic taxes. In a world of finite wealth, the reasoning went, assets must be concentrated in a small number of hands. Only this could enable the grand expenditures such as those needed to defend the realm, administer the government, and maintain social order. Mercantilism, in other words, did not aim at the prosperity of an entire people, nor did it think that possible to achieve. Rather, its purpose was to concentrate wealth among as few individuals as possible. The absolutist regimes perfected their policies over the 17th and 18th centuries—and in the process drove their own subjects into the direst poverty. (It is worth pointing out, by way of illustration, that the economic policies of China in the late 20th and early 21st centuries include many mercantilist elements.)

The classic statement in defense of mercantilism came from Thomas Mun (1571–1641), an English merchant and member of the board of directors of the English East India Company. He wrote *England's Treasure by Foreign Trade* in 1630, although it was not published until 1664. In it he argues, among other things, for the forced lowering of domestic wages. If the people of England cannot afford to purchase food, clothing, and other consumer goods, he points out, then the government will have larger amounts of those commodities available for export, which brings more money into the royal purse.

Modern thinking commonly regards mercantilism as nonsense, which raises the question of whether people in the early modern era were economic idiots. In reality they were far from it. Given the social bias against commerce as a "common" activity, Europe's nobility and most of its intelligentsia gave little thought to how economies function. The very idea of an economy as an existing, organic system remained a foreign concept. Money, goods, land, and raw resources were things one could put in one's hand, feel the heft of, and know to be real. An economy, on the other hand, is an abstraction, an invisible system of interactions that obeys supposedly fixed laws. Producing, selling, and consuming goods are aspects of human agency, but the notion of "an economy" or "a market" as an autonomous thing that determines human action requires a conceptual leap. And few people in early modern Europe were capable of or interested in making such a leap. Merchants understood that a scarcity of goods—as when, for example, a drought results in decreased crop yields—meant that they could charge a higher price. However, they interpreted this not as a scientific "law of the market" but simply as a scenario they could exploit. When 16th-century Spain imported tons of gold bullion taken from the New World, the country expected to acquire enormous wealth. What it got instead was an inflationary spiral unlike anything Europe had ever seen, the collapse of the currency, and the ruin of vast stretches of the peninsula. Compounding the problem, the Spanish rulers spent this money on a colossal scale—on palaces, museums, churches, artwork, and the army—rather than investing it in wealth-generating industry.[8] But no one at the time, in Spain or elsewhere, would have agreed that there was any connection. *That*, they would

---

[8]   Spain did not fully recover as an economic power until the late 20th century.

have insisted, makes as little sense as asserting that eating of massive amounts of food could result in a dramatic loss of weight.

MERCANTILISM AND POVERTY

Mercantilism served two specific purposes. First, it generated impressive amounts of revenue for the leading merchants and financiers of the age, who benefited from monopolies, protectionist policies that banned foreign competition, and the relative decline of domestic markets—thanks to the poverty of the bulk of the population. With captive markets in overseas colonies, too, high prices could be demanded with impunity. Second, mercantilism produced enormous returns for the governments, which made money from bribes and monopoly licenses, high tariffs on imported goods, onerous taxation of the common people, and investment in the commercial activities of the leading mercantile firms. If mercantilism did not create prosperity for the nation, that was never its aim. All that mattered was the preservation of the state and the institutions it controlled.

> If mercantilism did not create prosperity for the nation, that was never its aim. All that mattered was the preservation of the state and the institutions it controlled.

Mercantilism had been at work in France and Spain since the 1530s, in England since the reign of Elizabeth I, and in most of the rest of Europe after 1648. Its effects were stark. In contrast to the baroque splendor of aristocratic palaces and ornate churches was the grinding, humiliating poverty of the peasantry, village laborers, and local artisans and craftsmen. A French official's report on conditions among the rural populace of Normandy in 1651 paints a brutal picture:

> The most consistent food source here are the rats that the people hunt, so desperately hungry are they. They also eat plant roots that the farm animals will not touch. One can scarcely find words adequate to describing the horrors one sees everywhere. . . . This report, in fact, actually understates those horrors, rather than, as one might think, exaggerates them, for it describes only the tiniest fraction of the suffering in this district, suffering so dire that only those who have actually seen it can understand its scope. Hardly a single day passes in which at least two hundred people do not die. . . . I attest to having personally seen whole herds of people—men and women, that is, not cattle—wandering the fields between Rheims and Rethel, rooting in the dirt like pigs, and finding nothing edible, but only rotting fibers (and even these are only plentiful enough to feed half the herd), they collapse in exhaustion and have no strength left to continue searching for food. . . . The rest survive on a

Peasant Life   A small Dutch farm family prays before sharing
a single bowl of gruel. Note the absence of a table, but the
presence of an open fireplace—a common site of accidents,
especially involving infants. Two ladders serve as a staircase
leading up to the sleeping quarters. Though small, the home
is perfectly clean and well-ordered. The emphasis in this
engraving (1653) is not on the harshness of peasant life but the
spirit of simplicity and piety among the hardworking poor.

substitute for bread that does not deserve the name, made as it is from a
mixture of chopped straw and dirt.

As dire as these conditions were, they were an improvement from the last years
of the Religious Wars, for the simple reason that the people no longer had to
avoid marauding bands of desperate soldiers from nearly every nation in Europe.
Goethe's description of people "trapped between the land and the aristocracy as
between an anvil and a hammer" takes on new vividness.

The question must be asked: Given such unspeakable suffering, why did
people accept absolutist government—or at least not actively oppose it? The only
answer is that things were even worse during the Religious Wars. One can hardly
exaggerate the bloody, murderous horror that plagued Europe before 1648.

DOMESTICATING DYNAMISM: REGULATING CULTURE

European culture, too, was subject to a form of absolutism, but not simply as an extension of royal power. The whole of society became obsessed with rule making and breaking. Rules of etiquette, standards of spelling and usage, norms for musical composition and visual art, academic curricula, domestic architecture, even the subtle social demands of fashion—all these multiplied under the pressure to conform. All came to express explicit standards of value, certainty, decorum, and taste. Such standards have existed in every age, but they have seldom dominated life as they did in Old Regime Europe.

> The whole of society became obsessed with rule making and breaking. Rules of etiquette, standards of spelling and usage, norms for musical composition and visual art, academic curricula, domestic architecture, even the subtle social demands of fashion—all these multiplied under the pressure to conform.

The baroque style, which had emerged with the Catholic Counter-Reformation, had emphasized dynamic energy and raw emotional power. Roughly half the paintings by Peter Paul Rubens (1577–1640) glorify Catholic themes; most of the rest portray the magnificence of Europe's royals and high aristocrats. In music, the Baroque zenith was reached by the father-son team of Alessandro (1660–1725) and Domenico Scarlatti (1685–1757) and Antonio Vivaldi (1678–1741). Most music lovers today rank Johann Sebastian Bach (1686–1750) as the greatest baroque composer.[9]

Bach insisted that "all music should be for God" (*"Alle Musik soll für Gott sein"*). But as the style spread from Italy and Spain to the rest of Europe, its focus shifted to glorifying the monarchies. What else stood between the people and Hobbesian chaos? The courts slowly replaced the dynamism of the baroque with the controlled formal tone of **classicism**. In the visual arts this was the age of Nicolas Poussin (1594–1665) and Charles Le Brun (1619–1691); in theatre, of Pedro Calderón de la Barca (1600–1681), Pierre Corneille (1606–1684), and Jean Racine (1639–1699); in literature, of John Milton (1608–1674) and John Dryden (1631–1700). The strictures of formal classicism eased in the 18th century, but the insistence on proper composition, content, and form continued.

The Absolutist Age also saw the first comprehensive dictionaries of the European languages. Bilingual dictionaries, the sort to help English speakers learn French, or vice versa, had existed since the invention of the printing press. But dictionaries as normative reference works for native speakers and writers were another matter altogether. Nearly two dozen hastily produced English

---

[9]   In his own time, however, Bach was considered just a good provincial musician (especially as an organist). A figure of *real* stature would have composed operas, which Bach refused to do.

dictionaries had been published between 1550 and 1750, in a rush to capitalize on the dramatic spread of literacy made possible by print. Only with Samuel Johnson (1709–1784), however, was the extensive, critical, and prescriptive *Dictionary of the English Language* (1755) finally published.

Johnson's nine-year labor was a watershed event. A dictionary, after all, is a rulebook, one that asserts, for example, that the word *chair* is spelled C-H-A-I-R and in no other way—not chaar, chaire, chayr, chare, chaere, char, or any other phonetic estimation. (To date, for example, seven authentic signatures of William Shakespeare's have been found, and he spells his name differently each time.) It sets meanings and defines usage; it standardizes and regulates syntax.[10] Johnson's *Dictionary* succeeded where earlier efforts had failed, and it remained authoritative until the publication of the complete *Oxford English Dictionary* in 1928. In France, a team of scholars produced the *Dictionnaire de l'Académie française* in 1698. The *Vocabolario degli Accademici della Crusca* had appeared in Italy even earlier, in 1612, and the *Diccionario de la lengua española* arrived in 1780. The German language, by contrast, did not acquire a comparable dictionary until the Grimm brothers (of fairy-tale fame) began to compile their *Deutsches Wörterbuch* in 1838.

Ecstatic Divine Love   Gian Lorenzo Bernini (1598–1680) carved this famous statue of Saint Theresa of Avila in 1645. Theresa was a Carmelite nun whose mystical revelations formed the backbone of her books of confessional and theological writings. Her best-known books are *The Way to Perfection*, *The Inner Castle*, and her absorbing autobiography. In this last book (actually the first one she wrote) she describes one of her visions, this one of a heavenly angel: "In his hand I saw a long spear of gold, from the point of which a small flame showed. It was as though he thrust it repeatedly into my heart, piercing my innermost parts; and whenever he pulled the spear out it was as though he drew my heart out as well, leaving me all on fire with love for God. The pain was so great it made me moan—and yet this great pain was so sweet that I wanted it never to end."

---

10   Prior to Johnson, the spelling of English words was left to each writer's personal preference. So long as the reader could tell what word the writer meant, it meant little how the word used was spelled.

DECENCY AND MODESTY

If language needed standardization and control, so much more did daily behavior. Norms of social behavior had long been determined by local custom. Books of etiquette date back to the Middle Ages, when treatises on "courtesie" were required reading for the higher nobility of the late 12th and 13th centuries. Generalized works of etiquette for the urban classes, however, became increasingly common in post-Westphalia Europe. Richard Strathwaite (1588–1673) published a trilogy of guides—*The English Gentleman, The English Gentlewoman,* and *Description of a Good Wife*—that established norms of behavior that lasted a hundred years; Eleazar Moody's *School of Good Manners* (1715) was an enormously popular guide for parents who wanted to raise well-behaved children. In Italy, Baldassare Castiglione's *Il libro del cortegiano* (1528; in English as *The Book of the Courtier* in 1561) had established the norms for proper comportment in the Renaissance, but was overtaken in the 17th and 18th centuries by texts aimed at bourgeois society.

This is the society lampooned in the great comedy *The Middle-Class Gentleman* (*Le bourgeois gentilhomme,* 1670) by Molière (the pen name of Jean-Baptiste Poquelin [1622–1673]), whose very title is a part of the joke. A bourgeois commoner is attempting to behave with noble manners, as if one can become civilized by mimicking polite behavior. But a laughing matter in 1670 became serious business a generation later, as books on table etiquette, polite conversation, proper dress and comportment, and the rearing of well-behaved children grew in popularity. A French guide from 1729 helped explain the proper use of a new invention—the napkin:[11]

Table Knife and Fork   Most Europeans had traditionally used only knives and spoons at table. Forks, though known since Roman times, were used only as kitchen tools, if at all. Renaissance Italy reintroduced the use of table forks, although it is unclear whether this resulted from the desire to emulate the Romans or to limit one's exposure to disease—since people commonly carried their own knives and forks with them in a box. As a rule, the farther north and west from Italy, the slower the adoption of the fork. In Germany and England especially, forks were long considered effeminate affectations; and the people of the American colonies did not embrace them until the late 18th century. The knife and fork shown here were made in Germany in the 17th century.

---

[11]   Until the early 18th century, polite diners used the edges of the tablecloth to cover their laps and wipe their hands.

When at table one ought always to use a napkin, plate, knife, spoon, and fork; in fact it is now considered to be utterly improper to be without any one of these.

The proper thing is to wait until the highest-ranking dinner guest unfolds his napkin before unfolding one's own, but if everyone at table is a social equal, they should all unfold their napkins at the same time and without ceremony.

It is poor manners to use the napkin to wipe one's face, and even poorer manners to wipe one's teeth; but the grossest behavior of all is to use the napkin to blow one's nose.

This text from 1729 signals change in its very title: *La Salle: Les règles de la bienséance et de la civilité chrétienne* ("The Room: The Rules of Propriety and of Christian Civility"). And as for bodily comportment:

Decency and modesty demand that one keeps covered all the parts of the body, except the head and hands, when in society. Moreover, one should take every care never to touch with one's bare hand any part of the body that must remain properly covered; if one absolutely must do so, it must be done with the greatest discretion. A polite person simply must become accustomed to suffering small discomforts without twisting, rubbing, or scratching. . . .

When one needs to urinate, one should always withdraw to a private place—for it is permissible to perform natural functions (and this is true even for children) so long as one does it where one is not seen. It is nevertheless altogether impolite to emit wind from one's body—either from below or above—even if it is done without any sound.

Contrast an English guide from 1619, written in verse:

Let not your privy members be
laid open to be viewed;
it is most shameful and abhorr'd,
detestable and rude.

Retain not urine, nor the wind
which do thy body vex;
so [long as] it be done in secrecy,
let that not thee perplex.

The Teatro San Carlo in Naples   Built in 1737, then rebuilt after a fire in 1816, this is the oldest continuously used opera house in Europe. The original upholstery was blue; the red was used after a fire. Seen at the center here is the royal box, where members of the Bourbon dynasty sat. It was designed specifically for the staging of operas, with the auditorium built in a U-shape and tiered; an orchestra pit, so as not to overwhelm the singers; and all the backstage areas and equipment as needed for any theatrical production. Opera houses were expensive, and most of those built in the 17th and 18th centuries resulted from the patronage of royals and high aristocrats. By maintaining the system of tiered balconies as the reserve of the upper classes, the seats of the main floor could be opened to non-nobles. Thus opera, by its very popularity, helped to maintain the social system by embodying the privileged hierarchy while allowing the commoners to share in the delight made possible by aristocratic largesse.

Guidebooks laid out rules for conversation, letter writing, dress, the issuing of invitations, and behavior at occasions such as weddings, funerals, balls, and theaters.

Regulation reigned in other areas of life too. In music, most of the major compositional forms moved toward formal definition: fugues and sonatas initially, and eventually concertos and symphonies. Every opera had to have its text (libretto) approved by state censors before it could be staged, to make sure the plot carried no subversive messages. Just as significantly, popular pressure gradually demanded further norms in opera—such as the strict separation of comedy (opera buffa) and tragic opera (opera seria), the use of plots from classical drama or from French neoclassical theater, and the Italian language.[12]

---

[12]   Women were forbidden to take the stage in regular theater productions. Opera, however, offered them the chance to perform alongside men.

The period from 1680 to 1740 also saw the peak in popularity of castrati in the leading male roles. Castration before puberty prevented the natural deepening of the male voice, enabling the singer to sustain a high and flexible musical register. Moreover, the loss of testosterone production resulted in the weakening of the joints—which caused castrati to develop exceptionally long limbs and ribs. Their increased chest capacity allowed them extraordinary lung power, which aided their projection. So great was the demand for castrati and so lucrative were the potential rewards they could win that as many as three thousand young singers across Europe submitted to the operation annually during this peak period.

THE BIRTH OF PRIVATE LIFE

Aspects of domestic, even private, life became subject to innovative strictures, too. Societies were brought up on the idea of maintaining order at all costs. For most urban dwellers, living quarters by long tradition had been single open-space rooms above the workshop, tavern, or storefront in which they worked. The details of private life were conducted communally. Over the 17th and 18th centuries, however, domestic architecture took on interior walls, even among those with modest incomes. The activities of daily life—sleeping, cooking and eating, tending to hygiene, and socializing—were to be performed in discrete rooms. It is no accident that the word *privacy* was coined in the 17th century; before then, neither the word nor the concept existed. Even the human body became subject to a kind of control. Common people throughout the Middle Ages and Renaissance had worn simple garments that sheathed the body, whereas the 17th and 18th centuries saw the general introduction of underwear of various types. Henceforth, everyday dress for both men and women involved undergarments—not just to provide warmth but to support and control the body's movement. Cultural regulation like this was not imposed by government but arose naturally.

Henceforth, everyday dress for both men and women involved undergarments—not just to provide warmth but to support and control the body's movement. Cultural regulation like this was not imposed by government but arose naturally.

As standards of expected behavior rose, manners improved, and aesthetic values became defined and codified. In turn, attitudes toward those who failed to observe the new niceties grew harsher. Aristocratic culture had always prided itself on the chasm that separated it from the dirty masses, but a sense of cultural elitism began to emerge among bourgeois Europeans at this time as well. As a result, efforts spread to instill better behavior among the lower orders, some of them altruistic, others not. Centuries-old peasant entertainments like carnivals (rural festivals that usually preceded Lent) were discouraged from the pulpit and judicial bench alike.

A Clean, Well-lit Place   The interior of a well-to-do burgher's house in 17th-century Holland. The Dutch prided themselves on their sense of order and balance. The family that lived here was obviously wealthy but not ostentatious. The woman in the front room plays a harpsichord; to the left of the door is a four-posted bed. Each room opens onto the other, and each is filled with light.

English Puritan ministers railed against the evils of taverns, dances, country fairs, and popular folk songs. Protestant ministers in Germany struggled to stamp out rural irregularities in communal worship.

In the cities, the urban poor were no longer objects of pity and almsgiving but were denounced in sermons, speeches, broadsides, and newspapers (another invention of the age) as lazy, deceitful, uncouth, and potentially dangerous. New institutions arose to deal with them: poor houses, hospitals (hospices, that is), and reformatories. These institutions performed the valuable services of removing the unsightly destitute from polite society, and then either rehabilitating them (if possible) by teaching them a craft or effectively imprisoning them. In 1676 Louis XIV went so far as to order every city in France to build and maintain a hospital for warehousing the worst off of the urban poor.

In England, people whose behavior violated basic norms but who had not broken the law frequently ended up in Bedlam. Although the hospital dates back to the 13th century, in 1675 it became the first asylum for the mentally ill.[13] The

---

[13]   In 1725 Bedlam was divided into separate wings for those considered curable ("patients") and incurable ("lunatics").

idea caught on, and asylums soon dotted the European landscape. So too did prisons. Prior to the 18th century, jails or dungeons were simply holding areas for those waiting until judicial punishment (execution, lashing, maiming, or a simple fine) was carried out. But after 1700 state after state preferred to remove criminals (in noncapital cases, at least) from society altogether, and lengthy incarceration became the punishment of choice. Those whose presence offended polite society became isolated, institutionalized, and removed from the scene.

THE ENGLISH EXCEPTION

England rose to the top tier of European nations in the second half of the 16th century. When Elizabeth I died in 1603, however, a constitutional crisis threatened to undo the internal stability of the realm and endangered England's position in the international economy. In response, the new Stuart dynasty asserted greater absolutism, but it ended in civil war.

Elizabeth, of course, had never married, and so the Tudor dynasty ended. After some intrigue, the throne passed to James Stuart, the great-grandson of Henry VIII's sister. This marked the beginning of the trouble-plagued Stuart dynasty, which lasted, with interruptions, until 1714. Being Scottish, James I (r. 1603–1625) faced rude resistance from the start despite the legitimacy of his succession.[14] More than ethnic prejudice was at work in this, however, for James was a passionate advocate of royal absolutism. Before coming to power in England he had published a tendentious book called *The True Law of Free Monarchies* (1598), in which he argues that since kingship existed "before any estates or ranks of men . . . [and] before any parliaments were held or laws made," it is therefore unnatural for a king's power to be checked in any way. The argument is as weak as James's stubbornness was strong, and the struggle to balance royal ambitions and Parliamentary rights ultimately characterized the history of the entire Stuart dynasty.

James restated his position in a speech to the English Parliament in 1610:

> The state of monarchy is the supremest thing upon earth, for kings are not only God's lieutenants upon earth and sit upon God's throne, but even by God himself they are called gods. There be three principal [comparisons] that illustrate the state of monarchy: one taken out of the word of God, and the two other out of the grounds of policy and philosophy. In the Scriptures kings are called gods, and so their power after a certain relation compared to the Divine power. Kings are also compared to fathers of families; for a

---

[14] James, who ruled as James VI in Scotland (r. 1567–1603), was the first to style himself the king of "Great Britain."

king is truly *parens patriae*, the politic father of his people. And lastly, kings are compared to the head of this microcosm of the body of man. . . . I conclude then this point touching the power of kings with this axiom of divinity, that as to dispute what God may do is blasphemy . . . so is it sedition in subjects to dispute what a king may do in the height of his power.

Colossally and ideologically vain, James I also had a near-pathological fear of assassination.[15] His childhood in Scotland had been filled with political deceits, palace intrigues, kidnappings, and numerous murder plots. The horror of his early years made him distrustful of those around him, and once in power in Edinburgh and London he resolved that institutions like parliaments, courts, and churches were mere service organizations of the monarchy rather than sharers of power. Although he had been brought up as a Catholic, James found that Anglicanism suited his self-regard, for it identified the king as undisputed head of the church. He embraced the faith and endorsed the Act of Supremacy, which asserted that only an avowed Anglican could ever sit on the throne in England. His greatest achievement was his support for a new English translation of the Scriptures intended specifically for his newly adopted church—the so-called **King James Bible**, known officially as the Authorized Version.

The seldom-read dedication to the King James Bible provides a good example of absolutist ideology. It begins:

> Great and manifold were the blessings, most dread Sovereign, which Almighty God, the Father of all mercies, bestowed upon us the people of England, when first he sent Your Majesty's Royal Person to rule and reign over us. For whereas it was the expectation of many who wished not well unto our Sion, that, upon the setting of that bright Occidental Star, Queen Elizabeth, of most happy memory some thick and palpable clouds of darkness would so have overshadowed this land, that men should have been in doubt which way they were to walk, and that it should hardly be known who was to direct the unsettled State; the appearance of Your Majesty, as of the Sun in his strength, instantly dispelled those supposed and surmised mists, and gave unto all that were well affected exceeding cause of comfort; especially when we beheld the Government established in Your Highness and Your hopeful Seed, by an undoubted Title; and this also accompanied with peace and tranquility at home and abroad.

---

[15] In childhood, James had seen more than one family member cut down. He regularly wore a heavy dagger-proof tunic under his royal garments.

But among all our joys, there was no one that more filled our hearts than the blessed continuance of the preaching of God's sacred Word among us, which is that inestimable treasure which excelleth all the riches of earth; because the fruit thereof extendeth itself, not only to the time spent in this transitory world, but directeth and disposeth men unto that eternal happiness which is above in heaven.

Then not to suffer this to fall to the ground, but rather to take it up, and to continue it in that state wherein the famous Predecessor of Your Highness did leave it; nay, to go forward with the confidence and resolution of a man, in maintaining the truth of Christ, and propagating it far and near, is that which hath so

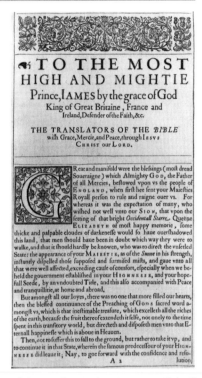

Divine Writ   Dedication page of the first edition of the Authorized (King James) Version of the Bible (1611).

bound and firmly knit the hearts of all Your Majesty's loyal and religious people unto You, that Your very name is precious among them: their eye doth behold You with comfort, and they bless You in their hearts, as that sanctified Person, who, under God, is the immediate author of their true happiness. And this their contentment doth not diminish or decay, but every day increaseth and taketh strength, when they observe that the zeal of Your Majesty toward the house of God doth not slack or go backward, but is more and more kindled, manifesting itself abroad in the farthest parts of Christendom, by writing in defence of the truth, (which hath given such a blow unto that Man of Sin as will not be healed,) and every day at home, by religious and learned discourse, by frequenting the house of God, by hearing the Word preached, by cherishing the teachers thereof, by caring for the Church, as a most tender and loving nursing father.

James fervently believed in mercantilism and followed its tenets in order to escape financial dependency on the Parliament. Wanting to increase English power in North America, he established the colonies at Jamestown (1607) and

Plymouth (1620), in what would eventually become the states of Virginia and Massachusetts. He also tried, though unsuccessfully, to arrange a marriage between his son Charles and a Spanish princess. He awarded many monopolies and collected enormous licensing fees, which raised opposition from the gentry; but he compensated them by creating (and selling to the highest bidders—most of whom came from the gentry) an unprecedented number of new noble titles. The "baronetcy" was his signature invention, and he happily bestowed this honor on anyone who would pay his asking price of 10,000 pounds. Many purchasers came forward. When James first came to the English throne in 1603 the House of Lords had fifty-nine members; when he died in 1625 the House had more than twice that number. He also granted more than two thousand knighthoods.

CIVIL WAR AND RESTORATION

When Charles I (r. 1625–1649) became king, opposition to the Stuarts had grown to the point where Parliament openly demanded constitutional reforms. Charles had inherited his father's vanity and stubbornness, however, in addition to his titles, and had no intention of compromising royal prerogatives. Unfortunately for him, he also inherited England's involvement in the Thirty Years' War. Meeting commitments to numerous parties in that struggle placed ever-greater pressure on royal finances, but Parliament passed a Petition for Right (1628) that denied the crown additional taxes and restricted the king's judicial authority. The following year Charles summoned a new Parliament, immediately arrested nine of its leaders, and dissolved the assembly; no new Parliament met for eleven years, during which time Charles bullied new fees and levies from the provinces. By 1640 king and country were wholly estranged. When Parliament did convene again in that year, the legislators prepared a "Grand Remonstrance"—a lengthy list of formal complaints about royal abuses of authority. Charles's troops again stormed the Parliament, but were resisted. Civil war had begun.

The Parliamentary forces were disorganized at first but soon came under the leadership of Oliver Cromwell (1599–1658), a Puritan in religion and a member of the gentry by social status. Without much military experience, he nevertheless rose quickly through the officer ranks of the Parliamentary forces. He was one of the three or four most powerful figures on the scene when the army defeated Charles in battle and took him prisoner in 1645. Few people wanted to abolish the monarchy altogether, and most hoped to force the king to some sort of compromise. When news came that Charles was in secret negotiations with Royalist sympathizers to launch a Scottish invasion of England, however, patience was at an end. Parliament placed Charles on trial for treason in 1648, and when the tribunal returned a guilty verdict Cromwell was one of the signatories to the king's death warrant. Charles was beheaded on January 30, 1649.

But the people who had opposed the monarchy soon found that, having removed the king, they could not agree on what to replace him with. Dissension broke out almost immediately; after several tense weeks, Cromwell took over the government by general acclamation. For the next eleven years he governed the Commonwealth of England, Europe's most radical experiment to date in representative government. Despite his best efforts, Cromwell failed to put together an administration that could outlast him. When he died in 1658, the Commonwealth quickly fell apart, and Parliament summoned Charles I's exiled son, who had taken refuge in Holland, to return to England and restore the monarchy. Charles II (r. 1660–1685), a carefree hedonist by nature, agreed to certain limits on royal power and took the throne amid a general sense of celebration. After twenty years of government by dour Puritans, the people welcomed Charles's love of pleasure and laughter and his reopening of the theater houses.

The party was short-lived, however, since an outbreak of bubonic plague in 1665 and the Great Fire of London in 1666 destroyed much of the city and took tens of thousands of lives. Charles now adopted a more serious approach, although he never managed to keep his living expenses within the budget the Parliament had set for him. In 1672 he attempted to force through a royal declaration that removed all legal penalties from the practice of Roman Catholicism, but backed down when Parliament resisted. Doubts about Charles's own religious loyalty filled the rest of his years on the throne.

Charles had no legitimate heir, since his wife's pregnancies had all ended in miscarriages and stillbirths. (He had married a Portuguese princess, Catarina de Bragança, who was unpopular with the English on account of her Catholicism and her lasting inability to learn English.) And so the crown passed in 1685 to Charles's brother James II (r. 1685–1688), who was openly Roman Catholic and determined to introduce absolutism.[16] James's short reign was filled with dissension, since the Parliament refused to remove the legal strictures that limited Catholic rights. Even more worrisome was the new king's desire for a much larger standing royal army. England had traditionally never kept soldiers in uniform and on the public payroll during peacetime. James's proposal, moreover, appeared too much in line with the actions of the post-Westphalian monarchs across Europe and stirred the Parliament into dramatic action.

In 1688 a group of leading members of Parliament invited the Protestant ruler of Holland, Prince William of Orange, to invade their realm and depose

---

[16]   Charles II was received in the Roman Catholic Church on his deathbed. James II had formally converted to Catholicism while growing up on the Continent during the Commonwealth.

James. (William was married to James II's daughter Mary.) William agreed. James initially thought he could defeat the invaders but soon realized otherwise, and so he fled the scene. He was soon captured by William's men, who, with William's consent, allowed him to escape to France—where he lived out his days in the court of Louis XIV. Since the coup proceeded without significant violence (James's soldiers deserted him en masse), it is known as the **Glorious Revolution**. Without shedding a drop of blood, England had staged a successful revolution, brought down an unpopular monarch, and brought to power a popular royal couple dedicated to Protestantism and constitutional rule.

OTTOMAN MIGHT AND ISLAMIC ABSOLUTISM

The Islamic world in the 17th and 18th centuries consisted of three empires that were also de facto absolutist states, although their regimes lacked the philosophical underpinnings found in Europe: the Ottoman Empire, Safavid Iran, and Mughal India (see Map 14.2). Language and culture distinguished them as much as political regimes. The Ottomans controlled the Arabic-speaking nations, the

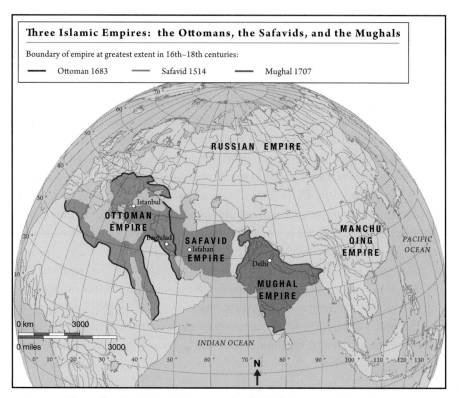

MAP 14.2   **Three Islamic Empires: the Ottomans, the Safavids, and the Mughals**

Safavids governed the Persian speakers, and the Mughal dynasty ruled over the numerous language groups of the vast Indian subcontinent. Important religious distinctions existed as well, with Sunni Islam dominating among the Arab peoples and Shi'ite Islam practiced by the bulk of Persian speakers. Though overwhelmingly Muslim, none of these states was religiously monolithic, for large Christian and Jewish populations continued to reside in them.

Ottoman military encroachments on Europe had continued well into the 17th century, and at least three times (1529, 1532, and 1683) their armies had advanced as far as Vienna. According to one tradition, the battle of 1683 was followed by a citywide celebration, for which the Viennese bakers' guild developed a new pastry—the croissant. This supposedly mocked the Islamic crescent that appeared on the Turkish army's banners. The powerful Ottoman forces were symbolically reduced to puff pastries.

After 1683 the Turks were put on the defensive for the first time in their history, a position exacerbated by the ascendancy of European merchant fleets in the Indian Ocean. Since they had previously lost control of the eastern Mediterranean at the battle of Lepanto in 1571, the new setbacks occasioned two new developments for the Turks. First, they gradually relinquished control over the furthest provinces of their empire—Morocco and Algeria, along the North African coast, which henceforth became independent states. To resist Spanish dominance in the western Mediterranean, these new states encouraged the "Barbary pirates" to attack ships on either side of the Gibraltarian Strait. Second, they delegated more power to provincial governors, with a system of tax farming that assigned local fiscal control to leading families. These steps were not, however, a complete capitulation of authority. Turkish autocracy had always differed from European absolutism in a fundamental way. Since the 15th century the monopoly of power was held by the dynastic house of Osman rather than by any specific individual. The sultan in Istanbul, as leader of the royal family, held primacy of place over his relatives, but power was rightfully held by every representative of Osman's line. The empire's system of government was therefore an oligarchical absolutism, but was no less absolutist for that.

Like that of its Western contemporaries, Ottoman absolutism was based on military might. The most important component of the army was the large corps of **Janissaries**, standing infantry units that resembled the military-religious orders of the Christian Middle Ages in their rigorous discipline, austerity, and spiritual vows. These "new soldiers" (the literal meaning of the Turkish word *yeniçeri*) were formed of Christian children from the Balkans and the Caucasus who were forced into military service and converted to Islam—just as had been the practice centuries before with the Mamluk slave-soldiers. They were sworn to celibacy during their years in the army, granted pensions and the right to marry upon retirement, and accorded exceptionally high social status. By the 17th century civil government was largely dominated by former Janissaries. At that time too the traditional practice of drafting Christian children into the corps (called *devşirme*) was abolished, as ethnically Turkish families sought to place their own children in the corps, in hopes of social advancement. Given the relative decrease in their military activity after 1683, the Janissaries were increasingly used (again like their European counterparts) as domestic police forces. In this role they maintained order, quelled revolts, and represented the ever-watchful eye of the sultan and his family.

SAFAVID PLEASURES

The Safavid dynasty in Iran had been established in 1501. It had established Shi'ism as the state religion and reasserted the Persian identity of the nation, after the Abbasid, Mongol, and Tatar interludes. The Safavids had emerged from a heterodox Sufi order and regarded themselves as either the earthly representatives of the Shi'i Hidden **Imam** or as the Hidden Imam himself. Given their religious origins, they were not likely to recognize any checks on their power. To be prudent, they complemented the religious basis of their claims to absolute authority by relying on the unwavering support of a large and potent army. Most of their army was composed of regular infantry units that served only as needed. More significant for maintaining the regime was a unique network of militant units known collectively as the **Qizilbash**. These companies—identifiable by the distinctive red-topped headpieces they wore (and from which they take their name)—regarded the Safavid ruler as divine. So great was their zeal that the Qizilbash customarily went into battle without any type of defensive armor. They were convinced that Allah and their Safavid lord's blessing would protect them from harm.[17]

Under the greatest Safavid **shah**, Abbas I [P] (r. 1587–1629), the Persians recaptured Baghdad and established commercial ties with both the British and Dutch East India Companies. Baghdad had never fully recovered from the devastation wreaked on it by the Mongols and may have held as few as fifty thousand people. An elaborate irrigation network had made the river valleys fertile since Sumerian times. Now that too lay in ruins, and most of Iraq had become a patchwork of scrubby pastoral zones loosely but violently controlled

---

[17]   The Qizilbash still exist as a distinct religious community in Afghanistan, Azerbaijan, Iran, and Pakistan. The third president of modern-day Pakistan, Agha Yahya Khan (1969–1971), was Qizilbash.

by rival tribes. But Baghdad itself still mattered as a forward defensive position against a renewed Ottoman offensive. Friendly ties with the East India Companies were vital, since conflicts over control of the sea-lanes had shifted commercial routes away from the Persian Gulf and toward the Red Sea, on the other side of the Arabian Peninsula. The shift threatened to cost the Iranians considerable revenue.

Like the European monarchs, the shahs centralized their nation's wealth as much as they did its political power, and they spent as lavishly on themselves as did Louis XIV. Magnificent palaces, pleasure gardens, libraries, astronomical observatories, and public adornments filled the cities. They built mosques and madrasas by the dozen and restored older centers of worship that had been damaged during the Mongol and Tatar years. In Iraq the holy shrines in the cities of Karbala and Najaf—dear to the Shi'a—were rebuilt and again became important sites of pilgrimage. Abbas II [P] (r. 1642–1666) extended his realm northward into Afghanistan, taking the strategic city of Kandahar from the Mughals, and ruled over a thriving and peaceable realm.

But the later Safavids gave in to the pleasures of their lavish lifestyle and spent more time enjoying themselves than in governing, which led to the dynasty's downfall in 1736. Several decades of turmoil ensued until, in 1796, a new dynasty took over—the **Qajar**—which held absolute power over Iran until 1925. The founder of the new dynasty, Muhammad Khan Qajar [P] (r. 1794–1797), had been castrated as a young boy by a rival for leadership of the Qajar tribe, and the experience contributed to his predilection for cruelty and violence.[18] While Muhammad was assassinated in 1797, the Qajar shahs still focused resolutely on maintaining their political power and the wealth that made it possible. Yet they also distanced themselves from the theocratic ideology of the Safavids. Religious and legal authority thus devolved from the court-appointed officials (qadis) of earlier times to the caste of scholars in shariah law produced by the madrasas. In the case of Shi'ite Islam, these were predominately clerics who held the title of **mullah** ("guardian"). Leadership of the mullahs fell to a higher office still, the **ayatollah** ("sign from God," literally). By the end of the 18th century, Iran had evolved into a dual absolutist state: political and military might was monopolized by the secular state under the autocratic control of the shah, while religious authority remained the preserve of an elite corps of mullahs led by their clerical superiors, the ayatollahs.

---

[18] Muhammad once ordered the blinding of twenty thousand men in a city that resisted his authority. He also had the Georgian city of Tbilisi burned to the ground and its entire Christian population put to death in 1795.

Isfahan   Isfahan, in central Iran, was the capital of Safavid Persia from 1598 to 1795. Located on a high plain just east of the Zagros Mountains, its high elevation—comparable to that of Denver, in the United States—makes for chilly winters. It snows usually once a year. Summers, though, are hot. Shown in this image is the Shah Mosque, built in 1611 and considered one of the great masterpieces of Persian architecture. The large square behind it (the Naqsh-e Jahan Square) was built to serve a purpose analogous to that of the Château de Versailles—that is, it housed all the Safavid rulers' leading nobles and ministers of state, keeping them all in his direct sight. The mosque itself comes off the square at a unique angle, so that the towering entrance arch (called an *iwan*) and the central dome of the mosque can both be seen from everywhere in the square. Visible to the right of the great dome is a smaller, lower dome that marks the "winter mosque"—a smaller, warmer site for use during the cold winters.

THE END OF ORDER

Absolutist Europe and constitutional England formed the center of a vast network of international trade (see Map 14.3). It proved a hybrid of commercial, colonial, mercantilist, and capitalist practices. It also turned on new markets, sustained by slavery and domestic labor, and it added enough uncertainty on top of sheer human misery to bring an end to order.

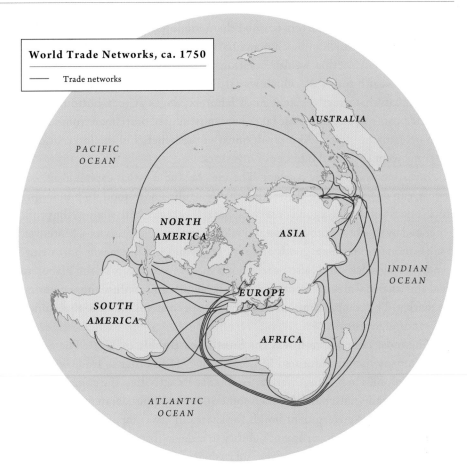

MAP 14.3   World Trade Networks, ca. 1750

Starting with Sweden in 1664, Europe's leading countries created royal or national banks that quickly developed systems of credit to finance manufacturing, commerce, and development. Strict mercantilism demanded the use of precious-metal coins, and aristocratic Europe's demand for Asian luxury goods never abated. Hence there was drainage of gold and silver from the West, which led to the introduction of paper money. Released from dependence on actual bullion, the new national banks dramatically increased loans, bonds, and other opportunities to invest. Credit now became available "on account," as promises to repay. National stock exchanges soon followed. Joint-stock companies like the British East India Company, the Dutch United East India Company, and the South Sea Company benefitted from the influx of investments. Their charters granted them monopolies on certain manufactures and trades, which allowed many to build impressive long-term returns. But involvement in this wealth creation was limited to those with excess capital, or wealth to invest, which was still a small percentage of the population. Mercantilist practices kept most laborers' wages at rock-bottom levels, and price controls and domestic taxes kept most skilled draftsmen from setting aside investment capital. As a result, most of the benefits of the international economy went to a small number of investors.

Investment was a new concept. The idea behind it—that capital itself, not people, can *do work*—is an abstraction that few fully understood. In purchasing stock, one is not buying a good or service, but rather the right to share in the profit generated by the future production and sale of those goods or services. Moreover, it takes money to produce goods and services, which usually means borrowing. In purchasing stock, one is also purchasing a share of a company's debt. Elaborate legal and financial arrangements can equally beguile and confuse those entering the market. The combination led frequently to speculative "bubbles" that ruined thousands of investors.

The most famous crash was the **South Sea Bubble** of 1720. The South Sea Company had been formed in London in 1711 in order to trade with the Spanish colonies in North America. To finance its activities, the company purchased England's national debt (then some 50 million pounds) in return for the right to exchange government bonds for shares in the company. Bondholders who despaired of the government's ability to redeem its bonds were thrilled by the possibility of New World riches and rushed to invest in the company. Soon a wave of speculation drove share prices to unprecedented heights, and the company encouraged the buying frenzy. It announced ever more spectacular ventures that it intended to undertake, like the manufacture of a (nonexistent) machine that could desalinate seawater—not to mention an ultrasecret "undertaking of great profit in due time to be revealed." Shares rose from 150 pounds each to over 1,000 pounds before the inevitable crash came and investors were wiped out.

THE SLAVE TRADE AND DOMESTIC SUBJUGATION

Among the most reliable investments were New World agriculture and the slave trade that enabled it. Until the 19th century, when settlers moved westward across the Great Plains, the New World did not produce food for export. Crops like potatoes, tomatoes, and corn (maize) were introduced into European farming and consequently were not shipped across the Atlantic. But sugar cane, cotton, and tobacco did not grow well in Europe. Being non-perishable, they could also be transported overseas to generate enormous profits, but they were labor-intensive crops. The need for slaves thus grew, as did the demand for the crops. Throughout the 18th century between seventy-five thousand and one hundred thousand African slaves were shipped across the Atlantic annually, until the slave trade was finally abolished (by France in 1793, England in 1807). Exact accounting is impossible, but somewhere around twelve million sub-Saharan Africans were brought to the New World in chains. The greatest number of them went to the Caribbean Islands, where they perished in horrifying numbers while working the sugarcane fields. Roughly a half million were sent to what eventually became the American South (see Map 14.4).

The profits generated by slave-produced New World agriculture were enormous. England's colonial profits rose from 10 million pounds to 40 million pounds between 1700 and 1776. France saw its revenues increase from 15 to 250 million livres in the same period. But the profits of the era were not distributed throughout society; they went to the highest social strata. Domestically, the rural economy was a ruin. As much as 20 percent of the European population lived in abject poverty.

The introduction of maize and potatoes alleviated famine in Europe, but also raised a new danger—alcoholism. Crops no longer needed for food could be converted into distilled spirits, which provided the poor with an escape from the dreariness and hardship of their lives. Before, liquor distillation had primarily been a secret of monasteries, which used it to support themselves. By now, however, the Protestant Reformation had advanced the knowledge of distillation across Europe. Gin became the hard liquor of choice among the poor, since it was so plentiful and cheap. By 1740, in England, gin production was nearly six times the nation's beer production—and all of it was drunk locally. The city of London alone had over six thousand gin shops, which sold cheap gin in bottles with rounded bottoms. This meant that the bottles could not be set down without risking a spill, which in turn urged the buyer to drink the entire bottle. When the government in 1736 tried to reduce consumption by imposing a heavy tax on gin, crowds took to the street by the thousands until they won a repeal of the tax.[19]

Those poor not killed off by drink often succumbed to disease, since the physical conditions in which the poor lived were appalling. In the district of

---

[19] As liquor became a favorite item for governments to tax, people operated their private stills at night, so that the smoke produced would not be seen. That is why homemade liquor is known as moonshine.

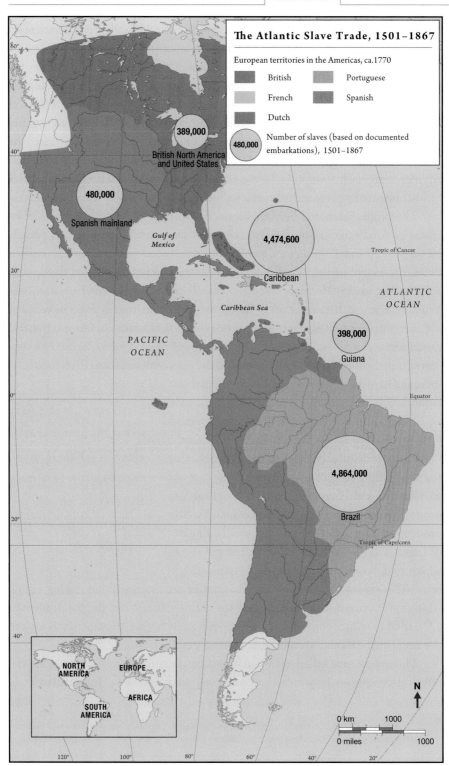

The Atlantic Slave Trade, 1501–1867

European territories in the Americas, ca.1770

British   Portuguese

French   Spanish

Dutch

480,000   Number of slaves (based on documented embarkations), 1501–1867

389,000

British North America and United States

480,000

Spanish mainland

Gulf of Mexico

4,474,600

Caribbean

Tropic of Cancer

ATLANTIC OCEAN

Caribbean Sea

398,000

Guiana

PACIFIC OCEAN

Equator

4,864,000

Brazil

Tropic of Capricorn

NORTH AMERICA   EUROPE

AFRICA

SOUTH AMERICA

N

0 km   1000

0 miles   1000

MAP 14.4   The Atlantic Slave Trade, 1501–1867

Brittany, in northwestern France, dysentery killed one hundred thousand in a single year (1779). Until the middle of the 18th century, only one-half of all children born lived to the age of ten, and only one-half of the females who made it to their tenth birthday survived until their fortieth. Pregnancy and childbirth were a death sentence for most of them.

Rural women became wage earners through the **putting-out system** of textile manufacture, which became increasingly widespread in the 18th century. Also known as **cottage industry**, this system transferred cloth production from towns to the countryside. Women had woven cloth for their families for centuries, but in the Middle Ages textile production had shifted to cities, where it came under the control of guilds that regulated production and set prices. The putting-out system returned the center of cloth making to the rural economy, as new merchants sought to avoid the urban guilds and improve profits. These entrepreneurs typically purchased bulk quantities of raw wool and cotton, which they distributed throughout rural districts, often following routes claimed by competing entrepreneurs. Then they retraced their steps, collecting the finished cloth from women and taking it to urban markets. Rural families needed this work desperately. Wages remained low, but by assigning tasks like carding or spinning to their children, countrywomen

The Working Poor   An example of cottage industry. In an attic room, an Irish family beats flax in order to expose the fibers contained within; once cracked open, the flax fibers are then soaked in water, removed, and spun by hand into linen thread.

were able to produce more finished cloth. Once redeemed, it often made the difference between life and death.[20]

THE RETURN OF UNCERTAINTY

Given the miseries of the age, the passivity of the people in the face of the excesses of absolutist society is striking. Even the most dramatic political action, like England's civil war and revolution, was undertaken by bourgeois and aristocratic factions. The underclass had seldom known prosperity and independence—and so had grown not to expect them. Disruptions could still spark them into action, as the rebellions of the 11th and 14th centuries showed. Yet as long as absolutism kept the peace, as it generally did between 1648 and 1700, peasants complained of their lot but seldom rose up against it.

The reappearance of warfare after 1700 added just the uncertainty, insecurity, and violence needed to trigger mass unrest. First came the War of the Spanish Succession (1702–1713). When King Carlos II died without an heir in 1700, France's Louis XIV and Austria's Leopold I—each of whom was married to a sister of Carlos's—greedily eyed the Spanish crown and its enormous overseas empire. Carlos's will had named an heir to the throne: the grandson of his sister, the closest male relative available. But Louis hoped to win the crown for himself before the young man, Felipe V, took power. Louis consequently invaded Spain; he also invaded the Spanish Netherlands, which brought him into a parallel war with England. The English army at this time was led by a career soldier named John Churchill, who defeated Louis's forces and brought the islands of Gibraltar and Menorca, plus France's New World territories of Newfoundland and Hudson's Bay, into England's possession.[21]

A subsequent conflict was the War of the Austrian Succession (1740–1748), which arose when ambitious outsiders challenged Maria Theresa's succession to the throne. Several countries joined into this fray, less to advance claims of their own than to do anything they could to weaken the Habsburg family in general. But the largest and most devastating conflict of the age was the **Seven Years' War** (1756–1763), which pitted Great Britain, Brandenburg-Prussia, and some smaller German principalities against an alliance of Austria, France, Russia, Saxony, and Sweden. This last war arose, in general, in response to the changes made to the Westphalian "balance of power" by the earlier two conflicts.

---

[20]   Cloth was the leading commodity in this system, but not the only one. Leatherwork, soap and candle making, and even metalwork formed part of the economy too.

[21]   His achievement resulted in his being created the First Duke of Marlborough, which raised the Churchills to the status of one of England's greatest noble families.

The War of the Spanish Succession had its North America parallel in Queen Anne's War. The War of the Austrian Succession correlated with King George's War. The Seven Years' War in Europe was matched with the French and Indian War. Together, these wars produced horrendous casualties. The Seven Years' War alone resulted in over a million deaths. Roused by the vast ruin of the country-side, the disruption of trade, the wasted expenditure, and the callous abuse of the peasantry, popular voices began to rise up and to demand change. Bread riots, calls for peace, and complaints over endless governmental deficits arose across Europe. Demonstrations against the treatment of the many by the very, very few sprouted from Ireland to Austria and from Sicily to Sweden. Surely something could be done to restore order. As the century progressed, new voices arose in response, voices dedicated to the idea that change was possible, necessary, and within reach. The world was a dark place that needed new light and hope.

WHO, WHAT, WHERE

absolutism	mercantilism
Ancien Régime	mullah
ayatollah	Peace of Westphalia
Baroque Age	protectionism
classicism	putting-out system
cottage industry	Qajar
Directory	Qizilbash
Fronde	Seven Years' War
Glorious Revolution	shah
Imam	social contract
Janissaries	South Sea Bubble
King James Bible	streltsi

SUGGESTED READINGS

Primary Sources

Fénelon, François. *The Adventures of Telemachus.*

Hobbes, Thomas. *Leviathan.*

Molière. *The Middle Class Gentleman.*

Tocqueville, Alexis de. *The Ancien Régime and the French Revolution.*

Saint-Simon. *Memoirs.*

Richelieu. *Political Testament.*

Anthologies

Beik, William. *Louis XIV and Absolutism: A Brief Study with Documents* (2000).

Gregg, Stephen H., ed. *Empire and Identity: An Eighteenth-Century Sourcebook* (2005).

Helfferich, Tryntje, ed. and trans. *The Thirty Years War: A Documentary History* (2009).

Wilson, Peter H., comp. *The Thirty Years War: A Sourcebook* (2010).

Studies

Bennett, Martyn. *Oliver Cromwell* (2006).

Bergin, Joseph. *Church, Society, and Religious Change in France, 1580–1730* (2009).

Casale, Giancarlo. *The Ottoman Age of Exploration* (2010).

Clark, Christopher. *Iron Kingdom: The Rise and Downfall of Prussia, 1600–1947* (2006).

Cracraft, James. *The Revolution of Peter the Great* (2006).

Dale, Stephen F. *The Muslim Empires of the Ottomans, Safavids, and Mughals* (2010).

Fowler, William M., Jr. *Empires at War: The Seven Years' War and the Struggle for North America, 1754–1763* (2005).

Harris, Tim. *Revolution: The Great Crisis of the British Monarchy, 1685–1720* (2006).

Hufton, Olwen. *Europe: Privilege and Protest, 1730–1788* (2001).

Hughes, Lindsey. *Russia in the Age of Peter the Great* (2000).

Ingrao, Charles. *The Habsburg Monarchy, 1618–1815* (2000).

Jones, Colin. *The Great Nation: France from Louis XV to Napoleon, 1715–99* (2003).

Levi, Anthony. *Louis XIV* (2004).

Linebaugh, Peter. *The London Hanged: Crime and Civil Society in the Eighteenth Century* (2006).

Martinich, A. P. *Hobbes* (2005).

Matthee, Rudolph P. *The Politics of Trade in Safavid Iran: Silk for Silver, 1600–1730* (2006).

Newman, Andrew J. *Safavid Iran: Rebirth of a Persian Empire* (2008).

Ormrod, David. *The Rise of Commercial Empires: England and the Netherlands in the Age of Mercantilism, 1650–1770* (2003).

Prak, Maarten. *The Dutch Republic in the Seventeenth Century: The Golden Age* (2005).

Quataert, Donald. *The Ottoman Empire, 1700–1822* (2000).

Rowlands, Guy. *The Dynastic State and the Army under Louis XIV: Royal Service and Private Interest, 1661–1701* (2002).

Smith, Jay M. *Nobility Reimagined: The Patriotic Nation in Eighteenth-Century France* (2005).

Streusand, Douglas E. *Islamic Gunpowder Empires: Ottomans, Safavids, and Mughals* (2010).

Szabo, Franz A. J. *The Seven Years' War in Europe, 1756–1763* (2007).

Wheatcroft, Andrew. *The Enemy at the Gate: Habsburgs, Ottomans, and the Battle for Europe* (2009).

Whisenhunt, William B., and Peter Stearns. *Catherine the Great: Enlightened Empress of Russia* (2006).

Zagorin, Perez. *Hobbes and the Law of Nature* (2009).

For additional resources, including maps, primary sources, visuals, web links, and quizzes, please go to **www.oup.com/us/backman**.

Reference Maps

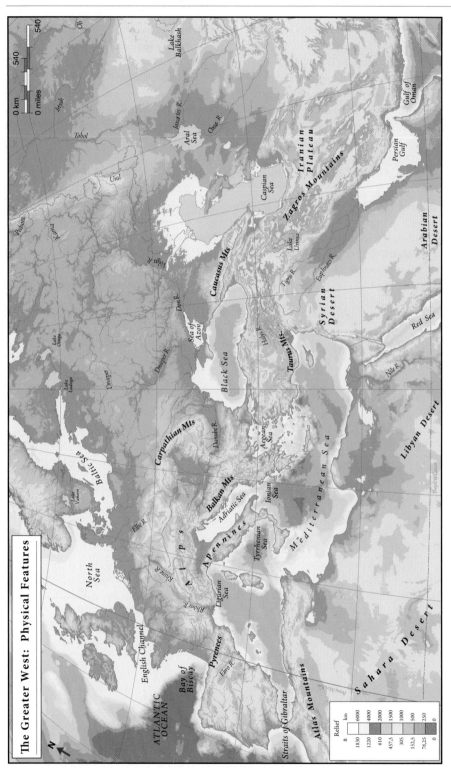

The Greater West: Physical Features

N

ATLANTIC OCEAN

Bay of Biscay

English Channel

Pyrenees

Ebro R.

Straits of Gibraltar

Atlas Mountains

North Sea

Baltic Sea

Lake Vänern

Elbe R.

Rhine R.

Rhône R.

A l p s

Apennines

Ligurian Sea

Tyrrhenian Sea

Ionian Sea

Adriatic Sea

Balkan Mts.

Carpathian Mts.

Danube R.

Lake Ladoga

Lake Onega

Dnieper R.

Dniepr R.

Don R.

Sea of Azov

Black Sea

Aegean Sea

Mediterranean Sea

Taurus Mts.

Halys R.

Caucasus Mts.

Volga R.

Pechora

Kama R.

Ural

Tobol

Irtysh

Ob

Lake Balkhash

Jaxartes R.

Oxus R.

Aral Sea

Caspian Sea

Lake Urmia

Iranian Plateau

Zagros Mountains

Persian Gulf

Gulf of Oman

Arabian Desert

Tigris R.

Euphrates R.

Syrian Desert

Red Sea

Nile R.

Libyan Desert

Sahara Desert

Prime Meridian

Tropic of Cancer

0 km   540   540
0 miles

Relief		
ft		km
1830	6000	
1220	4000	
610	2000	
457.5	1500	
305	1000	
152.5	500	
76.25	250	
0	0	

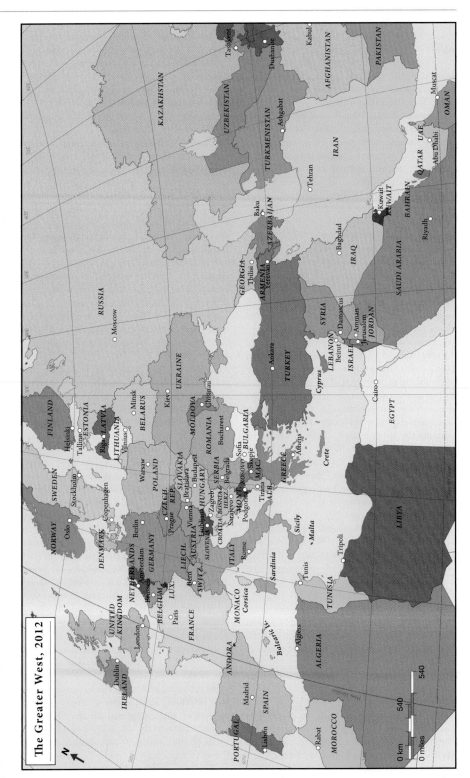

The Greater West, 2012

N

Glossary

A

Abbasids Dynasty of Islamic caliphs who came to power in 750 and remained titular heads of the Islamic empire until 1258, when they were unseated by the Mongols. Moved Islamic capital from Damascus to Baghdad.

absolutism Political theory granting limitless authority to a sovereign ruler, holding that a sovereign entrusted with absolute power will best protect the sovereign's subjects from disorder and chaos.

absurdity Postwar cultural concept, associated with the French-Algerian writer Albert Camus (1913–1960), that sees life as essentially meaningless.

Academy The school founded by the philosopher Plato in Athens in 385 BCE.

Act of Union Parliamentary acts (1800) that united Great Britain and Ireland.

Acts of Toleration Throughout the 17th and 18th centuries, laws promulgated to offer full or partial constitutional rights to Jews.

Afrikaners The descendants of the first Dutch settlers of South Africa; formerly known as the Boers; the language they speak is called Afrikaans.

Aggiornamento Among the issues addressed by the Second Vatican Council's meetings (1962–1965) were a reformation of the liturgy to allow for the participation of the congregation, a call for missionary work, an expression of regret for hostilities between the Catholic and Orthodox churches, and a rejection of the tradition of blaming the Jews for the killing of Christ. The word used by Pope John XXIII to describe his goal in summoning the Vatican II council—to bring the Church "up to date," literally.

Ahura Mazda The One Lord or eternal God, worshiped by Zoroastrians who believe he is the creator of all living things.

Almohads Reformist Islamic sect, made up chiefly of ethnic Berbers from North Africa, who invaded Muslim Spain in the 1170s.

amir al-umara' "Commander of commanders," a title held by those who seized civil authority from the Abbasid caliphs after 936.

Anabaptists Apocalyptic sect of Swiss exiles who rejected infant baptism, called for a second baptism in adulthood, and embraced a literal reading of Scripture and the imminent approach of Christ's Second Coming.

analytical geometry Developed by René Descartes, the application of algebra to the study of geometry.

analytic philosophy Branch of philosophy that emphasizes close and careful reasoning (as distinct from rationalist philosophy, which studies the movement of the human mind itself).

Ancien Régime The French aristocracy from 1648 to 1789, seen as a golden age (for those privileged enough to enjoy it) before the French Revolution.

anno Domini System of dating that reckons the years since the birth of Christ.

Annunaki Collective name for the gods and goddesses of the Sumerians.

Anschluss "Union," literally; the term has come to refer specifically to the political unification of Austria and Germany under the Nazi regime.

anti-Semitism Term coined in 1881 to describe the vicious hatred toward and persecution of Jews, both officially and unofficially, that emerged across Europe in the 19th century.

apartheid Official policy of racial segregation instituted in South Africa by the Afrikaner-dominated National Party in 1948.

appanage A land or estate held by a nobleman from the king of France without the requirement of performing feudal service in return.

Appeasement In the 1930s, the granting of political and territorial concessions to Hitler's Germany by many Western countries in order to preserve peace.

Arab Revolt Uprising (1916) of Middle Eastern Arab tribes against Turkish rule, which aimed to replace Ottoman imperial rule with autonomous Arab countries but instead furthered the European imperialist project by dividing the Middle East between England and France (see **Sykes-Picot Agreement**).

Arab Spring Wave of rebellions in ethnically Arab countries, beginning in Tunisia in December 2010 and rippling across Morocco, Yemen, Iraq, Bahrain, Egypt, and Kuwait. The rebellions turned violent in Libya, resulting in the eventual overthrow and death of dictator Muammar Qaddafi, and in Syria, which at the time of publication was on the brink of an all-out civil war.

Archaic period From 750 to 500 BCE, a time marked by the extension of networks of Greek colonies—primarily for peaceful, entrepreneurial purposes—around the Aegean rim, the Black Sea, and the entire perimeter of Asia Minor, across southern Italy and Sicily, and along the southern coast of France and the eastern coast of Spain, and along the northern coast of Africa.

Ark of the Covenant A chest containing the stone tables on which the Ten Commandments were inscribed, which Moses received from God on Mount Sinai. Captured by the Philistines around 1050 BCE, the ark was recovered by King David (r. 1005–965 BCE), whose son Solomon (r. 965–928 BCE) built a temple in Jerusalem to house it. The ark vanished after the Babylonians conquered Jerusalem in 586 BCE.

art nouveau   Popular style in art and design in the late 19th century, featuring flowing lines, flower-tracery, and gently erotic female forms.

Ashkenazim   Northern European Jewish cultural tradition uniquely focused on the preservation of Talmudic tradition.

askesis   Stoic term for the peace of mind acquired by the philosophical life. Later used to refer to the Christian "ascetics" who cut themselves off from society.

Assyrians   A strongly militaristic and powerful society (ca. 12th century BCE—612 BCE) of upper Mesopotamia, whose use of iron and steel for weaponry contributed to their formidable conquests.

Atheism   The rejection, or absence, of religious belief.

Augustus   Original title of the Roman emperors; given first to Octavius.

auto-da-fé   A Portuguese term meaning "act of faith." This was a public ritual of confession of sin and consequent humiliation for those deemed heretics by the Inquisition.

avant-garde   "Vanguard," literally. Term popularized by the Dada movement to describe bold artistic experimentation that questions the very idea of art.

Avesta   The holy book of the Zoroastrians.

ayatollah   Arabic, "sign from God"; the supreme clerical authority in Iran.

B

Ba'ath Party   Founded in 1947 by Arab Christian writer Michel Aflaq as the political representation of secular **Pan-Arabism**, applying socialist ideals of state-sponsored care for the masses (from the Arab word for "renaissance").

baby boom   Demographic bubble in the United States (1946–1964) when postwar prosperity and the return of soldiers from combat resulted in an elevated birthrate.

Babylonian Captivity   After the Chaldaeans destroyed Jerusalem and the Temple in 587, they took many of the surviving Jews back east as slaves, where they remained until they were released in 538 BCE by the Persian emperor Cyrus the Great (r. 576–530 BCE).

Balfour Declaration   Agreement (1917) that announced Britain's support for a national Jewish homeland in Palestine.

baptizein   Greek verb meaning "to baptize." Ritual of purification popularized by John the Baptist in 1st-century BCE Palestine. "To plunge or to dunk," literally.

barbaroi   General and pejorative term among ancient Greeks for any non-Greek peoples. English word "barbarian" derives from it.

Baroque Age   Concurrent with the **Ancien Régime**, an era in Europe of extraordinary artistic accomplishment in the service of the tremendously wealthy and privileged aristocratic class.

basileus   Title of the emperors of Byzantium.

Black Death   Successive outbreaks of bubonic plague, beginning in 1347, that killed up to a third of European and Muslim populations over the course of the 14th century.

Blitzkrieg   Nazi strategy of "lightning war" that used rapid motorized firepower to overwhelm an enemy before it could mount a defense.

Bloomsbury Group   Affiliation of writers, artists, and philosophers (including Virginia Woolf and John Maynard Keynes) who met socially in the Bloomsbury district of London in the first decades of the 20th century.

Bolsheviks   Political party led by Vladimir Lenin in the Russian Revolution that overthrew the Russian government in 1917, establishing a form of Communism that maintained power in the Soviet Union until 1991. A variation on classical Marxism, requiring the systematic use of violence, the establishment of a supposedly temporary dictatorship by Party members to effect the overthrow of prerevolutionary practices, and the violent exportation of revolution to other countries.

Book of the Dead   An anthology of prayers, poems, and similar texts collected during the Egyptian Middle Kingdom (2035 BCE–1640 BCE). Placed in the coffin, the Book of the Dead was believed to allow the deceased to enter paradise.

bourgeoisie   The prosperous and primarily urban middle class of Enlightenment Europe.

Boxer Rebellion   Violent attempt (1898–1901) by Chinese peasants, motivated by millennial Buddhist beliefs, to purge Westerners and Western influence from China.

Boyle's law   Discovered by Robert Boyle, states that the volume and pressure of a gas at constant temperature vary inversely.

Bronze Age   The period between 4000 and 1500 BCE characterized by the ability of early Near East inhabitants to smelt copper (and its alloy, bronze, which combines copper with tin) for weapons, farm implements, and tools.

Byzantine Empire   Eastern half of the Roman Empire, with its capital in Constantinople; at its height in the 4th and 5th centuries it included all of today's countries of Libya, Egypt, Israel, Jordan, Lebanon, Syria, Turkey, and most of the Balkan states.

C

caesar Title of the vice emperors under the constitutional reforms created by Diocletian. Later evolved into German and Russian terms for emperor (*kaiser* and *tsar*, respectively).

cahiers de doléances "Grievance notebooks," literally. Records of commoners' complaints compiled for the use of representatives to the Estates General in 1789.

Cairo Declaration on Human Rights Adopted in 1990 by the Organization of the Islamic Conference to replace the earlier (and secular) **Universal Declaration of Human Rights** with a specifically Islamic conceptualization.

caliph Successor to the Prophet Muhammad as political and religious leader of the Islamic world. Meaning "deputy" in the literal sense, in common usage it was roughly comparable to the English word "emperor."

capitulations Trade agreements between the Ottoman Empire and European nations that by the 19th century overwhelmingly favored European interests.

Carolingians Ambitious Frankish dynasty that overthrew the Merovingians, defended western Christendom against Muslim invaders, and united France.

Cathars Christian heresy that posited the existence of two equally strong but diametrically opposed gods—one absolutely good, who created human souls, and one absolutely evil, who created the physical world. Humans are trapped in a cycle of reincarnation until they overcome materialism.

censor A powerful office in the Roman Republic, whose duties were to maintain the census, to administer the state's finances for public works, and to preserve public morals.

census The official list of all citizens of Rome, their property, and legal class.

Central Intelligence Agency (CIA) American governmental agency originally created in 1947 to monitor and deter global Soviet influence. Its mission was officially limited to the gathering of intelligence but in practice the CIA has often engaged in direct political intervention.

chansons de geste Vernacular epic poems of the 11th to 13th century about the heroic deeds of knights. "Songs of deeds."

Chartist movement Labor movement begun by the London Working Men's Association in 1838.

chivalry In 12th-century Europe, an ethic that embraced ideal knightly behavior: comportment, noble demeanor, learning, and piety.

Chosen People The Hebrew Bible describes the Hebrews as God's "Chosen People," by which is meant not just the favor and protection God gives them but their obligation to obey God in all things and to live up to the high moral standards God expects of them.

Christian Democracy Western European ideological hybrid of social conservatism and economic liberalism.

Christian humanism Anticlerical movement of the northern Renaissance that emphasized the simple reading of Scripture (especially the New Testament), the singing of hymns, and communal prayer.

christianities The dozens of versions of early Christianity, each with its own beliefs, liturgical traditions, and customs, that emerged in the earliest years following the death of Jesus.

Church of England Protestant church founded by King Henry VIII of England when he broke with the Catholic Church in 1533. Also known as the Anglican Church; the monarchy is its supreme head.

Ciompi Rebellion Popular uprising in Italy in 1378.

citizenship As articulated by the 19th-century Egyptian reformer Rifa'a al-Tahtawi, a form of group identity that is not determined by race, creed, or ethnicity.

civil rights The guarantee of equal access to all parts of government and society for all members of a society. In the United States, the civil rights movement refers primarily to the struggle of African Americans in the 1960s for equal access.

Classical Age The era beginning with the defense of Greece against Persia lasting until the conquest of Persia by the Greeks under Alexander the Great (479–323 BCE), marked by vitality in civic life, economic prosperity, artistic expression, and literary achievement.

Classicism Artistic movement that replaced the flourishes of the Baroque with a more controlled and formal sensibility.

Cold War Term coined by American financier and presidential adviser Bernard Baruch to describe the relationship (1947–1991) between the Soviet bloc and western nations allied with the United States; each side possessed nuclear weapons, yet neither side dared to either use those weapons or disarm.

College of Cardinals Created by Pope Nicholas II (r. 1059–1061) and given sole power to elect the next pope.

comfort women Term used in imperial Japan for the quarter-million Chinese, Filipino, and other women captured and forced into sexual slavery in World War II.

comitatus An assembly or council of tribal elders among the early Germanic peoples. Term coined by Roman writer Tacitus.

comites Title of the regional governors ("counts") established under the Carolingian emperors in Europe. The term designated officeholders, not a hereditary class.

command economies Economies that aim to provide the highest possible yield for whoever held the raw materials and captive markets

Communism Socialist movement that advocates the destruction of capitalism and the development of a new, classless society of freedom.

The Communist Manifesto Book by Karl Marx and Friedrich Engels (1848) that presents a Marxist view of history as class struggle.

Concordat of Worms Established the independence of the papacy in 1122.

Conference of Berlin International conference (1884–1885) of European nations that established the standards by which any European country could claim an African territory over another European rival, touching off the "Scramble for Africa."

Congress of Vienna Conference of European diplomats convened from 1814 to 1815 to redraw boundaries and work toward peace after decades of conflict.

conquistadores The 16th-century Spanish forces that subdued South and Central America.

conservatism Political approach that values tradition and stability above the individual.

consul In the Roman Republic, the executive office in charge of the government.

Continental System Economic system, implemented by Napoleon, with two key aims: to create an integrated Continental economy and to bring about the collapse of Britain through the imposition of a strict trade embargo.

cottage industry The transfer of textile production from urban industry, where it was controlled by guilds, to rural producers, particularly women. Also known as the "putting-out system."

Council of Trent Ecumenical council convened from 1546 to 1563 to address the challenges of Protestantism by clarifying the teachings and practices of the Catholic church.

Counter-Reformation General reform of Catholic life initiated by the Council of Trent.

covenant The special promise God made to the Jews, symbolized by Moses's leading of the Hebrews out of bondage in Egypt and into the Promised Land; in return, the Jews agreed to live by the Torah.

credit default swap A new kind of financial instrument invented by the J.P. Morgan investment bank in 1994; misuse of the instrument contributed to the 2008 global economic collapse.

Crimean War Rooted in the long-standing desire of Russia to increase its influence over the Ottoman Empire, the immediate cause of the war had to do with Russian claims to protective oversight over Orthodox Christians in the Ottoman Empire, but more strategic goals were at stake. The war (1853–1856) pitted France and Britain, who were allied with the Ottomans, against Russia. While Russia accepted unfavorable terms at a conference in Paris in 1856 that ended the conflict, both sides performed ineptly, a fact that became widely known because the war was the first conflict to be covered by journalists and photographers.

crossbow Brutally efficient weapon, whose metal darts could pierce armor; it was the first weapon to be banned by the Catholic Church.

Cuban Missile Crisis Standoff between the Soviet Union and the United States in 1962, when Soviet leader Nikita Khrushchev built military bases in Cuba equipped with nuclear missiles. After two weeks of intense negotiations, Khrushchev withdrew the missiles.

cuius regio Full phrase is *Cuius regio, eius religio*, meaning "the religion of the ruler decides the religion of the realm." Compromise determined to settle the Wars of Religion in the 16th and 17th centuries. The policy guaranteed certain basic rights to the nonestablished religions.

cult of domesticity Sentimental cultural view in the 19th century that idealized women's role in the home, discouraging them from seeking work or other opportunities outside of their domestic duties.

cuneiform Technique of writing developed in Mesopotamia whereby wedge-shaped marks were impressed in clay tablets.

curiales The class of urban elites in ancient Rome who, though unsalaried, were responsible for municipal government and tax collection; obliged to make up any shortfalls in civic finance from their own personal wealth, they were entitled to retain a portion of the tax revenues they collected for personal use.

D

Dark Ages The period in Western Europe from the 4th to the 8th centuries, so named because of the chaos that reigned after the fall of the western Roman Empire and the endless depredations of various barbarian invasions.

decolonization European withdrawal during the 20th century from its former colonies.

Deism   Enlightenment-era belief in a single and possibly benevolent God who created the cosmos—but who plays no active role in it. As a result, a dual policy of religious freedom and of freedom from religious intolerance is essential to human progress.

Delian League   A military alliance formed in 478 BCE (Athens assumed control a year later) among all the Greek poleis, dedicated to maintaining a strong defense—particularly against Persia.

détente   A "loosening" of tensions between two nations. Used especially to describe efforts to improve diplomatic ties between the United States and the Soviet Union in the 1970s and 1980s. Ironically, *détente* is also a colloquial French term for the trigger of a gun.

dhimmi   Legal status of Jewish and Christian populations living under Muslim rule; officially granted freedom of religion, Jews and Christians had to accept certain restrictions on their communal practice and pay a poll tax (jizya) in return for Islamic protection. Restrictions include bans on any public expression of faith and curtailment of the ability to build or repair synagogues and churches.

dialectical materialism   In Marxist theory, the idea that history is driven forward by materialist concerns; to Lenin, this led inevitably to confrontation between the proletariat and the bourgeoisie.

Diaspora   The "exile" or "scattering" of the Hebrews after the Assyrians brutally conquered the Kingdom of Israel in 721 BCE and the Chaldaeans (or Neo-Babylonians) conquered Judah in 587 BCE.

Diet   The medieval German parliament.

Directory   In Prussia, companies of royal commissioners and civil servants who controlled financial and judicial affairs in the provinces on behalf of the king.

Documentary Hypothesis   The belief of many modern Biblical scholars that the Torah was compiled from four original sources: "J," by the Yahwist (ca. 950 BCE); "E," by the Elohist (ca. 750 BCE); "D," by the Deuteronomist (ca. 650 BCE); and "P," by the Priestly Author (ca. 550 BCE).

Dominicans   Mendicant order focused on education that established schools across Europe.

E

Edict of Milan   Issued by Constantine in 313 CE, legalizing Christianity and guaranteeing religious freedom for all faiths within the empire.

Edict of Nantes   Decree by Henri IV in 1598 that guaranteed religious freedom, with certain restrictions, throughout France.

Edict of Toleration   See **Edict of Milan**.

Elect   To Calvinists, those predestined for salvation.

emir   A military or naval commander, petty prince, or provincial governor.

enclosure movement   Trend of aristocratic landowners toward evicting small farmers (by enclosing formerly open fields with stone walls or hedges) and instead using those fields for the more profitable grazing of livestock, especially sheep.

Enlightenment   Term coined in the second half of the 18th century to describe an array of intellectual and cultural activities of the 1700s distinguished by a worldview informed by rational values and scientific inquiry.

Entente Cordiale   Diplomatic agreement between England and France in 1904, whereby each country recognized the other's spheres of influence in northern Africa.

Epic of Gilgamesh   One of the earliest known works of literature, originating in Sumer but first recorded by Babylonian scribes; relates the adventures of the semimythical Sumerian king Gilgamesh as he battles gods and monsters in pursuit of enlightenment.

Epicureanism   Philosophy based on the work of the Greek philosopher Epicurus (341 BCE—270 BCE) that promoted a life free of pain and fear as the way to happiness.

epistemology   The philosophical inquiry into the nature of knowledge (and, by extension, learning).

Essenes   An ascetic and eschatological sect within Second Temple Judaism.

Estates General   French parliament, established by the Capetian kings. Reestablished in 1789 (after having last met in 1614) at the behest of the French aristocracy. The three estates were the nobles, the clergy, and the common people.

Etruscans   A literate and prosperous people who associated with the Latins and profoundly influenced the emerging religious and moral culture of Rome.

European Union   United group of independent European nations established in 1993 to provide a process for coordinating policies formed at the level of member states.

evangelicalism   Protestant style of worship developed in Protestant church that emphasizes the work of the Holy Spirit in the world and the centrality of Biblical truth while retaining more of the traditional elements of Protestant denominations.

existentialism   Rationalist philosophy associated with Jean-Paul Sartre whose key tenet, "existence precedes essence," demands that we take action and make something of the world, or at least of our lives in it.

F

familia The essential social unit of the Roman Republic, comprising an entire household.

fasces Name of the symbol of Roman power over its citizenry—a battle-ax lashed to a bundle of birch rods. The root of the modern term **Fascism**.

Fascism The belief that force, directly applied to achieve a specific end, is the best form of government, exemplified by the dictatorships of Adolf Hitler (r. 1934–1945) and Benito Mussolini (r. 1922–1945).

Fatimids Dynasty of Shi'a rulers in 10th-century Egypt in parts of the Holy Land and Syria; they derived their name from Fatimah, the daughter of the Prophet Muhammad.

fatwa An Islamic legal pronouncement.

feminist movement A series of movements from the 19th century through the present day that aim to reform policies and practices that oppress the rights and well-being of women.

Fertile Crescent The region of the Middle East roughly framed by the Mediterranean to the west, the Arabian Peninsula to the south, and the Tarsus and Zagros Mountains to the north and east. The Tigris and Euphrates rivers flow through the center of this region, whose rich soils and abundant water gave rise to early agriculture. The Fertile Crescent connected central Asian and eastern Mediterranean economies.

feudal bonds The relationship between lord and vassal, whereby the lord granted dominion over property to the vassal in exchange for the vassal's pledge of service to the lord.

Final Solution Nazi program of systematic deportation and murder of Jews throughout Germany and all German-occupied territories during World War II.

al-fitnah "Rebellion." Used to describe an uprising against an impious ruler (not merely an unjust one).

Fourteen Points Woodrow Wilson's proposal, presented to the Paris Peace Conference (1919), for rebuilding Europe in the aftermath of World War I; ultimately rejected because of French and British concerns.

Franciscans Mendicant order established by Saint Francis of Assisi (1181–1226) dedicated to preaching and service to the urban poor.

Freemasonry Secret society that claimed its origins lay in medieval trade guilds; its members, wealthy bourgeoisie and noblemen alike, met in private clubs (or "lodges") to conduct business.

Freidenkerbund "Freethinkers' League." An early secularist group in Germany, formed in the 19th century.

Fronde Rebellion of French aristocrats against the tax policies of Cardinal Mazarin, during the regency for the underage King Louis XIV. Began in 1648.

fundamentalism American Protestant style of worship that insists on the presence of a fundamental Truth in every Scriptural passage and urges personal and societal reform before the approach of Armageddon; from the 1980s, fundamentalism has had considerable influence on American politics, particularly the Republican Party.

G

Gastarbeiter The "guestworkers," chiefly from Turkey, welcomed into Germany in the postwar era to rebuild the nation. German labor shortage necessitated the importing of workers.

General Theory of Relativity Einstein's theory (1915) describing gravity's relationship to space-time.

genocide Term coined in 1944 by Raphael Lemkin, a lawyer and Polish Jew, to describe the extermination of a particular racial or ethnic group, such as Germany's **Final Solution**.

Ghettos Segregated communities of Jews in European cities.

Gini coefficient Standard for measuring wealth and income distributions, named for Italian statistician Corrado Gini (1884–1965).

Girondins One of several factions during the French Revolution; a relatively moderate group, they championed a constitutional monarchy until they were driven from power by the more radical Jacobins.

glasnost "Openness," literally, in Russian. Specifically, the policy in the Soviet Union under Premier Mikhail Gorbachev to relax the traditional censorship of Soviet television, radio, and print media and to permit greater freedom of speech.

Glorious Revolution Coup in 1688 that deposed the Catholic king James II of England and replaced him with the popular Protestant ruler of Holland, William of Orange (who was married to James II's daughter Mary).

gold standard Monetary system, initially introduced in the West by Britain in 1821 and abandoned by most countries in the aftermath of the Great Depression, that pegs a currency to the price of gold.

Good Friday Accord Treaty signed in 1998 that ended eighty years of terrorist conflict in Northern Ireland.

Great Depression (1929–1936) Global economic depression that began with the crash of the New York Stock Exchange on October 29, 1929, resulting in massive unemployment and economic crises worldwide.

Greater West The matrix of European and Near Eastern cultures originating in the Fertile Crescent and still resonant today through bonds of trade, intellectual cross-fertilization, cultural overlap, and religious rivalry.

Great Purge Brutal efforts, beginning with show trials in 1936, by Josef Stalin (r. 1931–1953) to eliminate anyone he considered an enemy of the Soviet Union.

guild Artisanal and commercial trade associations that set prices, quality standards, methods and volume of production, and wages paid to workers. Guilds also assigned market shares to individual artisans or merchants.

gulag Network of Soviet Russian prison camps used to incarcerate political dissidents and enemies. Begun under Lenin and greatly expanded under Stalin, the gulag accounted for the deaths of roughly a million prisoners annually from the 1930s to the 1980s.

gynaeceum Area of a private home in ancient Greece restricted to women, their children, and their servants. Greek women were strictly segregated from public life and did not enter public areas of their own homes without the permission of their husbands.

H

hadith The written record of the actions and non-Qur'anic teachings of the Prophet Muhammad. The two most significant collections are those by al-Bukhari (d. 870) and al-Muslim (d. 875).

haeresis Term for the "philosophical sects" among the Jews of ancient Palestine (Pharisees, Sadducees, Essenes). Later used to refer to the "heresies" of post-Nicean Christianity.

hajj The pilgrimage of Muslims to Mecca, held annually. All able-bodied Muslims are expected to undertake the hajj at least once in their lives.

Hamas Conservative religious-political Palestinian group (and offshoot of the **Muslim Brotherhood**) equally devoted to charitable campaigns and social work among the Palestinians and to a terrorist war upon Israel.

Haredim The so-called Ultra-Orthodox Jews of Israel; they make up somewhere between 5 and 10 percent of the population.

Hasidim Adherents to a revivalist movement in Judaism, started in the mid-18th century in the Polish-Lithuanian Commonwealth by the Ba'al Shem Tov (d. 1760). Using highly emotive language and physical expression, Hasidic Judaism challenged the rather staid formalism of synagogue worship.

Haskalah Hebrew term for "enlightenment."

Hellenistic Age The era beginning with the death of Alexander the Great (323 BCE) and concluding with the conquest of the East by the Romans (327 BCE) and marked by a broader degree of cultural cohesion than previous eras, including the development of a common dialect of Greek (**Koine**) used across the territories. Although art and literature did not flourish as they did in the Classical Age, tremendous advances were made in the sciences.

heliocentrism First articulated by Copernicus, the observation that Earth is one of several planets that orbit around a stationary sun.

helot Slave owned by the city-state of ancient Sparta. Comprising roughly 75 percent of the Spartan population, they performed virtually all the labor, leaving the Spartans themselves free to perform military and civic service.

hetaera Ancient Greek courtesan, skilled in music and witty conversation in addition to her erotic services.

hieroglyphs System of writing used in ancient Egypt, especially in official records.

higher criticism Scholarly study of the Bible that seeks to determine the origins of the Biblical texts in time and place, in the process challenging long-held beliefs about the authority of Scripture. Synonymous with **historical criticism**.

hijab The "covering" of women required in Islamic society. Varies widely from country to country, depending on ethnicity, denomination, and to some extent to class. Least extensive covering is a simple headscarf; most extensive is the full-length burqa.

Hijrah The migration, or exodus, of Prophet Muhammad and his company of the faithful from Mecca to Madina in 622 CE. Marks Year 1 in the Islamic calendar (1 AH).

historical criticism See **higher criticism**.

historical materialism In Marxist theory, the process by which economic concerns propel historical change.

Hittites Indo-European group that settled in north-central Anatolia and by 1700 BCE had united into a single kingdom whose military repeatedly challenged Mesopotamia and Egypt.

Holocaust The systematic murder of six million Jews by the Nazis.

honestiores The senatorial and equestrian classes, municipal officials, and army veterans and their status entitling them to immunity from torture, lesser criminal fines, and, in capital crimes, exemption from crucifixion.

honor killings In some Muslim countries, and among some Arab immigrant communities in the

West, the murder of Arab women thought to have tarnished the honor of their families. The murder of these women by family members is believed to restore the family's honor.

hoplites   Ancient Greek infantrymen serving in a phalanx; name derives from Greek word (*hoplos*) for the smallish, circular shields they carried.

household gods   Family deities who watched over the family's farmland, household, and possessions. The daily worship of the household gods was the responsibility of the paterfamilias.

hubris   Arrogant self-pride, the deadliest of moral sins to the ancient Greeks; specifically, the delusional belief that one was in control of one's own fate. Frequently used as the plot device to trigger the dire events in Greek tragedy.

Huguenots   The Calvinists in 16th-century France, led by Henri de Navarre.

humiliores   Everyone in the Roman Empire apart from the honestiores and the slaves (the latter, in terms of the law, were counted as property rather than people). The humiliores were expected to obey the law, pay their taxes, participate in public religious rites, and hold to the ethical duties of family care and public service.

Hundred Years' War   From 1337 to 1453 CE; fought between England and France, beginning when England's king Edward III (r. 1327–1377) laid claim to the French throne; France (led, at one point, by the young girl Joan of Arc) eventually won.

Hyksos ascendancy   The Second Intermediate Period (1640–1570 BCE) of the Middle Kingdom, so named because of the revolt of foreign laborers against the Egyptian government.

I

Ideal Forms   In Plato's philosophy, the concept of a perfect and ultimate reality, of which our own perceived reality is but a flawed and flimsy reflection. Because we have a dualistic nature composed of an eternal soul temporarily housed in a flawed and mortal body, we can apprehend and aspire to that perfection.

ijma'   Arabic, "consensus"; in the Sunni tradition, a principle that embraced the use of reason to resolve a religious question among a community of scholars. Once the community's answer on any given questioned had been authoritatively expressed, the question was considered closed for all time.

The Iliad   Epic composed by Homer (ca. 750 BCE) recounting the events of the Trojan War in the Mycenaean age many centuries earlier. The epic evokes a lost, heroic, semimythological, and highly romanticized version of Greek history.

illuminationism   Twelfth-century Persian philosophical program that attempts to harmonize Sufism, Shi'ism, and rational philosophy.

imam   In Sunni Islam, a community leader who recites Qur'anic verses during prayer services. In Shi'ite Islam, a charismatic spiritual leader, a successor and descendant of Prophet Muhammad through the line of Fatima and Ali.

imperator   Title assumed by Augustus and all subsequent rulers of Rome; often translated as "emperor" but in the Republic referred to a triumphant military general.

imperialism   European (and, later, American as well) dominance of non-Western cultures for the exploitation of natural resources as well as political gain.

Index of Forbidden Books   A list of books proscribed by the Catholic Church, first published in 1599 and continually revised until its final suppression in 1966.

Indo-European   A horde of nomadic and herding nations, loosely related by their dialects of the language family, who began to migrate from their homeland near the Black Sea toward western Europe, the Aegean, and Asia Minor from about 2000 BCE. Other groups migrated eastward.

indulgences   Donations to the Catholic Church as a means of satisfying the requirements for the forgiveness of sin.

industrial revolution   The burgeoning 19th-century economy driven by mechanization, factories, an investment in infrastructure, and a growing workforce

Inquisition   Campaign by the Catholic Church to identify and correct heresy; heretics who would not admit their errors were punished, in some instances brutally.

intendants   Officials appointed by the royal court in Versailles to oversee the administrative work of the aristocracy during the Age of Absolutism.

intifada   "Uprising." Organized mass protests of Palestinians against Israeli occupation of the West Bank and Gaza (1987–1993). The Second Intifada lasted from 2000 to 2005.

Ionian League   An alliance (ca. 750 BCE) of several Greek coastal cities in Asia Minor organized by the vibrant and prosperous city of Miletus.

'ird   Arabic, "honor" or "purity"; in Islam, a quality that women either possessed or did not possess. If a woman lost that quality, the moral shame spread to her family; the only way to redeem the family's honor was to kill the woman who had transgressed.

Irish Republican Army   Terrorist group founded in the 1910s to fight what it saw as

English tyranny and Protestant oppression of Catholics in Northern Ireland

Iron Curtain Military and ideological barrier dividing the Soviet bloc from western Europe between 1945 and 1990.

Islam Religion founded by the Prophet Muhammad (570–632). In Arabic, the word "islam" means "surrender" and implies the fundamental duty of mankind to submit to the absolute authority of Allah.

isonomia Equality before the law. The term originates with the ancient Greek reformer Cleisthenes, but the notion of a single standard of behavior for all members of a community dates back to the ancient Hebrews.

Israel One of two Hebrew kingdoms (937–721 BCE), this one in the north of Palestine with Shechem as its capital.

J

Jacobins Radical party that seized power from the Girondists during the French Revolution. Resolutely antimonarchist, the Jacobins executed King Louis XVI and his family in 1793, outlawed Christianity, and sought to create a classless society based on radical principles.

Jacquerie Popular uprising in France (1358).

al-Jahiliyya Term (literally "Age of Ignorance" or "Age of Barbarism") used by Arab historians to describe the era between the death of Jesus and the birth of Muhammad.

Janissaries Elite military caste in the Ottoman Empire, 14th–19th centuries. The ranks of Janissaries were filled with Christian children, either orphaned or kidnapped from their parents, who were then converted and given a special, highly disciplined, military upbringing.

Jesuits Ecclesiastical order, founded by Saint Ignacio de Loyola in 1540, particularly devoted to education and missionary work.

jihad "Struggle," literally. Refers to any conscious, intentional, and persistent effort to advance the cause of Islam in the world. The term has a broad range of meanings, from something as innocuous as a personal vow to live a more committed Islamic life to a determination to wage religious war against the perceived enemies of God.

jizya Poll tax levied on all non-Muslims in an Islamic state.

Judah One of two Hebrew kingdoms (937—721 BCE), this one in the south of Palestine and centered on Jerusalem. (See **Israel**.)

judges As described in the Bible, the leaders of each of the twelve tribes of Hebrews who moved into Palestine around 1200 BCE, after being delivered from Egypt.

Junkers Landed aristocracy in Brandenburg-Prussia in the 17th–18th centuries. In popular usage the term came in the 19th century to designate all types of conservative, wealthy elites.

justification by faith alone Luther's understanding that one attains salvation not through the purchasing of **indulgences** or other outward acts but simply by having faith in Christ.

K

Ka'ba The holiest shrine of Islam. Temple in Mecca housing the stone believed to mark the site of Abraham's altar to Allah. Originally a pagan shrine dedicated to all the deities of the pre-Islamic Arab tribes. Site of the **hajj**.

Kabbala A mystical interpretation of scripture developed by rabbis that became newly popular in the 17th century in part via the influence of Sabbatai Zvi (1626–1676).

kalam "Theology." Unsystematic effort to provide rational explanation of basic religious mysteries in early Islam on the nature of the Qur'an and the attributes of Allah.

khalifah al-rasul Allah "Deputy of the Prophet of God," literally. Title of the ruler (caliph) of the Islamic empire.

khan The hereditary leader of a given tribe of Mongols.

King James Bible English translation of the Scriptures commissioned in 1604 by King James I of England.

Koine The demotic form of Greek used throughout the Middle East during the Hellenistic Age and the early Christian era.

Kristallnacht "Crystal Night," literally; the "Night of Broken Glass," poetically. The organized Nazi attacks on Jewish businesses, synagogues, and homes throughout Germany on November 9, 1938. Widely regarded as the turning point from Nazi anti-Semitic discrimination to blatant pursuit of genocide.

kulak "Fist," literally. Term popularized by Lenin and Stalin to designate relatively wealthy peasant freeholders who opposed the Communist regime in early 20th-century Russia.

Kulturkampf Otto von Bismarck's "cultural war" against Catholicism in Germany.

Kyoto Protocol International agreement, adopted in 1997, to combat global warming by reducing greenhouse gas emissions. The United States is not among the almost two hundred nations who have since signed and ratified the protocol.

L

laissez-faire "Leave it alone," literally. Term used to identify the economic doctrine of allowing markets to self-regulate, without government interference. First articulated by Adam Smith in *The Wealth of Nations* (1776).

Lares The ancestral household gods that protected homes in the Roman world; also the statuettes that represented them in family shrines.

Late Antiquity Term ancient historians use for the Dark Ages.

Lateran Agreement Agreement (1929) between Mussolini and Pope Pius XI that recognized the Vatican as a sovereign state in exchange for the Catholic Church's support of Mussolini's Fascist regime.

latifundia Slave-worked plantations in ancient Rome, especially during the republic.

Latins Name of the original settlers of the region of Latium.

League of Augsburg Alliance forged by Holy Roman emperor Leopold I in 1686 for defense against French expansionism; members included England, the Low Countries, Sweden, and several German principalities as well as the Holy Roman Empire.

League of Nations Woodrow Wilson's proposed international body that would arbitrate disputes, oversee demilitarization, and provide for collective security.

Lebensraum "Living space," literally. The conviction that the territorial losses forced upon Germany by the Treaty of Versailles (1919) had denied the German people sufficient space in which to live and thrive. Under the Nazis, it evolved into the policy of demanding the unification of all German-inhabited lands.

legatus Commander of a legion selected by the Roman emperor from members of the Senate. In smaller provinces, the legate also served as the provincial governor.

liberalism Political view calling for civil liberties, equality under the law, the right to vote, and a free market economy.

Libertas ecclesie "Freedom for the Church!" Popular rallying cry of the Peace of God reform movement in the 10th and 11th centuries.

libertarian Political stance that supports very small and highly limited government and opposes almost all forms of taxation.

Linear A Script used by Minoan culture on ancient Crete. Underlying language has not been identified, and hence the script has not been deciphered.

Linear B Syllabic script used by ancient Mycenaeans in Crete. Underlying Language is an early dialect of Greek, and the script was deciphered by 1953.

logos "Word," literally. Neoplatonic term for the spirit of wisdom that lies at the center of creation, from which emanate the **Ideal Forms** and all the elements of the cosmos. Term adopted by early Christians (see Gospel of John) to refer to Christ as the "Word of God" made flesh.

Lollards Anticlerical heretical group that condemned Catholic corruption and worldliness, believed in the right of nonpriests to preach, and taught that to live according to the spirit of Christ was more important than to follow the many letters of the church's laws.

longbow Fourteenth-century innovation in weapons technology that, by moving bow-and-arrow weapons from cavalry to infantry, allowed for the length of the bow to be greatly increased and therefore the range of its arrows considerably expanded.

lord In the feudal system, the figure who could grant vassals dominion over manors.

lugal Old Sumerian title of city-state kings in Mesopotamia.

Lyceum School founded by the philosopher Aristotle in Athens in 335 BCE.

M

ma'at Concept of cosmic order in ancient Egypt, everything being in perfect balance; includes the notions of meaning, justice, and truth, although in a passive sense, asking people not to upset divine harmony by attempting to alter the political and religious order.

madrasa Islamic religious school attached, administratively and often physically, to a mosque. Study focused on memorization of the Qur'an, with subsequent forays into Islamic law and literature.

magi Zoroastrian priests.

Maginot Line Barricade of artillery casements, machine-gun pillboxes, tank formations, barbed wire, minefields, and concrete bunkers built by France along its border with Germany.

Magna Carta Agreement in 1215 between the king of England and English lords, establishing certain constraints on royal power.

Magna Mater The "Great Mother," Cybele. There was a passionate religious cult dedicated to this life-giving goddess. A rival for popularity with Christianity.

Mahdi Messianic figure expected by Shi'ite Muslims; believed to be the return of the "Hidden Imam" who has gone into seclusion until the end of time.

mamluk   A slave-soldier in the medieval Islamic world.

mandates   Semi-independent states created in the Middle East by the League of Nations after World War I, dividing territories of the former Ottoman Empire between Britain and France.

Manhattan Project   Secret American program to develop an atomic bomb, begun in 1939 under the scientific direction of J. Robert Oppenheimer.

manors   In a feudal system, collective farms under the authority of lords.

Mare Nostrum   To Romans, the Mediterranean ("Our Sea" in Latin).

market   Term coined by economist Adam Smith (1776) to describe commerce as a rational pattern of human behavior.

Marshall Plan   American plan to rebuild western Europe after World War II by providing cash, credit, raw materials, and technical assistance to jump-start industrial production.

al-ma'siyah   "Disobedience." Justified resistance to a ruler or government who violates religious law.

maskilim   "Enlightened Ones," literally. Jewish religious scholars in the 18th century who worked to harmonize Jewish tradition with the principles of the Enlightenment.

mawali   Non-Arab Muslim converts in the Islamic empire.

medieval   In western Europe, the period between the end of the Dark Ages and the beginning of the Renaissance.

Mehmet Ali Pasha   Pro-Western dynastic leader of Egypt (r. 1805–1848) who built a powerful Egyptian military force, professionalized the government along Western lines, and developed both industry and education.

mendicant orders   Groups (such as the Dominicans and the Franciscans) dedicated to assisting the clergy in the performance of their evangelical mission.

Mensheviks   Faction of the Russian Revolution that was generally more moderate than Lenin's **Bolshevik** faction and was ultimately defeated by the Bolsheviks in 1917.

mercantilism   The economic policy of absolutism, defining economic wealth as tangible assets and promoting protectionism with the aim of concentrating wealth among as few individuals as possible.

Merovingians   Warrior dynasty who ruled as kings of the Franks from ca. 500 to the ascent of the Carolingians (ca. 754).

messiah   In the Jewish tradition, an earthly savior who would bring justice and create a safe, unified state for the Jews.

Midrash   Rabbinic literature that explicates Biblical texts.

miles/milites   Term for the warlord(s) of the 10th and 11th centuries who emerged from the breakup of the Carolingian Empire. By 12th century the term is translated as "knight(s)."

Minoan   An ancient and wealthy commercial culture that flourished from 2000 to 1500 BCE, centered on the island of Crete and named for its legendary founder, King Minos. Later Greek culture and mythology were profoundly influenced by the Minoans, and one of the two written scripts (called Linear B) used by Minoans records an early form of Greek.

missi dominici   Itinerant representatives of the Carolingian emperor, sent out to check on the job performance of the comites in the provinces.

modernism   1. To the Catholic Church in the early 20th century, a deplorable trend toward intellectual novelty that trivialized Scriptural truth and claimed "that there is nothing divine in sacred tradition [of the Church]." 2. Highly diverse cultural movement (roughly 1860–1950) that simultaneously rejects previous attitudes about how artists should work and resists the contemporary impersonality of mass-produced culture.

monasticism   In the rapidly Christianizing world, the movement to reject normal family and social life, along with the concern for wealth, status, and power, in favor of a harsh life of solitude and spiritual discipline in communities of other monks.

Mongols   Diverse group of nomadic Asian tribes that, through a series of brutal conquests in China, Russia, and the Muslim world, covered at its height in 1279 nearly one quarter of the Earth's land surface.

monotheism   The belief in a single, supreme deity.

Morgengab   The morning gift owed by a husband to his bride after the wedding night, in compensation for her lost virginity, among early Germanic peoples.

mullah   A Persian word used primarily in non-Arabic speaking Shi'i Muslim countries (e.g., Iran, Afghanistan, Pakistan) to designate a low-level cleric. It is a term of respect rather than a designation of office. With a literal meaning of "guardian" or "caretaker," it carries a colloquial sense analogous to the English word *reverend*, stripped of any ecclesial meaning. Used primarily by Shi'i Muslims and throughout Pakistan and India by both Sunnis and Shi'a.

Mulla Sadra The greatest Muslim philosopher of the modern era; his most important book is *The Four Journeys of the Intellect* (1638).

Muslim Brotherhood Religious-political group founded in Egypt in 1928 that, after years of repression by Egypt's military and secular regime, assumed power following elections in 2011.

mut'a A form of concubinage or "temporary marriage" permitted among Shi'i Muslims. Such marriages could be as short as twenty-four hours, as a means of legitimizing sexual activity.

Mu'tazilites Dissident Muslim scholars who, counter to the tradition of **ijma'**, believed that whenever tradition and reason were in conflict, the scale tipped in reason's favor.

Mycenaean Greece Society (1600 to 1200 BCE) marked by the dominance of mainland Hellenes in the Aegean region; named for the city of Mycenae, which according to tradition was the city ruled by the legendary King Agamemnon.

N

al-Nahda Arabic, "awakening" or "renaissance"; nineteenth-century Islamic intellectual and cultural movement centered in Egypt that advocated the integration of Islamic and European culture.

Napoleonic Code Systematic law code established by Napoleon that (among other principals) emphasized individuals' rights to property and standardized the legal structures for contracts, leases, and establishing stock corporations.

nationalism A collective consciousness or awareness that the members of an individual nation-group share a depth of feelings, values, and attitudes toward the world.

naturalism European literary movement (1850–1914) that aimed to depict the whole array of pressures, demands, irritations, and longings that shape human lives in as much specific and realistic detail as possible. Sometimes used (though inaccurately) as a synonym for Realism.

Neo-Lutheranism German religious movement of the mid-19th century that sought to reaffirm the distinctive Lutheran heritage. However, adherents were divided among conservatives who argued for scriptural inerrancy, moderates who privileged the institutional tradition of Lutheranism, and more liberally inclined believers who believed that traditional faith and the new sciences could be harmonized.

neoorthodoxy Protestant theology founded by Swiss Calvinist theologian Karl Barth (1886–1968) that emphasizes the absolute strangeness and "complete Otherness" of God.

Neoplatonism Spiritual philosophy derived from Plato that influenced both late Roman paganism and early Christian theologians.

New Deal American economic initiatives launched by Franklin Delano Roosevelt to help the nation recover from the Great Depression by increasing government spending to employ men and women, provide price supports for farmers, offer unemployment insurance and retirement benefits, and create welfare programs.

New Historians Young Jewish scholars and journalists, mostly born in Israel, whose archival research and writing has led to a more complex and less idealistic understanding of Zionism and the founding of Israel.

New Testament Canon of twenty-seven works written after the death of Christ by or about various apostles.

new woman The subject of innumerable journalistic and literary works in Europe, America, and parts of the Islamic world; a woman who, thanks to tremendous economic, cultural, and political shifts, was free to travel, get an education, and have a career.

Nicene Creed Statement of fundamental Christian beliefs issued by an ecumenical council convened by Constantine in 323–325.

nihilism Philosophical position of extreme skepticism that holds existence to be random, even meaningless.

Ninety-Five Theses A list, published by Martin Luther in 1517, of assertions condemning the theology of indulgences.

noble savage The idea, popularized by Jean Jacques Rousseau (1712–1778), that non-Europeans are untainted by civilization's corrupting influences.

nome An economic and administrative district in ancient Egypt, composed of towns and villages along defined segments of the Nile River. The chief administrator of each nome was called a *nomarch*.

North Atlantic Treaty Organization (NATO) Defensive alliance created by the United States in 1949 to protect Western Europe.

Nuremberg Trials Trials of Nazi leaders for war crimes before an international tribunal of judges and prosecutors from the Allied countries, held in 1945–1946 in Nuremberg, Germany.

O

Oath of Supremacy In Britain, an oath to recognize the monarch as the supreme head of the church within the realm. The oath effectively excluded Irish Catholics from holding public office or playing any part in public life.

Olympian deities   The numerous gods, worshipped by the ancient Greeks, whose passions and exploits are recounted in Greek mythology.
On the Origin of Species by Means of Natural Selection   Book by Charles Darwin (1859) that set forth his theory of natural selection as the means by which evolution occurs.
Organization of Petroleum Exporting Countries   Group of twelve oil-exporting countries that strongly influences both the production and the pricing of oil. A 1973 boycott by OPEC drove gas prices to record levels, disrupting the American economy.
Ottoman Turks   Dynasty founded by Osman (r. 1281–1324) that established a powerful state from the Balkans to Mesopotamia to North Africa.
Oxford Movement   Mid-19th-century English movement to reinforce the traditions of Anglican Christianity.

P

pacifism   In the aftermath of World War I, a term used to describe any principled and total rejection of violence as a means of resolving disputes.
Pale of Settlement   Region of Russian Empire where Jews were allowed to live (they were generally not allowed to live anywhere else in Russia), and the site of devastating pogroms in the late 19th century.
Palestinian Liberation Organization (PLO)   Political organization of Palestinian Arabs created in 1964 in opposition to the existence of the Jewish state of Israel.
Pan-Arabism   Ideology promoting the unification of all Arabs, particularly in opposition to Western imperialism. See **Ba'ath Party**.
Pan-Slavism   Populist approach of Tsar Aleksandr III (r. 1881–1894) that resulted in vicious persecution of Russian Jews, who were portrayed as exploiters of the common Russian people.
Pantheon   A temple built by the emperor Hadrian (r. 117–138 CE) in Rome and dedicated to the whole roster of major deities within the empire.
parlements   Ancient French aristocratic-led system of legal courts reestablished during the regency of Louis XV as a way to extend aristocratic privileges; Louis XV tried to overturn the parlements when he came of age.
paterfamilias   In the Roman Republic, the head (always male) of a household. The paterfamilias had complete authority over the familia and was the sole possessor of its property.

patria potestas   "Paternal power," the authority given by Roman law and custom to the male head of a household. Patria potestas gave the man possession of everything owned by the members of his household and gave him the power of life and death over every member except his wife.
patrilinear   Describes a social system in Mesopotamia and elsewhere, a society in which only men can inherit property.
Pax Romana   The "Roman Peace," a period of general peace and prosperity in the Roman Empire from Augustus (d. 14 CE) to Marcus Aurelius (d. 180 CE).
Peace of Augsburg   Compromise settlement (1555) between Charles V and Lutheran princes that granted Lutheranism legal recognition. With this policy, the religion of the local ruler determined the state religion of the principality, with certain guarantees offered of the rights of the religious minority.
Peace of God   Tenth-century rallies, initiated by peasants, for reform of the control warlords had over the church.
Peace of Westphalia   A collection of treaties (1648) negotiated by the first general diplomatic congress in Western history. Involving over one hundred delegations, it brought a century of European conflict to a close.
Peasants' Revolt   Popular uprising in England in 1381.
Peloponnesian War   (431–404 BCE)   Prolonged war between Athens, which sought to dominate all of Greece, and Sparta, one of the last holdouts against Athenian supremacy. An epidemic of typhus in 429 BCE weakened Athens, while the Spartans' alliance with Persia allowed them to challenge and defeat the Athenian navy.
Pentecostalism   American Protestant style of worship that is charismatic, even antiintellectual, in its emphasis on a mystical union with God manifested by the ability to speak in tongues and perform miraculous healings.
perestroika   Collective term for the economic policies of Mikhail Gorbachev in the Soviet Union that allowed for the limited introduction of free-market mechanisms. "Restructuring," literally.
phalanx   A fighting unit of Greek foot soldiers: eight horizontal lines of ten to twenty men each, who stood shoulder to shoulder and moved as a single unit.
Pharisees   One of three "philosophical sects" into which Judean society was divided. Unlike other Jews, they held a belief in the immortality of the soul and the resurrection of the dead; they also anticipated the arrival of a messiah.

phenomenology Philosophy associated with Edmund Husserl (1859–1938) and based on the belief that whereas the world may or may not be rationally ordered, our reactions to it are.

Philistines An urban, commercial people with origins in Mycenaean Greece who settled just south of Phoenicia and engaged in hostilities against the Hebrews.

philosophes Self-chosen term for the thinkers and writers of the Enlightenment, applied to all regardless of their ethnicity.

Phoenicians A seafaring culture that established a trade network across the islands of the Mediterranean and the northern coast of Africa; the Phoenician alphabet formed the basis of the later Greek alphabet, and their great city of Carthage (established in the 9th century BCE) later challenged Rome for domination of the entire Mediterranean.

picaresque Like *Gargantua and Pantagruel*, a literary work that is a series of loosely connected and frequently funny or scatological episodes.

plebeians The class of free landowning Roman citizens, represented in the government of the Roman Republic by the plebeian council.

plenitudo potestatis The Roman Catholic Church's "fullness of power." Describes the church's obligation to speak out on any aspect of life with a significant moral component and its right to be heard. The policy was fully enunciated in the 13th century.

pogroms Beginning in 1881, vicious attacks from 1648 on against entire Jewish communities in the **Pale of Settlement**.

polis The ancient Greek city-state (plural form *poleis*).

pontifex maximus In ancient Rome, a title ("chief priest") held by the pagan emperor; the Christian emperor Constantine used this precedent to declare himself the head of the Christian church as well.

populism As Lenin understood it, moral compromise dressed up as common sense; more generally, a political approach that pits (often cynically) the common people against an (often imaginary or exaggerated) elite. See **Pan-Slavism**.

post-structuralism Intellectual movement associated with French philosopher Jacques Derrida (1930–2004) that, by challenging the authority of language, allows feminists, ethnic minorities, and others to look for the hidden assumptions in the work of critical thinkers of the past.

Prague Spring Reforms initiated in 1968 Communist Czechoslovakia by moderate leader Alexander Dubček, who described it as "socialism with a human face"; the reforms were squashed by a Soviet military intervention in August 1968.

Princeps Epithet taken by the emperor Octavian, meaning "first in honor" (because his name appeared first on the censor's list of Roman citizens).

proletariat A term popularized by Marx to describe the working classes. A revolution of the proletariat, Marx believed, would bring about the end of capitalism and the birth of a classless society.

protectionism The blocking of imports by tariff barriers or other legal means in order to promote the interests of a domestic mercantilist economy.

Protestant Reformation Movement initiated by Martin Luther that sought to recreate what he believed to be Christian belief and practice as they had existed in the apostolic church.

psychoanalysis Technique associated with Sigmund Freud (1856–1939) that seeks to understand the unconscious mind.

Punic Wars Three wars Rome fought with Carthage between 264 and 146 BCE, resulting in Roman dominance of the entire western Mediterranean basin.

putting-out system See **cottage industry**.

Pythagoreans Group of philosophers named after Pythagoras (570–495 BCE), who had developed the famous theorem about right triangles. They sought to identify rational order and laws governing the natural world; hence their focus on mathematics.

Q

qadi Islamic religious judge.

al-Qaeda "The Base," literally. Islamic terrorist organization created in the late 1980s by former rebels against the Soviet Army in Afghanistan. Led by Usamah bin Laden until his death in 2011.

Qajar Dynasty that ruled Iran from 1796 to 1925.

Qizilbash Network of militant units who fought to defend and uphold the Safavid dynasty of Iran.

quantum theory New theory of physics proposed by Max Planck (1858–1947) suggesting that both light and matter exist as waves and as particles.

Qur'an The holy book of Islam, revealed to the Prophet Muhammad.

R

rabbi An honorific Hebrew word meaning "my master." Rabbis were originally teachers of Jewish law. During the Babylonian Captivity, far from their ruined temple, many Jews turned to their rabbis for religious guidance. Rabbis became leaders of the exiled Jews and during this time refined the laws governing Jewish life.

Rape of Nanjing Atrocities perpetrated by invading Japanese soldiers in the Chinese capital of Nanjing in December 1937–January 1938. Hundreds of thousands of Chinese civilians were brutally murdered.

rationalism The essential characteristic of Greek thought, from Mycenaean times to the earliest known philosophers of Miletus (Thales, Anaximander, and Anaximenes); attempts to explain the natural world through observation rather than through mythology.

rationalist philosophy Branch of philosophy that studies the movement of the human mind itself (as distinct from analytic philosophy, which emphasizes close and careful reasoning).

realist See **naturalist**.

Realpolitik Politics based on strategic and tactical realities instead of idealism.

Reconquista "Reconquest," in Spanish. Refers to the long struggle (985–1492) between Christian and Muslim warlord-princes for control of the Iberian Peninsula.

Reichstag Name of the lower parliamentary chamber in the German imperial government, 1871–1945.

Reign of Terror Brutal period of French Revolution (1792) during which, at the direction of Robespierre, tens of thousands of French citizens believed to be opposed in any way to the Revolution were executed.

relativity In physics, the concept that every vantage point in the universe, whether moving or stationary, is as valid as every other vantage point; as a cultural metaphor, the new and possibly frightening idea that there are no fixed points, no absolute time, and no absolute space.

religiones licitae The legally approved religions of ancient Rome. Christianity became one in 375.

Renaissance Literally "rebirth" (French); an era of tremendous cultural achievement as artists, scholars, and philosophers rediscovered the works of classical Greece and Rome and applied those ideas and aesthetics to contemporary arts, humanism, and modern statecraft.

Renaissance humanism Movement of philosophers such as Pico della Mirandola to develop human potential, to value the particular, and to assert the inherent dignity of each person.

Rerum Novarum (Latin, "of new things.") Encyclical issued by Pope Leo XIII (1891) that recognized the intrinsic rights of private property but insisted on the equal right of workers to form labor unions.

res publica Latin term for "republic" or "commonwealth"; a form of government based on a system of checks and balances that emerged in Rome in 509 BCE.

al-riddah "Insubordination" or "apostasy," depending on circumstance.

Risorgimento "Resurgence," literally. This was the name given to the 19th-century movement for Italian national reunification.

Romanticism Cultural and artistic movement in opposition to industrialization, preferring emotion and instinct over structural order and rational thought.

Rub' al-Khali The "Empty Quarter" of the Arabian peninsula. Area of vast and almost impenetrable desert.

Rule of Saint Benedict A communal handbook written by Saint Benedict of Nursia (480–547) to guide the monastery he had established; its focus on the physical and intellectual as well as spiritual well-being of monks led to its being widely adopted by monastic communities across medieval Europe.

Rumi Sufi poet (1207–1273) whose work championed Islam without disparaging other faiths.

S

Sadducees One of three "philosophical sects" into which Judean society was divided; an aristocratic party who were reputedly strict upholders of Temple ritual, dedicated to the literal reading of Scripture and the rejection of the Oral Torah.

Saint Bartholomew's Day Massacre Riot (August 23–29, 1572) between Catholics and Protestant Huguenots that began in Paris and spread across France, resulting in the deaths of thousands.

salons In urban, Enlightenment-era France, regular gatherings, often hosted by wealthy or aristocratic women in their own homes, to which philosophers, artists, and other cultural figures were invited to discuss ideas.

samizdat Secret literature of political dissidents in Soviet Russia and Communist Eastern Europe, who passed officially condemned information, literature, and uncensored documents; important especially in the 1960s and 1970s.

sans-culottes "Those without breeches," literally. Colloquial reference to political revolutionary militants in Paris drawn from the lower orders.

satire Literary genre, originally popular among the Romans, that flourished during the

Renaissance. Satirical writers use humor or figurative language to mock and criticize powerful people and institution.

Schlieffen Plan   Military strategy created by German chief of general staff Alfred Graf von Schlieffen in 1905 that called for German forces to circumvent French defenses by striking swiftly through Belgium and Luxembourg; this was exactly how Germany proceeded at the start of World War I nine years later.

scholasticism   Method of research and teaching in medieval universities, characterized by the application of Aristotelian logic and the attempt to harmonize all knowledge.

scientific management   Management theory that increases the productivity of labor by breaking down manufacturing into small, distinct steps.

Scientific Revolution   From 1500 to 1700, a cultural, philosophical, and intellectual shift from a view of the universe as divinely created to a concept of the natural world as a system that could be understood through study and observation.

Sea Peoples   Indo-European invaders (ca. 1200 BCE) who conquered the Hittites, ended the Egyptian dominance of Palestine, and wrought enormous destruction across southern and southeastern Europe before vanishing, possibly through assimilation into local groups.

Second Industrial Revolution   Continuation of the earlier industrial revolution but with a focus instead on producing capital goods (goods, such as steel and chemicals, used to produce other goods).

Second Vatican Council   Convened by Pope John XXIII (r. 1958–1963) as part of the effort to modernize the Church's teachings and governance.

second wave feminism   Women's movement in the 1960s and 1970s that focused on sexual health, access to abortion and contraception, equal rights in the workplace, childcare services, gender roles in society, and portrayals of women in popular culture. (The "first wave" of feminism had focused almost exclusively on women's suffrage.)

secularism   The declining power of religious beliefs and institutions and the subsequent decline in religious practice.

Sephardim   Jewish people centered around the Mediterranean, where they remained in constant contact with Arab, Greek, and Latin cultural developments.

Septuagint   A Greek translation of the Hebrew Bible created by a group of seventy-two scholars who convened in Alexandria around 260 BCE (the name is derived from the Greek word for "seventy". It includes several books later excluded from the Jewish canon.

serfs   Dependent farmers who performed labor on manors in exchange for the security and primitive justice provided by the landlord.

shah   Persian term for "emperor."

shari'ah   Islamic religious law.

She'ol   The underworld of the Hebrew Bible, to which all the dead are sent; not analogous to later Christian concepts of hell as a place of punishment.

Shi'a   Muslims who believe that political and religious legitimacy could pass only to members of the Prophet Muhammad's hereditary line.

Shoah   See **Holocaust**

simony   Paying money or presenting gifts in return for ecclesiastical office, a widespread abuse in the Roman Catholic Church in post-Carolingian era and inspiring the Gregorian Reform.

Six-Day War   Military action (June 5–June 10, 1967) initiated by Israel against Egypt, Jordan, and Syria; Israel seized the Gaza Strip, the Golan Heights along the Israeli border with Syria, the Sinai Peninsula, and the entire West Bank, including the eastern part of the then-divided city of Jerusalem. After the stunning defeat of Arab allies, much of Arab popular resentment turned toward the United States.

Social Catholicism   Nineteenth-century European Catholic movement founded on the idea that the challenge to Christian society under industrialism was structural rather than personal.

social contract   Articulated in Thomas Hobbes's *Leviathan* (1651), the theory that when people decide to live in community they enter a covenant with each other, compromising their individual free wills in return for the benefits of society. Government, which bears responsibility for preserving social stability, may therefore legitimately assert its will on the community whenever it deems it necessary to do so.

social Darwinism   Misuse of Darwin's theory of evolution by natural selection to morally justify imperialism as a healthy competition among societies.

sodalitia   Special "fellowships" within the Roman Catholic Church—that is, groups of less formal rank than religious orders, organized usually around a special theme or mission. In the debates over religious modernism, numerous sodalitia loyal to the pope were granted oversight authority of parish clergy.

sola fide   "By faith alone." Central concept in Martin Luther's theology—the notion that faith in Christ alone is sufficient to gain salvation.

sola Scriptura "By Scripture alone." Protestant belief, also originating with Luther, that the Bible is the sole source and sufficient authority (as opposed to tradition or the church) for divine teaching.

Sol Invictus The Unconquered Sun. Pagan cult devoted to the sun god in the Roman Empire. Identified with the emperor Constantine, who encouraged it despite his personal Christianity.

Song of Songs Biblical book, also known as the Song of Solomon, consisting of a poetic dialogue between a bride and bridegroom. Centuries of scholars have interpreted the Song of Songs as an allegory of the covenant between God and his people.

Sophists In Greece in the 5th century BCE, a group of thinkers who traveled from city to city teaching rhetoric and philosophy.

South Sea Bubble Economic crash (1720) sparked when the South Sea Company, an English company formed to trade with Spanish colonies in the New World, encouraged investors to speculate wildly on its supposed ventures but then could not make good on its unrealistic promises.

space-time Einstein's concept of time and space as elastic and therefore understood as different facets of a single dimension.

Spanish Civil War Internal conflict (1936–1939) between conservative and liberal forces in Spain that drew anti-Fascist support from around the world. The conservatives, under the Fascist dictator Francisco Franco (r. 1936–1975), won.

special theory of relativity Einstein's theory (1905) that maintains that all measurements of space and time are relative; the basis of the idea that nothing can go faster than the speed of light.

stadtholder Dutch term for "Head of State" in the 17th century, usually drawn from the noble house of Orange.

Stoicism Philosophy most famously described and taught by Seneca (4 BCE–65 CE) and Epictetus (55–135 CE) that conformed to Roman morals through an emphasis on duty, forbearance, self-discipline, and concern for others.

streltsi Semifeudalized noble cavalrymen who made up the Russian army until it was disbanded and reorganized by Tsar Piotr I in 1698.

structuralism Philosophy rooted in the work of Swiss linguist Ferdinand de Saussure (1857–1913) that emphasizes the structured ways in which we see, participate in, and comprehend the world.

subsidiarity Introduced by Pope Leo XIII, the principle that sought to preserve the dignity of persons and to help them recognize their own moral responsibilities and sought to safeguard against an overreaching centralized government.

suffrage The right to vote.

suffragettes European activists for women's rights who, in contrast with **suffragists**, favored confrontation, aggressive action, and, whenever they thought it necessary, even violence in order to change society.

suffragists Activists for women's rights who, in contrast with **suffragettes**, worked peaceably and within the legal system for women's rights.

Sufism A mystical, esoteric approach to Islam that flourished in the Ottoman Empire.

sultan "Commander," literally. Term for chief military officer in the Turkish empire. Under the Ottomans, the word came to represent the head of state.

Sultanate of Women Period (1640s and 1650s) of the Ottoman Empire when leading members of the imperial harem effectively controlled the state, directed foreign policy, and oversaw the fiscal system.

summa A "summary," or an encyclopedic effort to organize all thought on a given topic; a popular genre among the scholastic writers of the 13th and 14th centuries, representing the conviction that a rational order underlay all of human life.

sumptuary codes Dress codes in the cosmopolitan, diverse mercantile cultures of the Mediterranean that regulated styles of dress in order to establish the rules of engagement among different peoples.

sunnah The collected sayings and actions of Prophet Muhammad, used to establish Islamic legal precedents.

Sunni Muslims who regard selection by the community as the sole legitimate means to leadership of the Islamic world.

supermen Term used by Friedrich Nietzsche (1844–1900) to describe cultural, political, and intellectual figures with a will to power.

Sykes-Picot Agreement Pact between England and France (1916) that took advantage of the **Arab Revolt** to divide the dominions of the Middle East between the two nations.

Syllabus of Errors Sixty-five teachings Pope Pius X decreed irredeemably anti-Catholic in two 1907 encyclicals.

symposia All-male drinking parties in ancient Greece where philosophical ideas were discussed.

syncretism The union of religious doctrines.

T

taifas Petty princedoms in Muslim Spain, after the collapse of the caliphate in Cordoba in 1031.

takiyya "Concealment," literally. Practice of religious disguise permitted to Shi'i Muslims as a means to avoid persecution.

Talmud Codification of rabbinical law and commentary that became central to Jewish life starting in the Middle Ages. Two dominant forms exist: the Babylonian Talmud, compiled around 500 CE, and the Palestinian Talmud (also known as the Jerusalem Talmud), compiled around 400 CE. Reference to the "Talmud" usually means the Babylonian Talmud.

Tanakh A common name for the canonical Hebrew Bible—an acronym based on the letters T (for Torah, meaning "Instructions"), N (for Nevi'im, or "Prophets"), and K (for Ketuvim, or "Writings"). Traditionally believed to have been assembled by the "Men of the Great Assembly" around 450 BCE, modern scholars believe the compilation occurred later, between 200 BCE and 200 CE.

Tanzimat (Turkish, "reorganization"); a 19th-century movement by the Ottoman government to promote economic development and the integration of the empire's non-Muslims and non-Turks into civil society.

telos According to Aristotle, the intrinsic purpose or necessary role in the cosmic drama of every existing thing.

Tetrarchy Under Diocletian, a new system whereby the empire was formally divided into two halves with a separate emperor (**augustus**, in Latin) for each. Each half was further divided in half again, and each *augustus* therefore had a subordinate vice-emperor or *caesar.*

al-thawrah "Uprising," literally. Describes opposition to a government or ruler on account of the injustice of its rule. No directly religious overtone.

themes New system of organizing army under Byzantine emperor Heraclius in the 7th century that redistributed land to military officers and soldiers.

theory of evolution by natural selection As explained by Charles Darwin in his 1859 book *On the Origin of Species by Means of Natural Selection,* the process by which the superabundance of offspring produced by all living beings results in their competition for resources; over time, that competition favors traits in offspring that provide an advantage over their rivals.

Third Estate The branch of the French legislative body made up of elected representatives of the common people, including the bourgeoisie and wage earners. See **Estates General**.

Thirty Tyrants Committee of thirty Athenians appointed by the Spartan conquerors of Athens to rule the city.

Thirty Years' War Conflict that began in 1618 between Protestants and Catholics in Germany and gradually enveloped most of Europe, ending in 1648 after massive losses of life and property.

Tokyo Trials Trials (1946–1948) of Japanese officials for war crimes before an international tribunal of judges and prosecutors from the Allied countries.

Torah The first five books of the **Tanakh**, attributed to Moses.

totalitarianism A system of government that controls all aspects of society, using fear and intimidation to maintain power.

Treaty of Rome Treaty agreed to by Western European leaders in 1957 that established the European Economic Community to help postwar recovery and counterbalance American economic power.

Treaty of Versailles Controversial agreements that formally ended World War I on June 28, 1919, but ruinous concessions demanded from a defeated Germany were a contributing factor in the run-up to World War II.

Trinity For Christians, the doctrine in the existence of a single God in a union of three separate and divine "Persons."

trireme Ancient Greek warship with three tiers of oarsmen and a bronze-tipped battering ram on the prow.

troubadours Vernacular love poets popular in the aristocratic courts of southern France and northern Italy in the 12th and 13th centuries.

Truce of God An 11th-century decree by the reformed church banning warfare on holy days as well as the assault of religious pilgrims.

Twelve Tables The first written law code of the Roman Republic, ca. 450 BCE.

tyrant A person in a Greek polis who took power temporarily in order to bring about dramatic reform in a politically deadlocked state. In terms of social class, the tyrants were aristocrats but were allied with the masses.

U

'ulama Arab for "brotherhood" or "community," a central focus of Sunni life.

Umayyads Name of the ruling dynasty in the Islamic empire, 661–750. Governing the empire from their new capital at Damascus, the Umayyads were overthrown in 750 by the Abbasids, who transferred the capital to newly built Baghdad.

ummah   The community of Muslim believers.

uniformitarianism   Geologist James Hutton's theory that geological change consists of the slow accumulation of smaller changes—and these changes continue to happen in the present.

United Nations (UN)   Organization of member nations established in 1945, including a permanently standing International Court of Justice and International Criminal Court.

Universal Declaration of Human Rights   The first statement of global rights in history, drafted and promoted by American First Lady Eleanor Roosevelt and approved on December 10, 1948, by most members of the United Nations (Saudi Arabia, South Africa, and the Soviet Union abstained).

UN Women's Conference   International conferences sponsored by the United Nations to promote women's rights as *human* rights.

ushabti   Figures made of clay or wood, buried with well-to-do Egyptians, that represented servants who would work for one in the afterlife.

Utilitarianism   Philosopher John Stuart Mill's ethical principal that "holds that actions are right in proportion as they tend to promote happiness, wrong as they tend to produce the reverse of happiness"; based on this principle he argued that women should have the right to vote and determine their own destiny.

V

vassal   In a feudal system, a free man who pledged to serve a lord in exchange for dominion over a manor or manors bestowed by the lord.

vizier   Regional administrator under the Abbasid dynasty and later under the Ottomans. From the word meaning "burden sharer."

Volk   The German people. Related etymologically to the English word *folk* but with a different meaning.Used in a combined colloquial and mystical sense.

W

wadi   Seasonal river in Middle East.

Wahhabism   Conservative reform movement within Sunni Islam, taking its name from the 18th-century figure Muhammad ibn Abd al-Wahhab. The movement stresses returning to strict reliance on Qur'an and hadith, purging Islam of non-Arabic traditions, and restoring ethnic Arabs to leadership in international Islam.

The official sect in Saudi Arabia in the 20th and 21st centuries.

War of the Roses   English civil war for the throne (1455–1485) fought between the noble houses of York and Lancaster.

welfare states   In post–World War II Western Europe, societies in which the central government, funded by heavy taxation, provided all essential social services.

wergild   Old Germanic term—"man money," literally—for the compensation owed by an offender to his victim, according to custom.

will to power   Term used by Friedrich Nietzsche (1844–1900) to describe the passionate striving to make meaning and leave a mark on the world.

Women's International League for Peace and Freedom   Pacifist group founded in 1915 that campaigned for equal rights for all citizens, economic justice, and greater understanding and empathy between peoples.

World Economic Forum   Nonprofit foundation that encourages global political and business leaders to work together to address and resolve global business, industrial, and environmental issues.

World Trade Organization   Intergovernmental organization seeking to liberalize trade between nations.

Y

YHWH   The term for "God" used by the Yahwist author of the Torah (see **Documentary Hypothesis**), represented in English-language Bibles by the all-capitals word LORD.

Young Turks   Modernizing faction in Turkey that promoted pan-ethnic Islamic nationalism, overthrowing the sultan Abdul Hamid II in 1909 and replacing him with his half brother Mehmed V (r. 1909–1918).

Z

zakat   The giving of alms to the poor, required of Muslims.

ziggurat   Step-pyramid temples of ancient Mesopotamia, believed to be the dwelling places of the gods.

Zionism   From Hebrew *Tsiyon*, the name for the central portion of Jerusalem, but by extension referring to all of Israel/Palestine.Movement by Jews (especially from Eastern Europe) to establish a Jewish state in the Holy Land as a refuge from European persecution beginning in the 19th century.

Zollverein "Customs union." The free-trade zone established by Prussia in the early 19th century; an important early step in German unification.

Zoroastrianism Monotheistic religion founded by Zoroaster in Persia ca. 1300 BCE. In its emphasis on moral behavior, personal salvation, and the eventual victory of Good in a cosmic battle with Evil, Zoroastrianism is considered by many a precursor of Judaism (and, by extension, Christianity).

zunnar Identifying belt worn by non-Muslims in the early Islamic empire.

Credits

Index

Page numbers followed by *t* indicate a table. Page numbers followed by *m* indicate a map. Italicized page numbers indicate a figure or photo.